The Ancient City

*School for Advanced Research
Resident Scholar Series*

*James F. Brooks
General Editor*

The Ancient City

Contributors

Kathryn A. Bard
Department of Archaeology, Boston University

Karl W. Butzer
Department of Geography and the Environment, University of Texas, Austin

Janet DeLaine
Institute of Archaeology, Oxford University

Lothar von Falkenhausen
Department of Art History, University of California, Los Angeles

Mogens Herman Hansen
SAXO Institute, Faculty of Humanities, University of Copenhagen

Kenneth G. Hirth
Department of Anthropology, Pennsylvania State University

Michael J. Jones
Planning Department, City of Lincoln City Hall, Lincoln, United Kingdom

Jonathan Mark Kenoyer
Department of Anthropology, University of Wisconsin, Madison

Chapurukha M. Kusimba
Department of Anthropology, The Field Museum

Joyce Marcus
Museum of Anthropology, University of Michigan

Craig Morris
Division of Anthropology, American Museum of Natural History

K. Anne Pyburn
Department of Anthropology, Indiana University

Colin Renfrew
McDonald Institute for Archaeological Research, Cambridge University

Jeremy A. Sabloff
University of Pennsylvania Museum of Archaeology and Anthropology

Elizabeth C. Stone
Department of Anthropology, Stony Brook University, New York

Bruce G. Trigger
Department of Anthropology, McGill University

The Ancient City
*New Perspectives on Urbanism
in the Old and New World*

Edited by Joyce Marcus and Jeremy A. Sabloff

This publication results from an Arthur M. Sackler Colloquium
of the National Academy of Sciences, "Early Cities: New Perspectives on Pre-industrial
Urbanism," held May 18–20, 2005, at the National Academy of Sciences in Washington, DC.

Publication of this volume is made possible in part by generous support
from the National Academy of Sciences and the University of Pennsylvania.

SAR PRESS

A School for Advanced Research Resident Scholar Book

Santa Fe, New Mexico

School for Advanced Research Press
Post Office Box 2188
Santa Fe, New Mexico 87504-2188
www.sarpress.org

Co-director and Executive Editor: Catherine Cocks
Manuscript Editor: Judith Knight
Designer and Production Manager: Cynthia Dyer
Proofreader: Kate Whelan
Indexer: Catherine Fox
Printer: Publishers Graphics

Library of Congress Cataloging-in-Publication Data
The ancient city : new perspectives on urbanism in the old and new world / edited by Joyce Marcus and Jeremy A. Sabloff. -- 1st ed.
      p. cm.
  Includes bibliographical references and index.
  ISBN 978-1-934691-02-1 (pa : alk. paper)
  1. Cities and towns, Ancient. I. Marcus, Joyce. II. Sabloff, Jeremy A.

HT114.A537 2008
307.76--dc22

                              2007048199

Copyright © 2008 by the School for Advanced Research. All rights reserved.
Manufactured in the United States of America.
Library of Congress Catalog Card Number: 2007048199
International Standard Book Number 978-1-934691-02-1
First edition 2008. Sixth printing 2019.

Cover illustration: A view of the excavations of the ancient Sumerian city of Nippur, Iraq, 1899, from the top of the ziggurat (courtesy of the University of Pennsylvania Museum, image #139049). Back cover: Aerial photograph of the Postclassic Maya site of Tulum on the east coast of Yucatan, ca. 1920s–1930s (courtesy of the University of Pennsylvania Museum, image #18969).

To our late colleagues

Craig Morris
(1939–2006)

and

Bruce Trigger
(1937–2006)

We dedicate this book to Craig Morris and Bruce Trigger,
two outstanding scholars whose passing has saddened us all.
We truly wish that they were still with us
because both had so much more to contribute
to the study of prehistoric urbanism.

Contents

List of Figures	xi
List of Tables	xiv
Preface	xv
Joyce Marcus and Jeremy A. Sabloff	

Part I: The City's Past and Future

1. Introduction   3
   Joyce Marcus and Jeremy A. Sabloff

Part II: Overviews and Commentary on the Case Studies

2. The City through Time and Space: Transformations of Centrality   29
   Colin Renfrew

3. Early Cities: Craft Workers, Kings, and Controlling the Supernatural   53
   Bruce G. Trigger

4. Analyzing Cities   67
   Mogens Herman Hansen

5. Other Perspectives on Urbanism: Beyond the Disciplinary Boundaries   77
   Karl W. Butzer

Part III: Case Studies

6. Between Concept and Reality: Case Studies in the Development of Roman Cities in the Mediterranean   95
   Janet DeLaine

7. Urban Foundation, Planning, and Sustainability in the Roman Northwestern Provinces   117
   Michael J. Jones

8	A Tale of Two Cities: Lowland Mesopotamia and Highland Anatolia *Elizabeth C. Stone*	141
9	Royal Cities and Cult Centers, Administrative Towns, and Workmen's Settlements in Ancient Egypt *Kathryn A. Bard*	165
10	Indus Urbanism: New Perspectives on Its Origin and Character *Jonathan Mark Kenoyer*	183
11	Stages in the Development of "Cities" in Pre-Imperial China *Lothar von Falkenhausen*	209
12	Early African Cities: Their Role in the Shaping of Urban and Rural Interaction Spheres *Chapurukha M. Kusimba*	229
13	Pomp and Circumstance before Belize: Ancient Maya Commerce and the New River Conurbation *K. Anne Pyburn*	247
14	Incidental Urbanism: The Structure of the Prehispanic City in Central Mexico *Kenneth G. Hirth*	273
15	Links in the Chain of Inka Cities: Communication, Alliance, and the Cultural Production of Status, Value, and Power *Craig Morris*	299

Part IV: Central Themes and Future Directions

16	Cities and Urbanism: Central Themes and Future Directions *Joyce Marcus and Jeremy A. Sabloff*	323
	References	337
	Index	395

List of Figures

1.1	The concentric zone model	6
1.2	The sector model	7
1.3	Idealized diagram of a British city	8
1.4	The multiple nuclei model	9
1.5	Plan of Sesebi, a settlement in Nubia	14
1.6	Plan of Ikhmindi, a city in Nubia	15
1.7	The fort of Novaesium in Germany	16
1.8	Idealized city profile	16
1.9	The city of Pompeii, Italy	17
1.10	Plan of the Buhen fortress in Nubia	18
2.1	The idea of the city in fourteenth-century Renaissance Italy	32
2.2	Lorenzetti's depiction of citizens riding out from Siena	32
2.3	Transformation of the human skull	36
2.4	Comparison of the mediaeval monasteries of Cluny and St. Gall with the Minoan palace of Mallia	38
2.5	An early conceptualization of settlement hierarchy, as formulated by Al-Muqaddasi	39
2.6	Lancaster's imaginary reconstruction of Roman Drayneflete ca. AD 200	42
2.7	Lancaster's imaginary reconstruction of Drayneflete, soon after the Norman conquest, ca. AD 1070	42
2.8	Lancaster's imagined Drayneflete at the end of the seventeenth century	43
2.9	Lancaster's twentieth-century Drayneflete	43
2.10	Comparison of the New Kingdom Egyptian capital, Amarna, and late mediaeval London	48
6.1	Map of the Mediterranean	97
6.2	Ephesos, schematic city plan in the second century AD	100
6.3	Ostia, schematic city plan in the Republican period	101
6.4	Ostia, schematic plan of the civic center in the Julio-Claudian period	102
6.5	Ephesos, plan of the Augustan civic agora	105

6.6	Ephesos, Augustan gateway to the commercial agora dedicated by Mazaios and Mithradates	107
6.7	Lepcis Magna, schematic city plan at the time of Augustus	108
6.8	Lepcis Magna, bilingual inscription from the theater, AD 1–2	109
6.9	Lepcis Magna, schematic city plan at the end of the second century AD	110
6.10	Ostia, schematic city plan, second century AD	112
7.1	Map of the Roman Northwestern provinces showing sites in Gaul and Germany	118
7.2	The cities of Roman Britain and their tribal regions	120
7.3	Plans of selected cities in Gallia Belgica	123
7.4	Plan of Cologne showing the early city in relation to the later colonia	128
7.5	Plan of the early colonia at Colchester, with the line of the preceding legionary fortress marked	130
7.6a	Plan of the early city at Verulamium	131
7.6b	Plan of the late city at Verulamium	132
7.7	Reconstruction drawing of the walled city of Lincoln ca. AD 300	133
7.8	Plan of the developed city at Wroxeter (Viroconium Cornoviorum)	134
7.9	The city walls of Le Mans	136
8.1	Map showing the location of Mashkan-shapir	145
8.2	Plan of Mashkan-shapir	146
8.3	Digital Globe view of northern Mashkan-shapir and the plan of the Larsa palace	147
8.4	Manufacturing debris at Mashkan-shapir	148
8.5	Copper/bronze distribution at Mashkan-shapir	149
8.6	Cylinder seal distribution at Mashkan-shapir	149
8.7	Map of Urartu showing the location of Ayanis	151
8.8	Shovel test survey results	152
8.9	Plan of the outer town at Ayanis showing architectural traces	153
8.10	Magnetometry of Pınarbaşı showing excavated areas	154
8.11	Plan of excavated areas at Pınarbaşı	155
8.12	Magnetometry and plan of Köy	156
8.13	Magnetometry and photograph of Building 7, the stable	156
8.14	Plan of Building 6, the duplex	157
8.15	Plan of Buildings 1 and 3	158
8.16	Plan of Building 9	159
8.17	Plan of Buildings 10 and 11	159
8.18	Fine wares at Ayanis	160
8.19	Faunal remains from Ayanis	162
9.1	Map of ancient Egypt with nome divisions and some major towns and cities	167
9.2	Giza: plan of the Gallery Complex in the Fourth Dynasty royal production center	170

9.3	Giza: mortuary cult town of Queen Khentkawes	171
9.4	Plan of the Middle Kingdom pyramid town of Kahun	173
9.5	Plan of the New Kingdom workmen's town of Deir el-Medina	175
9.6	Plan of Akhenaten's royal city (Akhetaten) at Tell el-Amarna	176
9.7	Plan of the central city at Tell el-Amarna	177
9.8	Plan of the Eastern (workmen's) Village at Tell el-Amarna	179
10.1	Map of the major traditions	185
10.2	Major sites and regions of the Indus Tradition	187
10.3	Map of Harappa	190
10.4	Early Indus script	193
10.5	Indus script and writing	196
10.6	Map of Mohenjo-daro	199
10.7	Map of Dholavira	202
10.8	Map of Rakhigarhi	204
11.1	Section of the stamped-earth wall at Guchengzhai, Mi Xian (Henan)	211
11.2	Plans of selected Neolithic walled sites	213
11.3	Settlement pattern around Liangchengzhen, Rizhao (Shandong)	216
11.4	Plans of selected walled sites from the Shang period	217
11.5	Plans of selected unwalled Bronze Age dynastic capitals	219
11.6	Plans of selected walled sites from the Zhou period	220
11.7	Idealized layout of a Zhou capital from the "Kaogongji"	221
11.8	Plans of selected Warring States period capitals	224
11.9	Foundation of a Warring States period palace in the "palace city" at Linzi (Shandong)	226
11.10	Inlaid-bronze plan of the necropolis of King Cuo of Zhongshan	227
12.1	Great Zimbabwe wall	232
12.2	Plan of Songo Mnara	233
12.3	Plan of Gedi	234
12.4	Map of East African coast with all the cities and hinterland sites	238
12.5	Plan of Husuni Kubwa	240
12.6	Plan of the urban complex of Great Zimbabwe	244
12.7	Aerial view of Great Zimbabwe showing the perimeter wall	245
13.1	Map of the Maya lowlands	256
13.2	Lamanai, Belize	257
13.3	Altun Ha, Belize	258
13.4	Chau Hiix, Belize	259
13.5	Chau Hiix site center	261
14.1	The location of major urban sites in Central Mexico	274
14.2	Lockhart's model of the altepetl	279
14.3	What the altepetl might look like in terms of archaeological settlement patterns	280
14.4	Territory disarticulation: the location of lands of the three altepemeh of Teotihuacan, Acolman, and Tepexpan	282

14.5	Gibson's map of the population distribution of the three altepemeh of Teotihuacan, Acolman, and Tepexpan	283
14.6	The size and extent of the site of Xochicalco, Morelos, Mexico	287
14.7	The distribution of civic-ceremonial architecture at Xochicalco	288
14.8	The architectural layout of Structure X1-4, Xochicalco	289
14.9	The distribution of defensive precincts, systems mounds, and population clusters at Xochicalco	290
14.10	The location of Epiclassic defensive precincts at Xochicalco and neighboring sites in western Morelos	291
14.11	The location of the Tepeaca survey region in Central Mexico	292
14.12	Dispersed settlement patterns in the Tepeaca region during the Late Postclassic period	293
14.13	The Pyramid of the Plumed Serpent at Xochicalco	294
14.14	Four tribute panels from the north side of the Pyramid of the Plumed Serpent	295
14.15	The four payment panels from the east side of the Pyramid of the Plumed Serpent	295
15.1	The Inka empire and road system	300
15.2	General plan of the city of Huánuco Pampa	303
15.3	Zone IIB: the administrative palace at Huánuco Pampa	305
15.4	The great halls at the edge of the central plaza of Huánuco Pampa	307
15.5	The dressed stone ushnu platform in the central plaza of Huánuco Pampa	308
15.6	Compound VB5: the aqllawasi, or compound for the "chosen women," at Huánuco Pampa	311
15.7	The Chincha capital, now the site of La Centinela, as seen from the air in 1929	313
15.8	Sector III at La Centinela, built by the Inka with adobes	314
15.9	The Inka palace complex as seen from the stairway to the oracle of Chinchaycamac	315
15.10	Sector VIII: a Chincha compound with Inka alterations	317

List of Tables

10.1	Indus Tradition	186
10.2	Harappa Chronology	189
10.3	Mohenjo-daro Chronology	199
10.4	Dholavira Chronology	202
10.5	Rakhigarhi Chronology	204
12.1	The Nature of Trade Items through Time in Africa between the Hinterland, the Coast, and Overseas	242

Preface

This book is the result of the first Sackler Colloquium devoted to a topic in the social sciences. The colloquium, entitled "Early Cities: New Perspectives on Pre-industrial Urbanism," took place in Washington DC at the National Academy of Sciences Building from May 18 to 20, 2005.

Knowing that it would be impossible to present data from all the urban centers of the world, we selected a subset of them, focusing special attention on ancient cities where new field research was being conducted. We invited a broad range of scholars whose fieldwork in the New World and the Old World could offer diverse perspectives that would advance the comparative study of urbanism. We expected that such a comparative perspective would lead to the isolation of specific differences, as well as general similarities.

We hope that this book contributes to the ongoing debates and discussions about the impact of prehistoric urbanism, population growth, and occupational specialization on the tempo and mode of sociopolitical evolution.

There are many people who made the colloquium so successful. We are especially grateful to Jill Sackler (and to the Arthur M. Sackler Colloquia Fund) for supporting the colloquium; we were particularly happy that she was able to attend. Also in attendance was James Brooks, President of the School for Advanced Research, who has provided much-appreciated encouragement throughout the preparation and writing of this book.

We are very grateful to other key individuals: Alyssa Cruz, who shouldered much of the preparation for and organization of the colloquium, working tirelessly on the logistics and advertising; James Langer, who headed the National Academy of Sciences committee that selected and approved this as a Sackler Colloquium; Ken Fulton, who has been a very supportive and enthusiastic liaison between the National Academy of Sciences and James Brooks; and Brian J. L. Berry, who was the first person to suggest urbanism and cities as appropriate topics for a Sackler Colloquium. Although Berry's oral presentation at the Colloquium and those of Paul Hohenberg and Stephen Tobriner could not be included here, we very much appreciate their participation in the discussions that took place there.

We thank Dr. Catherine Cocks at the School for Advanced Research (SAR Press) and the anonymous reviewers for their constructive comments and advice on revising the book manuscript. In addition, we thank all the participants in this volume because they not only brought new data and novel insights to this endeavor but also were willing to follow the suggestions of several anonymous reviewers in revising their chapters. Our only regret is that the readers of this book will not have a chance to see all the fabulous color slides and creative Powerpoint images that accompanied the oral presentations in May of 2005.

Joyce Marcus and Jeremy A. Sabloff
Ann Arbor, Michigan, and Philadelphia
July 2008

part one
THE CITY'S PAST AND FUTURE

one
Introduction

Joyce Marcus and Jeremy A. Sabloff

> The most important issue confronting the social sciences is the extent to which human behavior is shaped by factors that operate cross-culturally as opposed to factors that are unique to particular cultures.
> —*Bruce Trigger,* Understanding Early Civilizations

Cities are so common today that we cannot imagine a world without them. In fact, more than half of the world's population lives in cities, and that number is expected to increase to two-thirds in the next century. For most of our history, however, there were no cities. Understandably, scholars want to know why, how, and when urban life began. Was the emergence of the city just a matter of nucleating previously scattered populations, or was it more? As the diverse case studies in this book show, it was much more.

When it came time to select a title for this book, we picked *The Ancient City* for two reasons. One was to honor the scholar who conceived the first book with that title. The second was to draw attention to ancient cities, many of them innovations for their era. These diverse settlements not only have much to tell us about the social, political, religious, and economic conditions of their times but also say something about our own. Since the literature on modern urbanism continues to be far more extensive than that which exists for ancient urbanism, this book contributes to correcting that imbalance.

The database on ancient cities has been expanding as a result of ongoing excavations all over the world, but much of that work remains unpublished. These excavations are enabling scholars to document intra-city changes through time, city-to-city interaction, and changing relations between cities and their respective hinterlands. Scholars now are able to speak more confidently about the founding and functions of ancient cities, their diverse trade networks, their heterogeneous city plans and layouts, and their diverse lifespans and trajectories.

Our sample of ancient cities—both in terms of total number and the kinds of data available on their internal diversity—is larger than ever, allowing us to reevaluate earlier assertions and inferences about specific differences and shared commonalities. Although both kinds of information are significant—data that demonstrate differences between cities and those that document recurrent patterns—recent studies show that the diversity is not infinite and that key units of analysis (such as houses and neighborhoods) can be compared from city to city in meaningful ways. Today's archaeologists are in a very favorable position to link data to models, to combine written texts with excavation data, and to compare a much larger body of data from both Old World and New World cities.

Historical and Comparative Analyses

Historians, sociologists, archaeologists, political scientists, demographers, and geographers who analyze ancient and modern cities share similar concerns, even though their datasets can vary considerably. This book focuses on ancient cities because we are interested in understanding the functions and services that early cities offered their residents and the residents of subordinate towns, villages, and farmsteads. This volume contributes the kinds of information that will broaden and deepen the comparative study of urban lifestyles and urban institutions.

The comparative study of cities began in earnest in the nineteenth century when Numa Denis Fustel de Coulanges published *La Cité Antique*. That book was later translated into English and published as *The Ancient City* (1864, 1872, 1963). Although written more than 140 years ago, Fustel de Coulanges' book has a very modern character. His focus was comparative (comparing Greek and Roman cities), historical (analyzing each city and society through time), and explanatory (discussing integrative forces such as religious beliefs, kinship, and tolerance of diversity, as well as disintegrative forces such as competition among economic classes and ethnic groups). Fustel de Coulanges discussed the roles of individuals, groups, and institutions and how all of them changed during the lifespan of a city. He noted:

> The social tie was not easy to establish between those human beings who were so diverse, so free, so inconstant. To bring them under the rules of a community, to institute commandments and ensure obedience, to cause passion to give way to reason, and individual right to public right, there certainly was something necessary, stronger than material force, more respectable than interest, surer than a philosophical theory, more unchangeable than a convention; something that should dwell equally in all hearts, and should be all-powerful there. [Fustel de Coulanges 1963:132]

For Fustel de Coulanges, those social ties were the worship of ancestors, the rise of laws, and a shared religion. He saw cities as the final development in an evolutionary scheme. Fustel de Coulanges' first era consisted of the family with its household gods; followed by the phratry with its god; then the tribe and its god; and finally the city, in which "men conceived a god whose providence embraced this entire city" (1963:132). In the end, the city itself was characterized by a hierarchy of creeds and a hierarchy of association.

> With the ancients, a city was never formed by degrees, by the slow increase of the number of men and houses. They founded a city at once, all entire in a day; but the elements of the city needed to be first ready, and this was the most difficult, and ordinarily the largest work. As soon as the families, the phratries, and the tribes had agreed to unite and have the same worship, they immediately founded the city as a sanctuary for this common worship, and thus the foundation of a city was always a religious act. [Fustel de Coulanges 1963:134]

Here Fustel de Coulanges was only partly right. While some ancient cities may have been founded as a religious act and "all entire in a day," others were *not* established in that way. Nevertheless, divine reasons were often added retrospectively to explain why and how a city was founded. Fustel de Coulanges noted that the Greeks, like the Italians, believed that the site of a city should be chosen by the gods and revealed by auguries. The short life of a city could be explained retrospectively by saying that the founder had dared to build a city without consulting the oracle; this was the explanation as to why the city founded by the Spartan Dorieus lasted only three years (Fustel de Coulanges 1963:138). Consider, as another example, Fustel de Coulanges' version of the founding of Rome: "Before coming to the Palatine, [the Romans] had lived in Alba, or some other neighboring city.... A man could not quit his dwelling-place without taking with him his soil and his ancestors" (1963:136). Thus, a circular pit was excavated on the Palatine Hill, and each man threw in a little earth brought from his former home. The clods of earth placed in the pit were believed to contain the souls of their ancestors, and these reunited souls kept guard over their descendants: "At this same place Romulus set up an altar, and lighted a fire upon it. This was the holy fire of the city" (1963:137).

Around this altar the city of Rome allegedly arose. To be sure, this may be revisionist history. So far, no circular pit and altar have been found, and without a written document no archaeologist could be sure that the soil in such a pit was brought from former settlements, nor that the clods of earth were thought to contain the souls of their ancestors. However, similar rites of dedication and sanctification are widely known from other times and places.

When colonists or conquerors settled in a preexisting city, they might also perform a ceremony such as establishing new sacred fires or fixing their native gods in their new home. Such rites and offerings are what we would expect to find in the Roman world, but they have been noted for other geographic areas as well.

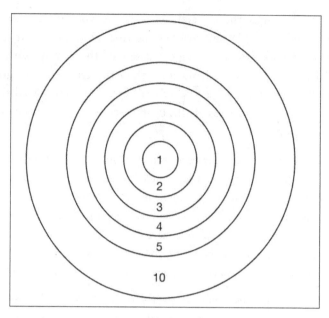

Figure 1.1. The concentric zone model consists of several rings: 1, city center; 2, factory district; 3, retrogressing neighborhoods; 4, workers' residences; 5, middle-class residences; and 10, commuters (redrawn from Burgess 1925:51).

How did the Romans view cities that fell into ruins? Camillus (cited by Fustel de Coulanges) says: "Our city was religiously founded; the gods themselves pointed out the place, and took up their abode here with our fathers. Ruined as it is, it still remains the dwelling of our national gods" (1963:141–142). Similar attitudes and explanations can be found in many parts of the world, from Italy to China to Mexico. Although both the founding and the abandonment of cities continue to be of enduring interest, most archaeologists can rarely isolate and confirm the causes. Indeed, Fustel de Coulanges was fortunate to have relevant and informative texts, an enormous advantage in understanding Greek, Roman, and other ancient cities of the world. When Fustel de Coulanges compared cities, he noted important similarities and differences, but it remained until the twentieth century for general models to emerge.

As the world became increasingly urbanized in the twentieth century, interest in the nature and development of cities grew correspondingly among social scientists. The models they developed have had a significant impact not only on scholarly studies of cities but also on practical policy making in the second half of the twentieth century. As we shall see, these studies also influenced the thinking of archaeologists who were actively assessing the effects of ancient urban growth during the later decades of the past century. We will discuss four of the most influential models (Berry and Wheeler 2005; Marcus 2000[1983b]).

1. In the 1920s and 1930s, the Department of Sociology at the University of Chicago had become home to several sociologists committed to the study of cities. Among these were Robert E. Park, Ernest W. Burgess, and Louis Wirth.

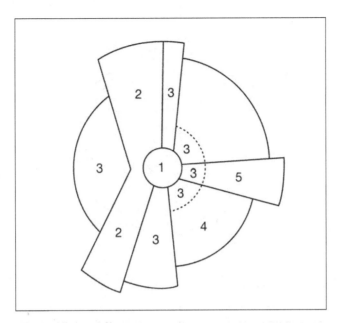

Figure 1.2. The sector model: 1, city center; 2, manufacturing district; 3, low-status residences; 4, medium-status residences; and 5, high-status residences (redrawn from Harris and Ullman 1945:figure 5).

The "Chicago School" saw the city as consisting of populations that had created a new environment. Some of the school's prominent advocates borrowed concepts from plant biology and animal ecology, such as competition and succession, and these concepts were applied in creative ways to the human environment of the city (Bulmer 1984; Burgess 1925, 1929; Park 1915; Park and Burgess 1924; Park et al. 1925; Wirth 1925, 1938).

Ernest Burgess (1925) developed the well-known "concentric zone model," based on the idea that the city has a single center from which growth proceeds outward (figure 1.1). His model—which featured Chicago and other modern cities—portrayed the city center as containing the central business district; outside of this, a zone (or ring) containing the factory district; then a zone of workers' residences; then a zone of middle- and upper-class residences; and, finally, an outer zone of commuters.

One of the key features of this concentric model was that socially and economically well-off individuals tended to move away from the center to occupy the outer ring. Critics of this model have noted that each zone is not as homogeneous as Burgess indicated. Nevertheless, as in all models, the staying power of Burgess's concentric zone model was that it was a simplified, idealized construct that was applicable to many different cities.

2. A second model, developed by the economist Homer Hoyt (1939), was the "sector model," today regarded as complementary to Burgess's concentric zone model. Hoyt's model (figure 1.2) showed that once there were differences in land use near the center of a city, those differences would often be maintained as the city expanded outward.

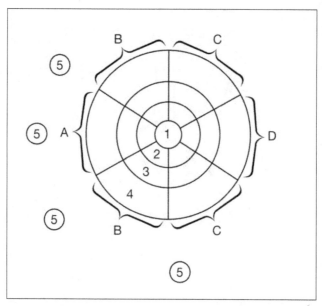

Figure 1.3. Idealized diagram of a British city that combines the principles of both the concentric zone model and the sector model: 1, city center; 2, transitional zone; 3, small houses in Sector B, large old houses in Sector A; 4, post-1918 residences, with post-1945 growth primarily on the periphery; 5, commuting-distance villages; Sector A, middle class; Sector B, lower middle class; Sector C, working class; and Sector D, industrial and lowest working class (redrawn from Mann 1965:96).

Thus, sectors of specific kinds of land use could grow outward as pie-shape wedges, crosscutting Burgess's concentric rings. Today's geographers have discovered that the sector model can be applied most readily to residential neighborhoods. For example, once an area of high-status houses has been established near a city center, new high-status residences will be constructed contiguous to them, perhaps growing outward axially along one of the major streets leading to and from the center or growing outward radially on all edges of the high-status zone. Another example comprises wards or quarters of the city that, while remaining relatively high-status, might come to be occupied by craftsmen, merchants, foreigners, or others. Within each sector there could also be gradations; for example, the sizes of factories, workshops, building lots, or houses might increase or decrease as one moves closer to the center.

Noting the value of both the concentric and sector models, later geographers sometimes combined them (figure 1.3), as Mann did (1965:96) to describe a British city.

3. A third model, developed by geographers Chauncy D. Harris and Edward L. Ullman (1945), was the "multiple nuclei model," which shows, as its name implies, that (a) a city can develop multiple nuclei and absorb pre-existing nuclei and (b) as a city grows, it can become decentralized and develop distinct manufacturing areas with specialized occupations and diverse personnel. Rather than have a single dominant nucleus or downtown, such cities can have a series of virtually equal nuclei that, once established, tend to be maintained (figure 1.4). In some cities, these nuclei have

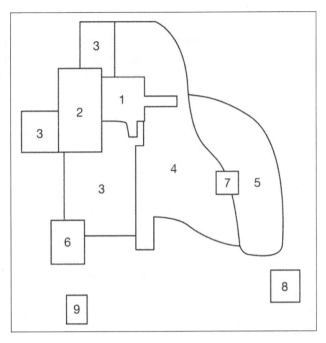

Figure 1.4. The multiple nuclei model: 1, central business district; 2, wholesale light manufacturing; 3, lower-status residences; 4, medium-status residences; 5, higher-status residences; 6, heavy manufacturing; 7, outlying business district; 8, residential suburb; and 9, industrial suburb (redrawn from Harris and Ullman 1945:figure 5).

existed from the city's beginning. In others, they developed as the growth of the city stimulated craft or occupational specialization that attracted more people to the same nucleus.

4. A fourth influential model, developed by Louis Wirth (1938), focused on residential areas in which people of similar origin, class, or occupation tended to live in the same neighborhood. Since these residents wanted to live with others of similar origin, occupation, or income, various parts of the city came to be identified with a particular social class, ethnic group, or occupation.

Each of these four models builds directly on its predecessor, and all highlight general principles that have enduring relevance to our understanding of ancient cities, even if some of their specific assumptions and applications do not fit all cities or all eras. All such models, however, have been subjected to criticism, usually when they fail to explain every case. According to some critiques, these models tend to pay too little attention to the roles played by individuals (human agents) and their decision making, as well as the important roles played by culture, symbolism, ritual, and religion. Ironically, these topics were the very strengths of early studies like Fustel de Coulanges' *The Ancient City*, in which he discussed individuals, sacred symbols, and rituals as conducted in ancient Greek and Roman cities.

In this burgeoning twentieth-century literature, we also find contrasts between scholars who saw the decision making of elites as crucial in city making and those more concerned with commoners. On the one hand, as the famous thirteenth-century and early fourteenth-century historian Ibn Khaldun once said, "dynasties and royal authority are absolutely necessary for the building of cities and the planning of towns" (quoted in Rosenthal 1958:235). On the other hand, Aston and Bond (1976:21) note: "Towns are built by and for people. Their regional and local sitings are the result of decisions taken by people and not of some inevitable physical control." Kevin Lynch (1981) affirms that cities are not organisms that reproduce or repair themselves, but rather entities built by people.

In today's postmodern intellectual atmosphere, studying an individual person or agent whose name we know is appealing, as is focusing on the unique qualities of a specific city. However, such an approach has its drawbacks, as noted by Anthony Orum and Xiangming Chen:

> Another danger is that each city, in particular, its history and institutions, is taken to be so unique that it becomes next to impossible to understand what general lessons it has to offer to the urban analyst. In brief, then, historical/institutional analyses must guard against the opposite danger of abstract theories—the danger of detail, of becoming convinced that history is all contingencies and no general process. [Orum and Chen 2003:55]

The complement to the study of individual agents was the comparative approach, as exemplified by V. Gordon Childe (1950) and Lewis Mumford (1961). These scholars sought to generalize and look for similarities and recurrent patterns. They were aware that the city shared many features inherited from towns and villages, but they isolated novel features that appeared for the first time in the urban matrix we call a city. Among the interrelated novelties discussed by Childe (1950) were greater community size, larger populations, higher densities of people, agricultural surpluses, truly monumental public buildings, full-time craft specialization, systems of counting and recordkeeping, a writing system, regular foreign trade and subsidized traders, officials, and priests. Similarly, "in the city specialized work became for the first time an all-day, year-round occupation" (Mumford 1961:103). Mumford went on to say, "With the growth of numbers and the increase of wealth in the city rose another kind of division: that between the rich and the poor, which came in with the next great innovation of urban life, the institution of property" (1961:107). Referring to the social constitution of the city, Mumford says:

> If it dismembered the whole man and forced him to spend a long lifetime at a single task, it re-assembled him in a new collective entity; so that while his individual life might be narrow and constrained, the urban pattern so woven was all the richer in texture because of the variegated threads that formed it. [Mumford 1961:109]

In addition to embracing the comparative approach of Childe and Mumford, scholars sought to describe evolutionary stages in the life of the city. A sequence of six stages was suggested by Leo F. Schnore (1965) and later evaluated and synthesized by David I. Scargill (1979:214–215), as follows:

1. First, a "reversed Burgess" pattern in which high-status groups live in the city center, with the poor on the periphery
2. Next, a stage in which the lowest-status groups are evenly spread throughout the city
3. Then, an intermediate stage in which the highest-status and lowest-status groups are concentrated in the center, while a middle class lives in the suburbs
4. Then, an "almost Burgess" city, which differs from Stage 5 in the concentration of the very highest-status groups in the center
5. Next, the "Burgess pattern," with low-status groups in the center and high-status groups in the suburbs
6. Finally, a stage in which low-status groups live in the suburbs

Even though Schnore's six evolutionary stages were designed to characterize modern cities, where people are able to choose where they want to live, some aspects of each stage (as well as the order of the changes) are worth evaluating against the developmental cycles and stages of ancient cities. Archaeologists are uniquely positioned to confirm, reject, or modify these stages and to formulate developmental sequences, based on the excavation of stratigraphic levels and the layout of superimposed cities.

The models developed by Burgess, Hoyt, Schnore, and others emphasized the downtown or city center. This emphasis led to the "principle of centrality," a general concept developed in several books by geographers and others. Examples of such books would be James Bird's *Centrality and Cities* (1977) and Nicos Polydorides' *The Concept of Centrality in Urban Form and Structure* (1983). This principle of centrality sought to explain the symbolic, economic, and administrative roles played by the city center and that center's impact on centripetal and centrifugal forces.

Polydorides (1983:1) defines the city center as "that particular area of the city in which urban activities and flows of people, vehicles, goods, and messages are most concentrated. The same area usually has a highly dense and conspicuous built form as well." He considers the city core to be the dependent variable, while the localization of authority is the independent variable. ("Authority" is here defined as the legitimate control of decision making in the political and economic processes of the city.) In Polydorides' model, authority and free choice are seen as complementary rather than exclusive, at least in the modern city. To be sure, some students of the ancient city have assumed that the royal family and top administrators controlled the city and made all the decisions. Other scholars, in contrast, would argue that we have continually underestimated the role of individual commoners, craftsmen, and ordinary city dwellers (Lohse and Valdez 2003; Marcus 2000 [1983b]; M. L. Smith 2003b).

In traditional or prehistoric cities, central authorities sometimes brought outside labor into the city center to construct public buildings. Among the Yoruba, for example, corvée labor was required of all those living near the city center, as well as those living in subordinate towns. Specifically, maintenance and repairs were the responsibility of men from an inner ring of nine settlements in close proximity to the palace, while actual new construction was undertaken by men brought in from settlements throughout the territory (Ojo 1966).

What a City Is and Isn't

In 1950 Childe said: "The concept of 'city' is notoriously hard to define." And in 1967 Horace Miner famously said, "Everyone knows what a city is, except the experts" (1967:3). Some scholars might still agree with both of these statements, even though significant progress has been made by archaeologists who continue to document key characteristics through the careful excavation of ancient cities.

Different disciplines and subfields, however, still define "city" in a variety of ways. Many sociologists consider cities to be *"places—that is, specific locations in space that provide an anchor and a meaning to who we are*. It is this quality of cities—this sense of their placeness and our own connection to places—that is one of the most fundamental but also most unacknowledged, concepts of urban social science" (Orum and Chen 2003:1). This sense of "placeness" becomes meaningful through a sense of individual identity, of who we are; a sense of community, of being a part of a larger group, whether a family or a neighborhood; a sense of a past and a future, of a place behind us and a place ahead of us; and a sense of being at home, of being comfortable, of being, as it were, in place (Orum and Chen 2003:11). Others have argued that "place" (as opposed to "space") can be thought of as the location where people live, work, and undertake activities (Relph 1976).

Many scholars, of course, see the city as an experience rather than simply a place. A few definitions will suggest the diversity of views. Louis Wirth (1938:8) defined a city as a "relatively large, dense, and permanent settlement of socially heterogeneous individuals." Gideon Sjöberg (1960:83) specified that it had "little more than 10,000 and perhaps only 5,000 persons." For other scholars, the total number of people involved is not the main concern. Spiro Kostof focused instead on the crowding and concentration of people:

> Cities are places where a certain energized crowding of people takes place. This has nothing to do with absolute size or with absolute numbers: it has to do with settlement density. The vast majority of towns in the pre-industrial world were small: a population of 2,000 or less was not uncommon, and one of 10,000 would be noteworthy. [Kostof 1991:37]

Scholars such as Anthony Leeds (1980) refused to distinguish between cities and towns, indicating that both cities and towns are in all aspects an urban society, with "rural" referring "only to a set of specialities of an urban society characterized by being linked (under any technology known) to specific geographical spaces" (as cited in Southall 1998). Southall (1973a:6) focused on the greater level of interaction in urban settings: "Cities and urban life have been distinguished in all times and places by a high density of social interaction relative to the wider society in which they were situated." Southall also considered the progressive differentiation of social roles, saying, "The great proliferation of differentiated roles has in the long run been more in the field of economic and occupational roles than anywhere else, with voluntary associations next in importance; so it is in these fields that the greatest heterogeneity of the urban social person has developed" (Southall 1973b:83).

As Renfrew and others emphasize (in this volume), it is not always a good idea to create an ideal category called *the* city, and one of the reasons is that there are many different kinds of cities. The diversity of cities is one theme, and so is their internal complexity and heterogeneity. This view is illustrated by Kostof's statements. "Cities are places where there is a specialized differentiation of work—whether people are priests or craftsmen or soldiers—and where wealth is not equally distributed among the citizens. These distinctions create social hierarchies: the rich are more powerful than the poor; the priest is more important than the artisan. Social heterogeneity is also axiomatic" (Kostof 1991:37–38). Kostof (1985), in particular, phrases his list of urban elements in a way that is especially useful to archaeologists, since they involve the ground plans of buildings that could be recognizable during excavation. "The city presents us with a new set of environmental ideas, such as the street, the public square, the defensive wall and its gates. It crowds our discussion with a score of building inventions—for example, the canal and the granary, the palace and the bath, the market, the bakery, shops, restaurants, and libraries" (Kostof 1985:43).

Here, then, are some of the elements often invoked in definitions of the city:

1. Heterogeneous people, occupations, crafts, classes, and statuses
2. Diverse political, social, religious, economic, and administrative buildings, institutions, wards, neighborhoods, and associated personnel (figures 1.5–1.7)
3. Dense packing or crowding of residential and nonresidential structures (figures 1.5–1.6)
4. A monumental core of unique buildings (for example, a cathedral or temple, a library, a palace, a central market, a courthouse, or a set of administrative buildings) (figures 1.6–1.7)
5. A skyline or "city profile" that shows maximum building height at the center of the city and less and less height as one moves away from the city center (figure 1.8)
6. A central focus—sometimes a sacred center, whose access was restricted and where temples predominated, and sometimes an administrative center where governmental buildings were concentrated (figures 1.6–1.8)
7. Special organizational features, such as grid-like modules like city blocks, streets, city walls, ward or barrio walls, canals, sewers, aqueducts, parks, and public squares (figures 1.7–1.10)

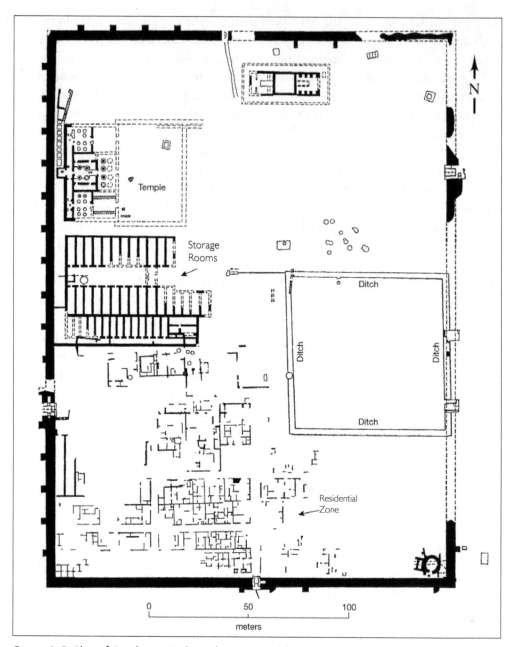

Figure 1.5. Plan of Sesebi, an Eighteenth Dynasty settlement in Nubia. Sesebi's streets were constructed on a grid, and the settlement was divided into various sectors: residential, storage, administrative, and religious. After the reign of Akhenaten, who founded the temples along the northwest wall, Sesebi grew in a more haphazard manner (redrawn from W. Y. Adams 1977:figure 34).

Inevitably, of course, scholars differ as to how these elements are linked to one another, and they differ in their explanation as to how and why such elements appear when these do in various cities. Some scholars have chosen to concentrate more on the

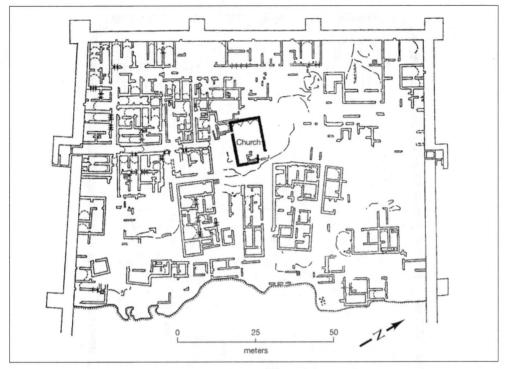

Figure 1.6. Plan of Ikhmindi, a walled city in the early Christian period, whose plan and construction differed significantly from those of ordinary medieval villages. Inside the walls we see evidence for the planning of residential units, which contrasted with the typically less structured "plan" of most contemporary Nubian communities. In addition, we see that a large square area was enclosed within a massive stone wall reinforced by external bastions and corner towers (redrawn from W. Y. Adams 1977:figure 76).

functions and roles of the city than on a list of elements. For example, in speaking of ancient Greek and Roman cities, Owens says:

> Within the Graeco-Roman world the city fulfilled various functions, and these functions affected its physical and architectural development. Until the reality of the pax Romana, the need for defence remained paramount. Cities were located with a view to the natural defensive qualities of the site.... The political, economic, social and religious functions of the city are reflected in its public buildings and their location within the urban environment. [Owens 1991:3]

The city, adds Eric Wolf (1966:11), is "a settlement in which a combination of functions are exercised, and which becomes useful because in time greater efficiency is obtained by having these functions concentrated in one site." Some scholars single out the symbolic and religious role of the city, showing how the city symbolizes the imposition of order on the landscape. For example, in speaking of the Chinese city, Tuan says:

Introduction   15

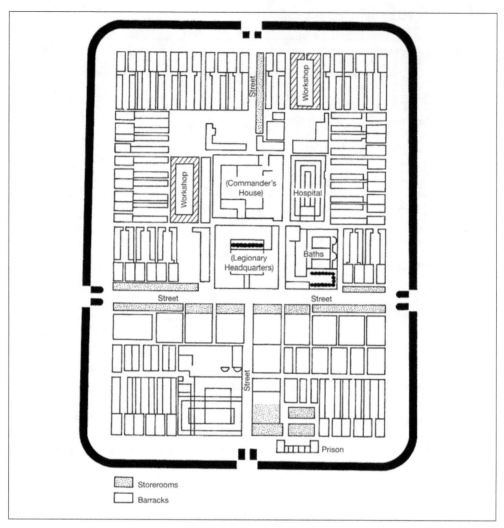

Figure 1.7. Army camps (castra) were established by the Romans throughout their territory, and this fort, Novaesium, in Germany, is a good example of a standardized plan with straight streets, the commander's headquarters in the center, and barracks and workshops around the periphery (redrawn by K. Clahassey from Gates 2003:figure 19.3).

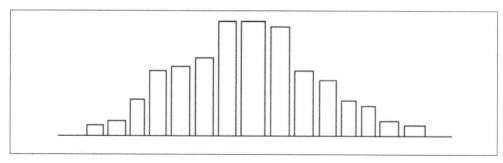

Figure 1.8. Idealized "city profile" that shows the tallest buildings in the center and decreasing building height as one moves away from the city center (created by K. Clahassey).

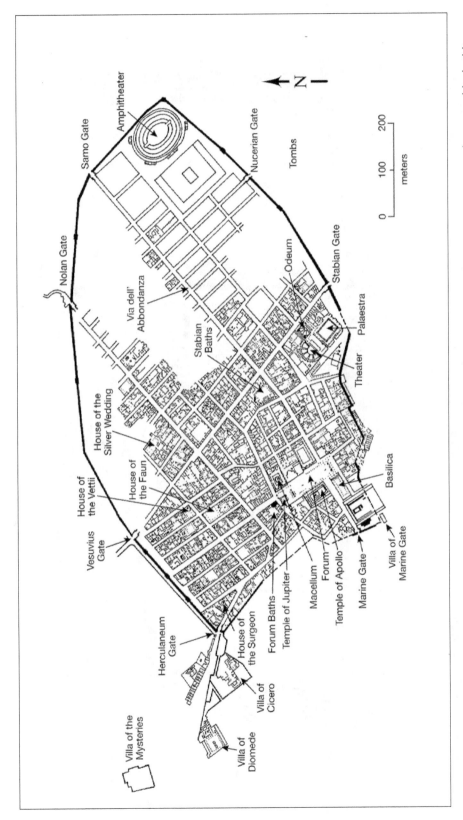

Figure 1.9. The city of Pompeii, with its ca. 15,000 people, was destroyed by a volcanic eruption ca. AD 79. Its streets, residences, public buildings, temples, baths, amphitheater, theater, and basilica all show planning (redrawn by K. Clahassey from Gates 2003:figure 21.2).

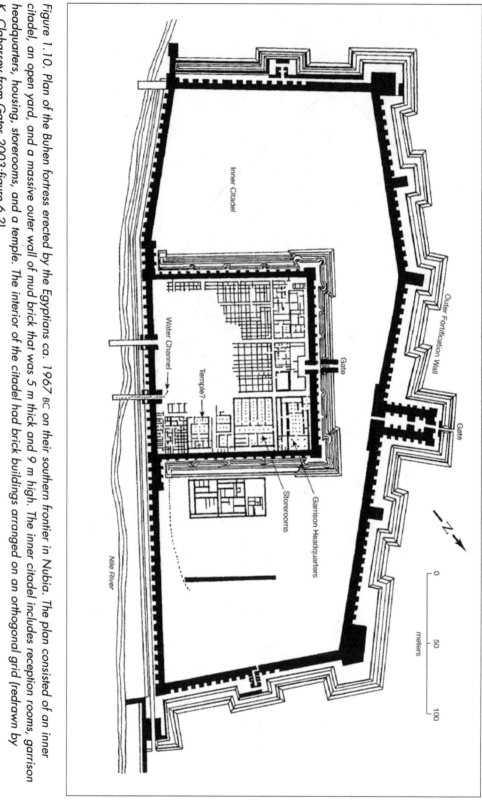

Figure 1.10. Plan of the Buhen fortress erected by the Egyptians ca. 1967 BC on their southern frontier in Nubia. The plan consisted of an inner citadel, an open yard, and a massive outer wall of mud brick that was 5 m thick and 9 m high. The inner citadel includes reception rooms, garrison headquarters, housing, storerooms, and a temple. The interior of the citadel had brick buildings arranged on an orthogonal grid (redrawn by K. Clahassey from Gates 2003:figure 6.2).

> The regular motions of the stars were to be translated architecturally and ritually to space and time on earth. The walled city oriented to the cardinal directions, the positioning of the twelve city gates, the location of the royal compound and the alignment of the principal axial street were given a geometric pattern that reflected the order to be found in heaven. The key concept was built on the related notions of rectilinearity, order, and rectitude. This key concept acquired architectural and social forms that were then imposed on earth, for the earth itself lacked paradigms of perfect order. [Tuan 1968:185]

Indeed, scholars like Wheatley (1971) have noted that a Chinese city can be thought of as a microcosm of the cosmos.

Inevitably, there have been scholars who find ancient and modern cities too different from one another to be classified in similar ways (Sjöberg 1960; Wheatley 1972). However, Monica Smith, who has studied South Asian cities, disagrees:

> Rather than seeing cities as fundamentally changed by the advent of the Industrial Revolution and the global connections of the modern world, new anthropological research suggests that both ancient and modern cities are the result of a limited range of configurations that structure human action in concentrated populations. [Smith 2003a:2]

If Monica Smith is correct, the majority of cities (one always hesitates to say "all") are the result of a limited range of configurations once people are concentrated in one place. This limited range of configurations will likely be evident to the readers of this volume, who will indeed see many similarities despite regional differences. The significance of this point is that if a limited range of configurations does exist, a single, widely agreed-upon definition for the city may one day be possible.

Sociologists and geographers have occasionally been able to characterize an entire city from the detailed information that can be gleaned from a city map; census data; lists of payrolls, taxpayers, or property owners; or comprehensive questionnaires covering all households, their occupants, and their incomes. Unfortunately, comparable data are virtually impossible for archaeologists to obtain, because they can never dig whole cities. Instead, archaeologists have to characterize a huge city from the small percentage (perhaps 1–10 percent) of the site that they have meticulously excavated.

One productive strategy has been to excavate units small enough to be exposed in their entirety—houses, features, and production areas of various kinds. Since some of the diversity within a city can be revealed by house-to-house inventories, such household data are providing insights on intra-neighborhood heterogeneity. We believe that more attention should be paid to the neighborhood, an intermediate-size unit that falls part way between the house and the city. Excavating neighborhoods complements both the data from the city as a whole (resulting from surface collections, aerial photos, and mapping) and the data from individual houses. So far, however, projects devoted to the excavation of whole neighborhoods are still rare (Stone 1987; Woolley and Mallowan 1976).

There was general agreement at the Sackler Colloquium that large size alone does not make a city. To be a city, a place has to have the services, public institutions, and internal diversity that set cities apart from large villages. While some writers have proclaimed Jericho on the West Bank, Khirokitia in Cyprus, and Çatal Höyük in Turkey to be "cities," most seminar participants did not agree. As Renfrew notes in chapter 2, Çatal Höyük lacks a monumental core and has no administrative center with public buildings and public administrators, simply a large number of residences. Reader (2004:16) had already called Çatal Höyük "more of an overgrown village than a city" and went on to say:

> The point is that for archaeologists and historians the most meaningful difference between a village and a city has nothing to do with size; it is instead a measure of social and economic differentiation within the communities. In this scheme of things, a place occupied exclusively by people who had left the land to become full-time craftsmen, merchants, priests and civil servants was a city, while anywhere occupied principally by farmers was a village. [Reader 2004:16]

For John Reader (2004:17), "the most remarkable feature of Çatal Höyük is that families lived in such close proximity to one another." While Reader would not necessarily agree, many Near Eastern archaeologists have pointed out that Çatal Höyük presented continuous blank, doorless walls to the outside world, as if defense were a consideration. In effect, the Neolithic farmers of the Konya Plain chose to live in one, large, less vulnerable settlement rather than in multiple, small, vulnerable villages (Hodder 2006).

The Origins of Cities

In addition to describing the form and function of cities, scholars are interested in determining why and how cities originated. "Precisely how it all started is unclear. Revolution implies a sudden break, but it may have been in several places at once, and with varying motives, that the idea of the city gradually took root. At this stage of our knowledge, we must assign the origin of the city-form to western Asia" (Kostof 1985:46).

Why would people leave a rural lifestyle characterized by open spaces and less crowding? In some parts of the world, such as 'Ubaid-Uruk Mesopotamia and highland Mesoamerican valleys in Oaxaca and Morelos, it is strongly suspected that one motivation was protection from raiding. The archaeological evidence sometimes consists of a defensive ditch, moat, palisade, or wall.

V. Gordon Childe (1950) saw cities arising where people lived next to rivers, where irrigation agriculture was practiced, and where agricultural surpluses could be produced to support craft specialists. Steady surpluses allowed some members of society to become full-time administrators, officials, scribes, and priests. The presence of elite residences and discrete types of monumental public buildings may suggest that urbanization was directed from the top down by political and religious leaders. Within the early city, craft specialization could lead to densely packed houses and associated workshops. Public temples could attract people to the center of an emerging city, where political agendas cloaked in religion were disseminated. In at least a few cases, the city itself was viewed as a sacred symbol or cosmogram to which people were drawn (Laur 2002; Malville 2000; Singh 1994; Wright 1977).

> The Chinese city was established only after an array of geomantic considerations had been satisfied; it was constructed as an axis mundi, an omphalos incorporating the powerful centripetality of that symbol; and it was laid out as a terrestrial image of the cosmos, a schema involving cardinal axiality and orientation, and, as a corollary, strong architectural emphasis on the main gates. [Wheatley 1971:481]

Thus, various concerns—the safety and defense of the rulers or general population, economic gain through craft production, the promotion of state religion through urban cosmograms, and the legitimization of new sociopolitical institutions—played greater or lesser roles at different times and places.

Another less tangible, but nonetheless important, motivation for migration to cities may have been the sheer concentration of diverse functions, services, and activities in the new urban centers. This magnet was the exciting variety of new experiences available (or what might be termed the "How are you going to keep them down on the farm once they have seen Paree?" perspective).

Even such archaeological features as city walls had diverse functions and changed over time. Some cities most likely had constructed walls for protection against attack (Flannery and Marcus 2003; Zou Heng 1987). Others did it to define sacred space at the center of a ceremonial center (Malville and Gujral 2000; Wheatley 1971) or to restrict access to the residence of the elite who occupied the inner city (Marcus 2000 [1983b]). In some settlements, the wall restricted access only to a monumental core or center; most of the private houses extended for a considerable distance outside the wall.

In some cases, "safety in numbers" resulted in cities so large that a wall was rendered unnecessary. Such cities deliberately became so large that they depopulated the surrounding hinterland, thereby creating a buffer zone that may also have discouraged attack. As von Falkenhausen notes in chapter 11, one of the largest unwalled settlements from China's Longshan period is Xinzhai in Mi Xian (Henan), which, with a size of 70 ha, is more than thirty times the size of the only known contemporaneous walled enclosure in the area, Wangchenggang. In Mesoamerica, Teotihuacan may have achieved the same level of invulnerability by growing to 20 sq km.

Conversely, having defensive works did not make a place a city. Many of the world's early villages had such works—a palisade at San José Mogote in Mexico, a wall at Tell Maghzaliyah in Iraq, and ditches and moats at the early Chinese villages of Banpocun and Jiangzhai.

How the Ancients Saw Cities

Kenneth Hirth's use of the term *altepetl* for the Aztec city and its hinterland (chapter 14) brings us to another important topic: ancient peoples saw their cities very differently from the way modern Western scholars see them. Indeed, a case could be made for using the ancients' own terms and definitions rather than our own. Let us look now at a sample of some of the ways non-Western cultures have defined their cities.

Among the Yoruba of West Africa, it was the presence of an *oba* (sacred king) living in a royal palace (*afin*) that defined the city (*ilú*). The Yoruba ilú did not stop at the walls of the city but extended out into farmland that supported and sustained it (Krapf-Askari 1969). This is reminiscent of the Aztec term *altepetl*, which referred simultaneously to the city and its province or political realm. The Aztecs' neighbors, the Zapotec, used the term *queche* for "city" or "populated center." *Queche* was also the root of other words, including *quechenatale*, which referred to the province headed by the city, showing us that, as in the Aztec case, a province was defined as the territory controlled by the ruler of a city.

Similarly, the Maya term *cacab* referred both to the town and to the land belonging to it. Like the Yoruba, the Maya consider the land, people, and minor settlements controlled by one ruler (who usually lived in a city) to be the meaningful unit. The fact that city and province could all be subsumed under the same term is important; it shows that the conceptual link between the ruler and his territory transcended urban space. Elsewhere in Mesoamerica it was equally difficult to remove the city from its political and economic landscape, including its regional hierarchy. Among the Quiché and Pokom of highland Guatemala, the term *tinamit* meant that "the town name extended over all the lands belonging to it; the names of hamlets and areas were subsumed" (Miles 1957:771).

In their hieroglyphic texts, the Classic Maya recorded the names of both the capital cities and the polities administered by their rulers. For example, the ruler of the city we call Calakmul (whose ancient name was Oxte Tun) controlled a state called Kaan. The ruler of Mutal (known today as Tikal) also controlled a state of the same name. These large Maya cities might have held 50,000 or more people at their peak, and estimates of their entire polities' populations would number in the hundreds of thousands, if not more.

Occasionally, some scholars have referred to such large states as "city-states," but we find it inappropriate. Such authorities on the polis as Mogens Hansen (2000a:17) define the "city-state" as a micro-state. Thus, "the city-state is what we today would call a specific type of micro-state and its smallness concerns the size of its territory as well as its population" (Hansen 2000a:17). Hansen goes on to say that "there is virtually no limit to how small a city-state can be, and city-states with a territory of less than 10 km^2 are attested"; at the upper end of the scale "the territory of a city-state may cover ca. 3,000 km^2 max. Larger city-states are indeed attested, but then they are no longer city-states to the same extent as their smaller neighbours" (2000a:17).

Clearly, the territories controlled by Tikal and Calakmul do *not* fit Hansen's definition of a "city-state," but there were some micro-states wedged in between some of the larger Maya states. To draw an analogy with Europe, consider Andorra, which Hansen (2000a:19) calls a micro-state and a city-state covering 470 sq km, whose entire population is only 46,000 people, wedged in between France and Spain. Similar micro-states were known among the Postclassic Mixtec and Aztec of Mexico and the Highland Maya of Guatemala. There is growing evidence that many of the city-states were created by the breakup of earlier large states (Marcus 1992a, 1998). Recently, Hansen (2000a:29) noted: "Emergence of a city-state culture by disintegration of a larger political unit is much more common than I imagined in 1991."

Separating a city from its politically controlled territory may be heuristically useful for the creation of a "city" category, but as we have seen, such an exercise does not conform to the reality of indigenous categories. The important point for many ethnic groups was that an individual belonged to a region controlled by a specific ruler, to whom he owed allegiance and tribute and from whom he received protection and civic-ceremonial leadership. Unless the city had a wall surrounding it, the boundary between "city" and "countryside" was far less striking to native peoples than to today's archaeologist. Indeed, the residence of the ruler (and the associated buildings in which he was active) was probably a more important unit for the purpose of determining the top of regional hierarchies than the mass of commoners.

To be sure, the dichotomies of urban/rural and urban/folk were important to scholars like Louis Wirth (1944) and Robert Redfield (1941) (see discussions in Miner 1952; Wilcox 2004). But Redfield later changed his dichotomy to a "folk–urban continuum" to emphasize the interdependent relationship of city and countryside. Yi-Fu Tuan (1978) also went beyond the dichotomy of "city" and "countryside," suggesting that we employ a continuous scale to evaluate each settlement along three dimensions—how close to nature and food production each city was, how close to the natural rhythms of day and night, and how much each city was affected by the seasons.

Others such as Dyos and Wolff (1973:899) have noted that even "in the nineteenth century no English city had severed itself from rural connections. The largest of them still conducted extensive backyard agriculture, not merely half-a-dozen hens in a coop of soapboxes, but cow-stalls, sheep-folds, pig-sties." Similarly, Kostof says:

> Cities are places that are intimately engaged with their countryside, that have a territory that feeds them and which they protect and provide services for. The separation of town and country...is thoroughly injudicious. Roman towns do not exist apart from their centuriated land roundabout; great Italian communes like Florence and Siena could not exist without their contado; and the same is true of New England towns and their fields and commons. Polis, civitas, commune, township—all these are terms that apply to an urban settlement and its region. [Kostof 1991:38]

Scholars are not in agreement as to whether a society can have urbanism before the state emerges or whether the state must come first (Possehl 1998). One reason for this lack of agreement is the diversity of cases worldwide. For the Middle Niger River of Africa, for example, McIntosh and McIntosh (2003:105) believe that cities appeared before the state and without a centralized hierarchy of any kind.

The Value of Comparative Studies

"Each city, like every other object in nature, is, in a sense, unique," said Louis Wirth (1925:175). Harris and Ullman (1945:7) agreed that "each city is unique in detail" but reminded us that each "resembles others in function and pattern." Most scholars today, with the exception of postmodernists, concur that while noting the differences between cities, we should also focus on similarities in pattern and function. Beyond this concurrence, however, lies a wide variety of cautionary statements, as the following sample of opinions would indicate:

> Comparative study of urbanism is of course essential, and when adequately informed about the Chinese case, it will be fruitful. Abstracting the seemingly comparable elements to construct broad generalizations, however, must be done with considerable understanding of peculiarly Chinese conditions. [Mote 1977:110]
>
> The sociology of urban history develops categories which are useful as guides in the study of cities. Without such guideposts, we would not be in a position to bring order and direction into the multitude of facts which we encounter. However, the directive principles are derived from a comparative study of the phenomena themselves and the accepted categories, in turn, must be subject to revision at all times. One might say that they are the forests which do not exist without the trees. [Comhaire 1962:39]
>
> The key, then, is to seek to enter the essence of each place at the time of its belle époque: to understand the precise conjuncture of forces that caused it to burst forth as it did. Out of that, it should be possible to tease out the general, the basic, the structural forces from those that are merely contingent and complementary; and then, as a result, to generalize as to the degree of commonality these places share, and on the other hand the residual forces that are special to each case. [Hall 1998:21]
>
> The fact is that the constructed-types approach assumes a coincidence in covariation among key variables that seldom obtains in the real world. In my view, a more productive approach to understanding phenomena within any domain is to ask what covaries with what. To what extent does a particular function vary with scale? How do morphological features change along with the different types of urban functions? If we could ascertain which empirical and analytical features of urban phenomena in China varied together in time and space, we would be in a better position to say something about cause and effect, about the direction of change, and about systemic relationship within

> the domain of Chinese cities. We would find, furthermore, that many propositions concerning covariation that hold for Chinese cities would also hold, or on first principles ought to hold, for analytically or geographically more inclusive urban domains. [Skinner 1977:5]
>
> If structural regularities are ultimately elucidated, then it is practically certain that they will be manifested in shared functions and in trends in systemic change rather than in form. [Wheatley 1972:601]

This book's case studies augment the growing database on ancient cities, allowing us to reevaluate what have been regarded as similarities and differences (Adams 1960, 1966, 1972; Andrews 1995; Arnauld and Michelet 2004; Benet 1963; Benevolo 1967, 1980; Braidwood and Willey 1962; Chakrabarti 1995; Doxiadis 1968; Fox 1977; Hall 1998; Hardoy 1968, 1973; Hauser and Schnore 1965; Kenoyer 1998; Kostof 1985, 1991, 1992; Kraeling and Adams 1960; Nas 1993; Nichols and Charlton 1997; Reader 2004; Redfield and Singer 1954; Robson and Regan 1972; Sanders et al. 2003; Scargill 1979; Sennett 1969; Sjöberg 1960; M. L. Smith 2003a, 2006; Southall 1998; Southall et al. 1985; Trigger 2003; van de Mieroop 1997; Weber 1962 [1958]; Wheatley 1978, 1983; Whitfield 1969).

Conclusion

Many scholars in fields as disparate as architecture and urban planning, economics and geography, history and archaeology, have expressed an increasing interest in the growth and development of ancient cities. One factor leading to this burgeoning interest was that much of the modern world was being converted into cities. A second factor was the growing intellectual curiosity about how many kinds of cities had existed in the past and how many diverse functions they had served. Still a third factor was an interest in trying to answer two major questions: how do cities operate, and why do some cities thrive while others shrivel?

It became clear that data from various parts of the world would allow us to modify or reject former "truths" and provide new inferences about the life cycle of the city, from its founding, through its growth and demise, and in some cases into the present. We therefore decided to invite ten scholars to discuss their recent fieldwork in different ancient cities, and these diverse case studies can be seen in chapters 6 through 15.

To put those case studies into comparative perspective, we asked two scholars (Renfrew and Trigger) to develop broad overviews (see chapters 2 and 3, respectively). We asked two scholars (Hansen and Butzer) to comment on the ten case studies in this book, as well as suggest new directions to enhance the study of prehistoric urbanism (see chapters 4 and 5, respectively).

The study of ancient cities is a field in which archaeologists are uniquely positioned to speak to a wider audience, one stretching far beyond the limits of their discipline. In this volume, anthropological and Classical archaeologists have worked side by side. Their efforts have been aided by geographers, geologists, historians, and philologists, as well as by participants who attended the colloquium. The resulting chapters will give the reader a worldwide perspective on the ancient city, and the understanding of future archaeologists—having been broadened by the aid of colleagues from other fields—will be lifted beyond its original confines.

part two
OVERVIEWS AND COMMENTARY ON THE CASE STUDIES

two
The City through Time and Space
Transformations of Centrality

Colin Renfrew

Literature on the ancient city is now vast, and several of this volume's contributors, not least Bruce Trigger (2003), command it more effectively than I. Is there something about the city that makes it a general (but not a universal) feature of the human condition, at least under certain conditions? Just what are the conditions that favor the emergence of cities? And, in particular, what do cities in very different times and places have in common? Are there features of urbanization that are a recurrent feature of human societies, and others that are not?

Can we see the city as a very general form, in the same sense that a galaxy, a planetary system, a living cell, or a complex living organism has form? Every city is, of course, unique, and "thick description" may emphasize the unique properties in each specific case. But to what extent can we make some generalizations that may have validity through time and across space? George Cowgill (2004:525), in a useful recent review, has cautioned against speaking of "the" city: "This leads us toward reification and essentialization of categories and creates unnecessary conceptual difficulties. It is far better to think of 'cities' or 'a' city, but never of 'the' city." But these are conceptual difficulties that must sometimes be faced, and I hope that we can do so here.

One of the central themes of the 2005 Sackler colloquium was the emergence of the city as a phenomenon seen at different times and places. Urbanism seems to occur spontaneously in a wide range of different contexts. It is a feature that, so far as we know, is restricted to our own species, although parallels with the complex societies of social insects have been noted since the days of the Ancient Greek dramatists Aeschylus' *Myrmidons* or Aristophanes' *The Wasps* (Henderson 1998). But it is not a feature universal to human communities, whereas social formations seen in other species are often universal features of the species in question. In this way the city is one of the most obvious and the most concrete, independently recurring (that is, independently emerging) features in human experience and thus perhaps indicative of what is latent and potential in all humans. Perhaps we can revisit that point together with an aspiration I first expressed more than twenty-five years ago (Renfrew 1979a:16): "The first lesson, if we want an *explanatory archaeology*, may be that we have to turn first to a *comparative archaeology*, and seek to observe affinities of form in whatever aspect, such as may indicate the working of fundamentally similar general processes."

It has been said that all archaeological lectures should begin with Stonehenge, our great Neolithic monument in southern England, dating from the third millennium BC. Looking at Stonehenge serves to focus attention on what a city is not. But Stonehenge, like other early monuments of prehistoric Europe, such as the Ring of Brodgar in Orkney, was certainly a center. We may regard it as a ritual center and probably the center also of a regional social unit, a deliberately planned monument representing an estimated 30 million hours of work. This and other prehistoric monuments might well be regarded as "cosmograms," thus anticipating a feature recognized for many early cities (Wheatley 1971). But there is no evidence of permanent residents at Stonehenge, and the population density was probably so low as to make urban settlement impractical at the time in Britain, before 2000 BC. Stonehenge reminds us that a food-producing economy sufficient to sustain a population density of perhaps a minimum of ten persons per square kilometer is a necessary condition for urbanization.

It may be pertinent also to take another site, several millennia earlier than Stonehenge, and offer it as a further example of what a city is not, namely, Çatal Höyük, the early Neolithic settlement in central Anatolia excavated by James Mellaart (1967) and more recently by Ian Hodder (1996, 2000). This was a settlement that has an agglomerate plan (agglutinated residences) within an area of approximately 32 acres, and it is not uncommonly referred to as a city by historical geographers (Southall 1998:23–27) and even as a "pre-agricultural metropolis" (Jacobs 1969:19). It is certainly the case that Çatal Höyük, like Jericho before it, represents a very large agglomeration of people at a remarkably early date, around 7000 BC, and in that sense is not unreasonably called a "large village" or a "town." But when Southall (1998:26) goes so far as to refer to the early Neolithic village of Jarmo in the context of "the emergence of urban life," we hit upon definitional problems that cannot be avoided. So far as we now know, the agglomerate plan of Çatal Höyük is made up of repeated individual units, some small and domestic, some larger and sometimes described as "shrines," but without any special buildings representing the separation of functions that one associates with centrality (or centralized institutions often located at the downtown or very center of a city). Until that case is made for Çatal Höyük, it seems inappropriate to see the site as a city in the sense in which we used that term during the colloquium. Site size and tight spacing of buildings are not enough.

Nonetheless, before the time of Stonehenge the "urban revolution" first effectively analyzed by Gordon Childe (1950) had taken place already in Sumer and in Egypt with the emergence of the first cities, such as Uruk and the major centers of the Egyptian Old Kingdom. A millennium later than these, at about the time of Stonehenge, urbanization was emerging in the Indus Valley, and within a few centuries the first urban centers are documented for Shang China. The subsequent emergence of urban societies, first in Mesoamerica and then in Andean South America, was discussed during the colloquium, as well as the subsequent development of urbanism in sub-Saharan Africa.

At this point, some modest definition of "a city" should be ventured, and that offered by Cowgill seems appropriate:

> A permanent settlement within the larger territory occupied by a society considered home by a significant number of residents whose activities, roles, practices, experiences, identities and attitudes to life differ significantly from those of other members of the society who identify most closely with "rural" lands outside such settlements...populations of at least a few thousand seem a necessary, if not sufficient, requirement for a settlement or a society to be urban.
> [Cowgill 2004:525]

More concisely, a city is a substantial population center offering specialized *services* to a wider society. Çatal Höyük and Jericho might make it in terms of size, being larger and more populous than the centers of some of the Greek city-states, but in other respects they probably do not.

For a first, perhaps more relevant image, I should like to turn to the *Allegory of Good and Bad Government* by the Sienese painter Ambrogio Lorenzetti, which decorates the Sala dei Nove (Council Chamber) in the Palazzo Pubblico in Siena (figures 2.1 and 2.2). Dating from around AD 1339, it offers graphic commentary on government and urban life in one of the leading city-states of Renaissance Italy (Chelazzi Dini et al. 1998:plate 68-81). It is worth recalling that the smaller regional territories of Italy—centered upon equally smaller cities such as Siena, Florence, or Venice—were not united into a nation-state until AD 1870.

The images can serve to remind us of many themes that will interest us. These include the relationship between urbanism and government, or between the city and the state. They illustrate the rural hinterland and the partially agricultural population of many cities. They illustrate the amenities of urban life, as well as the squalor and the overcrowding. They suggest the roles and identities that emerge and can exist only in an urban environment.

Figure 2.1. Lorenzetti's idea of the city in fourteenth-century Renaissance Italy. Townscape by the Sienese painter Ambrogio Lorenzetti in the Palazzo Pubblico, Siena.

Figure 2.2. Town and country: city and hinterland. Lorenzetti's depiction of citizens riding out from Siena (the city wall is seen on the left) into the productive fields surrounding the city.

City and State

> Man is by nature a political animal—H. *Rackham*, Aristotle, *Politics*

In general, the definition of the city has proved a simpler task than that of civilization (Childe 1950; Flannery 1994; Trigger 2003). Indeed, the difficulty of finding a workable definition for *civilization* has made that term unfashionable in recent years. Such was certainly one of the criticisms that could be pointed at the work of Arnold Toynbee. It might also prove a difficulty on a critical reading of Trigger's recent compendious study (2003), were it not for the circumstance that all the civilizations that he considered were urban: they had cities.

The term *city*, as noted earlier, is restricted—so far—to human societies. Cities within our solar system are inhabited by people, not by ants or bees. Clearly, there may be significant analogies or homologies between a beehive or an ant nest and a city in terms of various functional attributes, which could well be discussed in system terms. The analogies between more militaristic human societies and those of social insects were recognized already by Aristophanes in *The Wasps* (Henderson 1998).

Problems of terminology must obviously be dealt with. The term *city* derives from the Latin *civitas*, which gives rise also to the noun *citizen*. The two Latin terms *urbs* and *rus* (town and country) give rise to the English words *urban* and *rural*. The approximately equivalent Greek term is *polis*, again meaning the city but referring to the Greek city-state, which has a social or political (that is, pertaining to the polis) dimension. The nature of the Hellenic city-state has been well considered by Hansen (2000c, 2002b) in the context of his wider survey of city-state cultures. These distinctions lead naturally to a consideration of the anthropological or sociological notion of the state as a social form. Indeed, the three terms—*city*, *state*, and *civilization*—form a triad often reflecting different aspects (urban, social, and cultural) of a single concept. Their derivatives (*urbane*, *civilized*, *polite*) carry overtones that do not aid clarity in definition.

Curiously, there seems to be no term in English deriving from the word *state* to designate a member of a modern nation-state or indeed the early city-state. A Greek would say *politis*. In English we say "citizen," derived from *civitas*, and thus risk confusing the inhabitant of a city with the inhabitant of a state.

It cannot be avoided that many of our notions of the ubiquity of world cities are based upon our experience of the industrial city of the twentieth and twenty-first centuries. Their application to the pre-industrial era may be entirely illusory. Today, city life implies traffic lights, high-rise buildings with elevators, airports, banks, ground transportation, and telecommunication. All of these things rest upon a money economy, the product of the introduction of coinage in ancient Greece, of Renaissance banking, and the rise of capitalism. And while it might just be argued that Asian cities can be based upon monetary systems originating in Asia, the truth is that the modern world would not get very far without electricity and telecommunication. They all use a single technology, originating in Europe with Michael Faraday and James

Clark-Maxwell, developing in the United States with Hewlett-Packard, IBM, and Microsoft, and spreading to the developing economies of Asia. Even in the nineteenth century, the development of urban society was governed by the spread of railways and then of the internal combustion engine. That is the answer to Galton's problem —Galton having questioned whether the cross-cultural regularities observed by E. B. Tylor (1875) might not be the product of diffusion rather than of independent invention. In the modern world they are a result of diffusion. Many of the regularities recognized by modern urban geography are not applicable to the pre-industrial world, and this has, of course, long been recognized by historical geographers.

Yet that need not entirely demolish the possibility of generalizing more widely from modern urbanism. For although the invention and development of electrical power had a specific origin in the Western world, that need not necessarily have been so. Electric charge, a property of the electron, is a universal phenomenon in the universe, and so is the potential for its use. Do we really doubt that the use of electric power would have been invented elsewhere a few centuries later if Columbus and Cortés had not travelled to America, or Marco Polo to China, or Alexander the Great to India, thus uniting some of the trajectories of development? That the origins of modern telecommunications can be traced back to Faraday and Maxwell does not mean that these might not have been developed elsewhere.

Indeed, the widespread assumption that intelligent life on other galaxies may one day become known to us, on our planet, is founded upon such ideas. Yet such observation would be difficult if their intelligent denizens did not have their own Maxwell to establish the possible use of electromagnetic radiation for the purposes of communication.

A refreshing feature of the Sackler colloquium is that it returned to the notion of early cities rather than early states, because the theme of early states has been quite thoroughly examined in recent years (Feinman and Marcus 1998). One aspect of the discussion must be touched upon here. Most anthropologists today would agree that, in general, cities are a feature of state societies, yet the correspondence is not necessarily complete. For while the existence of a state society normally implies the presence within it of a capital city and perhaps others, the existence of a city does not imply the full range of features normally associated with the state, which often include settlement hierarchy.

The approach to settlement hierarchy developed by Greg Johnson (1972, 1982) has proved an influential one. Flannery (1998:16) concisely puts it: "In the Near East Wright and Johnson (1975) have suggested that chiefdoms tended to have only two or three levels (or tiers) of settlement, whereas states have tended to have a hierarchy with at least four levels: cities, towns, large villages and small villages." This view of settlement hierarchy is now a widespread one. But, ironically, its strict application would exclude from statehood the very entity where the phenomenon was first critically studied: the Greek polis or city. Political theory, first established in the writings of Plato and Aristotle, was applied by them to the *poleis* of ancient Greece. Their extent around 500 BC may be gauged approximately by the distribution of mints, because at that time coins were struck by independent city-states.

The case of ancient Melos, an island in the Cyclades of only 160 sq km is a celebrated one. Its claims to independent statehood, its siege, and its destruction in 416 BC by the Athenians were described in detail by the historian Thucydides (Sparkes 1982). The location of the polis of ancient Melos was investigated in the nineteenth century. The total population of the island, and therefore of the state, is estimated to be of the order of 2,000 to 3,000 (Wagstaff and Cherry 1982:145). And while ancient Melos must lie at the lower end of the size range for the Greek city-states, its tribute assessment in the Athenian Tribute Lists is fully half that of Paros and the same as that of Naxos (Renfrew 1982:280), both significant centers earlier, during the sixth century BC. None of these city-states could claim a settlement hierarchy beyond two tiers: the city itself and some outlying rural habitations. These were states with a single city, within which the administrative hierarchy was contained.

We are not in a position to provide an adequate city plan for these, but the city of Priene on the west coast of Asia Minor in the fifth century BC has been well investigated and would have been only a few times larger in population. Again, it is difficult to imagine more than a two-tier hierarchy for its small territory.

We must, therefore, recognize that the paradigm case in most discussions of the city, starting with Plato and Aristotle, namely the Greek polis, was in many cases the unique center of nucleation within a state society. In some cases, for instance, the Greek islands of Melos, Paros, and Naxos, the state gave its name to the city. Or the city gave its name to the state, as in the case of Athens. In the smaller Greek states, such as those of the Cycladic islands, with their well-defined constitutions and systems of government, there was no developed settlement hierarchy, but simply a single city center. And they were small: Plato formulated an ideal state with 5,040 citizens and therefore a total population of perhaps ten times that number. This contrasts markedly with the notion of the state as defined by at least a three-level settlement hierarchy (Wright and Johnson 1975) and clearly with a much larger population.

Fortunately, perhaps the apparent paradox revealed here is resolved by the dichotomy now widely proposed between territorial states and city-states (Marcus 1998; Trigger 2003:92–119), even if the distinction seems a slightly arbitrary one. Trigger's view that the distinction may be regarded as a dichotomy has been criticized by Marcus, who sees the two categories as endpoints of a continuum. Moreover, she perceives a diachronic element, seeing the so-called city-states often as the result of decentralization of earlier and pristine, large territorial states. Cowgill (2004:533) is also critical of the dichotomy that these terms create and observes that "the label unhappily invites us to confound issues of polities and kinds of settlements." Trigger's dichotomy is really about states or polities; our mission, in this book, is more about cities and urbanism and documenting intercity interaction.

The solution that the present book offers us is to stick primarily with settlements, with the concept of cities in the foreground and with definitions pertaining to social

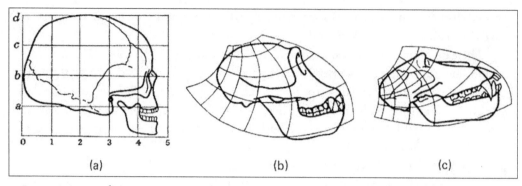

Figure 2.3. Transformation. Diagram by D'Arcy Thompson showing the transformation of (a) the human skull to that of (b) a chimpanzee and of (c) a baboon by a simple projection involving the continuous transformation of Cartesian coordinates (from Renfrew 1979a:23).

structures and polities (such as the state) in the background. Naturally, when we are considering the functions of cities, those of state societies may be very relevant, as indeed may be the settlement hierarchy at the head of which the city may sit. But when discussing and comparing ancient cities as places and as centers, we should not confuse the discussion with one about archaic states as social organizations.

Transformations

City plans often show striking similarities. That this should be so for some categories, such as Roman marching camps, may not be surprising: they have often been laid out according to the same preexisting plan. But the same property of predictability is often the case for mediaeval cities. Here, the similarity is often not one of deliberate urban design but arises from the need to accommodate a considerable range of very similar functions (cathedral, palace, market, mint, and so on) within a well-built city wall. More remarkably, comparable analogies or homologies can sometimes be seen between cities in different places, belonging to very different cultural traditions, where the similarities are unlikely to be due to direct contact or to the shared recognition of a specific, culturally determined plan. This is an important feature that is explored further in this book.

I suggest that a useful tool may be the concept of "transformation," derived from mathematics and long used in considerations of morphogenesis in the field of biology. D'Arcy Thompson in 1917 was one of the first to look in a coherent way at such similarities in form among biological species. He noted that in many cases they could be recognized as transformations (often embodying similar solutions to similar problems) (figure 2.3).

Such transformations involve elements of invariance. As the mathematician Bell put it:

> *Regularities* and *repetitions* in patterns at once suggest to a modern mathematician the *abstract groups* behind the patterns, and the various *transformations* of

> one problem, not necessarily mathematical, into another again spell *group* and raise the question, *what, if anything remains the same,* or invariant, *under all these transformations?* In technical phrase, what are the *invariants* of the *group of transformations?* [Bell 1951:95]

And he goes on to situate the notion of homologies of form within the wider field of topology:

> A *transformation* of one space S into another space S' is the assignment of a correspondence between the objects in S, S' such that to every object in S there corresponds at least one object in S' (as in mapping). The transformation of a subset A of S is the set of all correspondents under the transformation, of all objects in A. The transformation is said to be *uniform* or *single-valued* whenever it assigns a unique correspondent to every object in S: it is said to be continuous whenever the transform (the image on the map) of every open set A of S is an open set of S'. The transformation is said to be homomorphic when it is one-one and continuous both ways. [Bell 1951:156)]

This notion has, in effect, been applied in archaeology whenever we assert an equivalence of form between two cases, for instance, in speaking of a circular village of round huts (Flannery 1972). One can imagine the application of a formal analysis of this kind to the comparison of form and function made by Bintliff (1977) between mediaeval monasteries and the Minoan palace of Mallia in Crete (figure 2.4). Comparisons may show similar forms, but such forms may or may not be similar in function or meaning in the case of buildings or in the case of cities' layouts.

This approach has, I suspect, already been utilized by historical geographers, although I am not familiar with detailed treatments giving specific examples. Certainly, I make no claim to great originality with this proposal, but I would like to see how far we can develop it in the course of discussion. As will be seen below, its application between cities within a given culture or civilization, at approximately the same date, can often be appropriate. Also, its use diachronically, *within a continuous tradition*, can certainly be suggestive. The problem is greater when one seeks to apply it to different and indeed independent trajectories of growth. It is to these three cases that we shall now turn.

Imperial Identities and Imposed Structures

The cities within a given territory and period will often show marked similarities in form. For this, there may be several explanations. Within the boundaries of an empire, there will often be standardization that is the result of centralized control, imposed from above. In the Roman provinces, including Gallia and Britannia, Roman cities were often new foundations, even when placed at locations that had been settled during the preceding pre-Roman Iron Age.

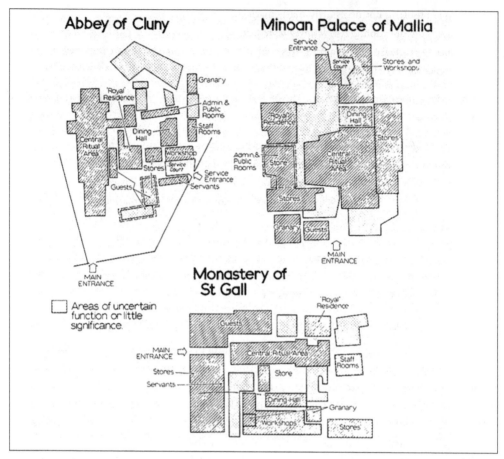

Figure 2.4. Transformation: analogy in form and function. Comparison (by John Bintliff) of the mediaeval monasteries of Cluny and St. Gall with the Minoan palace of Mallia (from Renfrew 1979a:29).

The urbanism of conquest and empire must often reflect the military necessities of the conquering authority, as well as the administrative forms it dictated. Moreover, after the imperial conquest, there is often a phase of building effectively *de novo*, which requires of the conquering authority the provision of a guiding plan. Deliberate urban planning rather than organic growth can thus be a common feature.

Much the same phenomenon is seen with the creation of a new (sometimes federal) capital, whether it be New Kingdom Amarna, at the wish of the pharaoh, or Washington DC, or Canberra.

Comparable phenomena of imposed structure are to be anticipated when one is speaking of subordinate centers within what is sometimes termed a "territorial state" (Marcus 1998; Trigger 2003). As noted above, the characteristic of the territorial state is that the territory of the polity is large, sometimes equivalent to that of the modern nation-state and often containing a considerable number of cities. Such cities are likely to show analogous features, operating as they will normally do as secondary centers,

a. Theoretical hierarchy of settlements:

   1. *Amsār* (sing. *miṣr*), metropolis.
   2. *Qaṣabat* (sing. *qaṣabah*), fortified provincial capitals.
   3. *Mudun* (sing. *madīnah*), provincial towns, a main town of a district, or a market town.
   4. *Qurā* (sing. *qaryah*), villages.

b. Theoretical hierarchy of regional units:

   1. *Aqālīm* (sing. *iqlīm*), regions.
   2. *Kuwar* (sing. *kūrah*), provinces.
   3. *Nawāhy* (sing. *nahiyah*), districts.
   4. *Rustaqāt* (sing. *rustāq*), agricultural units.

c. Theoretical spatial distribution of settlements:

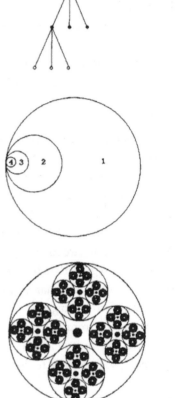

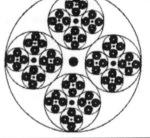

Figure 2.5. *An early conceptualization of settlement hierarchy, as formulated by the tenth-century Arab geographer Al-Muqaddasi (from Renfrew 1979a:33).*

subordinate to the primate administrative center or capital of the territory as a whole. The phenomenon of settlement hierarchy in this way was recognized by the tenth-century Arab geographer Al-Muqaddasi (figure 2.5).

To see the cities of a territorial state as transformations of a single model imposed from above may, however, overlook the historical dimension. For many territorial states are formed from the incorporation, often through conquest, of a number of local centers. In the case of the initial or primary state, these could be conquering chiefdoms. This is, in effect, the incorporation of a number of early-state modules within a single polity occupying the entire "region of cultural homogeneity" of the early civilization (Renfrew 1975), the equivalent of a peak in the Dynamic Model of Marcus (1998). The points of similarity, far from being imposed from above, come from the working of a number of processes.

Peer-Polity Homologies

In regions where there is no single centralized power, it is common that there should be a high degree of homology between the local autonomous centers, each often the urban capital of a city-state. The pattern there may be one of early-state modules (Renfrew 1975), where there are several essentially autonomous state units, each with its urban center. In such a case, where there may be a common language and often a common religion (albeit with local variants and local tutelary deities), the phenomena of symbolic entrainment and emulation can operate very strongly in the course of peer-polity interaction (Cherry 1986; Renfrew 1986). So it is that the Sumerian cities, each with its ziggurat and other comparable features, can be seen as transformations, one of another. The same is true of the poleis of Ancient Greece and then of Magna Graecia. The town planning attributed to Hippodamos of Miletos, well seen at Priene, is seen at other Greek cities, such as Rhodes (Ward-Perkins 1974:figures 12 and 13).

The concept of the early-state module may be a helpful one in considering the structure and patterning of a number of early-state societies. As the term implies, the social (and geographical) landscape is seen to be divided into a number of roughly equivalent units, each politically independent, and often of roughly equivalent size. They may be regarded, in a sense, as transformations of one another. Moreover, the cities of the region that has organized itself in this way share many points of similarity. As noted above, that was the case for the cities of Sumer. Those of Greece were again transformations, but of a different pattern or template. Indeed, in many early state societies, from Shang China in the fifteenth century BC to Etruria in the fourth century BC, or indeed among the Classic Maya, we observe closely comparable modular units. Within each region these units may be regarded as transformations of one another.

These similarities are not imposed. These early-state modules were politically autonomous. And the processes that formed them may be subsumed within the concept of peer-polity interaction (Cherry 1986; Renfrew 1986; Sabloff 1986; Snodgrass 1986). For the working of peer-polity interaction predicts that the cities at the centers of the early-state modules will increasingly come to resemble one another. Various processes combine to this end, including competitive emulation, warfare, symbolic entrainment, and an increasing flow in the exchange of goods. Moreover, these are processes endogenous to the region in question. There is, thus, a phenomenon of convergence operating in many early states that works to make their centers increasingly resemble one another. No doubt, at the moment of the emergence of each as a state polity, there will be peer-polity influences from neighboring polities that already work towards similarity. Then, over succeeding centuries, competition between centers resulting in emulation, plus a measure of symbolic entrainment, will result in increasing similarities. It should be remembered that in the "region of cultural homogeneity" shared by these early states (effectively, the region of the civilization that they share) it is likely that there will be one dominant language (Trigger 2003:101) and perhaps one dominant religion. This is thus the region that becomes the home to what is sometimes termed a "civilization." And this is, of course, the region that may at a later stage be united into a single "territorial state," as noted above.

The effect here is that the institutions of each neighboring early state will increasingly come to resemble one another and take forms that will likewise have resemblances. We can expect a converging similarity of forms among the early states in a region of cultural homogeneity. The working of peer-polity interaction among adjacent city-states will thus produce a similar outcome to the effects of imposed form in territorial states: convergent homology of form.

It would be interesting to undertake a formal analysis, employing the concept of transformation outlined here, for each of the case studies in this book. To what extent can the early cities of, say, Shang China, be seen as transformations of one another and thus perhaps of a more general idea?

The City through Time: Temporal Transformations

At Melania, every time you enter the square, you find yourself caught in a dialogue: the braggart soldier and the parasite coming from a door meets the young wastrel or else the miserly father from his threshold utters his final warnings to the amorous daughter and is interrupted by the foolish servant who is taking a note to the procuress. You return to Melania after years and you find the same dialogue still going on.—*I. Calvino,* Invisible Cities

The notion of transformation through time is perhaps also an unsurprising one. In the last section, we were comparing urban forms and early-state modules at different places within a single region, but (again, notionally at least) at much the same time period. Here, it is pertinent to consider diachronic change—change through time, occurring (again, notionally at least) at the same place. In some cases, there is cultural continuity, so the institutions of one period are seen to descend from those of the preceding. That may be seen even with new foundations, and it is often very much more in evidence when the surviving buildings of one period place strong constraints upon those of succeeding generations—a phenomenon particularly characteristic of "the Eternal City," Rome, but also seen in many other centers in Italy. In this case, the successive transformations may be seen as taking place along a single trajectory or along related trajectories of growth and change.

At this point, however, I wish to draw on the very valid, if greatly entertaining, insights provided by the late Sir Osbert Lancaster in his classic *Drayneflete Revealed* (1949). Drayneflete is, of course, both a minor English town and a figment of the imagination of Sir Osbert. Although Drayneflete perhaps only just ranks as a city in the sense intended here either in scale or in centrality, he has caught the notion of transformation through time effectively (figures 2.6–2.9).

In these urban images, we see the Roman temple, forum, imperial statue, and war chariot give way to the Norman church, open air market, Saxon cross, rural environment, and knight, and these by the fifteenth century to the Gothic church, fountain

Figure 2.6. Temporal transformation: time trajectory point A. Sir Osbert Lancaster's imaginary reconstruction of Roman Drayneflete ca. AD 200 (from Renfrew 1979a:40).

Figure 2.7. Temporal transformation (with invariant elements): time trajectory point B. Sir Osbert Lancaster's imaginary reconstruction of Drayneflete, soon after the Norman conquest, ca. AD 1070 (from Renfrew 1979a:40).

Figure 2.8. Temporal transformation (plus ça change…): time trajectory point C. Sir Osbert Lancaster's imagined Drayneflete at the end of the seventeenth century (after Renfrew 1979a:41).

Figure 2.9. Temporal transformation: continuity and contingency: time trajectory point D. Sir Osbert Lancaster's twentieth-century Drayneflete (from Lancaster 1949:44–45).

The City through Time and Space 43

building, market hall, and mounted knights. These are superseded by the cathedral, town hall, statue of Queen Victoria, and the motorized transport of the twentieth century, and with prophetic accuracy, by the Bauhaus civic center, the supermarket, the small historic building at the center of the traffic island, and the urban freeway of what has become today.

But these images have a further content: the transformations in the roles of individuals. Again, we can recognize stability and a constancy underlying the superficial changes effected by the transformation. The priest and the squire at the lower left and the lord and lady at the end of the seventeenth century in the foreground, with two soldiers and the beggar man at the right, find their counterparts in Roman and Norman Drayneflete, and most of these are seen transformed in the nineteenth- and twentieth-century versions.

These images remind us of the human realities that underlie the passage of time over the long-term trajectory in a single region or place.

The Great Encounter: Transformations across Space and Time

So far, the discussion has perhaps been rather predictable. It can be argued that within a single region and during a single time period, there is convergent homology of form among centers, so each can be regarded as the transformation of another. This was the first set of transformations that we considered. And we have noted, also, that over long trajectories through time, the structures of individual centers are transformed in a regular way, so one trajectory amounts to a series of transformations. The urban structures in the region at one point in time can thus still be seen as transformations of one another, comparable in very much the same way that they were several centuries or even millennia earlier, even though they are also, in other respects, very much changed. These were the diachronic transformations reviewed above, with the example of Osbert Lancaster's fictional Drayneflete.

But now we come to the really interesting part. In some senses, it seems that the urban centers seen across different and independent trajectories of growth and change show striking resemblances of form between trajectories and may even be considered as transformations of one another. But these are transformations across both space and time. If that is the case, in many instances it cannot be the product of contact and mutual influence in some geographically expanded sense of peer-polity interaction. Nor are the resemblances to be explained simply as the persistence of form, through time, along a single trajectory of development. For instance, the cities of Mesoamerica, which we can now consider, were remote from those of Europe and Western Asia with which we may seek to compare them. And, when we do note strong points of resemblance, the best comparisons may not be between contemporary states in Mesoamerica and in the Old World. The most persuasive homologies among the urban plans and urban functions of archaic states are not often contemporary. The most appropriate point of comparison for the Early Classic Maya will not necessarily be their precise contemporaries in Western Asia but rather cities and centers that flourished there very much earlier. These transformations across both space and time clearly cannot be explained away, either through direct contact or through the workings of traditions of long duration. If our juxtapositions among cities from different continents and at different times reveal structural homologies, these must be ascribed to some more fundamental cause.

The "Great Encounter" indicated at the head of this section is what I regard as one of the climactic moments in human history, when Cortés and the Conquistadores saw and then captured Tenochtitlan, the capital of the Aztec empire of Mexico. They were there as the representatives of the urban civilization of Europe, specifically of Spain. And through their agency, Europe conquered Aztec Mexico, forever ending (or at least fundamentally and discontinuously changing) the trajectory of development of Mesoamerican civilization. Everything the participants, European or Aztec, saw and encountered in the other was the product of a tradition entirely alien to their own. The same can, of course, be said of Captain Cook and the natives of the Friendly Islands, now the Kingdom of Tonga, in the course of that other great encounter, between Europe and Polynesia. Indeed, Cook found much to admire.

The case of Tenochtitlan was, however, even more remarkable because here was a great city—the rival of anything to be seen then in Europe. It ran on its own lines, followed its own faith, yet was recognizably a great city. It was a reality so rich that it exceeded imagination or fantasy, like some strange outpost in Italo Calvino's *Invisible Cities* (1974).

Cortés and his companions had no difficulty in "understanding" the workings of its government and its institutions, nor in recognizing the functioning of its urban components. Perhaps, in some cases, they simply imposed upon an alien reality their own assumptions as to working and function, based upon an internalized Eurocentric model. But the recognition was there and is strikingly documented by contemporary testimony:

> We...followed the causeway, which is eight yards wide and goes so straight to the city of Mexico that I do not think it curves at all. Wide though it was, it was so crowded with people that there was hardly room for them all. Some were going to Mexico and others coming away, besides those who had come out to see us, and we could hardly get through the crowds that were there. With such wonderful sights to gaze on we did not know what to say, or if this was real that we saw before our eyes. On the land side there were great cities, and on the lake many more. The lake was crowded with canoes. At intervals along the causeway there were many bridges, and before us was the great city of Mexico. [Díaz 1967:216]

In this striking passage we see the same recognition, by an observer in the early sixteenth century, that we are making today as anthropologists and archaeologists. He was seeing something that he recognized and that was, in a structural sense, a complex possessing features with which he was already familiar: the city.

Anthropologists, as we know, consider the most appropriate point of comparison for

Tenochtitlan not to be contemporary Spain in the sixteenth century AD, but rather the capital of some archaic territorial state, perhaps the Mesopotamia of the eighteenth century BC chosen by Robert McC. Adams (1966) for his illuminating comparative study.

Now the question arises, to what extent can Tenochtitlan (or perhaps, because that was the Great City, an enormous capital city, we should choose instead some second-order center) be considered as the product of a transformation of a city in Western Asia three or four millennia earlier? To what extent can the cities of archaic states, or at any rate of some archaic states, be considered as transformations of those of archaic states on different and independent trajectories of development?

There are indications that this might be so. The traveler who is welcomed from afar, from a distant continent, sitting in the shade and drinking a refreshing draught, may well ask a series of questions:

1. Where is the palace of the king? ("Take me to your leader.")
2. Which is the great temple of the greatest deity?
3. Is not the main street laid out towards the first of the four quarters?
4. Where is the vegetable market?
5. Where can we find livestock or poultry?
6. Where are the weavers and the garment industry?
7. Is there water transport—where is the main quay?
8. Where do the beasts of burden go?
9. How far from here are the quarries for the stone?
10. Are there scribes in the palace?
11. From how far do the exotic stones for the lapidary workers come?
12. Are there many foreigners among the workers?

Such questions would have meaning in most urban contexts, at very different times and places. From considerations like these, we might well develop a trait list of urban features that we might expect to reflect urban functions. We can begin by considering those that Childe (1950) listed as characteristic of urban society:

1. Increase in settlement size toward "urban proportions"
2. Centralized accumulation of capital resulting from the imposition of tribute or taxation
3. Monumental public works
4. Invention of writing
5. Advances towards exact and predictive sciences
6. Appearance and growth of long-distance trade in luxuries
7. Emergence of a class-stratified society
8. Freeing of a part of the population from subsistence tasks for full-time craft specialization

9. Substitution of a politically organized society based on territorial principles, the state, for one based on kin ties
10. Appearance of naturalistic or representational art

These features have been followed by later scholars. They refer, very properly, to urban functions rather than to urban structural features. Indeed, Childe was using them to indicate salient features of a state society, of what is sometimes termed a "civilization."

Taking a leaf from Childe's book, as it were, we can go on to suggest some broadly comparable features that are, instead, common aspects of urban structure and, as such, often directly visible in the archaeological record. Again, like Childe's checklist, they are of very wide, if not quite universal, applicability:

- Fortifications are a frequent feature of cities in most parts of the world, often defining what Lewis Mumford (1961) termed "the urban container." Trigger (2003:125) remarks, they are less frequent in the Americas than in the Old World.

- Urban blocks with residential accommodation are a common feature of cities. They occupy a considerable part of the area of the great center of Teotihuacán in the Valley of Mexico, just as they did in Ancient Rome.

- Axial principles, relating to cosmology, are seen in the layout of cities in many parts of the world. Their importance in China provided the title for Paul Wheatley's *The Pivot of the Four Quarters* (1971), and such symbolism, embodied and embedded in urban structure, is a common feature in Mesoamerica.

- Temple buildings are a recognizable feature in most ancient civilizations (to which that of the Indus is a notable exception). The crosscultural validity of the term *temple* is a shining example of a transform that retains its coherence (and its recognizability) in urban centers across space and time.

- Royal palaces for persons of high status are a widespread, but certainly not universal, feature of cities, particularly those that are primate cities in the sense of representing the capital and seat of power in an independent state or polity.

- Areas of craft production for a range of specialized products such as ceramics, metalworking, weaving, and lapidary work are a common feature of many cities.

- Burial places, where rich sumptuary goods accompany the burials of persons of high rank, are a feature of many cities, especially primate centers (although, again, the cities of the Indus appear to offer an exception).

- Places for public games, parades, and assemblies are a feature of urban life, the term *plaza* showing the wide applicability of the transform, from its origin in

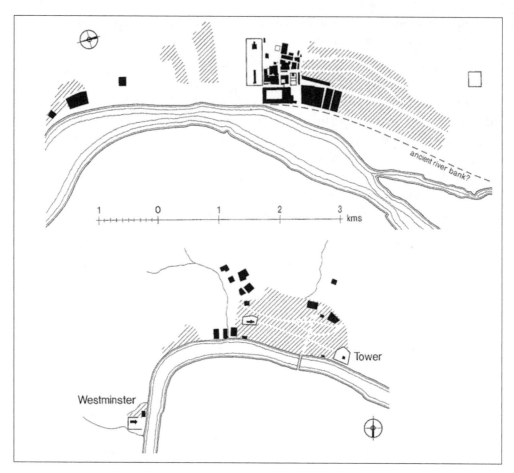

Figure 2.10. Transformation across space: comparison by Barry Kemp of the New Kingdom Egyptian capital Amarna (top) and late mediaeval London (bottom), drawn to the same scale. Buildings in solid black are those of controlling organizations: palaces, temples, and storehouses at Amarna; palaces, temples, and monasteries at London. Hatched areas are essentially residential. As Kemp notes (Carl et al. 2000:345): "Neither city displays a unified integration of the two spheres. Both cities arose from numerous local decisions, and both are images of societies with dispersed decision-making and a strong degree of self-organization. Despite the huge differences in the spans of time involved (fifteen years and a thousand) similar processes have converged towards a basically similar structure."

the urban centers of the Old World and its application to the ancient cities of Mesoamerica.

Some of these are features relating to the concept of the "urban container," noted above, as very effectively developed by Lewis Mumford (1961). Some of them relate also to the notion of intensification of production, an aspect emphasized by Jane Jacobs (1969), although her notion of what constitutes "a city" seems more flexible than that adopted here.

The notion that comparison across space and time may reveal structural similarities, themselves reflecting underlying processes, was suggested also by Carl and colleagues (2000:345) in their comparison of the city of Amarna in the Egyptian New Kingdom with late mediaeval London (figure 2.10). This offers a graphic example of the way that urban features can be recognized crossculturally. Such recognition may, in part, simply be an imposition on the part of the analyst or the beholder. But the very applicability of terms like *palace* or *temple* or *plaza* or indeed *fortification* to a wide range of cases across time and space does indicate the recurrence of structural features. Their recurrent association in such widely different contexts seems to justify the notion that, in some cases, a city in one specific context may be regarded as a transform of another situated in a very different location in both space and time.

Transformations of Trajectory: Allactic Form

In considering transformations, it is pertinent also to consider patterns of change, for it is as legitimate to identify or classify types of change as it is to classify system states. This allactic approach (from Greek *allagé*, change) is commonly used, for instance in the recognition of exponential or logistic growth patterns and in the consideration of cyclical processes. So far, we have considered transformations of urban form in three ways: between locations within a single time period, across time within a single region, and then between locations that are remote both in space and in time. But in the case of allactic form, it is no longer urban structures that are being compared with one another, but entire trajectories of urban growth and change.

I have suggested that system collapse may be seen as one of these (Renfrew 1979b). Marcus (1998) has developed the idea of cycles of change, and these, too, represent allactic form.

The pattern of the gradual increase in settlement size and functions, with a gradual increase in complexity, leading to the emergence of urban centers is a model commonly followed. It may be contrasted with the punctuated equilibrium approach of Gould, which has been discussed by Cherry in his description of the sudden emergence of the Minoan palaces (Cherry 1984).

Sudden shifts from dispersed to nucleated settlement patterns may be relevant to the phenomenon of urban formation, and the nature of such discontinuities has been discussed by Renfrew and Poston (1979), drawing upon catastrophe theory. Similar reasoning has been applied to early state formation, as well as to the collapse of state societies (Tainter 1988), the term *anastrophe* being proposed for episodes of sudden rise or growth, the opposite of instances of sudden catastrophic collapse.

Regularities and Irregularities

This chapter makes the case that the regularities observed when the urban centers of archaic states are compared may be sufficiently robust to warrant the recognition of a general category of "early city" that we might set alongside that of the "industrial city" of modern times. There may be developmental cycles, too, within a city's lifespan—the earliest era of its occupation, its middle phase, its growth cycles, and its collapse or recovery phases. As noted earlier, modern industrial cities are all inheritors of a single technology developed in the industrial West over the past two or three centuries, which has now become global. They can, in that sense, be regarded as manifestations (or indeed transformations) of a single phenomenon or structure. But early cities have undoubtedly arisen independently, and their similarities must have deep underlying causes.

In part, these similarities may be due to similar processes of change, and our discussion has perhaps centered too heavily upon structure, with too little emphasis upon process; the structures are the products of such processes, even if the processes themselves are conditioned by the existing structures. It may be, however, that the course of the argument and the recognition of similarities have been influenced somewhat by the examples usually chosen to sustain such discussion. I have concerns about two particular early cases of urbanization that may not fit the transformation model as well as the other cases, but we can still consider them as transformations. These two cases are the Indus civilization, with its remarkable cities, and the civilizations of pre-Columbian South America. These I know less well, but my concern is that they may not conform as closely to the general notion of "city as structure" than some other instances.

The great cities of the Indus Valley civilization, including Harappa and Mohenjodaro, certainly rank as cities in terms of size and "urban populations," their cramped accommodation for thousands of inhabitants in large street "insulae," and their large public buildings—the so-called "granaries" and the bath at Mohenjodaro. But they are conspicuously lacking in features common in early cities in many other cultures (Possehl 2000). There are no obvious residences for persons of high status ("palaces"). Indeed, there is very little direct evidence for persons of high rank—for example, no royal tombs have been found. There is no evidence for a centralized ruling elite (Kenoyer, chapter 10). As Kenoyer (chapter 10:201) puts it, "The lack of conspicuous temples or administrative buildings...indicates the lack of a highly centralized political and religious structure." Also, the iconographic repertoire is very poor. There are no obvious depictions of kings or deities. The representational repertoire on the Indus Valley seals is very limited. This society remains in large measure a faceless society, with no explicit evidence for persons of high rank. Analysis has not yet shown it to be a "class-stratified" society, although that remains possible. While these are undoubtedly cities, they fall outside the generalizations usually made about urban society. Clearly, there must indeed have been more modest systems of power and administration, perhaps with competing elites within a single city, but their works were less grandiloquent than in most other state societies and therefore less evident in the archaeological record. Unfortunately, this is a civilization that falls outside Trigger's large survey (2003:34), and this might well, if included, call some of his conclusions into question.

Conclusions

The case has been made for regarding the city as a universal form—universal, at least, to human societies that have moved beyond a certain threshold of growth and complexity. Nor, in the imagination, need one restrict the consideration to human societies. Science fiction is full of considerations of intelligent beings in other worlds, many of whom are imagined as living in what one might well define as cities. Such imaginings are not to be regarded as frivolous; many competent scientists would regard the possibility of such beings (and such centers) in other galaxies as being high. It remains to be seen how well the consideration given to specific cases in the course of this book will strengthen or diminish the view that their urban centers may be seen as examples of a more general form.

three
Early Cities
Craft Workers, Kings, and Controlling the Supernatural

Bruce G. Trigger

Archaeologists observe urban centers as a form of material culture, however much they seek to understand them in behavioral and cultural terms. Information about early cities has increased exponentially since the 1950s as a result of archaeological research carried out in many parts of the world. Yet the interpretation of this evidence has been caught up in a lengthy debate among archaeologists about how to explain products of human behavior. The first position, which became prominent in the 1960s and came to be known as processual archaeology, views human behavior largely as rational individual and collective responses to ecological constraints; post-processual archaeology, which began in the 1980s, sees human behavior as shaped by the historically contingent content of specific cultural traditions. Although these two approaches are gradually being transcended by broader and more sophisticated syntheses (A. Smith 2003; Trigger 2006:484–528), they have long influenced the questions that many archaeologists have asked about early cities, the sorts of research they have carried out, and the results they have expected. There were also, however, other archaeologists, including Joyce Marcus and Colin Renfrew, who already by the 1970s had adopted a more holistic approach to understanding the archaeological record.

Early cities were once regarded more as sources of archaeological data than as objects of archaeological study. Even painstaking early excavators, such as Robert

Koldewey at Babylon and German and then British archaeologists at Amarna, in Egypt, who gradually recovered the site plans of these major urban centers, made little effort to infer their social and political life from such data. Most ancient cities were excavated because their major buildings were viewed as being of art historical interest and were associated with concentrations of art objects and texts that could be displayed in museums and studied by art historians and epigraphers. Within the framework of the humanist approach that, until recently, dominated fields such as classical studies, Egyptology, and Assyriology, these sorts of finds were the means by which it was believed that the great cultural achievements of these ancient civilizations might best be understood. Few archaeologists bothered even to inquire why such material tended to be heavily concentrated in and around major buildings in early urban centers.

Although Fustel de Coulanges (1963[1864]) published detailed characterizations of cities in ancient Greece and Italy and Max Weber (1962[1958]) studied those of medieval Europe, using written sources, neither archaeologists nor geographers could agree on a generally acceptable, cross-cultural definition of urbanism. Arbitrary definitions based on population size or population density invariably succumbed to counter examples. Typological definitions that were useful for classifying archaeological artifacts or cultures did not work well for classifying cities. In 1950 Gordon Childe listed ten features that he claimed distinguished the earliest cities from Neolithic villages. His mixture of material culture and social organization as defining features marked an advance over previous, purely typological definitions, but his listing provided little insight into how early cities had functioned. Sociological definitions, which treated cities as "a state of mind," were highly ethnocentric and of little practical use to archaeologists (Park 1952).

Processual Approaches

The behaviorism that dominated the social sciences in the 1950s and 1960s led archaeologists to become interested in studying how ancient societies had functioned. Their attention was drawn to forms of locational analysis that were being developed by economists and human geographers (Chorley and Haggett 1967). This research, among other things, considered the role played by cities and smaller service communities as centers of marketing and trade. Much of it addressed modern communities and reflected the concerns of economists and management experts with using locational analysis to promote efficiency in the production and distribution of goods. Archaeologists, including Kent Flannery (1972), G. A. Johnson (1973), William Rathje (1975), and Sander van der Leeuw (1981), linked locational analysis with information theory to construct cost-based models of data processing and administration in early complex societies. Joyce Marcus (1973) used Central Place Theory to account for the hexagonal lattices of smaller centers that were evident around some Maya cities.

In 1972 I noted several premises underlying locational analysis derived from B. J. Garner's "Models of Urban Geography and Settlement Location" (1967) that seemed of special importance for understanding the growth of ancient cities. The first was the assumption of a tendency for human activities to be hierarchical in character and for this to be reflected in spatial organization. This assumption was based on the observation that, as more specialized activities develop, higher-level and more specialized functions are necessarily performed from a smaller number of centers. Second, with increasing complexity and specialization, different human activities tend to be located in the same place in order to minimize the need for movement of people, goods, and information. Because of this, single locations come to serve an increasing number of specialized functions. Third and finally, the size of communities tends to vary according to the number of functions they perform. This principle, combined with the hierarchical premise, explains why larger communities are exponentially less numerous within an interacting area than are smaller ones. Larger centers perform all or most of the types of functions carried out in smaller centers, but in addition they discharge the more specialized functions associated with a more restricted number of locations. A city can thus be defined as a community or settlement that performs numerous functions in relation to a broader hinterland (Mabogunje 1962:3–4). Because of the exploitive nature of the upper classes that lived primarily in urban centers, many of these functions were self-serving. While this definition distinguishes a city from a larger agricultural community or from a modern hamlet with a general store and a funeral parlor, which performs only a minimal number of fairly generalized services for a small surrounding area, it leaves service villages, towns, and cities as arbitrary divisions of a continuum. With respect to early civilizations, all three might appropriately be called urban centers, so I then proposed that factors that could lead to increases in the size of early urban populations included the following: overall population growth, rural unemployment, greater craft specialization, more marketing and trade, growing numbers of administrators, landowners choosing to live in urban centers to enjoy greater protection from commoners, need for defense against foreign enemies, more cult activities, tourism, a growing demand for education, and the employment of more retainers to serve expanding urban elites.

Overwhelmingly, all specialized functions, except for some forms of handicraft production that were very polluting or that created large amounts of nonrecyclable waste, were located within urban centers. Large temples, even those dedicated to major agricultural deities, were rarely located in the countryside. Not all of these factors were involved in the growth of any one urban center, and the importance of each factor could vary greatly from one urban center or one civilization to another. Yet, whatever the factors that encouraged specific examples of urban growth, the increasing size of cities would create pressure to devise the institutions of governance that were required for these cities to function. Kent Flannery (1972) perspicaciously observed that, under those conditions, explanations of the development of early civilizations had to focus more on defining the sorts of systemic change that shaped the archaeological record.

The application of locational analysis to explain the distribution and size of settlements in early civilizations assumed a similar concern to minimize the friction of distance, as is found in modern industrial societies. In other words, it was believed that people—then as now—sought, in a rational manner, to locate activities so that energy expenditures were minimized when it came to providing services and transporting goods and information.

Locational analysis helped archaeologists to define the general functions of early cities and to explain their distributions and relative sizes, but it did not account for much about their form, social composition, and the specific activities that occurred inside them. Answering these questions required analysis of community patterns from social, economic, and political points of view. The layouts of urban centers in early civilizations display considerable variation. If this variation were nonfunctional, it ought to have differed idiosyncratically from one early civilization to another, as happens with art styles. Recent work I have done comparing seven of the best-documented early civilizations (Trigger 2003) confirms earlier suggestions (Maisels 1990) that this variation is not random but correlates with two different types of political organization. The early civilizations I studied can be divided into what I have called city-state systems and territorial states. It has been argued that city-state systems may evolve into territorial states (Renfrew 1997) or that territorial states may devolve into city-state systems (Marcus 1989, 1998). Marcus proposes that initial states were territorial and evolved out of a network of competing chiefdoms. When those first-generation states broke down, they often fragmented into multiple polities sometimes called city-states. When second- and third-generation states broke down, they tended to become city-state systems. My own interpretation of the historical evidence suggests that both kinds of early civilizations developed independently from various sorts of early states and later evolved, if they did so at all, converging into a third, distinctive, and more complex form of political organization that I have labeled the regional state. Regional states combined large cities that were centers of craft production and commerce with extensive polities (Trigger 1985).

City-state systems took the form of a network of adjacent city-states whose elites tended to compete, often militarily, to control intervening territory, trade routes, and other resources while at the same time sharing common beliefs and symbols and making alliances with one another, often in the form of intermarriages among their ruling families. City-states varied in size, but most of them probably controlled a territory of only a few hundred square kilometers. Each city-state had a capital city usually near the center of its territory. Larger city-states might have a number of small, secondary administrative centers surrounding the capital, as well as numerous farming villages and hamlets. The capitals of these states tended to be relatively large communities, with populations ranging from a few thousand to more than 100,000 individuals, depending on the ability of a particular city-state to control and exact tribute from its neighbors. Considerable numbers of full-time farmers often lived in such centers, seeking greater protection for themselves and their possessions against the threats posed by endemic interstate warfare. It is estimated that in southern Iraq in Early Dynastic times (ca. 2900–2350 BC) more than 80 percent of the total population lived in urban centers (R. Adams 1981:90–94); elsewhere, the number varied from 15 to more than 50 percent.

Full-time craft producers generally lived in these cities and manufactured goods that were available to anyone who could afford to purchase them. This gave farmers, whether living in the city or the surrounding countryside, a chance to obtain well-made goods. A smaller number of craft specialists produced superior goods for the state and the upper classes. Interstate trade, which permitted yet more craft specialization, was often carried out by merchants who operated independently of the state, an arrangement that made it possible to obtain both luxury goods and necessary raw materials even during prolonged episodes of interstate warfare. As a result of widespread access to goods produced by full-time specialists and the development of more intensive agriculture within and close to cities in order to reduce the transport costs involved in feeding their populations, city-states were able to support a considerable number of nonfood producers, possibly amounting to between 10 and 20 percent of the total population.

Territorial states were much larger polities governed by hierarchies of officials operating at the central, regional, and local levels. Many combinations of representative and bureaucratic control were experimented with in efforts to hold such societies together. The various urban centers of territorial states were occupied by a much smaller portion of the total population than were those of city-states: usually less than 10 percent. Although individual territorial states often governed several million people, their capitals rarely had more than 50,000 inhabitants, with secondary and tertiary administrative centers much smaller. These centers were occupied only by members of the upper classes, government officials, craftworkers employed by the government, retainers, and their families. Farmers, being safer from foreign attack, could live in villages located conveniently near the fields they cultivated. The more dispersed nature of the farming population also meant that agricultural production was less intensive than in city-states. Farmers manufactured the goods they needed from locally available raw materials during slack work periods in the agricultural cycle. Because these goods were produced by part-time specialists, they were generally qualitatively inferior to the best that was available to farmers in city-states. Such goods were generally exchanged among rural families or bartered at local markets.

In territorial states, the central government controlled the procurement of valuable raw materials by monopolizing or carefully regulating mining operations and foreign trade. These materials were transformed into high-quality luxury goods that the king and his officials distributed among the upper classes and used to reward commoners who served the state well. Control of production and distribution of luxury goods by the central government played a major role in holding territorial states together. Thus developed a two-tier economy based on distinct urban and rural components. The basic resources to manage the state were obtained as taxes, rents, and corvées imposed on rural workers.

Functional relations, including those associated with the sorts of activities that occurred in early cities and the transportation links and other forms of articulation between higher- and lower-order centers, clearly played an important role in shaping urban settlements and urban life in early civilizations. Although the capitals of city-states provided services for many fewer people than did those of territorial states, they offered a much broader range of services. This explains why major cities in city-states were generally much larger in relation to the total population of these states than were the capitals of territorial states. Political arrangements also determined who lived in urban centers and the intensity of agriculture close to them. These correlations indicate the lasting importance of functional explanations of archaeological finds, despite the continuing dogmatic repudiation of this sort of explanation by some post-processual archaeologists. Such findings also question the wisdom of political economy having been divided into the more specialized disciplines of political science and economics, with the result that the one seeks to explain political behavior with little reference to economic factors and the other, economic activity without much reference to politics.

My distinction between the nature of cities in city-state systems and territorial states does not exclude the possibility that other types of cities may have developed in early civilizations (McIntosh 2005). However, clear evidence of other major variants has not been forthcoming, and research done in recent decades has ruled out the validity of a number of hypothesized types. It is no longer possible to regard early Iraqi cities, as Childe once did, as "regular industrial and commercial centres" inhabited by an "industrial proletariat" (Childe 1934:186) and hence similar in nature to urban centers in Western Europe. Maya cities have ceased to be regarded as vacant ceremonial centers, inhabited only by a small number of priests and visited periodically for religious celebrations by farmers who lived in the surrounding area—an interpretation that arose as a result of the misapplication of the direct historical approach (Becker 1979; Sabloff 1990). It is also no longer possible to describe Egypt during the Old and Middle Kingdoms as a "civilization without cities" (Wilson 1960; Bard, chapter 9). The first two examples have turned out to be city-state systems, within which larger political entities may have arisen from time to time, and Egypt is recognized as a normal territorial state. Each of these earlier interpretations was refuted as a result of the collection of more archaeological data.

Symbolic Approaches

Although addressed earlier by Paul Wheatley (1971), by the 1980s a growing interest in cultural studies had resulted in increasing attention being paid to the conceptual, as well as the functional, criteria that influenced the layout of cities and the nature and locations of different types of monumental buildings within them. Each early civilization has long been recognized as having developed its own distinctive monumental architectural style. Yet the limited cross-cultural variation in the uses to which such buildings were put has attracted less attention. Temples, palaces, and upper-class tombs all tended to evolve from earlier houses. In many early civilizations, these structures were literally called gods' houses, kings' houses, and houses of the dead. City walls, fortresses, and frontier defenses were derived from the fortifications of earlier times. Almost no buildings served specialized public functions in early civilizations, as did the libraries, stadia, arenas, theaters, and baths that first appeared in classical Western civilizations. Mesoamericans built elaborate stone ballcourts, but these were religious structures and invariably part of temple complexes. From a functional point of view, the monumental architecture of early civilizations was the domestic and defensive structures of earlier eras writ large.

Yet the development of monumental architecture in all the early civilizations seems contrary to what many cultural anthropologists and post-processual archaeologists might have predicted. Radical relativism would suggest that the creation or noncreation of structures that exceed in size and elaboration what was needed for practical purposes ought to reflect idiosyncratically variable cultural traditions. To account for the universality of monumental architecture in early civilizations, archaeologists have assumed that these buildings served a variety of vital symbolic functions. They are believed to have affirmed the social importance of those who ordered their construction—their size and splendor correlating with the power and wealth of those individuals. The centrality, imposing size, and distinctive style of such structures are also believed to have promoted social cohesion among the inhabitants of a state by enhancing their sense of belonging to a well-defined polity. At the same time, the upper classes controlled who had access to such buildings, what went on inside them, and how visible such activities were to ordinary people.

Very often, however, the largest single structures were erected at the time when the power of early rulers was being consolidated (Rathje 1975), a period that also witnessed lavish expenditures on rituals sponsored by the ruling class (Childe 1945). Monumental architecture also expressed dynastic ambitions and achievements, helped to legitimate and empower rulers who had usurped power or inherited office in an irregular manner, and served as a strategy for disguising political weakness and coping with disasters (Marcus 2003b). The Maya city of Tikal celebrated its defeat in AD 695 of the ruler of Calakmul by initiating an elaborate building program that was both innovative and expressive of Tikal's renewed power (Harrison 1999:125–146). Conversely, the Ur III rulers of southern Iraq expressed their hegemonic control over neighboring city-states by erecting a series of ziggurats, or temples built on solid brick platforms, of unprecedented size to honor the gods of these polities (Crawford 1991:57–81). The Late Classic rulers of the Maya state of Palenque compensated for their seemingly limited revenues and the small size of the buildings they were able to erect with the exceptional beauty and harmonious proportions that their architects gave to these structures (Freidel and Schele 1988:64–67). Although all the states belonging to a single city-state system shared the same general architectural canons, each member state tended to create a stylistic variant that visually expressed its own identity within the system.

In 1990 I proposed that in all early civilizations the construction by the state and the upper classes of buildings that were larger and more elaborate than functionally necessary suggests that conspicuous consumption, as originally defined by the economist Thorstein Veblen (1899), was universally viewed as an expression of wealth and political power in these societies (Trigger 1990). For ordinary people who possessed few labor-saving devices, the principle of "least effort" in relation to required results provided the key to all forms of ecological adaptation (Zipf 1949). The ability of rulers to amass great surpluses and expend them on projects that required vast amounts of human labor must have considerably enhanced the prestige of these rulers among their subjects. If commoners also believed that these structures increased the power of the rulers by winning them the favor of the gods, it was so much the better for these rulers. Yet, if conspicuous consumption on monumental architecture constituted a way of reinforcing political power in all early civilizations (a point that many culturally relativistic, post-processual archaeologists ought to be reluctant to accept), this effort was grounded, not simply on the rationalist ecological and adaptive considerations that constitute the focus of processual archaeology, but also on a highly specific metaphorical inversion of the principle of least effort that seems to have been no less widely understood (Lakoff 1987; Lakoff and Johnson 1980; Tilley 1999). This leads us into a realm of cross-cultural uniformities in human cognition of a sort long ignored by processual and post-processual archaeologists but which nineteenth-century archaeologists attributed to "psychic unity," a concept that we can now understand as designating a problem for study rather than an explanation of what happened.

More specific cross-cultural uniformities characterized urban centers associated with either city-states or territorial states, while differentiating these two types from one another. Cities associated with city-states were relatively compact, and their centers were marked by large buildings or complexes of buildings. In the Valley of Mexico, in Iraq, and among the Maya, these were temples, many erected on high platforms and hence visible from afar. Palaces, which functioned both as royal courts and as administrative centers, were located either adjacent to the central temple complex or elsewhere in the city. Generally, palaces were only one or two stories high. The centers of Yoruba cities were marked by the palace (*afin*), which contained major shrines and meeting places for hereditary government officials, as well as the royal residential complex. Thus, the central symbolism of the city focused on religious or other corporate themes rather than solely on the king. Temples or meeting places appear to have symbolized the unity of at least some of these communities prior to the development of kingship. In early times in Iraq, temple construction may have been the responsibility of individual temple corporations. Yet, in historical times, all monumental buildings were constructed and maintained in the name of the king. Nevertheless, temple complexes continued to dominate the urban landscape of Iraq in Neo-Babylonian times no less than they had done in the third millennium BC. Temples were also the most visible architectural symbols of Tenochtitlan and other cities in the Valley of Mexico in the Late Aztec period no less than they had been at Teotihuacán centuries earlier. Among the Classic Maya, where kings constructed major temples for their mortuary cults, the communal nature of such buildings was maintained by associating dead kings with major cosmic deities. It appears that, however powerful kings later became, symbols of urban unity established at an early stage of urban development in city-states were able to persist in these societies (Trigger 2003:123–131).

In territorial states, the layout of major urban centers tended to be dispersed rather than nucleated. Rulers, members of the nobility, and high-ranking officials sought to live apart from the rest of the urban population in residences separated from the settlements of elite specialists and retainers. Temples, palaces, and administrative buildings often were located within their own enclosure walls, which both protected and further isolated them from the rest of society. The most impressive structures associated with the Egyptian Old Kingdom administrative center at Mennefer (Memphis) were the royal pyramids and tombs of the upper classes constructed just beyond the western edge of the Nile Valley. The main administrative center consisted of an official palace and the temple of the local creator-god, surrounded by the residences of civil servants, soldiers, priests, artisans, and retainers. Royal residential palaces were located some distance away, near the pyramid of the reigning king (Trigger 2003:134–136).

At the center of the Inka capital of Cuzco, a zone between two small rivers was filled with stone palaces belonging to the reigning and former kings, temples, cloisters for celibate priestesses, and two large, contiguous squares where state rituals were performed. Adjacent to this central area was Saqsawaman, which served as both a fortress and a ritual center. Temples and palaces were not architecturally distinguished from each other; both consisted of single-room buildings constructed around the insides of a number of enclosed courtyards. Beyond the cultivated fields that surrounded the central core was a ring of settlements that housed nobles who were not related to the Inka kings, soldiers, craftworkers, and retainers. Still farther from the center were more farming communities and the elaborate rural residences of Inka rulers and high-ranking members of the royal family. The mummified bodies of dead kings and queens continued to reside in their palaces and rural residences, attended by descendants who had not become kings. The older royal palaces in central Cuzco also came to be used as centers for various cults of cosmic deities (Hyslop 1990).

The most imposing structures erected in northern China during the Shang Dynasty were huge enclosures with massive stamped-earth walls that appear to have served as elite-residence compounds and administrative centers. Within these compounds, stamped-earth platforms supported palaces and other elite buildings. Ancestor temples were located inside palaces. Around these enclosures were dispersed villages occupied by elite craftsmen, cemeteries for different classes of people, and at a greater distance, farm villages. The late Shang capital at Anyang seems to have been even more dispersed. Near its center was an elaborate palace complex but no evidence of a walled enclosure (Liu and Chen 2006; Trigger 2003:137–139).

In Old Kingdom Egypt, government construction appears to have been confined to the royal capital at Mennefer and to frontier regions. In most provincial centers, administrative offices, storage facilities, and temples appear to have been built in variable local styles, even if their construction and operation were paid for from government taxes (Kemp 1989:65–83). The greatest construction projects were the pyramid complexes of successive kings. Egypt was a small enough territorial state that most

Egyptian males were likely to visit or pass through the capital as corvée laborers at least once in their lifetime. Hence, Mennefer paralleled the king as a unique entity symbolizing the unity of Egypt itself.

By contrast, the Inka established regional centers throughout their kingdom, where major structures were built in Inka style. These centers were, like Cuzco, provided with all the buildings and ceremonial loci that the king needed in order to perform essential rituals when he was away from the capital waging war or inspecting provinces. While these communities did not closely resemble Cuzco visually, they had enough features in common to make them equivalent in the eyes of Inka ritualists. The Inka state covered much more territory than did ancient Egypt, and settled areas were separated by extensive tracts of uninhabited mountains and deserts. Because of this, the Inka rulers constructed Inka-style buildings as symbols of royal power in administrative centers throughout the kingdom (Hyslop 1990:174–176, 304–306). The contrast between how the Inka and Egyptian states distributed architectural symbols of royal power can thus be explained as adaptations to different ecological conditions. Although the Inka created the first large state based in the central highlands of Peru, they learned much from the successes and failures of many states that had preceded them in the Andean region. The even more striking, symbolic features that distinguished urban centers in territorial states from those in city-states reflect still more important differences in how class organization, political power, and social coherence were constituted in these different types of states.

If monumental architecture is a universal form of conspicuous consumption in complex societies, this constitutes an interesting expression of uniformity in human thinking. As metaphors go, however, it is a fairly straightforward one. The distinctive architectural expressions of power in city-states and territorial states carry cognitive parallels beyond the limits that either processual or post-processual archaeological theory can explain and suggest a sort of uniformity in human symbolic behavior that requires a different sort of explanation.

Emic Approaches

In recent years, post-processual archaeologists have sought to learn more about the culturally specific ideas that the inhabitants of particular ancient cities had about them. Long before the development of post-processual archaeology, this approach was pioneered by Joyce Marcus (1973, 1976, 1993:149–153), with her systematic study of what was meant by the Maya concept of "the four on high" (*kan kaanal*) when applied to the four Maya capitals (not always the same ones), each of which presided over a regional hierarchy of settlements. Adam T. Smith (2003:139–144) recently has proposed an alternative and more symbolic interpretation of these data.

Cultural approaches of this sort generally assume that, in the absence of historical contacts, there will be a vast amount of idiosyncratic variation in such beliefs from one early civilization to another. At the level of specific beliefs, this has probably been the case, yet not so in terms of general patterns of beliefs. Early cities generally appear to have been regarded as places where the human and divine realms came into especially close contact. Iraqi temples bore names such as the "House that is the Bond of the Sky and the Earth." The ancient Egyptians believed that the major shrine in every provincial center marked the location of the mound of creation, on which the god of that district had created the universe. This involved his fashioning not only cosmic order, the other gods, the universe, and human beings, but also cities, temples, and cult images (Meeks and Favard-Meeks 1996:13–32). Yoruba myths describe the god Oduduwa descending from the sky world to the site of his grove in the ancient city of Ife, where he created the terrestrial realm and the city of Ife itself. Oduduwa became the first ruler of Ife, and his immediate male descendants became the kings of the sixteen most prestigious Yoruba city-states (Awolalu 1979:12–13). In the Aztec myth of the Fifth Sun, the gods are described as re-creating the world in the ruins of the ancient city of Teotihuacán (León-Portilla 1963:54–61).

Archaeologists have read much specific cosmic imagery into ancient cities, especially ideas concerning centrality, directionality, and quadripartition. David O'Connor (1989b) maintains that, in the New Kingdom, Egyptian royal cities were laid out along a north-south axis associated with the king and the Nile River and an east-west axis associated with the sun. Where these two axes intersected, they built the main temple and just north of the approach to its western entrance constructed the official palace, where the king appeared as the earthly representative and incarnation of the sun god. At Waset (Thebes) during the flood season, the king and the cult statues of the local triad of deities were carried south to the temple of Luxor, where the king's life force was rejuvenated. At the end of the harvest, the god Amun proceeded westward to visit the royal mortuary temples on the opposite side of the Nile Valley. In the Aztec capital of Tenochtitlan, the Templo Mayor, located at the heart of the city, was believed to mark the center of the universe. Here, it was thought, the cosmic energy, which flowed down from the sky world and rose up from the underworld at the four quarters of the earth to make terrestrial life possible, returned to its source. Thus, for the Aztecs, the Templo Mayor was the most spiritually charged and important building in the world (Caso 1958:56–64). This pyramid temple's three tapered tiers, each with four sides, together with its top platform, represented the thirteen levels of the sky world, its supporting platform the earth, and its foundations the underworld, making it a cosmogram of the entire universe (Broda et al. 1987; van Zantwijk 1985).

Today more cross-cultural regularities are being found in the cosmic symbolism of early civilizations than many cultural anthropologists would have expected. Popular writers such as Graham Hancock (Hancock and Faiia 1998) interpret these similarities as being historically derived from a single mother civilization. If all early civilizations venerated a creator sun-god called Re, archaeologists might be inclined to take such ideas seriously. Yet many archaeologists follow the Romanian historian of religion Mircea Eliade (1954), a specialist on Siberian shamanism, in believing that a highly enduring and now worldwide representation of the cosmos originated in Upper Paleolithic shamanism. This representation postulated an *axis mundi* in the form of a centrally located cosmic tree or mountain that connected the terrestrial world with supernatural realms above and below it; around this axis, the human world was laid out in four quarters. Eliade's ideas are often used to read meaning into archaeological data in the absence of adequate, culturally specific documentation of what these data meant to their creators (Wheatley 1971:417–418), a practice that unwittingly may be exaggerating the extent of seeming cross-cultural uniformity in cosmic imagery. Concepts such as that of quadripartition were widespread in early civilizations, most of which saw either themselves or the terrestrial world of which they were a part as divided into four quarters. On closer inspection of what is known, however, it becomes clear that beliefs about centrality, verticality, and quadripartition display less specific uniformity from one early civilization to another than Eliade's followers believe. The desire to create cosmograms also does not appear to have been as obvious or widespread as Eliade's followers maintain (Trigger 2003:467–470). It is unclear how specific shamanic beliefs of an idiosyncratic cultural nature could have survived in any recognizable fashion for so long, in so many cultural traditions, or through so many dramatic economic and social transformations. It seems at least as likely that such shared beliefs as there are about cosmology reflect the basic sensory dynamics of how erect primates view the world around them (front/back, left/right, up/down) (Mithen 1996:235). The close identification in all early civilizations, and in still earlier societies, of what we differentiate as the natural and the supernatural would have made it relatively easy to use how the world was habitually perceived as a basis for speculating about its supernaturally determined structure.

We will gain accurate knowledge of how converging similar beliefs about the cosmic order were accepted in early civilizations and the extent to which cities were viewed as microcosms or cosmograms only after it has been determined, by means of detailed, case-by-case studies, what people living in individual early civilizations thought about such matters (Flannery and Marcus 1993; Kemp 2000; Marcus 1973, 2000 [1983b]; M. E. Smith 2003, 2005a). This must be done by studying texts that record the specific beliefs that people living in each early civilization held about such symbolism and by comparing these findings with archaeological data. Epigraphers in Egyptology, Assyriology, and classical studies are well trained to do this sort of work. Such investigations also accord with humanist traditions of research on early civilizations and with the belief of cultural anthropologists such as Clifford Geertz and postprocessual archaeologists that each culture must be understood on its own terms before comparing with another. Research along these lines is already providing fascinating insights into the various symbolic worlds of which ancient cities were a part. While much more research along these lines is necessary before a proper comparative study can be undertaken of what early cities meant to the people who lived in them, significant cross-cultural regularities are already emerging that require explanation.

Conclusion

Most archaeologists who are trained in anthropology agree that all human behavior is cognitively, and therefore culturally, mediated; that humans adapt to environments not as these really are but as they perceive and interpret these; and that a society's understanding of its environment must be sufficiently realistic to give most societies, their people, and their ideas a chance of surviving (Trigger 1998). That being so, it is not surprising that the findings of the adaptationist and functionalist studies of the 1960s and 1970s and of the investigations of the symbolic manipulation of material culture and its meaning that have flourished since the 1980s—and that began much earlier—are proving to be generally complementary rather than antithetical in nature. Although the prolonged confrontation between processual and post-processual archaeology sharpened an understanding of what each of these positions has to offer, both are now being seen as contributing in their own way to understanding early cities and other aspects of ancient cultures. There is also growing agreement that studies of ecological, social, and symbolic phenomena must be integrated into a holistic perspective. It is therefore no accident that many archaeologists are advocating replacing theoretical confrontation with attempts at a critical theoretical synthesis (Hegmon 2003; Marcus 2006; O'Brien 2005; Pauketat 2003; Schiffer 1996, 2000; Skibo and Feinman 1999; Skibo et al. 1995; Trigger 2003).

There are, however, many aspects of ancient cities and the archaeological record generally for which neither ecological-functionalist nor purely cultural explanations can account. Many of these take the form of cross-cultural regularities that nineteenth-century anthropologists would have discussed as examples of psychic unity. Explanations of this sort have in the past played only a limited and informally recognized role in archaeology. Roland Fletcher (1977, 1995) has suggested that the hominid mind possesses inherent proxemic interpretive abilities that produce significant uniformities, including cross-cultural uniformities, in the built environment. Anthony Forge (1972:374) has argued that in communities with more than 400 members, it becomes cognitively impossible to handle all relations on a face-to-face basis and that internal political segmentation and, therefore, more formal decision-making arrangements become necessary. Sander van der Leeuw (1981) has suggested that any time six or more social units need coordination, a new level of regulation is required. None of these promising propositions has been adequately studied and tested by archaeologists or other social scientists. To examine these and many other possible explanations and to account for many cross-cultural parallels in human behavior and material culture would require archaeologists and anthropologists to work more closely with psychologists, biologists, geneticists, and neuroscientists. These are fields in which experts have long been eager to offer biological explanations for uniformities relating to human behavior and cognition (Butterworth 1999; Dennett 2003; Donald 1991; Gazzaniga 1992, 1998; Low 2000; Pinker 2002; Wilson 1978). Yet little that is of scientific value, and much that is socially and politically dangerous, can result from such studies if they are not based on an informed understanding of the influences that culture exerts on human behavior. Hence, the involvement of anthropologists and archaeologists, with their broadly comparative perspective on human behavior, is vital for the success of such investigations. There is, however, the prospect that such research eventually may yield findings that are as interesting as is the recent demonstration by linguists and geneticists that the human ability to form plurals is controlled by a single gene (Gopnik 1997). I see this approach as a way of enhancing our understanding of cross-cultural uniformities shaping the archaeological record that so far have been ignored because they cannot be accounted for from an ecological-functional perspective. Many of these uniformities relate to symbolic aspects of cultures. Success in this endeavor would greatly expand the explanatory power of the cognitive-processual approach to archaeological interpretation (Renfrew and Zubrow 1994).

Acknowledgments

I deeply regret that I was prevented by illness from delivering this chapter as a Sackler lecture and from attending the conference on which this volume is based. I especially thank Joyce Marcus for her valuable editorial comments.

four
Analyzing Cities

Mogens Herman Hansen

In this very impressive cross-cultural volume on early urbanization are ten case studies that discuss cities in Mesopotamia, Egypt, India, and China. In Mesoamerica, the Maya and Aztec cities are covered and in South America, the Inka. A long contribution treats a wide range of early African cities, and Europe is represented by two studies of Roman cities.

Given that there were two contributions about Roman cities (chapters 6 and 7), I felt that it would be appropriate to have a case study on ancient Greek cities, and the editors of this volume agreed. Thus, wherever relevant, I will draw parallels between the ancient Greek cities and the other cities covered in the case studies (chapters 6–15). A discussion of the Neolithic city of Sesklo in Thessaly, for example, could complement Renfrew's chapter 2 and von Falkenhausen's chapter 11 discussion of Neolithic urbanization. Sesklo covered some 8–10 ha; it flourished from ca. 4800 to 4400 BC and had an estimated population of perhaps 3,000 (Demand 1996:9–12; Renfrew, chapter 2; von Falkenhausen, chapter 11).

We now know for sure that the Minoan Bronze Age palaces on Crete were not just palaces but centers of proper cities (Hansen 2002:7; Knappett 1999:621–624). Recent investigations have disclosed that the Mycenaean palaces were also centers of large nucleated settlements. Thebes covered at least 19 ha, Pylos some 20 ha, and Mykenai has been estimated at 32 ha. Each town seems to have controlled a territory of no more than 1,000–2,000 sq km (Bintliff 2002:156, 162, 173). That is important for ongoing discussions as to the extent of monumental architecture in Mesoamerica and South America and whether they were primarily political and religious centers or proper cities inhabited by a substantial number of permanent settlers. This issue is discussed in Morris's (chapter 15) contribution about the Inka cities.

Finally, the more than 1,000 *poleis* of the Greek world in the Archaic and Classical periods constitute one of the most impressive attestations of early urbanization (Hansen and Nielsen 2004). In his seminal paper, Kenneth Hirth advocates an emic approach to the Aztec *altepetl* and shows that "the *altepetl* included both rural and urban populations and no distinction was made between them by their inhabitants" and again that "the linguistic evidence equates city with the broader regional polity" (Hirth, chapter 14; Marcus 2000[1983b]:54–55). These observations fit the ancient Greek *polis* to perfection. One can simply exchange the word *altepetl* with the word *polis* and print the view in a book about Greek society in the Archaic and Classical periods (Hansen 2000c:152–154, 2002b:16). Also, membership of the polis, as well as of the altepetl, was not based on residential propinquity but on a different organization of the territory as a whole (Hirth, chapter 14). Hirth's emic approach reveals important similarities between two completely unrelated city-state cultures, one in Precolum-bian Mesoamerica and the other in ancient Europe.

My next point is about definitions. In order to conduct comparative studies, one must know what is being compared. The theme of this book is early cities and pre-industrial urbanism. Therefore, we must come to an agreement about some kind of working definition of the concept of urbanism and the concept of city. And, true enough, several of the chapters (Bard, chapter 9; Kusimba, chapter 12; Morris, chapter 15; Renfrew, chapter 2; Trigger, chapter 3; von Falkenhausen, chapter 11) open with a brief discussion of the question, What is a city?

All the case studies are archaeological, and, accordingly, several refer to Gordon Childe's study (1950) of the urban revolution and his ten criteria, which together form one of the best known and most frequently quoted definitions of what an early city is. All ten criteria are listed in Renfrew's chapter 2. Yet, the twelve studies presented in this book tend to question, or even disprove, at least five of the ten criteria (Bard, chapter 9; Hirth, chapter 14; Renfrew, chapter 2; Trigger, chapter 3).

(1) Writing was singled out by Childe as an essential aspect of urbanism. Following Childe, Sjöberg (1960:33) claimed that "the use of a writing system is the single firm criterion for distinguishing the city from other types of early settlement." But Uruk in Mesopotamia was a city several hundred years before cuneiform script emerged ca. 3200 BC (van de Mieroop 2004:19–23). The Inka civilization had cities but no script. The first major urban settlement in Africa was Jenne-jeno, which grew up in the third century BC and flourished in ca. AD 500–800, long before the population took up writing (Kusimba, chapter 12; McIntosh and McIntosh 1993:627–634). Also, if writing was a sine qua non for urbanism, there would be no reason to discuss Inka cities or large centers of the Neolithic period, such as Çatal Höyük in Turkey, or Sesklo in Thessaly, or the forty attested Neolithic cities in China (van Falkenhausen,

chapter 11). On the grounds that no special buildings testifying to a separation of function have been found, Renfrew (chapter 2) rejects the common view that Çatal Höyük was a city. But there may have been a separation of function and division of labor that does not show in the physical remains.

Conversely, writing is found in civilizations without cities. Thus, in writings on stone, bone, and wood, the Scandinavian runes were used for some 700 years before the earliest towns grew up in the southern part of Denmark (Knirk 1993:545–546).

(2) As Childe correctly observes, writing is a precondition for the development of sciences, but a consequence of this observation is that the existence of sciences as an urban characteristic disappears, along with writing, as a characteristic of urbanism.

(3) Truly monumental public buildings are indeed found all over the world in many early cities, from Mesoamerica to Mesopotamia, but no palaces or temples have been found in the cities of the Indus civilization (Kenoyer, chapter 10; Renfrew, chapter 2); von Falkenhausen (chapter 11) notes that numerous early Chinese cities had no monumental buildings, and Kusimba (chapter 12) makes the same observation for a number of early African cities. Allow me to add that dwellings in early Greek colonial settlements were huts or dugouts rather than houses, and it took a long time before temples were built in the sanctuaries (De Angelis 2003:17–39 for Megara Hyblaia; Tsetskhladze 1997:46–49 for Olbia). Other examples can be found, and we have to conclude that the presence of monumental public buildings is not an essential criterion to be used in a definition of what a city is.

Conversely, although we now know that both the Egyptians and the Maya had proper cities, some civilizations had monumental architecture but no cities. One example is early Medieval Ireland, where there were impressive monasteries but no cities until Norwegian Vikings in the early tenth century founded Dublin and the other Viking cities (Holm 2000). Again, Stonehenge, mentioned by Renfrew (chapter 2), counts as monumental architecture, but there is no sign of urbanism in the neighborhood.

(4) The division of labor and specialization of function are indisputably crucial aspects of urbanism, but, contra Childe, it is a moot point to what extent full-time specialists are required or whether we will allow early cities to have almost all part-time specialists, as Pyburn (chapter 13) has argued in her study of Maya cities.

(5) Childe takes it for granted that politically urbanized civilizations were organized as states. It is true that statehood and urbanism are often combined, but not always. There are cases of civilizations organized as states but without cities, although Trigger (2003:120) holds that "there is no evidence of a civilization without cities." Conversely, as mentioned in Renfrew's oral presentation at the colloquium (summarized in chapter 2), there have been urbanized civilizations not organized as states.

Examples of states without cities are the Anglo-Saxon kingdoms in their early period (ca. 500–700) (Arnold 1997:211–230) and most of the small Bantu-speaking kingdoms in Uganda, of which Ankole is the best known (Hansen 2000a:25–26; Oberg 1940; Steinhart 1978). Both the Anglo-Saxon and the Bantu kingdoms were certainly early states, but no cities were to be found.

Conversely, an example of cities without state organization is the Yako in Nigeria.

The Yako were settled in five towns or cities of 2,000–11,000 inhabitants each. These cities were governed by a crisscrossing system of patri- and matri-clans, but there was no central authority to enforce a legal order (Forde 1964; Hansen 2000a:26– 27). Here, in my opinion, is an obvious example of an urbanized civilization without state institutions. Also, in the age of Mohammed, Mecca and Medina were certainly cities situated along the caravan route from Palmyra to Aden, but it can be questioned to what extent they were states, that is, city-states. They were certainly not part of any larger state organization (Simonsen 2000:247).

Cities can be defined functionally, recognized as nucleated settlements distinguished from the hinterland, as centers of trade that gave rise to a considerable division of labor and specialization of function, as genuine central places, in the economic sense of the term. The title of this book is *The Ancient City*. No one will dispute that Uruk, Zhengzhou, Harappa, Athens, Rome, and Tenochtitlan were cities, but all the colloquium presenters presumed that the term *city* can be used as the general term for nucleated settlements larger than a village and correctly applied even to small early historical communities with a population of, say, just 1,000 inhabitants. Researchers have debated the synonymous use of *city* and *town*, and 1,000 inhabitants as the appropriate line of separation between city and village in ancient societies (Bairoch 1988:136; Horden and Purcell 2000:93; Kolb 1984:15). Smith (2005b:412) even includes two borderline cases of centers with 800 inhabitants. I endorse the view that to speak of a city or a town, a four-digit population is a requirement, but I also endorse the view that 1,000 inhabitants are enough to make an "early city" and that in exceptional cases we may go below 1,000 (Hansen 2000b:620, n. 108, 2004:26). This view conforms with V. Gordon Childe's study, in which he invariably speaks of cities and never of towns. I note that most contributors follow suit and speak of cities, not of towns. But in the Sackler Lecture, Colin Renfrew suggested that we should differentiate between town and city and should reserve the term *city* for large urban centers.

However, it is not just the size that lies behind the difference between towns and cities. We tend to speak of cities rather than towns when we have the administrative and political aspects of the settlement in mind. That distinction goes back to the Enlightenment, and a famous case is Rousseau's distinction in *Du contrat social* between *cité* and *ville*. Rousseau (1762:361) notes: "Le vrai sens de ce mot c'est presque entierement effacé chez les modernes; la plupart prennent une ville pour une Cité et un bourgeois pour un Citoyen. Ils ne savent pas que les maisons font la ville mais que les Citoyens font la cité." Similarly, according to the dictionaries, it is often the municipal autonomy that is emphasized when the term *city* is preferred to *town*.

As mentioned in Renfrew's lecture and in all the case studies, the urban aspects rather than the political aspects are in focus in this book on early cities. Nevertheless, all the contributors prefer *city* to *town*, although the term *city* suggests the political aspects. Apart from following Childe, one further reason may be that the majority of the case studies treat city-states—and several of them are about city-state civilizations—and in such a context the proper term is, of course, *city* rather than *town*.

In British English, a city is traditionally either a town with a cathedral or a town that has acquired the status of city by royal letter (Hornby 1995). Today, however, this distinction is largely forgotten, and the principal characteristic of a city is its size: a city is a large town. A city is defined as "a large and important town" (Hansen 2000a:25; Hornby 1995:201). Smith has the following definition:

> An urban settlement is defined here as one whose activities and institutions (whether economic, political, religious or cultural) affected areas outside of the settlement proper. Cities are large settlements with many urban functions that affect a larger hinterland, whereas towns are small settlements with fewer urban functionsaffecting a smaller region. [Smith 2005b:431, n. 14]

That is the distinction emphasized by Renfrew (chapter 2).

This point is not just a tedious discussion of terminology. It is inextricably linked to the question of whether, in studying nucleated settlements, we shall work with a two-tier model (distinguishing between cities and villages) or with a three-tier model (cities, towns, and villages), or even a four-tier system as suggested by Renfrew (cities, towns, villages, and hamlets). In his opinion, our choice of model is important if we want to know to what extent ancient Greece can be analyzed as an urbanized civilization.

A last important point is the common description of Childe's list as a "definition." A multithetic trait list comprising ten criteria, of which five are optional, can in no way be called a definition. It is—if anything—a Weberian ideal type (Weber 1973: 190–205, in particular, page 191), and as an ideal type, Childe's list may still be used in a modified form.

Instead of Childe's multithetic trait list, some prefer a functional approach: according to Trigger, a "city can be defined as a community or settlement that performs numerous functions in relation to a broader hinterland" (Trigger, chapter 3, 2003:120). For a similar definition, see Smith 2005b:432, n. 14. Similarly, quoting George Cowgill, Renfrew (chapter 2:31) notes that a city provides "specialized services to a wider society." Such an approach is linked with Central Place Theory, which goes back to Christaller's groundbreaking work (1933). The crucial aspect is to see nucleated centers as networks in which a city is placed at the top of a settlement hierarchy and the other nucleated centers farther down in accordance with their size and distance from the central place. The dominance of the city over the hinterland diminishes with the distance from the city, so there is an essential relationship between the size of a city and the size of the territory it controls.

The result is often too broad a definition of what a city is. Many villages fulfill the requirement of performing numerous functions in relation to a broader hinterland. As noted by Trigger and previously referenced, by this definition it is impossible to distinguish cities from towns and towns from villages.

One important aspect of this approach is the growing awareness of the view that cities must not be studied in isolation. A city must always be understood in relation to its hinterland. And this observation leads to my next point.

A combined analysis of urbanization and state formation supports the view that early civilizations roughly fall into two types: large, so-called territorial states (I prefer calling them "macro-states") each dotted with a number of cities and towns, and city-state civilizations (or "city-state cultures," as I have called them), in which a large region is broken up into city-states, each consisting of an urban center with its immediate hinterland.

This important distinction is a central point in Bruce Trigger's monumental study of early civilizations published in 2003, and it goes back to his earlier book published in 1993 (Trigger, chapter 3, 1993:8–14, 2003:92–119). Allow me here to state that I established this distinction as one of the fundamental aspects of the research program of the Copenhagen Polis Centre in 1991, and it was fully developed in the Centre's two comparative studies of thirty-five different city-state cultures, published in 2000 and 2002. The Copenhagen Polis Centre's research program of 1991 was published in Hansen 1994 and fully developed in Hansen 2000e and 2002b, in particular, Hansen 2000b:598; see also Yoffee 2005:45–46. This basic distinction between macro-states and city-state cultures, or—in Trigger's terminology—territorial states and city-state systems, is accepted by several of the contributors to this book and applied in their analysis; see chapters by Renfrew, Stone, Bard, and Pyburn. Without mentioning the opposition between territorial states and city-state cultures, the concept of city-state is discussed in chapters by DeLaine, Jones, Kenoyer, Kusimba, and Hirth. The only two contributions without any reference to city-states are those of von Falkenhausen and Morris.

One important observation that follows from distinguishing between territorial macro-states and city-state cultures concerns the percentage of the population settled in cities as compared with those settled in the hinterland. In territorial states, some 80 to 90 percent of the population lived in the countryside and no more than 10 to 20 percent in the cities. Bairoch (1988:137) reveals that, at 90 percent, 10 percent is based on the assumption that an urban center must have 5,000 inhabitants to count as a city. At 80 percent, 20 percent is my guesstimate of the proportion if we accept 1,000 as the minimum population (Jones, chapter 7; Trigger, chapter 3). In city-state cultures, the percentages were almost reversed. It is presumed that in some periods more than 80 percent of the Sumerian population lived behind the walls in urban centers of more than approximately 40 ha and only some 20 percent were settled in the hinterland (Adams 1981:90–94; Kuhrt 1995:31; Trigger 2003:124). Trigger suggests that in city-state systems at least 15 percent, and often more than 50 percent, of the population was urban (chapter 3, 2003:124). For the Greek polis, see Hansen 2004:11–16.

In early societies, at least some 80 percent of the population, and probably more, had to spend most of their time providing food for themselves and the remaining 10 to 20 percent of the population. If more than 50 percent of the population often lived behind the walls of the city, it is an inescapable inference that many of the citydwellers must have been farmers who had their house and family in the city and went out every morning to their fields in the hinterland (Childe 1950:11; Trigger 2003:125). They are what Max Weber (1999:67–68) called *Ackerbürger* and what I suggest calling "city-farmers." They constitute a crucial feature of the city-state cultures, and I note that they are duly mentioned and discussed in some of the chapters that treat city-state cultures (Kusimba, chapter 12; Pyburn, chapter 13; Trigger, chapter 3).

Let me add that in the ancient Greek city-state culture these city-farmers are abundantly attested in the literature (Hansen 1997:44–47, 2004:16–18) and that all the archaeological surveys that have been conducted during the past three decades—including Renfrew's survey of the island of Melos—show that in the fourth century BC the majority of the population of each small or middle-size polis lived in the urban center of the polis and the minority only in the hinterland. Only Athens and some other very large poleis had the majority of their population settled in the hinterland, either dispersed or in villages (Hansen 2004:11–16, 2006:16, 69–72, 80–82, 139–141).

One further consequence of having a large number of city-farmers is that the concept of the consumer city as invented by Werner Sombart and developed by Max Weber (Sombart 1902:2:198–205, 1916:1:142–154; Weber 1999:63–67) must be removed from analyses of city-state cultures and applied only in studies of territorial states.

The concept of the consumer city presupposes that (1) there is an opposition between the urban and the rural population; (2) the urban population constitutes a small part only of the total population of town plus hinterland; and (3) the core of the urban population comprises consumers who derive their maintenance not from what they produce, but from taxes and rents exacted from the rural population.

This model does not fit the typical city-state culture: (1) often the majority of the population lived in the urban center, not the minority; (2) because of the numerous city-farmers (Ackerbürger), there is no opposition between urban and rural population; and (3) the landowners who did not work as farmers themselves constituted a minority of the urban population, so the majority of the urban population was not maintained by taxes and rents exacted from a separate rural population (Hansen 2004:9–25; Trigger, chapter 3, 2003:131–141).

Thus, the concept of the consumer city should be removed from the study of city-state cultures and applied only in studies of territorial macro-states, where it often is a seminal concept and an excellent model that explains how a small urban elite of landowners exploited a much larger rural population of farmers settled in the countryside.

This picture of early cities in general and the Greek polis in particular is not universally accepted by ancient historians and classical archaeologists. Following Moses Finley, many still hold that the ancient economy was basically an agrarian subsistence economy. Trade played a small role, and long-distance trade was insignificant (Finley 1973; Hopkins 1983:xi). The overwhelming majority of the population was settled in the hinterland (Cartledge 1998:13), and the cities were the home of a small part of the population, of whom the majority were landowners who maintained themselves only by exacting taxes and rents from the much larger rural population. The urban population counted for no more than 10 percent of the total population of the polis, often less (Horden and Purcell 2000:92).

When this view seems to be contradicted by the rapidly growing number of landscape surveys, the answer has sometimes been that landscape surveys are unreliable sources for the demography of the settlement pattern (Corvisier 2004:15–17). Then, it is argued that before the Industrial Revolution it is a priori implausible that any urban population could outnumber the population settled in the countryside, either dispersed or in small villages. Bairoch (1976) holds that urban populations in early modern Europe could never have exceeded 25 percent of the whole.

But the a priori argument carries no weight. If we concentrate on the regions that in antiquity were broken up into city-states, we find that, in some cases at least, nucleated settlement seems to have persisted right up to the modern period, even long after the city-states had been transformed into urban centers of larger states. One example is Sicily in the nineteenth century. In 1871 the island had a population of two and a half million (2,584,099), of whom 176,004 lived dispersed in isolated farmsteads and 270,843 lived in nucleated settlements of up to 2,000 inhabitants each. More than two million (2,137,252) lived in towns with more than 2,000 inhabitants, and of these, close to a million and a half (1,377,819) lived in towns of more than 8,000 inhabitants. Thus, 30 percent of the Sicilian population lived in small towns (2,000–8,000 inhabitants), and 53 percent in large towns or cities of more than 8,000 inhabitants (Beloch 1886:476, n. 2). Yet, the overwhelming majority of the population were farmers who lived in the urban centers but worked in their fields outside the city wall. The Sicilian example shows that it was perfectly possible before the Industrial Revolution to have an urban population of close to 80 percent of the total population. Nineteenth-century Sicily is an unquestionable example of a people of whom the majority were Ackerbürger or city-farmers.

Precisely the same picture was found in Greece in the nineteenth century and still in the twentieth century wherever the pre-industrial settlement pattern survived. That has been demonstrated repeatedly by Renfrew and Wagstaff in their groundbreaking study of the island of Melos (Wagstaff and Auguston 1982).

To sum up, the large size of the urban population in city-state cultures, the importance of the Ackerbürger, and the resulting abolition of the consumer-city model being applied to city-state cultures are three very important insights brought into focus by this book.

Let me round off my comments by mentioning three further aspects of urbanism that are elucidated in this book.

(1) Trade, including long-distance trade, is an essential aspect of city life (Childe 1950:15, no. 9, in his trait list of urban characteristics): "Regular 'foreign' trade over quite long distances was a feature of all early civilizations" (Trigger 2003:342–355). Long-distance trade was an important aspect of the economy in about half of the thirty-five city-state cultures (Hansen 2000d:625, 2002b:140). Apart from defensive features and houses, the marketplace is the one physical feature that Weber (1999: 59–63) singles out in his definition of the city. I find it strange that Childe (1950) has no explicit mention of the market although he emphasizes trade as an essential characteristic of the city. Local trade in the marketplace is mentioned in almost all the case studies, and long-distance trade is emphasized in some of them (Kusimba, chapter 12; Pyburn, chapter 13.) The importance of long-distance trade for the emergence and

development of cities means that we cannot study the city just in relationship to its immediate hinterland. The long-distance trading networks are much larger and much more important for urbanization than often believed, and Central Place Theory cannot do justice to this aspect of urbanism (Hansen 2000b:609–610, 614–616). One example is Assur in the Old Assyrian period (ca. 1900–1800 BC) (Larsen 1976, 2000).

(2) Division of labor and specialization of function are crucial for urbanism, but, as I mentioned earlier, it is a moot point as to what extent full-time specialists are a necessary precondition for urban life (Pyburn, see chapter 13).

(3) Size and density of the population in the settlement are, in my opinion, indispensable requirements, although Trigger (chapter 3) disagrees. To name specific figures is, of course, arbitrary because all concepts are, in fact, artificial constructs pressed down upon a fluid world that has no "natural" dividing lines (Hansen 2000b:600–610). While a population of 5,000 or even 10,000 is a normal requirement in the modern world in order to speak of cities, it is almost universally believed that early cities could be much smaller. Sjöberg (1960), however, suggests a threshold of 10,000 inhabitants even for early cities, and de Vries (1981) insists on the same number for the period 1500–1800. For practical purposes, many studies of early cities suggest, as a rule of thumb, a four-digit figure as the minimum population size, which means that a nucleated center must have at least 1,000 inhabitants in order to count as a city (see above).

The other and trickier question is the density of population in the city. Many South American and Mesoamerican cities, some African cities, and some Asian cities—for example, the early Malay cities in Indonesia—were large open structures (Inka cities: Morris, chapter 15. Maya cities: Pyburn, chapter 13; Grube 2000:553–556. Precolonial Addis Ababa and Mbanza Congo: Kusimba, chapter 12. Indonesian cities: Reid 2000:421) very different from the European cities in which, to quote Max Weber (1999:59), "houses are built so densely that they stand wall to wall." Many of these open cities did not have a defensive wall, a characteristic of most ancient and Medieval European cities and one of the criteria listed in Weber's ideal type of *die Stadt*. From a strictly architectural and urban planning point of view, it can be questioned—and it has indeed been questioned—whether these settlements were cities. Yet, functionally, all these centers were undoubtedly cities. They can be recognized as nucleated settlements distinguished from the hinterland; they were centers of trade; they gave rise to a considerable division of labor and specialization of function; and they were genuine *Zentralorte*, in the economic sense of the term. Furthermore, they were admittedly open structures, but not more than they would count as cities even according to many modern definitions of what a city is. The modern Indian census requirements for being a city are often adduced in studies of urbanization. In modern India, the requirements for being a city are adduced by, for example, Wheatley (1972:620): (1) more than 5,000 inhabitants; (2) a population density exceeding 1,000 to the square mile; and (3) more than 75 percent of the adult males engaging in work other than agricultural. The required density of population is 1,000 inhabitants per square mile. That corresponds to a few more than four persons per ha. Maya cities were among the most open structures in Mesoamerica. Yet most of them seem to have had a population density of six to nine persons per ha (Grube 2000:553–556), and that is about twice the required minimum. When we distinguish between dispersed and nucleated settlement, the ancient South American, the Mesoamerican, some of the African, and some of the Asian cities belong with the nucleated settlements, in spite of the fact that a density of six to nine persons per ha is very different from historic cities in other parts of the world that have had population densities of 100 to sometimes more than 300 persons per ha. For European cities in the early modern period, Mols (1955) assumed an average of 175 persons per ha of inhabited urban space. The somewhat lower figures obtained by Russel (1958) for the period from ca. 1350 to 1550 are not reliable (Hollingsworth 1969:58). Furthermore, it must be kept in mind that some of the Mesoamerican cities were much larger and more densely settled than is traditionally believed (Smith 2005b).

five
Other Perspectives on Urbanism
Beyond the Disciplinary Boundaries

Karl W. Butzer

Lawrence Durrell's experimental *The Alexandria Quartet* (1957–1961) uses four novels to show how the same sets of events can be seen and interpreted very differently by people with dissimilar experience, perspective, and sociocultural background. Mountolive, a staid British civil servant, relates the happenings in an ostensibly objective way and in the third person. The indigenous Justine gives a wildly different, spicy, and intensely personal account that also diverges from the Levantine Balthasar's tawdry but much more complex rendition. Finally, the voice of expatriate Clea expands the temporal frame, putting the story into an unexpected political context.

This skilled apposition of outsider-insider (etic-emic) readings can be usefully applied to the study of urbanism, to highlight the distinction between "Western" and alternative interpretations. Urbanism is many things, depending on the question, the scale of vision, and the cultural background of a respondent. But the continuing effort to find general criteria for urbanism (Childe 1950) misses the point in that it implies that there is a single, rational answer. It would be much more creative to explore multiple facets such as religion, social values, and ethnicity at greater depth. Several of the contributions in this book illustrate the point, including the linguistically based study on ancient Chinese cities (Falkenhausen, chapter 11). Islamic urbanism, which had prehistoric roots and was in full bloom before the Maya Classic "collapse," represents another striking alternative to a single-mindedly "Western" perspective. Ethnographic or historical insight is a sine qua non to start a more etic investigation. Whenever possible, archaeology should be combined and contrasted with archival or historical research, as indeed many of the chapters in this book do. But there also has to be a greater cultural sensitivity, with regular recourse to cross-cultural and cross-temporal comparisons, if we are to grasp the insider perspective. To achieve that goal, we must transcend a preoccupation of urban archaeology with material evidence, something that will be possible only with a sustained, cross-disciplinary discourse among practitioners from all the subdisciplines concerned with early urbanism. As the short bibliography suggests, geographers are major contenders in historical and cross-cultural urbanism, and they contribute to identifying and understanding questions of contemporary relevance.

Long-term Settlement Histories and Discontinuities

Archaeologists who do not dichotomize town and country have recognized that within a particular region the number of settlements of all sizes increases and then decreases over time. In some instances, most of the larger and smaller places may appear to be abandoned. When the cycle waxes once again, many of the derelict sites may not be reoccupied, and the archaeological components may be different (Jameson et al. 1994; Potter 1979). Even when disjunctions are incomplete, such cycles of growth and decline are intriguing, if not challenging, to interpret (Enckell et al. 1979; Marcus 1998). They are common enough in European and Southwestern prehistory and find more dramatic analogs in the rise and decline of so-called high civilizations on different continents, where they involve urban sites, sociopolitical institutions, and possible ethnocultural identification.

In the more recent experience of the Modern demographic transition, explanations for growth would typically turn to a host of factors, both inputs and feedbacks, including disease; rural productivity; environmental resources and their management; urban market and labor demand; long-distance trade and economic integration; migration, insecurity, and war; and potential administrative incompetence or failed policies. The complexity of the issues may not even allow firm conclusions. In earlier ranges of historical or prehistoric time, these same factors remain material, but social unrest, dislocation, and cultural disillusionment probably weigh even more strongly. Nonetheless, a few archaeologists, historians, and even natural scientists have short-circuited these webs of reasoned explanation to assert "civilizational collapse" in response to mono-causal scenarios such as "abrupt climatic change" or environmental degradation. Never mind that co-occurrence or coincidence, even if it be true, does not prove causality.

"Collapse" is a very real part of urban prehistory and history, and it requires attention. Given the deductive proclivity of world-systems historians, who have a major interest in "rise and decline" (Chase-Dunn and Hall 1997), it is fortunate that there is a more cautious literature in geography about environmental vulnerability and social resilience (Bankoff et al. 2004; Endfield et al. 2004; Liverman 1999). But the critical facilities of anthropology must also be marshaled to challenge, rather than endorse, this new environmental determinism (Butzer 1997; McIntosh et al. 2000).

Long-term settlement histories serve to highlight a propensity for millennial long-waves in population history. We need only turn to the sixteenth-century demographic and social collapse of indigenous Mexico, in the context of earlier, archaeologically verified settlement histories (Sanders 1988), to see that population cycles are real. Such macroregional cycles deserve attention by more urban archaeologists and historians, reinforced by an explicit, cross-disciplinary discourse.

Population estimates pose a practical problem. Whatever their limitations, urban site sizes and site configurations offer the only semiquantitative access to prestatistical population aggregations, when used in conjunction with complementary data on smaller nucleated sites or dispersed settlement features (Butzer 1976, 1984), and their spatial relationships (Church and Bell 1988). Sometimes such non-urban sites are enumerated by religious or historical topographies (Timm 1984–1992), but more commonly they must be unraveled by regional archaeological surveys or related site-sampling procedures. As in the processual sphere of intensification and dis-intensification, with town and country tightly interwoven, ratios of urban to non-urban populations can sometimes be simulated from early statistics on preindustrial economic sectors.

Urban archaeology, in conjunction with archaeological survey and geo-archaeology, is uniquely equipped to address long-term settlement histories and discontinuities. These are of significant regional interest and help define the dynamic context of human settlement agglomerations. They also flag discontinuities that demand closer investigation. Such findings are relevant at a larger scale because both growth and decline foster questions about the range of factors that drive macroregional demographic change. This is interesting in historical terms and even more so in relation to the unprecedented global population expansion that began some 250 years ago. Will decline inevitably follow, and if so, why and how?

Urban Geo-archaeology

Switching from the regional to the site-specific frame, complex constructional histories are embedded in urban sites. In general terms, these will be picked up by traditional excavation methods. But specialized attention to urban sediments and their links to external, environmental processes may elucidate patterns of occupation within individual structures or in the course of changing urban land use, growth, and decay (Butzer 1982a). Surprisingly enough, such urban geo-archaeology still receives little attention. Beyond the standard issue of artifactual integrity, there is a microstratigraphy within and between structures that records accumulating "waste" under variable conditions of deposition and postdepositional transformation (Butzer 1981, 2005a; Butzer et al. 1982; Rosen 1986; Schuldenrein et al. 2004). This also has implications for the links between an early city and its changing environmental context. For example, the construction of cities and chinampas in the lacustrine Basin of Mexico may have been in response to repeated changes of lake level, as suggested by the research of Cordova (1997), rather than a deliberate reclamation of marshland, in other words, an opportunity as well as a challenge.

The most obvious case in point is the urban mound or tell, composed primarily of mud-brick (adobe). Building materials are liable to slow attrition and periodic collapse or destruction, followed by replacement or abandonment. Rooms may be swept clean or fall into disuse, with intrusion of floodwaters or blowing sands. Collapsed structures are built over or first cleaned out, to be dumped elsewhere. The sediment matrix accumulates sufficiently rapidly that appropriate study can identify the human and nonhuman agents responsible for particular sediment layers and can be used to reconstruct a settlement microhistory of growth or decline. Extended from a limited number of structures to a selection of wards or neighborhoods, urban geo-archaeology can identify demographic trends of growth and decline and can offer resolution on the processes of decay or abandonment (Butzer 1982a:table 6–1).

In the "Lost City of the Pyramids" at Giza (Lehner 2002a, 2004), it is possible to identify episodes of mud-brick meltdown and liquefaction, resulting in lateral mass movements of mud, or of major flood events that wreaked havoc within the site (Butzer 2005a). As a consequence, a part of this site complex had to be rebuilt at least three or four times within no more than thirty or forty years. This not only illustrates the dynamic nature of sites but also shows that phenomenal desert rains did not deter the powers-that-be from rebuilding the same structures in the same places. However, later mud-brick walls were placed on elaborate, rough-stone foundations, possibly stabilized by mortar. Such foundations later protected the site from deflation. In effect, the location was reused because of its advantages, illustrating an early response (ca. 2500 BC) to environmental vulnerability.

With adjustments, similar criteria can be applied to sites built of cut or crude rock, such as Ethiopia's Axum, with its prominent and durable collapse rubbles (Butzer 1981). For example, sediment accumulates after abandonment, even before the last of the superstructure tumbles down; the interior is opened up to slope-wash or eolian sands. Alternatively, structures or burial shafts may be overwhelmed by eroded soils from upslope, providing signposts for local landscape histories and land management. On a much larger scale, floodplain cities are affected by catastrophic floods, across time ranges of several centuries. Salvage study of foundations exposed by construction in cities of eastern Spain thus yields insights into urban settlement histories, and the rhythm of severe flooding becomes a proxy record of effective watershed disturbance (Butzer et al. 1983).

Cities are open systems—economically, demographically, and environmentally. Yet the common practice is for archaeologists, in the Mediterranean world and elsewhere, to shovel out the matrix between the architectural alignments, after the artifacts have been removed. But that "dirt" may be diagnostic of which parts of a site were or were not occupied at a particular time, and it can provide prima facie evidence for rise or demise. Sediments may also document direct links between site and environment, for example, down-slope of a settlement. All too many excavated urban sites are incompletely understood as a result of disciplinary introspection.

Rulership and Bureaucratic Integration

A different miscomprehension of early cities stems from a Eurocentric interpretation of how early states operated, namely, the assumption that hierarchical bureaucracies in capital cities were always effective in administering subordinate or distant towns. It is therefore helpful to draw attention to Ethiopia, a literate civilization with a history of precarious urbanism. Nineteenth-century kings traveled around the country, with their army and retainers, to collect tribute and live off the land (Kusimba, chapter 12; Pankhurst 1982). The pre-Modern written record of Ethiopia is largely limited to the religious chronicles of its kings (Tamrat 1972). Until the 1890s, there was nothing remotely similar to a civil service, a general accounting office, or an archive of decrees and other proclamations. Titles honored retainers of the negus at various levels, without creating regular officials or a permanent chain of authority. Any continuity was anchored in isolated monastic centers, in the physical projection of royal churches or residences (Butzer 1982b), and, above all, in oral tradition and its written transmission (Hable Selassie 1972).

Ethiopia is no analog for ancient Egypt, but this example suggests the need to reexamine some entrenched assumptions about institutional networking in early state formation (Lehner 2000). Until the second or third dynasties, tribute in Egypt appears to have been collected directly during periodic royal visitations to the provinces (Helck 1975; Martin-Pardey 1976:33–36). Some 2000 titles were awarded during the Old Kingdom, but almost none identify a function, implying that they were honorifics (Baer 1960). Bureaucratic delegation of authority appears to have been on a personal or idiosyncratic basis, raising legitimate questions about how authority was implemented, except within the pharaoh's residence and scattered royal estates (Quirke et al. 2001). Unfortunately, most of the preserved evidence for writing comes from mud sealings and stone inscriptions; little survives of the more explicit papyrus documents for the Old Kingdom.

In Egypt, the public religious realm was interwoven with the secular, and the early administrative role of the temples of the royal cult was quite unclear; the priesthood may, for example, have transmitted decrees to the provincial centers, while projecting the authority of divine kingship through temples and shrines and possibly keeping the accounts of the royal estates. Only towards the end of the Old Kingdom (Dynasty 6) is there evidence of secular agents supervising specific tasks (Martin-Pardey 1976:109–201; Quirke et al. 2001) or serving as intermediaries between the royal residence and the provinces. Officials for urban (as opposed to provincial) administration are not documented before the New Kingdom.

Although ancient Egypt does not offer a universal model for urban origins, it offers—as one of the very earliest complex societies (Lehner 2000)—an opportunity to rethink the accepted relationships between complexity and urbanism. Despite the belief that Memphis was the Old Kingdom capital, current evidence from both Giza (Lehner 2004) and Memphis (Jeffreys and Tavares 1994) suggests the presence of several large but short-term urban nucleations, linked to shifting royal residences, in proximity to different construction projects such as pyramids and their associated temples. This does not, of course, negate the possibility of a major, fixed ceremonial center, such as Ethiopia's Axum. Like the Boserupian dilemma, we do not know whether writing and putative administrative structures drove or were a consequence of rapid sociopolitical change and urbanization, restricted to the immediate proximity of the royal residence. Royal retainers and the priesthood may have been the two branches of an incompletely centralized but authoritarian, archaic state that probably depended heavily on kin relations. The phenomenal evolution of Egyptian artistic expression that began even before the unification of Egypt (perhaps ca. 3100 BC) appears to have been a function of royal prerogative. But royal power probably soon transcended provincial tribute and the agricultural production of royal estates, through monopolistic control of foreign trade for wine, oil, and timber, using Egypt's mineral wealth or military power (Butzer 1997; Warburton 2001:17–27).

We still do not really understand the emerging interrelationships between military power, official religion, writing, administrative institutions, a complex society, and urbanism during the millennium before the revival of Middle Kingdom Egypt. For Childe, the links were self-evident. Today, if we go beyond Eurocentric rationalism, we begin to recognize that explanation is far from simple. There is indeed much more to early urbanism than taxonomy.

Classical and Islamic Urbanism

City form, as a function of town planning, is of central interest to urban archaeology. At issue is not so much the economic relation of form and function, but the sociopolitical *momenta* that leave their imprint on urban morphology, as well as the ethnocultural tastes and imperatives that may limit formal geometries. Cityscapes project more than power, wealth, and style. They also reflect cultural values and the rituals of public social behavior, while accommodating the pushes and pulls of social segregation and neighborhood aggregation. These competing demands must be accommodated within optimizing solutions to economics and security. As a result, urban landscapes can be informative, even without explanatory texts, as to the many dialectical poles imprinted within an urban fabric.

After the death of Alexander the Great, the orthogonal grid-plan town bursts forth in the Hellenistic Near East, setting the tone for an "orderly" urban prototype that was perfected in Imperial Rome, dominating cities of the Mediterranean Basin for half a millennium; compare DeLaine (chapter 6), Fentress (2000), or Rich and Wallace-Hadrill (1991) with older taxonomies such as Grimal and Woloch (1983). We would now say that the new Hellenistic cities in the former Persian Empire were designed to communicate a Western meta-narrative that was fundamentally secular, rational, and propagandistic.

Although based on existing Greek prototypes (Owens 1991), the Hellenistic city was designed to project a New Order of enlightened polity and Greek civilization in non-Hellenic areas. The axial layout and formal architecture represented dynastic power, the official cult, and the centers of cultural and social interaction. Ethnic and assimilated Greeks clustered around the city core, lending prestige to the adjacent streets. The main body of indigenous people lived in peripheral "neighborhoods" that played only a subordinate role in urban life. The Hellenistic city was, in fact, designed to impress and to acculturate these indigenous, Near Eastern peoples.

Nonetheless, the planned Hellenistic or colonial model remained only one of two basic possibilities because indigenous urbanism reflected different principles. Traditional Near Eastern societies placed an inordinate emphasis on privacy. Family life was not exhibited on the street, nor were civic activities conducted in an agora or piazza. This is born out by the painstaking French excavations at Ugarit (Ras Shamra, Syria) (Yon 1997), where the Late Bronze site plan closely approximates that of an Islamic city of two millennia later. Ugarit was tightly packed, with narrow, winding streets and multiple blind alleys that provided semiprivate access to houses that were focused on home courtyards. Residential districts were based on social, primarily kin, groupings (Schloen 2001). Ugarit does not stand by itself, but as a well-studied prototype of cities emerging in greater Mesopotamia during the fourth millennium BC.

In Egypt, emphasis has been placed on top-down urban models, such as Lahun, Amarna, and Elephantine, which vaguely conform to Western expectations. The impression obtains that some orthogonal organization was imposed at certain times, but where organic evolution was possible, a different picture emerges. In the craftsmen's town at Deir el-Medina (McDowell 2001; Valbelle 1985), opposite Luxor in Upper Egypt, houses had air vents rather than windows facing the street, and during the town's final expansion, doorways began to open on new cul-de-sac alleys. Exteriors were plain, and whatever wealth there was, was displayed in the interior. Peaking shortly after 1200 BC, Deir el-Medina suggests that residential quarters in pre-Islamic Egypt may have been similar to the crowded, egalitarian Coptic settlements of a later time that were never recorded by excavators. Long before the Hellenistic era, indigenous Near Eastern neighborhoods already reflected different cultural values and rules. Given the compartmentalization of urban archaeology according to period, this fundamental characteristic has been essentially overlooked.

During the reign of Augustus, the city of Rome underwent a major makeover, with official investment and private wealth driving a frenzy of building activity, designed to glorify the deified emperor and to represent the power of the primate city. But the complex topography of the Seven Hills and existing architectural features precluded anything approaching an orthogonal grid. Contrary to widespread opinion, the architect Vitruvius (approximately 25 BC) played no tangible role in this rebuilding, other than as a conservative critic. New provincial cities sometimes implemented the norms of a chessboard geometry, but at least some of these were transformed military camps; even so, orientation with respect to the cardinal points was not the rule. The importance of Vitruvius is that he is one of the few surviving sources to document the architectural activity of a period in which architects planned on a large scale and helped create distinctive urban landscapes.

During the third century AD, the population of Roman provincial cities was declining rapidly as a result of epidemics, warfare, and economic disintegration. The original propagandistic role of the city to acculturate native peoples (see Jones, chapter 7) was forgotten as citizenship was extended to almost everyone. With the advent of Christianity under Constantine, the first churches were built outside the walls of Rome, creating new parish modules of nucleated settlement, while the core of Rome became a museum and decayed (Krautheimer 1983). Provincial cities of the fourth and fifth centuries AD saw a building-over of public spaces and conversion of elite residences into warrens of squalid slums (Carver 1996; Kennedy 1985). Piece by piece, all across the empire, the administrative structures that had once maintained city spaces and urban order failed.

The new Christian ideology certainly contributed to this transformation, as baths, circuses, and theaters were closed, temples razed, and administrative buildings converted into basilican churches. Commerce was unwelcome. Great cities such as Antioch did not recover after Justinian's plague of the 540s. The comprehensive architectural schemes of the Classical city were abandoned. Instead, rulers now sought to identify and glorify themselves through church construction on a monumental scale. Wherever cities did not die but evolved, they became differently grounded, in the transcendental symbolism of Christian redemption. This is clearly reflected in the Madaba mosaic map (ca. AD 550) of Jordan (Donner and Cüppers 1977), which shows a topography with few secular signposts but dominated by churches and focused on the city of Jerusalem.

The emergence of a Christian-Byzantine metropolis (Krautheimer 1969) in newly founded Constantinople remains to be comprehensively studied. Constantine's axial esplanade of power, pomp, and entertainment was modified under Justinian by construction of the "great" and "little" Hagia Sophias at either end. By 1204 the palace complex had been abandoned and only the churches remained, with the seat of government moved to modest buildings at the other end of town. As represented by city views drawn before 1453 (Manners 1997), Constantinople's hallmark was a host of parish churches at the center of neighborhood communities, possibly forming semi-autonomous social modules, that included foreign colonies. Neighborhoods or barrios form the building blocks of urban social living in many cultural contexts (Kaluzny 2004) and call for more explicit attention by urbanists. After the Ottoman conquest there mainly was continuity in the residential quarters, but with Muslim *mahallas* (quarters or sectors) of related kin groups clustered around their neighborhood mosques, interspersed among Orthodox, Armenian, and Latin modules.

The death of Muhammad, a millennium after that of Alexander, crystallized a counter-urban experience without formal geometries; it was nurtured in the Islamic "East," to remain characteristic well into the Industrial Era (Abu Lughod 1987). This city proclaimed the greatness of God, next to whom rulers and wealthy elites were insignificant. There was no division of the secular and the sacred because the existential realm was one and the same as the cognitive and religious. The urban environment was variably structured, for men and women, between what was forbidden and closed and what was open and accessible. It was a radically different city, the logic of which was based on religious tradition (Abu Lughod 1987; Eben Saleh 1998; Face 1984; Hakim 1986; Kaluzny 2004; Wheatley 1976; Wirth 1992), but its cultural roots were firmly embedded in its Near Eastern heritage. Small wonder that it was difficult to understand in Eurocentric terms.

In the Islamic city of the new Arab world, public buildings had to remain subordinate to mosques, and the spirit of egalitarianism did not tolerate ostentatious elite residences. There was little corporate identity (Lapidus 1984[1967]), and secular power was suspect, so public display of authority could lead to a negative backlash (Lindholm 1996). Bath houses were essential for personal cleanliness, rather than as sites of social intercourse. Commerce was a meritorious enterprise, and central spaces were used for semicovered *suqs* (bazaars). Open market places were likely to be found in outlying or extramural areas, to accommodate livestock and sometimes unruly tribal people. Commercial travelers were accommodated in prominent inns (*khans*). Family life was focused on the sequestered home courtyard, and streets were narrow and winding, possibly to accommodate camel rather than cart traffic. Alleys, stairways, or obstructed streets further served as an impediment to mounted raiders.

Religious schools (*madrasas*) extended the religious sphere beyond the mosque, which was surrounded by gardens and ablution facilities, whether modest or imposing. In many early mosques, the courtyard replaced the agora or forum as a center for discussion and legal decisions. The axis of the mosque was pointed towards Mecca, a sacred orientation (*qibla*) that could influence urban layouts as much as it did Islamic cartography.

The Islamic city as described here was an archetype best represented in conservative North Africa, and there were many regional and structural exceptions, for example, early Islamic, grid-plan military settlements. There also were planned cities, such as Abbasid Baghdad (circular) and Samarra (rectilinear) (Creswell 1958), but Islamic orthodoxy was always quick to condemn the trappings of secular power and such initiatives soon died. Interpretations of the *sharia* or even its prevalence varied a great deal, however, and Turkish Islam was more flexible in regard to the segregation of public and private space, which also may have been true for Islamic Spain. Whatever its ethnic variants, the resulting Islamic urban landscape, so often described as chaotic, is eminently logical but clearly non-Western.

But Islamic segregation of public and private spheres—and the view that women should be hidden—sustained a bottom-up dynamic based on kinship. The resulting neighborhood associations and households generated an irregular street plan, from a primary concern for the needs of the household and its immediate neighbors rather than for citywide organization (Schloen 2001:111). Mark Lehner (personal communication, 2000) argues that the nonlinear, nongeometric urban agglomeration reflects local impulses, constraints, and perceived needs, based on shared ideas and ideology. Islam put a significant spin on otherwise self-generating and self-regulating systems, in the sense of Schaur (1992).

In emphasizing alternative urbanisms, we are not dealing with academic esoterica but highlighting fundamental misconceptions about the "other" that have contemporary relevance. Some architectural historians or cultural geographers continue to equate adobe technology with Islamic urbanism, confusing material culture with a finely nuanced way of life. The misconception that New World adobe construction derives from Egypt via Morocco and Spain is commonplace (Butzer and Butzer 2000). Yet mud-brick was once used worldwide, wherever suitable muds were readily available. Large buildings of rammed earth were built in Medieval central Europe, yet four decades of Islamic archaeology in Spain reveal only cut-stone or rock construction in residential quarters, whether rural or urban (Butzer et al. 1986; Delaigue 1988; Valor Piechotta 1995). Such stereotypes and misrepresentation underscore the need for a better understanding of Islamic civilization and its visible manifestations. Given that Google, in 2007, had 40,000 hits for Islamic urbanism and 560,000 for Islamic archaeology, it is apparent that the cultural introversion of our dated, Western academic structures is out of line with the potential receptivity of an educated public.

Aix-la-Chapelle and Timbuktu

Rightly or wrongly, most of us are probably attracted to the idea that urbanism is somehow linked to artistic expression and intellectual activity. Childe saw it that way, and oft times that association was true. Limiting the issue to scholarship, I would argue that the preconditions are economic growth, enlightened patronage, and opportunities for scholarly exchange—through mobility and access to library sources or other prototypes (Butzer 1994).

Two examples may make the point. The Carolingian Renewal began under Charlemagne during the 780s and in a very unlikely place, a long abandoned Roman spa, which became the German city of Aachen, or Aix-la-Chapelle. Although there was no more than a set of sulfurous mineral springs on one of the scattered Carolingian dynastic properties, the emperor came here to "take the waters." A decade later, the site had been embellished by a strong keep, a small residential complex, and an innovative octagonal church that was modeled on Ravenna. There was no town. But Charlemagne managed to attract some of the best scholars of Britain, France, western Germany, and Italy to this isolated woodland site. Here they discussed education and the seven liberal arts, renewed inquiry into astronomy and mathematics, and obtained Classical manuscripts from Italy that were copied in monastic scriptoria and commented on or embellished by individual scholars (Butzer and Butzer 2003). By all accounts, this modest intellectual revival was driven by the emperor's penchant for discourse and the improvement of monastic education. He was fluent in Latin yet could neither read nor write. But he had the power, resources, and vision to make the Renewal possible. He became the first royal patron to sponsor scholarship since the Roman emperor Titus discussed science on power walks with Pliny during the late first century.

My second improbable case is the West African city of Timbuktu, or Tombouktou, near the River Niger in the unforgiving Sahel of modern Mali. Long synonymous with the end of the known world, Timbuktu nonetheless had 137,000 Google hits in 2007, reflecting its fame as a center of Islamic learning across 300 years, until the Moroccan conquest of 1591. To this gateway city connecting West Africa with the Saharan caravan routes to North Africa, Timbuktu's rulers—despite repeated dynastic and ethnic changes—attracted clusters of scholars from the Near East (Benjaminsen and Berge 2004; McIntosh and McIntosh 2003; Winters 1981). Its wealth of perhaps close to a million Medieval and early Modern manuscripts, now being gathered and preserved by an international effort, represents an inestimable resource for future research. In its time, this adobe city was very populous, its three grand mosques still visible today and its Islamic university revived.

The common threads with Aachen are wealth, mobility, and a critical mass of scholars, but the remarkably sustained patronage enjoyed by Timbuktu was beyond the vision of the last Carolingians. Even so, Charlemagne's image of a New Jerusalem still continues to define a palpable sacred space, visited daily by busloads of visitors from three countries.

Just as an international exchange sustained Timbuktu, our perspective on Medieval urbanism in Western Europe (Vance 1990) should emphasize the importance of *multiculturalism* in what is easily mistaken for an inchoate jumble of backward principalities. During a long wave of population growth, which began with the end of the Viking and Magyar depredations, European craftsmanship was stimulated by the misguided Crusading enterprise, which brought all walks of society into indirect contact with Islamic civilization. With the new flourish of specialized crafts came a demand for raw materials that was first met during the late 1100s by the market fairs of Champagne, attracting suppliers and merchants from all over Western Europe and Italy (Abu Lughod 1989). Trade became so lucrative that town charters followed, sometimes purchased from bankrupt local lords, emancipating the nascent cities from aristocratic interference. The common thread of such charters included market privileges, institutionalized craft guilds, and elected town councils that represented a first step to participatory government. By 1250, new town charters began to attract craftsmen and merchants to hundreds of small and large places all over east-central Europe (Quirin and Trillmich 1956:75, 86). Mining towns conferred more specific privileges, leading to an upsurge of mining activities.

Little appreciated is that most late Medieval towns of eastern Europe were multiethnic, drawing their new citizens from hundreds of kilometers away, with skilled weavers coming from distant Flanders or Wallonia (Quirin and Trillmich 1956:82–83).

The new cities provided safe havens not only for guilds of craftsmen but also for ethnic enclaves. The granting of urban privileges was economically profitable, and by 1300 the Serbian king was welcoming foreign merchants and craftsmen and especially the "Saxon" miners (Drennon 1998). Under Ottoman rule, craft guilds also became ecumenical, with adherents of different religions working together in a single confraternity (Inalcik 1993).

Like trade fairs, international pilgrimages, such as those to Compostela, Rome, or Jerusalem, further served to stir the ethnic pot, exposing people to new places, new people, and new ideas in an era without intercity trains or television. Grain from the Baltic helped feed the populace of Mediterranean cities. Bankers from Italy or Germany provided letters of credit in Paris or Bruges. Europe on the eve of 1492 was a surprisingly cosmopolitan place.

How can urban archaeology without written records do justice to the multicultural components of the urban experience? My former student Christine Drennon (1998) was able to show that traditional dress identified the "status" of women in multiethnic Macedonia, rather than their ethnicity. Kenoyer (chapter 10) points to a similar function for women's bangles in Harappa. Archaeological strategies to identify differences in burial practices, skeletal anomalies, or (isotopic) diet are not guaranteed to identify ethnic difference unless there were distinct belief systems and effective social segregation.

European and Mesoamerican Cities

Urbanism in Europe during the High Middle Ages was vibrant and diverse. There was no single master plan as cities evolved organically to accommodate new social and economic needs that transcended older defensive modes in the shadow of a strong fortress (Vance 1990), such as Prague, Brno, or Kraków. Larger cities might become multinodal, accommodating existing church-oriented quarters but also requiring a spacious marketplace. New city walls were added after the fact. It was around the market that leading citizens built their elaborate houses and where the most prominent buildings were to be found: guild halls, the mercantile exchange, and the council house. Many cities also embarked on ambitious church construction, beyond the ambit of traditional parishes, to provide both a religious and secular landmark that would signal the prestige of the city.

A similar diversity was found in the countryside, where the packed village nuclei of the earlier Middle Ages gave way on new sites to several kinds of linear villages, depending on the topography or economic function (Engel 1970:95–98). Here, too, spatial configurations were dictated by pragmatic priorities. Monasteries continued to be built or expanded, but the emphasis now was on display rather than redemption. The transcendental *mappaemundi* of an earlier time were being replaced by practical navigation charts or by illuminated maps of a wondrous, wider world inferred from travelers' rumors or the imagination (Harley and Woodward 1987). Religion mattered very much, but it had to take its place alongside secular pursuits. Church spires dominated the skylines, but most urban activity centered on the here and now. Unlike Islamic cities, which remained timeless except on the peripheries of Islam, West European urbanism continued to evolve and change without the anchor of a restraining ideology.

Historians of architecture are fascinated by the reemergence of the grid-plan town, parallel with the rediscovery of Classical architecture, towards 1500. Some attribute this to Leon Battista Alberti, writing in 1452, but the facts are otherwise. The first of the new chessboard towns were founded on new sites much earlier, after the reconquest of Valencia, in the mid-1200s. They were conceived by James I of Aragón, presumably as a compromise between a rectangular, defensive perimeter and a unified urban plan focused on a large plaza, where a main church stood across from the buildings of administration and commerce (Rosselló Verger 1987). The complementarity, rather than separation, of church and state was so proclaimed. Streets were broad, to accommodate religious processions and floats, and formed a perfect grid. James probably knew little of Classical antiquity and presumably had the plans for Castellón and Villarreal drawn up on rational and pragmatic grounds.

The grid-plan town, later attributed to Alberti and hailed as a product of the Italian Renaissance, had actually been born amid Medieval heterodoxy. The idea must have persisted in Spain as a strategy for building new towns, because in 1502 Santo Domingo was laid out in this manner, without instructions from the court. General directives, however, were given for the laying out of Panama City in 1513, and Puebla was planned in 1531 according to similar principles (Butzer 1992). Then, in 1538 Viceroy Mendoza had much of Mexico City razed and rebuilt on a rigid grid plan, and, indeed, he is known to have pondered Alberti (Tóvar de Teresa 1987). The colonial New World town had been born (Butzer 1989, 1992).

With the benefit of hindsight, it is ironic that the main cultural thrust of Spanish colonial policy was centered on *policía* (civilized behavior), which was to be exemplified by Mediterranean-style social ambience in properly planned new towns (Licate 1981). These were to be the model for relocated indigenous settlements, where the built environment and its social institutions were to "civilize" and acculturate the natives (Tacitus redux!) so that they might learn from the orderly temporal and spiritual living of their mentors. This all seems like a replay of the discussion on the new Hellenistic city.

Nonetheless, the imposed grid plan had more structural and functional similarities with Mesoamerican cities than differences. Indigenous urban centers in central Mexico were arranged according to astronomical bearings dictated by cosmological criteria (Hirth, chapter 14; Marcus 2000 [1983b]; Pyburn, chapter 13; Tichy 1991; Tyrakowski 1989). They were focused on great squares that served ceremonial, as well as commercial, needs or functions, close to prominent temples and palaces to project a particular social order and proclaim dynastic power. As the visible markers of wealth and status dissipated with increasing distance from the city center, crowded residential quarters for commoners were organized around more modest, sacred places. At the urban perimeter, the landscape dissolved into less structured villages and hamlets surrounded by market gardens (Butzer and Butzer 2000).

No major urban center in Spain had conformed to the unified grid-plan town imposed on the New World. That colonial model, whatever its thirteenth-century roots, was first applied in Mesoamerica during the early 1500s. It was to replace indigenous grid towns that had been laid out according to more exacting and regular criteria than any urban center in Western Europe. This is yet another example of Eurocentric arrogance and illusion.

Concluding Discussion

This commentary examines a half-dozen focal points or dichotomies that represent neglected questions, troublesome assumptions, or alternative perspectives on early urbanism. These can now be summed up and briefly elaborated.

(1) Cities have always been open, rather than closed, systems. I have singled out population growth and decline, as reflected in regional settlement histories, as a productive avenue to study long-term change. This, in turn, may be related to the articulation or integration of exchange systems. Such a macro-interpretation suggests world-system applications. It can also support or set strictures to the current cross-disciplinary interest in civilizational "rise and demise," especially the subject of discontinuity or collapse. Among other possible factors in such cyclic rhythms are abrupt climate change and environmental degradation, so today the metaphorical intersection of urban with environmental systems takes on even greater significance. This is where urban geo-archaeology comes in, as a methodology that can interrelate urban and environmental processes or identify growth or decline within the city, as at Giza or Axum. Urban geo-archaeology can deal explicitly with diverse and properly grounded, environmental perspectives. These would be germane to larger questions of sustainability (Butzer 2005b).

(2) Everyone seems to agree that religion is important in the study of urbanism. The question is, which kind of "religion"? Long after Buddhism disappeared from India, the city of Gaya in Bihar State continues to attract hundreds of thousands of pilgrims annually to the site of the Enlightenment of the Buddha. Many of the pilgrims are Buddhists from abroad, but most are Hindus who repeat a ritual without understanding its meaning. Nominally, this is an example of the imprint of formal religion, officiated by a Hindu priesthood, but its heterodox and bicultural roots make it a celebration of popular religion. How would one deal with such a city in strictly archaeological terms, without the advantages of tradition and written records? What analogs are there with the official cult of Old Kingdom Egypt? Did the eschatological shifts of the official Egyptian cult between Dynasties 4 and 5 affect or reflect popular religion? Could it be that the animal cults, especially of the Late Period, capture the spirit of Egyptian popular religion? Were the official cults of the Hellenistic kings and Roman emperors more than projections of authority or legitimacy designed to channel and regiment loyalty?

The Islamic city is not just an alternative cityscape but at once a physical, experiential, and transcendental realm that has no other counterpart in the ethnographic present. It draws heavily on prehistoric roots and on different cultural traditions from those of the Greco-Roman or Medieval Germanic city and requires a different epistemology. That is so not only because of distinct top-down ideologies, but also because of cultural preferences for the articulation of public and private space, which favor bottom-up self-organization and are expressed by diverging spatial configurations.

Further, in each kind of urbanism, the line between the secular and religious is differently conceived and expressed, as an indivisible duality, as an explicit complementarity, or even as a formal "separation." There is, then, a variable dialectic between the cultural and the political, with profound social, economic, and spatial implications. This has not yet been effectively recognized by comparative historical urbanists, despite its importance for understanding convergent or divergent urban evolution.

(3) The Early Modern model of a secular civil service (cleptocratic or not) is difficult to shake. A formal and rational bureaucracy centered at the pharaoh's court lagged behind state formation or urbanism by at least a millennium. The Egyptian case further suggests that the institutional structures responsible for administration and the channeling of power are particularly difficult to grasp. Entwined with the religious sphere and at once improvisational and culturally grounded, they also varied widely in time and space. Understanding such nuanced interrelationships is essential for hermeneutic purposes. In didactic terms, they are critical to model the energy and information flows within a city, to identify the positive and negative feedbacks of urban adaptation, and to explicate the rank-size hierarchy of urban networks. Economics and power are insufficient as the primary variables to interpret urbanism.

(4) Several examples developed here stress that urban centers commonly were multiethnic or at least bicultural. That pluralism applies to the population at large and the professional sectors represented, as well as the elite merchants, artists, and scholars. Ethnocultural complexity introduces different sets of tensions that may affect routine urban behavior, periodic social ferment, or decision making at the top. While the resulting behavioral patterns may find material expression, that is not necessarily so. Working models need to incorporate more experience from other kinds of historical, urban investigation.

My own dissatisfaction with an exclusively archaeological paradigm reflects a Medieval archaeology project that I directed in the Sierra of eastern Spain during the 1980s (Butzer et al. 1986). While I excavated a Muslim hamlet and two Islamic castles, Elisabeth Butzer searched the relevant archival records in Valencia. We found that the latter were biased and thematically incomplete, yet these archives added flesh to the bare bones of archaeological resolution, offering humanistic dimensions for the lifeways and hardships of an oppressed minority.

Unexpectedly, the archives also required different interpretations of deductions suggested by the archaeology. Some people from our mountain hamlet of twenty-some households had privileges to travel and trade, including Jusef Bar-Robe, a resident

Jew. The same food staples were sometimes bought and sometimes sold at market, questioning the assumption of self-sufficiency. Local craftsmen performed contract work in downtown Valencia. Our, supposedly simple, villagers did not just acquire their good tablewares by down-the-line trade or at local markets; they had close contacts with potters at an elite production center 50 km away, one of them even posting bail for such a potter.

If the goal is to understand a dynamic urban community in space and time, it is imperative to draw archival documentation into the discussion whenever possible—rather than shrink from studies that might be considered as "historical archaeology." In the absence of such documents, we should be sensitive to ethnographic experience and reluctant to engage in positivistic speculation.

(5) Last but not least, I am concerned about the Eurocentricity that partially blinds almost all of us, myself included, making it difficult to fully grasp alternative values and rationales or to give them their proper due (Marcus 2000 [1983b]). Urban archaeology should not be part of a Western meta-narrative. But unless we broaden our educational system to include more sophisticated study of non-Western civilizations or incorporate more non-Western practitioners into both discourse and praxis, there is a very real risk that we may fail to bridge that gap. Historical and comparative urbanism have significant applicability in an era of conflictive globalization and cultural incomprehension. Effective, cross-disciplinary collaboration could and should keep matters of contemporary relevance in focus.

Acknowledgments

For many years Elisabeth Butzer has stimulated me to develop an interest in Islamic urbanism, and I greatly appreciate her insights and discussions. Kay Ebel introduced us both to the city of Istanbul on a memorable series of walkabouts, and Christine Drennon educated us about the ethnic and religious diversity of Macedonia and its cities. Margaret Kaluzny recounted the religious and neighborhood components of historical Sevilla. The late Neville Chittick facilitated my study of Ethiopia's Axum. Mark Lehner elucidated the "Lost City of the Pyramids" at Giza for me on several occasions, exchanging ideas with uncommon enthusiasm. His critical suggestions on this manuscript are much appreciated. Finally, Juan Mateu, Vicens Rosselló, and other friends and colleagues from Valencia educated me in Mediterranean urbanism and town–country relationships, apart from making my excavations in the adjacent Sierra possible.

part three
CASE STUDIES

six
Between Concept and Reality
Case Studies in the Development of Roman Cities in the Mediterranean

Janet DeLaine

Although no two Roman town plans are identical, we are rarely in any doubt in identifying any particular city as Roman. The similarities reflect a common concept—or set of concepts—about what a city should be like and how it should function, based ultimately on the city of Rome itself, even if we need to abandon the old idea of some kind of mechanical blueprint endlessly repeated (Jones, chapter 7; Parrish 2001; Zanker 2000). The differences, however, reflect the unique set of conditions under which each city developed—local history, political role in the wider world, and economic circumstances. This is critical for those cities of the Roman Mediterranean that had independent histories as long as that of Rome itself and that managed to preserve something of their local identities through their changing relations with Rome and even under the empire. This chapter examines the diverse urban histories of three quite different cities—the Roman colony of Ostia at the mouth of the Tiber, the Greek city of Ephesos on the northwest coast of modern Turkey, and the Phoenician settlement of Lepcis Magna on the Syrtic Gulf of Libya—tracing their transformation into our recognizably Roman concept of a city and the economic implications of this transformation. For these cities, with further references, see Ostia (Meiggs 1973; Pavolini 1986); Ephesos (Scherrer 1995, 2001); and Lepcis Magna (Di Vita-Evrard 1999; Mattingly 1994:116–122; Savino 1999:95–152).

Ostia represents the purely Roman idea of a city, while Ephesos and Lepcis Magna have been chosen precisely for their early and mixed origins, to escape from the self-fulfilling formulation of just looking at "greenfield" Roman colonies. This latter type of colony has been much studied (Gros and Torelli 1988; Jones, chapter 7) and has given rise to the normalizing paradigm of the Roman city, based on the conceptual model established by Rome, at least as far as functions and the physical structures that go with them were concerned. But it was also influenced by the Roman military camp in the rectangular, orthogonally gridded plan, with main roads crossing at the central open space of the forum. The main civic buildings of Rome, and of Roman cities, derived ultimately from the evolved political structure of the Roman Republican state: the *curia* (senate house), the *comitium* (assembly place for the citizens), and the *basilica* (commercial hall and law court), the archetypes of which were in the Forum Romanum. Temples had always formed an important element of the civic landscape of the city—there were several fronting onto the Forum Romanum, but from the late Republic onwards they were increasingly set in monumental, porticoed spaces and made of marble, in response to models from the Hellenistic Greek world. This style became the norm for public buildings, especially under the empire, when major construction became the preserve of the emperors and their close families. The *fora* built by Julius Caesar, Augustus, and Trajan were along these lines and became important models for provincial cities. Places for games and performances in honor of the gods and in relation to major civic events, such as the Circus Maximus, existed from the early days, but only from the middle of the first century BC were these given permanent form as theaters and, eventually, amphitheaters. The last of the major buildings to be formalized were the baths, another area in which the emperors and their close associates invested lavishly from the early first century AD onwards. Other distinctive features of Rome that were imitated in the provinces were an established urban infrastructure, particularly in relation to paved streets, water supply and drainage, and the presence of luxurious houses for the land-owning elite.

By the second century AD, Ostia, Ephesos, and Lepcis Magna had all become large and important Roman cities that demonstrated these paradigmatic features, with both Ephesos and Lepcis being the preeminent cities in their regions. All were harbor towns in which both strategic and commercial considerations played important roles in determining historical and physical development alike. They were also cities in which urban life, albeit at a reduced scale, survived into the fifth century AD if not beyond. Although we have no contemporary written history for any of these settlements, the central core areas of each have been extensively excavated, at least in their imperial Roman levels, and all have left substantial epigraphic records that provide valuable information on the chronology and nature of public building, the changing political structure of the cities, and the varied ethnic and linguistic elements in the populations. Because a short chapter such as this cannot hope to be comprehensive, it will focus mainly on the last centuries BC and the first centuries AD. In this period there are three main trends. The first is the continued importance of a mythical or legendary foundation and the persistence of an ancient sacred topography, however transformed,

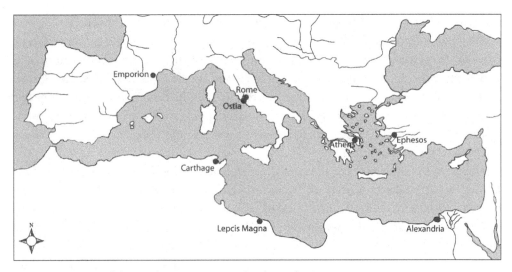

Figure 6.1. Map of the Mediterranean (map by the author).

across periods of political change. The second is the gradual evolution of a recognizably Roman civic center in its various guises and the concomitant shifts in the physical foci of urban life, with particular reference to the crucial transition to imperial rule under the first emperor Augustus between the late first century BC and the early first century AD. Lastly, there is the politico-economic nexus that allowed, in each case, an exceptional development in terms of the extent and quality of the built environment in the late first and second centuries AD.

Monuments and Memories: The Importance of the Legendary Past

The three Roman cities that form the focus of this chapter trace their origins back to the same Mediterranean-wide spread of urbanism that saw the emergence of Rome in the eighth to fifth centuries BC (figure 6.1). There were, of course, much earlier urban civilizations in Egypt, Mesopotamia, and Anatolia in the east. What set apart this particular wave of urbanization were its focus on the Mediterranean littoral, its western spread, and the gradual evolution in concept—if not in reality—of the autonomous city-state, comprising an urban political and administrative core and a peripheral supporting territory. The original opportunistic settlements appear to have been trade determined and polyglot, rather than restricted to any single ethnic, cultural, or even broad linguistic group (Gosden 2004:60–72; Osborne 1998), but by the fifth century, different versions had developed of the city-state principle, with clear individual identities. The main protagonists in this process were the Greeks and the Phoenicians, their spheres of influence roughly divided along a SE-NW axis from the Levant to northern Spain; the two met in Sicily, the great crossroads of the Mediterranean. Their subsequent growth varied with time and place, as did their relations with each other and with the original inhabitants. Carthage came to dominate the Phoenician *emporia* of the whole central North African coast, while the generally rich and powerful Greek cities of the western coast of Turkey, including Ephesos, remained independent of, and frequently at odds with, one another. Other sites remained as entrepôts, like Greek Emporion in southeast Spain, which coexisted with an increasingly Hellenized native population. The greatest visible impact on native populations, which can be demonstrated archaeologically, appears to have been in west-central Italy, among the Etruscans and Latins, including Rome.

These were not, however, entirely independent developments. Some of the similarities between the culturally different urban developments were the result of an ongoing process of interaction facilitated, if not necessitated, by the Mediterranean itself. For the historically best-attested and most important centers of these three spheres of influence—Athens, Rome, and Carthage—there is the clearest historical evidence of interaction, friendly and hostile, in varying combinations. About 507 BC, Carthage and Rome agreed to a bilateral treaty that defined spheres of influence in the Tyrrhenian Sea in the context of a power struggle for control between a Carthaginian–Etruscan alliance, on the one hand, and the combined forces of eastern and western Greek cities, on the other (Cornell 1995:210–214). A hundred years later it was Athens that made overtures to Carthage for help in her war against Syracuse (Thucydides VI, 88, 6). In the civil sphere, one tradition suggests that Rome looked to Athens to develop its law code in the fifth century BC (Dionysius of Halicarnassus, *Antiquitates Romanae* 10, 51–57; Livy 3:31–33), but it was the oligarchic, Carthaginian constitution that the fourth-century Greek philosopher Aristotle looked on with most approval (Aristotle, *Politics* II.xi.1–14). Unfortunately, Punic sources that might have given the Carthaginian point of view are extremely scarce, and we have to rely on the undoubtedly biased accounts of Greeks or Romans. Nevertheless, it is clear that with this kind of political and civic interaction, as well as through the trading activity attested in the archaeological record, came common knowledge of the physical structures of each others' settlements, and recognition of shared elements of the urban environment, such as the temples to the gods, the market place (agora, forum), and seats of government and law. By the time of the fully fledged city-states of the fifth century, it is clear that urban development and any new ventures of active colonization were within the context of a shared cultural milieu, to borrow Gosden's classification (2004:31–32).

This framework of early, urban settlement and multiple, interaction networks of the Mediterranean provides the context for the development of the three cities in question. Indeed, an alternative tradition makes Hermodoros of Ephesos one of those involved in drawing up the Twelve Tables of Roman law in the fifth century BC (Pliny, *Natural History* 34, 11, 21; Strabo, *Geography* 14, 1, 25 [C642]). The written traditions about the origins of these cities are clear, if late. The Greek city of Ephesos was said to have been founded by the mythical Athenian prince Androklos towards the beginning of the first millennium BC (Strabo, *Geography* 14.1.3, 4, 21). Lepcis Magna was said in later Latin sources to be a Phoenician settlement of the same period (Sallust, *Iugurtha*

78.1.4; Silus Italicus, *Punica* 3.256). The idea that Ostia was founded as the earliest Roman colony by Ancus Marcius, the legendary fourth king of Rome supposedly active in the seventh century BC, was already current in the third century BC (Ennius, *Annales* Ii, fr. 22, Vahlen). Archaeologically, however, these early dates have all proved elusive. The earliest signs of material culture relating to occupation are the mid eighth century BC at Ephesos (Scherrer 2001:58–59) and the mid seventh at Lepcis (De Miro and Polito 2005:121–123), and at Ostia it is the late sixth to fifth century BC (Zevi 2002a:12). What is important, however, is the role that the memory—however fictitious—of these legendary foundations played in the self-image of the cities of the Roman period (Alcock 2002; Gascó 1998). According to Plato (*Leges* 6.754a), a true Greek city had to have founders, which gave it legitimacy and identity. We need no better indication that Rome herself subscribed to the same philosophy from a relatively early date than the legends of Aeneas and Romulus.

It is, therefore, no surprise that Ostia continued to honor its legendary founder even into the empire. A fine marble dedicatory inscription to Ancus Marcius, probably from a second-century AD statue base, was found near the east gate of the mid-Republican settlement (ca. 300 BC), where the road from Rome once entered the town (*CIL* XIV S4338), proclaiming the community's privileged relation to the capital. We have no parallel from Lepcis Magna, but at Ephesos the mythical founder, Androklos, had a prominent cenotaph/heroön in the city (figure 6.2, no. 1) and a statue alongside that of the emperor in the monumental fountain honoring Trajan (Schowalter 1999:124). Another public statue of him was replaced in the early third century AD (Thür 1995:159–177). Thanks to a very long inscription of the early second century AD (*IvE* 27), it is clear that Androklos also had a more active role to play in Ephesian life. A donation by a wealthy Roman with strong connections to Ephesos provided for statues of him, together with those of Artemis, Lysimachos (the Hellenistic refounder of Ephesos), and the current Roman emperor, Trajan, to be carried in procession at regular intervals throughout the year (Alcock 2002:94–95; Rogers 1991).

The procession, in part, followed an older ritual pathway associated with the birth of Artemis the patron deity of the city, reinforcing the city's cumulative sacred history. It started from the ancient Temple of Artemis and followed a route that can be related archaeologically to the topography of the early Greek settlement (Scherrer 2001:58–61, 81), along a natural valley into the center of the Hellenistic and Roman city (where it is called the Embolos), passing a number of altars to Artemis (Knibbe 1995:144) and the monument to Androklos (see figure 6.2). The temple itself, on the site of a pre-Greek sanctuary northeast of the Greek and Roman city, was one of the wonders of the Hellenistic world and a site of pilgrimage. Over the centuries, this original processional route accumulated shrines, embellishments such as fountains, and funerary monuments of important citizens and benefactors, with particular concentrations in the earliest years of Roman influence (mid first century BC to early first century AD) and in the late first to mid second century AD, when the famous library and tomb of Celsus was erected (Thür 1995) (see figure 6.2, no. 10). The close relationship between procession, route, and monument created a constant in the urban layout that could be

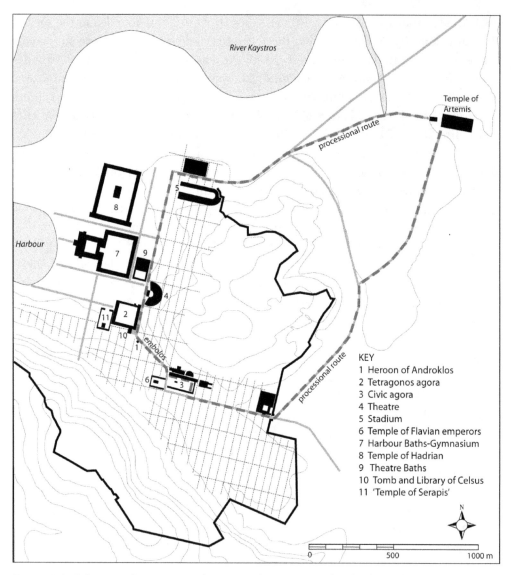

Figure 6.2. Ephesos, schematic city plan, second century AD (plan by the author).

modified but not radically altered. The central part of the route cut diagonally across the urban grids of the Hellenistic and Roman city, the one surviving relict of an earlier layout otherwise totally superseded by the second century AD.

Although our evidence is less secure, a similar type of early religious topography can be reconstructed at Ostia through consideration of non-orthogonal elements surviving in the later urban layout (figure 6.3). An early coastal route leading to the mouth of the Tiber from Lavinium, an important religious site incorporating the heroön of Aeneas, the first mythical founder of Rome, may have ended at the recently identified shrine of the Greek heroes Castor and Pollux (Heinzelmann and Martin 2002). To judge by a sixth-century BC dedication to them at Lavinium (*CIL* 1^2.2883;

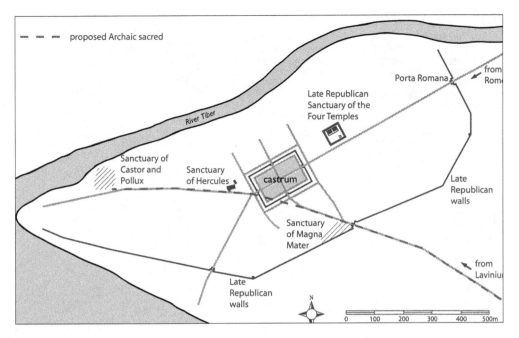

Figure 6.3. Ostia, schematic city plan, mid first century BC (plan by the author).

Torelli 1984:12, 163–164), this semi-divine pair was important in the region even before they were given a temple in the Forum at Rome in the early fifth century BC. At some point, Rome established sacred games in their honor at Ostia that were still being held in the fourth century AD (*Cosmographia Iuli Caesaris, Geographi Latini Minores* 83; *Ammianus Marcellinus* XIX, 10). From at least the third century BC, the coastal path also passed alongside the sacred spring and sanctuary of Hercules, a semi-divine hero associated both with Greek Herakles and with the Phoenician deity Melqart. Like Castor and Pollux, Hercules was much associated with seafaring and had important early shrines in Rome. Although in neither case can we date the origins of these cults at Ostia, there are strong arguments for assigning them to the period of the original colony or the very earliest years of the Roman Republic (Bispham 2000:162–164; Mar 1991:91; Zevi 1996:74–75). The walled *castrum*, which provides the earliest structural remains of the colony, was set just across this ancient route, but without hindering its viability or impinging on the sacred spaces. Indeed, it accumulated a third major and long-lived sanctuary—that of Cybele, the great Anatolian Mother Goddess—certainly by the Augustan period (Mar et al. 1999) but potentially as early as the end of the third century BC, when Ostia played a part in bringing the cult to Rome. All three of these cults show signs of activity into the later part of the fourth century AD, and as at Ephesos, the ancient diagonal route, modified only to take in the political heart of the later settlement, continued to form one of the major high-status streets in the city. In both Ephesos (figure 6.2) and Ostia (figure 6.3), the early sacred sites and processional routes were related to the natural topography and specific

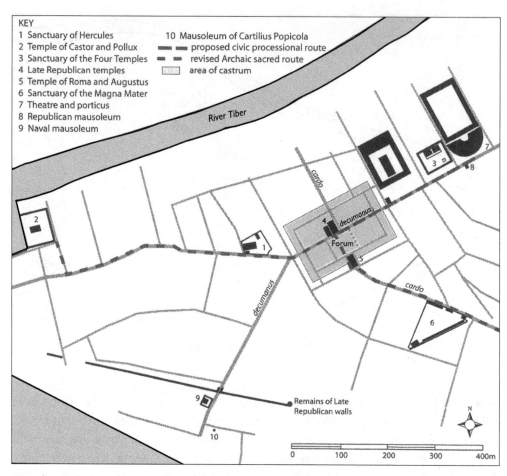

Figure 6.4. Ostia, schematic plan of the civic center, mid first century AD (drawn by the author).

features of the landscape. At Ephesos, and to a certain extent at Ostia, this created tension with the orthogonal plans of the later city, requiring efforts to maintain visual axes and to accommodate earlier "historic" sites, which, in turn, provided privileged locations for later religious or commemorative monuments.

Building on the Legend: The Formation of a Roman Civic Identity

In the centuries between the early foundations of the three cities and the formalization of the Roman empire under the first emperor, Augustus (31 BC–AD 14), after a long period of civil war, many changes in political and functional organization affected their physical layout and facilities, even if they did not always feature in the public version of civic history current in the Roman period. Ostia, despite being a Roman colony from the beginning, was exceptional in not being an autonomous settlement but governed directly by Rome. Even the precise location of this original settlement is much disputed (Zevi 2002b), but about 300 BC it became Rome's main naval base, at times supporting thirty war ships (triremes) needing some 6,000 men (Meiggs 1973:24–27, 580). It now seems very likely that the castrum, a small fort manned by Roman citizens, was built at this time (Martin 1996). Naval base and fort together provided security for goods, particularly the essential grain supplies going into Rome, and for armies setting off on campaign in Italy and the Mediterranean. Ephesos remained a nominally independent city but came and went under the control of various outside powers. The only one really recognized in the Roman period was Alexander the Great's general, Lysimachos, who in the early third century BC rebuilt the city on higher ground to avoid the constant flooding, probably laying out a grid plan for the first time, and enclosed the whole with fortifications (Hüber 1997; Scherrer 2001:61–68, 84). Like Ostia, Ephesus was an important naval base and center of commerce, with separate military and commercial harbors. Its subsequent relations with Rome were not always friendly or straightforward. A generation or two after coming under notional Roman control in the later second century BC, some inhabitants perpetrated a wholesale massacre of Roman citizens and their families (Canali De Rossi 1999), an episode conveniently omitted from later constructs of its past. Lepcis, in contrast, remained under the control of, and paid a heavy tribute to, Carthage until the middle of the second century BC. After Carthage was destroyed, Lepcis became virtually independent, if tenuously allied with Rome, and profited hugely by trade with sub-Saharan Africa and from markets in Alexandria (Savino 1999:95–98). Contact with Alexandria also opened Lepcis to the influence of the richest and most magnificent of the Hellenistic cities of the east. Not surprisingly, then, the first grid plan (Di Vita-Evrard 1999:51–54) and the few remnants of Hellenistic-style buildings at Lepcis appear to date precisely to the late second to early first century BC (De Miro and Polito 2005:121–127).

The later second and first centuries BC saw all three cities thriving commercially despite the vagaries of their political situations, while Rome's influence in the Mediterranean continued to increase. One notable result was the increasing presence of Italian/Roman merchants (*negotiatores*) in the cities of Asia Minor and North Africa, reinforcing the growing political relationships between the cities and Rome (Nicolet 1994:627–640). This was not a one-way process. One dedication from Rome, recording the gratitude of the Ephesians to the Roman people for help in war (*IvE* IV.1394; E. Weber 1999:139), implies the presence of an Ephesian embassy in Rome, and such embassies from both allied and foreign states were common events. We cannot be sure that the embassies passed through Ostia, but it is likely. Any visitors to Ostia from Ephesos and Lepcis, and vice versa, are likely to have noticed significant physical differences, in terms of overall layout and appearance, while recognizing common elements. The limited archaeological evidence for this period suggests that Ostia was the most different, especially in its lack of a formal political and commercial center (forum or agora), which would have made it difficult for outsiders even to recognize it as a city. In fact, despite the religious, political, and cultural differences, which had an impact on the built environment in terms of specific civic buildings and the vernacular style of domestic architecture, Lepcis Magna and Ephesos, as Hellenistic cities, probably had more in common with each other than with Ostia, even if the linguistic differences alone must have emphasized the foreignness. Overall, however, the combination of political alliance and commercial ties presumably widened the range of contact with other cities experienced by members of the urban elite and mercantile classes, reinforcing the cultural interaction that was such a vital feature of Mediterranean city-states from the beginning and preparing the way for the adoption of a more specifically Roman cultural vision of the city.

The Augustan Vision of Empire

The critical period of change towards a recognizably Roman urban form for all our cities is the hundred years from roughly 50 BC to AD 50, which politically marks a shift from an uncertain and variable hegemony with Rome at the top to a Rome-centered empire. Eventually, Julius Caesar's heir, Octavian (later the emperor Augustus), emerged to defeat all rivals and establish a dynasty in sole control of the Roman empire, at the same time creating a new visual language and image of empire in which the city was the paramount focus (Zanker 1988). As Rostovtzeff (1957:502–503) long ago noted, the success of the Roman empire may have lain, at least in part, in its harnessing of the practical advantages of the city-state to the needs of a territorial empire. Particularly associated with the Augustan age was the idea of "public magnificence," a concept that goes back, at least, to the late Republican and Hellenistic worlds (von Hesberg 1992) but which became one of the driving forces towards public building and the embellishment of cities of the empire with ever richer and more elaborate monuments. When the early second-century AD Greek philosopher Plutarch, a man at home both in Athens and in Rome, put into the mouth of Pericles a picture of the glory that the rebuilding of Athens in the fifth century BC would bring to the city (Plutarch, *Pericles* 12.4), he was clearly reflecting the conditions of his own times (DeLaine 2002a:222–224). Another Roman writer of the same period from the Greek-speaking eastern empire saw the embellishment of urban spaces as reflecting the harmony and order of the city itself (Aelius Aristides, *Orationes*, XVII, XXIII, XXVII). The status and glory embodied in magnificent public works thus formed another strand of civic identity, but one very much founded in the present rather than the past (Yegül 2000).

We can see the transformation of the urban fabric of Ostia in just these terms. The rapid physical and commercial expansion of the late Republic left the colony and naval base increasingly vulnerable to outside attack, leading to the erection of a new set of walls in the middle of the first century BC (Zevi 1996–1997). These enclosed a vastly greater area, incorporating the major religious sites discussed earlier. It is significant that this very expensive undertaking was given to Ostia by "the Senate and the People of Rome;" a monumental inscription on the main gate facing Rome advertised this gift and proudly declared Ostia's status as a Roman colony (figure 6.3). At some point

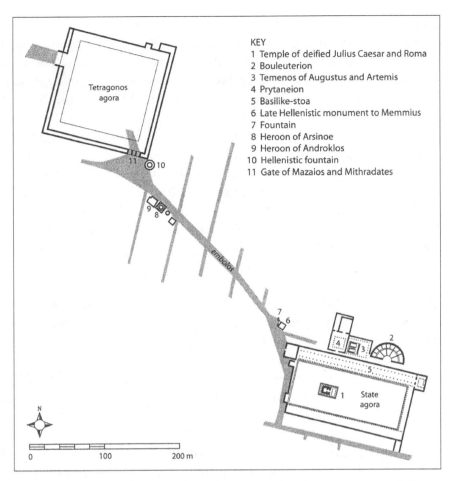

Figure 6.5. Ephesos, plan of the Embolos with commercial and state agoras, early first century AD (plan by the author).

in the first half of the first century BC, the city gained formal independence from Rome, having for the first time its own town council (Meiggs 1973:172–174). This is the most likely occasion for Ostia finally to be given a forum. The focus was originally a pair of small temples in local stone situated at the crossroads marking the center of the old castrum (figure 6.4, no. 4), with the open space extending to the south of the road from Rome and closed by a basilica-like structure. This public space took on a new resonance sometime in the next thirty years when a magnificent marble temple to the specifically imperial duo of the goddess Roma and the emperor Augustus, was added at the other end, at a time when such lavish use of marble was still rare (figure 6.4, no. 5) (Mar 2002:111–122; Pensabene 2004:105–107).

The removal of the fleet from Ostia after 31 BC allowed the city to consolidate its independent civic status, marked most notably by the erection of a large theater and an associated porticus about 18 BC (figure 6.4, no. 7). Because the theater was at the heart of Augustus's policy of civic and moral regeneration of the Roman state after half a century of civil war, being the main locus for the display of society ordered according to rank (Rawson 1987), this gave the reshaped city its own new politico-religious topography and created a new, more obviously civic, processional route. The theater's location alongside a preexisting group of four small temples, dedicated by P. Lucilius Gamala, one of Ostia's leading citizens of the late Republic (Coarelli 2004; Zevi 2004), and opposite a monumental tomb of the preceding century (Sole 2003; see figure 6.4, nos. 3, 8) does, however, suggest that existing local foci were not ignored, but assimilated into a wider imperial vision of the city. Similarly, the old cults were not forgotten. A new Temple of Castor and Pollux at the river's mouth was built in solid marble, almost certainly under imperial patronage (Heinzelmann and Martin 2002: 16–17). Also a major dedication was made to the Temple of Hercules by C. Cartilius Poplicola, the other most important Ostian of the period, who held the main public office for an unprecedented eight times under Augustus (Meiggs 1973:40). Poplicola's monumental tomb and that of another unknown Ostian, however, were located outside the sea gate of the Late Republican walls (see figure 6.4, nos. 9, 10), reflecting perhaps the importance of the Mediterranean as a whole in the fortunes of the city. These fundamental changes to the religious-political topography went hand in hand with more general development of the urban plan, the creation of a formal harbor basin at the river mouth, and the restructuring of Ostia's territory south of the city (Heinzelmann 1998).

The same period saw the transformation of Ephesos (Scherrer 2001:69–74), and the nature of the changes has parallels with Ostia. Early in his rule, Augustus made Ephesos the seat of the Roman governor of the province of Asia. The city was prompted to build a temple (or temples) to the goddess Roma and to deify Julius Caesar (Augustus's adopted father), in the revitalized "state" agora (figure 6.5). The seats of the town council (*pyrtaneion*) and assembly (*bouleuterion*) were rebuilt, and an important civic building was erected in the form of a hybrid between the Greek stoa and the Roman basilica (see figure 6.5, no. 5). At the center of the agora was a new temple, probably to deify Caesar and Roma, the whole in a very Roman arrangement even if many of the elements could be found in earlier Greek cities (Gros 1996b: 111–116). A further pair of small temples, to Augustus and the goddess Artemis, the patron deity of the city, were inserted in a small precinct behind the basilica-stoa. This agora lay across the old processional route from the Temple of Artemis, thereby incorporating the new temple to Rome and the divinity of its emperor into the existing ritual landscape of the city. The route also linked the new agora to the theater, now argued to have been begun around 50 BC but finished under Augustus (Scherrer 2001:84). Other civic buildings included a rebuilt commercial agora (the Tetragonos agora) and a gymnasium, the focus of citizen education in the Greek world, near the theater (see figure 6.2, nos. 2, 7).

In this nominally independent and largely autonomous city, most of these new buildings were, however, put up at the expense of wealthy Roman citizens, including freed slaves of the emperor and the "council of Roman merchants in Asia," rather than by a purely local Greek elite. Several of the highly visible building inscriptions that

Figure 6.6. Ephesos, gateway to the commercial agora dedicated by Mazaios and Mithradates, 4–2 BC (photo by the author).

record these acts of public munificence are in two languages, the Latin of the new regime and the native Greek (Weber 1999). The earliest known Latin inscriptions from Ephesos itself date to the early to mid first century BC, and these Augustan monumental inscriptions must have had a considerable impact on the local population. They were predominantly in Latin, peculiarly Roman in form and placement, and set prominently on major new buildings of at least partly Roman design, as can be seen in the monumental triple-arched entrance to the commercial agora built by the imperial freedmen Mazaios and Mithradates (*IvE* VII.1 3006; figure 6.6).

At Lepcis, the Augustan period also saw the expansion of the city beyond the area of the Punic city (Di Vita-Evrard 1999:54–76) (figure 6.7) and the erection of a series of monumental structures, including a theater with a portico behind, as at Ostia, here built over an earlier cemetery. The building of a formal market (the *macellum*) and a chalcidicum also has parallels at Ostia, although we know this only through inscriptions that inform us that the macellum was restored and a chalcidicum built in this same period at Ostia (Licordari 1984; Meiggs 1973:47). In Lepcis, as at Ephesos, the deeds of the benefactors were set forth in monumental inscriptions of Roman form. In the case of the theater (*IRT* 321, 322; *IPT* 24) and macellum (*IRT* 319; *IPT* 21), these were in Latin alone on the outside, but with Neo-Punic versions inside that emphasized the achievements of the local donor (figure 6.8). As at Ostia and Ephesos, a major addition to the religious landscape was a new temple dedicated to Roma and the emperor. This dominated the old Punic forum/agora from a central position, flanked on one side by an existing temple to Shadrapa, one of the protector deities of the Punic city, and on the other by a new temple to Milk'Ashtart (Melqart), the other

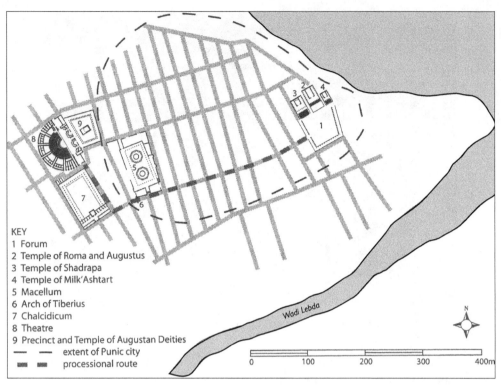

Figure 6.7. Lepcis Magna, schematic city plan, early first century AD (plan by the author).

civic deity (see figure 6.7, nos. 2–4) (Brouquier-Reddé 1992:81–91). In this case, the long dedicatory inscription to the emperor (*IPT* 22) appears to have been just in Neo-Punic. The new buildings all owed their creation to the local Libyo-Punic aristocracy, rather than to resident Roman citizens, although their names in the Latin texts are partly Romanized. They certainly appear to have been well-informed about contemporary public building in Rome and could command workmen skilled in masonry construction and trained in the Hellenistic East Mediterranean tradition. The theater was connected to the forum by a broad street leading from the coast and harbor to the main north-south road, once again creating the possibility of a processional route that linked the original civic center to the key ritual foci of the new regime, as we have already seen at Ostia and Ephesos. After the death of Augustus, a temple to the Augustan deities was set up in the portico behind the theater, and an honorific arch to his successor, Tiberius, erected along this route beside the macellum. In both subject and form, these two monuments further emphasized the importance of Roman imperial, rather than purely local, concerns.

Thus, in a very short space of time, the political changes introduced by the new imperial regime and its vision of empire provided not only the catalyst for modifications to the urban form in all three cities, but also a conceptual model for them in terms of the kind of monuments and urban developments to be given priority, based on the key structure of the city of Rome in its Augustan form (Zanker 2000).

Figure 6.8. Lepcis Magna, bilingual inscription from the theater, AD 1–2 (photo by A. Lane).

Although the cities differed in respect to who was responsible for the new monuments, all seemed to agree on the types of monuments required and the status these new buildings conferred.

The Cities at Their Height—Consolidation and Competition

If the Augustan period represents a single episode in which all the three cities began to take on specifically Roman imperial aspects, the completion of this process took place at different times over the ensuing two centuries and under different impetus. In each case, however, these were largely local—or, at most, regional—initiatives, but mediated through the constant of an overarching Roman imperial system.

In terms of large-scale projects, the relation of the individual city and its elite to the emperor still had the greatest impact, although the siting of monuments often further reinforced the existing sacred and political landscape. Ephesos and Lepcis, for example, had new temples to the imperial cult at the end of the first century, both of which can be associated with changes in status. The new temple at Ephesos was *the* main locus for the imperial cult in the whole province, a much sought-after honor that brought benefits in terms of prestige embodied in the newly important title *neokoros* (Boatwright 2000:94–104; Burrell 2004:59–70). Significantly, it was sited in a dominant position immediately above the Augustan state agora (see figure 6.2, no. 6). As well as the temple itself, local benefactors built a new gymnasium (for holding the Olympic-style games initiated at about this time) and associated baths, both on reclaimed land by the harbor (see figure 6.2, no. 7), and the stadium, begun possibly under Augustus, was completed. Once more, all these buildings were tied into the existing ritual landscape. A generation later, Ephesos was granted the rare honor of a second neokorate temple, dedicated to the emperor Hadrian, built on a vast scale on yet more reclaimed land by the harbor and stadium (see figure 6.2, no. 8), and with new or rededicated games. These honors, and the buildings that accompanied them, were strong cards in local intercity rivalries and set Ephesos in a league of its own. But they also reflect the wealth of the city and of its main citizens, many of whom also had Roman citizenship and some of whom had ties with other cities of the region and wider empire. At this time, such men began to appear as senators and consuls at Rome

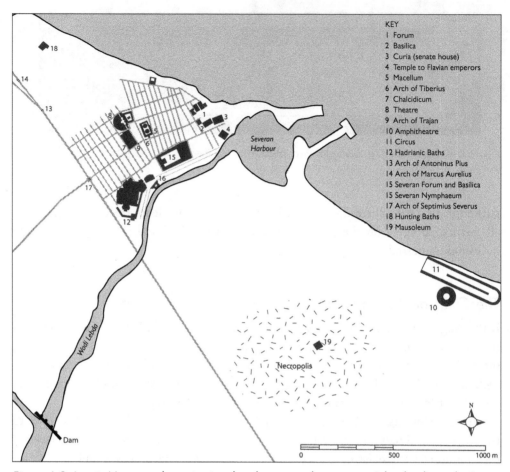

Figure 6.9. Lepcis Magna, schematic city plan, late second century AD (plan by the author).

and then as governors of provinces. T. Iulius Celsus Polemaeanus, originally from nearby Sardis, whose combined library and tomb formed the most lavish addition to the commemorative monuments along the processional route at Ephesos (see figure 6.2, no. 10), was one such provincial governor (Halfmann 2001; Scherrer 2001).

At Lepcis, the key events were the conferment, first of the honorary status of *municipium* on the city (AD 70s) and then, a generation later (ca. AD 109), that of colony (Di Vita-Evrard 1999:76–107). The first gave Roman citizenship to all the members of its town council, thus allowing them wider entry into the upper levels of the empire; their response, as at Ephesos, was to build a new temple for the imperial cult (figure 6.9, no. 4). This move recognized their loyalty to Rome, something demonstrated in no small way by the continuing tradition of public building, which had added further temples, a civic basilica and senate house, and an archetypically Roman amphitheater in the intervening years. Becoming a colony gave Lepcis the highest possible civic status in the empire, but one which required of the city the necessity of adopting the laws and institutions of Rome, although there was little change in the relationship between the local elites and Rome (Boatwright 2000:42–56). It did, however, confer wholesale Roman citizenship on all citizens of Lepcis, and the city and its people set up a commemorative arch in gratitude to the emperor Trajan, who granted them the honor. Thereafter, various local benefactors paid for an aqueduct and contributed to building a large set of baths (figure 6.9, no. 12) and finally built a large circus beside the amphitheater.

We have less evidence for interpreting the siting of these buildings than at Ephesos, but some suggestions can be made. The temple to the deified emperors sits in a prominent position between the forum and the harbor, combining the positions of the two neokorate temples at Ephesos, and the basilica and senate house (figure 6.9, nos. 2, 3) find their natural place in the forum. The amphitheater and circus are, however, well away from the monumental center, southeast of the harbor on the other side of the Wadi Lebda and beside an extensive necropolis including several large mausolea. Although this may simply represent the constraints of space in the expanding city, we have already seen that the theaters at both Ostia and Lepcis were associated with earlier cemeteries or funerary monuments and that at Ephesos the mausoleum or cenotaph of a founder or an important citizen also conferred ritual and civic importance to the spot. The hosting of gladiatorial and circus games during the empire was the gift of local dignitaries, as much in honor of the holding of magistracies and of imperial birthdays as in celebration of religious festivals, and we know of at least one benefactor at Lepcis specifically honored for, among other things, the lavish spectacles he provided (*IRT* 601). Locating the buildings to house such games beside the tombs of illustrious former benefactors and civic heroes may have added a special historical resonance to the events and even have raised the memory of times when gladiatorial games were still held at elite public funerals.

Because of its proximity to Rome and status as the earliest of all Roman colonies, there were no such obvious honors that could add to Ostia's prestige. Here the key additions are the imperial harbors built a few kilometers up the coast between the middle of the first century and the early years of the second century, which seem to have inspired Ostia's further expansion as a commercial city. As with the neokorate at Ephesos and the municipal and then colonial status at Lepcis, the harbors were something only the emperor could bestow, although this time more for the well-being and status of Rome than for Ostia. Nevertheless, Ostia gained. Towards the end of the first century AD, the main entrance to the city from Rome was rebuilt in marble at roughly the same time as a basilica was added to the forum, both of which could only enhance civic status (figure 6.10, nos. 11, 12). Shortly after, first the emperor Trajan and then his successor, Hadrian, agreed to act, nominally at least, as one of the two chief magistrates of the city. With this great honor went periods of new public building, particularly the large temple and its precinct, which extended the forum to the north (figure 6.10, no. 13), and two new and lavish sets of baths (figure 6.10, nos. 14, 15), all almost certainly financed by the imperial family (Pensabene 2002:220–253; Zevi 2000: 528–530). The final monumental structure of the second century AD was the even more

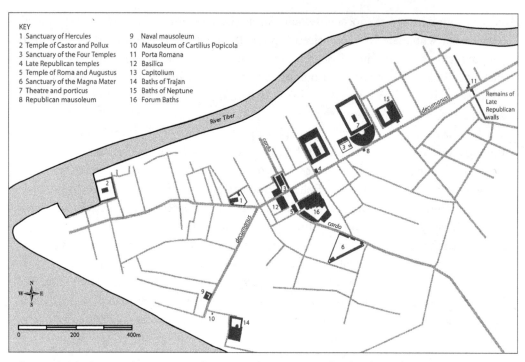

Figure 6.10. Ostia, schematic city plan, second century AD (plan by the author).

lavish Forum Baths, funded by the emperor Antoninus Pius's right-hand man, the prefect of the Praetorian Guard. At the same time, there was a vast rebuilding of the commercial and domestic fabric of the city at a higher level, probably to resolve long-term problems with flooding. We have little direct evidence for who was responsible for this aspect of Ostia's development, because of the paucity of relevant inscriptions, but a close analysis of the physical remains makes it likely that this was mainly "private enterprise" or, at the most, the responsibility of the town council (DeLaine 2002b; Heinzelmann 2002). Many of its members were not, in fact, of local origins, unlike at Lepcis, but represented the mercantile interests of other communities in the Mediterranean and beyond, above all the North African shippers and *negotiatores* (Cébeillac-Gervasoni 1996).

While we tend to think of urban development in terms of formal plans and specific monuments, it is worth noting that in all three cities the transformation of the civic landscape in the first and second centuries AD included wholesale changes to the natural topography. Extensive terracing to create new formal public squares and temple precincts, new harbor works, land reclamation allied to flood-management schemes, and new aqueducts bringing water from considerable distances were all hallmarks of the Roman development that enhanced the physical environment, as well as the economic basis, of the cities. They were also visual reminders of the Roman power over the ultimate force—nature—a power that symbolized the authority of the empire and was best exemplified in the greatest of all the wonders of the ancient world, the city of Rome itself (DeLaine 2002a).

By the end of the second century AD, all three cities had achieved a recognizably Roman urban form supplied with fundamentally Roman facilities, although following different trajectories and under largely local initiatives. The dual nature of the communities was a key factor. The town councils of these nominally independent cities were responsible for all day-to-day and most religious affairs, but they also acted within the wider sphere of province and empire, relation to which could add prestige and the possibility of real power on a larger scale for individual members of the elite. On a local level, what the individual benefactors gained was public recognition in the inscriptions, which were an integral part of the buildings themselves, and in the many statues set up by grateful town councils and other beneficiaries on inscribed bases, achieving a form of immortality that placed benefactors in the ranks of the city founders. That Lepcis Magna produced the first North African emperor at the end of the second century AD is wholly comprehensible. That he, in turn, embellished his native city with a totally unnecessary new temple, forum, and basilica complex modeled on one of the most famous monuments of Rome, the forum of the emperor Trajan (see figure 6.9, no. 15) (Ward-Perkins 1981:387–391), as well as with an equally unnecessary harbor based on Trajan's at Ostia, is quite in keeping with the models of public benefactors that go back ultimately to the conditions of the city-states of the fifth century BC.

The Cost of Urban Transformation

The reconciliation of local aspirations and ideals with the achievement of a wider Roman identity required not only the active will of the local and regional elites but also a deep pocket. The buildings and engineering works that provided the visual realities of these proud Roman cities did not come cheaply. For a city to maintain and demonstrate its importance, it was crucial that these monuments stand out in both a regional and an empire-wide context. Those members of the local elites who had achieved senatorial rank and/or played a part in the army or in governing the empire traveled widely and usually owned property in other provinces than that of their origins. They thus had plenty of models available for the monuments they donated to their home towns, including the monuments of Rome. But, in Rome the escalation in competitive public building to reinforce power and prestige, which had its origins in the Republic but still had an important role to play under the empire, raised the stakes for imitators in the provinces, as most easily demonstrated in the case of bath buildings (DeLaine 1992).

The increase in scale of buildings and the use of costly materials, especially marble brought from quarries all over the Mediterranean regions of the empire and granites from Upper Egypt and the western desert, inevitably increased construction costs, often beyond the resources of local town councils. Estimating on the basis of a series of building inscriptions from all over North Africa, compared with what can be reconstructed of the income of town councils of a medium-size city, it could have taken about thirty years' worth of disposable income for an ordinary town council to build a theater or a reasonably elaborate but medium-size set of public baths (Duncan-Jones 1990). Marble decoration was so expensive, even more so when it included statues, that it often formed a separate benefaction. Prices we have from Lepcis include 1 million sesterces for sixteen statues and 500,000 sesterces for redecorating the stage building of the theater (*IRT* 706, 534; Duncan-Jones 1982:68–69). In comparison, one of the major sets of baths at Ostia, the Baths of Neptune (see figure 6.10, no. 15), was built from a donation by the emperor of 2 million sesterces, but this was not enough to cover all its decoration (*CIL* XIV.98). A recent attempt to calculate the cost of marble for the Temple of Serapis at Ephesos has produced a figure of about 1.7 million sesterces, and for the Library of Celsus, one of the monuments along the processional route, a far more modest sum of about 50,000 sesterces (Barresi 2003:194, 203).

Not surprisingly, very little of the "public magnificence" of the imperial period in any of the three cities is known to have been paid for by the town councils, not even in the case of Lepcis, which was blessed with an exceptionally large and highly productive territory. At Ephesos, the Temple of Artemis was independently wealthy through the ownership of land and the taking of donations from visitors (Dignas 2002:169–177), and this temple acted to some extent as a treasury for the city, as temples had traditionally done in the Greek and Roman worlds for centuries. The presence of the Roman provincial governor in the city must also have brought an increase in visitors and the associated wealth, as well as encouraging local benefaction. Essential to all three cities, however, was their role in the commercial networks of the Roman Mediterranean and beyond. This is obvious for Ostia, where most of the richest citizens appear to have been merchants and shippers, many from the North African provinces. Markets at Ostia served not only the city itself but also Rome (particularly in grain and other comestibles), and the city was an entrepôt for selling and buying cargoes for the rest of the empire, as the exceptional richness of the ceramic record at the site attests. There were also human cargoes, from delegations to the emperor from different parts of the empire, to the military and civil entourages that maintained the empire, to slaves. Lepcis also had an exceptional position, not just shipping grain and olives widely across the Mediterranean but also serving the Roman army policing the frontier just 65 km to the south (Savino 1999:115–152). Perhaps most important was its position at the end of major trans-Saharan caravan routes that brought from outside the empire a wealth of rare—and thus high-value—trade items, from ivory and Nubian slaves to exotic animals for the arena. Ephesos, too, was a commercial city with a well-maintained harbor, also monumentalized under Trajan (Zabehlicky 1995).

Despite this, in all three cities, the cost of urban splendor was largely borne by individuals, usually members of the Roman elite with strong local ties, and sometimes the emperor. Many projects were simply beyond the pocket of communities with only local resources, based on land ownership and urban taxes. Instead, the wealth of those who created great monuments was often made at a regional or empire-wide level, either as individuals in the imperial service or from empire-wide land-holdings and commerce. What they chose to build thus, understandably, reflected empire and regional models, but the impact was modulated for local consumption and to reflect local civic pride by the choice of site within the existing civic and sacred topography and by references in the decorative programs or associated festivals to the legendary past.

Conclusions

In terms of the pattern of their development, Ostia, Ephesos, and Lepcis Magna were not unusual in the Roman Mediterranean except for their size and wealth. Most cities of even moderate size had a dual nature, formed from a local identity often going back before any existence as a Roman city, but overlaid by, or more often intertwined with, a Roman imperial one that led to a recognizably Roman, urban form through the addition of typically Roman facilities. For this to function, it was important that there was a common idea of what a city was, one that was shared with Rome itself (Gascó 1998). This softened the contrast between the autonomous past and the imperial present because Rome was recognizably part of that same Mediterranean past in a way that was not the case for the northwestern provinces and the peripheral parts of the empire (Alcock 2002).

Particularly in the Greek-speaking part of the empire, local identity was often closely tied with early sacred sites and with a line of benefactors going back to an original founder, however legendary. This local identity continued to provide a physical and emotional focus for civic, as well as religious, activity under the empire. If these provided the proof of antiquity so essential to civic identity in the Mediterranean world, they were also manipulated to provide an appearance of continuity into the imperial period, enhanced by the accumulation of monuments and dedications to current local benefactors and the emperors within the existing physical and ritual frameworks. The recognizably Roman global identity, on the other hand, appeared in the Augustan period and was tied very closely to the new political and social order. New or revamped civic centers, new temples to the goddess Roma and the emperor, and new or improved theaters appear in all these cities at this time, reinforcing the transformed urban focus of Roman life under the new regime. In the three cities we have looked at, the driving force for this change ranged from the emperor's close circle at Ostia, to the Italian commercial interests and imperial freedmen at Ephesos, to a Romanized but still strongly local elite at Lepcis. Despite the superficial differences in architectural form and in the languages of dedication that drew on local realities, a common underlying concept originating in Rome can still be clearly seen.

After the impetus towards a unifying Roman model provided by Augustus, subsequent development was left more to the demands of local and regional needs and desires, among which competition in terms of public magnificence was all-important. The escalating costs of these needs were increasingly met from the global resources of the imperial circle or those members of important families with local ties who operated at an empire-wide, rather than at a purely local, level. All three of the cities discussed here were involved in intersecting spheres of commercial activity at local, regional, and empire-wide levels. If the territory of Ostia was in many ways the whole empire and its market Rome, even Ephesos and Lepcis, which may have started as city-states with limited territories, eventually came to share in a wider imperial network of economic opportunities that contributed greatly to their wealth. That they chose to invest much of this in fulfilling a unifying Roman concept of the city, but through the filter of local traditions and realities, shows the importance of the city as a cultural form in which all forms of identity were simultaneously possible within the urban-based empire of Rome.

Abbreviations

CIL Corpus Inscriptionem Latinarum

IvE Inschriften von Ephesos

IPT Levi Della Vida, Giorgio and Maria Giulia Amadasi Guzzo, 1987, *Iscrizioni puniche della Tripolitania*. "L'Erma" di Bretschneider, Rome.

IRT Reynolds, Joyce M. and John B. Ward-Perkins (editors), 1952, *Inscriptions of Roman Tripolitania*. British School at Rome, Rome and London.

seven
Urban Foundation, Planning, and Sustainability in the Roman Northwestern Provinces

Michael J. Jones

The concern of this contribution is to analyze the process of establishing and developing cities in what became Rome's northwestern provinces. As Janet DeLaine (chapter 6) has demonstrated, urbanization already had strong roots in the Mediterranean before it came to play its part in the Roman imperial system. Here, at and near to its center, the empire had a sophisticated literary culture.

On its frontiers, however, the Roman army was encountering tribal societies, peoples that it was convenient to portray as "barbaric." In dealing with these groups, military force was used when necessary, but, where possible, diplomatic skills and a range of incentives were employed to win over hearts and minds. Native leaders were encouraged to recognize that it was in their best interests to adopt an ostensible Roman lifestyle in order to advertise their political status, and to enhance it by public service and munificence, including demonstrating their loyalty to the emperor. In this way, the traditional aristocratic rivalry for power and status was employed, where possible, to achieve the Roman objective of running the empire without having to pay for a huge bureaucracy (De Ligt et al. 2004; Mattingly 2004). A globalized system was created, but it was dependent on local networks for success (Hingley 2005).

Rome saw itself as representing *humanitas*—that is, cultivated, humane behavior—and fit to lead by example (Woolf 1998:54–60). There is an assumption of cultural superiority here, even though a major element was derived from Greek antecedents.

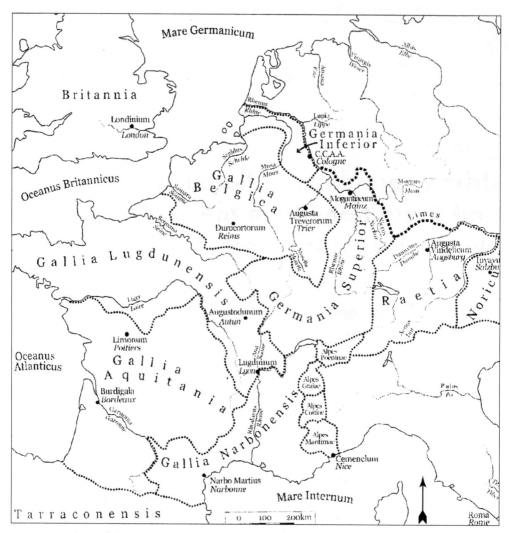

Figure 7.1. Map of the Roman northwestern provinces, showing sites in Gaul and Germany mentioned (courtesy of Maureen Carroll and Tempus Publishing).

The Romans saw their mission as bringing to the world their brand of "civilization," which they would have defined as peace and the dividend thereby afforded, enabling the optimal conditions for material prosperity and comfort. This involved city-based life. Those peoples faced with occupation and conquest responded to the prospect of integration into the empire in various ways. It was an opportunity for many, but there was a price to pay and some fought against it.

Roman Northwestern Provinces

The geographical scope of this chapter extends from the Pyrenees to northern England, covering the following areas (figure 7.1): Gaul, excluding the Mediterranean region, divided into three provinces; Upper and Lower Germany, later creations, largely out of

Gaul, in the 80s AD; and Britain, which was never completely pacified (and only southeast Britain was urbanized).

The northwestern provinces were conquered, not as land masses, but tribal state by tribal state, and, within the framework of each province, were largely administered by tribal region, Romanized as the *civitas*. Some cities were official plantations, notably the military colonies where retired legionaries were settled, probably together with some native peoples and immigrant craftsmen and traders (Hurst 1999b). Most, however, were founded principally as regional administrative centers. The Roman authorities required a single town—a capital—for the governance of each tribe or group of tribes forming the civitas and to which to devolve responsibility for tax collection.

A sharp contrast is apparent between the Mediterranean region and these northwestern provinces in terms of the numbers of cities founded. There were, for instance, about 250 cities each in Africa and in Italy, as opposed to fewer than 25 in Britain (figure 7.2). This discrepancy conceals the fact that in the northwestern provinces there was a network of hundreds of lesser towns with economic functions and a limited administrative role (Burnham and Wacher 1990). The culture of these provinces became a diluted form of that found already in the Mediterranean, but with a native admixture.

There is still some academic debate regarding the extent to which there was a formal urbanization policy and also whether and how the army was used in the process, both in advising on technical matters and in actual construction. Although the importance of the pre-Roman Gallic settlements underlying Roman towns has long been recognized, until recent decades the urbanization of these provinces was seen in Britain, particularly, as a purely Roman initiative. It was perceived from a Roman "imperialist" standpoint that dominated British academic approaches—as a former colonial power. Only in recent decades has the view prevailed that the development of the tribal capitals was left largely to the initiative of local aristocracies (Esmonde Cleary 1998; Jones 1987, 1991; Millett 1990). This reflects the newer, post-colonial perspective of a generation of scholarship not so constrained by the imperialist mindset and also more concerned with archaeological evidence and anthropological models as opposed to historical sources. The debate within the discipline continues: see James 2003 and Woolf 2004 for brief reviews.

The criteria for urbanization are recognized as having been linked to the level of socioeconomic organization (Groenmann-van Waateringe 1980). Some more recent analyses of the Lower Rhine region, using a theoretical framework based on the structuralist ideas of Louis Dumont and his pupils, identify the key factor as the ideology of the tribal leaders, that is, their traditional cosmology and value systems that viewed military skills and cattle rearing as badges of status (Roymans 1995, 1996). Here the landscape was a factor: good agricultural land on which productivity could be commercialized was more favorable to the adoption of Romanized forms. In these marginal cases, there was sometimes a need for more direct encouragement or a different Roman strategy.

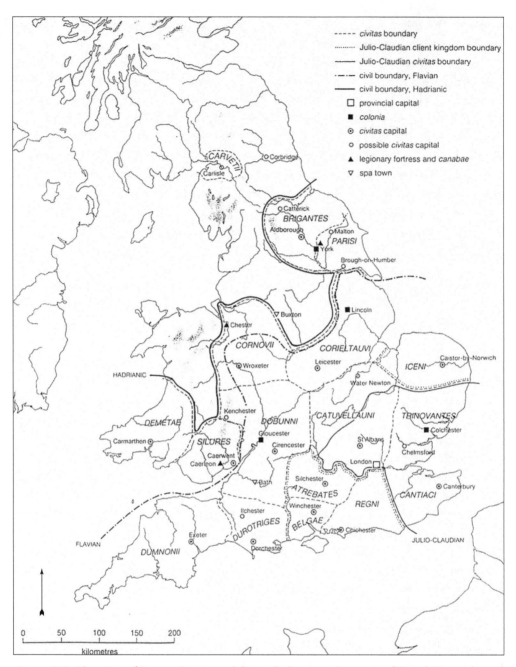

Figure 7.2. The cities of Roman Britain and their tribal regions (courtesy of David Mattingly and Oxbow Books).

The conditions for city foundation, then, were "primarily political and cultural," and there were "several species" of city (Reddé 2003). The most visible expression of the adoption of Roman forms was conspicuous spending on Roman-style public monuments and works: the Romans brought new ideas, techniques, and materials and the concept of monumentality. As long as serious problems did not occur, the Roman authorities did not interfere in local politics or religion. The interests of the Roman and native leaders therefore coincided, provided that some continuity of local traditions and identity could be maintained.

Urban Origins: The Pre-Roman Background

Some of the groups incorporated into the empire were already developing increasingly nucleated settlements, partly under the influence of contact with the Roman world. Coinage was introduced, and a process of urbanization was taking place at scattered but politically significant sites from the late second century BC in central Gaul, linked to trading contacts established following the Roman annexation of southern Gaul (Bedon 2003; Collis 1984). There was an upsurge in industrial production; iron and pottery artifacts, in particular, were becoming much more abundant. Merchants and travelers were bringing ideas and products from the Roman world and, no doubt, influenced attitudes towards material goods. The colonies incorporated some new elements of Roman culture—monumentality and imperial images—as introduced by the first emperor, Augustus (DeLaine, chapter 6; Zanker 1988, 2000).

One of the largest native sites in Gaul, containing an area of about 200 ha inside its ramparts, was Bibracte on Mt. Beuvray in Burgundy, central France (Bedon 2003; Gillaumet 2003). It was the capital of the Aedui tribe, which seem to have had a "special relationship" with the Roman authorities that allowed it particular privileges. Bibracte developed some Roman-style features in the first century BC, and wine was consumed in great quantities. Defended hilltops were sometimes retained in the new order, especially those like Paris and Lyon in convenient locations. Others were abandoned because it was difficult to provide the creature comforts of the Roman urban lifestyle to a site that was not on the road network and with good access to water. A planned replacement city at Autun (*Augustodunum*) was founded in a new location down in the plain 20 km (12 miles) away from Bibracte, adjacent to the river and at a communications crossroads. The city's name reflects the special favors with which the tribe was provided, as does the fact that it was given a rigid street grid from the start. Autun was, at the time, unique among noncolonial cities in the Three Gauls in being allowed to have fortifications, and the walls enclosed a larger area than was necessary. Moreover, it was soon promoted to colony. But there was some resistance to relocating: the hilltop site was not abandoned for at least a generation.

Developments in central Gaul provided the conditions for accelerating the process of "proto-urbanization" already under way—primarily as an indigenous development—farther north. Many of the later tribal centers—what became the civitas capitals—were based on native predecessors that had already experienced an increase in size and some spatial planning, although they would not have been recognized as cities in the Greco-Roman sense (Bedon 2003; Haselgrove 1996).

In southeast Britain, social changes leading to increasing nucleation were occurring well before the Roman conquest of AD 43, partly (but not exclusively) as a result of cross-channel trading, which gave access to luxuries like wine (Cunliffe 2004;

Haselgrove 2003). The effect of Julius Caesar's invasions of 55–54 BC, when formal diplomatic and trading agreements were reached with several tribes, was to accelerate those changes, both to increase the range of imported goods available and to encourage the notion of private property. Some of the tribal leaders may even have visited Rome and had their sons educated in Latin, an experience that can only have encouraged the adoption of a Roman lifestyle as a sign of prestige (Creighton 2000, 2005).

Functions and Planning

As in the Mediterranean region, the functions of the city councils included civic services, imperial propaganda, religious festivals, local administration and tax collection, social amenities, cultural events, and spectacles (Drinkwater 1987; Wacher 1995). There was also economic activity—markets, craft centers, and trading activity, especially at ports like Lyon and London—and industrial production. Some of these functions also served the people of the rural hinterland. The idea of the "consumer city" is one that has dominated approaches until recently but is now being challenged by a number of new studies, such as Mattingly 1997. Major urban settlements were also centers of education and training—for the propagation of classical culture and the use of the Latin language across the empire, which was later the basis for the spread of Christianity. The range of amenities provided the "good life" for the middle and, particularly, the upper classes; the poor, the vast majority, continued much as before, probably with increased burdens.

Although there was what has been called a "consistent family likeness" in terms of the layout and range of amenities to be found among the cities of the Roman west—and perhaps blueprints did exist—there was no one single model of urbanization but rather a firm set of preconceptions (Drinkwater 1987; King 1990:63–88; Wacher 1995; Wightman 1985:75–100). Much depended on existing settlement and topography, as well as local historical factors, and there was some local influence on methods and techniques. The models for the new cities were Mediterranean sites, including those of northern Italy (and, for Britain, those of Gaul), and it appears that military and civilian planning influenced each other. The principal characteristic of the developed Roman city of the northwestern provinces, as in the Mediterranean, was a regular street grid (figure 7.3), but even this could evolve, be modified and extended, or be curtailed (Davies 2002:127–140). There is no evidence that the plan of a whole city was conceived at the outset—this might perhaps be more likely at the military colonies—but it is likely that those planning new buildings were well aware of their visual impact. It appears that the sites for the principal public monuments were first selected and then others were slotted into available gaps as they could be financed. The similarities in form across the empire reinforced the sense of belonging to the Roman world, which was further strengthened by regular civic rituals.

The range of functions noted is reflected in the physical evidence, although, understandably, different cities displayed different emphases. A variety of building types is represented, for communal functions—government, religion, leisure, and

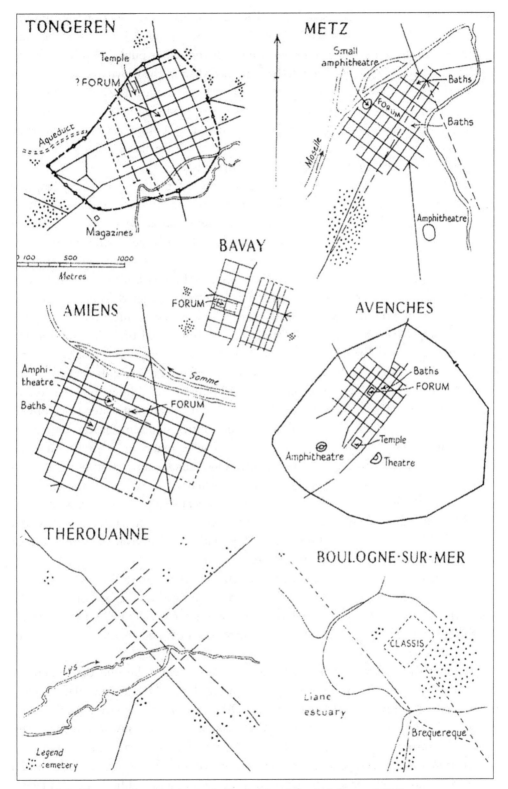

Figure 7.3. Plans of selected cities in Gallia Belgica (after Wightman 1985).

spectacle—as well as residences and specialized and industrial production (Drinkwater 1987; Gros 1996a; Wacher 1995:33–81). The two principal streets (*cardo* and *decumanus*) intersected at the center, with most of the major public buildings facing them. Streets were much less likely to be porticoed than in the provinces farther south and east, but many public buildings were faced with colonnades. The civic center, consisting of the forum (an open space), with offices and a council house and basilica (law court), was normally located at the principal junction and often at the highest point (Gros 1996a; Jones 1999). It was where the elite met to make decisions and where they advertised their status by dedicatory inscriptions.

There were usually several temples. One of classical form dedicated to the emperor or to the principal Roman deities might be found adjacent to the forum, especially in the *coloniae*, and this was a particular focus for ceremonial activity (Esmonde Cleary 2005). The majority, however, were of the Romano-Celtic type, dedicated to a local god (Jones and Mattingly 1990:285–295; King 1990:132–145). In the early years of urbanization, resources were devoted especially to religious buildings, rituals, and feasting as signs of status that replaced warrior symbols, rather than to the achievement of a formal grid. The public baths (a social and leisure center) represented the second principal indicator (after the forum) of the Romanized lifestyle (DeLaine and Johnston 1999). In addition, resources would have to be found to ensure a clean water supply, in some cases involving a costly aqueduct, fountains, and drainage systems (Burgers 2001; Hodge 1992; Wilson 2000). Other public buildings were devoted to culture and spectacle: a theater (for dramas) and/or an amphitheater (for "bloodsports"), or sometimes a hybrid of the two. At some cities, including at least one example in Britain at Colchester, space and resources were found for a circus, an arena for chariot racing (Humphrey 1986). Fortifications usually came later, but gates and arches—common in Gaul—were sometimes erected as separate monuments and clearly not for defensive purposes; the occurrence of walls had much to do with either colonial status or, later, civic pride, unless they were close to frontiers and considered vulnerable (Esmonde Cleary 2003). Here, especially, the survival of some regional building traditions is discernible in constructional details.

The range of accommodations included houses of the courtyard type for the aristocracy (although not commonly of the elaborate "atrium" type found in the Mediterranean), as well as simpler forms, and others for traders behind their street-front shops (Perring 2002). At some sites, there was a covered market in addition to individual shops.

Many of the traders were to be found outside the gates, beyond the cemeteries (Esmonde Cleary 1987). By traditional Roman law, burial always took place outside the official city limits (Pearce et al. 2000). Other activities, including noxious and extractive industries, required large areas close to sources of their raw materials, as well as ease of transportation. These were frequently to be found on the urban fringe.

Clearly differentiated zones are sometimes identifiable. Houses were often located in quieter areas on minor streets. Units in both houses and public buildings facing busier streets could also be utilized for commercial purposes (MacMahon 2006). Shops serving neighborhoods, such as bakeries and bars, were scattered around the city, but workshops tended to occur in clusters and metallurgical industries gathered towards the outskirts where there was access to water (Béal and Goyon 2002). Again, a streetfront location was essential so that they could market their products. At some cities, streets were later diverted or new ones added to allow freer passage through the city for wheeled vehicles (Davies 2002:127–140).

The cities produced vast amounts of waste, much of it water based and the product of industry (Ballet et al. 2003). Disposal of this waste was a managed process, and pragmatic considerations are sometimes apparent, for instance, in its being used for landfill, recycled as raw material, or scattered as fertilizer in the fields. As well as impressive architecture and engineering achievements, the city contained rubbish dumps, areas of unsightly weeds, dirt-ridden and dung-laden streets that had to be cleaned, graffiti-covered walls in the residential districts of the urban poor, and smoky and noxious industries on the edge of town. The benefits of analyses of environmental samples are clear but are still at an early stage (Dobney et al. 1999).

One aspect of current research that such sampling can illuminate is the experience of urban life—the ambience—and its impact on "mentalités." Monumental architecture could impress, overawe, and influence attitudes, especially when reinforced by ceremonial processions; it spread and encouraged appreciation of (and some resistance to) Roman civic values. There is plenty of documentary evidence from the Roman perspective, of course, that the offensive aspects—noises, smells, pests, some crime—were felt to be outweighed by the conveniences—opportunities for work, food, accommodation, amenities, public order and relative security, spectacles—which were not elsewhere available (Bedon 2002). The view from Rome was that civilized living—*urbanitas*—was to be cherished like peace. The city was a mix of differing densities, lifestyles, and diets, according to status. Finds of inscribed tombstones and burials, in particular, demonstrate that the cities of these former "fringe" provinces became cosmopolitan places. Detailed analyses of artifact and environmental collections still have a great deal to tell us about the populations and their cultural preferences. For instance, the provision of retail units in prestigious locations, such as on the street fronting the forum, reflects something of the products available and the attitudes of proprietors to their merchandise: precious metals were often to be found in these prime locations (MacMahon 2006).

Another recent approach has been to analyze city space in terms of social relations and how different groups used it during the course of the day (see Laurence 1994 on Pompeii). Modern theories of planning can also be applied to investigate the use of space as governed by social custom and to contrast elite behavior with that of other classes. Yet there are dangers, as well as benefits, inherent in using current theory. We must take care not to impose our modern values of what is attractive, acceptable, or offensive on ancient societies. We can achieve only glimpses of contemporary perceptions, and what is still difficult to establish in recent analyses is the response to all these changes of the mass of people and the influence they may have had. It is also difficult for us to appreciate the ritual thread that ran through daily life.

Provincial Comparisons

We can now analyze the evidence from the different provinces in turn, taking particular cities as examples.

Gaul

Following Julius Caesar's conquest, the two civil wars and the military campaigns on the German frontier inhibited further development for a few decades. It was the late Augustan period, in the late first century BC/early first century AD, before large-scale progress was apparent. The emperor's priority was the establishment of new colonies in southern Gaul; apart from some other colonial foundations, much of the rest of Gaul was left to its own initiative (Drinkwater 1985; Goudineau 1996, 2000). Some cities are particularly instructive of Roman or native attitudes.

Lyon was already an important center by the mid first century BC. It was favored commercially as an entrepôt for Mediterranean goods to be taken farther north and west by its location on the River Rhone at its junction with the Saône and became the core of the Gallic communications system. The steep slope made it necessary to build roads here at an angle, but those on the hilltop were laid out on a regular grid. Its elevated position required major aqueduct schemes to provide sufficient freshwater. Although Lyon was not situated centrally to the Three Gauls, the site across the Saône from the colony was chosen to be their capital because its promotion was less offensive to the Gallic tribes than being seen to favor an existing center of a particular tribe (Drinkwater 1975). Having made this decision, the emperor consolidated it by heavy investment: an altar to Rome and Augustus recognizing its status (as later at Cologne and Colchester) and an adjacent amphitheater. Political considerations were later overtaken by economic determinism: in the late Roman period, this area of the city was neglected in favor of the natural commercial focus close to the river. Lyon is one of several cities in Gaul in which excavations have identified artisans' quarters where artifacts were produced in great quantity. Those at Autun are typical, covering extensive areas on the edge of the city and revealing metal, glass, pottery, and bone (Béal and Goyon 2002; Gillaumet 2003). Shops in the city center could sell the products of these industries and undertake repairs.

Two cities in northern Gaul have revealed notable sequences and plans (see figure 7.3). Amiens may have originated from a military base at a strategic river crossing—the streets radiate from here. The street plan itself is of interest because the *insulae* are of two different sizes. How is this best explained? Were there two phases, the earlier of military origin? The authorities do not agree on this point. The city's forum was squeezed to fit into the grid. At Tongeren (Belgium), the latest discoveries have been interpreted to indicate that the army laid down the essentials of the city: street-grid, rampart, and early civic center. The natives then moved in, initially occupying native-style farmhouses but buying Mediterranean luxuries. It was the next generation that developed monumental buildings and Roman-style houses (Vanderhoeven 1996).

In general, the cities of Gaul were not packed with buildings from the start but instead were characterized by simple planning, clusters of first-phase public buildings and a number of houses, including traders' establishments, perhaps of timber (Goudineau 1996). Religious buildings appeared early in the process, and other new badges of status included rituals and feasting; only with the development of public buildings in stone was there a transfer of elite display to this medium (Haselgrove 1996). The great construction costs may have caused delays (awaiting the accumulation of adequate capital), but except where there was military influence (as suggested at Tongeren), the large-scale, orthogonal street grids arrived only as a secondary development, and probably one disruptive to the existing life of the town. It was accompanied by the steady and increasing monumentalization of the city center—a pattern now being suggested for Britain, as will be addressed later. The exact building forms and speed of change were left to local initiative (Goudineau 2000).

The Germanies

After Gaul had been subdued and the civil wars of 58–52 BC were over, campaigns were undertaken on the German frontier, including beyond the Rhine. While on campaign, the army established some new towns—presumably as markets for the local tribes. The evidence for this comes not only from the historian Cassius Dio but also from archaeological remains (Carroll 2001:37–40). The scheme was curtailed after the disaster of AD 9 and the loss of three legions. Henceforth, urbanization and conquest east of the Rhine were not attempted. Even beyond the frontier, tribal groups developed and maintained contact with the Roman world, and the material culture made available through this interaction encouraged the native elites to redefine their identities. In spite of these social changes, their settlements did not acquire the attributes of a Roman urban center (Wells 1999:174–258). In contrast with areas to the south and west, the natives lived in scattered farmsteads and settlements of longhouses and maintained a pastoral ideology. According to Tacitus (*Histories*, 4.64), some of the anti-Roman factions regarded urbanized life as a form of slavery.

The Batavian tribe presented a particular problem requiring a special strategy. Originating as legionary bases, Nijmegen and Xanten became important urban centers on the Lower Rhine. As noted above, in this region the local tribal aristocrats were not so enthusiastic about construction; therefore, urban development was slow. Here, the army's role in urbanization was crucial. The tribe actually set fire to the town of Nijmegen in a revolt in AD 69–70. The leaders who had inspired the rebellion were replaced, the town was abandoned, and a new site was chosen nearby for the replacement city (Carroll 2003; Enckevort and Thijssen 2003). The Batavians did, however, serve the Roman state by providing a stream of recruits for the army (Roymans 2005). An indication of the native elite's attitude is that the city council at Nijmegen contained a number of traders, who normally would have been excluded from such office. Like the early-second-century AD colony at Xanten, it developed into a full-fledged city only in the second century and did not survive to the end of the Roman period.

Tribes could be moved. For instance, the Ubii, loyal to Rome and unusually

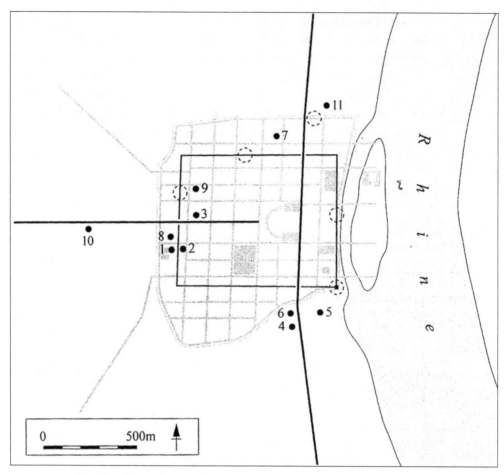

Figure 7.4. Plan of Cologne showing the early city in relation to later colonia. The dashed circles indicate sites where excavations have revealed remains of the defensive circuits. The numbered dots indicate excavated remains of occupation—houses, kilns, and other features (courtesy of Maureen Carroll and Tempus Publishing).

favored as a result, were brought from beyond the Rhine where they were under pressure from hostile tribes to fill the empty landscape and act as a "buffer" in the area around what became the city of Cologne, which served as their civitas capital. A city for the Ubii, and others, was established in the early first century AD on a regular plan with, as at Lyon, an altar to Rome and Augustus (figure 7.4). In AD 50 the city was promoted to the status of *colonia* and probably received an influx of veterans, and the walled area was later enlarged (Carroll 2001:123–131).

In Upper Germany, colonies were founded at Augst and Nyon, and Avenches was later promoted. All three preserve some evidence of their orthogonal planning and public buildings (Carroll 2001:41–61; Drack and Fellmann 1988). The provincial capital, Mainz, developed outside the gates of a legionary fortress and was not of significant civic status until the later Roman period.

Britain

Initially perceived in Rome as the "land beyond ocean," Britain displays a number of similarities to Gaul and Germany, including the diversity of patterns of development and the degree of acceptance of the Roman ideal. One important recent study has defined the social groups of the province as variously military, urban, and rural communities, but even this is believed to be a simplification because all varied across the province and through time (Mattingly 2006). The study of Romano-British towns has benefited from systematic excavation for more than a century. As a result, not only is the chronology of urbanization well understood, but also the pattern of regional diversity that has been revealed gives the same impression as in Gaul: the locals decided the exact form (Jones 1991; Millett 1990). As well as ongoing research at some abandoned sites and excavations ahead of urban renewal at the modern cities, several towns have been the subjects of detailed, GIS-based syntheses (Jones et al. 2003; Niblett and Thompson 2005). These, together with systematic study of artifactual and environmental assemblages, are beginning to allow us to address such issues as density, social and economic zonation, and the use of social space in private residences (Jones 2003; Millett 2001; Perring 2002).

Urban development in Britain began several decades later than in Gaul. The army remained throughout in the province and may have supported the process; technical expertise was also available from resident ex-military personnel. Cities established as the client-kingdoms of southeastern Britain were absorbed into the new province (Creighton 2005) or following conquest of other tribes as the army advanced north and westwards—but urbanization could be achieved over only part of the province (see figure 7.2). In the frontier regions, there were no cities, but rather central places for a provincial military-civilian culture distinct from that of southeast Britain: many soldiers came from more "Romanized" parts of the Empire (Millett 2001; Wells 1999, on the Rhine-Danube frontiers).

The models for town plans may have been provided by the military colonies, based to some extent on their previous existence as legionary fortresses (directly beneath the later towns), and from contacts with Gaul itself (Hurst 1999b). The insecurity of being a military province no doubt contributed to permission being granted for the provision of fortifications at an earlier date than for those in Gaul, but the primary motivation was still status (Esmonde Cleary 2003). In their construction, the earthen tradition of the second-century defenses was distinctively British.

Julius Caesar had noted that tribal centers in Britain were different from those in Gaul. One of the most important, Colchester, then developed into a dispersed "territorial" *oppidum*. Following the Roman army's arrival in AD 43, it became for a short period the focus of the conquest, housing a legionary fortress, and was the scene of the Emperor Claudius's victory celebration. The event was later marked by a temple to the deified Claudius, the center of the imperial cult in Britain. By this time, the army had moved on, and the fortress site had been converted to a colonia (figure 7.5). The new city partly incorporated the legionary grid system but also extended to the east, to the

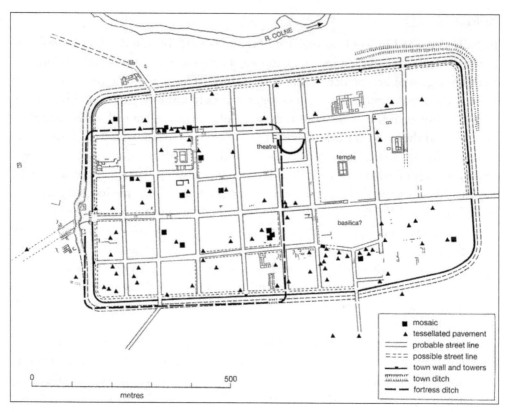

Figure 7.5. Plan of the early colonia at Colchester, with the line of the preceding legionary fortress marked (courtesy of Philip Crummy).

temple site: the two phases of streets are on slightly different alignments (Crummy 1997). The long-term excavator of Colchester, Philip Crummy, has identified a metrological system in its planning whereby it was laid out in blocks of standard units of Roman feet. Crummy has suggested (most recently in Crummy 1999) that this practice was widespread in Roman town planning. It is notable that at Colchester the early colonists—retired legionaries and a number of local people—lived in converted barracks (built only a few years earlier) and the major investment in the early years was in establishing a prominent imperial image. Tacitus tells us that the colony functioned as both an example of civic life and a bulwark against rebellion; in the second case, it was not entirely successful. The Roman authorities made the mistake of not fortifying the new colony, leaving it vulnerable during Boudicca's revolt of AD 60/61, when the new towns at London and Verulamium were also destroyed. This was remedied later in the century, but at least partly in order to emphasize the city's status.

Colchester was the early capital, but within a decade or so it was succeeded by London. Situated at the lowest bridging point of the River Thames, London was apparently unoccupied when the conquest took place, but like Lyon in Gaul, its favorable location soon made it the center of the road hub and the great entrepôt for the province—a place seething with both immigrant traders and native Britons, initially

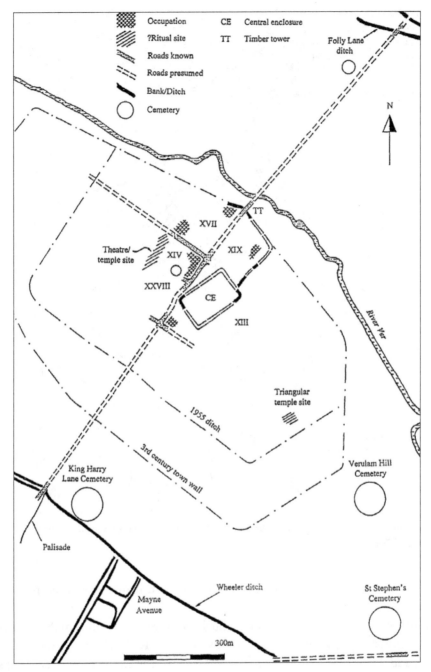

Figure 7.6a. Plan of the early city at Verulamium (courtesy of Rosalind Niblett and Tempus Publishing).

living in modest premises fronting dirt roads. In spite of setbacks, it grew at a faster rate and to a greater population size than any other Romano-British city. Its civic center was of huge scale, and there is some evidence that at least its core was planned from an early date (Milne 1995; Perring 1991; Watson 1998). London's status was initially

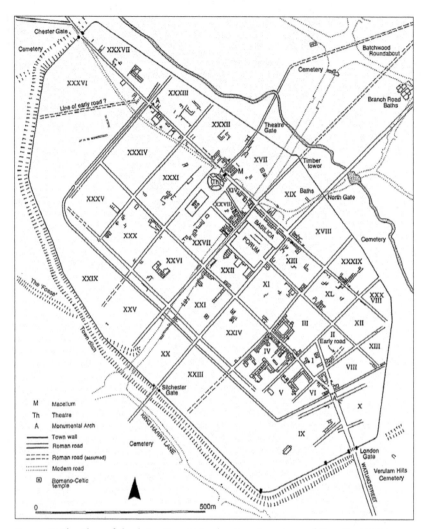

Figure 7.6b. Plan of the late city at Verulamium (courtesy of Rosalind Niblett and Tempus Publishing).

unusual, but when it became the seat of the governor, it may have been promoted to a colonia.

Another native center that has been much excavated, Verulamium (St Albans), has recently furnished some informative details on its early development (Niblett 2001; Niblett and Thompson 2005). The key elements of the earliest city were shops providing Roman-style goods and an early "Central Enclosure" that may have contained an aristocratic residence (figure 7.6a). The street grid came a generation later, together with the known forum and other public buildings (figure 7.6b). A similar pattern is now apparent at some other native centers. At Silchester, several phases of urban development can now be identified (Fulford 2003). Some organization of space is clear from the late first century BC, well before the Roman conquest. The settlement was growing throughout this period. Following the conquest, there appears to have been a new

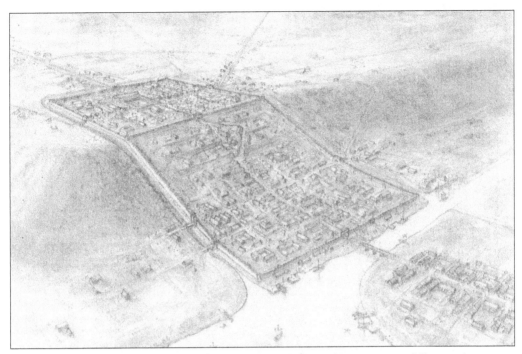

Figure 7.7. Reconstruction drawing of the walled city of Lincoln ca. AD 350, following the strengthening of the fortifications (by the late David Vale).

street alignment and Roman architectural forms, including houses similar in plan to some found in northern Gaul—a common source for Romano-British house forms. A generation later, a full grid was imposed on a different alignment. A combination of aerial photography and excavations has demonstrated that certain parts of the walled area were not filled until the third century.

There was an official obligation to accommodate a steady stream of retired legionaries in new colonies, and two more were created out of the former fortresses at Lincoln and Gloucester. Here, the legionary ramparts were left in position and soon faced in stone, and the military street systems were adapted as required. At both new colonies, a major state temple-precinct was also a prominent feature. The presence of a focus for displaying devotion to the emperor was clearly considered to be a priority. These colonies, which from their largely ex-military populations were seen as centers of loyalty to the emperor, represented the Roman concept of a provincial city. In the course of their first half-century, they developed a range of public amenities and some impressive architecture, and they continued to thrive (figure 7.7)—but even here the leading citizens had to fund the lion's share of their costs (Hurst 1999a, 2000; Jones 2002; Jones et al. 2003).

Two other former fortresses, at Exeter and Wroxeter, did not become colonies but tribal capitals. Wroxeter, on the border with Wales, lay some distance from the tribes of the southeast that experienced Roman influence a century before it (White and

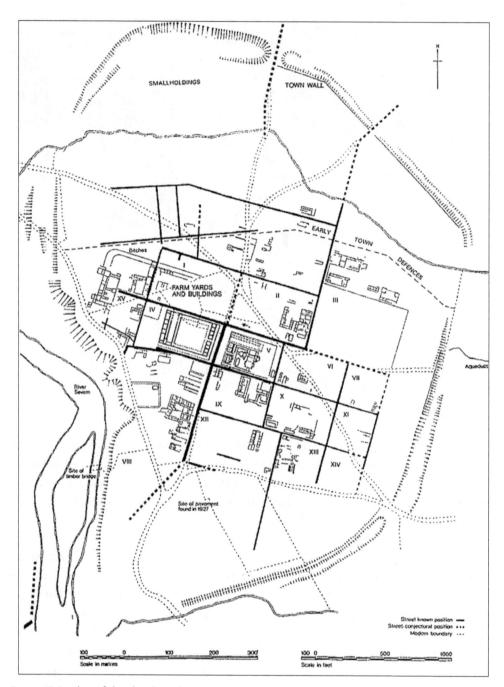

Figure 7.8. Plan of the developed city at Wroxeter (Viroconium Cornoviorum) (courtesy of Roger White and Birmingham Archaeology).

Barker 1998). Systematic field survey, using a range of up-to-date geophysical techniques, has recently been carried out on the deserted site of the city and its environs (White and Gaffney 2003). Although the geophysical results detected remains only at a superficial level, they did differentiate distinct social zones—public buildings, high status residences, artisan quarters, industrial workings (including extensive areas of open pits possibly used for tanning), and areas apparently little developed (figure 7.8). The picture of the environs gained is that market gardening was carried out adjacent to the city but the surrounding fields contained livestock and were not being used for agriculture. One problem with this site has always been the huge scale of its defended area. The latest attractive hypothesis to account for this paradox is that the enclosure extended to the top of a nearby hill, even enclosing a stream, which made for some eccentric street layouts in that part of the city. By doing so, it provided the sort of large fortified site with which the native aristocrats felt comfortable—in being similar to their earlier hill forts. The presence of the cattle around may be a further indication that, as well as adopting Roman architecture and other visible elements of the new culture, they maintained some existing status symbols—in the size of their livestock herds. The parallel with the Lower Rhine tribes discussed above is notable.

Apart from a few exceptions such as this, the evidence for the relationship of the British cities to their economic hinterlands is one that requires further study. It is difficult to establish the extent of each city's territory on present grounds, even at the coloniae; in the absence of good evidence, various hypotheses abound (Hurst 1999; Roskams 1999). Studies of coin-loss patterns, pottery distributions, animal bone and other biological assemblages, and landscapes, as well as the relationship between the city and nearby market centers, offer ways forward.

Growth, Maturity, and Decline (or "Transformation"?)

Cities were often sited for political reasons, but those that flourished in the long term, apart from capitals, were largely those on major routes and best placed to exploit trading activity, that is, at ports like Bordeaux, Lyon, and London. Some of the minor market centers also grew considerably, possibly as a result of the decentralization of commercial functions, but also because of economic growth. Few cities, especially in Britain, had populations of more than 10,000—although the principal centers could house several times this number—and only London had a walled area that covered more than 100 ha. It has often been stated, although it is merely an informed estimate, that 90 percent of the people still worked on the land. The elite that owned the land and had political power are likely to have amounted to less than 1 percent of the population (Mattingly 2006:293).

The investment in public works made by these aristocrats must, to some extent, have been recouped by an increase in the rents they charged, but expenditure on this level was unsustainable (Esmonde Cleary 1998). Marble veneers were very common, but their cost was exorbitant. An estimate of the cost of the water supply for Nimes, including its impressive aqueducts, has put it at the modern equivalent of many millions of dollars (Fabre et al. 1992:66–75). Some projects were never completed. Most of the expenditure on monumental buildings and public works poured out in the first and second centuries AD, so the cities reached their high point of such development by the beginning of the third century.

Figure 7.9. Photograph of the city wall of Le Mans, showing decorated masonry (photograph by Michael J. Jones).

Later events, including the third-century crisis in Gaul as a result of the Frankish invasions and the changes in taxation in the fourth century, shifted priorities. Public office became more of a financial burden and, as a result, was less popular. Personal surpluses were now more often devoted to private residences as the vehicle for establishing status. Public works were largely limited to the repair of monuments and amenities rather than replacements, leading to their ultimate abandonment or re-use for more utilitarian purposes. The vast majority of the public purse was devoted to fortifications, and these were now built or refurbished to reflect the city's status (Esmonde Cleary 1989; Faulkner 2000:121–130; see figure 7.8, figure 7.9). Sometimes, and especially in Gaul where only small parts of the cities were defended, this involved reusing the remains of public monuments and temples, and even burial monuments. At St. Bertrand-de-Comminges, in Aquitania, clear evidence has now been found that buildings in the city were being systematically demolished around AD 400 and the material taken up the hill to build the new fortifications (Esmonde Cleary and Wood 2006).

This was also the period when a formal organization of the Christian church and its new bishops was established in the principal cities, but churches, even those reusing existing buildings, were not common structures before the fifth century, even in Gaul. Few have come to light as yet in Britain (Petts 2003). Gradually, during the course of the fourth century, many of the cities were in terminal decline, or, to be more politically correct—but perhaps unduly so—in "transformation" (see Ward-Perkins 2005 for a stimulating recent discussion). They no longer existed by the middle of the fifth century in Britain and parts of Germany, where the Anglo-Saxon leaders had no use for towns, but in Gaul, especially, the new rulers did continue the Roman system and many sites retained some significance. In fact, some of the new Frankish invaders helped to sustain towns into the early medieval period—but only in areas where the idea of urbanism had earlier been warmly espoused. The late Roman diocesan city, led by a Christian bishop and characterized by strong walls and ecclesiastical establishments, was a common and significant feature of the so-called "Late Antique" period (fourth to seventh centuries: Knight 1999). Subsequently, the memory of a previous empire and its late Roman Christian associations could serve to legitimize the *"tyranni,"* the warlords who moved into the political vacuum left by the withdrawal of Roman authority, and structures including fora and amphitheaters—or merely the presence of city walls—were sometimes used as a symbolic focus for these new rulers (Carver 1993:19–33).

Conclusions

Roman urbanization of the northwest provinces was dependent on both imperial policy and local circumstances. It was achievable only where it could be imposed as a means of settling military veterans or with the positive involvement of native aristocracies whose ideologies were not hostile and who controlled their tribes sufficiently to enable urbanization to develop on the Roman model. Those tribal leaders had already begun to share some of the political and material benefits of contact with the empire. The Romans brought a particular view of the world in which "civilization" was based on city life, and they successfully exported this model to those societies whose leaders and organization were susceptible to what it offered, in terms of both political credentials and visible lifestyle.

But they did not possess the resources either to build all the cities themselves or to force the local communities to do so: a pragmatic approach is apparent. As in the Mediterranean, the cities were a means to govern provinces incorporated into the empire, and the functional aspect was balanced by the symbolic: rituals, images, and dedications were highly visible aspects of both emphasizing the imperial context and reinforcing the status quo. The process of developing the form of the cities was only achieved over a few generations, even at the coloniae—although some of these inherited a street grid from their previous existence as legionary fortresses. The natives interpreted the urban model presented to them according to their existing values, values that evolved through time: this explains the long gestation and the resulting diversity. Essential elements of the earliest phase of the new cities were major religious establishments, expressing devotion to the empire, and accommodation (much of it modest) for locals, immigrant traders, and craftsmen. Form was not initially so critical. The process of establishing a fully planned Roman city took at least an additional generation, partly because it may have been dependent on another generation of tribal leaders with a more Roman outlook, but also probably because of the heavy costs. Also, progress could have been affected by events elsewhere in the province. By the middle of the second century AD, the cities were largely complete in terms of their monumental cores—they had "become Roman," like their sponsors. They continued to grow as commercial centers but, apart from the great ports and some specialized centers, served only their regions, not the whole province. Urban society went with villa society, and in the third and fourth centuries large amounts of capital were devoted to residences in town and country.

The diversity of the physical evidence indicates that each city was of a similar pattern but also unique in terms of its exact planning and architecture. Decisions on detailed design were made locally from a range of options available. The natives interpreted the Roman forms from their own cultural perspective. Those who paid for the developments expected visible acknowledgment. What drove the process was aristocratic and intercity rivalry, supported by official encouragement but not coercion. The adoption of Roman building practice was one element of a changing culture that also affected diet and dining style, language, leisure, clothing and hairstyles, art, religion, and burial customs (Cool 2006; Henig 1995; King 2001; Pearce et al. 2000) and made available a vast range of material possessions for those who could afford them—a "consumer revolution" (Woolf 1998:181–205). But there was not a uniform pattern. Different groups had different experiences of the Roman presence and responded in different ways—whether it involved welcoming, acquiescing, or resisting—to the changes it brought, defining their own various new identities.

A number of points can be made about the nature of Roman urbanism, as described in this chapter and in the wider context of this volume. Cities of the Roman Empire incorporated all the elements used by Kostof to define a city and listed by the editors (Marcus and Sabloff, chapter 1), as well as those discussed by Trigger in his wide-ranging analysis of urbanism (2003:120–141). There are some notable comparisons between the social behavior of the Roman elite and that of the Maya (Pyburn, chapter 13): for instance, in the use of nonlocal resources—although of a purely mobile nature—for defining their status and in maintaining an urban residence, for access to particular services and commodities, and for social-networking purposes, at some distance from the primary source of their wealth in the countryside. Trigger (2003:141) has noted the second factor but addressed the possibility that the primary rural residences were located in situations affording considerable privacy and with limited access, so as to enhance the authority of their elite owners.

It was largely the aristocracy that created Roman cities; everyone had to live with their creations. Over the first few generations, the native elites became more and more integrated into the culture of the empire. The Roman city in northwestern Europe was not, however, a lasting phenomenon: political events, including imperatives on and beyond the frontiers, saw the cities of these provinces first change their character, then be reduced to a shadow of their former vitality.

Acknowledgments

I should like to thank the organizers for inviting me to present a version of this chapter at the colloquium, and I regret that ill health prevented me from doing so. Dr. Janet DeLaine kindly read it on my behalf. The version presented here has benefited from useful suggestions by Professor John Collis, Professor David Mattingly, Dr. Richard Reece, Dr. J. P. Wild, and Professor Roger Wilson. I also thank Professor Joyce Marcus and anonymous reviewers for their suggestions, and I have endeavored to respond positively to these.

Most of the illustrations included here were kindly provided by others. I should like to thank Dr. Maureen Carroll and Tempus Publishing for permission to use figures 7.1 and 7.4; Professor Mattingly and Oxbow Books for figure 7.2; Philip Crummy for figure 7.5; Dr. Rosalind Niblett for figures 7.6a and 7.6b; and Dr. Roger White for figure 7.8. Figure 7.3 is taken from Wightman 1985; figure 7.7 was the work of the late David Vale and is reproduced by permission of FLARE.

eight
A Tale of Two Cities
Lowland Mesopotamia and Highland Anatolia

Elizabeth C. Stone

Urban sociologists and city planners have developed a robust set of tools to understand the linkage between social variation and physical space within cities. Their models, of course, pertain to modern, industrialized cities, which are quite unlike those associated with early complex societies, but their work suggests that similar associations must have existed in the past. If we can find a way to understand the nature of the link between space and society in cities so very different from our own, it would enhance our endeavors to interpret the archaeological record of early complex societies. To identify such patterns in the past, the first step is to use descriptions of well-known premodern cities to document similar consistent relationships between space and society. Because the economies of these cities were much more closely tied to their agricultural hinterlands than is the case today, such an endeavor will need to take into account the environmental context within which these early cities developed.

Today, archaeologists are moving away from seeing all complex societies as having traveled along similar trajectories. Instead, a number of scholars have stressed variability. Trigger (1993, 2003) has drawn a distinction between city-states and territorial states. A complication of his approach is that he links the size of the polity with variations in the degree of urbanism and entrepreneurialism without developing causal links. As a result, the distinctions he drew in terms of the structure of these societies became lost in discussions regarding the size of their polities (Marcus 1998). Mogens Hansen's work on city-states is largely similar, but he argues that city-state societies maintain their distinctive identity even when incorporated into larger imperial structures (Hansen 2000b:613–614).

Other scholars have explored variability along single dimensions. Of these, the most interesting to my mind are those that explore whether all early complex societies were as hierarchical as they have so often been portrayed. Crumley (1987; Crumley and Marquardt 1987) introduced the concept of heterarchy to the archaeological literature. Blanton has presented a persuasive argument that some early states were based on "systematic exclusionary domination" (Blanton 1998: 144) and others were based on a "corporate power strategy" (Blanton 1998:145). My focus has been on the conditions that allowed the growth of complex societies lacking the high levels of social differentiation and low levels of social mobility typical of early complex societies based on exclusionary domination. I have argued that there are fundamental differences between early complex societies based on principles of hierarchy and those based on heterarchy and that this underlying social structure shaped the physical organization of ancient cities (Stone 1997, 1999). In this chapter, these differences are illustrated by the results of our fieldwork at the southern Mesopotamian city of Mashkan-shapir and the Urartian city of Ayanis.

Land, Labor, and Urban Planning

Most urban centers today are located in areas where arable land is both more or less permanent and more or less unbounded, but many of the earliest cities are found in areas with more restrictive environments. Associated with states with exclusionary domination, such as Egypt and Peru, is arable land that is both permanent and bounded —by desert in Egypt and by steep uplands in Peru. By contrast, those with corporate power strategies, such as among the Yoruba and Mesopotamia, have arable land that is readily available but only for short periods of time. Here land moves in and out of cultivation either through cycles of slash-and-burn in West Africa or as a result of the ravages of salinization and siltation in Mesopotamia. Both agricultural regimes represent unusual environmental conditions, but it may not be coincidental that many of the earliest state-level societies are to be found where land is either permanent and bounded or impermanent and unbounded.

Some of the differences between urban centers associated with Trigger's city-states and territorial states can, I think, be directly related to these differences in ecology. Bounded, limited, arable land makes it easy for elites to monopolize the means of production (to put this in Marxist terms) and thus control the larger population. Under these circumstances, elites were able to live apart in small enclaves that were separated from rural populations, whose material lives differed little from that of their Neolithic ancestors.

This kind of control over arable land is impossible in areas characterized by shifting agriculture. Here the key factor is control over labor rather than land (Stone 1997). This labor force dug the canals needed to replenish the agricultural hinterland as salinization took some areas out of cultivation in Mesopotamia, and it cleared the land for swidden agriculture in Yorubaland. Under these circumstances, the imperative for the rulers of these states was to attract labor rather than control arable land. The features that characterize these societies—large populous cities, high levels of entrepreneurial activity, high social mobility, more open decision making—can all be related to the importance of engaging the larger population so that it remained an integral part of that particular polity. Where the government cannot control all economic resources, power sharing and the provision of broad economic opportunities are needed to attract and maintain the labor force that is so crucial to its well-being. These conditions may also be related to the differences in the sizes of the polities noted by Trigger. Without modern communications, corporate power strategies require face-to-face interaction. This is most easily attained when the polity is small and a large segment of the population is living in the main city. The terminology coined by Trigger is unfortunate because it places emphasis on the differences in the sizes of the two types of polity. However, his descriptions of the differences between the elite enclaves that form the centers of territorial states and the populous, entrepreneurial, urban centers that lie at the heart of city-states are pertinent to any discussion of the differential effect of exclusionary and corporate governance. Moreover, even when united through military conquest into larger empires, both urban form and corporate power structures continue to exist on the local level of city-state societies.

As archaeologists, we can now go back to the work of urban planners and ask whether we can identify these differences in political organization on the basis of the layout of their cities. The urban centers of well-documented states based on exclusionary control, such as Cuzco (Bauer 2004:107–138; Hyslop 1990:29–68) and Tokugawa Edo (Jinnai 1990; Yazaki 1968:167–232), are characterized by relatively small size, the dominance of centralizing institutions, and occupation by elites and their servants. At Cuzco, the city was surrounded by suburbs occupied by dependent populations who were forcibly moved into the area, whereas at Edo these were scattered throughout the countryside. The small size and nature of these cities reflect the ability of these elites to dominate the economy.

By contrast, the capitals of city-states in Yorubaland (Krapf-Askari 1969) or in Medieval Syria (Abdel-Nour 1982; Lapidus 1984 [1967]) were dominated by political and religious institutions that were physically and structurally quite separate, a reflection of the power-sharing mechanisms that characterized their political systems. These cities were also large, with clearly defined neighborhoods. These were occupied by a mixture of different social classes and served as the locus for social mobility. At the center of these cities lay their entrepreneurial heart, the market, which served to connect people living in different neighborhoods. These features reflect the economic and political opportunities made available to the larger population as a means of attracting them to the city.

Most state societies, however, are to be found in geographical areas where arable land is both unbounded and permanent, lacking the ecological constraints described above. The rolling hills of Assyria are one example of this. There is clear evidence for corporate power at Assur in the second millennium BC, whereas exclusionary domination characterized the first-millennium Neo-Assyrian empire. It is not within the scope of this chapter to investigate whether the experience of Assyria and areas like it express variants not found where ecological conditions are more restrictive; rather, it investigates whether the coincidence between overall organizational type and urban plan described above can be identified as a consistent pattern in the archaeological record. To this end, we have been conducting archaeological fieldwork in two areas with restrictive environment—the southern Mesopotamian alluvium and the mountainous environment of Urartu.

Mesopotamia

The environmental conditions of southern Mesopotamia, with its arid alluvium made arable through irrigation systems that fall victim to salinization and siltation after a few decades (Adams 1965), suggest that its cities should resemble those of Yorubaland. Some of the features cited above as features of Yoruba cities—large size, the multiplicity of institutional foci, and residential neighborhoods including all classes—also exist in Mesopotamia (Stone 1995) and suggest the appropriateness of the model. However, no Mesopotamian site has come close to being completely excavated, and evidence for entrepreneurial activity is largely limited to written documents reflecting the interests of the state.

Mashkan-shapir

Our project at the site now known to be ancient Mashkan-shapir (Stone 1990; Stone and Zimansky 1995, 2004a; figure 8.1) was developed with the express aim of obtaining an understanding of at least one Mesopotamian city. Mashkan-shapir is an overwhelmingly early second-millennium BC site some 80 ha in size, most of it occupied for no more than 150 years. This means that an urban survey should provide evidence on its organization that could be tested against the model proposed above. Moreover, after the identification with Mashkan-shapir was made on the basis of inscriptions found at the site, we also knew that this was a planned city—so its morphology could not be ascribed to slow accretions developed over time. Mashkan-shapir was deliberately expanded from a small center (*mashkan* means "hamlet" or "encampment") when the king of Larsa, Sin-iddinam, built its city wall "in order to increase its dwellings," as expressed in the building inscription found associated with that wall. From that point onwards, Mashkan-shapir served as the second capital to the kingdom of Larsa.

The approach used to recover broad evidence of urban planning was simple. First, we conducted a detailed walking survey of the site, recording the locations of objects and architectural features and sketching the surface scatter. Second, we obtained a high-resolution aerial view of the site, using a kite as an aerial platform. Here not only could we relate our surface scatters to real patterns visible in the imagery, but also, in many instances—especially after a rain—traces of the underlying mud-brick architec-

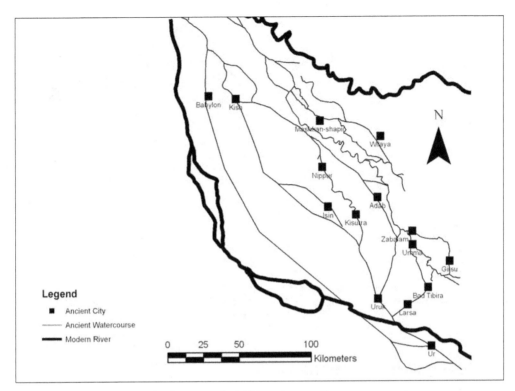

Figure 8.1. Map showing the location of Mashkan-shapir relative to contemporary watercourses and cities.

ture could be discerned. Third and finally, we planned to use the results of the survey to conduct excavations that would investigate the different parts of the site. This portion of the project was in its infancy when archaeological research in Iraq came to a halt in 1990.

The combination of the aerial photography and surface survey allowed us to identify the major features that served to divide the site, primarily the system of canals that flowed through the ancient city. We also identified the major walls that both surrounded the site and were built within it. Moreover, the modern isolation of the site meant that we were able to recover some 1,400 objects from the surface, enough that their distribution patterns could be used to assign function to the areas segregated one from the other by walls or canals.

The location of the main temple was made clear both by its topography of eroded mud-brick and baked-brick platforms and by the concentration of terracotta statuary—an artifact type associated exclusively with major temples at other Mesopotamian sites. Our temple shares with other Mesopotamian cities its location towards one edge of the site, here separated from the rest of the city by a canal.

We had a more difficult time identifying the administrative heart of the city. Until very recently, we were struck by the regularity of the architecture in the southwestern portion of the site and the presence of a large wall that segregated this area. We found many unbaked clay sealings in our excavations in the area. Because these are

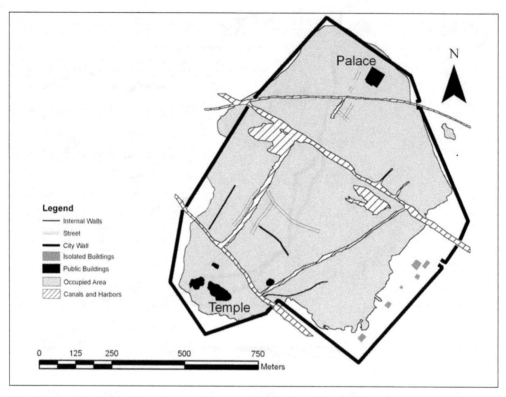

Figure 8.2. Plan of Mashkan-shapir indicating the location of major features.

used to control the contents of rooms and jars, their presence suggests that administrative activities were concentrated in this part of the site. In the absence of other candidates, we assumed that the palace referred to in the texts probably lies at lower levels within this area. However, we have recently obtained a high-resolution Digital Globe image of Mashkan-shapir. In addition to providing sad evidence for the destruction of much of the site by recent looting, the rise in the water table due to new irrigation projects has made subsurface architecture visible as salt marks. In an area in the far north of the site, where surface objects were relatively rare during the survey, we see an architectural pattern that is strongly reminiscent of the contemporary palace at Larsa (Margueron 1982:figure 257), albeit at a smaller scale. The administrative area and the temple were separated by a canal but otherwise were close together; the temple and the palace were at opposite edges of this ancient city (figures 8.2 and 8.3).

As noted above, it is the market, or center for entrepreneurial activity, that seems to form the heart of most urban centers of this kind. The rich written documentation on the Mesopotamian economy provides little light on this issue. We therefore emphasized the recording of indicators of manufacturing in our survey and searched for morphological features that might be related to entrepreneurial activities.

Although Woolley identified two harbors when he worked at Ur (Woolley and Mallowan 1976:plate 116) and it has been long known that major watercourses flowed through cities such as Nippur and Kish, the results of our work at Mashkan-shapir

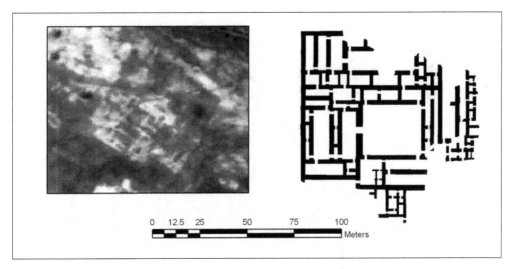

Figure 8.3. A comparison between the plan of the early second-millennium BC palace at Larsa and the traces of a large public building seen in imagery from Mashkan-shapir.

have led others to seek and find evidence for smaller canals and harbors within other Mesopotamian sites. Now high-resolution aerial and satellite photography has identified canals and harbors within a large number of sites in southern Iraq. The Mesopotamian texts describe their cities as bipartite, made up of the city and the quay or harbor, the latter being the place where external trade took place and where foreign merchants resided. These texts have been interpreted to indicate that there was a separate settlement beyond the city walls that was the focus of such trade, though no sites have been identified as likely candidates. However, if the texts refer to social rather than physical differences between the city and the quay, we might want to locate this center for commerce at the harbors.

Manufacturing debris has been found at many Mesopotamian sites, often clustered in one peripheral part of the city. The same is true for Mashkan-shapir (figure 8.4). Here the smokestack industries, such as pottery making, and the manufacture of synthetic basalt (Stone et al. 1998) are concentrated in the southeastern (leeward), part of the site. Many small grinding stones and fragments of exotic stones, which together must testify to lapidary work, were also found in this part of the city. Most interesting, though, are the clusters of copper fragments and cuprous slag that represent the locations of copper/bronze smithies. These were mostly scattered along a large east-west street—visible even from space—that ran through the city connecting the east gate with the (still unidentified) west gate. This road was important enough that baked-brick buttresses were built where it crossed one of the canals, doubtless to support a bridge or ease ferry traffic. Because metalwork is the only activity one would expect to find in a *suq* (market), that is likely to leave surface traces, it is not unreasonable to interpret these data as indicating the presence of a commercial street that linked two of the gates of the city, and such gates have long since been identified as

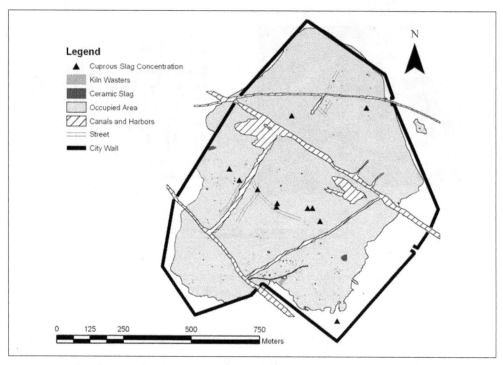

Figure 8.4. Plan showing the distribution of manufacturing debris at Mashkan-shapir.

seats of exchange (Oppenheim 1969). If our interpretation of our survey data is correct, then Mesopotamian cities would have been focused around something more akin to an American Main Street than a traditional Middle Eastern suq, because the crafts do not seem to have been clustered. This street, then, would represent the entrepreneurial heart of this Mesopo-tamian city, its central location similar to that of markets in other city-state societies.

The last question to be asked of the Mashkan-shapir survey is whether the data collected support the contention that residential districts were not segregated by wealth and power but rather that each neighborhood included all classes. Although architectural traces were identified within the city, these cannot be used to indicate whether residential patterns similar to those found at Ur, and elsewhere, existed at Mashkan-shapir. Instead, the objects recovered from the survey can be used to evaluate the distribution of wealth throughout the city. Two items can be used here. One is metal (figure 8.5)—a resource that had to be imported from some distance—and the second is the cylinder seal (figure 8.6), the ancient Mesopotamian badge of office. Both were quite evenly distributed across the surface of the site.

In sum, the data from Mashkan-shapir conform well to the patterns of urban organization associated with states based on corporate power as outlined above. Moreover, as a planned city, one transformed from a large village into a city by a royal act of construction, it is reasonable to assume that the spatial arrangement there reflected contemporary ideas of how cities should be organized. What we see is a city

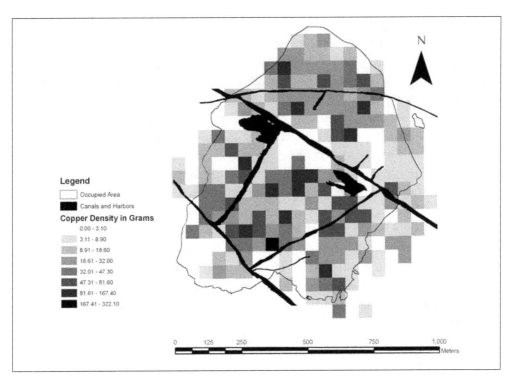

Figure 8.5. Plan showing the distribution of copper/bronze objects and fragments at Mashkan-shapir.

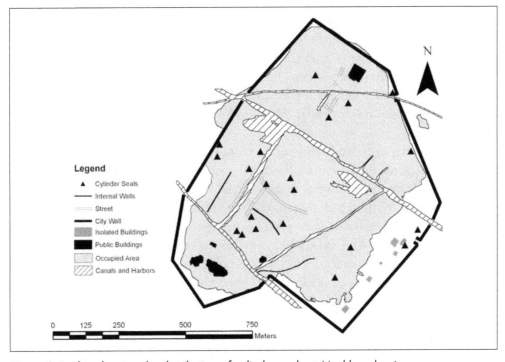

Figure 8.6. Plan showing the distribution of cylinder seals at Mashkan-shapir.

A Tale of Two Cities   149

where the two rival institutions, the palace and the temple, could not have been more distant from each other. The temple, especially, was isolated, separated by a large canal from the rest of the city. Other canals also served to subdivide the city. The western mound seems to have had an official character, at least within the walled portion; the southeastern mound was where much of the large-scale manufacturing activities took place. The center of the city held the cemetery (located on the old settlement mound) and residential districts, through which cut the large east-west thoroughfare where the shops of artisans were located. Because evidence for domestic housing has been found in all parts of the city, except perhaps in the religious quarter, it seems likely that if neighborhoods were not segregated by wealth, they were likely divided by their affiliation with the different foci of the city, associated with administration, exchange, palace, temple, and so on. Once again, this would parallel the evidence from Yorubaland, where these divisions were based on kinship, and medieval Aleppo, where they were based on a mixture of religion, kinship, place of origin, and occupation. Overall, the plan of Mashkan-shapir, and indeed what we know of other Mesopo-tamian cities, demonstrates strong similarities with the plans of urban centers associated with other city-state societies.

Urartu

The Kingdom of Urartu grew up in the mountainous areas of eastern Turkey, Armenia, and northwestern Iran (figure 8.7) in the first millennium BC, almost certainly in response to the growth of the Assyrian Empire farther south. Indeed, many of our key sources on Urartu come from descriptions of Assyrian military campaigns against them. In terms of landscape, the Urartian kingdom is similar to Peru, made up of rugged uplands occasionally interrupted by small pockets of alluvial soil suitable for agriculture, especially with the help of irrigation (Zimansky 1985:110–111). Indeed, the Urartians are justly famous for their water management—the Menua Canal still serves to bring fresh drinking water to the modern city of Van, located beside Urartu's ancient capital.

Until recently, little has been known of Urartian settlement beyond its fortresses, which have attracted the attention of archaeologists and treasure seekers for more than a century. Built on rocky eminences above areas of irrigable land, these were heavily fortified enclaves. Within, they contained extensive storage facilities, large tower temples, and columned halls that have been interpreted as palaces (Piotrovsky 1967; Zimansky 1985). The buildings within the fortresses were decorated with military implements—shields, quivers, helmets, and the like—and more weapons have been found in some of the storage areas. The columned halls and temples have evidence of elaborate wall paintings—with an emphasis on the artificial "Egyptian Blue" pigment—and might include inlaid or gold decoration. Everything about these fortresses speaks of wealth, militarism, and systematic exclusionary domination.

Perhaps because of the riches to be found within the fortresses, our information is much more limited when it comes to surrounding settlements. Urartian inscriptions

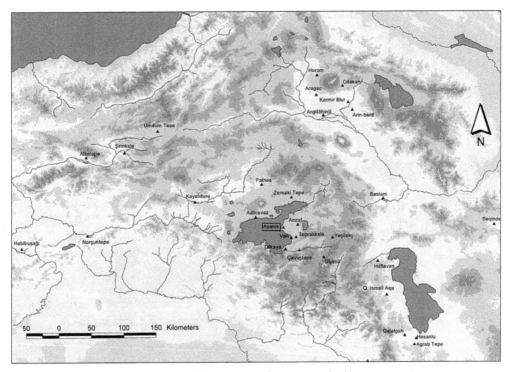

Figure 8.7. Map of Urartu showing the location of Ayanis and other major Urartian sites.

often refer to foreign deportees brought in to work on the construction of the fortresses, who then settled in the area. But only at Bastam (Kleiss 1988:11–28), Karmir Blur (Martirosjan 1961; Organesjan 1955:18–35), and Adiljivaz (Martirosjan 1974:35–73) have buildings beyond the citadels been excavated, and the publication of these finds remains spotty at best. Our project at Ayanis is therefore the first to examine the nature of a complete Urartian settlement, including both the fortress and the outer town. Information on the rural hinterland remains almost completely unknown.

The paucity of settlement data from other sites makes interpretation of our results more difficult. At Bastam, two areas were excavated beyond the fortress: a large public building containing stables (Kleiss 1988:19–28)—perhaps the royal chariot house—and a domestic area characterized by buildings with party walls (Kleiss 1988: 20–21). At Adiljivaz, a series of irregular houses, often with small columned halls, were excavated (Martirosjan 1974:35–73), and similar structures have been reported from Karmir Blur (Organesjan 1955:18–35). Also at Karmir Blur, but published only as part of the overall plan of the site, was a structure made up of a series of identical apartments, each one significantly larger than the average house. These data are very difficult to evaluate. The plan occurs only on the overview of the entire site, with no explanatory text (Piotrovsky 1967:177–178). We are provided with no information on the architecture, the associated artifacts, or even whether the buildings were excavated or simply extrapolated from surface traces.

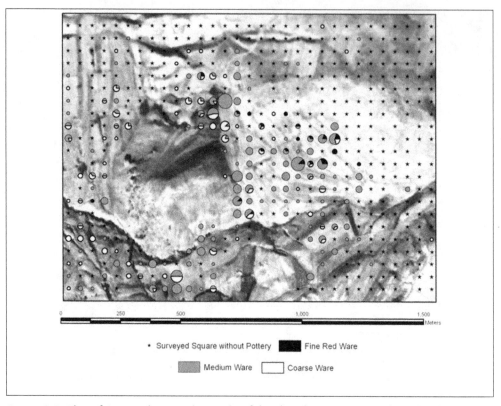

Figure 8.8. Plan of Ayanis showing the results of the shovel test survey conducted in the area around the fortress.

These data suggest the presence of both public buildings and private dwellings surrounding at least some Urartian sites. The houses seem to vary both in size and in plan, with some evidence for formal apartments, undoubtedly built by the state. None of the publications are sufficient to determine who was living in these areas and whether they were entirely foreign conscripts or included a mixture of lower-level Urartian elites. They provide no useful information on how the mixture of public and private structures was organized or on the purpose of the formal apartment-like buildings. If, as seemed likely, based on the wealth of the fortresses and their ecological contexts, these settlements were the elite enclaves we have come to expect from societies with exclusionary domination, then a more systematic exploration of an entire Urartian settlement was needed.

Ayanis

Our approach to our work in the outer town of Ayanis (see figure 8.7) was to gain as broad a picture of the settlement as possible and to use these data to sample different parts of the settlement. We began with a shovel test survey (figure 8.8), digging 40 liter holes every 50 m over an area 1.5 km by 1 km. We selected more than 25 ha of this larger area for magnetic gradiometry survey (figure 8.9). The latter was successful in indicating patterns of subsurface architecture with sufficient clarity that large, well-

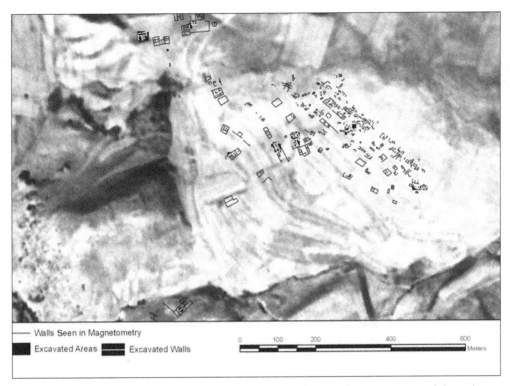

Figure 8.9. Plan of the outer town of Ayanis showing architectural traces recovered through magnetic gradiometry and excavation.

designed buildings can be distinguished from less formal architecture. Also useful is the ability of the magnetometry to identify areas with increased amounts of ash. These represent areas where trash was deposited, providing our best source of faunal and ceramic remains. Together, the magnetometry and shovel test survey suggest that the outer town of Ayanis was divided into three areas (figure 8.9): one, known locally as Pınarbaşı, located on a terraced promontory to the north of the fortress; another beside and probably continuing under the modern village to the south of the fortress (Köy); and a larger terraced hill, known as Güney Tepe, spread out to the east. The latter shows some internal differences: a number of larger structures built close to the fortress and a line of long narrow buildings a little farther up the slope. Still higher, several large squarish structures are surrounded by more scattered architectural traces. Similar traces of less well-organized structures continue high up the slope facing the fortress and follow the curve of the hill away to the south. To date, we have sampled all three areas, including multiple locations on Güney Tepe. I will discuss our results below, beginning with the architectural patterns, and then consider how these compare with both the fortress and one another in their ceramic, object, and faunal inventories. It is the overall context that will indicate how well the urban structure of Ayanis conforms to our ideas of urban patterning in societies based on exclusionary domination.

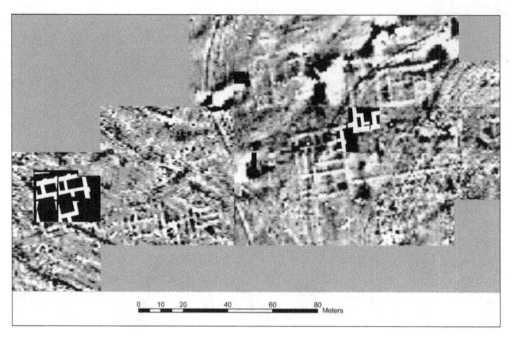

Figure 8.10. Magnetometry and excavated architecture at Pınarbaşı.

Architecture

The architecture of the fortress typically has wide, deep foundations built on bedrock that are continued above floor level with mud-brick walls (Çilingiroğlu and Salvini 2001:25-84). Of the architecture in the outer town, only that at Köy shares this feature. Elsewhere, the stone walls are narrower and continue well above floor level before being continued in mud brick—at least, we have assumed that they were using mud brick above the stone foundations. During the 2005–2007 excavations, however, we excavated one house using *muhre* rather than mud brick above the stone foundations. *Muhre* is the Turkish word used to describe a mixture of small stones and clay that was compressed within a frame. Because only the stone foundations were preserved in most of our excavation areas, we do not know how common this technique was in the outer town. It was certainly not used in the fortress. Construction styles varied within the outer town. In some cases, we found rectilinear buildings with foundations cut into the underlying bedrock, well-built walls, and exterior buttresses. We interpret these as reflecting the hand of the Urartian state architects. Elsewhere, the architecture was less formal, usually without buttresses and sometimes built over trash areas, evidence, we think, of domestic construction. Here building styles varied not only *between* buildings, but also *within* buildings in some instances. Most have features that we associate with domestic activities: rock-cut pits, troughs, bread ovens, grinding stones, and sandstone cheese-pressing stones. Identical features are found in the houses of the modern village.

We interpret Pınarbaşı and Köy as areas devoted to administrative functions of a

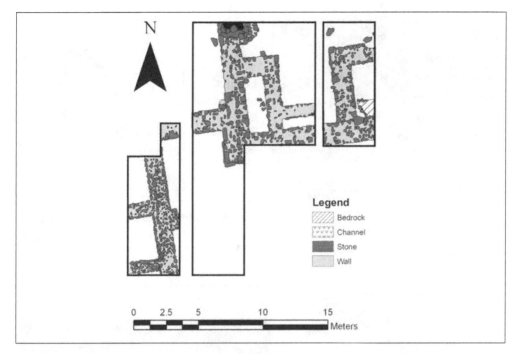

Figure 8.11. Plan of excavated areas at Pınarbaşı.

lower order than those within the walls of the fortress. The plans of five large buildings are visible in the Pınarbaşı magnetometry, three of which have been sampled through excavation (figures 8.10 and 8.11). Their architecture is very formal, and domestic features, other than fire installations, were absent. Also common at Pınarbaşı were large positive-magnetic anomalies. We have excavated two of these in Pınarbaşı and one in Güney Tepe, but these have all been empty holes. We suspect that these are sweep-out areas for smithies, but we cannot be certain.

The magnetic map of Köy (figure 8.12) shows one very large building made up of a series of rooms some 20 by 9 m in size. We have sampled only one 10-m square in this area, so our understanding is still limited. As indicated above, the architecture of this building more closely resembles that of the fortress than any other structure in the outer town, but exactly what this building was used for remains a mystery. The main floor was quite clean, with little in the way of ceramics, bones, or artifacts. Immediately above it, however, were a number of incomplete walls, two large ovens, and one room that was burned, together with the many pots within it. The whole appears to be very domestic and suggests that we are looking at a squatter occupation dating immediately after the destruction of the fortress. No comparable building has been identified within the outer towns of any other Urartian sites.

Most of our attention has been focused on Güney Tepe. Güney Tepe makes up the largest area of the outer town, and our magnetic map suggests considerable variability in architecture. It is also here that our shovel test survey suggested significant variation in ceramic distributions by elevation, with the larger concentrations of the fine

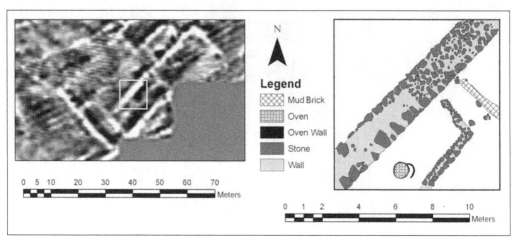

Figure 8.12. Magnetometry and plan of Köy.

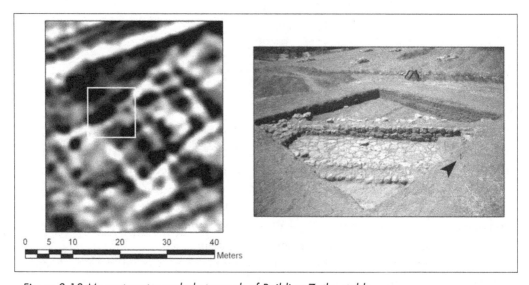

Figure 8.13 Magnetometry and photograph of Building 7, the stable.

red-polished wares usually associated with fortresses found farther up the slope. We have conducted excavations in six areas within Güney Tepe, five of them at different elevations in the main part of the settlement immediately in front of the fortress.

Close to the fortress, the magnetic map indicates the presence of a number of quite large buildings with considerable space between. We placed one 10-m square within one such building, siting our excavation so that it included both inside and outside space (figure 8.13). As at Pınarbaşı, it turned out to be a well-built structure, almost certainly the product of the Urartian state architects. The internal space was a paved stable, and trash deposits were recovered from outside the building. The discovery of the stable—and its location near the road leading up to the fortress—suggests parallels with the "Hallenbau" at Bastam (Kleiss 1988:19–28), a building that we would

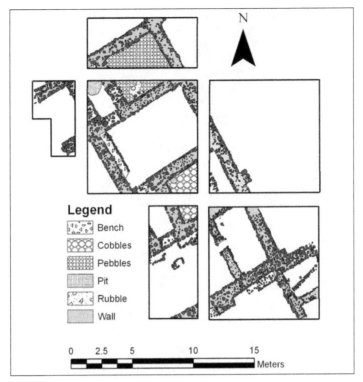

Figure 8.14. Plan of Building 6, the duplex.

interpret as the chariot house. The presence of spherolytes in the micromorphological samples, however, suggests that cattle and not horses were kept here (Wendy Matthews, personal communication, June 2004).

Farther up the slope, but still facing the fortress, is a series of terraces. The lowest is quite narrow, and the magnetometry suggests that it was occupied by a series of long, narrow buildings, one of which has been completely excavated. Like the other buildings discussed so far, it was well-built with external buttresses (figure 8.14). In plan, it may be interpreted as a duplex, made up of two units, each with a large room, a small, roughly paved room, and an ante-room. It shows evidence of later modification, using much less formal architecture, and, apart from one deep, ash-filled pit, had no domestic features. It is tempting to compare this duplex building with the apartments from Karmir Blur, although there are clear differences in both size and plan.

Within the next three terraces above the duplex, the magnetic map indicates a scattering of large, square buildings, with less clearly defined architecture between them. Farther up the slope and wrapping around the hill towards the south, we find a consistent pattern of architectural traces. We have excavated one of the square buildings, part of the more incomplete remains of the building next door, and a small section of the outer wall of the next large structure. We have also sampled one area farther up the slope and recovered two buildings in the southern part of the city, sampling a total of five houses. Although total excavation is limited to three of these structures,

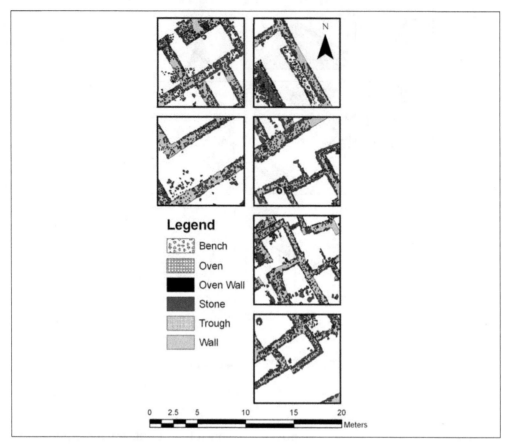

Figure 8.15. Plan of Buildings 1 (north) and 3 (south).

all exhibited evidence for the domestic features that we find in the modern village—bread ovens, grinding stones, troughs, paved stables, rock-cut pits, and so on.

There were, however, some differences in the architecture. Building 1 (figure 8.15), the only one of the square buildings that we have dug, was somewhat better built than the others, and its walls were founded on bedrock. The house next door, Building 3 (figure 8.15), had a mixture of architectural styles, all very informal, and some of its walls were built over trash deposits associated with Building 1. Building 9 (figure 8.16), situated farther up the slope facing the fortress, was founded on trash levels and evidenced multiple construction events, like Building 3. The last two houses (figure 8.17) were situated high on the far southern portion of Güney Tepe. Both were solidly built, with corner buttresses.

The outer town architecture at Ayanis can be divided first into the areas entirely devoted to public buildings (Pınarbaşı and Köy) and Güney Tepe, where architecture was more variable. The latter had public buildings (such as the stable) at the lower elevations, a well-built structure but without the usual domestic features (the duplex) on the lowest terrace, and houses with domestic features but varying in the formality of their architecture higher up the slope. Overall, the domestic structures are more sim-

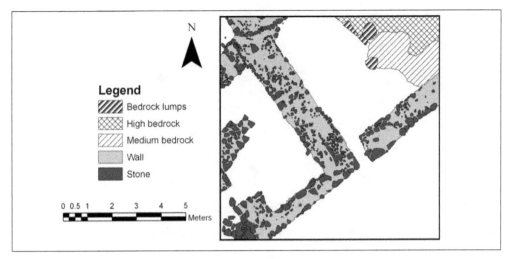

Figure 8.16. Plan of Building 9.

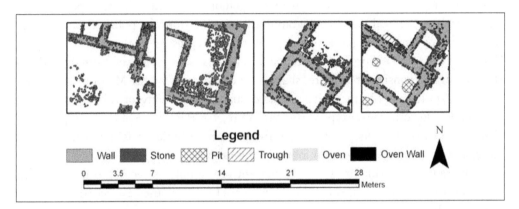

Figure 8.17. Plan of Buildings 10 and 11.

ilar than they are different. All are about the same size (approximately 200 m sq), all have evidence for domestic features, and all lack the formality of the architecture seen in the duplex and the public buildings.

Pottery

In general, pottery was relatively rare at Ayanis, and much of it is handmade. In the fortress, rooms filled with broken ceramics were found in two locations, perhaps testament to ritual disposal; otherwise, most of its pottery came in the form of complete vessels.

There are five significant Urartian wares. Petrographic analysis of the Ayanis ceramics was carried out by Melissa Moore, and neutron activation by Jeff Speakman and the Missouri reactor group (Speakman et al. 2004). Fine red-polished vessels served as the tableware within the fortress. Their consistency, as seen in the results of neutron

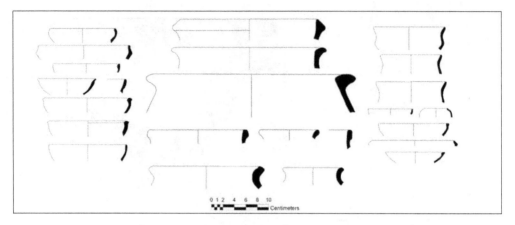

Figure 8.18. Assyrian style ceramics from Buildings 11 and 12, Ayanis.

activation and petrography, indicates that these were the product of professional potters' workshops. But in the outer town we also found examples of fine unpolished red wares that are chemically and petrographically distinct from the polished varieties but have the same shapes, suggesting that they might represent less professional copies. The other evidence for professionally made ceramics is found in the buff-slipped jars that are, again, consistent in ware, shape, and associated stamps. Medium and coarse wares are quite variable in their associated shapes, and many of these vessels were handmade. One other ware type, a fine buff ware, was found at Ayanis; both paste and shape are identical to Assyrian pottery from northern Syria. It is not made of local clays, and no examples have been found in the fortress.

Fine red wares made up nearly 20 percent of the pottery recovered from the fortress, most of which was of the red polished variety. The houses excavated in the area of Güney Tepe facing the fortress have similar percentages of fine red wares (figure 8.18), but all had much higher percentages of unpolished red wares. The pottery associated with House 1—seemingly one of the older buildings in the outer town—came closest to the pattern seen in the fortress. The two houses excavated in the southeast of Güney Tepe also have about 18 percent fine tablewares. There, however, the majority of these ceramics were not the red wares familiar to Urartu, but rather buff wares with both paste and shape similar to pottery from sites in Assyria.

Köy and Pınarbaşı are generally characterized by the small amount of fine red wares associated with these structures, with one exception. The trash area between two of the Pınarbaşı buildings had a small sample made up almost entirely of unpolished red ware. The Güney Tepe stable and duplex buildings also had quite low percentages of fine red wares.

In general, fine tablewares of various kinds were most common in the fortress and the domestic structures, whereas buff-slipped jars, which were also common in the fortress, show up in largest numbers in the structures we interpret as serving a more public function: Pınarbaşı, Köy, and the Güney Tepe stable.

Objects

The object classes of most significance for our understanding of the structure of settlement at Ayanis are those that might indicate a connection with the central government: bronze objects, and especially decorated bronze, sealed and inscribed bullae, Egyptian blue pigment, and perhaps iron implements. Objects were rare at Pınarbaşı and Köy, although two unbaked clay bullae with seal impressions were found at Pınarbaşı. These would tend to reinforce our impression that this area served an administrative function. Finds associated with the stable tend to be military in nature. These included a bronze, trilobate arrowhead, an iron arrowhead, and a bronze spearpoint—all of which are identical to examples from the fortress. These data tend to support the interpretation of this structure as associated with the Urartian military. The duplex had little in the way of objects, although a bronze fibula and an earring were found in the trash deposits outside the building. All of the more domestic-structure houses were similar in the presence of Egyptian blue pigment, pieces of bronze, and iron objects—especially thin arrowheads of the type never found on the fortress. Güney Tepe House 1, however, is the only domestic structure to have in its finds an inscribed bulla and pieces of decorated bronze, one quite elaborate.

Faunal Remains

Faunal samples were recovered from all contexts, but the sample from Köy is too small to be considered. The NISPs (numbers of identifiable specimens) from the different areas indicate that there were clear differences between the animals consumed in the fortress, Pınarbaşı, and Güney Tepe (figure 8.19). The faunal sample recovered from Köy was too small to be statistically meaningful. The faunal analysis of the Ayanis material was carried out under the supervision of Curtis Marean and Melinda Zeder. The bones from the fortress were dominated by ovi-caprids, almost all sheep, and had the only significant amount of wild species. The percentage of both cattle and goats increased somewhat in the Pınarbaşı sample and even more in the bones recovered from Güney Tepe. Dog and horse bones show up in more significant numbers in the Güney Tepe samples than in those from the fortress and Pınarbaşı, along with a few pig bones.

The differences between the faunal samples from the three areas are reinforced when we look at body part distributions. Whereas the sheep-size fauna from the fortress is dominated by the best cuts of meat, that from Pınarbaşı presents almost the opposite picture, suggesting, perhaps, that Pınarbaşı received those cuts of meat not consumed by the residents of the fortress. The sheep-size bones from Güney Tepe also show a lack of the best cuts of meat, but this is not so much the case for the cattle-size bones, suggesting that they had access to all parts of the carcass, minus perhaps some of the best cuts.

If we look at the faunal samples from different areas within Güney Tepe, these are generally quite similar, including those associated with the stable and the duplex. There are, however, two exceptions. Nearly 20 percent of the Building 3 sample is dog

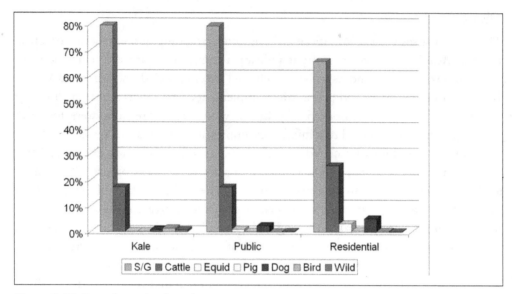

Figure 8.19. Faunal remains from Ayanis.

bones—generally, large animals with bones that have cut marks. Also unusual is the faunal collection from the houses in the southeast, where we had found the Assyrian pottery. Here the percentage of sheep to cattle is much higher than that elsewhere in Güney Tepe, similar to Pınarbaşı.

How can we evaluate these data from Ayanis? Certainly, the differences in architecture, ceramics, objects, fauna, and overall wealth indicate a great divide between the luxury associated with the fortress and the rest of the site. This difference cannot be ascribed to sampling error. Not only have we excavated a significant sample of the outer town, but also the kinds of architectural features associated with fortresses—temples, pillared halls, and large-scale storage rooms—would, had they been present in the outer town, have shown up clearly in the magnetometry. But it is not the domestic areas that yielded the most impoverished remains; this (except for architecture) is the prerogative of the public buildings of Pınarbaşı and Köy. The main residential area, Güney Tepe, also included some structures that we have interpreted as more closely associated with the fortress, such as the stable and the duplex. These, too, have fewer fine red wares, less Egyptian blue pigment, and fewer bronze and iron objects typical of the houses farther up the slope.

The houses themselves are in some ways very similar—in size; the presence of domestic features such as bread ovens, troughs, and stables; objects; fauna; and ceramics. But there are differences. The early House 1 is better built, had more red-polished ware, and was the only structure to have both writing and decorated bronze objects associated with it. The houses in the southeast replaced some of the fine red wares with pottery almost certainly imported from the Assyrian plains and had the only faunal sample from Güney Tepe dominated by sheep. The faunal sample from Building 3 had an extraordinarily high percentage of dog bones, with some evidence that they made up part of the diet. Given the temple inscription in the fortress describing the importation and settlement of people from areas around Urartu, including Mushki (where puppy burials have been found at both Gordion and Sardis) and Assyria (where sheep are the dominant meat source), it seems likely that the variation we see within the settlement may be attributable to ethnic differences playing out within a highly structured and centralized economy.

This evidence suggests that Ayanis is indeed comparable in organization to cities in other territorial states—perhaps most similar to Cuzco. The concentration of political and religious institutions in the cultural core, the significant differences in access to wealth objects exhibited, and an elite center surrounded by suburbs occupied by peoples imported to the area for their labor together form a striking parallel.

Conclusion

The two cities investigated have clear differences in plan—differences that complement the evidence derived from looking at well-documented instances of urban centers associated with exclusionary and corporate governance. These differences and their comparability with evidence for urban organization at sites such as Cuzco or the Yoruba cities suggest that the connection between polity type and urban structure posited at the outset of this chapter is quite robust. Ideally, such an investigation would encompass not just the nature of the urban centers, but also their relationship with the smaller centers and villages that made up their hinterlands, as well as the identifying features of those settlements. Few small Mesopotamian sites have been excavated, but those that have been suggest that many of the physical aspects of Mesopotamian cities were replicated within the smaller settlements (Stone 2005b:153–154). For Urartu, our information on small sites is nonexistent, and the activities of the PKK (the terrorist Kurdistan Worker's Party) in the area make survey impossible at present. Our model would predict this hinterland to have a mixture of small agricultural sites and occasional military establishments controlling the routes across this mountainous landscape, but we will need to establish whether this is, in fact, the case.

That the spatial data from the Mesopotamian city of Mashkan-shapir and the Urartian city of Ayanis show such strong correlations with those of Yorubaland and Cuzco does not mean that this pattern will fit urban centers associated with all types of states. These examples were specifically chosen for investigation because they existed within highly constraining environments. It seems likely that where those constraints are absent or, as may be the case in the later phases of the Maya, are overcome through the introduction of new technologies, sociopolitical forms may develop that will leave different imprints on the urban landscape. What this research has made clear is that the differences between these cities are substantial and can be measured along a series of axes: cities that house all elements within society or elite enclaves; institutional centers that are clustered or scattered; residential neighborhoods where rich and poor lived together or apart. These axes should make it possible to evaluate similarities and differences between the organization of cities from many times, places, and environments and associate these with variability in sociopolitical organization. After consistent associations between space and society have been developed for cities with written documents or ethnohistorical descriptions, the patterns observed should then be applicable to the centers of urban societies without decipherable written records, such as those found in Peru before the Incas and in the Indus Valley.

Acknowledgments

Our work at Mashkan-shapir was funded by grants from the National Science Foundation, the National Endowment for the Humanities, the National Geographic Society, the American Schools of Oriental Research, and private donations.

Our work at Ayanis is made possible by the generosity of the Ege University team directed by Dr. Altan Çilingiroğlu. It has been funded by the National Science Foundation, the National Geographic Society, and private donations.

nine
Royal Cities and Cult Centers, Administrative Towns, and Workmen's Settlements in Ancient Egypt

Kathryn A. Bard

In "The Urban Revolution," V. Gordon Childe (1950) included Egypt as one of the first centers of urban civilization in the Old World, along with Sumer and the Indus Valley. But the evidence of ancient Egyptian cities—and sociopolitical and economic organization there—is different from that in southern Mesopotamia and the Indus Valley. For much of the third and second millennia BC, Egypt was a large territorial state ruled by a king, who controlled an area of about 333,000 sq km, only 19,000 sq km of which were not desert (Trigger 2003:111). There were periods of strong, centralized control during the Old, Middle, and New Kingdoms, and the king exercised authority over vast resources, both material and human. Ideology justified the king's role, as did a monopoly of force. Although royal texts are frequently biased or exaggerated, there is impressive textual evidence for the high degree of bureaucratic organization of the state (especially during the Middle and New Kingdoms), which undoubtedly adds to what is known about Egyptian urbanization.

Most ancient Egyptian cities have not been well preserved, due to a number of factors—depositional, locational, and cultural. The best-preserved archaeological sites from ancient Egypt are the temples and tombs located beyond the floodplain in the very dry, low desert. Because of their relatively good preservation and monumental proportions, stone tombs and temples were also the focus of most early scholarly fieldwork in Egypt, as were well-preserved human burials and mummies. With the expansion and growth of Egypt's villages, many ancient settlements were destroyed or were covered by more recent ones. In the later nineteenth and twentieth centuries AD, with expanded cultivation, especially of cash crops such as cotton and sugar cane, and modern economic activity, such as factories and quarries, many ancient sites were destroyed. Many prehistoric and pharaonic sites within the floodplain have also been destroyed by millennia of cultivation. With meters of deposits of river alluvium (in both the valley and delta) over the millennia, a number of settlements have been covered or destroyed.

Although the poorly preserved settlement evidence may have suggested to Egyptologist John Wilson (1960:124) that ancient Egypt was a "civilization without cities," this is no longer believed to be true. More recent investigations have shown a wide range of different kinds of population centers in pharaonic Egypt, as have the settlement data recorded by earlier archaeologists working in Egypt.

With the emergence of the early state, ca. 3100–3000 BC, the crown imposed its control throughout Egypt. Town growth from the Early Dynastic period onward took place within the bureaucratic system of the state, but also through "direct government initiatives." The state sponsored the foundation of temples and associated "pious foundations" and constructed local redistributive centers, as well as "encouraging the building of walled towns" (Kemp 1977:199). The capital of the initial state was Memphis, founded in the north at the juncture between Upper and Lower Egypt. A fortified border town was established at Elephantine Island in the far south. The area of the earliest occupation at Memphis was probably near the elite tombs at North Saqqara, and in the Old Kingdom the city was located on high ground between the Nile on the east and the Bahr Libeini channel on the west (Jeffreys and Tavares 1994:159). No part of the Early Dynastic or Old Kingdom city has been found in situ (Jeffreys and Tavares 1994:159). Cemeteries have provided indirect evidence of the city's location, along with geo-archaeological investigations of changes in the course of the river and its channels by the Egypt Exploration Society's Survey of Memphis. Stones from monuments at Memphis were taken and reused in medieval Cairo, and most of what remains there now is from the New Kingdom and later (ca. 1550 BC onward). But excavations on Elephantine Island by German archaeologists have revealed an Early Dynastic fortress and somewhat later (Old Kingdom) administrative buildings, residences, and industrial areas (Kaiser et al. 1995; Seidlmayer 1996).

Ancient Egypt, the land of *Kemet*, consisted of the delta and a long narrow strip of floodplain from Cairo to Aswan at the First Cataract (figure 9.1). The written form of the word *Kmt* includes the hieroglyphic sign for the word *city* (*niwt*). Barry Kemp (2005:74–75) suggests that "the Egyptians regarded their country as fully urbanized, as if one large city." Spanning both sides of the Nile, provinces, which are often called "nomes," were established with nome centers (Butzer 1976:61–79; O'Connor 1972:684–688; Uphill 1988:14–20). The nomes functioned as "miniature states," with a principal town and surrounding field complexes, villages, estates, and households (Lehner 2000:305–306). But most people in ancient Egypt were peasant farmers who lived in rural communities and not in cities or towns, and their settlements are invisible archaeologically.

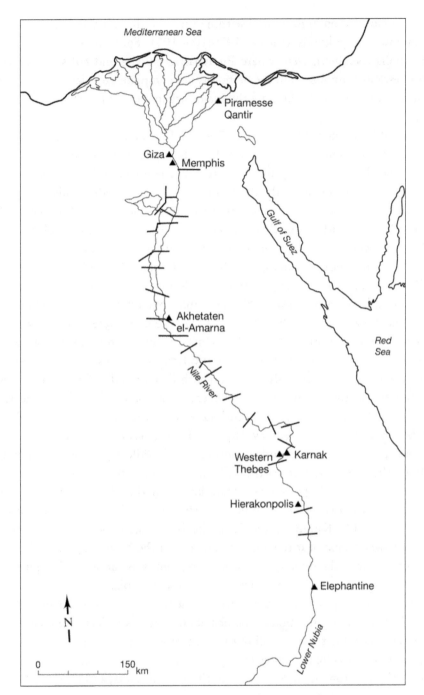

Figure 9.1. Map of ancient Egypt with nome divisions and some major towns and cities. The horizontal lines are the boundary lines between nomes (drawn by Kay Clahassey).

The Nile was the major artery of communication, which greatly facilitated control of this very large state. As a result, the settlement pattern is linear. Cities, towns, and villages were located on high ground within or next to the valley floodplain and in the delta on low sandy knolls (Bietak 1979:104–105). Some nome centers, such as Hierakonpolis (Nekhen), were where Predynastic polities and cults had arisen; the process of establishing nomes in the delta was not complete until later in the first millennium BC, when the delta became the major urban and commercial focus of Greco-Roman Egypt.

In the Old Kingdom (ca. 2686–2125 BC), "pious foundations," especially for the royal mortuary complexes, were established (Kemp 1983:85). A pious foundation included land donations set up for the perpetual maintenance by priests and personnel of a (statue) cult, of the gods, dead kings, and private individuals. Commodities and products from these estates supported the cult. From the Middle Kingdom (ca. 2055–1650 BC) onward, the settlement pattern in the Egyptian Nile Valley was dominated by a network of major towns—to exploit agricultural and human resources and to control communication along the Nile (O'Connor 1972:688). In the Middle Kingdom, the state took a more systematic role in construction of cult temples and associated buildings (Kemp 1989:157), although much more is known about temple towns in the New Kingdom (Bietak 1979:131). The main state cult center shifted to the Theban region (Temple of Amen-Ra), which became an important royal seat in the New Kingdom (ca. 1550–1069 BC). New royal cities were also founded in the New Kingdom, including the short-lived Eighteenth Dynasty city of Akhetaten (now the site of Tell el-Amarna), established by Akhenaten as his royal residence and the cult center of the god Aten, and the Nineteenth Dynasty city of Piramesse in the delta. Some of the best-preserved settlement evidence in Egypt, however, is from state-founded towns, built, in part, to house workers during Old, Middle, and New Kingdom times.

Above the First Cataract in the Nile was the land of Nubia, the major route through which exotic imported raw materials from the Horn of Africa came into Egypt—and to the east of Lower Nubia, in the Wadi Allaqi there were major gold mines. In the Middle Kingdom, the Egyptians built a series of large mud-brick forts, mainly in Lower Nubia near the Second Cataract. In the New Kingdom, after Egypt's major competitor in the region, the Kerma kingdom, was vanquished, Egyptian temple towns were established in both Upper and Lower Nubia.

Thus, different types of ancient Egyptian settlements functioned within the sociopolitical and economic organization of the pharaonic state, its beliefs, and its foreign relations. It is not possible to discuss all of these settlements in this chapter, but what both the textual and archaeological evidence suggest is a high degree of state organization and control through its towns, cities, administrative centers, cults, and forts.

Fourth Dynasty Giza: The Town of "Those Who Lived in Front of the Pyramid"

Richard Bussmann (2004) has documented seventeen different settlement sites near the Old Kingdom pyramids, including those at Giza. These sites include industrial ones, short-term settlements for workers, long-term settlements for workers and their families, priests' settlements, and pyramid towns. According to Bussmann (2004:39), although these pyramid settlements shared some of the characteristics of Egyptian towns, they differed in function.

Remains of the largest known pyramid town are now being excavated by Mark Lehner at Giza, to the southeast of the three pyramids. Lehner's excavations have revealed a complex of galleries, two towns (Eastern and Western Towns), and a royal administrative building with granaries (Lehner 2002a). Ceramics are all Fourth Dynasty (ca. 2613–2494 BC), the period during which the Giza pyramids were built, and the clay seal impressions are of Khafre and Menkaure, the kings who built the second and third Giza pyramids (Lehner 2002a:34). Missing from the excavated structures are sealings of Khufu, who built the Great Pyramid, suggesting that his pyramid town has yet to be located.

Administrators probably lived in the larger houses built in the Western Town (Lehner 2006:14). The Eastern Town, which has a fairly informal arrangement of houses with small rooms and thin mud-brick walls, may have been where craftsmen lived (Lehner 2002a:71–72, 2006:14). A large sunken courtyard in the administrative building contained the remains of circular mud-brick granaries, which probably supplied grain to the state bakeries that fed the pyramid workers (Lehner 2002a:59, 61–64).

A more formal plan is seen in the long rectangular rooms (approximately 35 m long) of the Gallery Complex, which covers 5 ha (figure 9.2). Three major east-west streets (North, Main, and South Streets) divided these structures, with an enclosure wall and gate houses controlling access to the complex (Lehner 2002a:36). The "Manor," a large house that may have been for an overseer, was located at the eastern end of Set II of the complex (Lehner 2002a:41–42, 71). Lehner (2002a:69–70, 2006:14) suggests that the galleries were barracks for a rotating labor force and could have housed 1,600–2,000 workers. One structure (Set III-4) contained sloping platforms, which may have been for sleeping, with the southern end walled off into a multi-room "house," possibly for a foreman, with a sleeping platform and a possible kitchen area (Lehner 2002a:38–41). The "Hypostyle Hall," with columns that supported a roof, may have been where food processing took place (Lehner 2002a:70–71). Some evidence in the Gallery Complex also suggests small-scale craft production, such as copper working and pigment preparation (Lehner 2002a:57, 2002b).

Excavated remains of towns associated with pious foundations have also been found at Giza. A town for Menkaure's pyramid cult was still in existence in his complex's valley temple about three centuries later (Kemp 1989:146; Reisner 1931:plate IX). Just to the north of this temple/town are the remains of an L-shape town for the personnel associated with Queen Khentkawes's mortuary cult (Hassan 1943:figure 1; Kemp 1989:144) (figure 9.3). The queen's town was 148 m long from east to west. Houses of three sizes were built: the largest were located in the southern "arm" of the plan, with medium-size houses on the west next to the queen's monument (Uphill 1988:40–42).

Thus, at Giza there is evidence of different settlements: towns for the cults of dead royalty, permanent workmen's towns, an administrative building with granaries, and

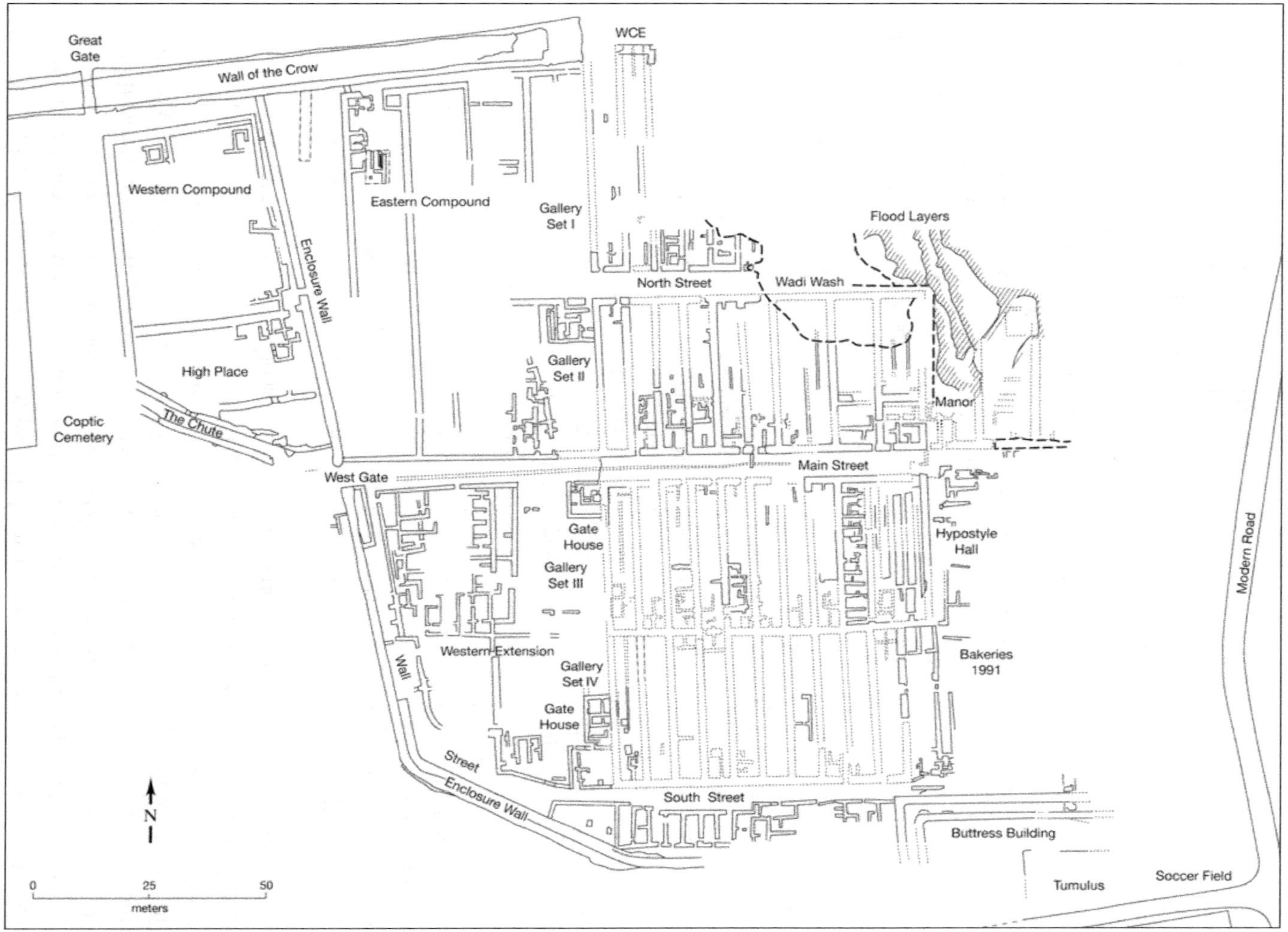

Figure 9.2. Giza: plan of the Gallery Complex in the Fourth Dynasty royal production center (redrawn from M. Lehner 2002a).

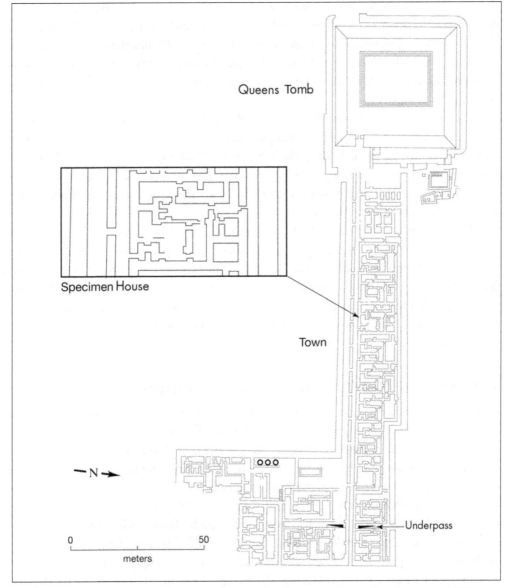

Figure 9.3. Giza: mortuary cult town of Queen Khentkawes (redrawn from B. Kemp 1989).

a possible barracks complex with associated bakeries, and some storage and craft production areas. These are specialized towns—organized for the construction of royal tombs and for the personnel of their mortuary cults. As known thus far, the Giza settlements are more a collection of special-purpose towns, some of which have highly formal plans. These towns did not grow and fuse together through time into a city. Some of the towns had a limited span of occupation (when the pyramids were being constructed), whereas the towns of the mortuary cults were to be used in perpetuity.

Missing from the Giza settlements are a royal palace and central administrative complex, a treasury, residences of the court and all other state officials, large industrial areas and workshops for specialized crafts (as found in high-status tombs), and residences of all other associated personnel and workers and their families. Presumably, these were located to the south, in and around Memphis. Within the capital, there was probably a formal palace, but the actual royal residences may have been near each king's pyramid site. There was probably also an important cult center of the god Ptah at Memphis at this time.

The most important state deity in the Old Kingdom, however, was the sun god, Ra, whose cult center was not at Memphis but across the river and farther north at Heliopolis (Quirke 2001). Most of the kings of the Fifth Dynasty (ca. 2494–2345 BC) built sun temples, in addition to their own pyramid complexes. Only two of these sun temples have been located: along the desert edge at Abu Gurob and northwest of the Memphis-Saqqara area at Abusir.

The impression one has of the Old Kingdom capital is of dispersed monuments and associated buildings farther west on the desert plateau and settlements in and to the north of Memphis. Some centralized functions probably took place at Memphis, but it was not a highly concentrated city with a large population. Although the Giza settlements do not suggest a functioning state capital, Lehner's excavations are providing a better understanding of the "Pyramid City" and how tens of thousands of workers lived and were organized for these huge state projects.

The Planned Middle Kingdom Town of Kahun

From the Middle Kingdom, there is evidence of a planned town associated with the pyramid of Senusret II (reigned ca. 1877–1870 BC) (figure 9.4). First excavated in the late 1880s by Flinders Petrie (1890, 1891), the town of Kahun was built next to the pyramid's valley temple. Priests and personnel for the king's mortuary cult lived there, and the many administrative papyri found at Kahun suggest a major administrative function of the town as well (Kemp 1989:149–151, 156–157).

Although some of the town had been destroyed by later cultivation in the floodplain, Petrie was able to make plans of more than half of its mud-brick houses, walls, and streets. The plan of the town was rectangular, 335 m long on the preserved west side and 384 m on the north (Kemp 1989:151), covering an area of 14 ha (Uphill 1988:66). Rectangular houses of different sizes were arranged in a grid along streets that ran east-west and north-south. The town was not fortified, but the rows of houses were surrounded by a thick wall, and another thick wall divided off part of the town on the west. One preserved gateway on the southwest was next to the royal mortuary temple, with another entrance on the northeast, leading to the street along which the largest houses were located. The purpose of these walls is uncertain; possibly, they controlled traffic in and out of different parts of the settlement.

Kahun was abandoned by the end of the Thirteenth Dynasty, and later occupants disturbed parts of the site, but Middle Kingdom artifacts were excavated in their original contexts in some houses. Petrie found tools used by builders (working in both mud brick and stone), carpenters, copper workers, farmers, fishermen, and weavers.

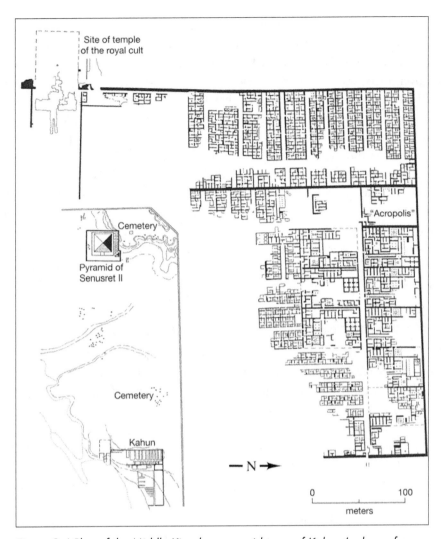

Figure 9.4 Plan of the Middle Kingdom pyramid town of Kahun (redrawn from B. Kemp 1989).

Although many materials would have been provided by the state, the agricultural tools suggest that some workers at Kahun cultivated their own food (David 1999:431).

Five large houses with many rooms, approximately 60 by 42 m in area, were located on the north side of the town. At the western end was an area that Petrie called the "Acropolis," built on a higher outcrop of rock with access via a rock-cut staircase. Three more large houses were located to the south. Kemp estimates that the granaries in the large houses could have held enough grain to support a population of 5,000 people, or 9,000 people on minimum rations (Kemp 1989:153–154). Many of the houses that Petrie excavated at Kahun (approximately 220 of them), however, were small ones arranged back to front in rows, with only four small rooms each. With up to six persons in a house, Kemp estimates that the entire community would have numbered fewer than 3,000 persons—a more likely population (Kemp 1989:155).

To the south of the Acropolis is an open space that may have been the location of the town's temple (for the cult of a god named Sepdu). Kemp suggests that this area (or the area just south of it) was where the town's administration was located. The town government was headed by a mayor, and although the vizier resided at the capital of Itj-tawy-Amenemhat ("Amenemhat [I] is the one who seizes/takes the Two Lands"), south of Memphis there was an office of the vizier at Kahun for legal business (Kemp 1989:156).

Hundreds of fragments of papyri were found at Kahun. There are lists of gangs of workmen, their dates of work and work details, and of officials and other personnel involved—including soldiers, priests, temple personnel, and scribes. Records of services rendered and payments were written on small pieces of papyrus. The so-called "census lists" (*aput*) recorded members of individual households with up to three generations and their servants, mostly females and their children (David 1986:116; Kemp 1989:157). Possibly, such lists were used by the state for purposes of taxation and conscription.

The New Kingdom Workmen's Town at Deir el-Medina

In the New Kingdom, kings were buried in hidden tombs in western Thebes, in the Valley of the Kings. A workmen's town was built nearby, at Deir el-Medina in the Theban hills. Begun in the early Eighteenth Dynasty, the village was occupied until the late New Kingdom, with the exception of the Amarna period, during Akhenaten's reign (McDowell 2001:18–23). Excavations at Deir el-Medina were conducted before the First World War by Italian and German archaeologists and subsequently by the French Archaeological Institute, Cairo (Bruyère 1924–1953; McDowell 2001:23–25).

Remains now visible at the site date to the Nineteenth Dynasty (ca. 1295–1186 BC), when the settlement was expanded (figure 9.5). With 68 houses in the final phase, the village covered approximately 0.65 ha (Uphill 1988:66). The village was walled in stone, with one entrance on the north, outside of which a few structures, possibly administrative buildings, were located. A second gate on the west side led to the main village cemetery. The long narrow houses, made of mud brick, with lower walls and foundations of stone, were laid out along a main north-south street and several east-west alleys (McDowell 2001:9–12).

There were at least twelve phases of construction at Deir el-Medina (Valbelle 1985:442). Houses varied in size from 40 to 120 sq. m and were one-story high, with a stairway to the roofed area in the back court (McDowell 2001:11–12). As households grew and/or changed in composition, houses were remodeled, but a fairly standardized house plan is seen, usually with four to six rooms aligned linearly, including an open-air back court where the cooking and food preparation were done. Lynn Meskell (2002:110–125) has suggested that there were different domains of women and men in these houses, in the first and second rooms, respectively, with the domain of female slaves or servants in the small rear rooms. In such small houses, however, it would be unlikely that any space was used exclusively for a single purpose.

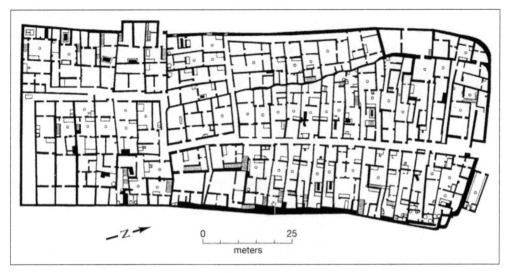

Figure 9.5. Plan of the New Kingdom workmen's town of Deir el-Medina (redrawn from McDowell 2001:xviii).

All of the villagers' basic needs, including clothing, firewood, pottery, water, and food (emmer wheat and barley, meat, fish, and vegetables), were supplied by the state. Payment was given in a monthly grain ration (McDowell 2001:5). Because the village lacked a source of water, even the villagers' laundry was state provided: laundry was picked up in the village and washed by launderers along the Nile (McDowell 2001:59). An attempt to locate well water near the village is seen in the excavation of the "Great Pit," to the east of a later (Ptolemaic) temple. The pit was excavated to approximately 50 m depth, but groundwater was never reached (McDowell 2001:16–18).

Tomb goods and many household items, especially furniture, were made by Deir el-Medina craftsmen in their spare time and obtained by villagers through barter and exchange. Goods were also obtained by reciprocal gift giving and loans—and through credit (McDowell 2001:7). Although poorly recorded, a few tools and some equipment possibly used for agriculture were found in the village, as were five granaries, which suggest that some farming was done, perhaps for profit by servants that some villagers are known to have had or by some of the villagers themselves (McDowell 1992:195, 202–206).

The Egyptian week consisted of ten days, and men who worked in the royal tomb spent eight of those days camping in huts along a ridge closer to the Valley of the Kings (McDowell 2001:7, 17). Much is known about the operations of the workmen's village from texts, including official documents on papyri, and from thousands of ostraca (Černý 2001; McDowell 2001:25–27). Appointed by the vizier, the Scribe of the Tomb issued rations to the workmen and kept daily attendance records (McDowell 2001:5–6, 219–220). Workmen's tools and materials were supplied by the state, and there is even a record of copper chisels being turned in to be reforged and resharpened (McDowell 2001:209–210, 231).

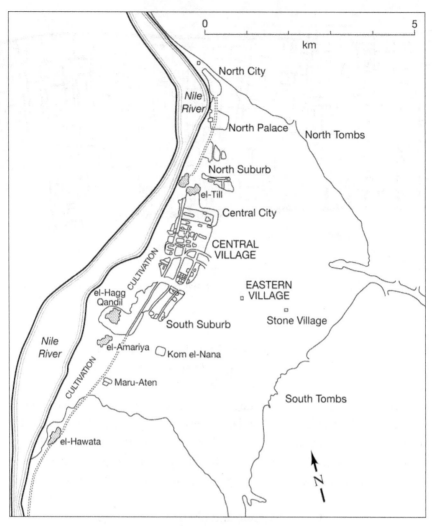

Figure 9.6. Plan of Akhenaten's royal city (Akhetaten) at Tell el-Amarna.

Toward the end of the New Kingdom, the outlying community of Deir el-Medina was no longer safe because of marauding desert peoples, and many of the villagers were relocated to Medinet Habu, the huge, walled mortuary-temple built in western Thebes for Rameses III (reigned ca. 1184–1153 BC). No more than 22 m wide, a village for temple priests, personnel, and officials was already in existence there, sandwiched in between the outer mud-brick walls of the enclosure and the north and south walls of the temple (Uphill 1988:43–46).

Akhenaten's Royal City at Tell el-Amarna

On the east bank in Middle Egypt, Akhetaten (the "Horizon of Aten") was the royal city of the heretical king Akhenaten (reigned ca. 1352–1336 BC) and the cult center of the god Aten (figure 9.6). Flinders Petrie conducted the first extensive excava-

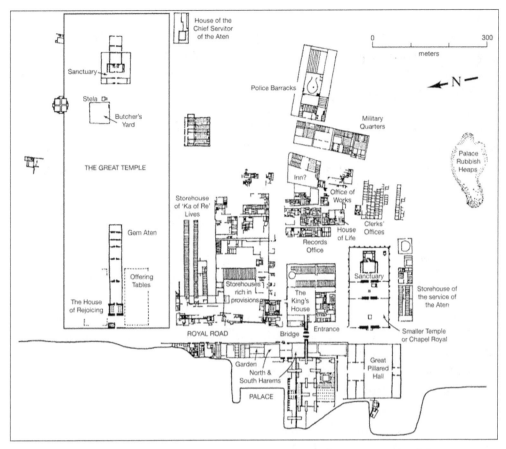

Figure 9.7. Plan of the central city at Tell el-Amarna (redrawn from J. D. S. Pendlebury 1951).

tions there in the 1890s, and after the First World War the site was excavated by the British Egypt Exploration Society, with ongoing excavations since 1977 directed by Barry Kemp.

The site has been fairly well preserved, in part because it is not near major population centers. Large parts of the city were also built in the low desert and were thus protected from disturbance by later cultivation. The city was occupied for only about eleven years and was abandoned by the court early in Tutankhamen's reign. Some occupation continued there in the Ninteenth Dynasty, when the stone temples were dismantled and statues smashed, but mud-brick buildings were simply left to decay.

The city of Akhetaten had no surrounding wall, but boundary stelae on both sides of the Nile define an area of approximately 16 by 13 km for the city limits (Kemp 1989:269). The city covered an area of approximately 440 ha, which does not include unexcavated areas (Uphill 1988:60). With population estimates of 20,000–30,000, but also 50,000 (Kemp 1989:269), the city was organized with a center planned on a grid, with administrative buildings and residences of different sizes extending southward to the River Temple (figure 9.7). To the north were the North City, North Suburb (with

298 houses), and two palaces. To the east was a walled workmen's village, and the mainly unfinished rock-cut tombs for high officials were in northern and southern groups in the eastern cliffs. The Royal Tomb was located up a central wadi in the eastern cliffs, near the mouth of which was a "stone village" where tomb workmen stayed.

The central city contained the Great Aten Temple, enclosed by a wall approximately 730 by 229 m (Kemp 1989:281). To the south of the Great Temple were associated structures, including more than 100 baking rooms nearby that are mounds with tens of thousands of sherds of bread molds (Kemp 1989:289). These were the bakeries that provided temple offerings, which were later redistributed to temple personnel and workers. There was also a small private palace (the "King's House"), which, according to Kemp (1989: 288–289), was associated with the largest granaries at Akhetaten (approximately 2,000 sq. m)—suggesting royal (and not temple) control of basic staples.

To the east of a small temple ("House of Aten") were administrative buildings, including the so-called Records Office, where the Amarna Letters were found. Farther east were quarters for the military police (which may have contained barracks like those that Lehner has excavated at Giza) and stables.

To the west of the Royal Road, which was spanned by a triple-arched bridge, was the Great Palace and an enormous royal hall with 510 mud-brick columns in 30 rows. Although much of the Great Palace has been destroyed by later cultivation, it may originally have been much larger, extending down to the river.

Houses were located in the North Suburb and to the south of the central city in the "Main City," which, according to Kemp (1989:294), consisted of "a series of joined villages." Although there was a hierarchy of house sizes, which suggests hierarchies of sociopolitical status at Akhetaten, there were no exclusive neighborhoods reserved just for high-status families. Large houses were next to small ones, and "rich and poor lived side by side" (Kemp 1989:294). One of the largest private houses at Akhetaten, which had 30 rooms—some only a few square meters in area—belonged to the vizier Nakht. But even the residence of one of the highest government officials was significantly smaller than any of the palaces of the royal family.

Houses were walled compounds made of mud brick. Larger houses probably had upper stories (Spence 2004:134). Kemp has described the basic elements of an Amarna house compound, which included circular grain silos in a court, but some houses also had larger vaulted rooms for grain storage (Kemp 1989:296–298). That grain was stored in private houses indicates some economic independence from the crown, which did not provide sustenance for all the inhabitants at Akhetaten, and probably private landholdings of such individuals.

In one area of the Main City, several sculptors' workshops were found, consisting of courtyards and small huts built against the walls (Kemp 1989:306, 308). The famous head of Nefertiti and other royal sculptures/models were left in the house of the sculptor Thutmose when the city was abandoned. Also in this area was a rectangular enclosure with four furnaces: one for firing pottery, another for ceramic or faience/pigment production, and the other two for glass making (Nicholson 2000:201). But these

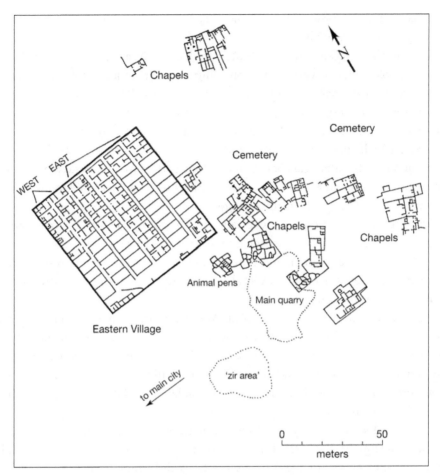

Figure 9.8. Plan of the Eastern (workmen's) Village at Tell el-Amarna (redrawn from I. Shaw 1995).

crafts were produced in the mainly residential Main City, in small-scale workshops next to houses. Some private houses were also where small-scale production facilities were located, including weaving and potting (Kemp 1989:309).

The eastern workmen's village—for tomb workers—was organized more rigidly along five north-south streets, with about 70 small houses, including one for an overseer (figure 9.8). Arranged in six blocks, the houses consisted of a hall or court, a living room, and two small rear rooms and a back staircase to the roof. A number of activities took place on the ground floor, such as weaving and food processing, and upper stories were probably added by the workmen to provide for family accommodation (Kemp 1987:25–26, 29; Spence 2004:139, 151). Unlike the city of Akhetaten, the village was surrounded by a thin wall. Water was brought from wells in the Main City to an area about 60 m south of the village (Kemp 1987:22, 24), and the state must also have provided the workers with grain, tools, and basic materials. A village pig industry, which included pig pens and areas for butchering and packing the salted meat in jars, probably provided supplementary income through the sale of meat to the Main City (Kemp 1989:256).

The new city of Akhetaten was built very hastily, in a region without the traditions of age-old cults or earlier cult buildings, which under normal circumstances would have been dismantled and remodeled or rebuilt. The art and architecture at Akhetaten are also very different, focusing on the cult of an obscure sun god with open-air temples and on an "extreme manifestation of the cult of the ruler" (Kemp 1989:285), which ignored the cults (and economic support) of other deities. Thus, Akhetaten represents a radical change in theology and its monumental manifestations, with major political and economic transformations in the society—demonstrating the role of royal agency in such culture change.

Akhetaten was not a typical Egyptian city, but Kemp (1989:317) maintains that "no royal city ever could be"—especially with the "separation" of the king and royal family in their palaces, ceremonial centers, and cults, which were always walled off from their settlements. Akhetaten was also a very atypical city in that it was occupied for only about eleven years.

Some aspects of city organization at Akhetaten are seen in earlier settlements, especially the planned community to house tomb workmen. The central city has a basic planned grid of temples and palaces aligned along processional routes—so important for royal display and something we would expect for such formal state architecture. But residential parts of the city display a less formal arrangement of rectangular house compounds.

In a general sense, the royal and temple architecture at Akhetaten reflect the role of the king in Egyptian society. But Akhenaten did not build a mortuary temple for his funerary cult closer (or next) to his tomb, as did kings from the Old Kingdom onward. Possibly, he intended his cult to be practiced within the city of the living. This was a radical change in the royal mortuary cult, which is also reflected in the private tombs at Akhetaten. Missing in these tombs are the traditional offering scenes and scenes of the tomb owner, his offices, and his estates. These are replaced by scenes of the living king and his family, his courtiers and soldiers—in the palace, temple, and along processional routes. Mortuary beliefs, the belief in a good burial, were very deeply rooted in Egypt—and were beliefs that affected all strata of the society. By ignoring these beliefs and focusing on the cult of the king and Aten, Akhenaten was surely courting rebellion against his new religion—which might be a major reason that it did not survive his death.

Although it reflects a major ideological aberration, Akhetaten may provide a general model of an ancient Egyptian royal city/capital. It had a highly formal plan in the central city, with a large palace (and other royal buildings), large cult temple, associated bakeries, and nearby administrative buildings and police barracks. Individual residences of the city were more dispersed outside the central district and were often associated with small-scale craft production, from pottery to the works of royal sculptors. Outside the city (to the east) were the elite and royal tombs, with a workmen's village (and camp) located between the city and tombs.

Conclusions

Ancient Egypt during the Old, Middle, and New Kingdoms was a large territorial state ruled by a king with great powers, through a highly organized bureaucracy. The bureaucracy functioned within the organization of urban centers, with capitals and royal seats, cult and nome centers, towns of workmen for state projects and royal mortuary cults, forts, and later towns/cult centers in Nubia. The capital city was where a number of specialized functions took place, but there were also special-purpose towns, ranging from nome centers to the towns of mortuary cults. Cereal cultivation within the floodplain ecology of the Nile provided not only basic subsistence for the Egyptians, but also a very large surplus that supported this state—and was extracted through the state's centers and temples, located throughout the country.

The urban organization in ancient Egypt was not centered on one huge city (as at Teotihuacan) but rather consisted of a network of cities and towns along a linear artery, the Nile. Although a number of towns had walls, they were not densely populated, walled communities with a thinly populated hinterland (as at Early Dynastic Uruk), because the Egyptian state controlled the internal order of the country. Nor were there separate communities of private or foreign merchants (as at Teotihuacan or the Old Assyrian trading colony at Kaneš/Kültepe), because the state controlled large-scale foreign trade and extraction of raw materials outside Egypt, which mainly went into the production of royal, elite, and cult goods.

Unlike the Early Dynastic cities in southern Mesopotamia, where the urban architecture was dominated by huge, walled-temple complexes built on high platforms, contemporaneous monuments in Egypt were the royal pyramids built on the solid bedrock of the low desert—to the west of areas of habitation. The institution of kingship in ancient Egypt was much stronger than that in Mesopotamian cultures, as reflected in Egyptian royal mortuary monuments, which symbolized Egyptian beliefs about the afterlife and the king's position in this. When royal tombs were hidden in the New Kingdom, the kings built large mortuary temples, where their cults were serviced by communities of priests and personnel. But these temples were also connected by ritual to the huge temple of Amen-Ra on the east bank of the Nile at Karnak. The Temple of Karnak became the main state center in Upper Egypt, with vast land holdings, and the state offices there controlled major functions in the south.

Because of factors of preservation, we have much less archaeological evidence for cities in Egypt during the third millennium BC than for those in southern Mesopotamia, which limits our understanding of early Egyptian urbanism. But even though there are no huge archives of texts, such as for the Ur III state, Egyptian bureaucratic texts (mainly from the second millennium BC) are helpful in filling in some of the gaps of information.

Although little remains of the architecture in major New Kingdom cities, such as Memphis and Piramesse, there is a wealth of textual evidence from this period. We know that the king was quite mobile, performing ceremonies in different centers and staying at different royal residences. Texts suggest that at Karnak there was a main governmental palace near the temple, which was the focus for royal ceremonies and state bureaucracy (at least, in the Eighteenth Dynasty; O'Connor 1995:279, 281). As at Akhetaten, there would have been large palaces at the royal capitals, although for the most part these have not been well preserved.

The king's officials and courtiers had estates in the provinces from which they extracted income, and cult temples owned land throughout the country. The Nile facilitated such economic exchange and control over a very large territory, and although there were desert tracks to mines and quarries, a road system was not necessary (as for the Inka state).

For communication and large-scale movement of goods and materials, the Egyptian state needed to control the importation of timbers for large ships, that is, cedar from Lebanon and northwest Syria, such as we found in December 2004 in a man-made cave at Wadi Gawasis on the Red Sea. Although Wadi Gawasis was a harbor, the evidence there of a temporary camp for seafaring expeditions to Punt in the southern Red Sea region is unlike the ancient Levantine port cities. Basic resources (especially food and freshwater) were scarce along the Red Sea coast, and food and materials were difficult to carry there through the desert wadis, especially when the expeditions were also carrying disassembled ships. The establishment of permanent settlements—ports and forts—on the Red Sea would require the logistical capabilities of the Romans, which were even more impressive than those of the pharaonic state, operating within a much larger trade network, from the Mediterranean to southern India.

Early civilizations had cities, and cities functioned within the sociopolitical organization, economic networks—and belief systems—of early civilizations. Thus, there were functional differences among early cities that also reflect location, extraction, and means of control of resources, both human and material.

ten
Indus Urbanism
New Perspectives on Its Origin and Character

Jonathan Mark Kenoyer

During the past two decades, a variety of archaeological research projects focused on the Indus civilization have made it possible to refine earlier models regarding the origin and character of this distinctive urban society. Excavations at the major city of Harappa have revealed a long developmental sequence from its origins to its eventual decline and subsequent transformation. Recent excavations at the large urban centers of Dholavira and Rakhigarhi, along with reexamination of the largest city of Mohenjo-daro, have shown that the development of urbanism was not uniform throughout the greater Indus region (Kenoyer 1998). Detailed studies within each city have revealed many shared characteristics, as well as some unique features, relating to the dynamic process of city growth and decline. In addition to the excavations of larger urban centers, regional surveys and extensive excavations at smaller settlements have provided a new perspective on the nature of interaction between large and small urban centers and even rural settlements.

The increase in radiocarbon dates from well-documented contexts in stratigraphic excavations has helped to refine the chronology of settlements in both core and rural areas (Meadow and Kenoyer 2005; Possehl 2002a, 2002b). On the basis of a more refined chronology and comparisons of the material culture, it appears that some rural settlements may have been directly linked to the major cities and others may have had relatively little direct contact during some time periods (Meadow and Kenoyer 2005). Such patterns can be interpreted as reflecting fluctuations in economic and political networks or alliances, providing an indication of economic and political organization. This dynamic quality is revealed only when sites of different sizes are excavated and when the regional chronology is sufficiently fine-grained.

The most significant advances in our understanding of the Indus civilization as a whole and the Indus cities in particular have been through the scientific study of subsistence, craft production, trade, and city planning. At sites such as Harappa, changes in these important components of urban centers can be traced over two millennia, from approximately 3900 to 1700 BC (Kenoyer 2003). The growth of cities such as Harappa appears to be directly linked to increase in regional and long-distance trade. The use of multiple sources for similar raw materials suggests that competition between merchants or local elites, as well as the heterogeneity of urban populations, may have stimulated more extensive trade networks, exploration for new resource areas, and possibly the colonization of distant regions. The importance of trade for the accumulation of wealth and power by a relatively small number of elites is further supported by the relatively restricted use of inscribed seals and tablets for economic and ideological purposes.

Although recent excavations have not revealed any bilingual texts to aid in deciphering the enigmatic Indus script, they have produced a larger sample of inscribed objects. These new inscriptions come from many types of sites and contexts, and it is now possible to define numerous distinct contextual uses of writing, as well as regional variations and changes in the nature of the writing system over time (Meadow and Kenoyer 2007). Writing in the Indus cities is clearly associated with both economic administration and ideology, which, in turn, appear to be linked to political organization. Although the names of ruling elites and lineages cannot be identified, the use of writing appears to be limited to the merchants and elite segments of the population. Ongoing studies of inscribed objects such as seals and tablets include the reanalysis of the signs and sign sequences chronologically and contextually.

Through a more comprehensive understanding of the nature of Indus urbanism, many earlier models for its decline have been replaced by models of transformation (Jarrige 1997; Kenoyer 2005; Mughal 1990a; Possehl 1997). Although some settlements were rapidly abandoned, many of the major cities continued to be inhabited for hundreds of years after the height of Indus urbanism. At Harappa, for example, there is evidence for continuity in settlement layout and internal spatial organization, regional and long-distance trade networks, and significant advances in technology (Kenoyer 2005). Even though there is continuity in some aspects of the city, during the final stage there are major changes in ideology, the Indus script disappears, and key indicators of merchants and elites, such as seals and standardized weights, also disappear. As with the origins of these cities, their decline and transformation are quite varied across the vast expanse of the greater Indus region.

Indus Tradition and Chronology

The Indus Tradition refers to the total phenomenon of human adaptations that resulted in the integration of diverse communities throughout the greater Indus

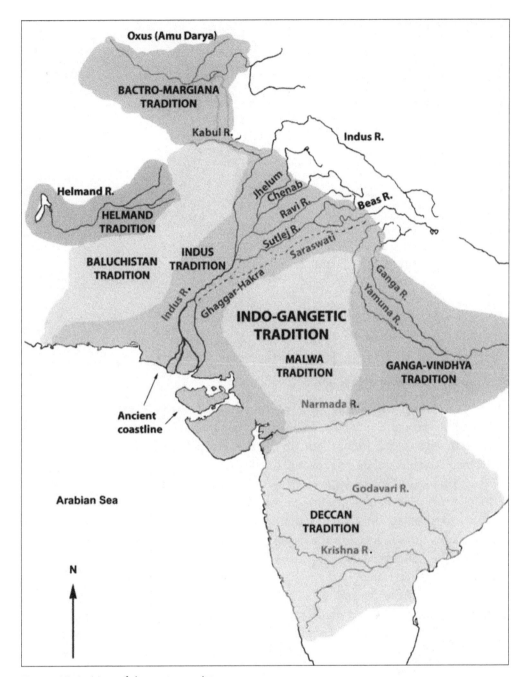

Figure 10.1. Map of the major traditions.

Valley and adjacent regions (figure 10.1). This tradition has also been called the Indus Valley Tradition (Kenoyer 1991a; Shaffer 1992) and Indus-Saraswati civilization (Gupta 1999; Lal 1997). The Indus Tradition has been divided into five eras and numerous phases that allow archaeologists to organize and compare materials from different periods and regions (table 10.1).

Table 10.1. Indus Tradition

Foraging Era	10,000–2000 BC	–
Mesolithic and Microlithic		
Early Food Producing Era	7000–5500 BC	–
Mehrgarh Phase		
Regionalization Era	5500–2600 BC	–
Early Harappan Phases		
Ravi, Hakra, Sheri Khan Tarakai,		
Balakot, Amri, Kot Diji, Sothi		
Integration Era		
Harappan Phase	2600–1900 BC	–
Harappa site, Period 3A	2600–2450 BC	–
Harappa site, Period 3B	2450–2200 BC	–
Harappa site, Period 3C	2200–1900 BC	–
Localization Era		
Late Harappan Phases	1900–1300 BC	
Punjab, Jhukar, Rangpur		

Geography and Climate

Most cities of the greater Indus Valley were established along two major river systems: the Indus River and the Saraswati-Ghaggar-Hakra-Nara River, which flowed along the eastern edges of the Indus plain. To the east and west, the alluvial plains are bordered by mountains and deserts that are filled with valuable mineral resources and seasonal grazing areas. Several large cities were located on islands in the Rann of Kutch and along major rivers in Saurashtra or mainland Gujarat. Smaller towns and villages were scattered along the coast, as well as along the major trade routes leading to resource areas surrounding the alluvial plain (figure 10.2)

The Indus Valley and adjacent regions are dominated by two major weather systems. The winter cyclonic system of the western highlands results in snowfall in Baluchistan and rainfall in parts of the Indus Valley. The summer monsoon brings moisture to the high mountains in the north and to the northern Indus plain. Scanty rainfall from both systems occurs in the southern Indus region and the deserts of Rajasthan. The climatic diversity resulting from these two weather systems is beneficial to the rise of large urban centers, and one system may provide water if the other fails.

Recent models of global climate indicate that, from around 18000 to 9000 BP (ca. 16000–7000 BC), southern Asia would have been cooler and drier than today, with a weak summer monsoon. From around 9000 to 7000 BP (ca. 7000–5000 BC), there appear to have been a stronger summer monsoon, warmer summers, and cooler winters. Although these models work at the macro level, they cannot be confirmed through detailed analysis of specific sites or regions. Generally speaking, there is no evidence for major changes in climate or rainfall since 9000 BP (ca. 7000 BC).

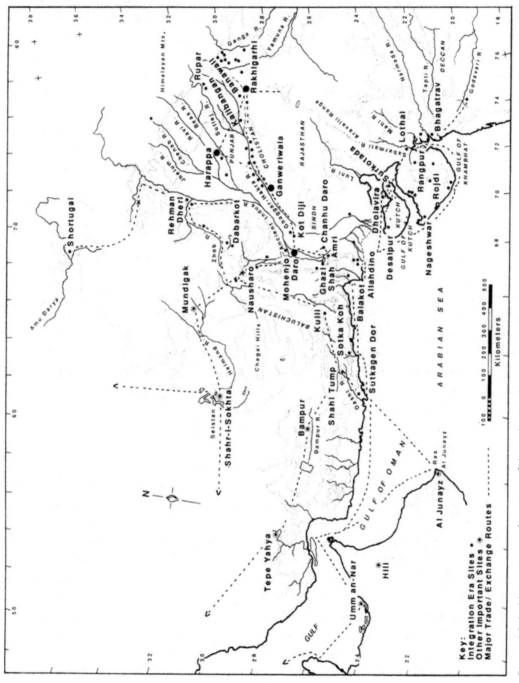

Figure 10.2. Major sites and regions of the Indus Tradition.

Origins of Indus Urbanism

The origin of Indus urbanism can be studied from either a general perspective of the Indus civilization as a whole or by looking at a few major urban centers. During the excavations of Harappa (Mackay 1938; Vats 1940) and Mohenjo-daro (Marshall 1931) in the 1920s–1930s, scholars had three different explanations for the origins of these cities and the urban civilization they represented. Some argued that they were the result of outside western influence (Wheeler 1968 [1953]); others claimed that they were the result of indigenous processes (Marshall 1931); and still others suggested that they emerged through a combination of internal and external factors (Allchin and Allchin 1982; Piggott 1952; Wheeler 1968 [1953]). All of these suggestions were based on indirect evidence because the earliest levels of these cities had never been excavated; in the case of Mohenjo-daro, it was because of a high water table, and at Harappa, because of a sampling problem. The interpretations for the origin of Indus cities therefore were based primarily on general comparisons between the fully urban phase of occupation with smaller regional settlements in the highlands to the west and excavations in Mesopotamia and Iran.

Not until the discovery and excavation of Mehrgarh from 1974 to 1986 (Jarrige 1991; Jarrige and Meadow 1980) were the foundations for the Indus civilization clearly established within the confines of the greater Indus Valley region. Subsequently, the reanalysis of the site of Kot Diji, Sindh, by Mohammad Rafique Mughal (1970) proposed that the emergence of the Harappan culture could be attributed to local cultural development rather than outside influence (see figure 10.2). Some scholars still suggest that the impetus for urbanism was the result of developments in Mesopotamia (Ratnagar 1991, 2001), but these suggestions cannot withstand rigorous critique (Lamberg-Karlovsky 2001) and cannot be supported by recent data.

Today most scholars support a model of indigenous development for Indus urbanism (Jarrige and Meadow 1980; Kenoyer 1998; Mughal 1991; Possehl 1990), but there is still no consensus regarding the role and contribution of different regions to the larger whole. In order to investigate the origins of individual urban settlements and their regional contributions to Indus urbanism, long-term excavations were begun at the site of Harappa in 1986 (Dales 1989) and continued through 2001 (Meadow and Kenoyer 2005; Meadow et al. 2001b). The results of these excavations can be compared with earlier excavations at the site of Mohenjo-daro, as well as more recent but not fully published excavations at the major urban centers of Dholavira and Rakhigarhi. These four settlements are the largest known urban centers of the Indus civilization, and each center dominated a part of the alluvial plain, or a coastal trade route, as in the case of Dholavira (see figure 10.2). In earlier publications, the site of Ganweriwala was included as a fifth major urban center (Kenoyer 1991a, 1998). After visiting the site in 2001 and examining the pottery and exposed stratigraphy, I do not believe that it should be ranked at the same scale as these other large cities until excavations have been undertaken. Many other smaller urban centers have been identified, but most have not been excavated. The site of Harappa has the most complete and

Table 10.2. Harappa Chronology

Early Food-Producing Era	
No traces of occupation	
Regionalization Era	
Ravi aspect of the Hakra Phase, Periods 1A–B	3900–2800 BC
Kot Diji Phase, Period 2	2800–2600 BC
Integration Era	
Harappan Phase	2600–1900 BC
Harappa Phase A, Period 3A	2600–2450 BC
Harappa Phase B, Period 3B	2450–2200 BC
Harappa Phase C, Period 3C	2200–1900 BC
Localization Era	
Harappa/Late Harappa Transitional Period 4	1900–1800 BC (?)
Late Harappa Phase, Period 5	1800 (?)–1300 BC

well-documented stratigraphic sequence, and it is presented first, followed by general summaries of the other major sites (table 10.2).

Harappa: Early Settlement

Harappa is situated on a low Pleistocene terrace between two major tributaries of the Indus River, the Ravi and ancient Beas (now the Sutlej) rivers. The ruins of ancient Harappa consist of three large, walled sectors and several smaller suburbs that cover approximately 150 ha (figure 10.3). One-third of the ancient site is occupied by the modern city of Harappa, and parts of the site may have been washed away by the Ravi River. Recent discoveries in a suburb of modern Harappa to the north of the old bed of the Ravi River suggest that there may be an extension of the ancient settlement in this area as well.

Excavations at Harappa have revealed a full sequence of occupations, beginning with an early village phase and continuing through the full urban phase. The Ravi phase village (Period 1, 3900–2800 BC) (Kenoyer and Meadow 2000) was probably divided into two parts, with one part along the northern edge of what is now Mound AB and the other at the northwest corner of Mound E; the two areas may have been separated by a low-lying area. The division of the settlement into adjacent but separate habitation areas is a pattern that continues in the subsequent proto-urban Kot Diji phase. The earliest architectural structures appear to have been huts oriented north-south and east-west and made of wooden posts, with walls of plastered reeds. Some mud-brick fragments from what may be a kiln have been found, but no mud-brick architecture has been found to date.

The earliest ceramic vessels at Harappa (Period 1A) are entirely handmade, with a range of decoration from plain to polychrome. Plain cooking pots have a coarse appliqué on the exterior made from clay and calcium carbonate nodules to avoid thermal stress. The Ravi phase pottery is quite distinct from pottery found at sites to the

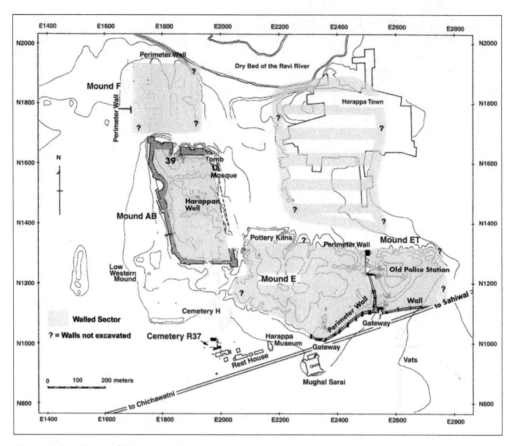

Figure 10.3. Map of Harappa.

southwest, such as Mehrgarh, but it has some similarities to pottery found at sites in the Suleiman range to the west and many more similarities to pottery in the Ghaggar-Hakra river valley region to the east (Mughal 1980, 1990b). This suggests that the overall ceramic tradition of the central and eastern alluvial plains evolved parallel to that of the southwestern plain and highlands. Towards the end of the Ravi phase (Period 1B), the potter's wheel began to be used, resulting in new and diverse vessel forms and rim shapes. Some of these forms became the basis for the pottery of the subsequent Kot Diji phase.

The use of pre-firing "potter's marks" and post-firing "graffiti" on pottery also indicates that concepts of graphic expression using abstract symbols were emerging. Many of the marks and signs consisted of a single character or symbol, but one example has three linked trident or plant shapes (figure 10.4a). Many marks and signs used during the Ravi phase continued to be employed through the Kot Diji phase and on into the Harappa phase, when some of them can be identified as elements of the Indus writing system (Meadow and Kenoyer 2007).

During the Ravi phase, there is evidence for local craft production in close proximity to domestic structures. A wide variety of craft production indicators and workshop areas have been found, including evidence for shell working, soft and hard stone-bead making, bone working, textile production (spindle whorls), and pottery making (Kenoyer and Miller 2007). Except for clay and bone, all other materials were brought to the site from distant resource areas. Marine shell came from the coast some 860 km to the south; lapis lazuli came from 800 km to the north in Afghanistan. Recent sourcing studies by Randall Law have traced gray cherts to the Suleiman Range, more than 300 km to the northwest (Law and Baqri 2003), and grinding stones to the Kirana hills (100 km to the north) and to the Suleiman Range to the west (Law 2005). The sources of many other materials, such as steatite, carnelian, and amazonite, are still being studied, but current evidence indicates that the people living at the site were connected to all major regions that became integrated into the later Indus urban phenomenon.

Other sites dating to this period have been found to the north and south of Harappa. The site of Jalilpur, some 75 km to the southwest of Harappa, has evidence for a Hakra/Ravi phase occupation in the earliest levels. During the subsequent phase, the site developed into a relatively large Kot Dijian settlement (13 ha). In the course of surface surveys by the Pakistan Department of Archaeology (A. Dogar, personal communication, 2001; Mughal et al. 1996), two Ravi phase settlements, Rajanpura and Hissoka, were located approximately 110 km northeast of Harappa on the opposite bank of the Ravi River.

On the basis of these initial surveys, Harappa appears to have been a central place in trade networks along the Ravi drainage. Although other sites were abandoned at the end of the Ravi phase or later Kot Diji phase, Harappa continued to grow in size and importance. Additional excavations will be needed at Harappa and other regional sites to understand the economic and political factors that made it possible for Harappa to become a regional urban center during the subsequent Kot Diji (Early Harappan) phase (Period 2, 2800–2600 BC).

Harappa: Incipient Urbanism

Early Harappan, or the Kot Dijian period, was first defined by Mughal (1970), who proposed on the basis of both artifact analysis and settlement pattern studies that this phase represented the initial urbanism in the greater Indus Valley (Mughal 1990b). This interpretation has been confirmed through excavations at Harappa (Meadow and Kenoyer 1997, 2001) and the discovery of numerous smaller, Kot Diji phase settlements in the Punjab and in the hinterland around Harappa (Dar 1983; Meadow et al. 1999; Mughal 1997; Mughal et al. 1996; Schuldenrein et al. 2004). It is now clear that initial urban development in the Indus region began between approximately 2800 and 2600 BC during the Early Harappan–Kot Diji phase (Harappa Period 2). The settlement data are still being analyzed, but they fit the general pattern described by Mughal, in which each major region sees the emergence of a three- or four-tiered settlement hierarchy of site sizes (Mughal 1990b, 1992a). The overall scale of the urban networks is smaller than that characteristic of the Harappa phase, but as noted below, many of the diagnostic features of Harappan society begin to appear during this phase.

The total area of the Early Harappan–Kot Diji phase settlement at Harappa is more than 25 ha and covers most of Mound AB, Mound E, and parts of Mound ET. Early city planning is reflected in the layout of north-south and east-west streets and houses and in the use of mud bricks of two sizes with 1:2:4 ratios to build houses, massive mud-brick platforms, and perimeter walls (Kenoyer 1993, 1995). The presence of wide streets running into the core areas of the city reveals the importance of vehicular traffic in these early urban centers.

The original Ravi phase division into two settlements was maintained (mounds AB and E), but during the Kot Diji phase these settlements appear to have been delimited by massive mud-brick perimeter walls. There is no evidence for conflict between the two settlements, so the walls may have been used for economic control and to reinforce political power or to protect both settlements from outsiders (Kenoyer 1991b). During this period, Harappa emerged as a major regional center, integrating its hinterland and obtaining materials from distant resource areas (Kenoyer 1997a).

During the Early Harappan–Kot Diji phase, an expansion of trade networks that were initiated during the Ravi phase brought not only new varieties of raw materials to the site, but also various qualities of similar materials used for the manufacture of utilitarian and elite objects. In addition to access to new sources of raw materials, this period sees the development of more efficient forms of transportation for heavy commodities by wheeled carts (Kenoyer 2004) and possibly by boat. The use of similar raw materials from different resource areas, such as gray-black chert from Baluchistan and tan chert from Sindh, indicates a competitive expansion of trade networks and the increasing importance of exotic items.

The production of glazed, steatite beads and seals, as well as faience ornaments, indicates an increase in technological complexity and new types of finished objects. Precious metals such as copper and gold were also employed for both utilitarian and decorative purposes. Many additional styles of bangles, beads, and pottery and other utilitarian objects reveal the need for increased variety for a more diverse urban population (Kenoyer 2000).

Wheel-made pottery became relatively common during this period and was probably made in large pottery kilns similar to those found at the site of Lal Shah near Nausharo, Baluchistan (Pracchia 1985). Smaller kilns were used for the production of figurines and bangles. Red-slip and black-painted designs replaced polychrome decorations of the Ravi phase. The motifs include horizontal bands, new styles of geometric and floral motifs, and the more traditional pipal leaf, fish scale, and intersecting motifs, which had their origins in the Ravi phase. Careful stratigraphic documentation of pottery forms and painted motifs has shown the development of the distinctive Kot Dijian–style pottery from earlier Ravi pottery and a gradual transformation into what is commonly referred to as Harappa phase pottery. When combined with the evidence of other artifact types, such as terracotta cakes, bangles, figurines, and even architecture, it is possible to confirm that the Harappan culture emerged from the earlier Kot Diji culture and that it was not introduced to this area from outside regions.

One of the most important developments documented at Harappa is the emergence

Figure 10.4. Early Indus script.

of the Early Indus script, incised on pottery and seals (figure 10.4). Although many Early Harappan–Kot Dijian sites have evidence for graffiti on pottery, the lack of proper documentation had led earlier scholars to dismiss these objects as irrelevant for the development of the Indus writing system (Parpola 1986). The discoveries at Harappa and similar evidence from Mehrgarh and Nausharo (Quivron 1997), Rehmandheri (Durrani et al. 1995), Kalibangan (Lal 1975), and possibly Dholavira suggest that regional styles of writing were developing at many sites throughout the Indus region.

Other indicators of control at Harappa are seen in the use of a cubical limestone weight that conforms to the later Harappan weight category, a clay sealing made by a square seal with Early Indus script, and an unfinished square steatite seal carved with an elephant motif (Kenoyer 2003; Meadow et al. 2001a). The emergence of writing, seals, and standardized weights implies the development of more complex social, economic, and political organizations that would have required these sophisticated tools, as well as techniques of communication and administration. During the late Kot Dijian phase, sites such as Harappa were probably organized as complex chiefdoms or early states.

The current evidence from Harappa and other Early Harappan sites suggests that the use of writing, stamp seals, and standardized weights developed over a period of 200 years prior to the Harappan phase, with the beginnings of writing possibly extending even earlier to the Ravi phase. Earlier models for abrupt change (Possehl 1990, 2002c) leading to the emergence of Indus cities and the Harappan phase are not supported by these new data.

Harappa: Urban Expansion

During the Harappa phase, which lasted around 700 years, the city grew to cover 150 ha and was made up of three large mounds and associated suburbs. At Harappa, three subphases can be defined on the basis of major rebuilding phases of the city walls and site expansion, changing artifact and pottery styles, and changes in styles of seals. Fired brick was used to construct multistory houses that were laid out along north-south and east-west streets. Houses were equipped with bathing areas, latrines, and sewage drains that were linked to larger drains, which eventually emptied wastewater outside the city walls. Massive mud-brick walls enclosed each of the mounds, with access limited to narrow gates that were wide enough only for a single oxcart to enter or leave. Major streets were more than 8 m wide, and some had central dividers, possibly to regulate two-way traffic of oxcarts. Major streets for cart traffic traversed the city, with wide streets present both interior and exterior of the city walls. This feature appears to be distinctive of Indus cities; it has not been documented in early urban centers of Mesopotamia or Egypt.

The city had links to smaller settlements in the surrounding hinterland, as well as to distant urban centers such as Mohenjo-daro. Raw materials from distant resource areas were brought to the city workshops to be transformed into valuable local commodities for everyday use and as wealth indicators for the urban elites. Special-ized crafts, such as stone bead making, steatite and faience ornament production, copper working, and pottery manufacture, and a variety of other crafts were carried out in workshops throughout each of the walled sectors of the city (Kenoyer 1997b; Miller 1999). All crafts practiced inside the city walls were indirectly controlled, but some crafts, such as weight manufacture and seal and tablet manufacture, appear to have been more directly regulated, because of their importance for merchants and the ruling elite.

The city was supported by a complex subsistence base that included wheat and barley agriculture (Weber 2003; Weber and Belcher 2003), cattle and water buffalo husbandry supplemented by sheep and goat herding (Meadow 1991; Miller 2003, 2004), and a well-organized fishing industry (Belcher 1998). The hunting of wild animals also contributed to the support of the urban populations, for food and for skins, ivory, and other animal products.

There is no evidence for warfare or a centralized ruling elite. Each of the walled areas may have been maintained by competing elites, merchants, landowners, or religious leaders. This type of decentralized, corporate rule has been documented during the later Early Historic period in northern South Asia (Kenoyer 1997a). No royal cemetery has been discovered, and only one relatively small cemetery of the Harappan period has been excavated; it is to the south of Mound AB and west of Mound E (Dales and Kenoyer 1991). Analysis of the burials and burial goods suggests that the individuals in this cemetery were members of one of the elite communities of the city but clearly do not represent the only elite community (Kenoyer 1998, 2000). Although the diversity of the urban population cannot be studied from the cemetery, comprehensive analysis of Harappan ornaments (Kenoyer 1992) and terracotta human figurines (Clark 2003) indicates the presence of many communities, who distinguished themselves by styles of ornaments, hairdos, and clothing. Harappa was clearly a meeting place for many different classes and ethnic communities.

At the beginning of the Harappa phase (Period 3A, 2600–2450 BC), the earlier division of the settlement into two walled sectors was maintained. A third habitation area, currently buried beneath Harappa town, may have been established at this time (see figure 10.3). In some sectors of ancient Harappa, such as Mound AB and the western edge of Mound E, the transition from the Kot Dijian to the Harappan phase appears as a gradual transformation of pottery and artifact forms, along with strong continuities in settlement planning. The Harappan city walls were constructed directly above or slightly offset from the Early Harappan walls. Houses and streets were constructed along the same general plans, with north-south and east-west orientation. The absolute sizes of bricks and the 1:2:4 ratios of the bricks remained the same in all parts of the site. In other areas of the site, there are distinct and relatively abrupt stratigraphic indicators of change, as well as architectural changes. On the eastern edge of Mound E, domestic structures were replaced by Harappan streets, and the Harappan city wall was constructed along a different plan. The city walls continued to be constructed of mud brick, but the architecture of the Harappan period is primarily made of fired brick with some wooden components. Fired brick has been reported from some Early Harappan sites, such as Kalibangan, where it was used in drains, but the widespread use of fired brick for architecture at Harappa does not begin until around 2600–2500 BC.

During Period 3B, from 2450 to 2200 BC, the city began to grow dramatically, with major walled suburbs constructed to the north and south of Mound AB and to the east of Mound E. Parts of the settlement currently buried under modern Harappa date to this same time period. The population increase was probably the result of an agglomeration of merchant and craft communities (Kenoyer 1989), some migration to the city from the surrounding countryside, and normal population growth. This process of urban growth appears to have been going on at all of the large urban centers in the greater Indus Valley.

The largest architectural feature of Harappa, commonly referred to as the "granary," was constructed at this time in one of the new walled suburbs called Mound F.

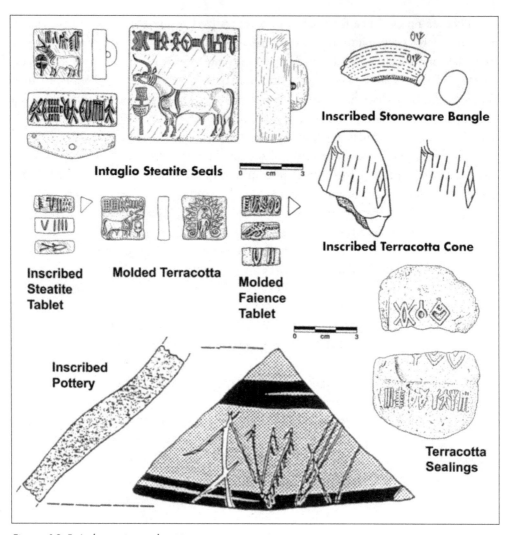

Figure 10.5. Indus script and writing.

Renewed excavations have shown three major building episodes for this structure and no evidence for its use as a "granary." Furthermore, this building, or "Great Hall," was built 200 years before the construction of circular brick platforms located to the south. These circular platforms were originally thought to have been used to process grain, but new excavations do not support this interpretation. The circular platforms were originally enclosed within small rooms and may have been used for some industrial purpose, possibly the production of indigo dye. They were constructed during the subsequent Period 3C, which dates from around 2200–1900 BC and represents the largest urban expansion of the city.

During Period 3C, Harappa appears to have been directly linked to surrounding rural settlements and to distant urban centers and resource areas. Impressed pointed-base goblets made at Harappa have been found at a small site called Lal Shah, located a day's walk (16 km) to the northeast (Wright et al. 1999). Analysis of stoneware bangles made at both Harappa and Mohenjo-daro shows that these distinctive ornaments were worn by elites who traveled between the two sites (Blackman and Vidale 1992). In addition to lapis lazuli and other minerals, the discovery of a pressure-flaked arrow point fragment and carved steatite figurine wig at Harappa provides evidence for close links to Central Asia (Meadow 2002). The trade in raw materials such as shell (Kenoyer 1983), carnelian, copper ingots, lead ore (Law and Burton 2006a), and carved limestone (Law and Burton 2006b) confirms that Harappa had trade items that provide evidence for contact with Gujarat, the Makran coast, Baluchistan, the foothills of the Himalayas, and possibly Rajasthan. The expanded trade contacts during this time may have been stimulated by intense competition for access to resources, the high demand of urban and regional consumers, and international trade. It is during this time period that the Indus script is executed on a wide variety of materials and in a broad range of public and private contexts.

Indus Script

Although the Indus script has not yet been deciphered, a brief discussion of its origin and character is necessary to demonstrate the complex bureaucratic, economic, and ideological role of writing in Indus cities. The Indus script did not appear abruptly but evolved from the Early Indus script over a period of 200 years. During the Harappa phase (2600–1900 BC), the Indus script became more standardized and widespread in all of the major urban centers of the Indus Valley (figure 10.5). The contexts in which script was used allow archaeologists to reconstruct the function of writing in the economy, politics, and ideology of the Indus cities. Discoveries of unfinished seals and an inscribed-tablet workshop at Harappa, combined with numerous finds from stratified contexts, have provided a new chronology for the writing and have helped scholars understand the wide range of contexts in which literate elites (traders, land owners, ritual specialists) used writing. Square seals with animal motifs and bold script across the top were used to seal goods for trade. Literate elites used writing on large jars filled with trade goods. They inscribed their names on small pieces of gold jewelry and developed a complex system of inscribed tokens for keeping accounts and maintaining trade contacts throughout the Indus Valley. Writing was also used in combination with narrative depictions of myths and religious ceremonies, possibly identifying the main characters, deities, or the name of the ritual. The production of distinctive copper tablets with script and animal motifs is possibly the earliest evidence for city coinage at the ancient cities of Harappa and Mohenjo-daro.

Square steatite seals with animal motifs and short inscriptions become more common in Period 3A and continue through Period 3C, but the carving style for both the animal motifs and the inscriptions shows stylistic changes. The greatest variation and widespread use of such seals appear to be during Period 3B. Small, rectangular, inscribed tablets made from steatite appear at the beginning of Period 3B, and by the end of 3B there is a wide variety of tiny tablets in many shapes and materials. They were made of fired steatite, molded terracotta, or glazed faience. These various forms of inscribed tablets continue into Period 3C, when we also find evidence for copper tablets, all bearing the same raised inscription. In contrast, copper tablets at Mohenjo-daro are incised and have several variations in terms of animal motifs on one side and inscriptions on the opposite side. Rectangular steatite seals with inscription only, glazed faience geometric seals, and stamped pottery (exclusively pointed-base or Indus goblets) appear to have been used only in Period 3C. During Period 3C, writing is found on steatite seals and various types of tokens or tablets, gold ornaments, bangles, bone and ivory objects, bronze tools, trade vessels, and storage containers. It was incised in the negative for making positive impressions and incised in the positive, molded and scratched into wet or fired clay, stamped, and painted. The nature of the writing in the different contexts suggests that the script was quite versatile and could be used to encode a range of messages.

At Harappa, the use of inscribed Indus seals disappears at the end of Period 3C, though there may have been some use of graffiti on pottery during the Late Harappan period.

Harappa: Urban Transformation

During the Late Harappa phase (1900–1300 BC), most of the walled mounds were fully inhabited. The encroachment of houses and workshops onto the streets suggest that the city was overcrowded, possibly as a result of refugees from regions to the east, where the Saraswati-Ghaggar-Hakra River was beginning to dry up. Although most of the Late Harappan occupation levels were destroyed by brick robbing, a few remaining areas and a large cemetery (Cemetery H) show a gradual transition from the Harappa to the Late Harappa phase (Kenoyer 2005). Continuities in some technologies and art styles and changes in other aspects of technology indicate that the transition was neither abrupt nor the result of replacement by new people.

This brief and selective treatment of Harappa is intended to provide a general comparative background for the evidence from the other excavated urban centers presented below. Although Harappa provides a relatively complete sequence, it was only one of several major urban centers of the larger Indus tradition.

Mohenjo-daro

The site of Mohenjo-daro is the largest and best-preserved urban center; this ancient city dominated the major trade routes and agricultural products of the southern Indus plain (figure 10.6, table 10.3). The ruins extend over 250 ha and are currently situated to the west of the Indus River in Sindh, Pakistan. Numerous mounds rise up above the plain. Others are partly buried by the silts of the encroaching Indus River. The earliest levels of the site currently lie buried below the water table, but small-scale excavations at the northwest corner of the western "citadel" mound by Wheeler (Alcock 1986) resulted in the recovery of pottery from these waterlogged levels. Many of the sherds from these early levels are similar to pottery found at the early levels of the nearby sites

Table 10.3. Mohenjo-daro Chronology

Regionalization Era	3500–2600 BC
Lowest levels of the site	
Integration Era	2600–1900 BC
Most of the occupation levels of the site	
Localization Era	1900–1700 BC
Mixed uppermost levels of the site	
Kushana Occupation	
(Indo-Gangetic Tradition—Localization Era)	AD 1–300

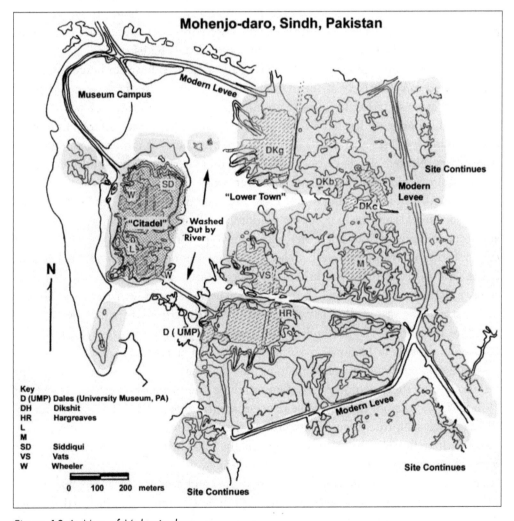

Figure 10.6. Map of Mohenjo-daro.

of Jhukar (Mughal 1992b) and Kot Diji (Mughal 1970), as well as the site of Amri (Casal 1964). On the basis of comparative analysis of this early pottery (Chaolong

1990), the origins of Mohenjo-daro may date to around 3500 BC, during the Kot Diji phase of the Regionalization era.

Most of the excavations carried out by Marshall and Mackay focused on the uppermost levels of the city, which correspond to the final occupation of the Integration era–Harappa phase and the Localization era–Late Harappan. Two radiocarbon dates from the mixed later levels place the final occupation between 2200 and 1900 BC (Dales 1973); the Late Harappan may continue much longer, to 1700 or even 1300 BC, based on dates from other regions.

The citadel mound on the west is the highest sector of the city and contains the famous "Great Bath" and so-called "granary," as well as numerous other large buildings and impressive streets with covered drains. One portion of the citadel mound has not been excavated because it is covered by a Buddhist stupa dating to the Kushana period, approximately second century AD. A massive mud-brick wall that had a large brick gateway in the southeast originally surrounded the citadel mound.

The other mounds of the city on the east are somewhat lower in height and have been referred to collectively as the "Lower Town," but they comprise several distinct habitation areas set apart by massive mud-brick walls, platforms, and wide streets. Additional suburbs are located farther to the east and south. Each sector has numerous large brick houses that could have been the mansions of powerful merchants or landowners. No temples have been identified, though there is one building with a double staircase that may have had a ritual function.

As noted for Harappa, important crafts were produced in different sectors of all the major mounds and include copper working, shell and ivory carving, and lapidary and stone tool production. There were also many types of furnaces for the manufacture of terracotta pottery, stoneware bangles, glazed faience ornaments, and fired steatite beads. Seal-manufacturing workshops have been discovered in very restricted locations, indicating strong control of production. The variety of raw materials at the site demonstrates the vast trading networks that linked the city to distant resource areas.

Rare discoveries of gold and silver ornaments provide evidence for a class of wealthy merchants or landowners similar to that seen at Harappa. At Mohenjo-daro, there are stone carvings of seated male figures that may represent some of the ancestral leaders of these communities. One of these fragmentary figures is called the "Priest-King," though there is no evidence that either priests or kings ruled the city. This bearded sculpture wears a fillet around the head, an armband, and a cloak decorated with trefoil patterns that were originally filled with red pigment. Male and female human figurines, as well as animal figurines, were made of terracotta, bronze, faience, or even shell. Different styles of ornaments and headdresses on the human figurines suggest that many classes and diverse ethnic communities inhabited the city. The painted pottery of Mohenjo-daro is very similar to that at Harappa, but there is some regional variation.

Towards the end of the Harappa phase, people using a slightly different type of pottery and new styles of geometric seals that did not have writing lived together with the latest Harappa-phase communities at Mohenjo-daro. The transition to the Late Harappan phase was gradual, as is the case at Harappa, and there is no evidence for a violent transition or an Indo-Aryan invasion. There appears to be a long hiatus after the Late Harappan, with the next major occupation of the site and the construction of a Buddhist stupa in the first and second centuries AD, during the Kushana period. The region around Mohenjo-daro continued to be inhabited throughout the Early Historic period, and a modern village is located near the mound today.

Dholavira

Dholavira (Kotada) is located on the Kadir Island just north of the large island of Kutch, Gujarat, India (Bisht 1989, 2000) (figure 10.7). The site, which extends over 100 ha, is situated on the slope of a low hill with two seasonal rivers flowing on the north and south of the walled settlement. The excavator has divided the occupation into seven stages (Bisht 1998–1999), beginning in the Regionalization era–Kot Diji phase and continuing through to the Localization era–Late Harappan phase, after which the site appears to have been largely abandoned.

The earliest settlement, Stage I, was located beneath the citadel and reveals the construction of a massive perimeter wall of mud brick and domestic architecture using both mud brick and dressed and undressed local stone (table 10.4). The perimeter wall was repaired and enlarged on the inner face during Stage II, and residential areas expanded to the north of the citadel. In the following Stage III, the wall was enlarged again, and the basic outline of the citadel was created. A smaller, walled area, called the bailey, was added to the west of the citadel. The residential areas adjacent to and north of the citadel were removed, and a large rectangular ceremonial ground or plaza was created. Stone-lined reservoirs excavated into the natural bedrock were added to the expanding settlement in the north, south, and west. Earthquake damage in Stage III resulted in major repairs of the city walls, and the walled settlement was expanded to the east. By the end of Stage III, the overall settlement plan had become established, with a series of three nested-rectangular city walls, the highest area being located in the south. This pattern suggests a different socioeconomic and political organization from that seen at the other large urban centers. The nested walls may reflect a hierarchy of internal settlement, a higher degree of control of access between different sectors of the settlement, and a need for defense against attack.

The outer wall enclosed an area approximately 771 m by 616.8 m (47 ha) (Bisht 1994) and was constructed entirely of mud brick. Large square bastions and two major gateways were located at the center of the northern and southern walls. Inside the outer wall is a fortified middle town (360 m by 250 m) with four gateways and an associated ceremonial ground with two gateways. The acropolis (300 m by 300 m) that rises approximately 13 m above the lower town has five gateways, and the small bailey on the west has two gates. A large, rectangular, open area—or plaza—and an entrance ramp are situated directly below the major north gateway of the acropolis,

Table 10.4. Dholavira Chronology

Regionalization Era	3500–2600 BC
Stages I–III	
Integration Era	2600–1900 BC
Stage IV–V	
Localization Era	
Stage VI	1900–1700 BC
Stage VII	>1700 BC

Figure 10.7. Map of Dholavira.

and numerous large open spaces are found within the different walled areas. Some of these open spaces appear to have functioned as reservoirs that would have been filled with seasonal rainwater. The sixteen or more reservoirs account for approximately 10 ha (10 percent) of the walled areas (Bisht 1998–1999). To the west, outside the walled city, are additional areas of habitation and a cemetery area, which bring the total area of the site to approximately 100 ha (Bisht 1989).

Large buildings in the acropolis area may represent administrative or ritual structures, and some of the open areas in the city could have functioned as markets or public gathering places. As in most sites in Kutch and Gujarat, the houses were made with sandstone blocks (dressed and undressed) combined with some mud-brick superstructures. Habitation and craft activity areas in the lower sectors of the city are organized in well-planned architectural blocks divided by north-south and east-west streets (Bisht 1998–1999). Small sewage drains made with stone were used to carry dirty water away from latrines and bathing areas to large sump pots placed on the streets. Various types of craft activity areas for agate bead making, shell working, and ceramic production have been located within the acropolis and in the lower town.

Rakhigarhi

Rakhigarhi is located along the south bank of the Chautang River (ancient Drishadvati or Saraswati River) in Haryana, India (Nath 1998, 2001) (figure 10.8). The overall site topography consists of a large east-west mound on the south (designated RG-4 and RG-5) that is currently occupied by two modern villages, Rakhishahpur and Rakhikhas. The current height of this mound is approximately 17 m. To the northwest are two smaller mounds separated by a north-south street. On the west is RG-2, which is called the "citadel mound" and stands around 14 m high. On the east is RG-3, approximately 12 m high and slightly smaller in area. Mud-brick perimeter walls have been noted around mounds RG-2, 3, and 4. These mounds appear to form the core of the urban center. The overall layout of the settlement, with multiple walled mounds, is generally comparable to that of Mohenjo-daro and Harappa, but the relationships between the mounds is unique.

Two additional mounds have been located to the north (RG-1) and northwest (RG-6) of the main settlement. Both of these mounds and the northern part of Mound RG-2 have Early Harappan occupation levels. Some 200 m to the north of RG-1 is another low mound, called RG-7, which appears to be a Harappan cemetery but also has some habitation deposits.

Limited excavations have been carried out at the site, and preliminary reports provide our only information on its nature. The earliest occupation recorded can be associated with the Regionalization era–Kot Diji phase, but so far no radiocarbon dates have been reported (table 10.5). The earliest architecture in Period 1A includes rectangular mud-brick structures and circular structures (1.9 m to 2 m in diameter) with doorways. The circular structures were made with mud brick, combined with postholes. A fired-brick paving has been reported for one circular structure, and another was made from wedge-shape mud bricks. During the subsequent Period 1B, more typical rectangular structures, with bricks made according to the 1:2:3 ratio, were constructed along a street that runs east-west. The pottery from this period is generally

Table 10.5. Rakhigarhi Chronology

Regionalization Era	3000–2600 BC
Early Harappan–Preformative, Period 1A	
Early Harappan–Formative, Period 1B	
Integration Era	2600–1900 BC
Harappa Phase, Period II	

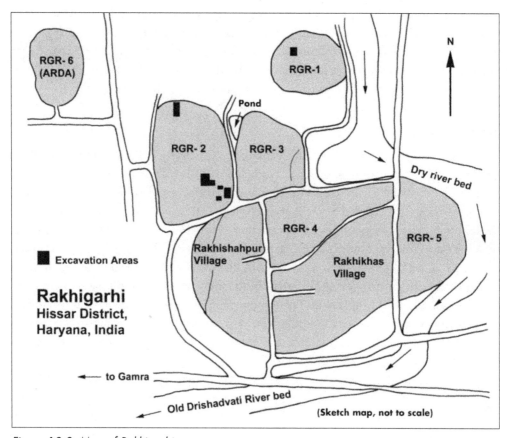

Figure 10.8. Map of Rakhigarhi.

similar to that found at the extensively excavated but much smaller site of Kalibangan and can be correlated to the local pottery traditions of the Indo-Gangetic divide (Sothi-Siswal Ware), as well as the Kot Dijian and Hakra pottery traditions. Around thirteen radiocarbon dates are attributed to the Period I Early Harappan occupation at Kalibangan, but they range from 5566 BC to 70 AD (calibrated), with a majority of the dates in the 3000–2600 BC range, which corresponds with the dates from Harappa and other Early Harappan sites.

Geometric seals—without script—were used, along with cubical stone weights, both of which are important indicators of the emergence of elites and centralized control. Some pottery with graffiti has been reported. Other artifacts include stone beads, terracotta bull figurines, toy carts and cartwheels, segmented bangles, and pottery discs. Detailed studies of these artifacts and the pottery are needed to determine whether they represent a distinctive regional style similar to Kalibangan or to the other larger urban centers of Harappa and Mohenjo-daro to the south.

The subsequent Period 2 occupation at Rakhigarhi represents the Integration era–Harappa phase, which is generally dated between 2600 and 1900 BC. The citadel mound (RG-2) has a massive perimeter wall along the western edge that is 12 m wide, with a preserved height of around 1.5 m to 2 m (15 to 18 courses), and can be traced for around 25 m. The wall is battered on the exterior, and the interior face is plastered. A large brick gateway is located in the north, and another one on the southwest with steps leading up to it from the exterior. The pathway leading to the southwestern gate is 1.1 m wide. The interior part of this mound has a large mud-brick platform and a brick-lined well. In the southwestern portion, excavations in 1997–1998 revealed a pillared corridor, with flanking rooms. Nearby was a craft-working area with shell-working debris from the manufacture of shell bangles (*Turbinella pyrum*). There is also evidence for steatite bead making, as well as agate or carnelian bead making. A circular potter's kiln may have been used to produce goblets, dishes, and terracotta bangles. A structure with small cell-like rooms with traces of barley has been identified as a granary. In front of the small rooms was a corridor with a bench, which has been called a "guard cell."

The drainage system included brick-lined public drains in the middle of the street, with terracotta pipes leading from the side streets. In domestic structures, smaller brick drains have been found associated with bathing platforms.

Various types of hearths have been identified, and one unique hearth with curved arms on either side has been identified as a fire altar. A rectangular mud-brick-lined pit, similar to sump pits at Mohenjo-daro, was found filled with debris and some animal bones. This pit has been designated a pit for animal sacrifice. An oval hearth with an upright mud brick in the center, identical to hearths and small kilns found at Harappa and Mohenjo-daro, has been called a fire altar. It is associated with a large storage jar. Such storage jars are commonly set into the ground near cooking areas for storage of goods, water, or garbage.

The largest mound (designated RG-4 and RG-5) is currently occupied by two villages, Rakhishahpur and Rakhikhas. Limited excavations on RG-4 revealed north-south streets and mud-brick platforms. A modern north-south road that may run along an ancient street separates RG-5 on the east. Small excavations on RG-5 have turned up evidence for the manufacture of bone, antler, and ivory artifacts, such as bone points, ivory combs, and needles.

All the typical Harappan styles of pottery and painted designs have been found, but a careful analysis of the pottery has not been undertaken yet. Terracotta cart fragments and wheels have been recovered. One wheel has an exterior surface with radiating ridges (resulting from the hand modeling) that appear to represent spokes of a wheel. The subsistence evidence includes wheat and barley, as well as cattle, water buffalo, fish, and a relatively low percentage of wild animal bones.

According to the published reports, inscribed seals and tablets have been found only in the excavations of the citadel mound (RG-2). Square steatite seals have the typical unicorn motif and Indus script on the front and a perforated boss on the back. A molded cylindrical faience tablet was discovered with a gharial (narrow-snout crocodile) and Indus script. Two circular terracotta sealings with plano-convex cross-sections had the impression of an elephant seal with Indus script. These molded terracotta tablets are similar to the ones found at Harappa and Mohenjo-daro.

Some 200 m to the north of mounds RG-1, 2, and 3 is a small mound (RG-7) that appears to be a Harappan cemetery. The location of the cemetery to the north of the site is unusual; most Indus cemeteries are located to the south or west of the settlement. Eleven extended burials were found in oblong pits, with the head to the north. Three phases of burial were indicated because some burials intruded into and disturbed other burials. Burial goods included pottery, and three female skeletons had shell bangles on their left wrists. One miniature gold amulet was found near the elbow of a female, and some of the burials had steatite beads around the skull, possibly the remains of a headdress or necklace.

Conclusion

This chapter provides new evidence for city origins by looking at the major Indus urban centers. At a very general level, Indus cities are similar to other early urban centers in terms of the concentration of a diverse and hierarchically organized population. Another similarity is that most cities have a long pre-urban settlement history. Each of the largest Indus cities appears to have had an Early Harappan component indicating that these cities were pristine urban settlements; they evolved over hundreds of years, through the internal competition of resident elites and the external influences of the rural hinterland and distant trading partners. In contrast to other urban cultures, the layout of Indus cities is quite unique. Each city had a distinct pattern of multiple-walled sectors that would have provided protection from small-scale raiding, but none of the large urban centers reveal destruction levels from warfare. The walls appear to have functioned primarily as a mechanism to control access into the city—possibly to tax goods coming into and out of the walled areas.

Although elites may have benefited at the expense of other lower-level communities, all people living in the city or its hinterland would have had increased opportunities for creating new economic and social networks. This phenomenon has been widely studied in the field of urban sociology and anthropology, and the concept of "small-world" networks that has been applied to Early Historic cities (M. L. Smith 2003b) could easily fit with the earlier Indus cities. Unfortunately, without the aid of literary texts, the nature of these small-world networks can be defined only on the basis of material culture and spatial organization.

Based on the distribution of distinctive artifacts and the layout of the cities, we can suggest that Mohenjo-daro, Harappa, and Rakhigarhi may have been ruled by competing elites, with fluctuating centers of power located in different walled sectors. The site of Dholavira is the only settlement that may have been administered by a small ruling class living in a central citadel area. The lack of conspicuous temples or administrative buildings is also a unique feature of the Indus cities and indicates the lack of a highly centralized political and religious structure. Although the cities did not have a single, central-administrative sector, each city as a whole can be seen as a central place for regional administration. Each city was linked to a network of smaller urban and rural settlements in the surrounding hinterland. All of these settlements were loosely integrated by a shared ideology and material culture, the use of a common writing system, and the use of a standardized system of weights, possibly for taxation. The relative uniformity of the material culture does not reflect an authoritarian society but can be explained through a variety of mechanisms, including a common belief system and conservative ideology that used material symbols to reinforce social hierarchy, as well as kin-based craft traditions that spread to all of the cities.

Many of the major features of the Indus cities are no longer a mystery, but there are still many areas that need further research. More information from smaller settlements in the hinterlands around the major cities and in distant resource areas is needed to understand fully the complexity and fluctuations in economic and political organization. Unfortunately, small sites in the heavily populated Indus Valley are rapidly being leveled to create agricultural land. In more remote areas, cemeteries and settlements are being looted for pottery, beads, figurines, and the isolated inscribed seal.

Ever since the independence of India and Pakistan, the sites that lie along the border between these two countries have been inaccessible for research. The area along the dried-up portion of the Ghaggar-Hakra River holds great potential for understanding the interactions between urban centers on the Indus River and its tributaries and the Thar Desert and Rajasthan to the east. In the other direction, the long drawn-out conflict in Afghanistan and recent disturbances in Baluchistan have made it difficult to investigate the relationships between the Indus settlements located on the alluvial plains and those scattered throughout the western highland regions. The nature of interaction between the Indus region and the farther regions of peninsular India, Central Asia, the Gulf, and Mesopotamia also needs to be investigated in order to test and refine models of external trade and core–periphery relations. Changes in political relations and the eventual stabilization of these various regions may begin to open up these areas for research.

Acknowledgments

I would first like to thank the organizers of the conference, Joyce and Jerry, for inviting me to participate in this important project. I would especially like to thank the Government of Pakistan, Department of Archaeology, and the numerous curators at the Harappa Museum for facilitating our continued work at Harappa. I would also like to thank the Archaeological Survey of India and especially R. S. Bisht and

K. C. Nauriyal, for allowing me to visit Dholavira to see the ongoing excavations and discuss their recent findings. Special thanks to all the colleagues who have participated in the research at Harappa and have helped to collect and analyze data: the late Dr. G. F. Dales, Dr. Richard Meadow, Dr. Rita Wright, Dr. M. Rafique Mughal, Mrs. Barbara Dales, Dr. Heather M.-L. Miller, Dr. William Belcher, Dr. Qassid Mallah, Dr. Laura Miller, Sharri Clark, Aasim Dogar, Nadeem Ghouri, Randy Law, Brad Chase, and all the other team members. Finally, I would like to thank the anonymous reviewers for their comments, which have helped to make this chapter more coherent.

My ongoing research at Harappa and on the Indus Valley Civilization has been supported by numerous organizations: the National Science Foundation, the National Endowment for the Humanities, the National Geographic Society, the Smithsonian Institution, the American School of Prehistoric Research (Peabody Museum of Archaeology and Ethnology, Harvard University), the University of Wisconsin, www.HARAPPA.com, and private donors.

eleven
Stages in the Development of "Cities" in Pre-Imperial China

Lothar von Falkenhausen

When inquiring into the archaeology of an area of the world in which English is not the scholarly language of reference, such as China, we are well advised to start by making every effort to comprehend the terminology used in the scholarly literature from which we derive our information. This is especially important when the results of our investigation are intended to serve, as is the case in this book, for cross-cultural comparison. If we are, for instance, to find out how ancient Chinese cities differ from, or correspond to, those of other early civilizations, we must first make sure that the semantic range of the word, or words, conventionally rendered as "city" capture phenomena that correspond at least more or less to those we are used to designating as "cities" elsewhere.

It is relevant to take note, in this connection, of the polysemy of the Chinese word (Ch) *cheng* 城, which is most commonly used to render such terms as (English) *city*; (German) *Stadt*; (Russian) *gorod*; (French) *ville*; and (Latin) *urbs*. Each of these Indo-European lexical items, of course, has its own distinct and highly evocative etymology, and so does *cheng*, which means both "city" and "city wall." The former meaning is undoubtedly derived from the latter, via a third, related meaning of "fortress." Of the Indo-European terms listed, only *gorod* (related to the English word *garden*, which designated, originally, a "guarded" enclosure) has a somewhat comparable semantic field. Also of relevance is the etymological connection of (Ch) *cheng* (reconstructed archaic pronunciation: *źjäŋ*) 城 *city* to the exactly homophonous *cheng* 成 *to establish*, which mirrors that of (German) *Stadt* (as well as [German] *Staat*, [English] *state*; and [French] *état*) to (German) *stehen*; (English) *to stand*; [Latin] *stare*; and so on).

In modern scholarship, the word *cheng* regularly turns up in connection with attempts to render into Chinese such larger concepts as (Greek) "polis"; (Latin) "civitas"; (German) "Stadtstaat"; and (English) "urbanism." Because, under the influence of Western anthropology, the presence of "cities" has come to be regarded as a leading indicator for the onset of "civilization" in China (Chang 1962, 1976:22–46; Okamura 2000; Shao Wangping 2000; Yang 2004a; Zhongguo 2003), Chinese archaeologists—linguistically conditioned to equate "cities" with "walls"—have focused their search for the origins of civilization in China single-mindedly on walled enclosures.

By comparison with other civilizations of the ancient world, however, sizable and important-looking walled settlements appear relatively late in the Chinese archaeological record. This has caused some psychological discomfort among scholars intent on establishing as early as possible an origin for Chinese civilization, and some have therefore embraced a very broad definition of "city" (Shao Wangping 2000:203–206, 216–219; Yang 2004a). I believe, however, that in order to understand the genesis of urbanism in early China, the equation of "cities" with walled settlements should probably be abandoned. More basically, as I will argue, it might be useful to question the linkage of "cities" and "civilization" in the case of China. China, I believe, presents us with a situation in which full-fledged and sophisticated state-level sociopolitical organization existed for many centuries in a spatial environment that lacked many crucial features of urbanism seen elsewhere. Full cities—and the crucial distinction between the urban and rural spheres—emerged only during the time of transition preceding the foundation of the first unified empire in 221 BC.

The surrounding walls of pre-Imperial Chinese settlements, where present, consist of stamped earth (*hangtu*), a durable but not particularly conspicuous material (figure 11.1). Stamped earth is also used for the platforms on which important buildings stood. The buildings themselves are highly impermanent, consisting mainly of a wooden frame, walls made of wattle and daub, stamped earth, or adobe bricks, and a thatched roof. Instead of thatch, wooden shingles may have been used on occasion. Roof tiles are first seen in the ninth century BC, and fired bricks appear only at the very end of the Bronze Age. Throughout pre-Imperial times, both tiles and bricks are restricted to very prominent buildings. Stone boulders are sometimes used as fill for the foundation pits of large wooden columns, and aprons of scattered pebbles surround some stamped-earth foundations; aside from this, stone is never used as a building material.

Until the middle of the first millennium BC, the vast majority of dwellings and other buildings at early settlements were semi-subterranean huts topped with simple thatched-roof structures. Such buildings, the forerunners of which can be traced back to the beginnings of settled life in China, enjoyed an even shorter use-life than the

Figure 11.1. Section of the stamped-earth wall at Guchengzhai, Mi Xian (Henan), third millennium BC (photo by the author, 2002).

wood-framed structures on their platforms. Hence, even settlements that were occupied only for a brief time tend to present the archaeologist with an impenetrable maze of intersecting pits. Some of these pits are the remains of deliberately constructed dwellings or storage buildings; many others are makeshift rubbis pits. Deliberately constructed buildings, as well, usually degenerated into rubbish pits at a secondary stage of their use-life. Stamped-earth foundations of aboveground buildings are often pockmarked to the point of near disappearance by pits dug into them after the buildings were abandoned. The foundations, in turn, often sit on top of filled-in pits from preceding episodes of settlement. Postholes, when preserved, can indicate the alignment of walls and structural supports, but more often than not, such alignments are obscured by successive phases of construction.

Despite the technical challenges these sites pose to their excavators, seven decades of fieldwork have now generated a fair amount of evidence that can be used to reconstruct the development of proto-urban and urban settlements in pre-Imperial China. Limiting myself to the core area of the early royal dynasties—the Yellow, Huai, and Middle Yangzi river basins and the Shandong peninsula—I shall trace this development through three principal stages: (1) an Incipient Stage in the third millennium BC (Late Neolithic); (2) a Formative Stage from ca. 2000 to ca. 600 BC, comprising most of China's great Bronze Age (including the historically documented Shang [ca. 1600–ca. 1046 BC] and Western Zhou [ca. 1046–771 BC] periods); and (3) an Advanced Stage, from ca. 600 BC to the Qin unification in 221 BC, which is largely, but not entirely, coterminous with the Warring States period in traditional historiography (ca. 450–221 BC). This periodization is for the purpose of presentation only and does not imply a teleological view of the evolution of "cities," which, over the course of this long time span and in the large territory that is China, was far less uniform and unilinear than my abbreviated narrative may suggest.

Xu Hong's (2000) excellent synthesis of archaeologically attested "cities" from pre-Imperial China documents 40 "cities" from the Incipient, 39 from the Formative, and 428 from the Advanced. Xu uses the term *chengshi* 城市, a neologism connecting the above-mentioned *cheng* with *shi* (market/market town). Even though Xu's criteria for inclusion into his list of "cities" may need some revision—as further discussed below—and future discoveries will undoubtedly modify his numbers, these figures do suggest a tremendous and possibly quite sudden expansion of urbanism about the middle of the first millennium BC. As I shall argue, it was only at that time that cities became a phenomenon of truly central importance to Chinese civilization. Even though settlements with some urban characteristics existed before that time, it might be a mistake to regard their existence as the crucial factor that defined early China as a state-level civilization.

Incipient Stage: Neolithic Proto-Urban Settlements

Villages surrounded by moats and, sometimes, low walls occur early on in the various neolithic cultures and phases of the Yellow River basin. The fifth-millennium sites of Banpo in Xi'an (Shaanxi) (Zhongguo Kexueyuan 1963) and Jiangzhai in Lintong (Shaanxi) (Xi'an 1988), both belonging to the Banpo phase of the Yangshao culture—or, according to Su Bingqi and associates (1994), to the Banpo culture of the Yangshao period—are well-known examples. They each contain a half-dozen or so clusters of semi-subterranean huts, with several small round huts surrounding one slightly larger square hut in each cluster. Each cluster perhaps corresponds to an extended (exogamous?) family group, and the small huts to a nuclear family. The surrounding walls consist of randomly accumulated earth, rather than being made by the labor-intensive stamping technique characteristic of later city walls. By all indications, sites of the Banpo phase do not form a three-tiered settlement hierarchy, commonly stipulated to be a defining characteristic of urbanism, nor is there an analogous hierarchy of burials at nearby cemeteries. The exclusion of walled villages like Banpo and Jiangzhai from the urban (indeed even from the proto-urban) category is therefore fairly uncontroversial.

Recent discoveries have, however, complicated our erstwhile picture of the fifth and fourth millennia BC as a pre-urban age. Large aboveground public buildings of possibly religious function have been found at some villages from the Yangshao culture, for example, at Dadiwan in Qin'an (Gansu) (Gansu 2006; Yang 2004b:2:46–49) and Xishan in Zhengzhou (Henan) (Yang Zhaoqing 1997; Yang 2004b:2:55–56). And to the surprise of its excavators, Xishan, which is associated with the fourth millennium BC Dahecun phase of the Yangshao culture, turned out to be surrounded by a substantial, stamped-earth wall of irregular contours. Settlements surrounded by mas-

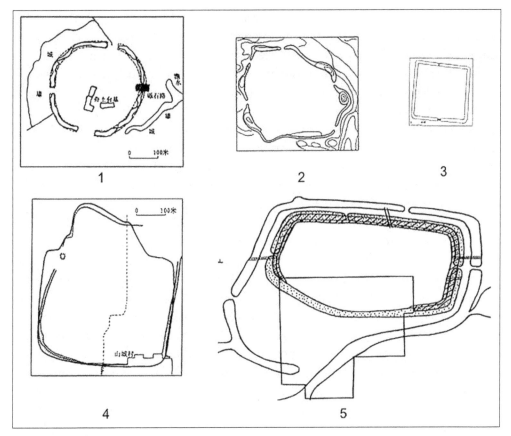

Figure 11.2. Plans of selected Neolithic walled sites: 1, Chengtoushan; 2, Zoumalou; 3, Pingliangtai; 4, Chengziyai; 5, Dantu (after Xu Hong 2000).

sive stamped-earth walls of surprisingly early date have also been found in southern China, for example, Chengtoushan in Li Xian (Hunan) (Hunan 1993; Yang 2004b:2: 94–95; figure 11.2[1]) and Zoumalou in Shishou (Hunan) (Zhang Xuqiu 1994b; and figure 11.2[2]), which belong to the fourth millennium BC Qujialing culture, and the even earlier Bashidang, also in Li Xian (Hunan) (Hunan 1996; Yang 2004b:2:79–81). It does not seem at present that these sites were lodged at the top of a complex settlement hierarchy (with a corresponding burial hierarchy), as one would expect in an urban or proto-urban context, but this impression may be due to insufficient fieldwork. Technologically, in any case, the mode of construction of the large building foundations and of the walled enclosures is ancestral to those attested by proto-urban and urban sites of later periods.

From the third millennium BC, we now know approximately two dozen stamped-earth walled enclosures pertaining to various local phases of the Longshan culture. One example is the site of Pingliangtai, Huaiyang (Henan) (Henan 1983; Xu Hong 2000:15; Yang 2004b:2:60–61; figure 11.2[3]). Its enclosure is square in shape (185 by 185 m, making for a surface area of some 3.5 ha), and it is oriented to the cardinal directions. The two gates piercing the walls are not aligned with each other. The more prominent of the two gates is the south gate, which is situated in the exact center of the south wall. Its guard buildings, constructed of adobe bricks, testify to a concern with restricted access. Excavation and subsurface sounding inside the enclosure have revealed an as yet undetermined number of rectangular multiroom buildings with adobe walls, standing on low stamped-earth platforms and oriented to the cardinal directions. Their spatial layout has not yet been reported. Though modest by modern standards, such architecture was imposing by comparison with the predominant semi-subterranean dwellings. Buildings constructed in this way may have served as elite residences and/or for religious practices connected with the cult of ancestors, used since about 3000 BC to legitimize a kin-based social hierarchy (Liu Li 2000). Given the continuing importance of ritual display in the exercise of political authority, palace and temple functions were to remain united in elite architecture throughout the Bronze Age.

Even though we cannot be sure whether such temple/palaces were, in their time, restricted to walled settlements, their prominent presence at Pingliangtai adds greatly to the impression that Pingliangtai was a privileged space—a "gated community" for an elite social stratum that kept itself and its activities self-consciously apart from the common fray. Given the relatively small size of the Pingliangtai enclosure (about four soccer fields), most of the non-elite population that sustained this elite stratum must have lived elsewhere. Whether there was any non-elite settlement in the "suburban" areas around the enclosure (as there was later around walled sites during the Bronze Age) is so far unknown, and we know nothing about the settlement pattern in the wider surroundings of the site. Data from comparable settlements elsewhere in North China are, however, beginning to show indications of three-tiered settlement-cum-burial hierarchies. Pingliangtai seems to have been one in a network of elite-activity centers spread across much of what was to become the core area of the early Chinese dynasties.

The evidence is still quite fragmentary on neolithic settlement systems in China. Liu Li (1994, 2004) provides important theoretical considerations, but they are proleptic rather than firmly based in presently available data. Xu Hong (2000:31–47) courageously and judiciously summarizes the incomplete data available at the time of his writing; for lesser treatments of the same subject in English, see DeMattè 1999 and Yang 2004a. Full-coverage survey data are now gradually being generated, for example, by the Sino-foreign archaeological collaboration projects at Gongyi in central Henan (Chen Xingcan et al. 2003; Liu Li et al. 2002–2004), Liangchengzhen in coastal southwestern Shandong (Fang Hui et al. 2004; Underhill et al. 1998; Zhongmei 1997), and Chifeng in Inner Mongolia (Chifeng 2003; Shelach 1999).

One should caution that the Longshan period walled enclosures differ from one another in many respects. Xu Hong (2000) wisely treats them under separate regional rubrics. Their predominant functions may not have been the same in each case. Reflecting an increasingly violent political climate, some sites may have been walled for defense purposes (Zou Heng 1987); in other cases, the main goal in constructing a wall may have been to define the sacred space of a ceremonial center (Wheatley 1971).

Because most of the settlements in question remain unexcavated, the main criteria by which one might classify them are shape and size. Pingliangtai, for instance, is relatively small in size and unusually regular in shape; at the opposite side of the size spectrum are such sites as Chengziyai in Zhangqiu (Shandong), the type site of the Longshan culture (Li Ji et al. 1934; Xu Hong 2000:16–17; Yang 2004b:2:71–73), with an enclosed area of 20 ha (see figure 11.2[4]).

In my opinion, it is debatable whether a site like Pingliangtai—or even Chengziyai—should be considered as a "city" merely on the basis of its obvious evolutionary continuity with the more unambiguously urban, walled settlements of the Bronze Age. Instead, in searching for evidence of Late Neolithic urbanism, one should arguably expand the focus beyond walled settlements. It is surely significant, for instance, that some walled settlements are much smaller than nearby unwalled settlements. One of the largest known unwalled settlements from the Longshan period is Xinzhai in Mi Xian (Henan) (Zhongguo 1981), which, with 70 ha, is more than thirty times the size of the only known contemporaneous walled enclosure in the area, Wangchenggang in Dengfeng (Henan) (Henan 1992). Recently, an outer wall enclosing a larger area appears to have been found at Wangchenggang, which would reduce the size difference (Chen Xingcan, personal communication, 2005). Even clearer is the case of Liangchengzhen in Rizhao (Shandong), where the settlement context is better known than at any other Neolithic settlement in China, thanks to the ongoing long-term survey project by Shandong University and the Field Museum. Liangchengzhen —at about 90 ha, one of the largest known prehistoric sites in China—was a significant manufacturing center and place of residence, yet it does not seem to have been surrounded by a wall. An approximately contemporaneous walled settlement has, however, been found at Dantu, 1 km from Liangchengzhen (Luo Xunzhang 1998; Xu Hong 2000:17–18; see figure 11.2[5]). With a size of 23 ha, Dantu is significantly smaller than Liangchengzhen. The Liangchengzhen Survey has classified Liangchengzhen as the sole site in the top tier, and Dantu as a second-tier site, of a four-tiered settlement hierarchy (figure 11.3). In terms of archaeologically attested activities, Liangchengzhen was by far the most diversified site in the area (Bennett 2002). Despite the lack of surrounding walls, it seems a more likely candidate than Dantu for being a "city." Or perhaps Dantu and Liangchengzhen were two interdependent components of one site lodged at the top of a three-tier settlement hierarchy. One might imagine a small, castle-dwelling aristocracy that exerted authority over a subject population inhabiting a large, unenclosed, yet proto-urban, center. Mutatis mutandis, the same situation may have prevailed at Xinzhai. Xu Hong (2000), in his listing of Late Neolithic "cities," includes Dantu, but not Liangchengzhen, and Wangchenggang, but not Xinzhai. Xu furthermore excludes Taosi, perhaps the largest and most important Terminal Neolithic settlement in North China, probably because no walled enclosure had been identified there at the time of Xu's writing. Now that a wall has been found there (Guojia Wenwuju 2002–2001:24–27; Yang 2004b:2:64–66), Taosi presumably would be included. Such inconsistencies illustrate the lexically induced conceptual problems outlined at the beginning of this chapter. Yang's (2004a:138–143)

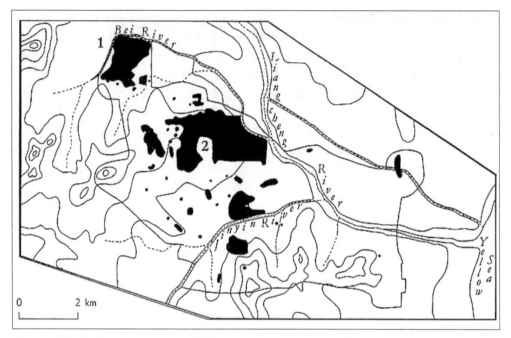

Figure 11.3. Settlement pattern around Liangchengzhen, Rizhao (Shandong): 1, Dantu; 2, Liangchengzhen (after Underhill et al. 1998).

useful list of "Earthen-Walled Sites in Prehistoric China" includes Taosi, as well as Liangchengzhen, noting that "ramparts have not been identified, but the site covers between 1 and 2 million sq. meters" (Yang 2004a:139).

Formative Stage: Early Bronze Age Lineage Seats

The difference between Neolithic and Bronze Age "cities" is, first and foremost, one of scale. At more than 20 sq km (if one includes its as yet incompletely traced outer enclosure), the Early Shang city at Erligang in Zhengzhou (Henan) may have been, during the time of its florescence in the fifteenth century BC, the largest agglomeration of people anywhere in the world (Yoffee and Li 2005), and it was more than fifteen times the size of Liangchengzhen and Dantu combined. Its inner enclosure, more than 3 sq km in area (figure 11.4[1]), was almost a hundred times as large as Pingliangtai and more than ten times as large as the largest known Longshan period enclosures. Like Pingliangtai, but at an incomparably more vast scale, this enclosure was filled by temples/palaces and elite residences, most of them, unfortunately, overbuilt later on (for archaeological reports, see Henan 1993; Henan 2001; in English, see An 1986; Yang 2004b:2:120–123). Comparable settlements existed contemporaneously in distant areas but loosely connected with the Shang state; Sanxingdui in the remote Sichuan Basin, for instance, had an approximately 3-sq-km walled core surrounded by more than 10 sq km of densely inhabited suburbs (Chen De'an 1991; Sichuan et al.1987; Zhao Dianzeng 1989; figure 11.4[2]). Medium-size regional cen-

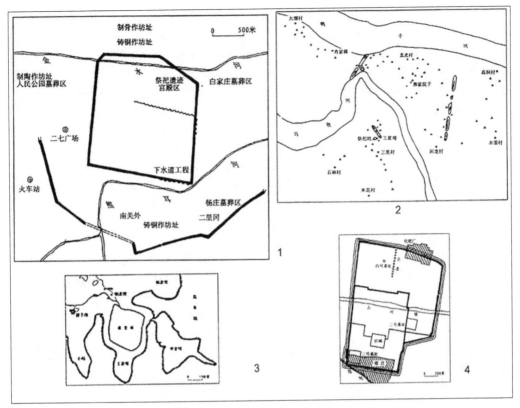

Figure 11.4. Plans of selected walled sites from the Shang period: 1, Erligang; 2, Sanxingdui; 3, Panlongcheng; 4, Shixianggou (after Xu Hong 2000).

ters with walled enclosures are also known, such as Panlongcheng in Huangpi (Hubei), in the Middle Yangzi region (Hubei 2001; Yang 2004b:2:124–136; figure 11.4[3]), and Yuanqu (Shanxi) on the north bank of the Yellow River (Yang 2004b: 2:127–128; Zhongguo et al. 1996, 2001; for a study of the settlement system around Yuanqu, see Railey 1999). Because these two sites were located on the peripheries of the Shang realm, the presence of walls conceivably may have been motivated by defense needs.

The most comprehensively excavated walled settlement from the Chinese Bronze Age to date is Shixianggou in Yanshi (Henan), better known as the "Yanshi Shang City" (Du Jinpeng 2003; Du and Wang 2004; Yang 2004b:2:118–119; Zhongguo 2003:203–218; figure 11.4[4]). It dates to the first half of the Shang dynasty, approximately contemporaneous with Erligang. Measuring about 1 sq km in area, it was enclosed by stamped-earth walls 16–17 m thick and an outer moat 6–7 m wide. The earliest part of the settlement was the rectangular "inner enclosure" in the southern part of the site, which was later extended on the north and east by an L-shape "outer enclosure." Five gates and remains of roadways have been found, attesting the cardinal orientation of the urban layout. The southern third of the site was filled with more than ten large temple/palace compounds, three of which had their own enclosing walls.

Stages in the Development of "Cities" in China   217

The largest building, Structure 2 in the western part of the central enclosed compound, measured 90 m in length during its most extensive construction phase. In the northern part of the "inner enclosure," excavations have revealed remains of elite buildings in association with what appear to have been ponds and gardens. The "outer enclosure" contained ceramic and metal workshops, as well as other manufacturing sites, probably producing especially for the resident elite; some tombs were also found there.

Current evidence suggests that Shixianggou served principally as a place of elite settlement, religious activity, and manufacture of prestige goods. The inhabitants were apparently either persons of elevated status or retainers and servants attached to elite households. The ordinary population lived elsewhere; its settlements have not been archaeologically located. A similar situation seems likely for Erligang, where, likewise, there was significant manufacturing activity in the vast outer-walled zone surrounding the central enclosure.

In a curious parallel to what we have observed to be the case in the Late Neolithic, however, walled enclosures are absent from some of Bronze Age China's largest settlement sites, including some that are known to have been the capitals of major polities. An early example—located less than 10 km from Shixianggou—is the pre-Shang site of Erlitou in Yanshi (Henan) (Yang 2004b:2:112–114; Zhongguo 1999; figure 11.5[1]), perhaps the earliest capital of a full-fledged dynastic state in the North China Plain (Allan 2007; Liu Li 2004:229–232; Liu and Chen 2003; Thorp 1991). Likewise, at the Late Shang (ca. 1325–ca. 1046 BC) capital of Yinxu at Anyang (Henan), probably pre-Imperial China's best-known archaeological site, almost eight decades of excavation have failed to yield any evidence of a stamped-earth enclosure (Chang 1980; Li Chi 1977; Yang 2004b:2:133–140; Zhongguo 1994, 2003; figure 11.5[2]). Instead, archaeologists found extensive remains of temples/palaces, residential quarters, workshops, ritual sites, and cemeteries spread out without any discernible pattern over an area of 24 sq km on both sides of the Huan River. Adding to the puzzle, a collaborative Sino-Canadian settlement survey of the Anyang area has recently discovered the remains of a large rectangular walled city just predating the Yinxu capital on the north bank of the Huan River (Guojia Wenwuju 2001–1999:37–39, 2003–2002:26–29; Yang 2004b:2:130–132). The need for defense seems inadequate to explain why Shixianggou had a walled enclosure but nearby Erlitou did not (unless historical circumstances changed and the invading Shang needed greater military protection than their "Xia" predecessors…but this is a just-so story of a kind archaeologists should avoid) or why the Shang walled the city on the north bank of the Huan River but not nearby Yinxu.

From the Western Zhou period, remains of walled enclosures are particularly scarce. None of the various Western Zhou capitals (at Zhouyuan in Fufeng and Qishan [Shaanxi; figure 11.5(3)], Feng/Hao in Chang'an [Shaanxi], and Luoyang [Henan] [Chen Quanfang 1988; Iijima 2004; Xu Hong 2000:61–65; Yang 2004b:2:152–157; Ye Wansong 1992) was walled. Neither, apparently, were most of the capitals of the regional polities of the time. One example of a large unwalled political center is the

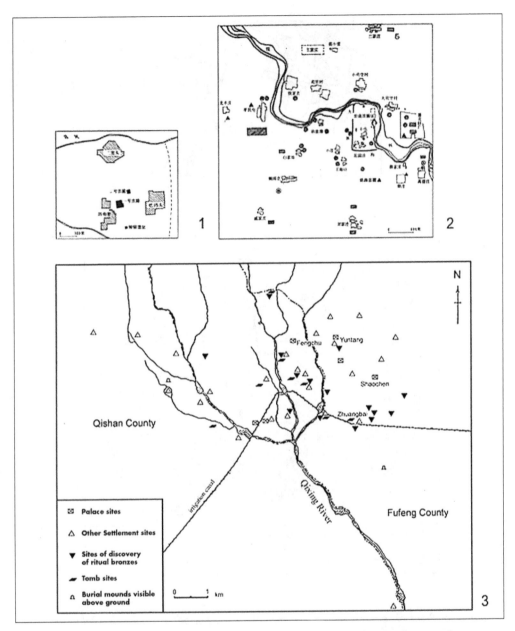

Figure 11.5. Plans of selected unwalled Bronze Age dynastic capitals: 1, Erlitou; 2, Anyang; 3, Zhouyuan (after Xu Hong 2000).

first capital of the Jin polity at Qucun in Quwo (Shanxi), which flourished between ca. 1000 and 589 BC (Beijing 2000). Based on the estimated number of tombs at the surrounding cemeteries, the adult core population of Qucun can be calculated to have numbered just below 2,000 on average over the more than four centuries of the site's occupation (Falkenhausen 2006:133 n. 10); the total population probably exceeded 5,000, perhaps considerably during the most florescent phases of occupation. Xu Hong

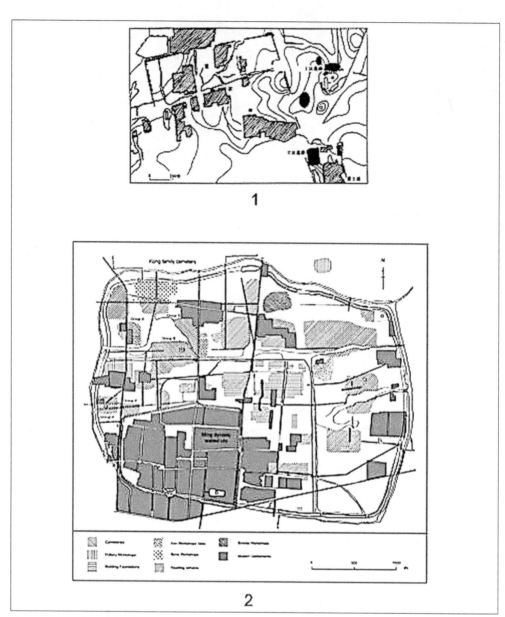

Figure 11.6. Plans of selected walled sites from the Zhou period: 1, Liulihe; 2, Qufu (after Xu Hong 2000).

(2000) includes Zhouyuan, Feng/Hao, and Luoyang (as well as Erlitou and Yinxu) as "cities" even though they are unwalled, but not Qucun, in spite of its considerable extent and population. Despite their sizable populations, these settlements apparently consisted only of scattered elite temple/palace compounds surrounded by a haphazard scatter of still largely semi-subterranean vernacular structures.

The only known instance of a wall-enclosed settlement dating to Early Western Zhou (ca. 1050–ca. 950 BC) is the capital of the Yan polity at Liulihe in Fangshan (Beijing)

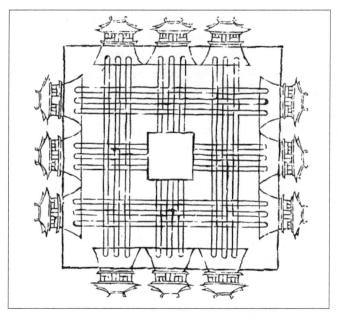

Figure 11.7. Idealized layout of a Zhou capital from the "Kaogongji" (after Sanli tu, 1676 edition).

(Beijing 1995; Xu Hong 2000:69–70; Yang 2004b:2:161–163; figure 11.6[1]). As Yan was a remote northeastern outpost of the Zhou realm, defense may be the main reason for the presence of a wall here. Perhaps for military reasons, the Yan capital was abandoned at the end of the Early Western Zhou period. No walled enclosures are currently known that were built, or indeed even occupied, anywhere in China during the following 150 years. Future archaeological discoveries will undoubtedly fill this lacuna.

In spite of well-published views to the contrary (Shandong et al. 1982; Yang 2004b: 2:171–172), the walled enclosure of Confucius's hometown, the seat of the ancient polity of Lu at present-day Qufu (Shandong), goes back no further than ca. 800 BC at the earliest (Xu Hong 2000:95–97). It measures about 10 sq km in size—more than four times the Late Imperial county seat that eventually came to occupy its southwest corner (figure 11.6[2]). Even though the Lu capital is sometimes referred to as the paradigm of a Zhou period city, Xu Hong (2000:171–184) has shown that its plan and layout actually show little correspondence to the blueprint presented in the "Kaogongji" ("Notes on Examining the Artisans"), a third-century text now preserved as an appendix to the Confucian ritual classic *Zhou li* (*Rites of Zhou*) (figure 11.7). The shape of the walled enclosure is irregular, rather than rectangular as stipulated by the "Kaogongji." Eleven city gates have been located, two on the south wall and three each on the east, west, and north walls; the "Kaogongji" calls for three gates on each side. Moreover, at variance with the "Kaogongji," the gateways of the Lu capital are not aligned with one another, and the five roadways that have been traced within the enclosure do not form a grid pattern; in fact, they do not even always cross at right angles. The only (surely fortuitous) point of correspondence with the "Kaogongji" is that the major temples/palaces and elite residences were located approximately at the center of the site. It is possible that they had their own enclosing walls (as the "Kaogongji" stipulates), but the remains so far traced are ambiguous because the entire temple/palace complex was overbuilt later on, so little is known about its appearance during the Zhou period. In fact, the "Kaogongji" is not a reliable guide to the standard layout of cities in any archaeologically attested period of Chinese history. It does not appear to represent, even in idealized form, any concepts in the minds of actual city builders in pre-Imperial China.

Surrounding the temples/palaces of the Lu capital, excavations and survey have revealed extensive remains of workshops, where ceramic, metal, and bone objects were manufactured for elite consumption. Moreover, the Lu capital contained several elite cemeteries; in this respect, it saliently differed from Imperial period Chinese cities, where the dead were invariably buried outside the walls. Various ritual sites are known to have existed in the immediate surroundings of the Lu capital; whether these suburban areas also featured (non-elite) settlements of any significance has not been archaeologically tested.

Walled or unwalled, the urban (or perhaps still largely proto-urban) agglomerations of the Formative Stage were invariably the seats of corporate lineages that controlled the areas around them (Falkenhausen 2006). As such, they were nodes of sociopolitical organization and centers of religious activity, thus conforming to some of the criteria of "city states" as stipulated by Hansen (2000e). But Chinese cities lack the special aura associated with the Greek polis and the free cities of medieval Europe, and there is no indication that they stood culturally apart from the surrounding rural areas, which were populated, as far as we know, by members of the same group that inhabited the urban sites. Another aspect that distinguishes these sites from early cities in other parts of the world is their relative impermanence. In contradistinction to the Near East, ancient China has no tells or tepes. Few of the Neolithic and Bronze Age settlements covered by Xu Hong (2000) were inhabited over a long time. The huge walled center of Erligang, for instance, seems to have been occupied for just over a century, and Yinxu, with an occupation of some 273 years, is on the long side. It is true that at the site, in Tengzhou (Shandong), that served as the capital of the Xue polity during Eastern Zhou times, walled settlements seem to have existed continually—but perhaps not as the seat of one continuous lineage—from Neolithic through Warring States times (Xu Hong 2000:18). At Xinzheng (Henan), one site served successively as the capital of two distinct polities, Zheng (from the eighth century to 375 BC) and Hán (until 230 BC) (Yang 2004b:2:176–279). But these appear to have been exceptions. One of the key deliberate characteristics of early Chinese lineage seats was that they could be easily moved. Such a concern may well be one reason that, in cross-cultural comparison, pre–Warring States settlements in China stand out for their lack of truly monumental architecture.

Early historical texts attest that capitals were moved often (Price 1995). The Shang kings, for instance, are recorded to have relocated their capital seven times, though they also apparently maintained a permanent ritual center (the Great City Shang) in eastern Henan (Chang 1980). The Zhou court, as well, moved incessantly between several coexisting capitals before eventually settling at Luoyang, and within the Luoyang area, the location of the royal settlement shifted considerably between the eleventh and the third centuries BC. The many local polities of the Zhou period also variously changed their locations. The reasons a polity might move were manifold—ecological, economical, political, or religious. A move could occur voluntarily or under duress. Significantly, in any case, political legitimacy was not bound up with the control of any particular location (or, as seems often to have been the case in the Near East, with the cult of a local deity), but with the correct performance of the ancestral cult. The paraphernalia needed were portable and, if destroyed, replaceable, and the temples were relatively modest by international standards (and needed frequent rebuilding even if they remained in the same location). Political power, in early China, emanated primarily from the internal social organization of the lineage system, not from any tangible manifestation of authority in a particular place. Such cultural priorities, which may be part of what makes ancient Chinese civilization unique, probably go a long way toward explaining the appearance of proto-urban and urban settlements in China during our Incipient and Formative Phases.

Advanced Stage: Late Bronze Age Cities

The expansion of urban settlement evident from Xu Hong's figures, quoted at the beginning of this chapter, approximately coincides with the removal of the capital of the Jin polity from the above-mentioned Qucun to Xintian at present-day Houma (Shanxi) in 589 BC. During the following two centuries, until its abandonment in ca. 403, Xintian was perhaps, in terms of its urban morphology, China's most modern city (Shanxi 1996; Xu Hong 2000:86–89; Yang 2004b:2:184–187; figure 11.8[1]). Concentrated settlement at Xintian was dispersed over an area of some 60 sq km. In the center, the ruling house of Jin had its seat in a triple-walled enclosure, altogether some 3.5 sq km in size. Why there were three enclosures rather than a single one is unknown; they may have represented successive episodes of expansion. Interestingly, the same configuration was later replicated at Anyi (Shanxi province) and Handan (Hebei province), the capitals of two of the Warring States period successor states of Jin (Xu Hong 2000:97–98, 100–101; figure 11.8[2], [3]), which may suggest that the three enclosures had different functions. Xintian contained, furthermore, at least three smaller enclosures (in two cases, double enclosures), each measuring approximately 2 ha. These are thought to have been the residences of ministerial lineages unrelated to the ruling house, which wielded increasing political power in Jin during the sixth and fifth centuries BC. At an earlier stage of sociopolitical development, these lineages would have resided in their own respective appended domains at some distance from the Jin capital. Their manifest presence at Xintian signals an incipient tendency away from single-lineage to multi-lineage "cities."

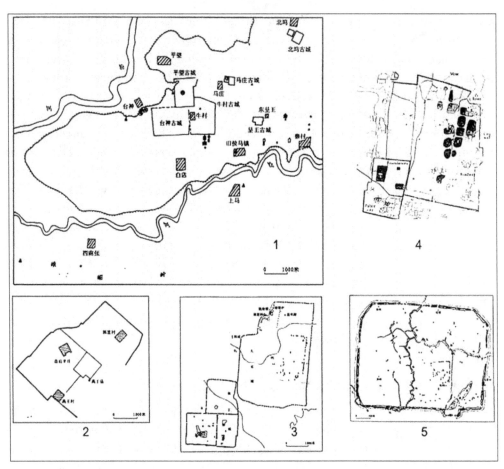

Figure 11.8 Plans of selected Warring States period capitals: 1, Xintian; 2, Anyi; 3, Handan; 4, Linzi; 5, Jinancheng (after Xu Hong 2000).

The various enclosures at Xintian were surrounded by the densely populated living quarters of a substantial non-elite population. Interspersed with the settlements were extensive cemeteries and sites of ritual activity. In addition, Xintian contained large and elaborate manufacturing workshops, which now no longer produced merely for local elite consumption, but for far-flung commercial trade. This situation is clearest in the case of the famous Houma bronze foundry (Institute of Archaeology 1996; Shanxi 1993). Xintian also features the earliest known incidence of buildings placed on towering stamped-earth mounds, which were China's first attempts at a truly monumental architecture. Such buildings were constructed both at the rulers' temple/palace compounds and surmounting the rulers' tombs in the suburbs. They were hugely labor-intensive to construct, and their splendor, contrasting with the modesty of non-elite remains, reflects the breakdown of the traditional segmentary-lineage structure and an increasing social chasm between the ruling stratum and the subject population (Falkenhausen 2006:326–369).

By comparison with "cities" from the Formative Stage, Houma was thus not only more extensive, but also significantly more diverse in the composition of its inhabitants. To a much larger extent than earlier lineage sites, which were predominantly ceremonial in character, Xintian was a commercial center, reflecting new economic and technological trends that were to transform China completely during the subsequent centuries.

From the fifth century BC onward, the capitals of the Warring States period kingdoms grew to unprecedented size and population. Simultaneously, a network of secondary cities, administratively dependent on the capitals, took shape in the various kingdoms of the time. Sites of this latter category constitute the bulk of the many "cities" from this period listed by Xu Hong (2000). Of course, the various lineage seats of the Incipient and Formative stages, as well, differed greatly in their sizes, but it was only during the Advanced Stage that we begin to perceive a consistent hierarchy of cities of different ranks and sizes. This reflects the transformation of the erstwhile kin-centered patrimonial polities into territorial states.

The most often-mentioned Warring States period capital is Linzi, the capital of the mighty kingdom of Qi in present-day northern Shandong (Qunli 1972; Xu Hong 2000:98–100; Yang 2004b:2:173–175; figure 11.8[4]). With perhaps as many as half a million inhabitants, Linzi was the most populous city in the world during the fourth and early third centuries BC—a bustling commercial hub, as well as a great center of learning. The Qi capital had been moved to this location in 859 BC, but the early stages of urban development are as yet obscure. During the Warring States period, Linzi occupied an area of some 20 sq km. The entire urban area was walled—different from Xintian, but in keeping with most contemporaneous capitals in north China—doubtless due to military threats. Also like most other Warring States period capitals, Linzi comprised a "palace city" (*gongcheng*) of some 3 sq km in the southwestern part of the settlement and a much larger "outer enclosure" (*waiguo*). Conventional wisdom has it that the gongcheng of Warring States period capitals are the genetic descendants of the elite enclosures seen during the Incipient and Formative stages and the waiguo came into being by walling the erstwhile suburbs. But excavations have shown that at Linzi, the construction of the walls around the now extant gongcheng actually postdates that of the waiguo. In any case, the dichotomy of gongcheng and waiguo encapsulates the separation of elite activity from the life of the ordinary population, and it reflects the binary division of Warring States period society into increasingly despotic rulers and an undifferentiated mass of commoners.

The inner layout of Linzi is still incompletely known. The gongcheng contained a huge elevated platform that served as the foundation of the main royal palace (figure 11.9). A stone-built watergate facilitating the city's water supply, but constructed in such a way that intruders could not have entered through it, has been made visible in the northwestern part of the waiguo. Moreover, the waiguo contained the enormous (unfortunately, looted) tombs of some pre–Warring States period rulers of Qi. The Warring States period kings of Qi, by contrast, built their large necropolises outside

Figure 11.9. Foundation of a Warring States period palace (popularly but anachronistically called "Duke Huan's Terrace") in the "palace city" at Linzi (Shandong) (photo by the author, 1986).

the capital. As constructions of a predominantly ritual character, these necropolises bring out more fully than any architectural remains within Warring States period cities the textually attested preoccupation with the cosmological dimensions of built architecture and of the urban form (Falkenhausen 2006:293–325; figure 11.10).

Among the major Warring States period capitals, the only one to lack the gongcheng/waiguo division is Jinancheng, in Jiangling (Hubei), the capital of the southern kingdom of Chu, which, to judge by the furnishings of its cemeteries, must have been one of the richest cities of its day (Höllmann 1986; Hubei 1980; Yang 2004b:2:193–196; figure 11.8[5]). Like other contemporaneous capitals, Jinancheng was a major commercial center with a diverse population. Indeed, the most important new ingredient in these capitals was their substantial population of commoners, who, without being direct dependents of the rulers' courts (although, to some extent, perhaps developed out of an earlier stratum of attached craftsmen), pursued commerce and artisanry. I must rather ashamedly note that we know this mainly from texts. All that archaeology can so far contribute by way of verification is mortuary evidence showing strong signs that the traditional lineage order was collapsing and that ancestral prestige apparently played less and less of a role in determining the social position of individuals (Falkenhausen 2003, 2004, 2006). While one should not jump to the conclusion that kinship was no longer important as the basic element of social organization (or indeed as a determinant of residence within urban settlements), it does

Figure 11.10. Inlaid-bronze plan of the necropolis of King Cuo of Zhongshan, found in his tomb at Sanji, Pingshan (Hebei) (after Hebei 1995:2:plate 69).

appear that the new social reality enabled (and/or reflected) new ways of social interaction and new ways of acting out one's social relationships spatially.

The Warring States period capitals thus were the first places in China where a specifically urban culture—a veritable "city life"—could develop. The Warring States period capitals were, however, very different from "cities" in ancient or medieval Europe: they do not seem to have enjoyed a special legal status, nor did their commoner inhabitants possess rights that set them apart from rural dwellers by virtue of dwelling in a city. If this were the crucial defining criterion of a city, then it would follow (absurdly, in my opinion) that China never had any true cities, even during later historical periods.

Final Remarks

Residence in settlements with proto-urban or urban characteristics became progressively more common during the final centuries of pre-Imperial China. This is evident not only from the exponential increase of urban sites about the middle of the first millennium BC, but also from the expansion of the functional range of cities, which from sites of elite activity developed into bustling centers of commercial and production activity. Although there is no harm in labeling as "cities" the large (walled and unwalled) lineage seats from the Formative Stage and even perhaps some of the major sites from the Incipient Stage, it was only at the Advanced Stage—in a time when state-level civilization had been established in China for more than 1,500 years—that the presence of cities became a defining ingredient of Chinese civilization and cities became showcases for its highest cultural achievements.

Could it be that in ancient China, social organization, expressed through ritual enactments that reaffirmed the internal hierarchy of human relationships within kin groups, mattered more than spatial control. Could it be that, as a result, outward manifestations of power in the abstract were less strongly expressed than in other civilizations of the ancient world? If so, this would be remarkable and should be retained as distinctive. But even if such a distinction vis-à-vis other civilizations were real during the Neolithic and most of the Bronze Age, it disappeared by the Warring States period. One might wonder whether any sort of "influence" from across Eurasia played a role in the transformation (Barnhart 2004). This question, albeit unanswerable with current evidence, should no longer be considered heretical.

twelve
Early African Cities
Their Role in the Shaping of Urban and Rural Interaction Spheres

Chapurukha M. Kusimba

This chapter discusses what we know about early urbanism in Africa: the factors influencing the growth, size, and location of early African cities and the strategies used by urban elites to control demand-and-supply channels of goods and services that were the life of the city itself. The similarities in the formation processes of urbanism and urban culture in Africa and the rest of the world severely weaken the prevailing stubborn notion that early manifestations of African urbanism were somehow different from those of other regions. My two case studies are the Swahili coastal towns and Great Zimbabwe.

Introduction

Scholars have argued that patterns of population and urbanism in Africa are unique (Fletcher 1986, 1998; O'Connor 1983). Since the Victorian era they have argued that Africa's hostile climates and diseases discouraged urbanism. Recent syntheses of African history blame Africa's harsh environment, especially its endemic diseases, for discouraging population growth, complexity, and urbanism (Iliffe 1995:1; Reader 1997:254):

> The very vastness of the African continent, with a diluted and therefore readily itinerant population living in a nature at once generous with its fruits and

minerals, but cruel with its endemic and epidemic diseases, prevented it from reaching the threshold of demographic concentration that has almost always been one of the preconditions of major qualitative changes in the social, political, and economic spheres. [Reader 1997:266]

The idea that something intrinsic to Africa retarded the development of population and urbanism is long embedded in Western historiography and closely tied to the idea that Africa lacks history in general (Holl 1990, 1995). Numerous factors have been isolated as the cause of Africa's lack of cities, including climate, soil, diet, and isolation, making known cities a product of foreigners (Bent 1892; Delafosse 1922, 1924; Kirkman 1964; Levitzion 1988; Mauny 1961; Stigand 1913). Other scholars have argued that Africa's abundant resources and gentle climate discouraged urbanism (Clark 1962).

Although environmental determinism cannot sustain continent-wide generalizations, environmental factors are apparent. Urbanism in Africa and elsewhere arose in regions of high ecological and economic potential, including ancient Egypt (the middle Nile towns of Nubia, such as Kerma, Napata, and Meroe); the Ethiopian highlands; the East African Coast; the Zimbabwean plateau; the Great Lakes region of East Africa; the Sahelian region of West Africa; and the West African forest zone (Holl 2003). These areas all gave humans who possessed the right technologies the potential to produce a storable and transportable food surplus.

Three of Africa's most successful state societies, Ghana, Mali, and Songhai, and cities such as Timbuktu, Walata, Jenne-jeno, and Gao are found on or near the Inland Niger Delta and the upper and middle zones of the Niger (Holl 1985, 2003; Hunwick 1999; Insoll 1996, 1999, 2000; McIntosh 1998; McIntosh and McIntosh 1984, 1993). This region allowed the recessional cultivation of rice, as well as a position on interregional trade routes and long-distance trade in gold and salt; evidence of pre-Islamic trade dates back to Roman periods, when we see rock paintings of chariots (for trade, raiding, or exploration). Potash Silica beads, two Roman and one South Asian, found in Jenne-jeno point to Roman trade (Insoll 2003:211). Jenne-jeno was already a significant town by 300–200 BC, and the site peaked between AD 500 and 800. The sites of Koumbi Saleh, Tegdoust, and Gao were all established by AD 600, and the kingdom of Ghana showed early urbanism in the Mema area of Mali by AD 500 (Insoll 2003:212–213). This early urbanism is in line with excavations at Dhar Tichitt in Mauritania, which show a large village complex, possibly a pristine chiefdom, between 1500 and 500 BC (Holl 1985; Munson 1971, 1980). The prosperity of the Western Sahel served to attract Arab and Berber traders from North Africa, who discovered a complex trade system already in place (Holl 2003; Insoll 2003:213).

In the Ethiopian highlands, the emergence of hierarchical society and cities such as Aksum and Adulis, as well as many other regional centers of trade and ceremony, is attributed to population pressure on the productive, volcanic soils of the area, which supported agriculture much better than in the surrounding area (Butzer 1981).

Similarly, the well-watered but narrow East African coast had numerous resources that its arid hinterlands lacked. In Iron Age cities of the East African coast, competition for productive land and access to ocean resources is demonstrated by the presence of territorial markers such as mounds and burial tumuli, a system of land tenure in which clan leaders determined access and mediated land disputes and clan land was demarcated into sacred and ritual areas to ensure ownership through time (Chittick 1974, 1984; Horton 1996; Kusimba 1999a). In architecture, Swahili towns are closely built villages and towns with two-story houses, which suggest competition for land (Connah 1987:176–177).

Like any continent, Africa includes areas more or less amenable to productivity and population growth. In many areas, urban development took advantage of marginal zones and the opportunity to transport goods and services to depleted areas. Cities such as Kumbi Saleh and Awdahgust of the eighth through twelfth centuries AD and the Sahelian Ghana kingdom developed near oases, to serve as entrepôts to trans-Saharan trade (Berthier 1997; Devisse 1983, 1993; Mauny 1961; Robert-Chaleix 1989).

The Nature and Types of African Cities

Urbanization has been an important feature of Africa's history for more than two thousand years (Anderson and Rathbone 2000:1; Holl 2000; O'Connor 1983:25). Most cities remained small and were associated with the rulers and thus had brief life spans (Fletcher 1998; Krapf-Askari 1969:25; O'Connor 1983:26). In physical terms, they were relatively discrete entities but were surrounded by a peri-urban zone—determining the boundaries separating "urban" and "hinterland" landscapes remains archaeologically elusive (O'Connor 1983:299; Trigger 2003:124). However, ethnographic research shows the peoples' awareness of urban and rural differences and how these shaped their interactions. For example, the Yoruba and Swahili, who are perhaps the most urbanized peoples in sub-Saharan Africa, distinguish themselves as town people from culturally inferior "country people" (Bascom 1955, 1969; Krapf-Askari 1969; Lloyd 1974:32; Stigand 1913; Trigger 2003:124). As in other areas, African cities were centers of economic activity, loci of political authority and militarism, and sites of ritual power (Anderson and Rathbone 2000:1).

Typically, early African cities were compact, with a high density of settlements and relatively abrupt edges, often surrounded by a wall (O'Connor 1983:195). City walls protected the residents from surprise attack, slowed down the enemy, differentiated the elite from commoners, and also impressed visitors with the city's grandeur and status (Insoll 2003; Trigger 2003:125; figure 12.1). In Old Oyo, the center of the city was dominated by the palace of the king, from whence roads radiated out to the rest of the city (Agbaje-Williams 1986; Southall 1998:327). Swahili and Hausa cities were divided into several wards, each with its own identity but outwardly very similar in appearance (Allen 1993; Insoll 2003; Middleton 1992, 2004; figure 12.2). Many are built of the same construction materials. Beyond the walls were the farm plots tended by the city's residents (Krapf-Askari 1969; O'Connor 1983:195).

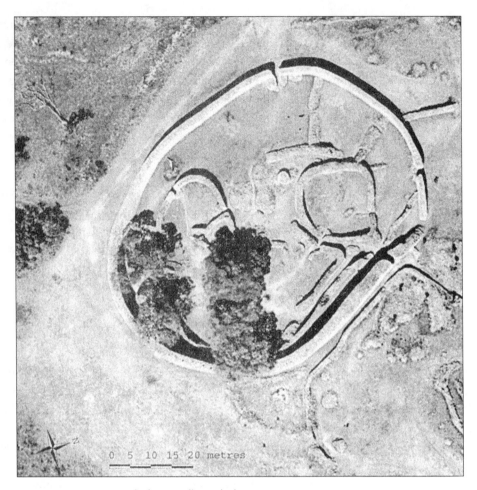

Figure 12.1. Great Zimbabwe wall, Zimbabwe.

African cities' social organization still relied on kinship and lineage ties. Residential differences, based on status and income in many long-inhabited towns, have been difficult to discern archaeologically in spite of extensive excavations (Horton 1996; Kusimba 1999a). Trading and crafts are widely dispersed, so there are no distinct functional and residential zones. For example, O'Connor's description of Hausa cities is typical of African Islamic cities:

> Traditional Hausa cities have a clearly identifiable focal center, a bounding wall, and building of fairly uniform character occupying most of the land between. There is usually a triple focus, for in addition to the Emir's palace and the main city market there is the Grand Mosque, often an imposing building rising above the generally even skyline.... The city is divided into wards or quarters, and further sub-divided into compounds, in each of which rights of occupation are passed down within a family. All compounds once included some cultivated land, though most families also had fields within and outside

Figure 12.2. Plan of Songo Mnara, Tanzania.

the city wall: but as the population has grown, ever more dwellings have been built within each compound. Narrow winding paths run between the compound walls, which often remain intact, broken only by a single doorway.... Minor markets and small mosques are spread through the various wards, and craft industries are also widely scattered, so that for many people residence and workplace are the same. [O'Conner 1983:196–197]

Fletcher (2000) has recognized two types of African cities. The first are nucleated settlements of around 1 sq km (Krapf-Askari 1969). These include the nucleated settlements of the East African coast and Madagascar, such as Kilwa (47 ha), Zanzibar (60 ha), and Antananarivo (88 ha) (Chittick 1974; Juma 2004; Radimilahy 1998) and the Yoruba cities of Nigeria (Agbaje-Williams 1986; Bascom 1969: 29–30; Krapf-Askari 1969; Mabogunje 1962; Usman 2001). For example, individual Yoruba urban center populations ranged from 5,000 to 70,000 inhabitants. Benin City had a population of 50,000 (Agbaje-Williams 1986; Trigger 2003:129).

The second group includes low-population areas of patchy and clumped settlements with an extensive skirt of low-density occupations. Often, these settlements do not have marked boundaries, and many times subsistence farming enclaves are important parts of the settlements (Connah 1987; McIntosh 1995). Often, they lack stone

Early African Cities   233

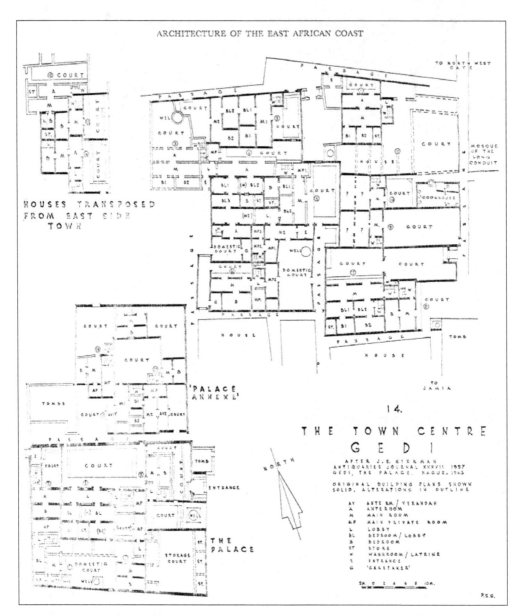

Figure 12.3. Plan of Gedi, Kenya.

buildings, and the chief's enclave is also made of wattle and daub and is simply a much larger compound than the rest of the settlement (Southall 1998). Often, these settlements are temporary or shifting, perhaps suggesting the political maneuvers that are typical of early state societies. Given the importance of agricultural activities in these settlements, one might correctly call them, as de Maret (2000) has, "giant villages."

An example of a giant village is pre-colonial Addis Ababa, which included a mobile imperial capital with dispersed settlements around it. Addis Ababa and other Ethiopian cities often covered 30–40 sq km and contained 30,000 to 40,000 people.

Their Amharic rulers frequently relocated their capital cities when firewood became exhausted (Butzer 1976; Munro-Hay 1994; Pankhurst 1998; Phillipson 1998). Settlements of the kings of the Kongo kingdom of central Africa, called *mbanza*, were large, low-density settlements of around four persons per sq km; they evolved as a result of trade, refugee settlement, or concentration of power. Mbanza Kongo is a famous example (de Maret 2000; Thornton 2000). Areas of denser settlement were surrounded by cultivated fields. Often, the king's residence was an especially large compound of wattle and daub with more ornate decorations (de Maret 2000). The lack of monumental or stone architecture at many African settlements and their semi-permanent nature lower their archaeological visibility (de Maret 2000).

Many dispersed settlements included walled areas for the king, such as seen among Benin, Old Oyo, Awdaghoust, Begho, and Ouagadougou (Connah 1975, 1987; Devisse 1983; Polet 1985; Robert et al. 1970; Robert-Chaleix 1989; Vanacker 1979). Fez had two walled areas and surrounding occupation, but the whole area covered 3.5 sq km. Forty other mounds that were functionally differentiated and probably traded with one another surround Jenne-Jeno's main mound of 33 ha; the full area covered 100 ha (McIntosh 1998). The stone "core" of Great Zimbabwe is about 1 sq km; the total site area is more than 25 sq km and includes a palimpsest of dispersed settlements around it (Garlake 1973, 1982; Huffman 1996; Ndoro 2001; Pikirayi 2001). Great Zimbabwe population estimates have ranged from 1,000–5,000 to 10,000–18,000 persons (Connah 1987; McIntosh 1997; Sinclair et al. 1993). The dispersed "giant village" is not limited to sub-Saharan Africa. In ancient Egypt, Karnak and Luxor (1500–2000 BC) and Memphis (500 BC), spread 15 km along the Nile, might be called dispersed (Fletcher 1993, 1998). Often agglomerations of people occurred in acephalous societies for defense. South African defensive towns such as Molokwane housed 10,000–16,000 people. Fortification offered some advantages, chief among which was safety, security, and privacy. Many walled towns in North, West, and East Africa developed into centers of Islamic learning and high culture (Hunwick 1999; Insoll 2003).

Early cities also shared similar constraints, including subsistence, waste disposal, and disease (Trigger 2003:123; Zeder 1991). In his survey, Glenn Storey (1992) found that preindustrial urbanism faced similar constraints: "The phenomenon of preindustrial urbanism is uniform throughout the world. Similar numbers of people could be fed and housed given the existing technology, transport systems, hinterland productivity, and administrative structures available in the preindustrial era, which, despite local variations, were similar all over the world" (Storey 1992:119). Similar limitations affected all pre-colonial city sizes, especially on transport technology (Hassan 1993). The amount of food and other goods available from the hinterland depends on transportation, and this was uniformly limited in early cities. Tribute exaction is a major factor in chiefly power and city size. In the early city, the size depended primarily on the chief's power to exact tribute and command resources from the surrounding hinterland (Marcus 2000[1983b]). Dominion over, or connection with, the countryside did not exceed a walking distance, usually around 5 km, even when donkeys or boats, for example on the Nile, could be used for transport (Hassan 1993:557). As Hassan notes, large-scale urbanism only began in the European Renaissance with large-scale manufacture, trade, industry, and worldwide commerce.

The Cities' Relationships with Their Countrysides

Cities grew out of rural settings. They have sought to maintain peaceful relationships with their hinterlands because their citizens often have long-term relationships with those hinterlands (Khaldun 1967). The interdependence of urban and rural peoples is beneficial to both. Urban elites retained close contact with the rural economy, as well as participated in local commerce and longer-distance trade (Anderson and Rathbone 2000:2). Rural people often lack the technical skills, labor, and resources to engage competitively in large-scale craft and industrial operations and thus need cities to provide them with finished goods and services (Bronson 1977).

People moving into and out of the city, whether permanently or temporarily, bind the city and its countryside together (O'Connor 1983:271). Cities' welfare and survival must be sought in the nature of the relationships they forge with their rural surroundings, on which they are dependent. How much produce comes from the rural area to the cities? What kinds of ideas are transmitted, and what patterns of political relationships or domination exist? Did urban areas bring benefits to the rural areas, or did they prosper at the expense of the rural areas? Or both?

The hinterland played several different roles in exchange networks with cities (Bronson 1977; Holl 2003). They functioned both as an ultimate producer of one trade item, for example, iron, salt, gold, and ivory, and as collection centers for items from farther inland, such as skins, cola nut, and enslaved persons (Reefe 1993:122; Vansina 1993:120). Relationships between the city and its hinterland were of three kinds.

First, they were relatively egalitarian, including debt patronage, fictive or real kinship, friendships and gift exchange, and client or trade partnerships (Nicholls 1971:42, 56). This was the case on the East African coast where the hinterland populations were relatively dispersed and mobile (Kusimba 1999a). The city provided finished manufactured goods in exchange for hinterland products, inducing the hinterland to enter into the regional economy voluntarily. In order to get the maximum profit from trade proceeds, a city would have sought to produce as many goods as possible, through techniques that hinterland peoples could not duplicate (Bronson 1977:44). For example, Swahili craft specialists produced textiles, cowrie shells, sugar, brass wire, iron tools, and shell beads specifically for hinterland markets. Another person-to-person trade relationship was between client and patron, although urban patrons often held the upper hand when possible.

Second, the urban–hinterland relationship was unequal, with the city exercising economic and political control over hinterland centers and exacting manufactured goods as tribute. This was the case in West African savannah cities, where hinterland production was undertaken in relatively concentrated and permanent facilities that the city-state could easily control. For example, the emirs of cities such as Kano, Katsina, and Sokoto exercised strong powers over the people living in the surrounding villages, which were part of the small state. Their powers were weaker over rural people (O'Connor 1983:296). The political and cultural influence of the Yoruba city of Old Oyo, which thrived from the twelfth to the early nineteenth centuries in the open grassland area of Nigeria, was vast, extending into other Yorubaland and non-Yoruba territories. Old Oyo's leaders used a web of political (including military), kinship, ideological, and economic interactions with northern Yoruba groups such as the Igbomina to sustain the state capital (Usman 2001).

Third, the city may have entered into trade partnerships with some communities and into coercive relationships with others. Lunda state capitals had little authority over many parts of their area, from which leaders only exacted tribute. The capital of 10,000 people in 1875 lived off tribute, but had little direct control of the hinterlands (Vansina 1993). Institutions of kingship in central African kingdoms include the ruler at the apex of the political structure in the capital. The hinterlands were relatively autonomous; they may have paid tribute, but any attempts to militarily secure their loyalty often resulted in voting with their legs, leading to the weakening of the city's economy.

The Shaba-Kasai trade spanned a 1,000-km north-south network, which connected the peoples of central Africa in a complex trading system ranging from basic everyday essentials to highly specialized and luxurious items. The Shaba-Kasai trading zone was one of the largest in Africa and developed independently of the international ivory/slave trade (Reefe 1993). The organization of this complex exchange network provides an excellent example of homegrown leadership and networking. Rural villagers organized themselves into ad hoc groups for a single trip under a designated leader, and after having solicited the protection of spirits, they traveled to near or distant capitals to trade. These groups, which ranged in size from about five to twenty individuals, consisted of adult males accompanied by their clients and by women who carried and prepared their food. Once at their destination, people might manufacture, or at least process, some of the products they needed, such as salt, and remit a portion to local earth-priests (Bakari 1981). However, the smelting of ore and even lake fishing required technology that visitors often did not possess or specialized materials they could not bring with them, in which case they had to trade with local producers for all the goods they sought (Reefe 1993:122). I now present two case studies from the East African coast and Zimbabwe, whose development is intimately connected with long-distance exchange with the coast.

East African Coastal Cities

Five decades of archaeological study document the long-term processes of urbanization and origins of complex society in eastern and southeastern Africa; archaeologists and historians have accumulated enormous data on the development of urbanism in the region (Abungu 1998; Allen 1993; Fleisher 2003; Garlake 1966; Horton 1996; Horton and Middleton 2000; Juma 2004; Kusimba 1999a; LaViolette and Fleisher 2005;

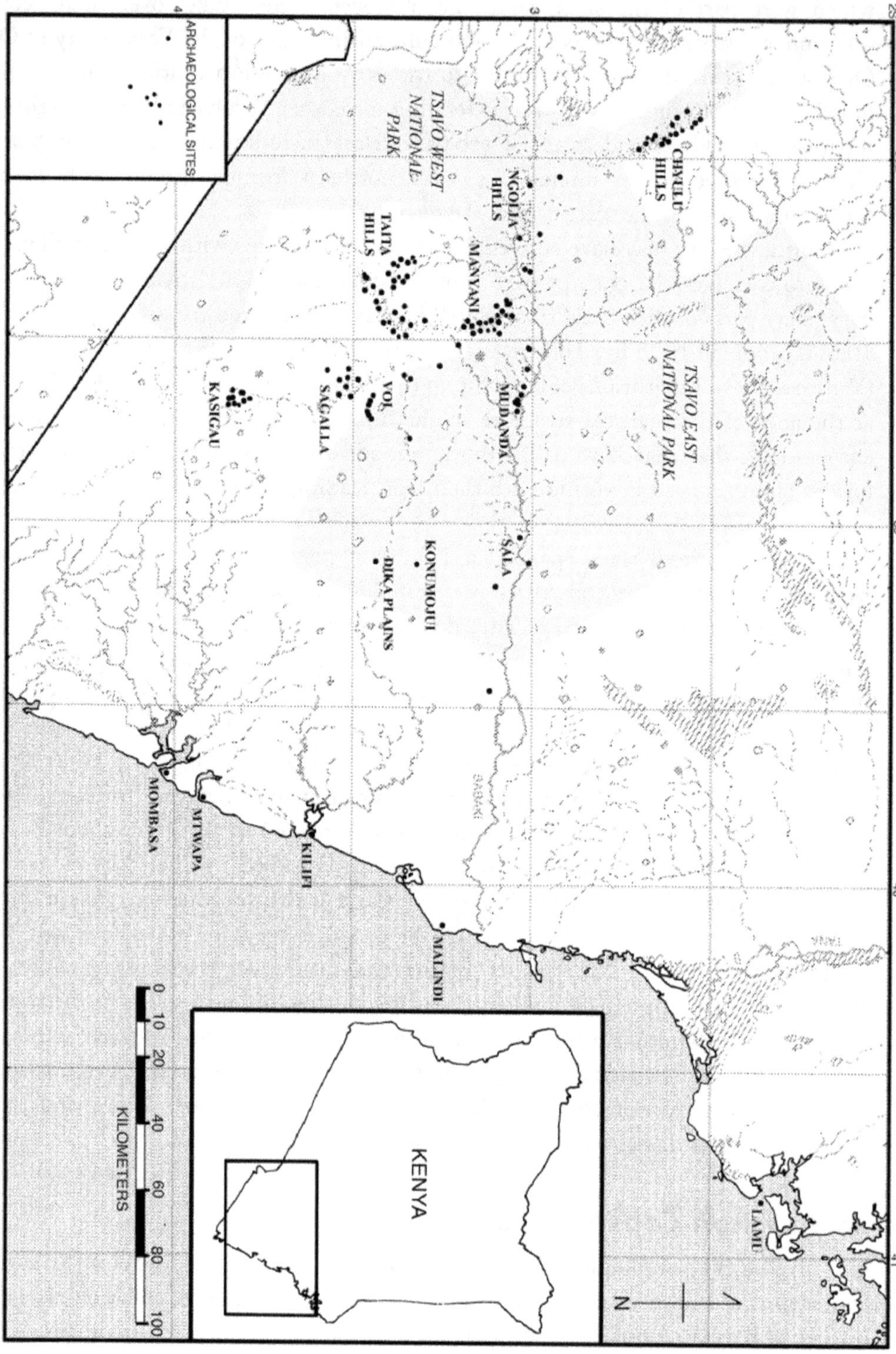

Figure 12.4. Map of East African coast with all the cities and hinterland sites.

238   Chapurukha M. Kusimba

Middleton 1992; Pikirayi 1993, 2001; Pwiti 2005; Sinclair and Hakansson 2000). These studies have shown that early cities emerged along the East African coast from Somalia to Mozambique around AD 500 (figure 12.4). Coastal residents were farmers, fishers, traders, scribes, rulers, and enslaved persons. Wealth from Indian Ocean trade was the main catalyst for the rapid development of urbanization (Middleton 2004). Equally important in its emergence was the commercial and cultural dialogue maintained between the coast and hinterland (Mutoro 1998; Pearson 1998). The residents of these cities and states were initially drawn from different language groups, but in time, one language, Kiswahili, became the dominant language. Introduced around AD 800, Islam gradually expanded to become the primary religion and means of elite cultural expression by the time of European contact in early AD 1500.

Economic and social interaction amongst diverse groups who made their living from hunting, herding, farming, and iron working laid the foundation from which international trade exchange systems interlocked (Kusimba and Kusimba 2005). By the end of the first millennium AD, the coast had become a regular partner in the millennium-old long-distance exchanges that reached as far as the Arabian Peninsula, India, Sri Lanka, and China (Allen 1993; Mitchell 2005; Pearson 1998). By the thirteenth century, there had emerged an African urban elite that financed, managed, and controlled local, regional, and interregional trade and communications (Fleisher 2003; Helm 2000; Kusimba 1999a, 1999b). Innovations in ironworking aided agricultural intensification and specialization in hunting, fishing, and herding (Abungu 1998; Horton 1996; Kusimba 1999a). These changes improved the quality of life and precipitated population growth and economic prosperity. In the late fifteenth century, however, the coast became embroiled in long-standing conflict between Christendom and Islam, represented by the Portuguese and Omani Arab mercantile interests. The Portuguese and Muslim rivalry for control of Indian Ocean commerce was economically crippling for East Africa (Kusimba 1999a, 2004).

Large urban sites were often located at the mouths of rivers or near estuaries, inlets, and offshore islands (Horton 1996; figure 12.5). However, within the hinterlands of these large urban areas were smaller rural village communities that were linked to the large settlements. Beyond the hinterlands, these cities were connected to wider eastern, central, and southeastern African forager, agrarian, and pastoral chiefdoms and states through a complex network of interaction spheres (Kusimba and Kusimba 2005). What was the relationship between the coastal cities and their more rural hinterland?

The Cities' Relationships with the Hinterland

Trade between hinterland societies and the coastal towns and cities dates to 1000 BC (Kusimba et al. 2005; Pearson 1998). In later years, some hinterland trading communities gained a monopoly on direct trade: the Giriama, Akamba, and Oromo in Kenya and the Nyamwezi, Yao, and Makua in Tanzania and Mozambique. In Kenya, regional

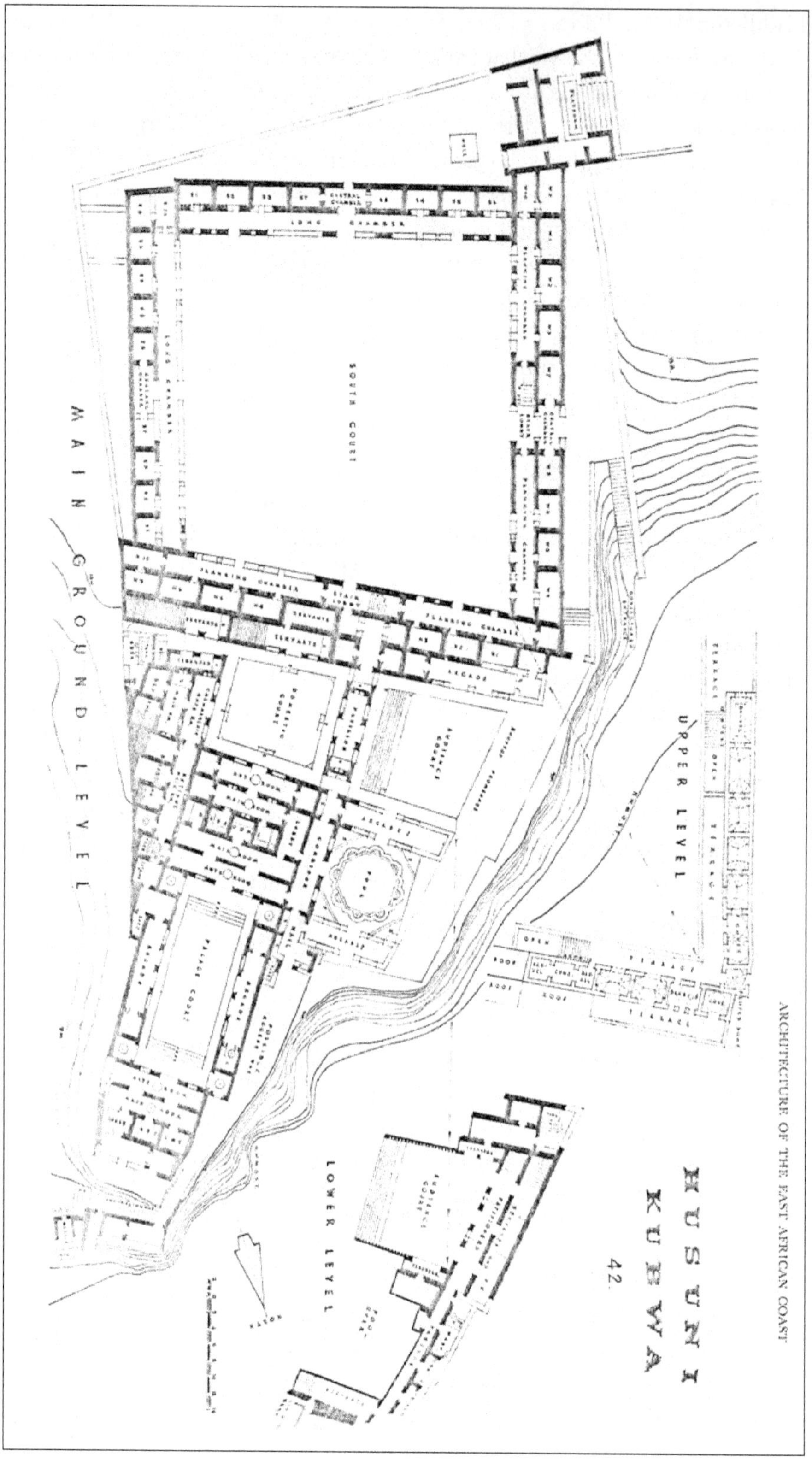

Figure 12.5. Plan of Husuni Kubwa, Kilwa, Tanzania.

and interregional trade was carried out among the Akamba, Oromo, Taita, Waata, Giriama, and Swahili from earlier times (Mutoro 1998). The Waata foragers of Tsavo hunted game such as elephant, rhino, zebra, buffalo, and ostrich and sold the skins, dried meat, and ivory to coastal Mijikenda in exchange for palm wine, cloth, grain, and beads. The Oromo pastoralists traded ivory and cattle with Pokomo, Giriama, and Swahili. The Taita agropastoralists visited the coast to sell sun-dried vegetables, meat, ivory, and grains in exchange for palm wine, cloth, beads, and hardware. The Taita farmers would travel to Jomvu Market, near Mombasa, to sell ivory and cattle directly to Swahili, Arab, and Indian merchants. The Akamba agropastoralists were trading partners with Giriama, Taita, and Waata. The Akamba would come to coastal markets, and Giriama traders would travel to Akamba land for ivory and cattle.

These trade relationships were dependent on fictive kin ties called *undugu wa chale* (blood brotherhoods) in Kiswahili (Herlehy 1984:293–294). Brotherhoods provided opportunities for people who were otherwise strangers, competitors, and potential enemies to enter into fictive ties that legitimized their relationship and partnership beyond the family to the wider community. Membership into the community conferred certain advantages: freedom to exploit resources while enjoying the protection of the whole community. In this sense, brotherhoods served to reduce tensions and suspicions arising from competition for resources while simultaneously providing opportunities for access to technical and sacred knowledge (Herlehy 1984; Kusimba and Kusimba 2005).

Coast–hinterland interactions are coming to light. Survey within the southern highlands of the Rufiji drainage system in the Mtare, Kihansi, and Ruhunji areas have discovered many sites dating from the LSA through the Iron Working to modern times. Msemwa (2001:44) "suggests contact between Mwangia people of the coast of Rufiji, the Miharawa culture and that of the people of Malawi and Zimbabwe who produced Nkope/Gokomere/Nkazi pottery tradition between 400–600 AD." This interaction sphere is affirmed by "old mango trees, which mark ancient trade routes that linked the coast and the interior," (Msemwa 2001:44) and by oral accounts and historical sources. Comparisons between coastal and inland pottery traditions here and in the Tana Delta have confirmed the cultural connections across the hinterland of the coast (Kiriama et al. 1996).

At Engaruka, 200 km inland from the coast, ornaments of shell and bone, cowrie shells, glass beads, and copper objects attest to trade with the East African coast. Engaruka's population exceeded 5,000 people in seven villages on a hilltop above the complex maze of irrigation fields (Sutton 1998). Similarly, Kasigau, located 150 km from the coast, an important stop on trade routes, likely served as a collecting and distributing center (Wakefield 1870) of diverse trade items—ivory (raw and cut), iron bloom, rhinoceros horn, rock crystals, poison, bows and arrows, hides and skins, honey and beeswax, milk, butter, buttermilk, and other animal products. The trade items desired by the peoples in Kasigau were beaded products, cloth (both South Asian textiles and Swahili), marine shells, ostrich eggshell, and glass beads (Kusimba 2004; Kusimba and Kusimba 2001, 2005; Kusimba et al. 2005).

Table 12.1. The Nature of Trade Items through Time between the Hinterland, the Coast, and Overseas

Time	Hinterland–Coast	Coast–Hinterland	Coast–Overseas	Overseas–Coast
1750–1900	Raw ivory, slaves, rhino horn, animal skins, gum Arabic, rock crystal	Grains, iron tools, guns for hunting, imported cloth	Cut and raw ivory, slaves, rhino horn, animal skins, gum Arabic, rock crystal	Prestige goods (ceramics, crafts), iron and steel tools, guns, cloth for direct use, grains, cereals, cattle
1650–1750	Raw ivory, animal skins, rhino horn, slaves, gum Arabic, rock crystal	Grains, iron tools, dried fish, imported cloth, beads and beadwork, marine products	Cut ivory, animal skins, timber, gold, slaves, rock crystal, gum Arabic	Prestige goods (ceramics, crafts), iron and steel tools, cloth for direct use, grains, cereals, cattle
1550–1650	Raw ivory, iron bloom, animal skins, rhino horn, slaves, gum Arabic, rock crystal	Grains, iron tools, dried fish, local and imported cloth, beads and beadwork, marine products	Cut and worked ivory, animal skins, timber, gold, slaves, rock crystal, gum Arabic	Prestige goods (ceramics, crafts), iron and steel tools, monochrome and colored cloth for reweaving, grains, cereals
pre-1550	Iron bloom, animal skins, rhino horn, cut and raw ivory, slaves, gum Arabic, rock crystal	Grains, iron tools, dried fish, local cloth, beads and beadwork, marine products	Iron bloom, wootz steel, cut and worked ivory, processed animal skins, cut timber, gold, slaves, rock crystal, gum Arabic	Prestige goods (ceramics, crafts), iron and steel tools, monochrome and colored cloth for reweaving, grains, cereals

Archaeological surveys in the Kasigau have located more than 250 sites. We have mapped and extensively excavated eight, including a terrace and an iron-smelting site. Excavations at Kirongwe turned up evidence for intensive iron production spanning 800 years. The volumes of slag demonstrate that the most intensive iron smelting occurred during the deposition of these levels, dating from AD 700 to AD 1380, a time when urban growth was intensifying on the coast (Kusimba et al. 2005).

Iron was an important craft and exchange item. Kirongwe's iron was probably used in the manufacture of household and farm implements, as well as weapons used primarily for hunting and, therefore, meeting the demand for hinterland items from the coast. Iron accelerated intensification in terrace farming and livestock husbandry in the hinterland (Kusimba and Kusimba 2001, 2005) and enabled people to kill elephants, whose ivory was in high demand in Eurasia. This early demand for ivory was conducted largely by peripatetics such as the Waata and Okiek hunters, who had patron–client relationships with the more dominant pastoralists, who in turn supplied ivory to the coastal trading partners (S. Kusimba 2003).

City hinterland relationships in East Africa before AD 1500 were more inclusive, more accommodating, and less coercive. The period between AD 1500 and AD 1900 was characterized by warfare and the slave trade, which combined to undercut the trading networks that had developed earlier (Kusimba 2004). By the eighteenth century, many towns and cities were abandoned because of the failure to withstand international competition and conquest (see table 12.1).

Great Zimbabwe

Southeastern Africa saw the development of at least five successive polities on the Zambezi plateau that were based on trade and supported by a close relationship with agriculturally rich hinterlands (Pikirayi 2001). Elites traded cattle for gold and passed it on to coastal traders at Sofala and other entrepôts and in return received cloth, glass beads, and Asian ceramics. Copper was also traded, beginning in the fourteenth century AD. An early city at Mapungubwe was eventually eclipsed by Great Zimbabwe, the largest of the pre-colonial Zambezi states. Chivowa and Gumanye Hills were among the first areas of settlement in the tenth century AD (Sinclair 1987). By the twelfth century, control of Indian Ocean trade shows up in imported goods and dry masonry architecture, which became even more significant in the subsequent centuries as Great Zimbabwe became an urban complex and the center of a state (figure 12.6).

Great Zimbabwe's elites controlled coast-bound trade in gold, ivory, and, later, copper by taxing traffic through their territories. The regional economy's basis, however, was vast herds of cattle, kept for meat and milk but also as a form of wealth, distributed to the hinterland in exchange for tradable luxuries and as a means of forging alliances. Zimbabwe was the locus of the butchering and social distribution of cattle meat, which probably accompanied feasting.

The city of Great Zimbabwe, covering 720 ha, was one of the largest in sub-Saharan Africa (Sinclair et al. 1993). A perimeter wall enclosed two stone features, the Hill Complex and Great Enclosure, both encircled by a large perimeter wall (figure 12.7). Outside these elite residences lived 11,000–18,000 people, doubtless commoners or vassals of the elites. Significant evidence of ritual is found in elite residences of the Hill Complex, including six soapstone birds distinctive to this site. Spatial segregation, stone architecture, and the prominence of the Zimbabwe Hill were all meant to establish and separate elite spaces and elite decision making.

The extent of the Great Zimbabwe state has been estimated at 50,000 sq km, including much of the Save river system of south-central Zimbabwe, which was a major coastal conduit to the port of Sofala. This hinterland is dotted with stone ruins, home to vassals that controlled distinct territories and exchanged gold for cattle, cloth, and beads with the kings of Zimbabwe.

Great Zimbabwe was but one of the chiefdoms cycling into states in southeastern

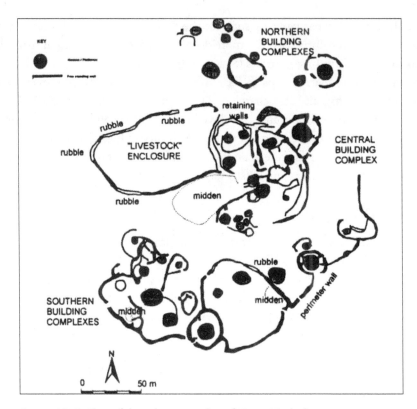

Figure 12.6. Plan of the urban complex of Great Zimbabwe.

Africa between AD 1100 and 1600, beginning with Mapungubwe to the south. At Torwa and Khami, 300 km away, stone compounds built from the beginning of the fourteenth century eventually expanded to rival and challenge Great Zimbabwe and began to manage coastal trade. These later, smaller states were the breakdown product after the Great Zimbabwe state collapsed. Great Zimbabwe thus repeats a common theme of collapse at polities by fissioning at the margins, followed by a shift in the locus of power (Pikirayi 2001).

Discussion and Conclusions

From the archaeological evidence, large quantities of Islamic and Chinese ceramics and beads occur at coastal cities such as Shanga, Mtwapa, Kilwa, and Manda and at hinterland cities such as Mutapa and Great Zimbabwe, supporting the notion that trade played a crucial role in the development of cities in eastern and southern Africa (Pwiti 2005; Sinclair and Hakansson 2000). The analyses further indicate that the economic and social interaction among disparate groups, who made their living from hunting, herding, farming, and iron working, laid the firm foundation from which international trade-exchange systems interlocked. By the end of the first millennium AD, the East African coast and southeast Africa had become regular partners in the millennium-old

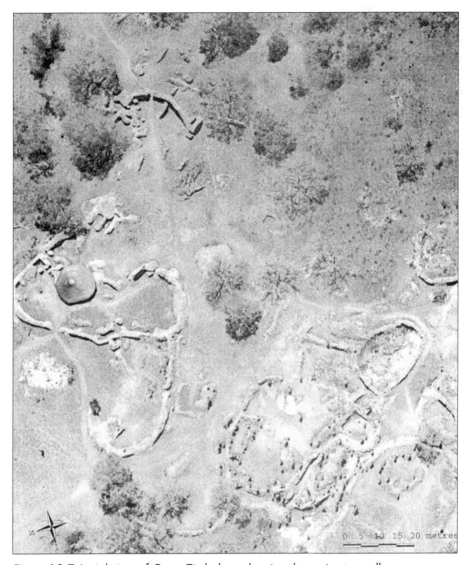

Figure 12.7 Aerial view of Great Zimbabwe showing the perimeter wall.

long-distance exchanges that reached as far as the Arabian Peninsula, India, Sri Lanka, and China (Kusimba 1999a; Pearson 1998).

Innovations in ironworking aided agricultural intensification and specialization in hunting, fishing, and herding. These changes improved the quality of life, precipitated population growth, and created economic prosperity that culminated in the flourishing of urbanism in the region. In the late fifteenth century, however, Africa became embroiled in a violent encounter with Europe (which has not ended); details are best known by history, not archaeology. Hence began the slow but steady decline in African cities and hinterlands, visible even today.

In conclusion, recent research on urbanism in Africa has shown unequivocally that Africans built most preindustrial cities and that indigenous African initiatives were dominant at each stage of their growth (Holl 1985, 2003, personal communication 2003; Kusimba 1999a; McIntosh 1998; Pikirayi 2001). However, those cities that survived longest were those which became major centers of regional and international trade (Allen 1993; Anderson and Rathbone 2000; O'Connor 1983:31; Pearson 1998). Some African cities thrived as capitals of empires, others partly as religious centers, and others as terminals in long-distance trade—trans-Saharan, Indian Ocean, and trans-Atlantic—(Curtin 1984; Pearson 1998; Ringrose 2001; Thornton 1992). African cities show much cultural continuity with the surrounding rural area, although they always housed distinct elite (Allen 1993; Middleton 1992, 2004; O'Connor 1983:32). In this sense, African cities were in many ways similar to other cities worldwide (Marcus 2000 [1983b]) and were easily recognized as such by Arab and European visitors.

thirteen
Pomp and Circumstance before Belize
*Ancient Maya Commerce
and the New River Conurbation*

K. Anne Pyburn

In this chapter, I consider commercialism as a stimulus to the development of ancient Maya cities. I shift focus from production and prestige economy, which have been the subject of much archaeological research and theorizing, to consumption by ordinary households, which is less often discussed. I do not propose consumerism as a prime mover for the rise of cities, nor do I visualize ancient Maya traders as canoe-borne capitalists. I do propose that consumer culture is not exclusively a product of modern capitalism, though some researchers disagree (Campbell 1987; McCracken 1988), and that certain archaeological patterns suggest that a healthy trade in commodities contributed to Maya urbanism.

Urban Maya

Although mounds left behind by Maya houses are evenly distributed over Maya settlements, this even spread rarely represents the configuration of any single period but is accumulated from the construction (and destruction) of houses occupied and abandoned throughout the life of a city. When careful chronology is applied to house remains including those not represented by mounds, some sites show a more uneven distribution and an increased nucleation of houses (and probably population) over time (Pyburn et al. 1998). Because households are not corporate groups, but economic units that vary in composition and residence pattern across both time and space (Netting

1993; Wilk 1988), house remains do not directly reflect functioning households, which makes archaeological reconstructions of changes in ancient Maya population density extremely speculative. Because most early urban centers in other parts of the world were not as densely populated as archaeologists once thought (Hansen 2000a, 2000b; Sjoberg 1960; M E. Smith 2004; M. L. Smith 2003c; Trigger 2003; Yoffee 2005), calculations of absolute density command less attention.

Abundant data, particularly on site-size hierarchies and multifunctionality, have demonstrated that Maya cities, towns, and villages were linked economically and through a range of sociopolitical and cultural ties. The weight of Polanyi's "dogmatic misconceptions" (Trigger 2003:59) has been lifted, and archaeologists no longer automatically accept that in pre-capitalist cities the economy was subsumed by the political structure, that reciprocity and redistribution are on the primitive side of an impenetrable barrier that divides pre-capitalism from capitalism, or that non-capitalist economies are fundamentally different (Masson 2002a; M. E. Smith 2004; M. L. Smith 1999; Trigger 2003; Wilk 1996; Yoffee 2005). A spate of new work revisiting the familiar idea that ancient Maya cities were linked through commercial systems (Rathje 1971, 1975; Renfrew 1975; Sabloff 1975; Sabloff and Freidel 1975; Sabloff and Lamberg-Karlovsky 1975; Sabloff and Rathje 1975) has again opened up new and better ways of understanding archaeological data (Marcus 1995b, 2003a; Masson and Freidel 2002; Rathje 2002; Sabloff 2004, 2007).

Tracing the interrelations among states by documenting the volume and flow of various commodities has led us away from the expectation that early states were invariably territorial (Charlton and Nichols 1997; Trigger 2003) or macro-states (Hansen 2000a) that subsumed multiple urban centers in an integrated political economy. Hansen's concept of "city-state culture" (2000a:16), composed of multiple self-governing but not self-sufficient cities that are economically specialized but still primarily agrarian, has gained footing (M. E. Smith 2004; M. L. Smith 2003c; Trigger 2003; Yoffee 2005) as cross-culturally valid and testable.

The city-state culture model, echoing theories of peer-polity interaction (Renfrew and Cherry 1986; Sabloff 1986), renews the focus on the role of interdependent commercialism among similar communities in the rise of cities (Flannery 1968; Rathje 1972, 1975; Sabloff 1977; Sabloff and Rathje 1975). Archaeologists often characterize the Maya economy as lacking full-time commercial specialists except those who were "attached" to elite patrons (Freidel and Schele 1984; Webster 2001; Yaeger 2003). Along with the red herring of absolute population density, this presumed lack of commercial specialists has been one of the most consistent points of contrast between the Maya and other early urban cultures (see Masson 2002a for an excellent summary). As it turns out, most early cities had few full-time specialists (Skinner 1977:277; M. E. Smith 2004:83), but many did have attached, as well as semi-independent, semi-specialized producers. Specialist workshops were probably exceptional everywhere (Costin and Hagstrum 1995; M. E. Smith 2004) and not crucial for commerce, which can include multiple variations of barter, trade, and exchange.

Clearly, although all cities have some things in common, many types of settlement can be included in this term. Past models that characterized cities as resulting from a particular evolutionary trajectory and performing specific functions in a standardized social and cultural framework have been overturned by identification of the very wide range of urban forms and functions that exist even within a single culture (Marcus 1989, 1993, 1998). It may even be true in some cases that the variation between contemporary cities provides the interaction and tension required to develop and sustain them (Hansen 2000a).

The recognition that there were multiple types of cities and many interacting states means that regional analysis is key to understanding the functioning of cities, but the fact that interrelationships among polities are flexible and complex makes it difficult to determine which "region" is relevant or large enough to document all interaction and interrelationships. I think that this is especially problematic for the Maya. First of all, the boundaries of the regions that define Maya cities are not merely geographical; they are ideological, economic, political, and social (Ashmore 1989; Ashmore and Sabloff 2002, 2003; Ball 1993; Marcus 1974, 1976, 1983b, 1993, 1998, 2000[1983b], 2003a) and may be impossible to document and are thus invisible to archaeologists. This is a point Marcus (1984) has made in her discussion of the cosmological significance of the distribution of Maya cities. To some extent, regions create cities (Hansen 2000a; Trigger 2003; Yoffee 2005), but cities also create and define their regions: for example, a city can have a cosmological locus that is not geographically "accurate" (Ashmore and Sabloff 2002; Marcus 1983b, 1984, 1993).

A city can also have an economically or politically important relationship with a distant city or region (Marcus 1993). The assumption that transport costs precluded the exchange of subsistence goods applies only to some Maya cities because certainly those located on arterial rivers could have depended on bulk transport of corn or other subsistence items. In fact, riverine transport might create a tighter link between cities than proximity if the nearer city must be reached overland or through inhospitable territory. Commercialization is a means of buffering the periodic local shortfalls that face all farmers via access to nonlocal resources; the desirability of connections across resource zones is obvious. Such connections might also be brought to bear on conflicts between neighboring cities.

Archaeologists and others have considered these sorts of interrelationships as evidence of ancient-world systems (Gunder-Frank and Gills 1993; Hall and Chase-Dunn 1993; Upham 1990; Wallerstein 1977), but it is possible for external influences to be significant and even generative without being systematic. Individual agency, especially among political figures (Flannery 1999), historical events, such as the conquest of the New World (Wolf 1982), and environmental catastrophes, which, contrary to the assumptions of prime-mover models (Gill 2001), are likely to have unpredictable and varied results at a micro-environmental level (Pyburn 1998), all regularly influence early states. Such factors have systemic consequences, but individuals and unique events are not systems, though archaeological recognition of the distinction can be difficult. Galactic polities, interaction spheres, and core buffers are difficult to disprove; arguments identifying them tend to become circular.

Archaeologists identify "basic needs" as basic because they were widely traded—and widely traded because they were basic (Rathje 1972, 1975). Obsidian is useful, but people will not die without it, nor would the demise of obsidian trade have destroyed Maya civilization. The same is true of hard stone; I have seen plenty of teeth from Classic-period Maya people who made do without it. Salt is more crucial, but very few populations were demonstrably unable to provision themselves (Marcus 1983a:477). As it happens, there appears to have been a variety of types of salt (Andrews and Mock 2002; Dahlin and Ardren 2002; Dillon et al. 1988; Kepecs 1999; Masson 2002b; McKillop 2002, 2005; Nance 1992) and probably regional, ethnic, or even personal preferences, as was the case for salt trade in other parts of the ancient world.

Elites and Production

Despite Polanyi's (1944, 1957) current unpopularity amongst anthropologists (but see Halperin 1994 for a holdout), many archaeologists still recognize a split between prestige economy and market economy. Conventionally, Mayanists argue that people settle on land best suited to their needs (McAnany 1995:110) but then fall under the sway of elites, who squeeze them for support by forcing them to produce surpluses and tribute through intensification and specialization (Chase and Chase 1996; Foias 2002). The goal of the elites is to control surplus production to aggrandize themselves both at home and abroad. Access to nonlocal resources is important for the establishment and maintenance of elite status. Some archaeologists have proposed that prestige and market economies coexisted in parallel universes (Abrams 1994; Feldman 1985; Foias 2002; McAnany 1993), but this might be a false dichotomy (Inomata 2001). Certainly, cities and states will have to be evaluated individually for evidence of how separate or interrelated were various strands of their economies.

The idea of a two-tiered economy of elite trade in ritual or symbolic commodities and household trade in "needs" (Trigger 2003:404) is fueled by the idea that elites supported full-time specialists only to provide material reification of their status. This suggests a closed system, in which people turn a blind eye to obvious commercial opportunities. The empirical difficulty with this proposition is that, although Maya prestige goods show up in prestigious contexts (not all these arguments are circular), examples of nearly all prestige goods also show up in ordinary burials and houses (West 2002). Even if this distribution began as the result of elite-controlled redistribution (Masson 2002a), it is still the case that ordinary people had high-status goods, which they themselves could "redistribute." This access to high-status goods undermines the idea that prestige goods served to aggrandize only elites and reify an absolute difference between elites and everyone else. A more convincing argument that better fits the archaeological data on Maya commodities would be that elites had better quality, and a larger quantity, of goods that everybody wanted and that aggrandizement served the elite by allowing them to define and advertise the most desirable goods.

I am unconvinced that elites controlled very much production because there would be so much effort involved that there would be little point in being elite. If elite control is taken to mean that the elite were actually the producers (Foias 2002:229; McAnany 1993; McAnany et al. 2002), most types of unmechanized production require investment and coordination of a significant amount of labor. Elizabeth Graham has pointed out:

> If elites painted polychromes, they also needed body clays, slip clays, paints, brushes, holders, resins, cleaners, paper for designs, mineral pigments, stands, wooden rollers, tempers, kilns, firewood, and sponges, not to mention help in preparing surfaces, preparing ingredients, stoking fires, regulating airflow, getting lunch on time, settling clays, toting water, ordering supplies, keeping track of transactions, training and feeding apprentices, and cleaning up the mess at the end of the production day. [Graham 2002:414]

According to Trigger, elites in all early civilizations "controlled a disproportionate amount of the wealth of their societies, avoided physical labor, enjoyed an opulent lifestyle, and indulged in conspicuous consumption" (Trigger 2003:153). But (with apologies to Marx) controlling wealth does not require control of production. A prestige-economy model does not explain the complexity of the archaeological record of the Maya, either in the variety or in the distribution of commodities (Masson 2002b; West 2002).

In addition to requiring considerable administration and non-elite labor, control of production is difficult and inefficient. As Janusek (2002) has pointed out, the diversity of interest groups may be both the foundation of urban life and a threat to it. Thinking from the archaeological record has given us an impoverished idea of pre-industrial specializations. In the cities in late imperial China, where 80 percent of the residents were farmers and specialists were mostly part-time (Skinner 1977:265), there was an immense variety of specializations, including various types of musicians, diviners, messengers, gamblers, traders, charlatans, pettifoggers, and scribes, most of whose efforts would be archaeologically invisible. In these cities, the residences of crafts and trades people of many specialties were intermingled with residences of their wealthy patrons and merchants. Because all production took place within households whose economy was primarily agrarian (both elite and non-elite), very small amounts of evidence of this sort of production would be detectable in midden and activity areas. Associations between producers, such as guilds, were formed precisely because their dispersed members had little physical contact. Undoubtedly, late imperial China had some of the most commercialized of all pre-industrial cities, so this example shows the archaeological invisibility of specialists even when prevalent. Early cities would not need many practitioners of each specialty; usually one or two in each craft would be sufficient. Control of such diversity could be difficult.

Elites who are supported by landholdings have administrative problems. Life is often better and more interesting for the upper classes in large urban centers, where there is more access to commodities and where they can curry favor with other elites (Skinner 1977; Trigger 2003). Finding someone reliable and trustworthy to watch over their rural estates without slacking or skimming was difficult. Japanese history is replete with examples of complications arising from this situation (Sansom 1963); usually family members are drafted for the job, but even sons and daughters can be treacherous.

I see producers' private ownership of land as an important early stimulus to urbanism and elites, as more inspirational than omnipotent. This is completely compatible with the probability that some elites in early cities were supported by controlling production on their estates as absentee landlords and by production from collectively owned or institutional land (Trigger 2003:662; Yoffee 2005). However, cross-cultural data overwhelmingly indicate that small family farms are much more efficient producers than collectives, sharecroppers, or coerced labor for estates. Profit motives of landowning families, combined with their micro-environmentally specific knowledge, make for levels of productivity with which no communal or coercive authority can compete (Netting 1993). Considering the small proportion of a city that had any sort of special status—less than 20 percent (Trigger 2003:155)—the mechanism for forced production on a significant scale is difficult to envision. There is no evidence that the Maya had the elaborate administrative hierarchies or standing armies used in Chinese, Inka, or Mexican cities; pomp and circumstance hardly seem sufficient to create a Foucaultian (Foucault 1995) internalized hegemonic ideology (Demarest 1992; Houston et al. 2003). The distribution of trade goods may indicate, as Freidel (1981) and West (2002) have suggested, that elites controlled distribution, but how did they do it? Household middens at most Maya sites contain evidence of at least a few luxury goods. How did elites profit from the purchasing power of smallholders who had everything they needed? Why do smallholders buy things they do not need? How do elites gain political and economic power and hold on to it by controlling the distribution of non-essential goods? The answer is that they define needs and do everything they can to inspire and orchestrate *consumption*. Elite displays of exotic or manufactured consumer goods serve to foment "need" and emulation by non-elites.

Smallholders, Peasants, and Production

Overemphasis on elite control of production stems from a misunderstanding of how most agrarian households function. Certainly, several types of land tenure and various methods of food production were operating among ancient Maya communities, including corporately held village lands, share cropping, wealthy estates, and so on. However, understanding the very efficient production strategies of *smallholders*, individual farming households working on hereditary land (Netting 1993), is key to understanding Maya urbanism. Smallholders improve their land to intensify production, thereby making less land produce more and enabling populations to live closer together. Smallholders form communal workgroups to help one another during brief periods, adding another layer of logic to their tendency to cluster. Investment increases the value of land, so families become place-bound even in situations where unimproved land is not scarce (thereby answering Trigger's [2003] question about why the Maya did not occupy more territory than they did).

Netting came up with the concept of smallholders in contradistinction to the Marxist evolutionary model developed by Chayanov (1966 [1925]). Netting collected his data from the Alpine Swiss and the Nigerian Kofyar, where he expected to find peasants laboring just enough to meet the subsistence needs of their lineages and the disruptive external demands resulting from their incorporation into the market economy of the modern world system. Instead, he found that the unit of economic organization was the household, not the lineage, and that market participation was long-standing (traditional) and motivated at the household level. In both cultures, the social unit of consumption and production, the household, was not defined by kinship; instead, he found kin relations generated and defined by the ownership and divisibility of resources and land. The Kofyar say, "Our parents are the people who feed us."

Although Netting worked with extant cultures, he saw a major part of the difficulty with Marxist models resulting from assumptions about a primordial system, similarly assumed by Sahlins (1972), which was interrupted and turned into a system of peasant exploitation by the rise of class-based society. Though Netting agreed that farmers are often exploited, he found that exploitation and external pressure were not prerequisites of intensive agriculture, nor did he find intensification exclusively the outcome of population growth. Instead, he found farmers voluntarily diversifying and intensifying their production for reasons of their own, such as the maximization of profits, hedging against inflation and poor harvests, long-term sustainability, permanent residence, and increasing the quality of life.

Netting (1993:7) argued that evolutionary models "pigeonholed farmers by contrasting technologies," relegating systems with simpler tools, fragmented fields, greater labor input, and "pre-scientific knowledge" into an earlier and lower category of subsistence. He felt that this reified false contrasts because the comparison between mechanized and unmechanized farming failed to account for the difference in productivity possible with different types of land and technology. Mechanization on Alpine farms, for example, would simply not allow the intensity of production that Swiss smallholders generate: the amount of hours of labor per unit of land might fall with mechanization, but the hours *per unit of production* would actually rise.

Similarly, production on a scale beyond the capacity of smallholders, such as the working of huge estates by slaves or laborers, could never be as efficient or as productive in terms of hours of labor per unit of production as a more fragmented and more autonomous smallholder strategy. Seasonal and micro-zonal variation can be handled more reliably with local strategies, and people will agree to a greater degree of effort within their households if the profits will ultimately be their own. Land improvements and maintenance are more reliably and cheaply accomplished by a skilled workforce that will inherit the benefits of its own efforts, than by slaves or micromanaged labor. This argument is not only logical; Netting collected convincing empirical data to support it. The key, he believed, was land: land rights, land ownership, land value, and land improvability.

The Chayanovian model, which is most familiar to archaeologists, was based on peasant farmers living in an environment where land was not scarce (the Russian

Steppe) and where the improvement of fields was not possible. Steppe requires little clearing, and draft animals were available to break up the soil. The steppe climate is such that no amount of improvement will allow more than one crop per year, because the growing season is determined by long, cold winters. In contrast, the Kofyar and the Swiss work a circumscribed amount of land that repays investment. This means that rather than deplete the land, as with extensive swidden, land use over time requires improvements and maintenance that actually increase its productivity and value. This may mean more than one crop per year, which is tantamount to increasing or even doubling the amount of available land. Land value is related less to ease of exploitation than to improvability and to attachment to place. Stone, Netting, and Stone (1990) describe a situation in which Kofyar moved into an uninhabited area and farmed in a much more extensive way than they had in their previous overcrowded context. But within a few years of their move, the repayment of obligations and the integration of their society through the formation of task groups stimulated them to reestablish intensive strategies that allowed them to continue normal relations with the relatives and friends they had left behind. Social structure had a self-perpetuating effect on subsistence strategy by encouraging intensification, land improvements, and an attachment to place. Perpetual reuse of house sites and long sequences of burial and reburial in house floors convincingly argue that Maya householders felt a similarly strong attachment to place (McAnany 1993) as do people in many parts of the world (Goody 1962).

Smallholders have three particularly important characteristics that relate to the origin of cities. Foremost is that they *love* surpluses. Agriculture is never a safe enterprise, and any sort of cushion is desirable, so smallholders voluntarily produce as much as they can. Of course, many factors affect how much this will be, including the health and composition of any household, unpredictable weather, and the choice of crops, which may vary from year to year. But as long as smallholders control their own productivity and benefit from it, they will produce as much surplus as is feasible. Such farmers produce much more, in fact, than farmers working for a community or for an absentee landlord, because being forced to produce a surplus for a landlord offers limited benefit and can set a taxation standard impossible to sustain in all years.

There are other ways to create an economic cushion, and smallholders also love to diversify: any household with sufficient labor will add crafts to food production or acquire specialized skills to accumulate resources and stimulate reciprocal obligations among producers. Availability of extra hands is the only requirement for specialization. Weaving, pottery making, tool making, midwifery, necromancy, and so on, are all strategies of accumulation of either real wealth or social indebtedness that mitigate the effects of bad weather, family tragedy, political upheaval, and crop failure that plague all agricultural communities. No coercion is involved, except perhaps between family members, in order for craft production to emerge. But, obviously, there is a limit to how much diversification can cushion one household among many, all subject to the same pressures. If everybody's crop succumbs to drought, the fact that one neighbor owes another a bushel of corn makes little difference, and nobody will be interested in ready-made pots. So smallholders love markets. They go great distances to reach them, and there is even some indication that they can create them (Netting 1993). Elites do not need to control or force surplus production of foods or crafts: there are more efficient ways to profit.

Although Netting (1993) saw smallholding as a robust cross-cultural pattern, he did not see smallholding as an evolutionary stage, and he was not interested in explaining social change. His data showed that smallholders exist today within the world system in cultures that have been called tribes and chiefdoms, as well as those characterized as states. Smallholders in all sociopolitical contexts endure household fortunes that oscillate dramatically from generation to generation. His longitudinal study documented that a smallholding economy was stable and did not produce hereditary elites, because no household was ever able to sustain an economic advantage beyond a single generation. But under the conditions of social life at the start of urbanism, efficient, productive, concentrated, and vulnerably place-bound smallholders seem like an excellent foundation, and a perfect fertilizer, for a city. Urbanism may involve elite control of production but surely also results from elites reaping the benefits of smallholder enthusiasm for surpluses, diversification, and markets by stimulating consumption. In my conclusions, I discuss how this was done, but first I will show how this argument applies to archaeological data.

Chau Hiix, Altun Ha, and Lamanai:
A conurbation on the New River

Maya speakers settled three communities between New River Lagoon and the Caribbean Ocean during the Preclassic period in what is today north-central Belize. The three communities—Lamanai, Altun Ha, and Chau Hiix—are geographically contiguous and historically and politically interrelated, so I have chosen to call their territory a *conurbation*, which refers to a number of cities or towns that form one continuous settlement area (figure 13.1). Areas of the New River Conurbation that have no evidence of settlement are inhospitable environments or places where site formation processes conceal and destroy archaeological remains. Comparison of the history and interrelations of these three settlements offers some compelling arguments for the significance of smallholders and commerce to the development of cities.

Chau Hiix, the site of my own research for the past fifteen years, lies slightly to the southwest of the center point of a straight line drawn across the 40 km of territory between the monumental centers of Altun Ha and Lamanai. The three sites are at different stages of investigation and reporting. Altun Ha is the most completely reported of the three (Pendergast 1979, 1982, 1984, 1990, 1992, 1998). Lamanai, having been under investigation and published widely since the 1970s, is also well known. Chau Hiix was discovered only in 1989 (Pyburn 1991) but has been continuously researched since then and has appeared in a variety of publications (Pyburn 1996, 1997, 1998, 2003, 2004, 2005) and theses (Andres 2000, 2005; Cook 1997; Cuddy 2000; Goldsmith 2004; Meier 2003; Metcalfe 2005; Sweely 1996, 2005; Wille 2007; Wrobel 2004).

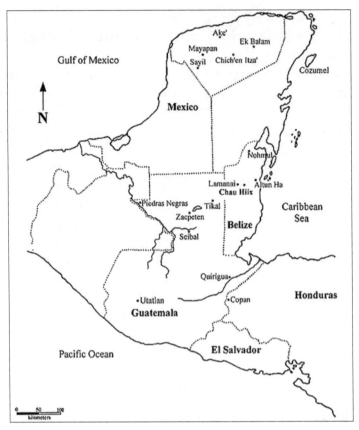

Figure 13.1. Map of the Maya lowlands.

Despite their proximity and obvious connection, the three settlements have distinct archaeological patterns and historical trajectories. Although all three were settled in the Preclassic period, Lamanai—the westernmost city—was still occupied during the Spanish Conquest, and its history includes a Spanish church (Graham 2004; Pendergast 1991, 1993). Chau Hiix, the smallest settlement, also lasted into the Spanish Conquest. In contrast, Altun Ha was depopulated after the ninth century AD (Pendergast 1979), a period of Maya history that has long fascinated archaeologists (Sabloff 1992, 1994; Wilk 1985).

Lamanai (Submerged Crocodile) (figure 13.2), some 40 km from Altun Ha and 15 km from Chau Hiix, is situated on the western edge of New River Lagoon, with immediate access to the New River's arterial connection to the ocean and the Petén. Settlement is aligned with the lagoon edge, and all the plaza groups in the urban core are aligned north-south (Pendergast 1992). Lamanai is by far the largest of the three cities; the nine courtyards (Adams and Jones 1981) in its monumental core cover more area (1.5 km) and contain larger buildings than exist at either Altun Ha or Chau Hiix. The known settlement of Lamanai covers 4.5 km, encompassing 720 structures, though house mounds are rarely absent where land types permit farming.

Despite their consistent north-south orientation, plaza distribution in the site cen-

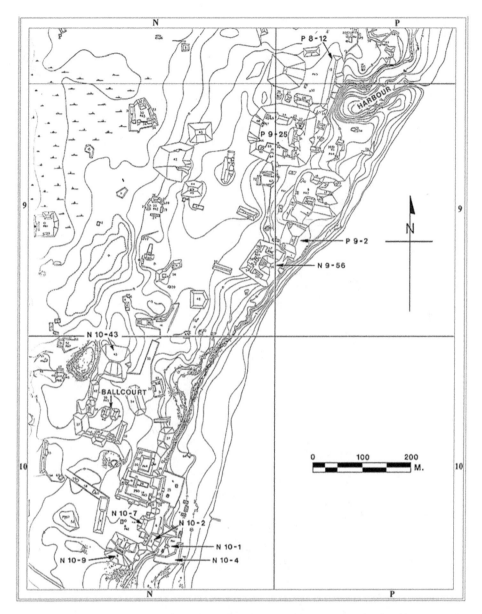

Figure 13.2. Lamanai: map of the central settlement area showing the final layout and the number designations of the main buildings. Contour interval is 1 meter (after Pendergast 1981:33, figure 3).

ter seems to follow no preexisting plan (Pendergast 1992). The settlement appears to have developed haphazardly by accretion rather than according to an urban plan. Similarly, the distribution of settlement outside the center follows no recognizable pattern. Soils in this locus are some of the finest in northern Belize (Wright et al. 1959), and there is evidence that wetlands along the river were modified for agricultural use (Pendergast, personal communication, 1991).

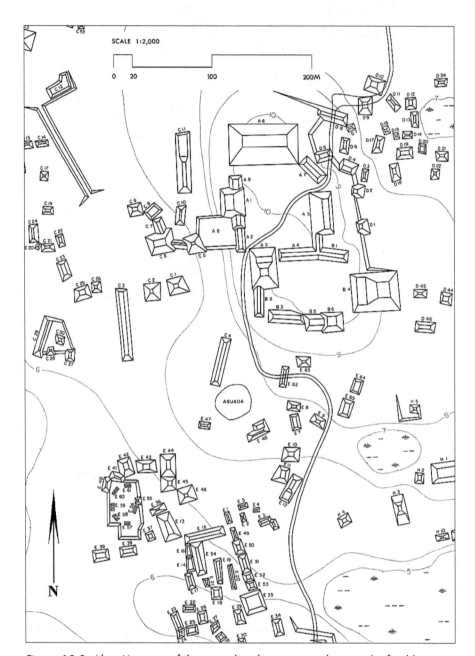

Figure 13.3. Altun Ha: map of the central settlement area showing the final layout and the number designations of the main buildings (excerpted from Pendergast 1979: Altun Ha base map, map 2).

Altun Ha (Rock Stone Pond; figure 13.3) lies 25 km east of Chau Hiix, 12 km west of the Caribbean Ocean, and 8.3 km from Midwinter Lagoon, the nearest standing freshwater source. Although characterized as "effectively coastal" (Pendergast 1979), Altun Ha's location suggests a compromise between access to waterborne trade, which would have required a significant (though reasonable) hike, and protection from

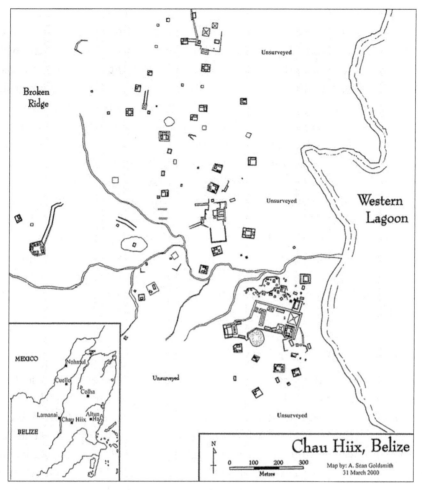

Figure 13.4. Chau Hiix: map of the central settlement area showing the final layout of the main buildings (map by A. S. Goldsmith).

ocean-transported marauders and weather. Unlike other members of the conurbation, Altun Ha has no watercourse to hug; its settlement plan is relatively concentric. The orientation of its monumental buildings is inconsistent, but their layout appears to be more planned than that of Lamanai. In all standard measures of site size, Altun Ha is second to Lamanai, with five courtyards in its site core covering only half a kilometer (Andres 2005; Pendergast 1984). Though large and ornate, none of Altun Ha's buildings are as massive as the great structures of central Lamanai.

Altun Ha's known settlement area is estimated at 2.33 km, encompassing 516 structures in an unplanned distribution. Though considerably larger in almost all respects than Chau Hiix, Altun Ha has less high-quality arable land directly associated with its settlement than does either of its neighbors. It also has no reported evidence of agricultural intensification.

Chau Hiix (*jaguarundi*, figure 13.4) settlement follows the western shore of a seasonal watercourse known as Western Lagoon, which is fed by Spanish Creek, giving its residents New River access to waterborne traffic passing Lamanai. The importance of this connection is demonstrated by enormous dams and canals dug during the Classic period to create a year-round channel to Spanish Creek. Although the settlement parallels the north-south line of the lagoon, both plazas in the site center are oriented east-west (Andres 2005). The site center covers only .2 km, and though the known site area is now at 2.5 km, slightly larger than Altun Ha, the structure count to date is at 375, making Chau Hiix undeniably the smallest city in the New River Conurbation.

Nevertheless, Chau Hiix has immediate access to the best (and the most) agricultural land of the three communities (Pyburn 2003, 2005; Wright et al. 1959). It also has abundant evidence of raised-bed terraces west of site center (Cuddy 2000; Goldsmith 2004), suggesting intensification through water control and fertility management as documented at other Belize sites (Scarborough et al. 1995). Further, the canals and dams that modified the hydrology of Western Lagoon (Andres and Pyburn 2004; Pyburn 2003) improved both access to trade routes and agricultural production; Chau Hiix has significant evidence of drained, raised, and possibly island fields. Its hydrological modifications may have made it possible to grow two crops per year (Pyburn 2004).

Consumption at Chau Hiix

Chau Hiix's access to trade routes allowed residents to consume the usual suite of exotic goods, including small amounts of pearls, hematite mirrors, and carved slate, jadeite, and *Spondylus* shell. In terms of locally available resources, Chau Hiix appears to have had everything essential, which may explain why the site was settled as early as any known Maya community. Chert, though not particularly high quality but certainly adequate for making any sort of tool, is so abundant in the natural substrate that the monumental structures of the site are built from chalcedony boulders. Local clays are suitable for making pottery; experiments by my students have achieved reasonable success with little attention to temper or firing.

Requirements for intensive and sustainable agriculture were more than met. Reliable water from natural springs, rivers, and the seasonal lagoon was supplemented by a system of reservoirs designed to catch runoff from the main platform. Smaller reservoirs appear to be scattered among the agricultural terraces west of the site center, seasonal water shortages to accommodate (Cuddy 2000; Goldsmith 2004). In addition to excellent local soils suitable for intensified agriculture through terracing, modifications to the adjacent lagoon and river system provided still more control of water resources and made it possible to produce an even greater agricultural surplus (Pyburn 2003).

This same system also brought water transport directly to the site entrance and connected Chau Hiix to an inland water route between the central Petén and the Belize Valley that passes by Lamanai. The passage is open much of the year but would have been especially easy to navigate (the rivers flow backward) when hurricanes made sea trade risky (Pyburn 2003). Best of all, the entrance to the site on the water would be easy to conceal and defend. The site's main monument (figure 13.5) overlooks this

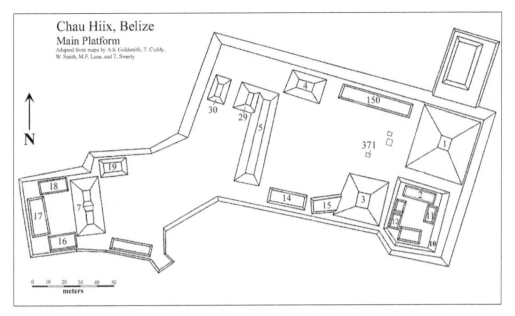

Figure 13.5. Chau Hiix: map of the central platform showing the Terminal to Early Postclassic layout and the number designations of the main buildings.

entrance from a distance of about a kilometer, so unwelcome guests who had managed to get past Lamanai could be spotted and intercepted (Andres and Pyburn 2004; Pyburn 2003). It is possible to see the tallest buildings of Lamanai from the top of Structure 1 at Chau Hiix. A small quantity of Chau Hiix obsidian was sourced in 1997; 9 pieces were from Ixtepeque, 33 were from El Chayal, and a single artifact was from San Martín Jilotepeque.

Despite local abundance, Chau Hiix's consumption patterns suggest dependence on importation of ordinary household goods, not just exotic elite wares, and imply that the settlement was not economically self-sufficient for much of its history. Chau Hiix, literally drowning in chalcedony, is full of imported chert. I have resisted this as nonsense for years, but Beverly Chiarulli, the lithic analyst for the project, has finally convinced me that there are no local sources for the sort of chert used for many finer tools at Chau Hiix. There are expedient flake tools, chunky bifaces, and occasional pressure-flaked masterpieces made of Chau Hiix chalcedony, but a surprising percentage of the assemblage, including that from house mounds, is chert from somewhere besides Chau Hiix. Much of it is the fine-grained banded or honey-colored stone thought to come from Colha, suspected to be a supplier of tools (Hester et al. 1994) and boats (Wilk 1976). We have no complete reduction sequences for Colha-type chert at Chau Hiix (Chiarulli 2006), despite years of screening middens in search of such data.

In addition to imported chert, Chau Hiix residents consumed huge quantities of obsidian. We find it everywhere, all over the ground, in every excavation, in every burial. Tomb 1 was covered with sacks of it (and also with a bushel of flakes of imported honey-colored chert). Tombs 2 and 3 had polyhedral obsidian cores.

Chau Hiix residents also imported quantities of sea shells, especially conch, which they carved into beads, scoops, and decorative plaques. Six of the seven largest plazuela groups nearest the site center yielded evidence of shell carving in the Terminal Classic (Cook 1997). Postclassic surface offerings often include whole conch shells of varying species and sizes.

Chau Hiix residents apparently also purchased ceramics. Chau Hiix has an unusual quantity of blackware pottery. According to the project ceramic analyst, Bob Fry (personal communication, 2003), blackware is so abundant at Chau Hiix that it was almost certainly locally produced, though perhaps not at the household level. Although it has often been suggested that fancy wares were made by specialists and traded or presented to ordinary people by elites, specialist production of plainwares (whether or not local) is less frequently argued and not easy to demonstrate. However, ordinary ceramics were probably not a household product at Chau Hiix, because the variety of plainware shapes and sizes is more limited than we might expect from idiosyncratic production (almost every excavation turns up one of about three to four types of redware bowl, each era having its own set). But more convincing in this regard is the frequency with which ordinary vessels were mended (holes were drilled in adjoining pieces, and the broken pots were tied together). Unfortunately, I cannot say how commonly this mending occurs at Lamanai and Altun Ha, but the practice is relatively uncommon at other Belize sites where I have excavated.

We have kept track of all mend holes found at Chau Hiix and have discovered that blackwares were almost never mended, as we might expect if they were readily available, nor usually were polychromes, which might be prestigious and valuable but perhaps not essential to daily life. What is most surprising is that the redware or even plainware pots have frequently been mended, suggesting that these were harder to replace or do without than either blackwares or polychromes and were not the product of casual and ongoing household production. Mended pots appear in all types of deposit at Chau Hiix, but the greatest quantity of mended pots was discovered in a Terminal Classic "problematic deposit" (Iglesias Ponce de León 2003) that also contained jade beads, modeled vessels, obsidian blades and cores, whole and broken tools, carved bone and shell, and human teeth (Wille 2007).

Buying Power at Lamanai

These consumption patterns do not appear to be unique to Chau Hiix. After digging at Chau Hiix for fifteen years, I cannot quantify the difference, but the magnitude of commodities from caches, burials, and tombs from Lamanai dwarfs the discoveries at Chau Hiix to insignificance. We have a single example of several types of elaborate pottery at Chau Hiix that are known from multiple examples at Lamanai. So far, we have not found anything at Chau Hiix that has not been found (in greater quantity) at Lamanai. Lamanai's material cultural record, in terms of its portable artifacts, easily rivals that of Altun Ha, with the caveat that many of the most dramatic commodities from Lamanai are from the Postclassic, after Altun Ha was depopulated.

Lamanai is, of course, by far the biggest of these three sites. Chau Hiix's site center would probably fit into Structure P 9-25, which is a single courtyard group at Lamanai. I suspect that when settlement areas are better known, Chau Hiix will prove to cover as much territory as either Lamanai or Altun Ha, but its downtown would not have impressed its neighbors. In terms of masks, stelae, architectural volume, and elaborate exotic caches, Lamanai is the clear winner. Not only does it have a ball court, but also the ball-court marker was dedicated over a bowl of mercury (Pendergast 1998). The Chau Hiix ball-court marker is round and flat and had nothing buried under it.

Over time, all three sites became more crowded with buildings, and the individual buildings became more massive. This would occur from simple accretion as architecture was added over time, but because there was no obvious spatial constraint on any of the three centers, there seems to have been some intentional crowding. Andres (2005) has recently shown that during the Terminal Classic the central precincts of all three sites were made less accessible and less visible to casual observers. Enclosure was achieved through the addition of buildings and walls to block open spaces, the filling in of windows and doorways, and the raising of platform height so that the level of occupation was above the ordinary line of sight across the central platform.

Altun Ha: The Cost of Success

Imported goods are similarly common at Altun Ha; in fact, they are more prevalent than at Chau Hiix. It is hard to know what the per capita consumption of exotic or manufactured goods was, because the number of people in each community at any point in time is unknown. Overall, Altun Ha was obviously more prosperous than Chau Hiix; where Chau Hiix has yielded about ten eccentric chert objects from tombs and offerings, Altun Ha excavators have recovered dozens. The abundance of obsidian at Altun Ha includes eccentrics and green obsidian (Pendergast 2003), both unknown at Chau Hiix. Various pieces of carved jade have been recovered from burials at Chau Hiix; the quantity from Altun Ha is probably twenty times greater, including, of course, the 4.42-kilo jade head.

The entire central precinct of Chau Hiix would fit into the 200-m expanse between B6 and A6 at Altun Ha, and Altun Ha has a second courtyard almost as large. To date, Chau Hiix has no architectural masks; Altun Ha does. Interestingly, Chau Hiix does have a ball court; Altun Ha apparently does not.

After its crescendo of construction and wealth display, Altun Ha was depopulated rather rapidly after the ninth century. Lamanai, in contrast, kept right on flaunting its wealth and flourished into the Postclassic, as did Chau Hiix, perhaps by incorporating people moving in (or returning) from other places (Metcalfe 2005; Wrobel 2004).

At Altun Ha, abandonment of monumental buildings was followed by the intentional desecration of four royal tombs, suggesting an "inside job" (Pendergast 1992), and deposition of garbage onto the floors of beautifully vaulted rooms (Pendergast 1982). These buildings were eventually left to collapse on their own. In contrast, vaulted buildings were abandoned at Chau Hiix and Lamanai but were first strewn with offerings and then carefully filled in through their opened vaults so that the room interiors were preserved. The exterior of some of these buildings was buried under a layer of chert boulders, which offered a second layer of protection.

It is tempting to suggest that respectful treatment of ancestral architecture indicates a continuity with the past that averted Postclassic disaster; unfortunately for this scenario, similar infilling and burial of monuments occurred at nearby La Milpa and at Xunantunich and its satellite Minanha (Iannone 2005), all of which were abandoned. Whatever community changes are signified by the burial of buildings, they were not necessarily fatal.

The fate of Altun Ha probably cannot be understood in terms of its immediate neighborhood; otherwise, Chau Hiix and Lamanai would have changed more dramatically. Following Flannery's idea of "hypercoherence" (1972, after Rappaport 1971), I have argued (Pyburn 1998) that the drama at the end of the ninth century AD resulted when the self-governing interdependence that characterized Maya states briefly gave way to larger macro-states, or perhaps a hegemonic state (Marcus 1993; Trigger 2003:113). The widespread changes archaeologists have documented over a wide area of the Maya lowlands, occurring during a short period and including resource shortages, drought, and warfare, were not the causes of political change, for these problems had been dealt with successfully during the preceding centuries. Instead, the inability to cope with these exigencies at the appropriately micro-environmental level possible under self-government, foreclosed on cities bound to a centralized authority. In particular, interference with the direct intercity collaboration crucial for settlement continuity through times of resource stress and political disagreement would account for the sudden archaeological visibility of a variety of local difficulties.

But the question remains, why was Altun Ha unable to call on its neighbors? We can speculate that it had done so in the past, when Chau Hiix's central monument looked more like B-4 at Altun Ha (Pendergast, personal communication, 1991) and when it received a stucco cylinder vase from central Mexico at roughly the same time that Altun Ha received its cache of central Mexican green obsidian (Pendergast 1998). I suspect that Chau Hiix's single carved stela appeared, though it is currently fragmentary and illegible, about the time Altun Ha got into difficulties. Marcus's (1993, 1995a) idea that the sudden appearance of emblem glyphs among small communities indicates competitive sublords seeking autonomy from larger political units could be seen as a support for my suggestion that there was a new political element to resist. At the same time that stelae suggest independence, they also indicate participation in a wider system; these monuments tacitly recognize a preexisting authority by employing its symbols.

Superficially, this is an inversion of the more widely accepted argument that the proliferation of emblem glyphs, stelae, and the iconography of kingship in local areas indicates increased competition for power amongst upstart local kings. I am proposing instead that the appearance of these monuments in local areas indicates increasing control—or attempts at control—by a centralized authority, because they signify tighter inclusion of ever-smaller polities and towns into an overarching political economy with at least some degree of centralized authority. For example, building a post office in a small rural town does not signify independence of the town, but a closer tie to a centralized authority. Naming of towns and kings can aggrandize them—or help delegate responsibility, delineate authority, and increase control. However, this small twist to received wisdom has only minor explanatory value because the external imposition of a nonlocal authority structure could immediately result in just the sort of local rebellion and resistance envisioned in the original scenario. The only question is, who put up the stelae? Marcus notes (personal communication, 2005) that "given our timeframe, both incorporation strategies and resistance or succession strategies could be in motion."

Discussion: Smallholder Sustainability and the Success of Cities

Netting (1993) noted that smallholding frequently coexists with extensive agriculture; it is not simply land quality that dictates economy. History, culture, and technology, combined with climatic possibilities and human agency, also promote smallholding, not because of the raw productivity of land but because of its potential for improvement through investment. He also noted that though political upheaval and family fortunes may have short-term effects, in the long term, smallholder production remains stable (barring absolute natural or political catastrophe) and though surpluses remain high and the fortunes of individuals may vary, permanent class distinctions do not arise.

Where land investment is not feasible or not practiced, Chayanovian rules apply; productivity and the size of farms are tied directly to the need for food or to outside pressure by absentee landlords or hegemonic political regimes. Unlike smallholders, Chayanovian peasants have so much land available, they have no incentive to improve it and no reason to bequeath it, which also removes the means of improvement—the investment by place-bound family members into the property they will inherit. Netting also suggested that extensive systems are more vulnerable to outside pressures than are smallholders, whose land-tenure system, established surplus production, and economic diversification help them weather political and economic storms. Free from the leveling mechanisms of smallholding economies, Chayanovian peasants are a more likely locus of the origin of social classes, but also more vulnerable to the fate of the larger political economy in which they are embedded (Pyburn 1998).

Following Netting's predictions, I see Altun Ha populated by fewer smallholders and a relatively high percentage of Chayanovian peasants practicing more extensive forms of agriculture, probably as members of a wealthy estate. I see them most likely working for an absentee landlord with political ties and responsibilities to the power centers of the central Petén. This is why the trappings of elite status (large quantities of exotic sumptuary objects and significantly more baroque architecture and royally appointed tombs) are so visible at Altun Ha and why the distinctions between the "haves" and the "have nots" reach such a crescendo at Altun Ha in the Late Classic (Andres 2005; Pendergast 1992). Wealth and power bestowed land ownership, whereas for smallholders, it is land tenure that creates stability and limits power. Producers at Altun Ha worked as hard as necessary for themselves and their masters and sought status through political and economic maneuvers that were not grounded in a resilient smallholder strategy. The predominance of extensive land-use strategies would have made Altun Ha more vulnerable to political forces than were its western neighbors. And exploitation by outsiders not only cut farmers off from the fruits of their labor but also diminished both their ability and their incentive to produce a surplus or actively diversify in order to seek markets and participate in trade.

Chau Hiix, on the other hand, was clearly a smallholder paradise. Though excellent land would have attracted settlers to both Lamanai and Chau Hiix, land offering a very high return on investment would have emphasized smallholding at Chau Hiix over time. Chau Hiix's smallholders would have had easy access to markets through Lamanai and would have benefited from its protection, but Chau Hiix residents would also have been subject to Lamanai's control of their consumption of imports. Lamanai, like Chau Hiix and Altun Ha, went through a Late Classic flurry of construction that created barriers between the rulers and the ruled and increased the control of movement within the monumental centers. But just as Altun Ha was "closing up shop," Lamanai and Chau Hiix razed walls, lowered building platforms, and produced evidence of new forms of power structure deemphasizing hierarchy; that is, a *popol na* (council house) was introduced into the main platform at each site (Andres 2005; Graham 2002). Construction, population, and production continued to be strong at Postclassic Lamanai and Chau Hiix, and trade continued to fill household middens with consumer goods.

Chau Hiix was the key to Lamanai's Postclassic success. By stimulating consumption at Chau Hiix and controlling its access to trade, Lamanai would have had a captive market and a source of surplus not easily disrupted by the route changes affecting other inland trade systems. Despite the local wealth and agricultural surplus Chau Hiix did produce, its elites do not appear to have competed with Lamanai or Altun Ha but may have underwritten their competition with one another. In the Postclassic, Chau Hiix's access to trade, long controlled by Lamanai, was also protected by it; Lamanai, however, with access to a reliable source of surplus that could be protected and concealed, was able to continue thriving in an era when such alliances were breaking down at other cities.

Pomp and Circumstance: Buying into the System

Although it is not revolutionary to suggest that elites succeeded where they were able to stimulate, sustain, and protect markets (Marcus 1993), not much has been written about this strategy as a motive for Maya architecture and city planning (Becker 2003; Loten 2003; Marcus 2003b; Sabloff 2003). Most discussions of site center defensibility focus on protection of the residents, either from the public or from marauders, not protection of producers, consumers, and commercial interests. But this sort of environmental control might have been quite important.

Mayanists overemphasize elite aggrandizement and creation of Marxian false consciousness as the reason for monumental constructions. Individual aggrandizement was certainly intended, but these monuments are advertising the power of rulers and their families to do something. Their status as aggressive warriors and conquerors is much displayed, but why? Who was the audience for the claims of conquest over the neighbors? Was the visiting ruler from the next-door kingdom supposed to see the stele and become too frightened to invade? Were local farmers supposed to look at these advertisements and lay down tribute more willingly?

I think that we have been missing the phenomenological impact of Maya city centers, which we rarely juxtapose with the residences of ordinary farmers as they would have been in the Classic period. *National Geographic* has clouded our imaginations with paintings of tree-covered grounds around palaces and orderly kitchen gardens around thatched huts. And epigraphers have been too credulous of the documents they translate (Marcus 1992b), suggesting that Maya symbolism identifies rulership with natural symbols of power in the rainforest.

Actually, tropical gardens are not neat, and by the height of the Classic period, orchards were probably a commodity for wealthy people, if they existed at all, within city centers. In the tropics, insect infestations are a constant problem, and thatched houses attract vermin of all sorts: rats, bats, snakes, opossums, and vultures. Pelting rain melts buildings, and unremitting moisture rots food, clothing, documents—everything. An ordinary household would spend a tremendous amount of time trying to keep themselves and their possessions dry and free of insects and their food stores safe from mold, rats, and poor relations.

Bearing this situation in mind, the aspect of a large, elevated platform, plastered and painted, where not a single squirrel or sneak thief could pass unnoticed, must have been impressive to a rural visitor. From the center of the platform of even a small site like Chau Hiix, only human-created features would have been visible. Indeed, Maya architecture refers to nature, but not to respect for it, to domination of it. Maya rulers were advertising—and delivering—a controlled environment, safe from both natural elements and human raiders who would interfere with commerce.

Seeing Maya city centers as market enclaves makes sense of their layout, which, although variable, generally includes at least one open area that could be easily controlled and protected by surrounding towering structures. The stelae that decorate these venues do display the achievements of rulers and record their conquests, but they also emphasize the protective authority of rulership (Joyce 2000) and they certainly display the control of commodities to great advantage.

What clusters of smallholders offered elites was not just the chance to control production, but also a source of economic diversity and a concentration of active consumers. People will exploit their own households more thoroughly than any external authority if their surplus accrues to their advantage. Trade allows the conversion of agricultural surplus into wealth and prestige, both buffers against misfortune but also opportunities for indulgence. The way elite are portrayed by most Mayanists makes it hard to see why anyone would want to be elite. They sacrificed and accumulated ritual objects for display and to propitiate deities. They struggled to dominate lazy and resistant, or else magnificently credulous, farmers in order to get control of a surplus that gave them power to distribute it to get more power. Power is seen as intrinsically valuable, rather than being the power to do or to have something (Pohl 1985).

Maya elites displayed their status goods because these were available to non-elites and elites benefited from making consumption desirable, possible, and safe. Not as much as elites, who controlled the system, ordinary people had some of just about anything available. The wide distribution of exotic items, including Rathje's (1972) basic needs (obsidian, hard stone, and salt), as well as the jade and polychromes found in the fill of the humblest house mounds in every Maya site, does not mean that there were no social strata. The surprising number of mended plainwares or simple redwares that might be assumed to be household produce shows that these items were avidly salvaged. This suggests, along with their profound uniformity, that they were acquired from specialists. Promoting consumption encourages specialization and is in the interests of people who want to increase their own wealth, as well as their power and political control over the rest of the population.

Most units of anthropological analysis—age groups, genders, warriors, weavers, households, families, lineages, regions, cities, and states—are at least partly units of consumption. In fact, we really have a modest amount of data on Maya production; what we have is an immense amount of data on consumption and some reliable ways of determining who consumed what. Consumption is an interesting process to look at during the formation of cities because it tends to be hierarchical and competitive in all societies; Gandhi's India is the only example I can think of where voluntary simplicity contributed to the formation of a new state, and that a reactionary one. If the thing to be consumed is unlimited, it does not motivate or explain social organization; water figures in societies in the desert. But there are improvements and motives that can make water figure elsewhere, such as proximity and "taste." These are the economic factors that elites try to control. Rathje has recently argued (2002) that this is why elites destroy wealth—to keep consumer goods scarce and under their control. This seems pretty inefficient, and there are easier ways to keep consumers interested in the market.

The ancient Maya elite were certainly involved in a prestige economy, but to a degree, all economies are prestige economies. Trade is very distantly connected to biological needs, but it is also tightly connected to social and political needs at all levels of society. Elite political motives do not forge an economy, but sociopolitical motives interact with economic motives to forge a city. One thing that elites do, both to hold on to their elite status and to stimulate consumption, is vary their repertoire. There is a very good reason why Maya kings look similar to one another but always significantly different and why ceramic styles sometimes create a "horizon." Masson (2002a) has suggested that Classic period regionalization in pottery styles implies elite control of regionalized markets in domestic wares, but a close inspection of individual cities shows constant fluctuation in what appear to us to be minor differences. Rather than simply control distribution, I suggest that the elite influence the popularity of goods whose distribution they benefit from. Controlling access to places like Chau Hiix would certainly be rewarding and require minimal effort once the canals were dug and maintenance work assigned. Chau Hiix certainly had significant quantities of imported goods people did not *need*.

Consumption practices create both local and regional identities, proclaim independence and allegiance, and claim superiority or democratic standards at all levels of society. Elites maintain elite status not only by having the best or by controlling distribution, but by defining what the best is (Wilk 2004). Of course, material-culture distribution and variation are what archaeologists mostly see, but there are other types of consumption that are costly and elite, such as the acquisition of education, connoisseurship, and palate (Goody 1982).

One way elites stimulate markets and consumption is by sponsoring pageants, including sporting events, feasts, public displays, pilgrimages, and various sorts of aesthetic competition (Wilk 1995). The participants in these events accrue status, but it is the elites who sponsor them and retain the right to pick the winners, who implicitly verify their right to set standards of excellence and taste and motivate consumer practices to their own advantage (Pyburn 2004; Wilk 2004). Pageants and competitions seem more likely than "ritual ballgames and ceremonial battles" (Schele and Freidel 1990). Viewed in this light, the fact that Chau Hiix and Lamanai have similar ball courts might suggest one type of pageant. The "problematic deposit," described above with reference to the heavily mended redwares at Chau Hiix, suggests another, perhaps competitive feasting (Wille 2007). There is a similar deposit at Lamanai (Elizabeth Graham, personal communication, 2005).

Returning to my original argument, rather than cause increasing social complexity and the rise of urban centers and although probably tempting to elites, controlling production can create economic stress. Interference with local systems of production that have long, adaptive histories by top-down edicts has caused problems for many cultures in recent history (Pyburn 1997). Reduced diversification may make it possible to corner a market temporarily but reintroduces the vulnerability that smallholders diversify to avoid. It is important to remember that smallholders diversify on an agrarian base that they never willingly jeopardize. As long as elites focused on stimulating and controlling consumption, cities flourished in the Maya lowlands. But where elites managed to gain control of production to a degree that affected the subsistence economy, disaster followed. The demise of this sort of economic hegemony would account for the rapid rise of new trading systems often said to characterize the secularized Postclassic.

Taking a last look at Altun Ha, I want to revisit my earlier point that the term *city* is a general term that includes many types of settlement. Cities, like states, wax and wane over time (Marcus 1992a; Marcus and Feinman 1998). Although Altun Ha certainly participated in trade—and, no doubt, hosted regular markets—the timing, significance, and contents of Altun Ha's markets may not have been the same as those that fueled Chau Hiix and Lamanai. Exchange at Altun Ha may have looked more like the elite-controlled deployment of status goods than what was hawked to all comers at Chau Hiix; Lamanai had a more balanced combination of market styles and merchant types. But I hypothesize that elites at Altun Ha probably had more control of production, deciding what should be planted, and when, from afar. Such strategies are expensive, unstable, and dangerously disengaged from the micro-environmental factors that smallholders exploit. Elite landowners lack the local knowledge and the investment required for sustainability, and their estates easily fall victim to greed, mismanagement, and collapse.

Considering the broader issues addressed in this book about the nature of early cities and where they come from, it seems important to try to discern whether one city along the New River was an overarching political power stimulating, cajoling, and sometimes controlling the conurbation. Of course, there may have been no political center, with each site tied to the others in shifting ways fueled by complementary roles and specialties. But the very different sizes and trajectories of the three, combined with the data and speculations presented here, do suggest some interesting possibilities.

If Lamanai, by all measures the largest of the three cities, was the Classic period political apex, why was Altun Ha, its middle-range subordinate center, abandoned? Quite a few other cities, including some that were definitely not "middle range," such as Tikal, also were depopulated. Why were Altun Ha's elite tombs robbed and Lamanai and Chau Hiix's left intact?

If Altun Ha was the political center of a multi-city state, why would a city controlling the agricultural output of some of the most productive farmers in the Maya world change so radically while its subordinate cities kept going on just as before, giving little appearance of having escaped a political or economic yoke? The reason is that the producers at Altun Ha were land poor because of their less intensive and less sustainable strategies and their lack of personal investment in the land. Their relationship with Chau Hiix and Lamanai was partly political, partly pomp and circumstance choreographed by nonresident elites with an eye on profits and little local investment. All Maya agriculture was intensive by the Classic period. But the production on wealthy estates was less efficient and less productive than smallholding, and estates were probably constantly trying to expand. Netting (1993) mentions that the Ibo, extensive agriculturalists living near the smallholder Kofyar, are constantly trying to move in on Kofyar land. Wealthy landowners, especially under conditions of political stress, would be more likely to make decisions about land use with short-term benefits that were ultimately unsustainable. Altun Ha probably did have access to produce from Chau Hiix and Altun Ha but did not control production and only benefited from some control of distribution to and from the central Petén via less reliable ocean routes. Bulk trade in mass-produced goods or food was relatively limited by Altun Ha's landlocked locus. These distribution channels were dependent on Petén connections, and when these declined, Lamanai easily stepped in to incorporate the distribution system engineered by Altun Ha into its already healthy mercantile economy.

Many burials at Chau Hiix contain extra bones that show from their condition that human bones were recovered and reburied with people more recently dead (Della Cook, personal communication, 1996). Tomb 1, an Early Classic tomb built into the base of the Structure 1 staircase (figure 13.5), contained a bundle of bones from at least twelve individuals that was obviously a secondary burial (Della Cook, personal communication, 2005). The tomb was reopened, and the bundle was substituted for the bones of the left leg of the primary inhumation. In the Terminal Classic and Early Postclassic, Structure 2, judged to be an elite residence because of its size and location immediately south of Structure 1, Chau Hiix's largest monument, became a necropolis, despite the fact that it continued to be used by the living, as evidenced by the perpetual reconstruction of its floor above the dead. In all, at least 70 individuals were buried in Structure 2 in family clusters (Wrobel 2004); isotope analysis of their bones indicates that they were not foreigners (Metcalfe 2005). This was a new practice at Chau Hiix, not known from earlier periods, when interments were isolated; at most, three or four people were buried over time in house floors. McAnany (1995) and others have argued that the Maya were ancestor worshippers, but I would add to this the importance of "place" to smallholders, whose strategy hinges on their ownership of land. Ancestral burials in many cultures both signify and establish land tenure.

Perhaps the disturbance of elite tombs at Altun Ha was not so much desecration as an indication of a change in land ownership. The failure of wealthy estates would lead to a withdrawal of retainers and possibly a change in the system of land tenure; smallholders do readily move into newly available land (Stone et al. 1990). Perhaps new residents eradicated evidence of former owners, or maybe the elite moved their dead to join family members where land tenure was still secured by perpetual residence. We cannot guess where they were moved, but if the political economy of the conurbation was secured by the residence of representatives from Chau Hiix and Lamanai at Altun Ha, perhaps some of the burials, and secondary burials that appear in Structure 2 during the Terminal and Early Postclassic, were simply people returning home. With this in mind, it might one day be possible to find the reburial places of the elite of Altun Ha.

To a certain extent, many of our constructions of ancient cities come out of our personal folk models of human behavior. Are people always unwilling to produce more than they need? Are they basically rational or irrational, normally social, selfish, or moral, inherently gullible or suspicious, predictably hierarchical or democratic? On the premise that such characteristics ought to be the subject of research questions instead of the assumptions that underlie them, Richard Wilk argues that people's motives and choices are never very clear and that these define types of behavior, not types of people (Wilk 1996:150). Whatever else we may conclude about urban life, I feel confident that new suites of motives and behaviors were brought into more intense proximity, which no doubt created alliances and feuds, synergy and disintegration, elitism and democracy, and a never-ending conversation about what it means to be urban, such as the one we partake of here.

Acknowledgments

Many of my students are acknowledged in this chapter, and I hope it is clear that I have depended on them for inspiration, ideas, and a good deal of old-fashioned hard work. I must especially thank Christopher (Kip) Andres for all his good ideas and good humor; he provided the maps for this chapter and contributed a great deal of insight. I would also like to give special acknowledgment to Patti Cook, Tom Cuddy, Sean Goldsmith, Sarah Wille, and Gabriel Wrobel, who have given a great deal of themselves to the Chau Hiix Project over the years. My colleagues Caroline Beebe, Beverly Chiarulli, Della Cook, and Robert Fry have added immeasurably to the project with their expertise. These students and colleagues are the people who are most responsible for what we know about Chau Hiix today. I have also had the great fortune to benefit from the friendly encouragement and the editorial comments of Joyce Marcus and Jeremy Sabloff, whose generosity to me over the years has been unfailing and considerable. All my ideas have been discussed, argued, invented, and reworked in conversations with Richard Wilk. Finally, Christine Hastorf, who once asked me to clarify what I meant when I suggested that pageants could affect the rise of elites, and Daniel Miller, who asked me why archaeologists ignore consumption, sparked the ideas in this chapter. The errors are the only part for which I claim full credit.

fourteen
Incidental Urbanism
The Structure of the Prehispanic City in Central Mexico

Kenneth G. Hirth

> Gazing on such wonderful sights, we did not know what to say, or whether what appeared before us was real, for on one side on the land there were great cities, and in the lake ever so many more,...and in front of us the great City of Mexico.
>
> —*Bernal Díaz del Castillo,* The Discovery and Conquest of Mexico, 1517–1521

The epigraph by Bernal Díaz captures the impression the early Spanish conquistadors had of the Central Mexican landscape as they approached the Aztec capital of Tenochtitlan. Central Mexico was a land of many marvels, and first among them was the numerous, large, nucleated communities found in the area around modern-day Mexico City. Many of the conquistadors had traveled widely throughout Spain and had seen the thriving cities of the Iberian Peninsula. What impressed them about Central Mexican communities were the scale of construction, the cleanliness and organization of urban areas, and most of all, the size and density of their populations. The Spanish undoubtedly confused the throngs of people visiting urban markets for permanent city residents, but this distinction may be more important to us than it was for them. In the eyes of most Spanish conquistadors, the indigenous societies of Central Mexico were highly urbanized (figure 14.1).

It is an interesting paradox that despite an intense interest in the structure of prehispanic cities, archaeologists appear to be less certain about the urban character of Mesoamerican cities than were the Spanish who saw them firsthand. Archaeologists continue to debate fundamental issues about what the Mesoamerican city was and what areas did or did not have cities (Chase et al. 1990; Sanders and Webster 1988; M. E. Smith 1989). I believe that the reason for this confusion stems from a misunderstanding about

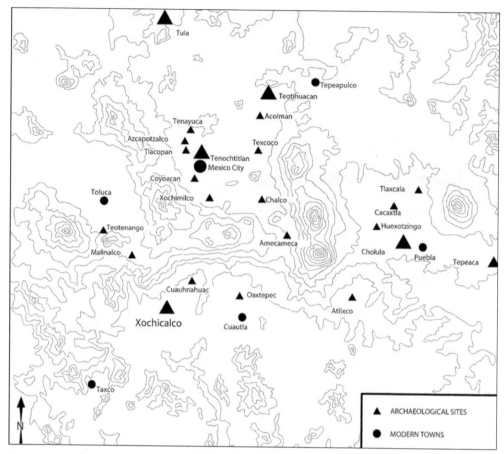

Figure 14.1. The location of major urban sites in Central Mexico.

what prehispanic urban centers were and how they were structured. I argue here that many Mesoamerican cities were the by-product of incidental urbanism; nucleated populations were a secondary result of developing regional sociopolitical systems. Cities in this context were secondary features, both structurally and developmentally, of the systems that produced them. Cities developed in concert with institutions of centralized authority, but in Mesoamerica they did not necessarily represent unique and separate corporate communities within their regions.

The discussion presented here differs from others in this volume in two ways. First, it examines the *structure* of Central Mexican urban centers instead of their origin and development. The focus on structure forces me to address the question of emic (insider) versus etic (outsider) views of the city. Although both views are necessary, I adopt a more emic-oriented view of the city to portray what I feel are the important features of prehispanic urban structure. Second, the discussion examines late examples of urbanism from the Postclassic period, at or just before the Spanish Conquest, instead of early cases. This permits a more thorough reconstruction of indigenous urban structure by combining archaeological data with ethnohistoric descriptions of urban communities.

The presentation that follows examines three aspects of urban structure in prehispanic Central Mexico. First, it reviews approaches and concepts used by archaeologists to study urban structure in Mesoamerica. I believe that in the process of applying Western interdisciplinary, and primarily etic, approaches to the study of urbanism, researchers have overlooked some essential features of prehispanic population organization. Second, I draw upon ethnohistoric information and present what I believe is a more indigenous or emic view of Central Mexican urban structure. I argue that large nucleated communities at the time of the Conquest were primarily epiphenomena and an incidental result of the development of large regional city-states, called *altepetl*. This perspective departs from the established tradition of viewing Central Mexican cities as large, integrated, corporate communities. The altepetl had a segmental and heterarchical population structure, and I identify three physical manifestations that characterize it: territory disarticulation, population dispersion, and service rotation. Third and finally, this chapter examines some of the archaeological evidence for segmental urban structure in Central Mexico, using information from Xochicalco, Morelos, and Tepeaca, Puebla. Physical evidence for territory disarticulation, population dispersion, and service rotation is identified, suggesting that the altepetl, and its form of incidental urbanism, was a common feature of the prehispanic urban landscape throughout Central Mexico.

The Study of Mesoamerican Urbanism

A fundamental starting point for studying prehispanic urbanism is to establish a working definition for what constitutes an urban community. Archaeologists in Mesoamerica have addressed this issue using two approaches. The oldest and most common method for studying prehispanic urbanism is the trait-complex or *typological* approach (Childe 1950; Weber 1962[1958]; Wheatley 1972). In this approach, urban communities are defined in terms of specific criteria with which archaeological remains can be compared. In Central Mexico, urban communities are often defined by the size and density of their resident populations. The starting point for this approach is Louis Wirth's (1938:8) definition of the city as a "relatively large, dense, and permanent settlement of heterogeneous individuals." The attractiveness of this approach is that information on prehispanic population size and residential density can be readily collected from careful archaeological mapping and settlement pattern analysis.

An example of this approach is Sanders and Webster's (1988) analysis of the Mesoamerican urban tradition using Fox's (1977) typology of urban places. Sanders and Webster propose that large, dense cities were rare in Mesoamerica because of energetic constraints to urban growth. They argue that most Mesoamerican cities were regal-ritual centers organized around the household of the ruler. They contend that except for their larger size, most Mesoamerican cities were largely indistinguishable from communities in the rural countryside. A major criticism of this typological approach is that it uses overly generalized analytical categories that hide, rather than highlight, differences in urban structure (Chase et al. 1990; M. E. Smith 1989).

More recently, archaeologists have advocated the use of a *functional* (hierarchical) approach for studying urban structure (Blanton 1976; Marcus 2000[1983b]). This approach defines cities as high-ranking central places within systems of regional interaction (Blanton 1981; Blanton et al. 1981; Marcus 1973; M. E. Smith 1979). Urban rank from this perspective is a function of the sociopolitical, religious, and economic functions that a center provides for its surrounding hinterland. Urban institutions are seen as a by-product of the political and economic forces that shape socioeconomic systems (Blanton 1981:392). The strength of this approach lies in its recognition of regional symbiosis as the foundation of urban economy and the incorporation of concepts of regional hierarchy and integration from Central Place Theory (Berry 1961; Berry and Garrison 1958; Chorley and Haggett 1967; Haggett et al. 1977; Hoselitz 1955; Jefferson 1939; C. A. Smith 1976a, 1976b).

The functional approach has been readily adopted by archaeologists in the Maya area (Chase et al. 1990). The reason is that Maya cities are small and can be defined as high-ordered central places without a large resident population (M. E. Smith 1989:454). This approach shifts the focus of urbanism away from specific criteria such as population size or density, to the formation of site hierarchies at the regional level (C. A. Smith 1976a). The drawback of this approach is that the definition for an urban center is not clear-cut but depends on a site's relative position in the regional-settlement hierarchy. Likewise, hierarchies may not exist as researchers propose (see below), and defining and quantifying higher-order functions using archaeological data is a difficult task.

One of the consistent features of Mesoamerican research has been the use of interdisciplinary studies of urbanism to interpret prehispanic communities. Archaeologists have relied on urban sociology, history, and cultural geography for many conceptual approaches. Although archaeology has benefited from the theoretical richness that interdisciplinary studies provide, researchers have not always recognized the inherent problems involved in using Western views of urbanism. I have argued elsewhere (Hirth 2003, 2004) that Mesoamerican archaeologists often fall victim to a Weberian view of urbanism. The Weberian view of urbanism tends to study cities as discretely bounded and integrated autonomous communities with distinctive forms of internal governance (Hirth 2003; Weber 1962[1958]:81). This perspective emphasizes the unique characteristics of urban communities and how they differ from their supporting rural hinterlands (Jacobs 1969, 1985; Sjoberg 1960). Urban sociology has contributed to this view by emphasizing the uniqueness of urban environments and their effect on the behavior and creativity of their residents (Bookchin 1992; Park 1915; Wirth 1969). Within anthropology, concepts like the closed, corporate community (Wolf 1957, 1986) have also contributed to viewing cities as isolated entities.

The challenge for archaeologists is to link the definitions, concepts, and processes of urban development with the material remains available to study them. The topic of urbanism naturally focuses attention on the largest or most-prominent archaeological sites. We identify sites, define their boundaries, estimate their populations, and reconstruct urban functions using a combination of survey and excavation techniques.

Unfortunately, even the simple process of isolating boundaries and defining cities can distort our reconstructions of urban communities. Spatial boundaries of archaeological sites often are morphed into social boundaries (Chang 1968; Millon 1973), and cities take on the mantle of autonomous communities in the process of investigating them.

The result is that most interpretations of prehispanic urban structure in Mesoamerica are shaped by Western concepts of what the city is and how it was structured. As noted by Uzzell (1979:335), the tendency to view cities as bounded communities is a perspective that permeates all studies of urbanism. This Western bias has hindered rather than enhanced our understanding of prehispanic communities. Although Joyce Marcus (2000[1983b]:241) identified this problem more than twenty years ago, research has not evaluated whether Western concepts of urban structure accurately describe Mesoamerican community structure. I believe that they do not. What is needed is an *emic* model of the prehispanic community that accurately characterizes indigenous urban structure before we engage in comparative analyses.

The discussion that follows uses ethnohistoric information to reconstruct the organization of urban communities in Central Mexico at the Spanish Conquest. I propose that the large, highly nucleated urban communities of Central Mexico were a secondary by-product of large regional city-states (*altepemeh* is plural of *altepetl*). They were *not* tightly integrated autonomous communities. Instead, they were open, segmented, and unbounded settlements with loose structures of internal social control. Despite their size, highland cities lacked clear corporate boundaries or political integrity. Central Mexican urbanism is best thought of as a form of *incidental urbanism*, a secondary aspect of the altepetl's segmentary community structure. Recognizing the structure of these communities is important because it shifts attention away from the physical manifestations of size and density, to a discussion of the organizational principles on which Central Mexican urban centers were based.

Incidental Urbanism and the Altepetl in Central Mexico

The Spanish were impressed with the large-scale public architecture, the well-organized urban design, and the large size and density of prehispanic cities. Because these three features can be examined using archaeological data, they have become hallmarks for etic definitions of Central Mexican cities.

Public architecture refers to the temples, plaza groups, and other civic-ceremonial structures that were prominent in the ritual life and daily administrative operation of the state. Included here are the many large, sumptuous homes and elite palaces that the conquistadors lived in during their travels throughout Central Mexico. The Spaniards were also impressed with the organization and cleanliness of urban areas. In Central Mexican cities, a large public marketplace was usually held either daily or on a rotating schedule in a large open plaza. Archaeologists studying urban design have identified the use of orthogonal grids and directional alignments to plan the layout of public and residential space in large cities such as Teotihuacan, Tula, and Tenochtitlan (Calnek 2003; Mastache et al. 2002; Millon 1973; Sanders 2003). Likewise, there is good ethnohistoric and archaeological evidence for the organization of towns and cities into ward and barrio units of different size (Calnek 2003; Hirth 1995; M. E. Smith 1996; van Zantwijk 1985).

Finally, Central Mexican cities are often described by the Spanish as large, densely nucleated settlements, and this has been reiterated by archaeological investigation. The two largest cities to develop in Central Mexico were Teotihuacan (AD 150–650) and Tenochtitlan-Tlatelolco (AD 1400–1521), each with resident populations of 100,000–150,000 (Calnek 1976, 2003; Millon 1973; Sanders 2003; see figure 14.1). Despite these large centers, most urban centers in Central Mexico were intermediate-size settlements of 10,000–20,000 persons. In all cases, large nucleated settlements were administrative centers of regional city-states called *altepemeh*. The overall archaeological impression is that Central Mexican cities were large, well-integrated, corporate communities. Unfortunately, I believe that this impression is largely incorrect.

I believe that the indigenous emic view of urban communities in sixteenth-century Central Mexico was quite a bit different from the one adopted by archaeologists. The urban/rural dichotomy often used by archaeologists to define and discuss regional community relationships did not exist in the minds of indigenous people. Many of the settlements that archaeologists have identified as cities were segments of the larger altepetl and did not have identities or organizational structures separate from those of this larger political body. The altepetl was the *primary* organizational entity in Central Mexico, and cities were *secondary* features of their development. This is *not* a subtle distinction, and Central Mexican cities cannot be understood except within this context. Although we define cities in a variety of ways, there is no indigenous Nahuatl word for the city to distinguish it from the larger altepetl! This should tell us that attempts to define cities apart from the altepetl are not a productive or informative enterprise. According to Marcus (2000[1983b]:208), "the archaeologist or geographer that draws a line separating the 'city' from its politically controlled territory may be performing an act that is heuristically useful for his…analysis, but that does not conform to the reality of the Mesoamerican Indian world."

The altepetl in Central Mexico consisted of the royal household and the land and people of the ruler (Hirth 2003:61; Hodge 1984). Conceptually, the altepetl included both rural and urban populations, and no distinction was made between them by their inhabitants. The 1571 dictionary of Fray Alonso de Molina defines the altepetl as *pueblo o rey* (town or king). Similarly, the Siméon dictionary of 1885 translates *altepetl* as *poblado, ciudad, estado, rey, soberano* (settlement, city, state, king, sovereign) (Hodge 1984:17). The linguistic evidence equates "city" with the broader regional polity, instead of defining it as a special, large community within the altepetl. This broader view of *altepetl* is represented by other word usages, such as *altepeua* (inhabitant of a city, of a country) and *altepetlalli* (land in common), which emphasize the polity's corporate structure (de Molina 1977; Hirth 2000:272). This pattern is found throughout Mesoamerica in the Valley of Oaxaca, the Yucatan peninsula, the Huasteca, and the Mixteca (Gutiérrez Mendoza 2003; Hirth 2003; Marcus 2000[1983b]:207; Restall 1997:26).

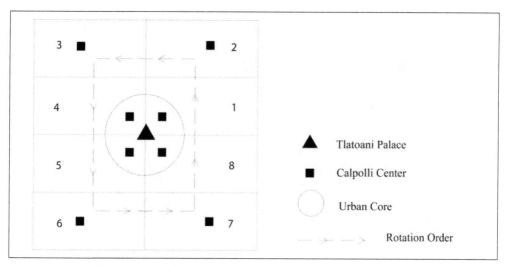

Figure 14.2. Lockhart's model of the altepetl. Numbered boxes represent calpolli within the altepetl and the order of their service rotation to the ruler.

James Lockhart (1992) was the first to recognize and identify the spatial structure of the altepetl. According to Lockhart (1992:14), the altepetl was the primary administrative unit of indigenous society and was composed of a number of secondary, relatively equal, self-contained territorial/population subunits referred to as *calpolli* and *tlaxilacalli*, among other terms. The altepetl's internal organization was cellular and segmental rather than hierarchical. Territorial/population segments within the altepetl were ordered for tribute payment but were not ranked hierarchically with respect to one another. Altepetl segments all had the same rank, and tribute obligations were ordered and carried out on a rotational basis. The order of rotation was fixed and repeating and provided the thread of life within the altepetl. What is particularly important is that any large city or large nucleated settlement within the altepetl did not exist as a separate, integrated jurisdiction (Lockhart 1992:19). Instead, it was an artifact of incidental nucleation of calpolli and tlaxilacalli segments within the altepetl.

Figure 14.2 reproduces Lockhart's model of the altepetl and depicts how nucleated population clusters were organized within it. It illustrates three important aspects of altepetl structure. The first is its cellular, segmental structure. In figure 14.2, the altepetl is composed of eight separate calpolli, each with its own land allocations. Second, the model depicts how population within each calpolli could be distributed over space. The four outlying calpolli have population clusters located at the center of their territorial lands, whereas the population of the four central calpolli is clustered together to create a nucleated settlement at the center. Although this central, nucleated settlement might look like a city in terms of population size and density, it lacked the formal organization that would set it apart as a distinct social or juridical entity within the altepetl. Third, the model illustrates the rotational pattern of obligations within the altepetl. All calpolli units have equivalent ranks, and a system of rotating obligations provided the means of integrating the altepetl's regional population.

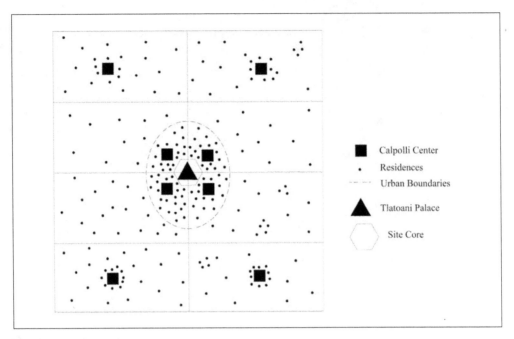

Figure 14.3. What the altepetl might look like in terms of archaeological settlement patterns.

Figure 14.3 transforms this model into a hypothetical settlement pattern that this type of structure could create. At the center would be public architecture that defines the altepetl's civic-ceremonial core. This would include the palace of the ruler (*tlatoani*) and other important civil-religious structures, including temples, ballcourts, and a central marketplace. Around the civic-ceremonial core would be the administrative buildings and population associated with the four innermost calpolli. From an archaeological perspective, this central settlement would strongly resemble a large, integrated community when it was not. This figure also illustrates how the population of each calpolli segment could vary in the degree of nucleation or dispersion across the lands of the altepetl.

Archaeologists could misinterpret this settlement pattern in several ways. First and most important, the population concentrated at the center of the altepetl could be interpreted as an autonomous urban community organized internally into four distinct wards or administrative segments. Second, the regional distribution of population and the administrative structures create the appearance of urban-rural differences in community structure within the altepetl. Third, differences in the size and distribution of population clusters produce the impression that the altepetl was organized into a three-tier administrative hierarchy of city, town, and homestead, instead of being a single political entity with a segmented residential organization. Although this reconstruction is hypothetical, it illustrates the type of errors that can be made when the wrong analytical concepts about community structure are used in analysis. Developing more informed models of indigenous community organization is the only way to avoid this problem.

Community and the Spatial Organization of Central Mexican Altepemeh

Central Mexican altepemeh had segmental structures that permitted great variation in how population aggregates were organized and distributed over space. The altepetl was the primary, regional administrative entity in Central Mexico, and its three components were its ruler (*tlatoani*), its supporting population, and the land or geographic territory that composed the altepetl. Although boundaries between altepemeh could be precisely defined using boundary markers, there was no conceptual, internal boundary or division between rural and urban space. The segmental structure of the altepetl permitted great fluidity in how regional territory was defined and manipulated. This meant that territory and population could be added, or removed, from the altepetl with little difficulty.

The unit of importance within the altepetl was the land or resource-holding body. This unit had different names (*calpolli*, *tlahtocayo*, *tlaxilacalli*, and so on) and varied in how it was organized. What is important is that land-holding units could, but did not necessarily, correspond to residential groups. Land-holding units were corporate groups throughout Central Mexico, but their populations did not necessarily reside together in a single settlement. The result was a segmented community structure in which territory, not residence, was the primary organizational feature. This type of segmented organization permitted great variation in how land-holding units were integrated or added to altepetl holdings. Two common variants in settlement structure associated with altepemeh were territory disarticulation and population dispersion, both of which are discussed below.

Territory disarticulation refers to the creation of an altepetl with noncontiguous rather than contiguous boundaries. Disarticulation was not a problem under conditions of segmented-community structure because all population segments within the altepetl had equivalent status irrespective of their physical location. Although altepemeh ideally were defined by contiguous territory, disarticulation occurred over time through expansion, annexation, migration, and affiliation of groups to rulers and regional altepetl. Noncontiguous territories were created as plots of land outside the altepetl were added to the patrimonial or pre-bendal estates of ruling elite (Weber 1947; Wolf 1966) through marriage, inheritance, and conquest (Spores 1984:131). One place where disarticulated altepemeh are well documented is the Teotihuacan Valley, located northeast of Mexico City (Munch 1976). Here the three altepemeh of Teotihuacan, Acolman, and Tepexpan illustrate the range of variation possible in the territorial structure of altepemeh at the time of the Spanish Conquest (figure 14.4).

The *Relación Geográfica de Teccisztlán e su Partido* of 1580 provides a comprehensive list and map of rural settlements in the Teotihuacan Valley and the names of the *cabeceras* (principal towns) to which they paid tribute (Sanders et al. 2001:map 240, table 92). The altepetl of Teotihuacan consisted of approximately twenty tributary settlements. Seventeen of these were located in the area immediately surrounding the town of Teotihuacan, where its ruler lived. The other three were located in the Temascalapa

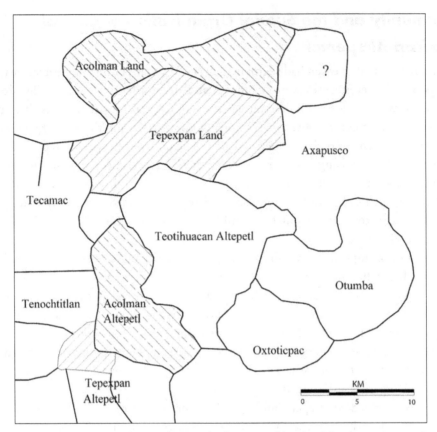

Figure 14.4. Territory disarticulation: The location of lands of the three altepemeh of Teotihuacan, Acolman, and Tepexpan in the northeastern Basin of Mexico.

region, 15 km north and outside the Teotihuacan Valley. Most of the Teotihuacan altepetl was defined by contiguous territory, with only a small percentage of its land and people located outside its immediate domain (figure 14.4).

The altepetl of Acolman, by contrast, was characterized by strong disarticulation of territory. This altepetl consisted of twenty-six tributary settlements that were divided relatively equally in two separate blocks. The main block consisted of the productive irrigated land surrounding the settlement of Acolman. The second block consisted of the rainfall agricultural lands located north and outside the Teotihuacan Valley in the Temascalapa region. These two blocks of land were separated from each other by intervening lands of the Teotihuacan and Tepexpan altepemeh (figure 14.4).

Finally, the altepetl of Tepexpan consisted of twelve dependent-tribute settlements and is characterized by extreme disarticulation; most of its territorial land was separate from the land cluster containing the main settlement of Tepexpan. The town of Tepexpan was located on the lower alluvial plain of the Teotihuacan Valley, but its land here was limited. Most of the altepetl's dependent territory was located on the north slope of Cerro Gordo in the Temascalapa region and the Xaltocan plain (figure 14.4).

Figure 14.5. Map of the distribution of the population of the three altepemeh of Teotihuacan, Acolman, and Tepexpan (redrawn from Gibson 1964:figure 2).

In this case, the majority of Tepexpan's territory was disarticulated from the central territorial domain of its ruler. Gibson (1964:figure 2) feels that the pattern was even more complex than that presented here, with considerable intermingling of individual lands and communities within and between the different altepemeh (figure 14.5).

The principle of disarticulation also operated in the formation of patrimonial and pre-bendal estates of ruling elite. Patrimonial estates are the land and people assigned to ruling families for their individual support. They are not private property per se, but land under the supervision and patronage of specific elite that stays with the family from generation to generation. Pre-bendal estates consist of the land and people assigned to support the costs of specific offices and institutions of the state. These lands were temporarily assigned to support individuals while they held special offices. The assignments were not permanent and would change hands as the individuals holding these offices changed.

Land was added to the patrimonial estate of Teotihuacan in 1437 when its ruler married the daughter of the ruler of Texcoco (Münch 1976; Sanders et al. 2001:906). This new land was located in Chalco, 50 km south of Teotihuacan. It was removed from the patrimonial household of Nezahualcoyotl, the ruler of Texcoco, and was added as a disarticulated property to the household of Quetzalmanalitzin in Teotihuacan. This pattern is found throughout the highlands. The pre-bendal estate of the altepetl of Yanhuitlán in the Mixteca Alta consisted of 102 fields, 68 of which were located in the altepetl of Yanhuitlán and 34 distributed throughout four other neighboring altepemeh (Spores 1967:164–168). The modular structure of the altepetl made it possible to integrate noncontiguous areas without difficulty. As a result, we find disarticulated territories at many levels of society.

Population dispersion is the second predictable feature of settlement structure within the altepetl. The absence of strong corporate-community structure produced fluid settlement boundaries and resulted in the dispersion of households across the landscape. Although population dispersion is found throughout Mesoamerica at different times and places, it is particularly prominent during the Late Postclassic period immediately prior to Spanish Conquest. This is important because altepetl-like forms of organization dominated the Postclassic Mesoamerican landscape and thus permitted the widespread dispersion of regional population. Although Drennan (1988) has argued that population dispersion was an adaptation to swidden agriculture, I believe that it also reflects the principles of broader community structure.

Archaeologists in Central Mexico often model community organization in terms of ward, barrio, or calpolli segments (Carrasco 1971; Sanders et al. 1979). I will not review this literature here (Carrasco 1971, 1976a, 1976b; Monzón Estrada 1949; Reyes García 1996; Zorita 1963, 1994), but they are examples of the primary land-holding units that compose the altepetl. Research has demonstrated that the calpolli was not a universal feature of Central Mexican settlement organization. It is rarer in the Puebla-Tlaxcala region than in the Valley of Mexico (Hicks 1982:244) and apparently did not exist in the Tepeaca region of the eastern Valley of Puebla (Martínez 1984). In Tepeaca, the altepetl was subdivided into four *tlahtocayo* or royal households (*casas señoriales*) located in three separate communities (Tepeaca, Acatzingo, Oxtoticpac). This form or organization changed the basis for residential structure and permitted considerable latitude in where individuals could be located within the altepetl.

In Tepeaca, regional populations were not organized by co-resident settlement groupings, but as more abstractly constructed tribute groups (*cuadrillas*) organized to produce goods and services for elite households. Although people lived in settlements with their own distinct toponymic identity, this was not the administrative structure that integrated altepetl population. Instead, populations were organized through the three-tier administrative hierarchy of the tribute cuadrilla system. The smallest administrative unit in the cuadrilla system was the *centecpantin*, a group of twenty households (de Molina 1977; Siméon 1991) supervised by an individual with the title of *centecpanpixqui* (Martínez 1984:104; Rojas Rabiela 1986:140). The next level in the administrative hierarchy was the *macuillamantli*, a group of five centecpantin. This represented a grouping of 100 households and was supervised by a *macuiltecpanpixqui*, who coordinated tribute activities (Katz 1966:100; Martínez 1984:103). At the highest level of the cuadrilla hierarchy was the *calpixque*, who supervised the macuillamantli tribute units placed under him (Rojas Rabiela 1986:140–141). The number of macuillamantli that a calpixque supervised depended on the size of the tlahtocayo and the way tribute households were organized by work or craft specialization (Ixtlilxóchitl 1975:1:380, 393).

Two things are important here. First, the cuadrilla system was not based on residential propinquity, and, second, settlement location did not provide the structure for organizing regional population within the altepetl. In Tepeaca, centecpantin tribute units did not necessarily correspond to residential groupings. Instead, centecpantin tribute units often cut across the settlements, wards, and barrios that people lived in. Martínez (1984:table 2) has summarized the tribute cuadrillas listed for 111 settlements distributed between fourteen elite households in the Tepeaca altepetl. The results show that roughly 60 percent of these 111 settlements were subdivided into centecpantin that crosscut the natural organization of residential groupings. That is, many adjacent households in the same ward or barrio were divided into tribute cuadrillas assigned to different lords within the same or different tlahtocayo (Martínez 1984:106).

Because residential settlements were not important political or administrative units in the Puebla-Tlaxcala region, population nucleation provided no effective organizational advantage for its residents. The result was a gradual drift away from nucleated settlements toward residential dispersion. People resided directly on the land they worked for their subsistence, permitting efficient agricultural cultivation (Drennan 1988) without sacrificing social control.

The Archaeological Evidence for Segmental Urban Structure

The question for archaeologists is whether there is physical evidence for the type of segmented-community structure documented in ethnohistoric sources. No matter how plausible or probable a model may be, if it is empirically invisible and unable to be measured in the archaeological record, then it has little utility for researching the past. The remainder of this chapter examines the archaeological evidence for segmented-community structure in Central Mexico. I draw on evidence collected in archaeological projects in the western Valley of Morelos at Xochicalco and the eastern Valley of Puebla at Tepeaca.

Evidence for segmented-community structure is found in three types of archaeological data. The first is the existence of a segmental organizational structure at both the community and regional levels. Intensive surface mapping at the prehispanic urban center of Xochicalco identified evidence for segmental urban structure and the *disarticulation* of regional population within the context of the site's urban plan. The second line of evidence examines Late Postclassic settlement patterns within the former altepetl of Tepeaca, Puebla. Here weak settlement boundaries and the *dispersion* of population across the landscape conform to predictions of a population integrated through the cuadrilla system. Third and finally, integration of population segments within the altepetl was based on their position within the rotational-service cycle, rather than their rank order by size or some other hierarchical criteria. My discussion here focuses simply on whether evidence for rotational service can be found in the highlands. If it can, then we know that all the structural components of segmental altepetl community structure were present in Central Mexico at least by AD 700.

Segmental Urban Structure and Population Disarticulation at Xochicalco

Research and mapping at the site of Xochicalco, Morelos, have revealed an urban structure that I believe is a product of segmented-community organization. The site of Xochicalco dates to the Epiclassic period (AD 650–900), when it was the center of a powerful regional-conquest state that included most of western Morelos and northern Guerrero. Systematic site mapping indicates that Xochicalco covered a maximum of 4 sq km during the Epiclassic (figure 14.6) and had a population of 10,000–15,000 (Hirth 2000). Surface reconnaissance was used to define Xochicalco's maximal site limit, and site growth was reconstructed using surface collections and excavations to date phases of occupation.

Initially, Xochicalco appeared to be a corporate urban community organized internally into a series of small residential wards (Hirth 1995). The more we studied the site plan, however, the clearer it became that Xochicalco actually was a cluster of loosely articulated site segments instead of a single, integrated urban center (Hirth 2000). These site segments were contemporary in age and appear to represent clusters of administrative structures constructed and used by populations residing outside of Xochicalco.

The distribution of administrative structures and defensive architecture at Xochicalco provides good evidence for a segmental community structure. Xochicalco, like other major sites in Mesoamerica, has the majority of its civic-ceremonial architecture located in and around the central site core (figure 14.7). At the center of the site is the palace complex of Xochicalco's ruler, which was surrounded, in turn, by temples, ballcourts, the institutional facilities associated with a public market, and administrative buildings of various kinds (Hirth 2000).

Although we are only beginning to understand the functions of the different types of public buildings at Xochicalco, one architectural arrangement, the systems mound, stands out as distinct from the rest. Systems mounds are large, free-standing platforms

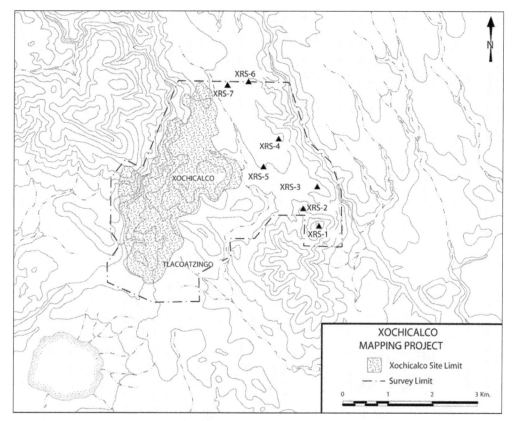

Figure 14.6. The size and extent of the site of Xochicalco, Morelos, Mexico. Outlying triangles indicate the location of small rural settlements during the Epiclassic period.

that supported a complex of buildings on their summits. One of these structures (building X1-4) was excavated in the central site core by Cesar Sáenz (1964a, 1964b; figure 14.8). This structure had a group of buildings organized around a central patio on its summit that had an administrative function. Excavations recovered three carved stelae commemorating the life histories of three of Xochicalco's rulers (V. Smith 1988, 2000a) in a subfloor crypt of the group's main building. The architectural layout of this and other systems mounds throughout the site suggests that these structures all supported small room complexes that had administrative functions.

Unlike other architectural constructions, systems mounds at Xochicalco were not concentrated in the central site core. In fact, most systems mounds were distributed across adjacent hillsides outside the main site core on Cerro Xochicalco. They occur either alone or as the central building in small architectural complexes; examples can be found in the administrative precincts at Tlacoatzingo, Cerro Temascal, and La Maqueta (figure 14.7). Systems mounds are always located in topographically prominent and/or defensible locations underscoring their importance in Xochicalco's internal administrative organization. Systems mounds at Tlacoatzingo and La Maqueta are located at the center of two large population clusters. Most systems mounds, however,

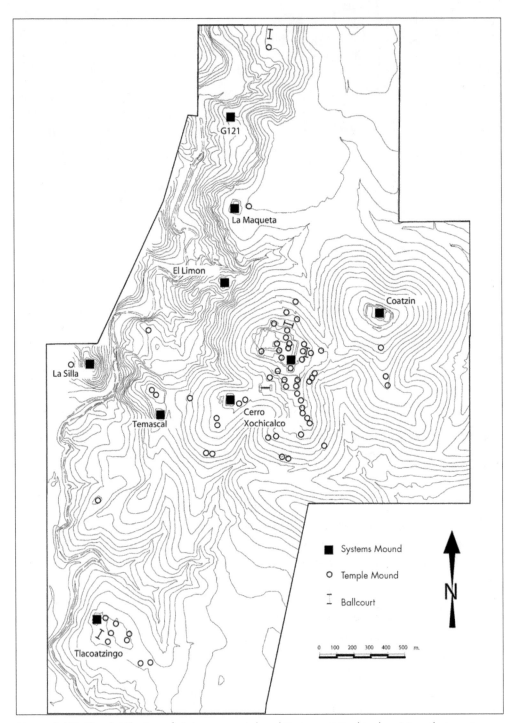

Figure 14.7. The distribution of civic-ceremonial architecture at Xochicalco. Note that most systems mounds are outside the main site core on Cerro Xochicalco.

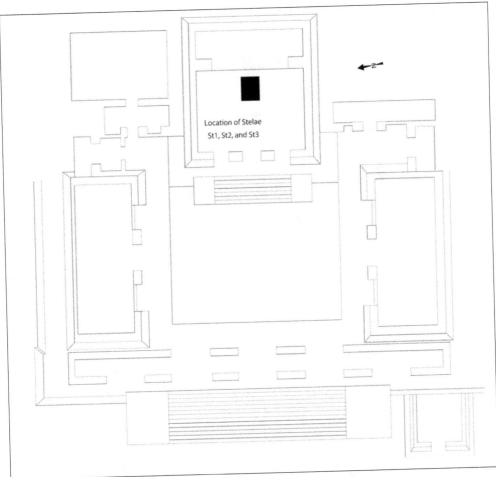

Figure 14.8. The architectural layout of Structure X1-4, the systems mound excavated by Cesar Sáenz in the central site core of Cerro Xochicalco.

were part of administrative complexes that did not have associated resident population; examples include the architectural complexes of Coatzin, Temascal, La Silla, El Limón, and Group G121 (figure 14.9).

The defensive architecture constructed at Xochicalco also provides evidence for the site's segmented organizational structure. The defensive character of Xochicalco has long been recognized (Armillas 1948); its prehispanic residents used walls, moats, ditches, ramparts, and defensive terraces, together with the natural slope, to fortify and protect areas of the site. What is most striking about Xochicalco's defensive plan is that the site is subdivided into seven separate and distinctive defensive precincts. Cerro Xochicalco is the largest and most heavily fortified of these defensive precincts. Although Cerro Xochicalco was large enough to provide safe refuge for all of the site's resident population, six other defensive precincts were constructed on adjacent hillsides. The seven defensive precincts, when combined with the distribution of systems mounds at Xochicalco, allow us to identify nine areas within the urban zone

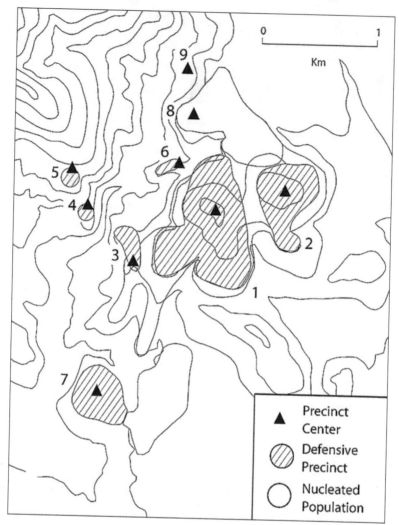

Figure 14.9. The distribution of defensive precincts, systems mounds, and population clusters at Xochicalco: 1, Cerro Xochicalco; 2, Coatzin; 3, Temascal; 4, La Silla; 5, La Fosa; 6, El Limón; 7, Tlacoatzingo; 8, La Maqueta; 9, Group G121.

that appear to represent semi-autonomous administrative precincts (figure 14.9). Three of these precincts (Cerro Xochicalco, Tlacoatzingo, and La Maqueta) have residential populations that account for 80 percent of the site's resident population. The other six precincts have either no population (Coatzin, La Fosa), or very low associated population (La Silla, Temascal, El Limón, Group G121). Two of these nine administrative zones (La Maqueta, G121) are located in semi-defensible areas but lack the special defensive constructions and features associated with the other seven (figure 14.9).

In prehispanic Mesoamerica, military organization paralleled social organization. Military units were created from the barrios and calpolli where people lived and were

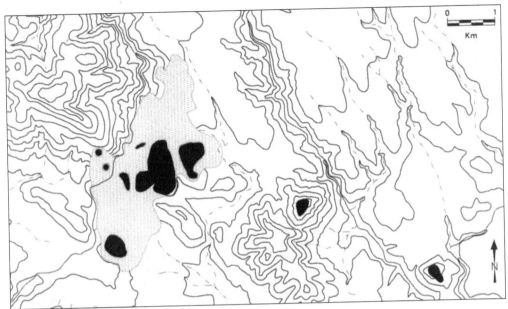

Figure 14.10. The location of Epiclassic defensive precincts at Xochicalco and neighboring sites in western Morelos.

society's primary social units (Hassig 1988:55–56). The presence of multiple defensive precincts at Xochicalco indicates that social groups here defended themselves as *independent but coordinated* segments rather than as a single, integrated, corporate body (Hirth 2000:241). Groups apparently worked together for their mutual defense rather than supported a single, centralized defensive strategy through the central state. Some Epiclassic sites in the surrounding region also had defensive precincts and did not rely on Xochicalco for their protection (figure 14.10). As mentioned above, most defensive precincts at Xochicalco did not have resident populations that would have used them. Instead, the populations that constructed and used the vacant defensive precincts at Xochicalco must have resided in its surrounding hinterland and came together only in times of common defense. Cerro Coatzin and Cerro La Fosa are good examples of defensive precincts without associated population.

These data indicate that the populations represented by the administrative and defensive precincts at Xochicalco were part of the community and integrated into its overall urban plan. But their populations did not reside together at Xochicalco! Representation of these population segments in the site center without having to be physically present represents a form of *disarticulation* associated with the emergence of a segmental model of altepetl organization like that discussed above.

Late Postclassic Settlement Dispersion in the Tepeaca Altepetl

One predictable feature of community structure within the altepetl is that settlements may have fluid boundaries. This is because primary affiliation is to the altepetl and not the population aggregate where people reside. In archaeological terms, this could be

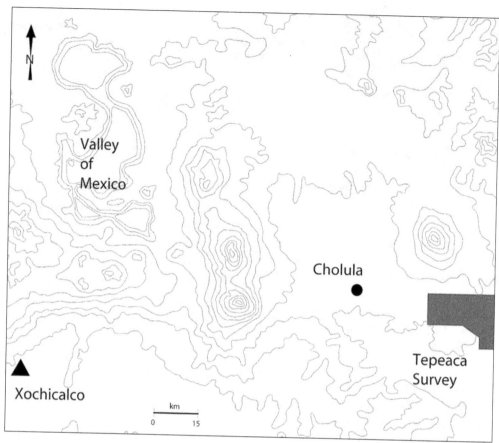

Figure 14.11. The location of the Tepeaca survey region in Central Mexico.

represented by low-density settlement clusters and a general *dispersion* of residential population across the landscape.

Settlement pattern analysis was used to evaluate whether population dispersion was a specific feature of altepetl organization in the area around Tepeaca, Puebla (figure 14.11). Settlement surveys have documented dispersed settlement patterns during the Late Postclassic period elsewhere in the highlands (Kowalewski et al. 1989; Parsons 1971; Parsons et al. 1982). Ethnohistoric research has established the broad outline of community structure and provided the background for testing the altepetl model using archaeological data. In Tepeaca, for instance, the altepetl was organized into four tlahtocayo (patrimonial estates), the partial boundaries for which were known (Yoneda 1991). We also know that populations in this region were organized into tribute cuadrillas that cut across residential groupings within the valley (Martínez 1984). Under these conditions, we would expect that regional population would be dispersed rather than located in tightly nucleated residential communities.

The Late Postclassic settlement pattern in the Tepeaca region is illustrated in figure 14.12. Two things are evident from this pattern. First, the Late Postclassic population is very dispersed; tightly nucleated communities were not found anywhere in

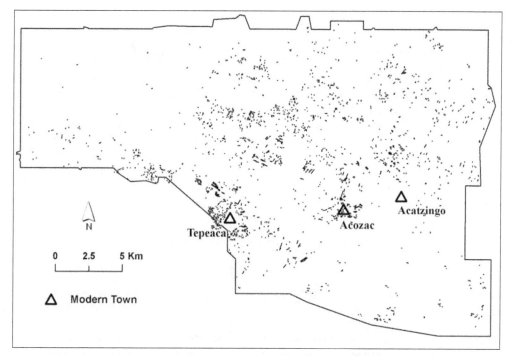

Figure 14.12. Dispersed settlement patterns in the Tepeaca region during the Late Postclassic period. Please see figure 14.11 for the specific location of the Tepeaca survey region.

the region outside the principle site of Tepeaca. Second, no breaks were observed in the distribution of settlement that would mark the divisions within or between altepemeh. Mapa de Cuauhtinchan No. 4 shows the boundaries *between* the patrimonial territory of the tlahtocayo of Tepeaca and the tlahtocayo of Acatzingo and Oxtoticpac (Yoneda 1991). Although the boundaries of the altepetl were established in AD 1467 by the Aztec king of Axayacatl (Martínez 1984:47), there is no evidence for any break in the distribution of archaeological settlements that would reflect these territorial divisions. Following the prediction of the model, regional population was dispersed in low-density settlements throughout both the Tepeaca and Acatzingo tlahtocayo.

Evidence for Rotational Service at Xochicalco

Ethnohistoric evidence indicates that population segments within altepemeh were ordered and integrated through a system of rotational service. Although the *principle* of rotation provided the structure for many aspects of prehispanic life, identifying rotational-service obligations using archaeological data is difficult. This notwithstanding, it is possible to document the principle of rotational obligations on which the structure of the altepetl was based. At Xochicalco, rotational obligations were depicted in the monumental art associated with meeting tribute obligations. Tribute payments, like the rotational services that supported the altepetl, were fixed to calendar cycles and reflect the organizational principle underlying segmental structures.

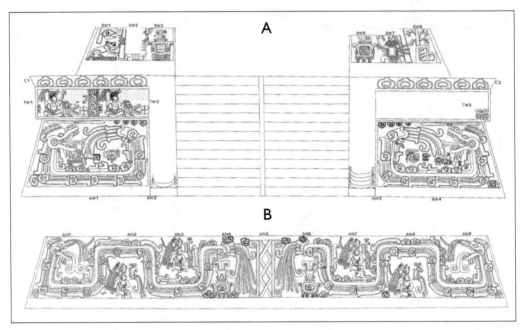

Figure 14.13. The Pyramid of the Plumed Serpent at Xochicalco: A, The west stairway to the Pyramid of the Plumed Serpent; B, The northern talud of the pyramid showing ruler images interspersed between the coils of the serpent.

Evidence for conquest tribute at Xochicalco was found on the bas-relief carvings covering the sides of the Pyramid of the Plumed Serpent (Structure X1-1) (figure 14.13a). The dominant imagery on this structure consists of large undulating serpents located on the lower sides of the platform mound (the talud) (figure 14.13b). Serpent imagery was associated with rulership; images of the ruler in the coils of the serpent emphasize the political character of this structure. Twenty-eight panels located on the upper portion of the basal platform (the tablero) depict the collection of tribute from conquered places. The temple on the summit of the platform is largely destroyed, but the remaining portions are covered with bas-relief images of warriors, emphasizing the political theme of this structure.

The twenty-eight tribute panels of the Pyramid of the Plumed Serpent can be subdivided into two groups. Twenty-four panels contain the names of conquered places paying tribute; the four others contain calendar dates during the year that tribute was paid. The twenty-four tribute panels each contain the figure of a warrior holding a tribute bag (figure 14.14). A speech scroll emanates from the warrior's mouth, and the word for tribute (*nitlacalaquia*) is glossed in rebus form by the open teeth shown eating the *kan* symbol, representing the idea of something precious (Hirth 1989). What is different in each panel is the toponym, that is, the name of the place paying tribute, located directly above the word for tribute. Taken in their entirety, these twenty-four panels provided a list of the tribute domain for Xochicalco during the height of its political power. Unfortunately, most of the toponyms on these panels are destroyed;

Figure 14.14. Four tribute panels from the north side (tablero) of the Pyramid of the Plumed Serpent.

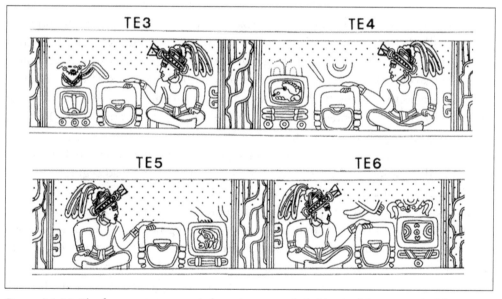

Figure 14.15. The four payment panels from the east side (tablero) of the Pyramid of the Plumed Serpent.

only seven can be read and identified with any certainty (Hirth 1989; V. Smith 2000b).

The four payment panels are important for this discussion. These panels are located together on the east side of the structure. Each panel depicts a seated warrior holding a large sealed vessel or stoppered jar (figure 14.15). The implied meaning seems to be one of storage or collection. The figures lack speech scrolls, and, in place of the symbol for tribute, there is a cartouche with bar-and-dot numerals representing a calendar glyph (V. Smith 2000b:72). The four dates (3 Reed, 13 Monkey, 5 Death, and 6 Twisted) are from the highland ritual calendar. The association of calendar dates with tribute collection is important. At the time of the Conquest, the Aztecs collected tribute four times a year from conquered provinces. It would have been nice if these four dates corresponded to ninety-day intervals within the annual calendar, but they do not. Nevertheless, the presence of four dates in this context is not coincidental. Bas-relief carvings were positioned above the calendar glyphs, and although they are too badly destroyed to be read, they resemble the toponyms found on the tribute panels. They probably represent places where tribute was collected.

The collection of tribute from conquered groups was structured following the same organizational principles as service tribute within the altepetl. Evidence for the periodic and rotating collection of conquest tribute at Xochicalco suggests that the principle of rotational service was well established between AD 650 and 900 and was a fundamental feature in the organization of altepemeh elsewhere in Central Mexico at this time.

Conclusions

Large, nucleated, urban centers were found throughout Central Mexico at the time of the Conquest. These cities, despite their size and density, were not formal corporate entities with distinct identities or jurisdictions. Large communities were, to a great extent, an incidental by-product of the growth of their altepetl and the socioeconomic forces that shaped them. What this underscores is the importance of maintaining a regional perspective when studying Mesoamerican urbanism, because the form of Central Mexican urban centers was shaped by the size, organization, and development of their respective political regions.

This chapter has explored the prehispanic altepetl and how it affected the structure and organization of the settlements within it. Altepemeh had segmental structures that provided great flexibility in the way populations could be organized at the regional level. They were composed of a series of independent, corporate segments (for example, calpolli, tlaxilacalli, and tlahtocayo). These segments held land in common and were of equal rank within the altepetl irrespective of their location in rural or urban settings. Although these population segments could be clustered together to form a nucleated settlement, they did not constitute an integrated community. Instead, large settlements were the incidental by-product of altepetl development and did not, by themselves, constitute corporate municipal communities.

The organization of populations within the altepetl was by segmentary unit, rather than by residential locale. Populations of the same calpolli, for instance, could reside together or be dispersed; the spatial distribution of the population did not affect the organization of the altepetl. As a result, altepemeh vary widely in how their populations were distributed across the landscape. Three organizational features of Central Mexican altepemeh were territory disarticulation, population dispersion, and rotational integration. All three of these characteristics can be identified in the archaeological record, dating back to the Epiclassic period at Xochicalco, Morelos. This suggests that incidental urbanism within the context of altepetl development was a long-standing feature of Central Mexican community structure.

This chapter challenges the traditional understanding of Mesoamerican urban centers in two important ways. First, it argues that the city, as we commonly refer to it, does not represent a separate and specific institution within Mesoamerica. Instead, cities were embedded within, and dependent upon, the broader altepetl of which they were a part. Mesoamerican cities were not corporate entities with their own independent municipal identities. Rather, they were by-products of altepetl development and the processes that governed its size and structure (Sanders and Webster 1988). I have referred to this process as incidental urbanism and believe that it was a fundamental feature of urban structure throughout prehispanic Mesoamerica. Second, this chapter contends that the tendency for archaeologists to define cities as separate and unique social institutions is incorrect and is strongly influenced by Western views of the urban community. In Mesoamerica, the community was not defined by the limit of the built environment, even though it can be useful (under certain situations) to study this as if it were. Recognition of this fact creates a number of methodological problems for archaeologists, who must define sites on the basis of material remains. Despite these difficulties, accurate modeling of Mesoamerican urban centers is a necessary first step to interpreting their form and structure from archaeological remains. Only then will it be possible to study the development of Mesoamerican urban centers throughout prehistory with the archaeological tools at our disposal.

Urban communities varied greatly in form across Mesoamerica, from the nucleated towns of Central Mexico to the dispersed centers of the Maya lowlands. Despite these differences, a common set of organizational structures underlies population organization at the regional level. These organizational structures are represented by a range of similar indigenous concepts, such as the altepetl in Central Mexico, the *nu'u* in the Mixteca, the *bichou* among the Huastec, and the *cacab* in the Yucatecan Maya region (Gutiérrez Mendoza 2003; Hirth 2003; Marcus 2000[1983b]). In Mesoamerica, cities were an incidental by-product of these larger structures and the way they were organized. Unless we begin our investigations by asking what the indigenous view of community structure was for the people who resided in them, we will never acquire a truly meaningful understanding of what Mesoamerican urbanism was and how it evolved over time. This work is intended as a first step in that direction.

fifteen
Links in the Chain of Inka Cities
Communication, Alliance, and the Cultural Production of Status, Value, and Power

Craig Morris

Evidence for the expansion of the Inka empire stretches for more than 4,000 km, from near the border of modern Ecuador and Colombia in the north through highland and coastal Peru and highland Bolivia into northwestern Argentina and through the northern half of Chile (figure 15.1). The Inka empire was by far the largest empire of the New World.

Since the sixteenth century AD when the Spaniards first described the settlements they saw, there has been little doubt that the Inka built great cities. Pedro Sancho de la Hoz (1968[1538]:176), secretary to the conquistador Francisco Pizarro, saw the Inka capital in 1534 and exclaimed: "The city of Cuzco...is so large and so beautiful that it would be worthy to appear even in Spain." Unfortunately for archaeologists, modern Cuzco now covers much of the ancient capital, but the walls that remain show incredible construction and architectural skills, justifying the effusive reactions of the sixteenth-century observers. Certainly, the ruins of the largest Inka settlements look like cities, covering a square kilometer or more and consisting of thousands of structures with impressive architectural diversity and planning. The archaeological evidence also leaves little doubt that these sites displayed quintessentially urban features, including palaces, public ceremonial precincts, and manufacturing zones.

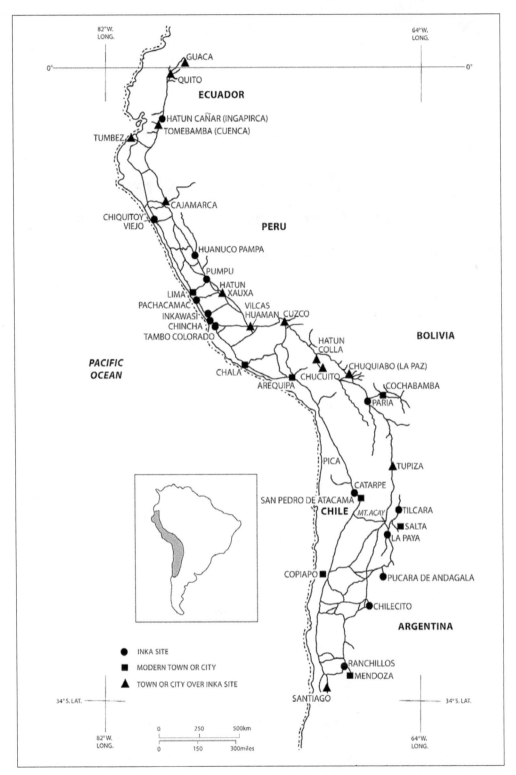

Figure 15.1. The Inka empire and road system (based on Hyslop 1984).

Even the earliest observers, however, hint that Inka cities departed somewhat from our usual conceptions of urbanism. Perhaps for this reason, Inka specialists (including me) often use terms like "center," avoiding full commitment to the notion of an Inka "city." Cieza de León (1959[1553]:109) notes, with his usual precision, that more than 30,000 people "served" Huánuco Pampa, one of the Inka sites discussed below. He did not choose terms that implied permanent "residence." The notion of service also fits well with John Murra's (1980) studies of the non-trade-based Inka economy, showing that the state and its ruling elite were supported by tribute in labor rather than goods. Most, if not all, cities housed substantial numbers of transients. But in the Inka case, as we will see, there are suggestions that in many cities transients and people fulfilling short-term labor obligations may have substantially outnumbered permanent residents. There seems, nevertheless, to have been a significant core of long-term residents that would distinguish such cities from what have been called "empty" ceremonial centers.

In 1972 Murra (1972, 1985) outlined a theory of Andean "vertical ecological complementarity" in which political units of various sizes established colonies in differing ecological zones, maintaining direct access to varied critical resources. These colonies were often interspersed among lands of other groups, resulting in what Murra called an archipelago model of resource exploitation and economic and political organization. The evidence suggests that the archipelago pattern was distributed unevenly across the central Andean highlands but was not a major feature of the coast, except for some intrusive highland colonies. This chapter is not the place for a full exploration of the political and economic dynamics of such a system of dispersed and interspersed political units. It is important, however, to consider the potential consequences of the large-scale expansion of such a system as the Inka state extended its territorial and economic reach. How would a settlement system based on resource exploitation and "archipelago" principles bring about "urban" settlements?

A heavily mobile population tied to a labor-tribute system, a political and religious ceremonial focus, non-trade exchange, state-controlled production of key goods, and large-scale storage are all characteristics of Inka cities, as indicated by a careful reading of the written sources and confirmed by archaeology. Studies of the Inka road system (Hyslop 1984) and some of the large sites it links (D'Altroy 1992; Hyslop 1990; Morris 1972, 1982) suggest that individual cities were not as pertinent to the Inka pattern as was the overall network that formed a great web over an intricately planned empire (figure 15.1).

We are still in the early stages of investigation of the enormous Inka settlement network, but some of its salient features have already emerged. For example, many of the cities were planned by the state and built on previously vacant land, well away from existing, pre-Inka, settlements. Even when the Inkas inserted themselves directly into existing cities, they created a spatially separate, official Inka sector, clearly marked by its own architectural style. In this chapter I explore two cities: Huánuco Pampa, built by the Inkas on virgin land, and another, built before Inka times as the capital of the pre-Inka Chincha kingdom, a capital the Inka later adapted to their own agenda.

Huánuco Pampa

Feasts and Rituals, Production and Storage, Political and Cultural Transformation

> In what is known as Huánuco there was an admirably built royal palace, made of very large stones artfully joined. This palace or lodging was the capital of the provinces bordering on the Andes, and beside it there was a temple to the sun with many vestals and priests. It was so important in the times of the Incas that there were always over thirty thousand Indians to serve it. The stewards of the Incas who were in charge of collection of the regular tributes in the region served this palace.
>
> —*Pedro de Cieza de León,* The Incas of Pedro de Cieza de Léon

Huánuco Pampa; an administrative city on the great highland road that linked the settlements of the empire, lies on a wide *pampa* (plain), at an altitude of about 3,800 m in the central Peruvian highlands. It covers almost 3 sq km (figure 15.2) and has 497 storehouses built in neat rows on a hill to the south overlooking the settlement. The site is unusually well preserved, and in the late 1960s and 1970s we excavated almost 300 of the nearly 4,000 structures whose foundations can still be seen. In the 1980s we studied nearly a million pottery sherds, as well as animal bones and other remains, found on the floors and in the refuse areas of the city.

Our studies of the resulting database continue, but our conclusions to date show several dimensions of the activities in the city and how they related to Inka economics, statecraft, and urban planning. They confirm many of our expectations. We did not locate any areas where we believe a formal marketplace might have functioned. However, storage was abundant, and we now have a good understanding of its technological sophistication (Morris 1981) and the purposes for which stored goods were used (Morris 1986). We also are beginning to understand which areas were used by transients and which were used by longer-term residents. Most important, the evidence shows what people were doing in the city, the kind of city it was, how it advanced the strategies of the Inka, and how it can help us grasp broader patterns of variation in urban life.

Both written and archaeological evidence indicates that three, ranked, public-ceremonial areas were, in various senses, the core of the city. These areas were vital to the political and economic expansion of the empire—by redistributing prestige goods, by building and communicating (through ritual and ceremony) an ideology of compliance with Inka rule, and by helping create a hierarchical political structure that made a politically fragmented area governable. These areas were the key to understanding the urban population structure and principal urban economic activities, namely, storage and the production of cloth and beer. These economic activities enabled the city to supply the items for its elaborate ritual calendar and meet its agenda of imperial "generosity."

Figure 15.2. General plan of the city of Huánuco Pampa.

The architectural evidence for the three ranked areas consists of three plazas of decreasing size, each with its associated public buildings, located on the east-west axis of the city. I have suggested in an earlier publication (Morris 1987) how these three plaza sectors may relate to a complex overall city plan that reflects some of the organizational principles outlined by Zuidema (1964) and others (Wachtel 1973) based on studies of the written sources. The three plazas are still not well understood, though tripartite organization likely constituted an important mechanism of empire building. One of its features appears to have been the creation of a mechanism to designate an intermediate social class (in addition to the royal kin groups and the commoners) that could link the kin groups of Cuzco rulers to those of local leaders. The three resulting classes were named *collana*, *payan*, and *cayao* and apparently reflect kinship hierarchies. Collana was associated with the Cuzco kin groups of the rulers and the most important officials. The lowest rank was cayao, the commoners who comprised hundreds of non-Inka groups incorporated into the empire. Members of the third, the middle group, payan, had connections to both collana and cayao through intermarriage and mechanisms of fictive kinship. Membership in the payan category was likely expanding as a result of the need for an ever-larger intermediate elite to govern the growing empire, as well as the importance of cementing relationships between Inkas and local elites through marriage ties.

Ethnohistorians (Wachtel 1973:32) believe that the three ranked classes were represented spatially primarily by a concentric pattern, and the three main plaza groups with related buildings extending eastward from the center of Huánuco Pampa (see figure 15.1) is consistent with that suggestion. The order is understandably the reverse of that described for Cuzco. The great central plaza was probably the space for the common cayao class. A large, two-part administrative palace (Morris 2004) that occupied much of the eastern part of the city provided enclosed and restricted public plaza areas for the payan and collana groups.

The Administrative Palace: Ranked Spaces for the Cuzco Rulers and an Intermediate Elite

A brief description by Martín de Murúa (1946[1590–1609]:165–166) of a palace in Cuzco and the people entering and using its spaces allows us to construct a model of an Inka administrative palace that may also help us understand the well-preserved architecture and excavated artifacts of the Huánuco Pampa palace (figure 15.3). The most restricted part of the palace (Unit IIB4) contained a group of six badly looted structures, partly built of dressed stone masonry; this highly restricted area was likely intended for royal lodging. A group of smaller and more rustic buildings within the same compound, which yielded evidence of small-scale cooking, possibly served as kitchen and service spaces for the royal quarters. The overall compound overlooks a large pond fed by a spring through an underground canal. Other underground canals brought water from the spring to other water features, perhaps ceremonial "baths." This least accessible part of the palace merited a comment by Murúa regarding the Cuzco palace: "And going farther in were the salons and rooms where the Inca lived. And this was all full of delights, since various areas were planted with trees and gardens, and the royal lodgings were spacious and built with marvelous artistry" (Murúa 1946[1590–1609]:166).

Elaborate dressed-stone gateways separate the private compound from a plaza

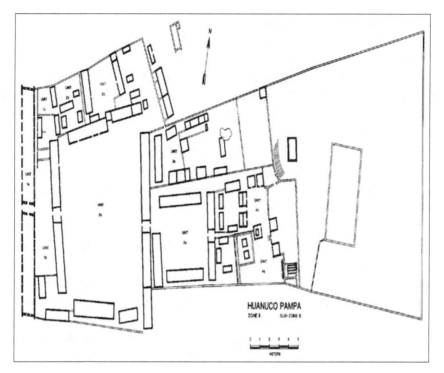

Figure 15.3. Zone IIB: the administrative palace at Huánuco Pampa.

surrounded by long buildings (Unit IIB3a; figure 15.3) that served as the public sector of the collana complex. The trapezoidal enclosing wall that surrounds both the private compound and the more public plaza areas imply that they were probably two conceptually related parts of a single entity, each part quite different in access and function.

The basis of the Andean labor economy, which the Inka had stretched to an imperial scale, obliged the recipient of labor to reciprocate with feasts and gifts. Indeed, the cycle of obligations was probably initiated with royal generosity. The critical ingredient of the feasts was maize beer—explaining the Inka drive to terrace and irrigate the slopes of warm valleys and use other means to increase maize production (Morris 1986, 1987; Murra 1960). There is evidence of food and beer consumption in the buildings surrounding the main plaza at Huánuco Pampa, as we will see below, but the plazas and buildings of the palace, which we ascribe to the royal (collana) and intermediate (payan) classes, are what produced the greatest concentration.

The public space of the collana complex—with its abundance of sherds from plates and the large jars used for storing shelled maize, maize beer, and other products—served as a setting for large-scale consumption of food and drink. The quantitative study of the ceramics has also revealed interesting and unanticipated distribution patterns of ceramic decorative motifs. Most notable is the presence of an unusually high percentage of sherds with two designs that are local adaptations of Cuzco motifs. One of these is Cuzco Polychrome A, and the other, a local variant of Cuzco White on Red (Julien 2004; Miller 2004; Rowe 1944:46–47). The percentage in both cases is approximately double that found in the public plaza area directly to the west (Unit IIB2a; see figure 15.3), discussed below. Although the third of the principal Imperial Inka decorative motifs, Cuzco Polychrome B, is also common in the collana-associated unit, its occurrence is far lower than in the less elite area (Unit IIB2a) to the west. Our tentative interpretation is that Cuzco White on Red and Polychrome A are somehow associated with the more exclusive of the elite groups that used the administrative palace. Although it must still be regarded as a working hypothesis, based in part on the Murúa account, it seems likely that Unit IIB3a was linked to the royal groups associated with the Cuzco rulers (collana) and that Polychrome A and Cuzco White on Red pottery also related to that group. White on Red and Polychrome A and B designs occur primarily on the large vessels used for maize beer, so they may have been used to mark or label supplies of that prestigious drink.

A more spacious public area (Unit IIB2a; see figure 15.3) is encountered on entering the administrative palace from the city's central plaza. It consists of ten long buildings and, including its large plaza, covers about three times the area of the Unit IIB3a, just described. Based in part on the Murúa account, we hypothesize that this area was probably associated with the intermediate (payan) status group. The size, location, and layout of the intermediate plaza area all suggest that it served a larger number of people than did IIB3a. There are also indications that the larger unit was used by more numerous groups but the smaller and more restricted collana area may have been used more intensively and regularly, perhaps even continuously.

In terms of decorated ceramics in IIB2a, 57 percent were of the Polychrome B variety. Polychrome A and White on Red accounted for only about 13 percent each. It is also of note that a local incised pottery, which is very rare throughout the city, accounted for about 7.5 percent of the decorated ceramics in the unit. Only four sherds of this pottery were found in Unit IIB3a. In terms of vessel shape assemblages, the two palace units are remarkably similar, suggesting nearly identical activities—the serving of food and drink. The differences that distinguish the areas are likely related to the social identities of the people who used them.

These differences in the decoration on ceramic serving wares would almost certainly have been matched by differences in the clothing and adornment worn by the people in the two areas, because the state is known to have issued gifts of cloth that bore emblems of social categories to important subjects (Murra 1962). Architecture, ceramics, cloth, and metals were all media in an artistic sense, but the symbol-laden objects made from them were also media of communication. Images and encoded information were communicated to critical audiences in order to influence perceptions and actions. The messages communicated were reinforced by human associations and ceremonial performances effective in achieving social, political, and economic impact. People advanced in status; goods increased in value; and the state grew in size and power. The scenarios in the Huánuco Pampa palace were designed as part of what Geertz (1980) christened in Bali as "the theater state" and involved what Victor Turner

Figure 15.4. The great halls at the edge of the central plaza of Huánuco Pampa.

(1969) labeled "ritual processes." At Huánuco Pampa, the Inka built an elaborate palace complex as an architectural backdrop to symbolically rich props and costumes, coordinated with music, dance, food, and inebriating drink to create transformative rituals that turned guests into subjects.

The Central Plaza and the Common Sectors: Bringing the Diverse Hinterland inside the City and the State

The third of the ranked public ceremonial spaces at Huánuco Pampa was the enormous central plaza. More than half a kilometer in length (see figure 15.2), the main plaza was so large and so much the centerpiece of the city plan that the four zones of structures that surround it almost seem to cling to the plaza's edges, instead of the plaza being simply an open space where the city's neighborhoods come together. It was surrounded by long multi-door halls (figure 15.4) along much of its periphery. The royal highway from Cuzco to Quito crossed it, and the "streets" that separate many of the city's twelve sectors opened into it. The evidence for large-scale cooking in most of the long buildings suggests that they served as communal, probably transient, housing. They likely provided facilities for visits by commoners from the surrounding hinterland to Huánuco Pampa for rituals and ceremonies and for short-term labor tribute.

Near the center of the plaza is a stepped, three-level platform accessed by a wide stairway and adorned with images of pumas (figure 15.5). Because of its impressive construction and the pumas, the so-called *ushnu* platform, or at least its massive upper

Figure 15.5. The dressed stone ushnu platform in the central plaza of Huánuco Pampa.

level, was probably meant to be emblematic of the Inka state and its rulers, whereas the plaza itself and the various building sectors around it (except for the two-part palace described above) related to the incorporated groups.

Because Huánuco Pampa was a city built and furnished by the state, we have only occasional material evidence for the many groups that would have inhabited these non-elite areas on their occasional visits and longer sojourns. We know from other evidence that there was substantial diversity among the groups, both in ethnicity and in scale. The *visita* (inspection report), of Iñigo Ortiz de Zúñiga (1967[1562], 1972 [1562]) informs us that many members of the Chupaychu and Yacha groups, with whom the report mainly deals, spent time in labor service at Huánuco Pampa, and we presume that several other, less well-documented groups from nearby regions visited and sometimes lived in the city as well. For instance, the upper Marañon Valley, between Huánuco Pampa and the areas of the Chupaychu and Yacha, would likely have formed an important part of Huánuco Pampa's sphere of control. The impressive upper Marañon sites, such as Garu, indicate that the polity of which they were part may have been larger and more centralized than their Chupaychu and Yacha neighbors, (Morris and Thompson 1985:151–160). Other groups presumably occupied regions west of Huánuco Pampa. All of this points to a hinterland of considerable political complexity.

Representatives of these various peoples must have made up the bulk of the population of Huánuco Pampa. The length of time they resided in the city probably varied greatly. Most would have provided their labor tax, possibly working to build the city and at the same time participating in its urban ceremonial life. Many of them probably occupied the thousands of irregularly arranged, small structures back from the edges of the plaza. The most transient of the representatives were probably housed in the long halls. Although intriguing, the evidence for the specific organization of the various sectors surrounding the plaza is very incomplete and beyond the scope of this chapter (Morris 1987; Morris and Thompson 1985:63–73).

What use did the enormous central plaza itself serve? Unfortunately, we have no direct evidence, except for the imprint of the road, the eating and drinking in the surrounding great halls, and the likelihood that Inka officials witnessed or officiated over the plaza's activities from their elevated position on the top of the ushnu platform. It seems likely that the central plaza, somewhat like the smaller plazas within the palace, was used for many of the political and religious rituals that punctuated the elaborate ceremonial calendar providing a blueprint for activities throughout the year. Rowe (1946:308–312) contains a brief summary. It was the primary ceremonial area for the city's non-elite residents and visitors. In a recent study, R. Alan Covey and I (Morris and Covey 2005) proposed that the great plaza might have been the scene of an unexpected activity: ritual warfare. Violent forms of competition took place within other ancient states, and a tradition of ritualized fighting with frequent death was common throughout the recorded history of native Andean groups. Recent studies of Andean warfare and violence in its social and ideological contexts (Arkush and Stanish 2005; Redmond 1994; Swenson 2003; Topic and Topic 1997) are beginning to move us closer to understanding the vital, but extremely complex, role of war in sociopolitical transformation. The hypothesis of ritual warfare postdates our field research; we did not systematically test the hypothesis for ritualized fighting in the center of Huánuco Pampa. However, this important practice could have been conducted in such an open space.

Inka stories and legends characterize most of the groups they incorporated as warlike and uncivilized before these were brought into the empire. Given the Inkas's penchant for casting themselves as great pacifiers, as well as valiant warriors, and the Spanish tendency to see everything through their own lens of war and coercive conquest, a picture has emerged of the Inka empire as a conquest state in a more or less European sense. When we look more closely at Andean conflict and warfare (Hartmann 1971, 1979; Topic and Topic 1987, 1997; Urton 1993), however, the picture is much less clear-cut. Chroniclers recorded ritual battles fought with some regularity but limited to certain times of the year. The battles contained strong elements of religion, often focusing on the importance of spilling blood on the earth. More recent ritual battles, with their bewildering combinations of ceremonies, feasts, violence, and death, have been described in detail by ethnographers (Cama Ttito and Ttito Tica 2003; Valencia Espinoza and Valencia Becerra 2003). Sometimes economic exchanges take place, elements of prestige and rank (both within and between groups) are involved, and the results are often predicted based on previous experience, but predictions do not always match the results. Loss of life is low in comparison with fully coercive warfare, but it is, nevertheless, a routine part of the outcome.

Warfare in Inka times, although strategic in its implications, was probably much more embedded in the broader context of social relations and ritual than our analyses have typically assumed. In a way analogous to exchange—in which there was little institutionalized trade—military matters were likely so ritualized that they become hard to separate from the political, economic, and religious aspects of social affairs. Given these Andean traditions, warfare may have been one of the uses of the great central space at Huánuco Pampa—a place where the many small groups from the surrounding hinterland could test their strength and arrive at tentative positions in an emerging hierarchy. The Inkas and their soldiers may often have participated, and the results would have been a way of creating a pattern of winners and losers, helping build a multilevel hierarchical order in a region known for fragmentation and political chaos.

In this scenario of ritualized warfare, battles would be regularly refought, and no solution was final. Although lack of "finality" has its limits, it would have tended to thwart the emergence of strong local rivals to the Inka. Rule, at least in the early stages, would have been a matter of maintaining a precarious balance. Perhaps this precarious balance is inherent in archipelago systems, in which groups are interspersed among one another, a situation Murra (1986:50) has described as "intense, temporary truces." A tense coexistence among the diverse groups the Inka brought together around Huánuco Pampa's main plaza may have been a major aspect of the "administrative" management of that hinterland. Of course, the Inka's own participation—from their palace on the eastern side of the plaza—would almost certainly have been included as part of this set of tense and "tentative" alliances. Sallnow (1987:141) has noted the importance of ritual battles fought between groups considered in some sense as insiders. The ambivalence of alliances and a somewhat shifting notion of inside and outside may have been characteristic of the early phases of Inka expansion into an area. War, religion, exchange, and the manipulation of prestige and hierarchy were all carefully linked. Expansion of scale involved the careful management of periods of ambivalence and transition. The political process in this case was not one of simple conquest and coercion, but a slower one involving the special facilities of an administrative city where complex and varied strategies of communication could be carried out to convince and motivate potential subjects.

Chosen Women and Chosen Goods

Certain material goods needed to be produced in the city for the mechanisms of royal generosity and labor service to function. Production of the symbol-laden goods in stone, cloth, metal, and ceramics needed to be monitored to ensure quality and appropriate symbolic content. The crucial maize beer was highly perishable and thus needed to be produced near the place of consumption. The massive storage complex at Huánuco Pampa ensured the availability of much of the city's supplies, but Inka planners also provided critical manufacturing facilities within the city.

Architect Emilio Harth-Terré (1964) proposed that the walled compound of fifty buildings bordering the north side of Huánuco Pampa's main plaza (figure 15.6) served as barracks. Its very regular layout and obvious concern with security and control do indeed suggest a military installation. Harth-Terré's interpretation thus served

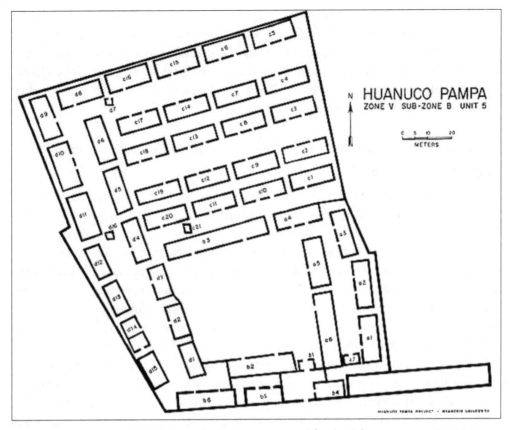

Figure 15.6. Compound VB5: the aqllawasi or compound for the "chosen women," at Huánuco Pampa.

as our working hypothesis. But our excavations uncovered sherds from large jars usually associated with brewing, as well as spinning and weaving tools and the occasional copper pin used by women to fasten their garments. We found not a single weapon among the several tons of material (Morris 1974).

The intensive use, probably continuous occupation, brewing of substantial quantities of maize beer, production of cloth, and presence of women were obviously not what we expected of a barracks. Nevertheless, extraordinary security and control were confirmed by the surrounding wall with a single entrance leading past an apparent checkpoint. Of the Inka's known population groups, the closest fit for the occupants of the compound would be the famous *aqlla*—the cloistered women who brewed maize beer and wove cloth for the Inka state (Murra 1966). The chroniclers' emphasis on seclusion and religious service for aqllas led to confusion with "vestal virgins," and a few of the young women were even honored to become sacrificial offerings (Reinhard and Ceruti 2006). Irene Silverblatt (1987), however, has argued convincingly that one of the principal roles these women served was as high-status brides who cemented political ties with important local leaders; this role, along with their importance as brewers and weavers, probably explains their presence in the city.

Given the amount of space in the compound and its intensity of use, the number of aqlla could have exceeded 200. The impressive "house of chosen women" gives us a much expanded notion of the scale of the aqlla institution. Its true importance, however, lies in what it produced and provided for the Inka state: prestigious clothes marked with labels of status for imperial gifts, the prestige drink for royal hospitality, and prestigious women for marriage exchange.

Assembly, Communication, and Labor Service to Promote Political and Economic Growth

Huánuco Pampa was a place designed to facilitate social, political, and economic change, and growth. It was politically created and "artificial," in some ways not unlike Brasilia, a modern political creation. But it was not built primarily to house a relatively static and self-perpetuating bureaucracy. The *khipu* knot records, the key indicators of bureaucratic activities (Ascher and Ascher 1981; Urton and Brezine 2005), are not preserved, and although administrative "bureaucrats" must have been present, they were not the most visible feature of Inka "reciprocal administration." Instead, what we see at Huánuco Pampa are the old traditions of reciprocity, including labor service, expanded to an urban scale. We also see a city with a mobile population accustomed to a system of multiple settlements—moving, for varying amounts of time, between them. Huánuco Pampa was essentially an urban island in an archipelago of ecological "complementarity." It provided a place of assembly and communication, with its core functions being discharged around the set of three plazas. The aim was to convince, to create new sets of relationships and attitudes. A context of royal hospitality and generosity was one of the hallmarks of this political process; a context of ritual warfare may have been another. Most of the rest of the city supported those core communications functions—497 storehouses (with a capacity of 37,000 cubic meters) were a source of food and other goods, and a large, well-ordered, walled compound were a source of women, beer, and fine cloth.

The Chincha Capital

The Cultivation of a Grand Alliance

The archaeological site of La Centinela (figure 15.7), the former capital of the wealthy Chincha kingdom on Peru's south coast, is dramatically different from Huánuco Pampa. It was built mainly of coursed adobe, called *tapia*, and painted gleaming white. Its most notable architectural features are stepped pyramids, and many of its monumental structures had stood for at least a century before the Inkas. Little is known of Chincha's founding and early growth, but certainly it was not an "artificial" creation of a distant empire. A major oracle made the capital a religious pilgrimage center, but most of the people related to the city either were permanent residents or lived in smaller sites throughout the Chincha Valley.

Chincha was the subject of an anonymous sixteenth-century AD report known sim-

Figure 15.7. The Chincha capital, now the site of La Centinela, as seen from the air in 1929.

ply as an "Aviso" (Rostworowski 1970). It confirms some information found in other sources. According to Pedro Pizarro (1917[1571]:32), the lord of Chincha was such a close ally that he rode in a litter close to the Inka ruler on the day the Inka empire fell to the Spaniards. But the Aviso also tells us that Chincha had three highly specialized groups: one devoted to agriculture, a second to fishing, and a third to long-distance trading with the coastal regions of what is now Ecuador, as well as with the southern highlands. In her analysis, María Rostworowski indicated that the principal commodity acquired in the north was probably *Spondylus* shell and, in the south, metal ores.

So far, our studies have found little hard evidence for Chincha's far-flung trade contacts. Only very small amounts of *Spondylus* have appeared, most of it worked into finished objects, and nothing so far indicates port facilities or large-scale warehousing. Likewise, there are few hints that the goods supposedly traded found their way into the quarters or refuse of the local or Inka elites, as we had predicted. It may well be that the reports of Chincha's long-distance exchange reflect more of a blueprint for a developing strategy than a fully implemented movement of goods.

The results of our studies of political ties between Chincha and the Inkas have been far more positive. Information from La Centinela's elite areas suggests some of the intricate details of a complex form of parallel rule involving the Lord of Chincha. Menzel's (1959, 1966) observations on the notable effects of Inka ceramics on the local pottery styles carry through to virtually all of the evidence we have uncovered. The influence was profound and not limited to the highest levels of leadership.

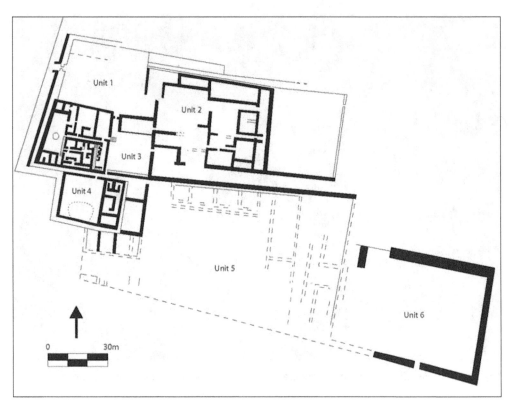

Figure 15.8. Sector III at La Centinela, built by the Inka with adobes, showing the entrance plaza to the shrine of Chinchaycamac (Unit 1), the possible sun temple and house of the "chosen women" (Unit 2), the Inka palace (Unit 3), the palace of the Chincha lord (Unit 4), and the dual public plazas (Units 5 and 6).

Because our research focus has mainly been the Inka period, our understanding of the Chincha capital before it became part of the empire is very incomplete. The evidence suggests that the compounds dominated by stepped pyramids with platforms and forecourts were not primarily residential. Rather, they likely served a mainly ceremonial role, perhaps related to local descent groups. There was almost certainly a large permanent population living in modest dwellings between La Centinela and the neighboring site of Tambo de Mora. The two sites were probably part of the same urban complex (Lumbreras 2001). Recently, Javier Alcalde, Carlos Del Aguila, Fernando Fujita, and Enrique Retamozo (2002) uncovered extensive evidence for the production of shell, gourd, and metal products in Tambo de Mora.

The Chincha capital was home to the oracle of Chinchaycamac, said to be a "son" of the great oracle of Pachacamac (Rostworowski 1992:52), a pilgrimage center of pan-Andean renown more than 100 km north of Chincha. A critical feature of the Inka's transformation of the Chincha capital was their co-option of the oracle, probably associated with La Centinela's tallest pyramid complex (Sector II). They re-oriented access to the shrine through their newly built imperial compound (see figure 15.7; figure 15.8), associating it with their own dominance. As was their practice in newly incor-

Figure 15.9. The Inka palace complex (Sector III, Unit 3) as seen from the stairway to the oracle of Chinchaycamac (Sector II) at La Centinela.

porated territories, the Inkas built a temple to the Sun, their imperial religion, in Chincha (Cieza de León 1959[1553]:136). It seems that proper, but almost token, respect was paid to the official Sun cult, with the major effort and emphasis being reserved for the long-established shrine of the local oracle. In part, this reflects the Inka's own beliefs in oracles (Gose 1996), but political motivations toward good relations with an ally must have been a primary factor.

The Seats of Rulership

A double-jamb imperial doorway led into the new Inka palace (Unit 3; figure 15.8; figure 15.9) from the plaza that served as entrance to the oracle complex. The doorway enters a small plaza that, in terms of its position, is analogous to the much larger plaza for the intermediate elite at Huánuco Pampa. A stairway links the plaza to the most restricted part of the palace complex, with its public area and the royal lodgings. The striking difference between Chincha's two-part palace and its equivalent at Huánuco Pampa is the great reduction in public space. In the Huánuco region, the intermediate group, the leaders of the many small local polities, was a virtual multitude, requiring ample public spaces in both sectors of the palace. In Chincha, the critical local leadership could almost be reduced to a single person, and royal hospitality could thus be provided in a far smaller space.

The most notable feature of the whole complex the Inkas added to La Centinela is the compound (Unit 4; figure 15.8) built—in signature Inka adobes—as a palace for the local lord directly adjacent to their own palace. It sat on a pyramid-shape platform, apparently a reference to a traditional Chincha architectural form and to its intended occupant. In the local palace, the residential rooms occupied the position appropriate for the "intermediate" elite, whereas a largely open plaza was in the position of the space designated for Inka rulers. The entrance to that plaza was through a double-jamb Inka doorway. Notably, the doorway into the intermediate plaza of the adjacent Inka palace was a plain doorway, typical of Chincha construction. The representatives of royal Inka power had access to a space marked for them by its doorway in the compound they had built for the local leader, and the local leader had reciprocal access through a doorway suitable for him into a space, designated for people of his rank, in the royal palace. The adjoining palaces with their paired, interlocking spaces allowed the allied leaders, as both hosts and guests, to interact in surroundings appropriate to the circumstances and to their ranks.

After laboring to figure out this intricate architectural puzzle, I came across the following in Fernando de Santillán (1927[1563]:14–15) referring to cooperative local leaders: "To them [the Inka] bestowed favors and gave gifts, both gold cups and clothing from Cuzco, and in honor of their obedience he ordered that in each of those provinces a house be built for the said lord beside that which he had built for himself."

A relatively large public plaza was part of the Inka addition to La Centinela and related to the paired palaces, but unlike the Huánuco plaza, it was not the central element of the plan. The plaza appears to have consisted of two parts (Units 5 and 6; see figure 15.8). The tall enclosing wall of Unit 6 (Unit 5 is very poorly preserved) had a single course of tapia at its top, a probable reference to Chincha architecture, perhaps denoting use of the area primarily by the local populace. Placement of the dual plazas and other architectural details suggest that they were used both by people from the city and by other residents of the valley. It is unlikely that the plazas were used for ritual battles, as proposed for Huánuco Pampa. Such battles would probably not have been among the political mechanisms of a long centralized kingdom; furthermore, the space simply does not seem adequate.

Critical to the planning and use of the dual plazas is the perspective of the two palaces as seen by people assembled in them. The eastern end of the Chincha palace is a forecourt facing the large plaza that probably functioned much like a stage for public events. The Inka palace was imposing, but it sat to the side. The most visible ceremonies would have been associated with the stage-like platform of the local palace—with the Inka palace playing the role of the more silent, yet principal, partner.

Inka Participation in a Subsidiary Compound

In making a detailed study of one of the local compounds from Chincha times that had been slightly modified by the Inkas, we discovered that the modest architectural changes had a profound impact on the organization and use of the compound. The changes consisted of the expansion of a public plaza on the side of the pyramid complex and the extension of a wall on the upper pyramid construction, effectively divid-

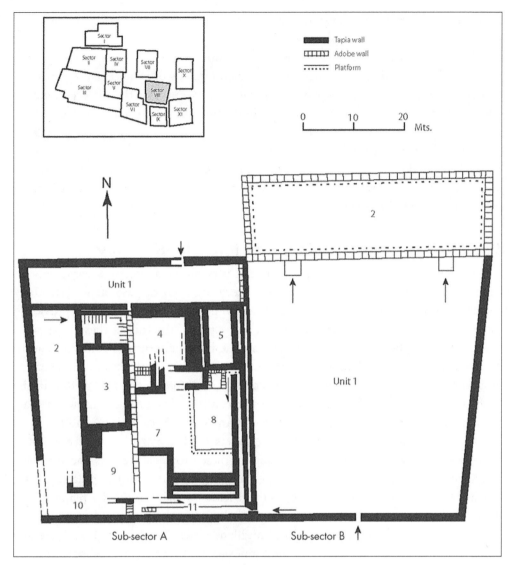

Figure 15.10. Sector VIII: a Chincha compound with Inka alterations.

ing it into two parts (figure 15.10). Differences in ceramics confirmed the new dual character of the compound, with one side having more Inka material than the other. The changes demonstrate both an increased emphasis on public ceremonies and a significant Inka influence at middle levels of Chincha society.

In their modifications of Sector VIII, as in their newly built Sector III, the Inkas had focused on building new public spaces, indicating an emphasis on ceremony in their collaborative rule of the wealthy valley. But the architecture suggests that ceremony and communication links were targeted rather precisely and specifically to a limited number of individuals and groups in an already hierarchical and tightly structured polity. Many of the details of the relationships cannot be reconstructed, but the archaeological remains demonstrate an intricate alliance, supported by religion and carefully articulated at multiple points.

Dorothy Menzel's (1959) conclusions regarding the enduring quality of Inka influence on Chincha bear out the impact of their strategy of alliance using new ceremonial elements at multiple levels of Chincha society. Neither the material remains nor the written sources point to such lasting influences in the Huánuco region. In spite of the elaborate city they had built, the Inka bond did not survive the Spanish Conquest. Creating hierarchy may be more difficult, or at least require more time, than joining and permeating an existing one. A permanent urban population may also be easier to transform than one that is heavily transient and accustomed to refighting battles and reforming alliances.

Urbanism, Communication, and Imperial Strategy

Anyone familiar with the Andes is aware that very large architectural complexes go back thousands of years before the Inkas—predating even the use of pottery. Many archaeologists call these sites cities, but research needs to proceed further, providing more details on the size, internal diversity, and activity structure of these large sites. Several centuries before the rise of the Inkas, the basic patterns of Andean urbanism outlined above were in place. Chan Chan, on the Peruvian north coast, is perhaps the best and most studied example of a large coastal city (Moseley and Day 1982). In the highlands, the pattern of establishing urban enclaves far from the capital was a characteristic of the Tiwanaku empire in the southern Andes (Kolata 1993) and the Wari empire in the central and northern Andes (Anders 1991; Isbell 1991; McEwan 2005; Schreiber 1991) well before AD 1000. Many of these provincial centers had the characteristics of rigid urban planning—and perhaps also the fluctuating populations—we saw at Huánuco Pampa. The Wari centers, at least, probably formed a planned network or chain of cities, similar to that built by the Inkas along the Andean cordillera. I also suspect that all of these coastal and highland cities, like the two Inka cities discussed here, were great centers of cultural innovation, dispersal, and transmission.

Huánuco Pampa and La Centinela are, in a sense, a study in contrasts. Environmentally, architecturally, politically, and economically, they were worlds apart. Yet the Inkas envisioned them as parts of a vast and diverse empire, an empire in which controlling a wide range of resources and the varied capacities of people to exploit those resources was fundamental. It was not just the end of a trajectory of political expansion, but a centuries-old strategy of adaptation.

Huánuco Pampa was planned as an effort to structure a fragmented region using an administrative capital built on neutral ground, some distance from local population centers. There, as guests working part-time for the state, the peoples of the region could participate in a rich ceremonial life that promoted an emerging hierarchy of groups in tense alliance. Through lavish, beer-drenched feasts in symbol-laden settings, gifts of coded clothing, marriage to prestigious women, and, perhaps in some cases, tests in ritual battles, the local groups gained rank and position in a complex imperial system. La Centinela was an already stratified and centralized city with a large and populous capital. The Inkas built a ritual administrative complex at the edge of the city's most important and monumental sector. With carefully interlocking architectural spaces and the encouragement of a composite style of ceramics, they signaled a carefully nuanced approach to manipulating the religious, political, and ceremonial life of the kingdom. Various points in the existing political hierarchy were targeted for alliance. The alliance achieved was probably of great mutual benefit. Even if the long-distance exchange network was not yet fully realized, evidence for prosperity and great wealth abounds in both the written and archaeological records.

In both of these two vastly different regions, the emphasis was on installing administrative and ceremonial facilities designed to redefine political, economic, and religious relationships by creating and dispersing new patterns of interaction and integration. The two cases begin to illustrate how various patterns of communication at multiple positions in the web of social and cultural interactions motivate and modify behavior—leading to changed perspectives, new alliances, and, eventually, a new political and economic landscape. Elaborate settings brought the appropriate people together to instill in them the cultural templates of a revised social and economic order. With society and empire building as their premise, the cities functioned almost like sociopolitical machines designed to produce the patterns of human interaction that added status to individuals and value to goods. Whether or not conscious, the intention was to form a more centralized and ranked, though still diverse, society that effectively managed space, time, natural resources, and human labor. The goal was to increase overall wealth, directing much of it to support the increasingly large elite and to investments in the production of the symbolic goods, places, and ceremonies that ensured continued growth. The goal was also to increase the power of the central authority through the new interpersonal and intergroup links and relationships—making the cities an essential feature of the empire they promoted.

part four

CENTRAL THEMES AND FUTURE DIRECTIONS

sixteen
Cities and Urbanism
Central Themes and Future Directions

Joyce Marcus and Jeremy A. Sabloff

During the past two decades, archaeologists have been excavating ancient cities all over the world. Some were found immediately below modern cities, and others are situated in remote areas. These excavations have created a critical mass of data that can now be subjected to new analyses to reassess, refute, and expand on previous inferences and models of urbanism. One of our goals in this book is to show the diversity of cities, a task that can be more fully appreciated today because our sample of ancient cities is far larger than it was even two decades ago. The contributors to this volume have been active participants in this endeavor because they have all excavated or intensively studied two or more cities. We selected these scholars precisely because they were in a position to compare those cities with one another, as well as with others in different parts of the world.

Rather than recapitulate the results of their excavations and the insights they offer in their chapters, we have selected ten topics that we believe should be productive avenues for future research. Although we will discuss each topic in turn, we predict that significant progress will be made only when several of them are combined in creative research designs.

These ten topics are (1) analyzing the diversity of city plans; (2) documenting the multifunctional roles of city walls; (3) establishing the stratigraphic history of a city's center, that concentration of temples, palaces, plazas, schools, marketplaces, and amphitheaters; (4) linking building plans to institutions and personnel; (5) assessing the division of labor and the evolution of specialized workers; (6) determining the city's ability to attract and control the mobile populations who came to work and attend festivals in the city; (7) documenting the subdivisions or building blocks of a city, that is, the houses, residential clusters, neighborhoods, craft wards, business quarters, manufacturing districts, and so on; (8) assessing the interdependence or complementarity of city and rural populations, for example, urban artisans and bureaucrats versus pastoralists and village farmers; (9) studying the roads and trade networks that linked cities to one another across the landscape; and (10) connecting written documents to archaeological remains.

Analyzing the Diversity of City Plans

Obtaining a large sample of complete city plans is a major challenge. Ancient cities can sometimes be extensively mapped, but, more often than not, the earliest cities are so deeply buried that they cannot be mapped in their entirety, precluding our recovery of complete plans.

As a result, our sample of the earliest cities for every part of the world remains small. Because these cities were "emergent novelties"—significant departures from what came before—we will continue to find it difficult to explain city origins without more plans of the earliest cases. An example of a city that was an emergent novelty would be Teotihuacan in highland Mexico, which emerged at ca. 100 BC. Teotihuacan's origin, as well as its complete plan at the time it first became urban, remains to be fully documented (Millon 1981, 1992). Some of the formal layout from its apogee has been documented, but with so many later constructions to obscure our view, it is impossible to draw a complete plan of the earliest stage of Teotihuacan.

We should remind ourselves that the processes and motivations that led to the establishment of the first cities may well be different from the processes and motivations that led to the founding of secondary cities in those same parts of the world. When texts occur with secondary (or later) cities, there is always the temptation to extend them back to the first city, which may well be an error. The causes for the earliest urban centers lie in pre-urban times, not in the reaction to a preexisting city.

To what extent can complete plans answer the question of a city's emergence? City plans can suggest population growth by revealing the expansion of residential occupation, period by period, but there are also cases in which the *extent* of residential occupation does not increase but the *density* of residences does. If the spacing between residences decreased or if one-story residences added a second story, we need to be able to document those changes. Even when such increases in population density can be demonstrated, it remains for us to determine whether that crowding, packing, or aggregation was voluntary or forced.

Internal growth can be difficult to distinguish from in-migration unless excavations are careful and extensive. When population growth was the product of in-migration, excavation may detect the presence of different ethnic or occupational groups. Such immigrants' material culture, or tombs and burial practices, might vary; their skeletons might even indicate some distinctive characteristics.

When it can be shown that a city's hinterland lost population at the same time that the city gained population, a plausible case for in-migration can be made. For example, for the city of Teotihuacan, a case of in-migration can be made because its Late Formative gain in population coincided with its hinterland's loss of population. There are even suggestions that streets were extended in anticipation of the influx.

A town reorganized to function as a city might yield evidence to that effect over several building levels. One clue might be that former residential space was reorganized into streets, plazas, and patios or new and different kinds of public buildings. Another clue might be that residential zones were reorganized so that people could reside in areas grouped according to profession, ethnic affiliation, or craft specialization. A third line of evidence might be the imposition of a main square and standardized monumental public buildings on a settlement that formerly had no monumental core. Such changes could imply the emergence of new elite personnel and decision makers who had the authority to remake the city core into a new kind of public space.

The latter change is considered to be "top-down," with elites directing it. Such top-down directives, however, might be complemented with "bottom-up" decisions made by commoners. For example, non-elite townsmen or villagers could elect to leave their hinterland settlements, moving to the city for greater security or for social, political, economic, and religious advantages. It is often difficult to determine specific reasons without texts.

Mapping the complete plans of cities for successive periods of occupation could change many of our current ideas—especially our generalizations about the degree to which specific cities were formed by "top-down" or "bottom-up" decision making. Although many archaeologists know that their city plans are palimpsests, they sometimes find it more convenient to treat them as if they were "snapshots," that is, complete plans for a single time period.

Given the ongoing destruction of so many of the world's ancient cities by development and wars, there is an urgent need to continue intensive mapping and excavation projects to provide more data on the evolution of each city. Only a concerted effort will allow us to determine the principles of city planning, patterns of city growth, and planned and unplanned change in each region. Because one of the impressive aspects of city plans is their diversity, we must set as a major goal the mapping of more initial cities in each part of the world. We cannot simply retrospectively project the data from our much larger sample of later cities or use data from the later parts of cities to understand the earliest cities.

The Multifunctional Roles of Walls

Whereas many city walls had only a single obvious role, others served multiple functions during their lifespans. A wall originally constructed for defense might later be used to segregate sacred space from secular or residential space. Sometimes as population grew, it expanded beyond the limits of an earlier wall, one that ultimately served to separate elites from commoners.

Many archaeologists are reluctant to acknowledge the role of warfare in creating early walled cities. In the middle of the twentieth century, some scholars were even loath to see walls as indicative of violence and warfare. In his list of the ten processes that led to urbanism, the pacifist V. Gordon Childe did not include warfare or the need to live in large groups behind defensive walls (Childe 1950; Flannery 1994:105). Even today, there are archaeologists who try to see walls as "symbolic" even when the evidence for war is compelling. We have little doubt that the need for security often led to population aggregation, precocious urbanism, and the construction of walls, ditches, moats, ramparts, and watchtowers.

Even Neolithic villages might have defensive walls of mud brick, wooden planks, or even wooden palisades. In other cases, it appears that normally dispersed populations aggregated to create safety in numbers. The large village of Çatal Höyük in Anatolia packed houses together in such a way that its windowless outer walls provided no entry to outsiders.

Some city walls protected most, but not all, of their citizens. For example, the outer wall at the Maya city of Mayapan surrounded temples, public buildings, nobles' residences, and many lower-status residences. The wall's circumference was 9.1 km, enclosing an area of 4.2 sq km; inside the wall were more than 3,500 individual structures (Jones 1952; Shook 1952), at least 2,100 of them residences (Pollock et al. 1962:204).

Additional residential units, however, occurred outside the wall, and more recent work by Masson and colleagues (2006) has shown that they extended outward for some distance. Who were these people outside Mayapan's walls? Were they lower-status people, forced by population growth to move to a location outside the walls, or were they squatters arriving from other settlements? We do not as yet know. One explanation offered for the Mayapan wall is that it protected the seat of government, other specialized institutions, and associated high-status personnel. A second explanation (not mutually exclusive from the first) was that the wall defined the limits of the city for administrative purposes.

To be sure, not all walls were for defense; some were, in fact, constructed to ensure privacy for the elite or to decrease accessibility to sacred locations. For example, some of the huge walled enclosures constructed by the Egyptian ruler Khasekhemwy of Dynasty 2 (ca. 2686 BC) served to set off sacred space from the profane (Naville et al. 1914; O'Connor 1989). Khasekhemwy's mud-brick enclosure at Hierakonpolis measured 67 by 57 m; its walls were 5 m thick and reached at least 9 m in height. His mud-brick enclosure at Abydos was even larger—122 by 65 m, with walls 5.5 m thick, reaching a height of 20 m (Kemp 1989:53–55). Constructing mud-brick walls that reached 20 m in height was a real feat.

Some ancient cities had multiple concentric walls, with an outer wall for defense functions and an inner wall serving other functions. The Maya city of Tulum is one example. Tulum had an outer wall, called the Great Wall, with three sides forming a rectangular space that enclosed temples, palaces, and public buildings; the fourth side of the rectangle was a steep cliff overlooking the Caribbean Sea. Inside the Great Wall was another walled area, called the Inner Enclosure, which contained seven structures, most of them religious in function. According to Lothrop (1924:90), the wall of the Inner Enclosure merely served to separate religious structures from the more secular parts of the city, thereby ensuring that the former were less accessible and more private. Lothrop argued that the wall of the Inner Enclosure played no defensive role but the Great Wall did. Indeed, the Great Wall was 717 m long, 6 m wide, and as much as 4.5 m high in places.

Because walls are often well preserved and yield key information, their functions should continue to intrigue archaeologists for the foreseeable future. Cases like that of Mayapan warn us that although excavations within a city's walls are the norm, we should also excavate outside the walls to see whether there is also occupation there and, if so, how it differs from the intramural occupation. It might also be productive to compare and contrast early cities with and without walls to see whether any useful patterns emerge. One obvious question would be, Are walled cities regularly associated with regional warfare, whereas nonwalled cities lack such evidence?

Establishing the Stratigraphic History of a City's Center

Understandably, the monumental center of the city is where archaeologists usually have placed most of their excavation units, and the results have been very informative, especially when a long stratigraphic sequence of buildings and monumental constructions has been exposed.

Unlike the periphery of a city, the center of a city usually has a dense concentration of public spaces and public buildings such as temples, palaces, platforms, plazas, marketplaces, ballcourts, and amphitheaters. Together, all those public spaces and buildings often form a monumental core or set of tall edifices that serves as a beacon or magnet for residents of both the city and its hinterland.

At the center of some ancient and modern cities are royal temples, courts, and palaces. For instance, at the center of the modern Nepalese city of Bhaktapur are the palace of the Malla king and the temple of the king's lineage deity. Centrally located to the south of the palace are the residences of the Pajopadhyaya Brahmans, including those families who were the king's priests. Intermingled with the Brahmans were the former royal officials and suppliers. Farther out from the center were farming families, then the butchers' homes, and finally the homes of the untouchables (Levy 1990: 174–180). From the center with the king and his associates out to the Brahmans, farmers, butchers, and untouchables, Levy sees a kind of "geometrically idealized Bhaktapur" that is "organized in a series of concentric circles from a center out, and at the same time, as it is built on a hill, from top down" (Levy 1990:176).

This kind of idealized concentric model is similar to that described by E. W. Burgess (1925), whose model of a city had a single center from which growth moves outward, with poorer people left behind in the center and wealthier people moving to the city's periphery. Many ancient cities are a "reverse Burgess" because the highest-status people live at the center. Similarly, Bhaktapur has the highest-status people at the center of the city at the top of the mountain, with the lowest-status people and untouchables occupying the periphery of the city.

By documenting changes in a city's monumental core—its layout, degree of planning, or increasing diversity of building types—we can discern the range of functions and services that the inner city offered over time. The initial emergence of new and distinctive building types can tell us much about a city, its administrators, and its specialized personnel. Most telling is when these distinctive new types of buildings also contain distinctive artifacts.

One of the problems with excavating the monumental center of a city is that well-preserved buildings are often found in the uppermost levels and they can rarely be removed. Furthermore, when the uppermost buildings are consolidated, we can obtain only a partial view of earlier buildings below them. For example, at the Zapotec city of Monte Albán in Mexico, visitors see the latest buildings because these have been consolidated for tourism. The sequence of buildings that lies below them cannot be fully exposed, so we cannot see its full extent or record its complete plan.

Nevertheless, in the case of Monte Albán, we do know something about the development of its monumental main plaza and the immense stone buildings that surround it. At 500 BC at least 2,000 people moved abruptly to the top of a mountain, now called Monte Albán. They arrived on this previously unoccupied mountain with no master plan for converting a rocky mountaintop into an orderly city with a symmetrical layout. Instead, the new residents simply built themselves houses, began to build a defensive wall, and selected areas where they would build three public buildings, choosing locations where they could take advantage of natural stone outcrops as the core inside those monumental structures (Acosta 1965; Caso et al. 1967; Flannery and Marcus 1983:figure 4.3).

By 100 BC the outlines of a master plan had begun to appear. By then, they had leveled a huge area that would serve as the Great Plaza. They had decreased access to that plaza by building monumental structures around it. They had created the overall semblance of perfect symmetry, which is precisely what one notes when entering the Great Plaza today. They also had created distinctive building plans—palaces, ballcourts, an arrowhead-shape building, and colonnaded two-room temples, all of which suggests the emergence of specialized personnel and administrators.

The monumental core of many ancient cities features temples, leading some investigators to regard the ancient city as more sacred and religious than its modern counterpart. As emphasized by Karl Butzer (chapter 5), the Islamic city of the new Arab world also features religious structures. In such cities, other buildings should be subordinate to the mosques, and the egalitarian ethos does not tolerate any ostentatious residences of the elite. Indeed, in such cities, secular power and authority are often regarded as suspect. Although some modern cities, such as Jerusalem, Banaras, and

Mecca, are often considered sacred cities, we should not assume that all modern cities are less sacred than their ancient counterparts.

In the monumental centers of many ancient cities, there was a sacred or holy structure, sometimes several of them. Routledge (1997:232) concluded that the Egyptian temple "was a central organizational principle of the city, both conceptually and practically."

Still other cities are thought to have resembled a sacred cosmogram (Ashmore 1991; O'Connor 2005). Wheatley (1971), for example, saw the Chinese city as a cosmogram divided into four quadrants. Other cities with sacred overtones were also composed of four quadrants. Examples include the Aztec capital of Tenochtitlan, the Inka capital of Cuzco, and Egyptian cities such as Per Ramesses. Uphill (1969) concludes that each of the four quarters at the Egyptian delta city of Per Ramesses was focused on a temple, with a deity in charge of each quarter (Uphill 1969:30-31:figure 4; 1984:figures 5 and 6). Routledge (1997:230) indicates that the archetypal form of the Eighteenth Dynasty royal Egyptian city was a square divided into four quarters, with processional routes leading from one temple in each of the four quadrants to the others.

In the Mesoamerican worldview, each of the four quarters was associated with a specific color, tree, wind, or other attribute (Marcus 1983c:356; Thompson 1934). This principle was so ancient that by the time the Aztec displayed it, it had already been used by countless earlier Mesoamerican cultures. This *principle of quadripartition* was replicated at various levels, from the household unit to the territorial state.

In the Maya region, for example, one hieroglyphic text associates the four world directions with four lords and four capital cities. A passage dating to AD 731 on Stela A at the Honduran city of Copán refers to four types of skies and heavens, then to four world directions, and then to four hereditary lords who ruled four different cities (Marcus 1976, 1993).

It is no surprise, therefore, that by the time of the Aztec period, such principles were widespread. The Aztec divided their capital, Tenochtitlan, into four quadrants (*nauhcampa*), each associated with a color and patron deity. The main plaza at Tenochtitlan was considered to be the navel (*tlalxico*) or center of the empire, with four quadrants extending out from it. Many Aztec rituals required that the same item be offered to each of the four world directions and then to the center. Such rites could be replicated on several levels—in offering boxes, houses, temples, and the main plaza of the city.

In some respects, the US capital is similar to an ancient royal city. Meyer (2001:2) says that the District of Columbia "was laid out as a perfect square, ten miles on a side (the limits imposed by Article 1 of the US Constitution), with its four corners pointing to each of the cardinal directions, like the ancient cities of Ur and Babylon in Mesopotamia." Washington's four quadrants are simply referred to as NW, NE, SW, and SE today.

In many parts of the ancient world, the monumental temples at the center of the city were not only the focus of city residents but also a destination for those in the hinterland. Careful study of the monumental core of ancient cities allows scholars to examine the complex interaction of religious and political authority in these early urban centers. Such monumental structures demonstrate an impressive investment of labor, and they can create a central city skyline that influences our ideas about how a city should look.

Linking Building Plans to Institutions and Specialized Personnel

Distinctive or standardized building plans, such as those of many palaces and temples, have led investigators to regard them as centralized institutions. In Crete, for example, "a Minoan palace is understood as a central administrative organism to which flows the produce of the surrounding land for storage and redistribution" (Tsipopoulou 1997:263). A similar position has been assigned to the Mesopotamian temple, although today some would argue that the temple's role has been overemphasized relative to that of royal families.

The rise or increased importance, of certain kinds of economic specialization has often been seen as closely associated with the process of urbanism (Childe 1950). Specialization can be detected in many areas, from evidence of large-scale manufacturing and craft production, to the organization of labor, to a hierarchy of administrators, or to clusters of artifacts or paraphernalia associated with institutions (Cowgill 2007; Manzanilla 1993, 1996).

In some parts of the ancient world, recent work on labor, guilds, production stages, and the residential quarters occupied by craft specialists is helping us understand that each commodity (for example, shell, obsidian, pottery, ivory, lapis lazuli, stone bowls, seals, bullae, and other artifacts) can have different histories of procurement and loci of manufacture. At the Aztec capital of Tenochtitlan, craftsmen are known to have lived in different sectors of the city. Some of these craft specialists (goldsmiths, feather workers, lapidaries) had been brought to the capital from different provinces. Though they now resided in the capital, they were allowed to worship their own patron deities and participate in their own provincial festivals and rituals.

In many cities, specialists clustered by ward. The traditional Hindu city was divided into wards called *gramas*, a term that means "village" in some of the local languages. Every ward was set aside for a caste or trade guild that enjoyed autonomy (Dutt 1977[1925]:147); some 100 to 500 houses made up a grama (Slusser 1982:84). Each ward had at least one crossing point (more if it was a large ward), and these crossing points divided each ward into neighborhoods. Major crossing points were the loci for large, uncarved stones, usually partly buried in the ground.

In many ancient cities, standardized and distinctive building types and spaces—plazas or courts, marketplaces, palaces, temples—were created and then staffed by specialized personnel. To determine the functions of such special places, one must often depend on finding associated artifacts; written tablets are, of course, particularly useful. A couple of rooms in the Palace of Pylos had economic tablets (written in Linear

B) that reveal how the Mycenaeans managed their hinterland, keeping track of what entered and left the palace. For example, the palace not only had storage rooms with tablets recording data on oil, but investigators also found oil stored there, ready to be disbursed in transport vessels. Other storerooms in the same palace had tablets showing inventories of vases, furniture, and disbursements (Palaima and Wright 1985). Linear B tablets give us particularly rich insights into administration because they reveal standardized units of weights and measures. They also provide data on male landholders, ration lists for women and children, lists of women involved in textile work, and inventories of vases, livestock, agricultural produce, leather, ivory, and wine. To be sure, the distinct building plan of the Mycenaean palace was enough to indicate the presence of specialized personnel. However, not until the Linear B tablets were deciphered were we able to determine the specific quantities of commodities received.

But a word of warning is in order. In the past, scholars often assumed a one-to-one correspondence between structure form and function. As numerous recent examples show, such assumptions do not always hold up. Moreover, many structural forms can be multifunctional. The reluctance today of Maya archaeologists to use the term *palace* is just one instance of the weakness of older functional assumptions.

Assessing the Division of Labor and the Evolution of Specialized Workers

This topic sounds fairly simple and straightforward. Unfortunately, it is not, largely because archaeologists usually recover finished items, instead of every stage in the production sequence, from procurement of raw materials to the manufacture of the final product. Furthermore, as Rosen has said,

> While it is clear that there must be a general correlation between economic and socio-political complexity, the more interesting aspects of this relationship lie in the disconformities between the two. Thus, the rise of specialization in the Levant, as reflected in the archaeological record, in some cases seems clearly to predate the first cities, and seems to take several different forms.
> [Rosen 1997:85]

In areas such as Mesoamerica and the Near East, a wide range of crafts were produced in the houses of the earliest villages long before the world witnessed the emergence of the first cities. Early villagers in Mexico's Oaxaca Valley were making a series of shell ornaments, mica inlays, and iron-ore mirrors to be circulated among wards of the same village or traded well beyond the valley in which the village lay (Flannery and Marcus 2005). Villagers at Beidha in Jordan produced stone, bone, and antler artifacts in what look very much like the first-floor workshops of two-story houses (Kirkbride 1966).

Although specialization began before cities, it certainly escalated in ancient cities. Mesopotamian cities had large weaving establishments staffed by women (R. Wright

1996). The Inka also had establishments, called *acllahuasi*, where women were expected to turn camelid fibers into different classes of woven cloth, from gauze-like fabrics to more mundane textiles (Murra 1962). Women were also expected to produce maize beer in great volume to reward the male laborers who both farmed and dug canals for the Inka state. Although archaeologists have been able to identify the ground plans of weaving or brewing establishments in Egypt, Mesopotamia, and the Andes, Mesoamerica has lagged behind by comparison.

Determining the Unique Services a City Offered

By combining three lines of information—texts, building plans, and specialized artifacts associated with specific buildings—we are sometimes able to document the unique services that a city might afford its residents and others. Cities were often able to offer their hinterlands unique services and public performances—especially capital cities, which conducted events such as a ruler's inauguration, the consecration of a national temple with its patron deity, or an annual festival. To accommodate such grand performances or major events, some capital cities set aside a large open space. For example, we read the following about the main plaza of the Aztec capital, Tenochtitlan:

> [The main plaza was immense] for it accommodated eight thousand six hundred men, dancing in a circle. This courtyard had four doors or entrances, one on the east, another on the west, one on the south, and another on the north. From each one of these began one of the four causeways: one to Tlacopan; another toward Guadalupe; another toward Coyoacan; and yet another toward the lake and the canoe dock. The four main temples had entrances facing the directions I have mentioned, and the four gods standing in them also faced the same directions. [Durán 1977:78]

Also unique to the Aztec capital were certain annual festivals. For example, according to Sahagún (1981:66, 68), the human impersonator of a deity named Tezcatlipoca was sacrificed during an annual ceremony held in the capital. As soon as one impersonator was sacrificed, a new one was chosen to represent Tezcatlipoca during the coming year. Although this rite took place in the city, it was not an isolated request, but part of a series of rituals involving pilgrimages to outlying mountains, where children were sacrificed. This cycle of rituals, some inside the city and some outside, was intended to end the dry season and inaugurate a new agricultural cycle by bringing rain (Broda 1971; Carrasco 1976c; Heyden 1991).

For the archaeologist, assessing a city's ability to attract hinterland populations can be difficult because such people may come for only a short time. One clue to such visits would be the presence of an area for public assembly that seems too large to have served the city alone, accompanied by the mass discard of specific items such as drinking vessels (Moseley et al. 2005).

Documenting the Building Blocks of a City

Archaeologists might well be able to design better excavation strategies if they can figure out how to isolate the building blocks of a city. Such building blocks might be houses, multifamily compounds, neighborhoods, wards, or quadrants, and each of these units might be nested within a larger unit. For example, in the case of the already mentioned city of Bhaktapur in Nepal, there are successively inclusive levels, from the nuclear family, to the extended household, to a patrilineally related group of households that acts as a ritual and social unit, to the residential ward, to the mandalic section, to people living in one of the two halves of the city, and on to the whole city (Levy 1990:197).

In many cities, the smallest building block is the house, but houses can vary tremendously, not only between cultures but also over time within the same culture. In Classic period Teotihuacan in the Basin of Mexico, for example, residence seems to have taken the form of large walled compounds that may have held more than 100 people who shared an occupational specialty (Millon 1981, 1992). In the Postclassic, or Aztec, period in the same valley, the compounds had been replaced by what appear to have been nuclear family or extended family households (M. E. Smith 1997).

In the city of Eshnunna in Mesopotamia's Diyala River basin, there were clear city blocks delimited by streets. Large houses along the main streets appear to have been occupied by wealthy merchants who displayed their wares in front rooms and lived above or in the rear. Poorer residents lived in the interior of a street block in smaller houses that did not face the street; these people had access to main streets only via a series of narrow, twisting alleyways (Delougaz et al. 1967:plate 26).

To be sure, the examples given above come from regions where stone or mud brick are the preferred building materials. In tropical areas where a great many residences are of wattle and daub or some equally perishable material, defining building blocks will be more challenging.

Taking a Broad Regional Focus to Assess the Interdependence or Complementarity of City Dwellers and Non-City Dwellers (Pastoralists, Farmers, Traders, and so forth)

The relationship between city dwellers and their hinterland's populations can be complementary, interdependent, separate, or even antagonistic. Most scholars today would argue that a city must be seen in its regional and macro-regional context in order to appreciate its relationships with towns and villages in its hinterland.

The city is, of course, often dependent in some way on its hinterland. In chapter 15, for example, Morris discusses the role of temporary residents who came into the Inka city from the hinterland to perform labor service and be recompensed with lavish beer drinking. At Huánuco Pampa, one of the cities built by the Inka state in highland

Peru, members of at least two groups—the Chupaychu and the Yacha—came to the city to pay tribute in the form of labor. Morris deduces that many of these temporary residents occupied thousands of irregularly arranged, small structures at Huánuco Pampa.

Even though we know that the populations of many modern cities fluctuate seasonally (beach and ski resorts come to mind), we sometimes forget that ancient cities experienced major seasonal influxes as well. In addition, some state-sponsored events may even have required the attendance and participation of hinterland populations. Such short-term residency would be difficult to demonstrate without ethnohistoric documents. To provide archaeological verification for the presence of diverse ethnic groups, hundreds of residences in several wards or sectors would need to be excavated. That is just what was done at Huánuco Pampa (Morris and Covey 2006; Morris and Thompson 1985).

In Bhaktapur, the bounded city was considered "safe," and the world beyond the city was considered "dangerous." This apprehension notwithstanding, the hinterland of Bhaktapur was full of significant shrines and sacred spots, each marking a place where city dwellers would visit on their sacred pilgrimages. A similar pattern was displayed by Aztec pilgrims, who left the capital city in processions to conduct hinterland rites at mountaintop shrines. Throughout the dry season, for example, the Aztec performed a series of rites to ask for rain; several of these involved the sacrifice of children (Broda 1971:table 1; Sahagún 1981:8). One such Aztec rite was the festival Huey Tozoztli, in which rulers from the Basin of Mexico cities of Tenochtitlan, Texcoco, Xochimilco, and Tlacopan ascended the slopes of Mount Tlaloc to make offerings on its 4,100-m summit. There they called forth rain from the mountain's interior, and to ensure that those rains would arrive on time, the four rulers sacrificed children. Other important pilgrims from the city, including participants dressed to impersonate the mountain deity, also ascended to the summit (Broda 1971:281).

Studying the Roads Linking Cities to One Another and Their Hinterland

There are really two topics here: intra-site streets and roads linking sectors of the city and inter-site roads or causeways linking cities to their hinterland or to other cities. Such routes may be either formal or informal, with the former requiring a greater labor investment (Trombold 1991:3). We should perhaps not make this a rigid dichotomy, because part of the same road could be formal and then, farther along, become a simple path.

Examples of both can be found in Mexico's Oaxaca Valley during the occupation of the city of Monte Albán (Blanton 1978). Alignments of occupied residential terraces suggest that several major routes traversed the city virtually from its founding at 500 BC; by AD 600 many of these routes had become formalized roads with detectable roadbeds, built up where they crossed gullies and contoured to the mountainside. Some of these roads clearly extended north and west from Monte Albán proper to the satellite hills of Mogotillo, El Gallo, and Atzompa, but in the intervening low-lying areas, they became so informal that they cannot be traced accurately by archaeologists.

Some 10 km south of Monte Albán lay site SMT-23, Cerro Tilcajete, a secondary administrative center that flourished at AD 100 (Elson 2006; Spencer 2006). Leading off toward Monte Albán from the summit of SMT-23 was a formal road that became too informal to trace archaeologically as it descended the slopes of the hill. The evidence suggests that some kind of road connected Monte Albán to this second-tier administrative center. In the Maya region, some large centers are linked to subordinate centers by roads. For example, Folan and others (1995) recovered evidence that a series of roads led from Calakmul, a Maya capital, to satellite centers such as Uxul, Sasilhá, and Naachtún.

Archaeologists often complain that most studies of roads give distances in miles or kilometers when actual travel times might be more meaningful. Better studies of pedestrian traffic could be done using a range of GIS (Geographic Information Systems) analyses. For example, GIS can simulate the movement of people or materials along a network of roads and can analyze the spatial relationships among mapped phenomena such as cities, roads, and natural obstacles such as rivers, irrigation canals, and mountain ranges. On a broader scale, the study of water transport routes such as rivers and canals, combined with terrestrial trade routes, could contribute to our understanding of a city and its hinterland. Like walls, roads could be multifunctional, serving military and economic roles, as well as symbolic, ceremonial, and social ones.

Roads enabled pilgrims and merchants to travel to the city; they also allowed kings and their courts to go on processions to subordinate towns and to make a wide range of trips with ritual, symbolic, and economic impact. Presumably for this reason, some roads were wider and more elaborate than one might expect if the only concern had been creating a road for merchants and commodities. Many rulers knew that having good roads between the capital city and the provinces could help maintain order, quell revolt, reassert political control, and reestablish the boundaries of their realms. So important was this activity that the Egyptian ruler, during a jubilee ceremony held every thirty years, ran a course between cairns to show that he was still vigorous enough to travel to the limits of his realm (Kemp 1989:58–59; Uphill 1965).

In addition to roads, the study of other transport routes and associated facilities that linked cities and hinterlands, or cities to other cities, also would be fruitful. We have in mind the further study of rivers, lakes, or sea coasts, which might provide insights into the regional linkages of cities.

Linking Written Documents to Archaeological Remains

Although texts have played a major role in our interpretation of ancient cities, there is nothing like being able to combine text, survey, and excavation. Only from multiple levels of superimposed occupations can we really see changes in city layouts and building plans. Texts, for their part, can supply the names and functions of rooms and buildings, the names of architects, the names of artisans, and many details that we could not recover in any other way (Palaima 2003; Schele and Mathews 1998; Sweet 1997).

To be sure, texts have their biases and limitations. In much of the world, they tend to be biased in the direction of royals and nobles, so to retrieve data on the much more numerous commoners, we must turn to the archaeological record. Texts can sometimes provide evidence on what motivated the founding of a city and provide some of the richest details about the beliefs and behaviors of a city's occupants. But only by combining texts, maps, and excavations can archaeologists discern recurrent patterns and regularities, as well as unique behaviors, that might be missing from the texts.

Conclusion

Urbanism was a long process, with many fits and starts in different regions of the world (Adams 1966; Andrews 1994; Marcus 1983b, 2003b; Sabloff 1997; Sjoberg 1960; M. L. Smith 2003a, 2006; Stone 1987, 2007; Wheatley 1972). One of our many challenges is to convert static city plans into populated places with economies, politics, rituals, and beliefs. Although each city is unique in numerous ways (Wirth 1925:175), taking a comparative approach can help us answer such questions as Why did cities emerge? and What functions did cities serve? Despite their diversity, cities had a finite number of patterns, functions, and explanations. Once cities existed, they often became destinations, landmarks that attracted more and more population until they became demographic centers of gravity.

Many of today's cities are dynamic places, full of sounds, hustle and bustle, heterogeneous groups of people, modern and older buildings, and evidence of ongoing change and innovation. Others are seen as cultural sinks, depressing and dangerous. To what extent were ancient cities the same? Archaeologists who try to answer that question have both advantages and disadvantages.

Two of the biggest disadvantages are that we cannot interview informants about their attitudes and beliefs and we cannot excavate cities in their entirety, making it very difficult to characterize the city as a whole.

Our principal advantage is that excavation may allow us to recover evidence both from the initial founding of a city and from its later forms. The documenting of hundreds or even thousands of years of change in a single city is the special role of the archaeologist, sometimes aided by written documents that add data we would not be able to recover in any other way.

At various points in the past, for millions of people, urban living replaced the village and farmstead. A way of life artificially created by humans drew them away from a life seemingly more embedded in nature. One of the paradoxes of this transformation is that although cities in the Third World continue to act as irresistible magnets, the citizens of many developed countries now flee the city in droves, abandoning their neighborhoods to immigrants and urban decay. Only if archaeologists, geographers, sociologists, and historians join in the quest will we come to understand the paradox that makes the city both a brave new world and a potential destroyer of all that was appealing in village life.

References

Abdel-Nour, Antoine
1982 Introduction a l'Histoire urbaine de la Syria ottomane (XVIème–XVIIIème). Publications de l'Université Libanaise, section des Études historiques XXV. Beirut: Librairie Orientale.

Abrams, Elliott M.
1994 How the Maya Built Their World: Energetics and Ancient Architecture. Austin: University of Texas Press.

Abu Lughod, Janet
1987 The Islamic City: Historic Myth, Islamic Essence, and Contemporary Relevance. International Journal of Middle East Studies 19:155–176.
1989 Before European Hegemony: The World System AD 1250–1350. New York: Oxford University Press.

Abungu, George H. O.
1998 City States of the East African Coast and Their Maritime Contacts. In Transformations in Africa: Essays on Africa's Later Past, edited by Graham Connah, pp. 204–218. Leicester: Leicester University Press.

Acosta, Jorge R.
1965 Preclassic and Classic Architecture of Oaxaca. In Handbook of Middle American Indians, vol. 3, edited by Robert Wauchope and Gordon R. Willey, pp. 814–836. Austin: University of Texas Press.

Adams, Richard E. W., and Richard C. Jones
1981 Spatial Patterns and Regional Growth among Maya Cities. American Antiquity 46(2):301–322.

Adams, Robert McCormick
1960 The Origin of Cities. Scientific American 230(3):153–168.
1965 Land behind Baghdad. Chicago: University of Chicago Press.
1966 The Evolution of Urban Society: Early Mesopotamia and Prehispanic Mexico. Chicago: Aldine.
1972 Patterns of Urbanization in Early Southern Mesopotamia. In Man, Settlement and Urbanism, edited by Peter J. Ucko, Ruth Tringham, and G. W. Dimbleby, pp. 735–749. London: Duckworth.
1981 Heartland of Cities: Surveys of Ancient Settlement and Land Use on the Central Floodplain of the Euphrates. Chicago: University of Chicago Press.

Adams, William Y.
1977 Nubia: Corridor to Africa. Princeton, NJ: Princeton University Press.

Agbaje-Williams, Babatunde
1986 Estimating the Population of Old Oyo. Odu: A Journal of West African Studies 30:3–15.

Alcalde de Gonzales, Javier, Carlos del Águila Chávez, Fernando Fujita Alarcón, and Enrique Retamozo Rondón
2002 "Plateros" precoloniales tardíos en Tambo de Mora, Valle de Chincha (Siglos XIV–XVI). Anales del Museo de América, pp. 43–57. Madrid.

Alcock, Leslie
1986 A Pottery Sequence from Mohenjo Daro: R. E. M. Wheeler's 1950 "Citadel Mound" Excavations. *In* Excavations at Mohenjo Daro, Pakistan: The Pottery, edited by George F. Dales and Jonathan Mark Kenoyer, pp. 493–551. Philadelphia: University Museum Press.

Alcock, Susan E.
2002 Archaeologies of the Greek Past: Landscape, Monuments and Memories. Cambridge: Cambridge University Press.

Allan, Sarah
2007 Erlitou and the Formation of Chinese Civilization: Toward a New Paradigm. Journal of Asian Studies 66(2):461–496.

Allchin, Bridget, and Frank Raymond Allchin
1982 The Rise of Civilization in India and Pakistan. Cambridge: Cambridge University Press.

Allen, James de Vere
1993 Swahili Origins: Swahili Culture and the Shungwaya Phenomenon. London: James Currey.

An, Chin-huai
1986 The Shang City at Cheng-chou and Related Problems. *In* Studies of Shang Archaeology, edited by Kwang-chih Chang, pp. 15–48. New Haven, CT, and London: Yale University Press.

Anders, Martha B.
1991 Structure and Function at the Planned Site of Azangaro: Cautionary Notes for the Model of Huari as a Centralized Secular State. *In* Huari Administrative Structure: Prehistoric Monumental Architecture and State Government, edited by William H. Isbell and Gordon F. McEwan, pp. 165–197. Washington, DC: Dumbarton Oaks Research Library and Collection.

Anderson, David M., and Richard Rathbone
2000 Introduction: Urban Africa Histories in the Making. *In* Africa's Urban Past, edited by David M. Anderson and Richard Rathbone, pp. 1–17. London: James Currey.

Andres, Christopher R.
2000 Caches, Censers, Monuments, and Burials: Archaeological Evidence of Postclassic Ritual Activity in Northern Belize. Unpublished MA thesis, Southern Illinois University, Carbondale.
2005 Building Negotiation: Architecture and Sociopolitical Transformation at Chau Hiix, Lamanai, and Altun Ha, Belize. Unpublished Ph.D. dissertation, Indiana University, Bloomington.

Andres, Christopher R., and K. Anne Pyburn
2004 Out of Sight: The Postclassic and Early Colonial Periods at Chau Hiix, Belize. *In* The Terminal Classic in the Maya Lowlands: Collapse, Transition, and Transformation, edited by Arthur A. Demarest, Prudence M. Rice, and Don S. Rice, pp. 402–423. Boulder: University of Colorado Press.

Andrews, Anthony P.
1995 First Cities. Smithsonian Exploring the Ancient World, Jeremy A. Sabloff, series editor. Washington, DC: Smithsonian Books.

Andrews, Anthony P., and Shirley B. Mock
2002 New Perspectives on the Salt Trade. *In* Ancient Maya Political Economies, edited by Marilyn A. Masson and David A. Freidel, pp. 307–334. Boston: Rowman and Littlefield.

Arkush, Elizabeth, and Charles Stanish
2005 Interpreting Conflict in the Ancient Andes: Implications for the Archaeology of Warfare. Current Anthropology 46(1):3–28.

Armillas, Pedro
1948 Fortalezas Mexicanas. Cuadernos Americanos 7:143–163.

Arnauld, M.-Charlotte, and Dominique Michelet
2004 Nature et dynamique des cités mayas. Annales Histoire Sciences Sociales 59(1):73–108.

Arnold, Christopher J.
1997   An Archaeology of the Early Anglo-Saxon Kingdoms. 2nd. ed. London and New York: Routledge.

Ascher, Marcia, and Robert Ascher
1981   Code of the Quipu. Ann Arbor: University of Michigan Press.

Ashmore, Wendy
1989   Construction and Cosmology: Politics and Ideology in Lowland Maya Settlement Patterns. *In* Word and Image in Maya Culture: Explorations in Language, Writing, and Representation, edited by William F. Hanks and Don S. Rice, pp. 272–284. Salt Lake City: University of Utah Press.
1991   Site-Planning Principles and Concepts of Directionality among the Ancient Maya. Latin American Antiquity 2:199–226.

Ashmore, Wendy, and Jeremy A. Sabloff
2002   Spatial Orders in Maya Civic Plans. Latin American Antiquity 13(2):201–216.
2003   Interpreting Ancient Maya Civic Plans: Reply to Smith. Latin American Antiquity 14(2):229–237.

Aston, Mick, and James Bond
1976   The Landscape of Towns. London: Dent.

Awolalu, J. O.
1979   Yoruba Beliefs and Sacrificial Rites. London: Longman.

Baer, Klaus
1960   Rank and Title in the Old Kingdom: The Structure of the Egyptian Administration in the 5th and 6th Dynasties. Chicago: University of Chicago Press.

Bairoch, Paul
1976   Population urbaine et taille des villes en Europe de 1600 à 1970. Revue d'histoire économique et sociale 54:304–335.
1988   Cities and Economic Development from the Dawn of History to the Present. Chicago: University of Chicago Press.

Bakari, Mtoro B.
1981   Customs of the Swahili People. Berkeley: University of California Press.

Ball, Joseph W.
1993   Pottery, Potters, Palaces, and Polities: Some Socioeconomic and Political Implications of Late Classic Maya Ceramic Industries. *In* Lowland Maya Civilization in the Eighth Century AD, edited by Jeremy A. Sabloff and John S. Henderson, pp. 243–272. Washington, DC: Dumbarton Oaks Research Library and Collection.

Ballet, Pascale, Pierre Cordier, and Nadine Dieudonné-Glad (editors)
2003   La ville et ses déchets dans le monde romain: Rébuts et recyclages. Montagnac: Monique Mergoil.

Bankoff, Greg, Georg Frerks, and Dorothea Hilhorst
2004   Mapping Vulnerability: Disasters, Development and People. London: Earthscan.

Barnhart, Richard M.
2004   Alexander in China? Questions for Chinese Archaeology. *In* Chinese Archaeology in the Twentieth Century, edited by Yang Xiaoneng, vol. 1, pp. 329–343. New Haven, CT: Yale University Press.

Barresi, Paolo
2003   Province dell'Asia Minore. Costo dei marmi, architettura pubblica e committenza. Rome: "l'Erma" di Bretschneider.

Bascom, William
1955   Urbanization among the Yoruba. American Journal of Sociology 60:446–454.
1969   The Yoruba of Southwestern Nigeria. New York: Holt, Rinehart and Winston.

Bauer, Brian S.
2004   Ancient Cuzco: Heartland of the Inca. Austin: University of Texas Press.

Béal, Jean-Claude, and Jean-Claude Goyon (editors)
2002   Les Artisans dans la Ville Antique. Lyon: Université Lumière-Lyon 2.

Becker, Marshall J.
1979   Priests, Peasants, and Ceremonial Centers: The Intellectual History of a Model. *In* Maya Archaeology and Ethnohistory, edited by N. Hammond and G. Willey, pp. 3–20. Austin: University of Texas Press.
2003   Plaza Plans at Tikal: A Research Strategy for Inferring Social Organization and Processes of Culture Change at Lowland Maya Sites. *In* Tikal: Dynasties, Foreigners, and Affairs of State Advancing Maya Archaeology, edited by Jeremy A. Sabloff, pp. 253–280. Santa Fe, NM: SAR Press.

Bedon, Robert (editor)
2002   Amoenitas urbium: Les agréments de la vie urbaine en gaule romaine et dans les régions voisines. Caesarodunum xxxv–xxxvi. Limoges: Presses Universitaires de Limoges.
2003   La naissance des premières villes en gaule intérieure durant la période de La Tène finale. *In* La naissance de la ville dans l'antiquité, edited by Michel Reddé, pp. 195–214. Paris: De Boccard.

Beijing Daxue Kaoguxue Xi Shang Zhou Zu and Shanxi Sheng Kaogu Yanjiusuo (Zou Heng)
2000   Tianma-Qucun 1980–1989. 4 vols. Beijing: Kexue Chubanshe.

Beijing Shi Wenwu Yanjiusuo
1995   Liulihe Xi Zhou Yan guo mudi, 1973–1977. Beijing: Wenwu Chubanshe.

Belcher, William R.
1998   Fish Exploitation of the Baluchistan and Indus Valley Tradition: An Ethnoarchaeological Approach to the Study of Fish Remains. Unpublished Ph.D. dissertation, University of Wisconsin, Madison.

Bell, E. T.
1951   Mathematics, Queen and Servant of Science. New York: McGraw-Hill.

Beloch, K. J.
1886   Die Bevölkerung der griechisch-roemischen Welt. Leipzig: Duncker und Humblot.

Benet, F.
1963   The Ideology of Islamic Urbanization. International Journal of Comparative Sociology 4(2):211–226.

Benevolo, Leonardo
1967   The Origins of Modern Town Planning. Translated by Judith Landry. Cambridge, MA: MIT Press.
1980   The History of the City. Translated by Geoffrey Culverwell. Cambridge, MA: MIT Press.

Benjaminsen, Tor A., and Gunnvor Berge
2004   Une histoire de Tombouctou. Paris: Actes Sud.

Bennett, Gwen P.
2002   The Organization of Lithic Tool Production during the Longshan Period (ca. 2600–2000 BC) in Southeastern Shandong Province, China. Unpublished Ph.D. dissertation, University of California, Los Angeles.

Bent, Theodore
1892   The Ruined Cities of Mashonaland. Bulawayo: Books of Rhodesia.

Berry, Brian
1961   City Size Distributions and Economic Development. Economic Development and Culture Change 9:575–587.

Berry, Brian, and W. Garrison
1958   The Functional Basis of the Central Place Hierarchy. Economic Geography 34:145–154.

Berry, Brian J. L., and James O. Wheeler (editors)
2005   Urban Geography in America, 1950–2000. New York: Routledge.

Berthier, Sophie
1997   Recherches archeologiques sur la capitale de l'empire de Ghana. Etude d'un secteur d'habitat a Kumbi Saleh (Mauritanie). British Archaeological Reports #680. Oxford: Archaeopress.

Bietak, Manfred
1979   Urban Archaeology and the "Town Problem" in Ancient Egypt. *In* Egyptology and the Social Sciences, edited by Kent R. Weeks, pp. 97–144. Cairo: American University in Cairo Press.

Bintliff, John L.
1977 New Approaches to Human Geography: Prehistoric Greece, a Case Study. *In* A Historical Geography of the Balkans, edited by F. E. Carter, pp. 59–114. London: Academic Press.
2002 Rethinking Early Mediterranean Urbanism. Mauerschau 1:153–177.

Bird, James
1977 Centrality and Cities. London: Routledge and Kegan Paul.

Bisht, Ranvir Singh
1989 A New Model of the Harappan Town Planning as Revealed at Dholavira in Kutch: A Surface Study of Its Plan and Architecture. *In* History and Archaeology, edited by B. Chatterjee, pp. 397–408. Delhi: Ramanand Vidhya Bhawan.
1994 Secrets of the Water Fort. Down to Earth (May):25–31.
1998–1999 Dholavira and Banawali: Two Different Paradigms for the Harappan Urbis Forma. Puratattva 29:14–32.
2000 Urban Planning at Dholavira: A Harappan City. *In* Ancient Cities, Sacred Skies: Cosmic Geometries and City Planning in Ancient India, edited by J. M. Malville and L. M. Gujral, pp. 11–23. Delhi: Aryan Books International.

Bispham, Edward
2000 Mimic? A Case Study in the Context of Early Roman Colonisation. *In* The Emergence of State Identities in Italy in the First Millennium BC, edited by Edward Herring and Katherine Lomas, pp. 157–186. London: Accordia Research Institute, University of London.

Blackman, M. James, and Massimo Vidale
1992 The Production and Distribution of Stoneware Bangles at Mohenjo-daro and Harappa as Monitored by Chemical Characterization Studies. *In* South Asian Archaeology 1989, edited by Catherine Jarrige, pp. 37–44. Madison, WI: Prehistory Press.

Blanton, Richard E.
1976 Anthropological Studies of Cities. Annual Review of Anthropology 5:249–264.
1978 Monte Albán: Settlement Patterns at the Ancient Zapotec Capital. New York: Academic Press.
1981 The Rise of Cities. *In* Supplement to the Handbook of Middle American Indians, vol. 1: Archaeology, edited by Jeremy A. Sabloff, pp. 392–400. Austin: University of Texas Press.
1998 Beyond Centralization: Steps toward a Theory of Egalitarian Behavior in Archaic States. *In* Archaic States, edited by Gary M. Feinman and Joyce Marcus, pp. 135–172. Santa Fe, NM: SAR Press.

Blanton, Richard, Stephen Kowalewski, Gary Feinman, and Jill Appel
1981 Ancient Mesoamerica. New York: Cambridge University Press.

Boatwright, Mary T.
2000 Hadrian and the Cities of the Roman Empire. Princeton, NJ: Princeton University Press.

Bookchin, Murray
1992 Urbanization without Cities: The Rise and Decline of Citizenship. Montreal: Black Rose Books.

Braidwood, Robert J., and Gordon R. Willey (editors)
1962 Courses toward Urban Life. Viking Fund Publications in Anthropology, no. 32. New York: Wenner-Gren Foundation.

Broda, Johanna
1971 Las fiestas aztecas de los dioses de la lluvia: Una reconstrucción según las fuentes del siglo XVI. Revista Española de Antropología Americana 6:245–327.

Broda, Johanna, David Carrasco, and Eduardo Matos Moctezuma
1987 The Great Temple of Tenochtitlan: Center and Periphery in the Aztec World. Berkeley: University of California Press.

Bronson, Bennet
1977 Exchange at the Upstream and Downstream Ends: Notes towards a Functional Model of the State in Southeast Asia. *In* Economic Exchange and Social Interaction in Southeast Asia, edited by Karl L. Hutterer, pp. 39–52. Michigan Papers on South and Southeast Asia, no. 13. Ann Arbor.

Brouquier-Reddé, Véronique
1992   Temples et Cultes de Tripolitaine. Paris: Éditions du Centre National de la Recherche Scientifique.

Bruyère, Bernard
1924–1953   Rapport sur les Fouilles de Deir el Médina. Cairo: Fouilles de l'Institut français d'archéologie orientale.

Bulmer, Martin
1984   The Chicago School of Sociology: Institutionalization, Diversity, and the Rise of Sociological Research. Chicago: University of Chicago Press.

Burgers, Alfonso
2001   The Water Supplies and Related Structures of Roman Britain. British Archaeological Reports, British Series 324. Oxford: Archaeopress.

Burgess, Ernest W.
1925   The Growth of the City: An Introduction to a Research Project. In The City, edited by Robert E. Park, Ernest W. Burgess, and Roderick D. McKenzie, pp. 47–62. Chicago: University of Chicago Press.
1929   Urban Areas. In Chicago: An Experiment in Social Science Research, edited by T. V. Smith and Leonard V. White, pp. 113–138. Chicago: University of Chicago Press.

Burnham, Barry, and John S. Wacher
1990   The Small Towns of Roman Britain. London: Batsford.

Burrell, Barbara
2004   Neokoroi: Greek Cities and Roman Emperors. Leiden: E. J. Brill.

Bussmann, Richard
2004   Siedlungen im Kontext der Pyramiden des Alten Reiches. Mitteilungen für Deutschen Archäologischen Instituts, Abteilung Kairo 60:17–39.

Butterworth, Brian
1999   What Counts: How Every Brain Is Hardwired for Math. New York: Free Press.

Butzer, Karl W.
1976   Early Hydraulic Civilizations in Egypt: A Study in Cultural Ecology. Chicago: University of Chicago Press.
1981   Rise and Fall of Axum, Ethiopia: A Geo-archaeological Interpretation. American Antiquity 46:471–495.
1982a   Archaeology as Human Ecology. New York: Cambridge University Press.
1982b   Empires, Capitals and Landscapes of Ancient Ethiopia. Archaeology 35(5):30–37.
1984   Siedlungsgeographie (Settlement Geography). Lexikon der Ägyptologie 4:924–933.
1989   Historical Querétaro: Interpretation of a Colonial City. In Field Trip Guide, 1989 Conference of Latin American Geographers, Querétaro, Mexico 1989, pp. 3–27. Austin: University of Texas, Department of Geography.
1992   From Columbus to Acosta: Science, Geography, and the New World. Annals, Association of American Geographers 82:543–565.
1994   The Islamic Tradition of Agro-ecology: Cross-cultural Experience, Ideas, and Innovation. Ecumene 1:7–50.
1997   Sociopolitical Discontinuity in the Near East ca. 2200 BCE: Scenarios from Palestine and Egypt. In Third Millennium BC Climate Change and Old World Collapse, edited by H. N. Dalfes, G. Kukla, and H. Weiss, pp. 245–296. Berlin: Springer.
2005a   Desert Floods and Shifting Floodplain Margins at Giza, Egypt: Construction and Destruction of the Pyramid Workmen's Town. Abstract, Annual Meeting, Association of American Geographers, Denver, CO, p. 71.
2005b   Environmental History in the Mediterranean World: Cross-disciplinary Investigation of Cause-and-Effect for Degradation and Soil Erosion. Journal of Archaeological Science 32:1773–1800.

Butzer, Karl W., and Elisabeth K. Butzer
2000   Domestic Architecture in Early Colonial Mexico: Material Culture as (Sub)Text In Cultural Encounters with the Environment, edited by A. B. Murphy and D. L. Johnson, pp. 17–39. Lanham, MD: Rowman and Littlefield.

Butzer, Karl W., Elisabeth K. Butzer, and Juan F. Mateu
1986   Medieval Muslim Communities of the Sierra de Espadán, Kingdom of Valencia. Viator 17:339–413.

Butzer, Karl W., Ismael Miralles, and Juan F. Mateu
1983   Urban Geo-archaeology in Medieval Alzira (Prov. Valencia, Spain). Journal of Archaeological Science 10:333–349.

Butzer, Paul L., and Karl W. Butzer
2003   Mathematics at Charlemagne's Court and Its Transmission. *In* Court Culture in the Early Middle Ages, edited by Catherine Cubitt, pp. 77–90. Turnhout: Brepols.

Calnek, Edward
1976   The Internal Structure of Tenochtitlan. *In* The Valley of Mexico, edited by Eric R. Wolf, pp. 287–302. Albuquerque: University of New Mexico Press.
2003   Tenochtitlan-Tlatelolco. The Natural History of the City. *In* Urbanism in Mesoamerica, edited by William T. Sanders, Alba Guadalupe Mastache, and Robert Cobean, pp. 149–202. México, D. F.: INAH; University Park: Pennsylvania State University.

Calvino, I.
1974   Invisible Cities. London: Pan.

Cama Ttito, Máximo, and Alejandra Ttito Tica
2003   Batallas rituales: Tupay o Tinkuy en Chiaraje y Tocto. *In* Ritos de competición en los Andes: Luchas y contiendas en el Cuzco. Colección Etnográfica, vol. 1, pp. 19–50. Lima: Fondo Editorial de la Pontificia Universidad Católica del Perú.

Campbell, Colin
1987   The Romantic Ethic and the Spirit of Modern Consumerism. Oxford: Basil Blackwell.

Canali De Rossi, Filippo
1999   Da ermodoro ad ermocrate: Relazioni fra Efeso e Roma in età repubblicana. *In* 100 jahre Österreichische forschungen in Ephesos. Akten des Symposions Wien 1995, edited by Herwig Friesinger and Fritz Krinzinger, pp. 93–98. Vienna: Verlag der Österreichischen Akademie der Wissenschaften.

Carl, P., Barry Kemp, R. Laurence, R. Coningham, Charles Higham, and George L. Cowgill
2000   Were Cities Built as Images? Cambridge Archaeological Journal 10(2):327–365.

Carrasco, Pedro
1971   Social Organization of Ancient Mexico. *In* Archaeology of North Mesoamerica, pt. 1, edited by Gordon Ekholm and Ignacio Bernal, pp. 349–375. Handbook of Middle American Indians, vol. 10. Austin: University of Texas Press.
1976a   The Joint Family in Ancient Mexico: The Case of Molotla. *In* Essays on Mexican Kinship, edited by Hugo Nutini, Pedro Carrasco, and James Taggart, pp. 45–64. Pittsburgh: University of Pittsburgh Press.
1976b   Estratificación social indígena en Morelos durante el siglo XVI. *In* Estratificación social en la Mesoamérica prehispánica, edited by Pedro Carrasco and Johanna Broda, pp. 102–117. México, D. F.: SEP-INAH.
1976c   La sociedad mexicana antes de la conquista. *In* Historia General de México, vol. 1, edited by Bernardo García Martínez, José Luis Lorenzo, Ignacio Bernal, and Pedro Carrasco, pp. 165–286. México, D. F: El Colegio de México.

Carroll, Maureen
2001   Romans, Celts & Germans: The German Provinces of Rome. Stroud: Tempus.
2003   The Genesis of Roman Towns on the Lower Rhine. *In* The Archaeology of Roman Towns: Studies in Honour of John S. Wacher, edited by Peter R. Wilson, pp. 22–30. Oxford: Oxbow Books.

Cartledge, Paul
1998   The Economy (Economies) of Ancient Greece. Dialogos 5:4–24.

Carver, Martin O. H.
1993   Arguments in Stone: Archaeological Research and the European Town in the First Millennium. Oxford: Oxbow Books.

1996 Transitions to Islam: Urban Roles in the East and South Mediterranean, Fifth to Tenth Centuries AD. *In* Towns in Transition: Urban Evolution in Late Antiquity and the Early Middle Ages, edited by Neil Christie and Simon T. Loseby, pp. 184–212. Aldershot, UK: Scolar Press.

Casal, Jean Marie
1964 Fouilles D'Amri. Paris: Commission des Fouilles Archaeologiques.

Caso, Alfonso
1958 The Aztecs: People of the Sun. Norman: University of Oklahoma Press.

Caso, Alfonso, Ignacio Bernal, and Jorge R. Acosta
1967 La Cerámica de Monte Albán. Memorias del Instituto Nacional de Antropología e Historia, no. 13. México, D. F.

Cébeillac-Gervasoni, Mireille
1996 Gli "Africani" ad Ostia ovvero "Le mani sulla città." *In* l'incidenza dell'antico. Studia in memoria di Ettore Lepore, vol. 3, pp. 557–567. Naples.

Černý, Jaroslav
2001 A Community of Workmen at Thebes in the Ramesside Period. 2nd ed. Bibliothèque d'Étude 50. Cairo: Institut français d'archéologie orientale.

Chakrabarti, Dilip K.
1995 The Archaeology of Ancient Indian Cities. Delhi and London: Oxford University Press.

Chang, Kwang-chih
1962 China toward Urban Life. *In* Courses toward Urban Life, edited by Robert J. Braidwood and Gordon R. Willey, pp. 177–192. New York: Viking Fund Publications in Anthropology.
1968 Settlement Archaeology. Palo Alto, CA: National Press.
1976 Early Chinese Civilization: Anthropological Perspectives. Cambridge, MA: Harvard University Press.
1980 Shang Civilization. New Haven, CT: Yale University Press.

Chaolong, X.
1990 The Kot Dijians and the Harappans: Their Simultaneity, Another Possible Interpretation. *In* South Asian Archaeology 1987, edited by M. Taddei, pp. 157–202. Rome: IsMEO.

Charlton, Thomas H., and Deborah L. Nichols
1997 The City-State Concept: Development and Applications. *In* The Archaeology of City-States: Cross Cultural Approaches, edited by Deborah L. Nichols and Thomas H. Charlton, pp. 1–14. Washington, DC: Smithsonian Institution Press.

Chase, Arlen F., and Diane Z. Chase
1996 More Than Kin and King: Centralized Political Organization among the Late Classic Maya. Current Anthropology 37(5):803–810.

Chase, Diane, Arlen Chase, and William Haviland
1990 The Classic Maya City: Reconsidering the "Mesoamerican Urban Tradition." American Anthropologist 92:499–506.

Chase-Dunn, Christopher, and Thomas D. Hall
1997 Rise and Demise: Comparing World Systems. Boulder, CO: Westview.

Chayanov, A. V.
1966 Peasant Farm Organization. *In* A. V. Chayanov on the Theory of Peasant Economy, edited by
[1925] D. Thorner, B. Kerblay, and R. E. F. Smith, pp. 29–270. Homewood, IL: Richard D. Irwin.

Chelazzi Dini, Giulietta, Alessandro Angelini, and Bernardina Sani
1998 Sienese Painting from Duccio to the Birth of the Baroque. New York: Harry N. Abrams.

Chen De'an
1991 Sanxingdui yizhi. Sichuan wenwu 1:63–66.

Chen Quanfang
1988 Zhouyuan yu Zhou wenhua. Shanghai: Shanghai Renmin Chubanshe.

Chen Xingcan, Liu Li, Li Runquan, Henry T. Wright, and Arlene Miller Rosen
2003 Zhongguo wenming fudi de shehui fuzahua jincheng: Yiluohe diqu de juluoxingtai yanjiu. Kaogu xuebao 2:161–218.

Cherry, John F.
1984   The Emergence of the State in the Prehistoric Aegean. Proceedings of the Cambridge Philological Society 30:18–48.
1986   Polities and Palaces: Some Problems in Minoan State Formation. *In* Peer Polity Interaction and Socio-political Change, edited by Colin Renfrew and John F. Cherry, pp. 19–46. Cambridge: Cambridge University Press.

Chiarulli, Beverly
2006   Transformations of Lithic Technology at Chau Hiix, Belize. Paper presented at the Society for American Archaeology Annual Meeting, San Juan, Puerto Rico.

Chifeng Zhongmei Lianhe Kaogu Yanjiu Xiangmu (The Chifeng International Collaborative Archaeological Research Project)
2003   Neimenggu dongbu (Chifeng) quyu kaogu diaocha jieduanxing baogao, (Regional Archaeology in Eastern Inner Mongolia: A Methodological Exploration). Beijing: Kexue Chubanshe.

Childe, V. Gordon
1934   New Light on the Most Ancient East: The Oriental Prelude to European Prehistory. London: Kegan Paul.
1945   Directional Changes in Funerary Practices during 50,000 Years. Man 45:13–19.
1950   The Urban Revolution. Town Planning Review 21:3–17.

Chittick, H. Neville
1974   Kilwa: An Islamic Trading City on the East African Coast. British Institute in Eastern Africa, Memoir no. 5. Nairobi.
1984   Manda: Excavations at an Island Port on the Kenya Coast. British Institute in Eastern Africa, Memoir no. 9. Nairobi.

Chorley, Richard J., and Peter Haggett (editors)
1967   Models in Geography. London: Methuen.

Christaller, Walter
1933   Die zentralen orte in Süddeutschland: Eine ökonomisch-geographische untersuchung über die gesetzmässigkeit der verbreitung und entwicklung der siedlungen mit städtische funk-tionen. Jena.

Church, Richard L., and Thomas L. Bell
1988   An Analysis of Ancient Egyptian Settlement Patterns Using Location-Allocation Covering Models. Annals, Association of American Geographers 78:701–714.

Cieza de León, Pedro de
1959   The Incas of Pedro de Cieza de León. Translated by Harriet de Onis, edited by Victor W.
[1553]   von Hagen. Norman: University of Oklahoma Press.

Çilingiroğlu, Altan, and Mirjo Salvini
2001   Ayanis I: Ten Years' Excavations at Rusahinili Eiduru-kai 1989–1998. Rome: Istituto per gli Studi Micenei ed Egeo-Aatolici.

Clark, John Desmond
1962   Africa, South of the Sahara. *In* Courses toward Urban Life, edited by Robert J. Braidwood and Gordon R. Willey, pp. 1–33. New York: Wenner-Gren Foundation.

Clark, Sharri
2003   Representing the Indus Body: Sex, Gender, Sexuality, and the Anthropomorphic Terracotta Figurines from Harappa. Asian Perspectives 42(2):304–328.

Coarelli, Filippo
2004   Per una "topografia gamaliana" di Ostia. *In* Ostia, Cicero, Gamala, Feasts and the Economy. Papers in Memory of John H. D'Arms, edited by Anna Gallina Zevi and John H. Humphrey, pp. 89–98. Journal of Roman Archaeology, supplementary series 57.

Collis, John R.
1984   Oppida: Earliest Towns North of the Alps. Sheffield, UK: University of Sheffield.

Comhaire, Jean
1962   Part Two. *In* How Cities Grew: The Historical Sociology of Cities, by Jean Comhaire and Werner J. Cahnman, pp. 39–119. Madison, NJ: The Florham Park Press.

Connah, Graham
1975 The Archaeology of Benin. Oxford: Oxford University Press.
1981 Three Thousand Years in Africa. Cambridge: Cambridge University Press.
1987 African Civilizations: Precolonial Cities and States in Tropical Africa. Cambridge: Cambridge University Press.

Cook, P. M.
1997 Basal Platform Mounds at Chau Hiix: Evidence for Ancient Maya Social Structure and Cottage Industry Manufacturing. Unpublished Ph.D. dissertation, University of Arizona, Tucson.

Cool, Hilary E. M.
2006 Eating and Drinking in Roman Britain. Cambridge: Cambridge University Press.

Cordova, Carlos E.
1997 Landscape Transformation in Aztec and Spanish Colonial Texcoco, Mexico. Unpublished Ph.D. dissertation, University of Texas, Austin.

Cornell, Timothy J.
1995 The Beginnings of Rome. Italy from the Bronze Age to the Punic Wars (ca. 1000–264 BC). London: Routledge.

Corvisier, Jean-Nicolas
2004 Le bilan des land surveys pour la Grèce: Apports et limites. Pallas 64:15–33.

Costin, Cathy L., and Melissa B. Hagstrum
1995 Standardization, Labor Investment, Skill, and the Organization of Ceramic Production in Late Prehispanic Highland Peru. American Antiquity 60(4):619–639.

Cowgill, George L.
2004 Origins and Development of Urbanism: Archaeological Perspectives. Annual Review of Anthropology 33:525–549.
2007 The Urban Organization of Teotihuacan, Mexico. In Settlement and Society: Essays Dedicated to Robert McCormick Adams, edited by Elizabeth C. Stone, pp. 261–295. Los Angeles: Cotsen Institute of Archaeology, University of California.

Crawford, Harriet E. W.
1991 Sumer and the Sumerians. Cambridge: Cambridge University Press.

Creighton, John
2000 Coins and Power in Late Iron Age Britain. Cambridge: Cambridge University Press.
2005 Britannia: The Creation of a Roman Province. Abingdon, UK: Routledge.

Creswell, K. C.
1958 A Short Account of Early Muslim Architecture. Harmondsworth, UK: Penguin.

Crumley, Carole L.
1987 A Dialectical Critique of Hierarchy. In Power Relations and State Formation, edited by Thomas C. Patterson and Christine Ward Gailey, pp. 155–168. Washington, DC: American Anthropological Association.

Crumley, Carole L., and William Marquardt
1987 Regional Dynamics in Burgundy. In Regional Landscapes in Historical Perspective, edited by Carole L. Crumley and William H. Marquardt, pp. 609–623. New York: Academic Press.

Crummy, Philip
1997 City of Victory: The Story of Colchester—Britain's First Roman Town. Colchester, UK: Colchester Archaeological Trust.
1999 Colchester: Making Towns out of Fortresses and the First Urban Fortifications in Britain. In The Coloniae of Roman Britain: New Studies and a Review, edited by Henry R. Hurst, pp. 88–100. Journal of Roman Archaeology, supplementary series 36.

Cuddy, Thomas
2000 Socioeconomic Integration of the Classic Maya State: Political and Domestic Economies in a Residential Neighborhood, Chau Hiix, Belize. Unpublished Ph.D. dissertation. Columbia University, New York.

Cunliffe, Barry W.
2004 Iron Age Communities in Britain. 4th ed. London: Routledge.

Curtin, Phillip D.
1984 Cross-cultural Trade in World History. Cambridge: Cambridge University Press.

Dahlin, Bruce, and Traci Ardren
2002 Modes of exchange and regional patterns: Chunchucmil, Yucatan. *In* Ancient Maya Political Economies, edited by Marilyn A. Masson and David A. Freidel, pp. 249–284. Boston: Rowman and Littlefield.

Dales, George F.
1973 Archaeological and Radiocarbon Chronologies for Protohistoric South Asia. *In* South Asian Archaeology 1971, edited by N. Hammond, pp. 157–169. London: Duckworth.
1989 Harappa: A New Look at the Type Site of the Indus Civilization. *In* Old Problems and New Perspectives in the Archaeology of South Asia, edited by J. M. Kenoyer, pp. 127–132. Madison: Wisconsin Archaeological Reports.

Dales, George F., and Jonathan Mark Kenoyer
1991 Summaries of Five Seasons of Research at Harappa (District Sahiwal, Punjab, Pakistan) 1986–1990. *In* Harappa Excavations 1986–1990, edited by R. H. Meadow, pp. 185–262. Madison, WI: Prehistory Press.

D'Altroy, Terence N.
1992 Provincial Power in the Inka Empire. Washington, DC: Smithsonian Institution Press.

Dar, Saifur Rahman
1983 Khadin-Wala, the First Kot Dijian Site Discovered on the Right Bank of the River Ravi. Journal of Central Asia 6(1):17–34.

David, A. R.
1986 The Pyramid Builders of Ancient Egypt. London: Routledge and Kegan Paul.
1999 Lahun, Town. *In* Encyclopedia of the Archaeology of Ancient Egypt, edited by Kathryn A. Bard, pp. 430–432. London: Routledge.

Davies, Hugh
2002 Roads in Roman Britain. Stroud: Tempus.

De Angelis, Franco
2003 Megara Hyblaia and Selinous. The Development of Two Greek City-States in Archaic Sicily. Oxford: Oxford University Press.

Delafosse, Maurice
1922 Les Noirs de l'Afrique. Paris:Payot.
1924 Le Gana et le Mali et l'emplacement de leurs capitales. Bulletin du Comite d'etudes historiques et scientifiques de l'A.O.F. 9:479–542.

Delaigue, Marie-Christine
1988 Capileira, Village Andalous: Un habitat montagnard à toits plats. British Archaeological Reports, International Series 466. Oxford: Archaeopress.

DeLaine, Janet
1992 New Models, Old Modes: Continuity and Change in the Design of Public Baths. *In* Die römische Stadt im 2. Jahrhundert n. Chr.. Der Funktionswandel des öffentlichen Raumes. Kolloquium in Xanten vom 2. bis 4. Mai 1990, edited by Henner von Hesberg, Hans-Joachim Schalles, and Paul Zanker, pp. 257–275. Cologne: Xantener Berichte Band 2. Rheinland-Verlag GmbH.
2002a The Temple of Hadrian at Cyzicus and Roman Attitudes to Exceptional Construction. Papers of the British School at Rome 70, pp. 205–230.
2002b Building Activity in Ostia in the Second Century AD. *In* Ostia e Portus nelle loro relazioni con Roma, edited by Christer Bruun and Anna Gallina Zevi, pp. 41–101. Acta Instituti Romani Finlandiae 27. Rome.

DeLaine, Janet, and David E. Johnston (editors)
1999 Roman Baths and Bathing. Proceedings of the First International Conference on Roman Baths. 2 vols. Journal of Roman Archaeology, supplementary series 37.

De Ligt, Luuk, Emily Hemerlrijk, and Henricus Singor (editors)
2004 Roman Rule and Civic Life: Local and Regional Perspectives. Amsterdam: J. C. Gieben.

Delougaz, Pinhas, Harold D. Hill, and Seton Lloyd
1967 Private Houses and Graves in the Diyala Region. University of Chicago Oriental Institute Publications, vol. 88. Chicago: University of Chicago Press.

Demand, Nancy H.
1996 A History of Ancient Greece. New York: McGraw Hill.

Demarest, Arthur A.
1992 Ideology in Ancient Maya Cultural Evolution: The Dynamics of Galactic Polities. *In* Ideology and Pre-Columbian Civilizations, edited by Arthur A. Demarest and Geoffrey W. Conrad, pp. 135–158. School of American Research. Santa Fe, NM: SAR Press.

de Maret, Pierre
2000 Urban Origins in Central Africa: The Case of Kongo. *In* Comparative Study of Thirty City-State Cultures, edited by Mogens Herman Hansen, pp. 461–482. Copenhagen: Det Kongelige Danske Videnskabernes Selskab.

DeMattè, Paola
1999 Longshan-Era Urbanism: The Role of Cities in Predynastic China. Asian Perspectives 39:119–153.

De Miro, Ernesto, and Antonelle Polito
2005 Leptis Magna: Dieci anni di scavi archeologici nell'area del Foro vecchio: I livelli fenici, punici e romani (Missione dell'Università di Messina). Rome: "l'Erma" di Bretschneider.

de Molina, fray Alfonso
1977 Vocabulario en lengua Castellana y Mexicana y Mexicana y Castellana. México, D. F.: Porrúa.

Dennett, Daniel Clement
1967 The Conquest of New Spain. Translated by J. M. Cohen. Harmondsworth, UK: Penguin Books.
2003 Freedom Evolves. New York: Viking.

Devisse, Jean (editor)
1983 Tegdaoust III: Recherches sur Ouadaghost: Campagnes 1960/65, Enquetes Generales. Paris: Editions Recherches sur les Civilisations.
1993 Vallees du Niger. Paris: Association des Musees Nationaux.

Díaz del Castillo, Bernal
1956 The Discovery and Conquest of Mexico 1517–1521. New York: Farrar, Straus and Cudahy.

Dignas, Beate
2002 Economy of the Sacred in Hellenistic and Roman Asia Minor. Oxford: Oxford University Press.

Dillon, Brian D., Kevin O. Pope, and Michael W. Love
1988 An Ancient Extractive Industry: Maya Salt Making at Salinas de los Nueve Cerros, Guatemala. Journal of New World Archaeology 7(2/3):37–58.

Di Vita-Evrard, Ginette
1999 Lepcis. *In* Libya. The Lost Cities of the Roman Empire, edited by Antonio Di Vita, Ginette Di Vita-Evrard, and Lidiano Bacchielli, pp. 44–145. Cologne: Könemann.

Dobney, Keith, Allan Hall, and Harry Kenward
1999 It's All Garbage…A Review of Bioarchaeology in the Four English Colonia Towns. *In* The Coloniae of Roman Britain: New Studies and a Review, edited by Henry R. Hurst, pp. 15–35. Journal of Roman Archaeology, supplementary series 36.

Donald, Merlin
1991 Origins of the Modern Mind: Three Stages in the Evolution of Culture and Cognition. Cambridge, MA: Harvard University Press.

Donner, Herbert, and H. Cüppers
1977 Die Mosaikkarte von Madeba. Wiesbaden: Harrassowitz.

Doxiadis, Constantinos A.
1968 Ekistics: An Introduction to the Science of Human Settlements. New York: Norton.

Drack, Walter, and Rudolf Fellmann
1988   Die Römer in der Schweiz. Stuttgart: Theiss-Raggi.

Drennan, Robert D.
1988   Household Location and Compact versus Dispersed Settlement in Prehispanic Mesoamerica. *In* Household and Community in the Mesoamerican Past, edited by Richard Wilk and Wendy Ashmore, pp. 273–298. Albuquerque: University of New Mexico Press.

Drennon, Christine M.
1998   (Re)Inventing Macedonia: The Passage from Religious to Territorial Identity. Unpublished Ph.D. dissertation, University of Texas, Austin.

Drinkwater, John F.
1975   Lugdunum: "Natural Capital" of Gaul? Britannia 6:133–140.
1985   Urbanization in the Three Gauls: Some Observations. *In* Roman Urban Topography in Britain and the Western Empire, edited by F. Grew and B. Hobley, pp. 49–55. Council for British Archaeology, Research Report 59. London.
1987   Urbanization in Italy and the Western Empire. *In* The Roman World, edited by John S. Wacher, pp. 345–387. London and Boston: Routledge and Kegan Paul.

Du Jinpeng
2003   Yanshi Shang cheng chutan. Beijing: Zhongguo Shehuikexueyuan Chubanshe.

Du Jinpeng and Wang Xuerong (editors)
2004   Yanshi Shang cheng yizhi yanjiu. Beijing: Kexue Chubanshe.

Duncan-Jones, Richard
1982   The Economy of the Roman Empire. Cambridge: Cambridge University Press.
1990   Structure and Scale in the Roman Economy. Cambridge: Cambridge University Press.

Durán, fray Diego
1977   Book of the Gods and Rites and the Ancient Calendar. Translated and edited by Fernando Horcasitas and Doris Heyden. Norman: University of Oklahoma Press.

Durrani, F. A., I. Ali, and George Erdosy
1995   Seals and Inscribed Sherds of Rehman Dheri. Ancient Pakistan 10:198–233.

Durrell, Lawrence
1957–   The Alexandria Quartet. New York: Dutton.
1961

Dutt, Binode
1977   Town Planning in Ancient India. Delhi: New Asian Publishers.
[1925]

Dyos, Harold James, and Michael Wolff
1973   The Way We Live. *In* The Victorian City: Images and Reality, edited by Harold J. Dyos and Michael Wolff, vol. 2, pp. 893–907. London: Routledge and Kegan Paul.

Eben Saleh, M. A.
1998   Transformation of the Traditional Settlements of Southwest South Arabia. Planning Perspectives 13:195–215.

Eliade, Mircea
1954   The Myth of the Eternal Return. New York: Pantheon Books.

Elson, Christina M.
2006   Intermediate Elites and the Political Landscape of the Early Zapotec State. *In* Intermediate Elites in Pre-Columbian States and Empires, edited by Christina M. Elson and Ronald Alan Covey, pp. 44–67. Tucson: University of Arizona Press.

Enckell, Pehr H., E. S. Königsson, and L. K. Königsson
1979   Ecological Instability of a Roman Iron Age Community. Oikos 33:328–349.

Enckevort, Harry van, and Jan Thijssen
2003   Nijmegen—A Roman Town in the Frontier Zone of Germania Inferior. *In* The Archaeology of Roman Towns: Studies in Honour of John S. Wacher, edited by Peter R. Wilson, pp. 59–71. Oxford: Oxbow Books.

Endfield, Georgina H., I. Fernández Tejedo, and S. L. O'Hara
2004 Drought and Dispute, Deluge and Dearth. Journal of Historical Geography 30:249–276.

Engel, Josef (editor)
1970 Grosser historicher Weltatlas, II. Mittelalter. Munich: Bayerischer Schulbuch-Verlag.

Esmonde Cleary, A. Simon
1987 Extra Mural Areas of Romano-British Towns. British Archaeological Reports, British Series 169. Oxford: British Archaeological Reports.
1989 The Ending of Roman Britain. London: Batsford.
1998 The Origins of Towns in Roman Britain: The Contributions of Romans and of Britons. *In* Los Orígenes de la ciudad en el Noroeste Hispánico, edited by Antonio Rodríguez Colmenero, pp. 35–54. Lugo: Diputación Provincial de Lugo.
2003 Civil Defences in the West under the High Empire. *In* The Archaeology of Roman Towns: Studies in Honour of John S. Wacher, edited by Peter R. Wilson, pp. 72–85. Oxford: Oxbow Books.
2005 Beating the Bounds: Ritual and the Articulation of Urban Space in Roman Britain. *In* Roman Working Lives and Urban Living, edited by Ardle MacMahon and Jennifer Price, pp. 1–17. Oxford: Oxbow Books.

Esmonde Cleary, A. Simon, and Jason J. B. Wood
2006 St Bertrand-de-Comminges III: Le Rempart de l'Antiquité Tardive de la Ville Haute. Bordeaux: Fédération Aquitania.

Fabre, Guilhem, Jean-Luc Fiches, Philippe Leveau, and Jean-Louis Paillet
1992 The Pont du Gard: Water and the Roman Town. Paris: CNRS.

Face, Mario
1984 Architektur und Städtebau. *In* Tunesien, edited by K. Schiephake, pp. 321–337. Stuttgart: Thienemann.

Falkenhausen, Lothar von
2003 Social Ranking in Chu Tombs: The Mortuary Background of the Warring States Manuscript Finds. Monumenta Serica 51:439–526.
2004 Mortuary Behavior in Pre-Imperial Qin: A Religious Interpretation. *In* Chinese Religion and Society, edited by John Lagerwey, vol. 1, pp. 109–172. Hong Kong: Chinese University Press.
2006 Chinese Society in the Age of Confucius (ca. 1050–ca. 250 BC): The Archaeological Evidence. Los Angeles: Cotsen Institute of Archaeology, University of California.

Fang Hui, Gary M. Feinman, Anne P. Underhill, and Linda M. Nicholas
2004 Rizhao Liangcheng diqu juluo kaogu: Renkou wenti. Hua Xia kaogu 2:37–40.

Faulkner, Neil
2000 The Decline and Fall of Roman Britain. Stroud: Tempus.

Feinman, Gary M., and Joyce Marcus (editors)
1998 Archaic States. School of American Research. Santa Fe, NM: SAR Press.

Feldman, Lawrence
1985 A Tumpline Economy: Production and Distribution Systems in 16th-Century Eastern Guatemala. Malibu, CA: Labyrinthos.

Fentress, Elizabeth (editor)
2000 Romanization and the City: Creation, Transformations, Failure. Journal of Roman Archaeology, supplementary series 38.

Finley, Moses I.
1973 The Ancient Economy. Berkeley: University of California Press.

Flannery, Kent V.
1968 The Olmec and the Valley of Oaxaca: A Model for Interregional Interaction in Formative Times. *In* Dumbarton Oaks Conference on the Olmec, edited by Elizabeth P. Benson, pp. 79–110. Washington, DC: Dumbarton Oaks.
1972 The Cultural Evolution of Civilizations. Annual Review of Ecology and Systematics 3:399–426.
1994 Childe the Evolutionist: A Perspective from Nuclear America. *In* The Archaeology of V. Gordon Childe, edited by David R. Harris, pp. 101–119. University College London: The Prehistoric Society.

1998   The Ground Plans of Archaic States. *In* Archaic States, edited by Gary M. Feinman and Joyce Marcus, pp. 15–58. Santa Fe, NM: SAR Press.
1999   Process and Agency in Early State Formation. Cambridge Archaeological Journal 9(1):3–21.

Flannery, Kent V., and Joyce Marcus
1983   The Earliest Public Buildings, Tombs, and Monuments at Monte Albán, with notes on the internal chronology of Period I. *In* The Cloud People, edited by Kent V. Flannery and Joyce Marcus, pp. 87–91. New York: Academic Press.
1993   Cognitive Archaeology. Cambridge Archaeological Journal 3:260–270.
2003   The Origin of War: New ^{14}C Dates from Ancient Mexico. Proceedings of the National Academy of Sciences 100(20):11801–11805.
2005   Excavations at San José Mogote 1: The Household Archaeology. Memoirs of the Museum of Anthropology, no. 40. Ann Arbor: Museum of Anthropology, University of Michigan.

Fleisher, Jeffrey B.
2003   Viewing Stonetowns from the Countryside: An Archaeological Approach to Swahili Regions, AD 800–1500. Unpublished Ph.D. dissertation, University of Virginia, Charlottesville.

Fletcher, Roland J.
1977   Settlement Studies (Micro and Semi-Micro). *In* Spatial Archaeology, edited by David L. Clarke, pp. 47–162. London: Academic Press.
1986   People and Space. *In* Patterns of the Past, edited by Ian Hodder, Glynn L. Isaac, and Norman Hammond, pp. 97–128. Cambridge: Cambridge University Press.
1993   Settlement Area and Communication in African Towns and Cities. *In* The Archaeology of Africa, edited by Thurston Shaw, Paul Sinclair, Bassey Andah, and Alex Okpoko, pp. 732–749. London: Routledge.
1995   The Limits of Settlement Growth: A Theoretical Outline. Cambridge: Cambridge University Press.
1998   African Urbanism: Scale, Mobility, and Transformations. *In* Transformations in Africa, edited by Graham Connah, pp. 104–138. London: Leicester University Press.
2000   Diversity and Dispersal in African Urbanism: A Global Perspective. *In* Development of Urbanism from a Global Perspective, edited by P. J. J. Sinclair. http://www.arkeologi.uu.se/afr/BOOK/Fletcher/Flecherframe.htm. Uppsala: Department of Archaeology and Ancient History, University of Uppsala.

Foias, Antonia
2002   At the Crossroads: The Economic Basis of Political Power in the Petexbatun Region. *In* Ancient Maya Political Economies, edited by Marilyn A. Masson and David A. Freidel, pp. 223–248. Boston: Rowman and Littlefield.

Folan, William J., Joyce Marcus, and W. Frank Miller
1995   Verification of a Maya Settlement Model through Remote Sensing. Cambridge Archaeological Journal 5(2):277–283.

Forde, Cyril Daryll
1964   Yakö Studies. Oxford: Oxford University Press.

Forge, Anthony
1972   Normative Factors in the Settlement Size of Neolithic Cultivators (New Guinea). *In* Man, Settlement and Urbanism, edited by Peter J. Ucko, Ruth Tringham, and G. W. Dimbleby, pp. 363–376. London: Duckworth.

Foucault, Michel
1995   Discipline and Punish: The Birth of the Prison. Translated by A. Sheridan. New York: Vintage Books.

Fox, Richard
1977   Urban Anthropology: Cities in Their Cultural Settings. Englewood Cliffs, NJ: Prentice-Hall Inc.

Freidel, David A.
1981   Civilization as a State of Mind: The Cultural Evolution of the Lowland Maya. *In* The Transition to Statehood in the New World, edited by Grant D. Jones and Robert R. Kautz, pp. 188–227. Cambridge: Cambridge University Press.

Freidel, David A., and Linda Schele
1984   Kingship in the Late Preclassic Lowlands: The Instruments and Places of Ritual Power. American Anthropologist 90(3):547–567.
1988   Symbol and Power: A History of the Lowland Maya Cosmogram. *In* Maya Iconography, edited by Elizabeth P. Benson and G. G. Griffin, pp. 44–93. Princeton, NJ: Princeton University Press.

Fulford, Michael G.
2003   Julio-Claudian and Early Flavian Calleva. *In* The Archaeology of Roman Towns: Studies in Honour of John S. Wacher, edited by Peter R. Wilson, pp. 95–104. Oxford: Oxbow Books.

Fustel de Coulanges, Numa Denis
1864   La Cité Antique. Paris: Librairie Hachette.
1872   La Cité Antique: etude sur le culte, le droit, les institutions de la Grèce et de Rome. 4th ed. Paris: Hachette.
1963   The Ancient City. New York: Doubleday.

Gansu Sheng Wenwu Kaogu Yanjiusuo
2006   Qin'an Dadiwan: Xinshiqishidai yizhi fajue baogao. 2 vols. Beijing: Wenwu Chubanshe.

Garlake, Peter S.
1966   The Early Islamic Architecture of the East African Coast. British Institute of History and Archaeology in East Africa, Memoir no. 1. Nairobi and London: Oxford University Press.
1973   Great Zimbabwe. London: Thames and Hudson.
1982   Great Zimbabwe: Described and Explained. Harare: Zimbabwe Publishing House.

Garner, Barry J.
1967   Models of Urban Geography and Settlement Location. *In* Models in Geography, edited by Richard J. Chorley and Peter Haggett, pp. 303–360. London: Methuen.

Gascó, Fernando
1998   Vita della polis di età romana e memoria della polis classica. *In* I greci. 2. Una storia greca. III. Trasformazioni, edited by Salvatore Settis, pp. 1147–1164. Turin: G. Einaudi.

Gates, Charles
2003   Ancient Cities: The Archaeology of Urban Life in the Ancient Near East and Egypt, Greece, and Rome. London and New York: Routledge.

Gazzaniga, Michael S.
1992   Nature's Mind: The Biological Roots of Thinking, Emotions, Sexuality, Language, and Intelligence. New York: Basic Books.
1998   The Mind's Past. Berkeley: University of California Press.

Geertz, Clifford
1980   Negara: The Theatre State in Nineteenth-Century Bali. Princeton, NJ: Princeton University Press.

Gibson, Charles
1964   The Aztecs under Spanish Rule. Stanford, CA: Stanford University Press.

Gill, Richardson B.
2001   The Great Maya Droughts: Water, Life, and Death. Albuquerque: University of New Mexico Press.

Gillaumet, Jean-Paul
2003   De la naissance de Bibracte à la naissance d'Autun. *In* La naissance de la ville dans l'antiquité, edited by Michel Reddé, pp. 215–225. Paris: De Boccard.

Goldsmith, A. S.
2004   Houselots at Chau Hiix: A Spatial Approach to Non-elite Domestic Variability at a Small Maya City. Unpublished Ph.D. dissertation, University of Calgary.

Goody, Jack
1962   Death, Property and the Ancestors: A Study of the Mortuary Customs of the LoDagaa of West Africa. Stanford, CA: Stanford University Press.
1982   Cooking, Cuisine, and Class: A Study in Comparative Sociology. Cambridge and New York: Cambridge University Press.

Gopnik, Myrna (editor)
1997   The Inheritance and Innateness of Grammars. Oxford: Oxford University Press.

Gosden, Chris
2004 Archaeology and Colonialism. Cambridge: Cambridge University Press.

Gose, Peter
1996 Oracles, Divine Kingship, and Political Representation in the Inka State. Ethnohistory 43(1):1–32.

Goudineau, Christian
1996 Gaul. In The Cambridge Ancient History, vol. X: The Augustan Empire, 43 BC–AD 69, edited by Alan K Bowman, Edward Champlin, and Andrew Lintott, 2nd ed., pp. 464–502. Cambridge and New York: Cambridge University Press.
2000 Gaul. In The Cambridge Ancient History, vol. XI: The High Empire, AD 70–192, edited by Alan K Bowman, Peter Garnsey, and Dominic Rathbone, 2nd ed., pp. 462–495. Cambridge and New York: Cambridge University Press.

Graham, Elizabeth
2002 Perspectives on Economy and Theory. In Ancient Maya Political Economies, edited by Marilyn A. Masson and David A. Freidel, pp. 398–418. Boston: Rowman and Littlefield.
2004 Lamanai Reloaded: Alive and Well in the Early Postclassic. In Archaeological Investigations in the Eastern Maya Lowlands: Papers of the 2003 Belize Archaeology Symposium, Research Papers in Belizean Archaeology, vol. 1, edited by Jaime Awe, John Morris, and Sherilyn Jones, pp. 223–242. Belmopan, Belize: Institute of Archaeology and the National Institute of Culture and History.

Grimal, Pierre, and G. Woloch
1983 Roman Cities. Madison: University of Wisconsin Press.

Groenman-van Waateringe, Willy
1980 Urbanization and the North-west Frontier of the Roman Empire. In Roman Frontier Studies 1979. British Archaeological Reports, International Series 71, edited by S. Hanson and L. J. F. Keppie, pp. 1037–1044.

Gros, Pierre
1996a L'architecture romaine I: les monuments publics. Paris: Picard.
1996b Les nouveaux espaces civiques du debut de l'Empire en Asia Mineure: Les exemples d'Ephése, Iasos et Aphrodisias. In Aphrodisias Papers 3, edited by Charlotte Roueche and Robert R. R. Smith, pp. 111–121. Journal of Roman Archaeology, supplementary series 20.

Gros, Pierre, and Mario Torelli
1988 Storia dell'urbanistica. Il mondo romano. Bari: Laterza.

Grube, Nikolai
2000 The City-States of the Maya. In A Comparative Study of Thirty City-State Cultures, edited by Mogens H. Hansen, pp. 547–565. Copenhagen: Det Kongelige Danske Videnskabernes Selskab.

Gunder-Frank, Andre, and B. Gills (editors)
1993 The World System: Five Hundred Years or Five Thousand. New York and London: Routledge.

Guojia Wenwuju
1999–2001 Zhongguo zhongyao kaogu faxian. Beijing: Wenwu Chubanshe.
2001–2002 Zhongguo zhongyao kaogu faxian. Beijing: Wenwu Chubanshe.
2002–2003 Zhongguo zhongyao kaogu faxian. Beijing: Wenwu Chubanshe.

Gupta, S. P.
1999 The Indus-Sarasvati Civilization: Beginnings and Development. In The Dawn of Indian Civiliza-tion (up to ca. 600 B.C.), edited by G. C. Pande, pp. 269–375. Delhi: Munshiram Manoharlal.

Gutiérrez Mendoza, Gerardo
2003 Territorial Structure and Urbanism in Mesoamerica: The Huaxtec and Mixtec-Tlapanec-Nahua Cases. In Urbanism in Mesoamerica, edited by William T. Sanders, Alba Guadalupe Mastache, and Robert Cobean, pp. 85–118. México, D. F.: INAH; University Park: Pennsylvania State University.

Hable Selassie, Sergew
1972 Ancient and Medieval Ethiopian History to 1270. Addis Ababa: Haile Selassie University Press.

Haggett, Peter, Andrew Cliff, and Allan Frey
1977 Locational Analysis in Human Geography. London: Edward Arnold.

Hakim, Besim Selim
1986 Arabic-Islamic Cities, Building and Planning Principles. London: KPI Limited.

Halfmann, Helmut
2001 Städtebau und Bauherren in römische Kleinasien. Ein Vergleich Zwischen Ephesus und Pergamon. Istanbuler Mitteilungen, Beihaft 43. Tübingen: Wasmuth.

Hall, Sir Peter
1998 Cities in Civilisation. London: Weidenfeld and Nicolson.

Hall, Thomas D., and Christopher Chase-Dunn
1993 The World-Systems Perspective and Archaeology: Forward into the Past. Journal of Archaeological Research 1(2):121–143.

Halperin, Rhoda H.
1994 Cultural Economies Past and Present. Texas Press Sourcebooks in Anthropology, no. 18. Austin: University of Texas Press.

Hancock, Graham, and S. Faiia
1998 Heaven's Mirror: Quest for the Lost Civilization. London: Michael Joseph.

Hansen, Mogens H.
1994 Poleis and City-States, 600–323 BC A Comprehensive Research Programme. *In* From Political Architecture to Stephanus Byzantius, edited by David Whitehead, pp. 9–17. Stuttgart: Steiner.
1997 The Polis as an Urban Centre. The Literary and Epigraphical Evidence. *In* The Polis as an Urban Centre and as a Political Community, edited by M. H. Hansen, pp. 9–86. Copenhagen: Det Kongelige Danske Videnskabernes Selskab.
2000a Introduction: The Concepts of City-State and City-State Culture. *In* A Comparative Study of Thirty City-State Cultures: An Investigation Conducted by the Copenhagen Polis Centre, edited by Mogens H. Hansen, pp. 11–34. Copenhagen: Det Kongelige Danske Videnskabernes Selskab.
2000b Conclusion: The Impact of City-State Cultures on World History. *In* A Comparative Study of Thirty City-State Cultures: An Investigation Conducted by the Copenhagen Polis Centre, edited by Mogens H. Hansen, pp. 597–623. Copenhagen: Det Kongelige Danske Videnskabernes Selskab.
2000c The Hellenic Polis. *In* A Comparative Study of Thirty City-State Cultures (Historisk-filosofiske Skrifter 21), edited by Mogens H. Hansen, pp. 143–187. Copenhagen: Det Kongelige Danske Videnskabernes Selskab.
2000d General Index. *In* A Comparative Study of Thirty City-State Cultures: An Investigation Conducted by the Copenhagen Polis Centre, edited by Mogens H. Hansen, pp. 624–25. Copenhagen: Det Kongelige Danske Videnskabernes Selskab.
2002a Introduction. *In* A Comparative Study of Six City-State Cultures, edited by M. H. Hansen, pp. 7–21. Copenhagen: Det Kongelige Danske Videnskabernes Selskab.
2004 The Concept of the Consumption City Applied to the Greek Polis. *In* Once Again: Studies in the Ancient Greek Polis, edited by Thomas H. Nielsen, pp. 9–47. Stuttgart: Steiner.
2006 Polis: An Introduction to the Ancient Greek City-State. Oxford: Oxford University Press.

Hansen, Mogens Herman (editor)
2000e A Comparative Study of Thirty City-State Cultures: An Investigation Conducted by the Copenhagen Polis Centre. Copenhagen: Det Kongelige Danske Videnskabernes Selskab.
2002b A Comparative Study of Six City-State Cultures. Copenhagen: Det Kongelige Danske Videnskabernes Selskab.

Hansen, Mogens H., and Thomas H. Nielsen
2004 An Inventory of Archaic and Classical Poleis. Oxford: Oxford University Press.

Hardoy, Jorge E.
1968 Urban Planning in Pre-Columbian America. New York: Braziller.
1973 Pre-Columbian Cities. New York: Walker.

Harley, John B., and David Woodward (editors)
1987 The History of Cartography, I. Cartography in Prehistory, Ancient, and Medieval Europe and the Mediterranean. Chicago: University of Chicago Press.

Harris, Chauncy D., and Edward L. Ullman
1945 The Nature of Cities. Annals of the American Academy of Political and Social Science 242:7–17.

Harrison, Peter D.
1999 The Lords of Tikal: Rulers of an Ancient Maya City. London: Thames and Hudson.

Harth-Terré, Emilio
1964 El pueblo de Huánuco-Viejo. Arquitecto Peruano 320–321:1–22.

Hartmann, Roswith
1971 Mercados y ferias prehispánicas en el área Andina. Boletín de la Academia Nacional de Historia (Quito) 54(118):214–236.
1979 Más noticias sobre el "Juego del Pucara." In Amerikanistische Studien (Estudios americanistas), vol. 20, edited by Roswith Hartmann and Udo Oberem, pp. 202–218. Collectanea Instituti Anthropos. St. Augustin: Haus Völker u Kulturen.

Haselgrove, Colin
1996 Roman Impact on Rural Settlement and Society in Southern Picardy. In From the Sword to the Plough: Three Studies in the Earliest Romanisation of Northern Gaul, edited by Nico Roymans, pp. 127–185. Luxembourg: Musée National d'Histoire d'Art; Amsterdam: Amsterdam University Press.
2003 Society and Polity in Late Iron Age Britain. In A Companion to Roman Britain, edited by Malcolm Todd, pp. 12–29. Oxford: Blackwell.

Hassan, Fekri
1993 Town and Village in Ancient Egypt: Ecology, Society, and Urbanization. In The Archaeology of Africa: Food, Metals and Towns, edited by Thurston Shaw, Paul Sinclair, Bassey Andah, and Alex Okpoko, pp. 551–569. London: Routledge.

Hassan, Selim
1943 Excavations at Giza IV (1932–1933). Cairo: Faculty of Arts, Egyptian University.

Hassig, Ross
1988 Aztec Warfare. Norman: University of Oklahoma Press.

Hauser, Philip M., and Leo F. Schnore
1965 The Study of Urbanization. New York: Wiley.

Hebei Sheng Wenwu Yanjiusuo
1995 Cuo mu: Zhanguo Zhongshan guo guowang zhi mu. 2 vols. Beijing: Wenwu Chubanshe.

Hegmon, Michelle
2003 Setting Theoretical Egos Aside: Issues and Theory in North American Archaeology. American Antiquity 68:213–243.

Heinzelmann, Michael
1998 Beobachtungen zur suburbanen topographie Ostias. Ein orthogonales Strassensystem im Bereich der Pianabella. Mitteilungen des Deutsches Archäologisches Instituts, Römische Abteilung 105:175–225.
2002 Bauboom und urbanistische Defizite–zur städtebaulichen Entwicklung Ostias im 2. Jh. In Ostia e Portus nelle loro relazioni con Roma, edited by Christer Bruun and Anna Gallina Zevi, pp. 103–121. Acta Instituti Romani Finlandiae 27, Rome.

Heinzelmann, Michael, and Archer Martin
2002 River Port, Navalia and Harbour Temple at Ostia: New Results of a DAI-AAR Project. Journal of Roman Archaeology 15:5–19.

Helck, Wolfgang
1975 Domänen: Abgaben und Steuern. Lexikon der Ägyptologie 1:3–12, 1117–1120.

Helm, Richard
2000 Conflicting Histories: The Archaeology of the Iron Working Farming Communities in the Central and Southern Coast of Kenya. Unpublished Ph.D. dissertation, University of Bristol, England.

Henan Sheng Wenwu Kaogu Yanjiusuo
2001 Zhengzhou Shang cheng: Yijiuwusannian—Yijiubawunian kaogu fajue baogao. 2 vols. Beijing: Wenwu Chubanshe.

Henan Sheng Wenwu Yanjiusuo
1993 Zhengzhou Shang cheng kaogu xin faxian yu yanjiu, 1985–1992. Zhengzhou: Zhongzhou Guji Chubanshe.

Henan Sheng Wenwu Yanjiusuo and Zhongguo Lishi Bowuguan Kaogubu
1992 Dengfeng Wangchenggang yu Yangcheng. Beijing: Wenwu Chubanshe.

Henan Sheng Wenwu Yanjiusuo and Zhoukou Daiqu Wenhuaju Wenwuke
1983 Henan Huaiyang Pingliangtai Longshan wenhua chengzhi shijue jianbao. Wenwu 3:21–36.

Henderson, J. (translator)
1998 Aristophanes: The Acharnanians, the Clouds, the Knights, the Wasps (Loeb Classical Library). Cambridge, MA: Harvard University Press.

Henig, Martin
1995 The Art of Roman Britain. Ann Arbor: University of Michigan Press.

Herlehy, T. J.
1984 Ties That Bind. International Journal of African Historical Studies 17:285–308.

Hester, Thomas H., Harry Shafer, and Jack D. Eaton (editors)
1994 Continuing Archeology at Colha, Belize. Austin: Texas Archeological Research Laboratory, University of Texas.

Heyden, Doris
1991 Dryness before the Rains: Toxcatl and Tezcatlipoca. In To Change Place: Aztec Ceremonial Landscapes, edited by Davíd Carrasco, pp. 188–202. Niwot: University Press of Colorado.

Hicks, Frederic
1982 Tetzcoco in the Early 16th Century: The State, the City, and the Calpolli. American Ethnologist 9:230–249.

Hingley, Richard
2005 Globalizing Roman Culture—Unity, Diversity, and Empire. London: Routledge.

Hirth, Kenneth
1989 Militarism and Social Organization at Xochicalco, Morelos. In Mesoamerica after the Collapse of Teotihuacan AD 700–900, edited by Richard A. Diehl and Janet Catherine Berlo, pp. 69–81. Washington, DC: Dumbarton Oaks Research Library and Collection.
1995 Urbanism, Militarism, and Architectural Design: An Analysis of Epiclassic Sociopolitical Structure at Xochicalco. Ancient Mesoamerica 6:223–250.
2000 Ancient Urbanism at Xochicalco: The Evolution and Organization of a Pre-Hispanic Society. Archaeological Research at Xochicalco, vol. 1. Salt Lake City: University of Utah Press.
2003 The Altepetl and Urban Structure in Prehispanic Mesoamerica. In Urbanism in Mesoamerica, edited by William T. Sanders, Alba Guadalupe Mastache, and Robert Cobean, pp. 57–84. México, D. F.: INAH; University Park: Pennsylvania State University.
2004 Comunidad y altepetl en Mesoamérica prehispánica: Una perspectiva arqueológica. Paper presented at the CIESAS conference Territorios y Estructura Socio-Política de los Indios de México: Siglos XVI al XVIII. Mérida, Mexico.

Hodder, Ian (editor)
1996 On the Surface: Çatalhöyük 1993–1995. Cambridge, UK: McDonald Institute.
2000 Towards Reflexive Method in Archaeology: The Example at Çatalhöyük. Cambridge, UK: McDonald Institute.
2006 The Leopard's Tale: Revealing the Mysteries of Catalhöyük. London: Thames and Hudson.

Hodge, A. Trevor
1992 Roman Aqueducts and Water Supply. London: Duckworth.

Hodge, Mary G.
1984 Aztec City-States. Museum of Anthropology, Memoir no. 18. Ann Arbor: University of Michigan.

Holl, Augustin F. C.
1985 Background to the Ghana Empire: Archaeological Investigations on the Transition to Statehood in the Dhar Tichitt Region (Mauritania). Journal of Anthropological Archaeology 4:73–115.
1990 West African Archaeology: Colonialism and Nationalism. *In* A History of African Archaeology, edited by Peter Robertshaw, pp. 296–308. London: James Currey Ltd.
1995 African History: Past, Present, and Future—The Unending Quest for Alternatives. *In* Making Alternative Histories: The Practice of Archaeology and History in Non-Western Settings, edited by Peter R. Schmidt and Thomas C. Patterson, pp. 183–212. Santa Fe, NM: SAR Press.
2000 The Diwan Revisited: Literacy, State Formation, and the Rise of Kanuri Domination (AD 1200–1600). New York: Kegan Paul International.
2003 The Land of Houlouf: Genesis of a Chadic Chiefdom (1900 BC–1800 AD). Ann Arbor: Museum of Anthropology, University of Michigan .

Hollingsworth, Thomas Henry
1969 Historical Demography. Ithaca, NY: Cornell University Press.

Höllmann, Thomas O.
1986 Jinan: Die Chu-Hauptstadt Ying im China der Späteren Zhou-Zeit. Materialien zur Allgemeinen und Vergleichenden Archäologie, vol. 48. München: C. H. Beck.

Holm, Poul
2000 Viking Dublin and the City-State Concept. Parameters and Significance of the Hiberno-Norse Settlement. *In* A Comparative Study of Thirty City-State Cultures, edited by Mogens H. Hansen, pp. 251–262. Copenhagen: Det Kongelige Danske Videnskabernes Selskab.

Hopkins, Keith
1983 Introduction. *In* Trade in the Ancient Economy, edited by P. Garnsey, Keith Hopkins, and R. C. Whittaker, pp. ix–xxv. London: Chatto and Windus.

Horden, Peregrine, and Nicholas Purcell
2000 The Corrupting Sea. A Study in Mediterranean History. Malden, MA: Blackwell Publishers.

Hornby, A. S. (editor)
1995 Oxford Advanced Learner's Dictionary of Current English. Oxford and New York: Oxford University Press.

Horton, Mark
1996 Shanga: The Archaeology of a Muslim Trading Community on the Coast of East Africa. British Institute in Eastern Africa. Memoir no. 14. London: British Institute in Eastern Africa.

Horton, Mark, and John Middleton
2000 The Swahili: The Social Landscape of a Mercantile Society. Oxford: Blackwell Publishers.

Hoselitz, Bert
1955 Generative and Parasitic Cities. Economic Development and Culture Change 3:279–294.

Houston, Stephen D., Héctor Escobedo, Mark Child, and René Muñoz
2003 The Moral Community: Maya Settlement Transformation at Piedras Negras, Guatemala. *In* The Social Construction of Ancient Cities, edited by Monica L. Smith, pp. 212–253. Washington and London: Smithsonian Books.

Hoyt, Homer
1939 The Structure and Growth of Residential Neighborhoods in American Cities. Washington, DC: US Federal Housing Administration, US Government Printing Office.

Hubei Sheng Bowuguan
1980 Chu du Jinancheng kaogu ziliao huibian. Wuhan: Hubei Sheng Bowuguan.

Hubei Sheng Wenwu Kaogu Yanjiusuo
2001 Panlongcheng: Yijiuliusannian—Yijiujiusinian kaogu fajue baogao. 2 vols. Beijing: Wenwu Chubanshe.

Hüber, Friedmund
1997 Zur städtebaulichen Entwicklung des hellenistisch-römischen Ephesos. Mitteilungen des Deutsches Archäologisches Institut, Istanbuler Abteilung 47:251–269.

Huffman, Thomas N.
1996   Snakes and Crocodiles: Power and Symbolism in Ancient Zimbabwe. Johannesburg: Witwatersrand University Press.

Humphrey, John H.
1986   Roman Circuses: Arenas for Chariot Racing. London and Berkeley: University of California Press.

Hunan Sheng Wenwu Kaogu Yanjiusuo
1993   Li Xian Chengtongshan Qujialing wenhua chengzhi diaocha yu shijue. Wenwu 12:19–30.
1996   Hunan Li Xian Mengxi Bashidang Xinshiqishidai zaoqi yizhi fajue jianbao. Wenwu 12:26–39.

Hunwick, John
1999   Timbuktu and the Songhay Empire. Leiden: Brill.

Hurst, Henry R.
1999a   Topography and Identity in Glevum Colonia. *In* The Coloniae of Roman Britain: New Studies and a Review. Journal of Roman Archaeology, supplementary series 36, pp. 113–135.
2000   The Fortress Coloniae of Roman Britain: Colchester, Lincoln and Gloucester. *In* Romanization and the City: Creations, Transformations and Failures, edited by Elizabeth Fentress, pp. 105–114. Journal of Roman Archaeology, supplementary series 38.

Hurst, Henry R. (editor)
1999b   The Coloniae of Roman Britain: New Studies and a Review. Journal of Roman Archaeology, supplementary series 36.

Hyslop, John
1984   The Inka Road System. Orlando, FL: Academic Press.
1990   Inka Settlement Planning. Austin: University of Texas Press.

Iannone, Gyles
2005   The Rise and Fall of an Ancient Maya Petty Royal Court. Latin American Antiquity 16(1):26–44.

Ibn, Khaldun
1967   The Muqaddimah: An Introduction to History. Princeton, NJ: Princeton University Press.

Iglesias Ponce de León, María Josefa
2003   Problematical Deposits and the Problem of Interaction: The Material Culture of Tikal during the Early Classic Period. *In* The Maya and Teotihuacan: Reinterpreting Early Classic Interaction, edited by Geoffrey E. Braswell, pp. 167–198. The Linda Schele Series in Maya and Pre-Columbian Studies. Austin: University of Texas Press.

Iijima Taketsugu
2004   An Investigation of the Western Zhou Capital at Luoyang. *In* Chinese Archaeology in the Twentieth Century, edited by Yang Xiaoneng, vol. 1, pp. 247–253. New Haven, CT: Yale University Press.

Iliffe, J.
1995   Africans: History of a Continent. Cambridge: Cambridge University Press.

Inalcik, Halil
1993   The Middle East and the Balkans under the Ottoman Empire. Bloomington: Indiana University Press.

Inomata, Takeshi
2001   The Power and Ideology of Artistic Creation. Current Anthropology 42(2):321–349.

Insoll, Timothy
1996   Islam, Archaeology, and History: Gao Region (Mali) ca. 900–1250. British Archaeological Reports 647. Oxford: Tempus Reparatum.
1999   The Archaeology of Islam. Oxford: Blackwell.
2000   Urbanism, Archaeology, and Trade: Further Observations on the Gao Region (Mali). British Archaeological Reports. Oxford: Archaeopress.
2003   The Archaeology of Islam in Africa. Cambridge: Cambridge University Press.

Institute of Archaeology of Shanxi Province
1996   Art of the Houma Foundry. Princeton, NJ: Princeton University Press.

Isbell, William H.
1991 Huari Administration and the Orthogonal Cellular Architecture Horizon. *In* Huari Administrative Structure: Prehistoric Monumental Architecture and State Government, edited by William H. Isbell and Gordon F. McEwan, pp. 293–315. Washington, DC: Dumbarton Oaks Research Library and Collection.

Ixtlilxóchitl, Fernando de Alva
1975 Obras Históricas. Vol 1. México, D. F.: Universidad Nacional Autónoma de México.

Jacobs, Jane
1969 The Economy of Cities. New York: Random House.
1985 Cities and the Wealth of Nations: Principles of Economic Life. New York: Vintage Books.

James, Simon
2003 Roman Archaeology: Crisis and Revolution. Antiquity 77:178–184.

Jameson, Michael H., Curtis N. Runnels, and Tjeerd H. van Andel
1994 A Greek Countryside: The Southern Argolid from Prehistory to the Present Day. Stanford, CA: Stanford University Press.

Janusek, John Wayne
2002 Out of Many, One: Style and Social Boundaries in Tiwanaku. Latin American Antiquity 13(1):35–61.

Jarrige, Jean-François
1991 Mehrgarh: Its Place in the Development of Ancient Cultures in Pakistan. *In* Forgotten Cities on the Indus, edited by M. Jansen, M. Mulloy, and G. Urban, pp. 34–49. Mainz am Rhein: Phillip von Zabern.
1997 From Nausharo to Pirak: Continuity and Change in the Kachi/Bolan Region from the 3rd to the 2nd Millennium BC. *In* South Asian Archaeology 1995, edited by Bridget Allchin, pp. 11–32. Bombay: Oxford University Press and IBH.

Jarrige, Jean-François, and Richard H. Meadow
1980 The Antecedents of Civilization in the Indus Valley. Scientific American 243(2):122–133.

Jefferson, Mark
1939 The Law of the Primate City. The Geographical Review 29:226–232.

Jeffreys, David, and Ana Tavares
1994 The Historic Landscape of Early Dynastic Memphis. Mitteilungen, Deutsches Archäologisches Institut, Kairo 50:143–173.

Jinnai, Hidenobu
1990 The Spatial Structure of Edo. *In* Tokugawa Japan, edited by C. Nakane and S. Oishi, pp. 124–146. Tokyo: University of Tokyo Press.

Johnson, Gregory A.
1972 A Test of the Utility of Central Place Theory. *In* Man, Settlement and Urbanism, edited by Peter J. Ucko, Ruth Tringham, and G. W. Dimbleby, pp. 769–785. London: Duckworth.
1973 Local Exchange and Early State Development in Southwestern Iran. Anthropological Papers 51. Ann Arbor: University of Michigan, Museum of Anthropology.
1982 Organizational Structure and Scalar Stress. *In* Theory and Explanation in Archaeology: The Southampton Conference, edited by Colin Renfrew, Michael Rowlands, and B. A. Segraves, pp. 389–421. New York: Academic Press.

Jones, Barri, and David Mattingly
1990 An Atlas of Roman Britain. Oxford: Blackwell.

Jones, Michael J.
1999 Lincoln and the British Fora in Context. *In* The Coloniae of Roman Britain: New Studies and a Review, edited by Henry R. Hurst, pp. 167–174. Journal of Roman Archaeology, supplementary series 36.
2002 Roman Lincoln: Conquest, Colony and Capital. Stroud: Tempus.
2003 Cities and Urban Settlements. *In* A Companion to Roman Britain, edited by Malcolm Todd, pp. 162–192. Oxford: Blackwell.

Jones, Michael J., David Stocker, and Alan Vince
2003   The City by the Pool: Assessing the Archaeology of the City of Lincoln, edited by David Stocker. Lincoln Archaeological Studies 10. Oxford: Oxbow Books.

Jones, Morris R.
1952   Map of the Ruins of Mayapan, Yucatan, Mexico. Carnegie Institution of Washington, Department of Archaeology, Current Reports no. 1. Washington, DC.

Jones, Richard F. J.
1987   Romano-British Urbanization: A False Start? World Archaeology 19(1):47–57.
1991   The Urbanization of Roman Britain. In Britain in the Roman Period: Recent Trends, edited by R. F. J. Jones, pp. 53–66. Sheffield, UK: University of Sheffield.

Joyce, Rosemary
2000   Gender and Power in Prehispanic Mesoamerica. Austin: University of Texas Press.

Julien, Catherine J.
2004   Las Tumbas de Sacsahuaman y el estilo Cuzco-Inca. Ñawpa Pacha 25–28(1987–1989):1–125. Berkeley, CA: Institute of Andean Studies.

Juma, Abdulrahman
2004   Unguja Ukuu on Zanzibar: An Archaeological Study of Early Urbanism. Uppsala: Department of Archaeology and Ancient History, University of Uppsala.

Kaiser, Werner, Peter Becker, Martin Bommas, Friedhelm Hoffmann, Horst Jaritz, Sven Müntel, Jean-Pierre Pätznick, and Martin Ziermann
1995   Stadt und Tempel von Elephantine. 21/22. Grabungsbericht. Mitteilungen des Deutschen Archäologischen Instituts, Kairo 51:99–187.

Kaluzny, Margaret A.
2004   From Islamic Ishbiliya to Christian Sevilla: Transformation and Continuity in a Multicultural City. Unpublished Ph.D. dissertation, University of Texas, Austin.

Katz, Friedrich
1966   Situación social y económica de los Aztecas durante los siglos XV y XVI. México, D. F.: Universidad Nacional Autónoma de México.

Kemp, Barry J.
1977   The Early Development of Towns in Egypt. Antiquity 51:185–200.
1983   Old Kingdom, Middle Kingdom and Second Intermediate Period ca. 2686–1552 BC. In Ancient Egypt: A Social History, edited by Bruce G. Trigger, Barry J. Kemp, David O'Connor, and A. B. Lloyd, pp. 71–182. Cambridge: Cambridge University Press.
1987   The Amarna Workmen's Village in Retrospect. Journal of Egyptian Archaeology 73:21–50.
1989   Ancient Egypt: Anatomy of a Civilization. London: Routledge.
2000   Bricks and Metaphor. In Viewpoint: Were Cities Built as Images? Cambridge Archaeological Journal 10: 335–346.
2005   100 Hieroglyphs: Think Like an Egyptian. London: Granta Books.

Kennedy, Hugh
1985   From Polis to Medina: Urban Change in Late Antique and Early Islamic Syria. Past and Present 106:3–27.

Kenoyer, Jonathan Mark
1983   Shell Working Industries of the Indus Civilization: An Archaeological and Ethnographic Perspective. Unpublished Ph.D. dissertation, University of California, Berkeley.
1989   Socio-economic Structures of the Indus Civilization as Reflected in Specialized Crafts and the Question of Ritual Segregation. In Old Problems and New Perspectives in the Archaeology of South Asia, edited by J. M. Kenoyer, pp. 183–192. Madison: Department of Anthropology, University of Wisconsin.
1991a   The Indus Valley Tradition of Pakistan and Western India. Journal of World Prehistory 5(4):331–385.
1991b   Urban Process in the Indus Tradition: A Preliminary Model from Harappa. In Harappa Excavations 1986–1990, edited by R. H. Meadow, pp. 29–60. Madison, WI: Prehistory Press.

1992   Ornament Styles of the Indus Tradition: Evidence from Recent Excavations at Harappa, Pakistan. Paléorient 17(2):79–98.

1993   Excavations on Mound E, Harappa: A Systematic Approach to the Study of Indus Urbanism. *In* South Asian Archaeology, 1991, edited by A. J. Gail and G. J. R. Mevissen, pp. 165–194. Stuttgart: F. S. Verlag.

1995   Interaction Systems, Specialized Crafts and Culture Change: The Indus Valley Tradition and the Indo-Gangetic Tradition in South Asia. *In* The Indo-Aryans of Ancient South Asia: Language, Material Culture and Ethnicity, edited by G. Erdosy, pp. 213–257. Berlin: W. DeGruyter.

1997a   Early City-States in South Asia: Comparing the Harappan Phase and the Early Historic Period. *In* The Archaeology of City-States: Cross Cultural Approaches, edited by D. L. Nichols and T. H. Charlton, pp. 51–70. Washington, DC: Smithsonian Institution Press.

1997b   Trade and Technology of the Indus Valley: New Insights from Harappa, Pakistan. World Archaeology 29(2):262–280.

1998   Ancient Cities of the Indus Valley Civilization. Karachi: Oxford University Press.

2000   Wealth and Socio-economic Hierarchies of the Indus Valley Civilization. *In* Order, Legitimacy and Wealth in Early States, edited by J. Richards and M. Van Buren, pp. 90–112. Cambridge: Cambridge University Press.

2003   Uncovering the Keys to the Lost Indus Cities. Scientific American 289, July(1): 67–75.

2004   Die Karren der Induskultur Pakistans und Indiens (Wheeled Vehicles of the Indus Valley Civilization of Pakistan and India). *In* Rad und Wagen: Der Ursprung einer Innovation Wagen im Vorderen Orient und Europa (Wheel and Wagon—Origins of an Innovation), edited by M. Fansa and S. Burmeister, pp. 87–106. Mainz am Rhein: Verlag Philipp von Zabern.

2005   Culture Change during the Late Harappan Period at Harappa: New Insights on Vedic Aryan Issues. *In* Indo-Aryan Controversy: Evidence and Inference in Indian History, edited by L. L. Patton and E. F. Bryant, pp. 21–49. London: Routledge Curzon.

Kenoyer, Jonathan Mark, and Richard H. Meadow

2000   The Ravi Phase: A New Cultural Manifestation at Harappa. *In* South Asian Archaeology 1997, edited by M. Taddei and G. De Marco, pp. 55–76. Rome, Istituto Italiano per l'Africa e l'Oriente; Naples: Istituto Universitario Orientale.

Kenoyer, Jonathan Mark, and Heather M.-L. Miller

2007   Multiple Crafts and Socio-economic Associations in the Indus Civilization: New Perspectives from Harappa, Pakistan. *In* Craft Production in Complex Societies: Multicraft and Producer Perspectives, edited by I. Shimada, pp. 152–183. Salt Lake City: University of Utah Press.

Kepecs, Susan

1999   The Political Economy of Chikinchel, Yucatan: A Diachronic Analysis from the Prehispanic Era to the Age of Spanish Administration. Unpublished Ph.D. dissertation, University of Wisconsin.

King, Anthony C.

1990   Roman Gaul and Germany. London: British Museum Press.

2001   The Romanization of Diet in the Western Empire. *In* Italy and the West: Comparative Issues in Romanization, edited by Simon Keay and Nicola Terrenato, pp. 210–223. Oxford: Oxbow Books.

Kiriama, H. O., H. Mutoro, and L. Ngari

1996   Ironworking in the Upper Tana Valley. *In* Aspects of African Archaeology: Papers from the 10th Congress of the PanAfrican Association for Prehistory and Related Studies, edited by Gilbert Pwiti and Robert Soper, pp. 505–508. Harare: University of Zimbabwe Publications.

Kirkbride, Diana

1966   Five Seasons at the Pre-pottery Neolithic Village of Beidha in Jordan. Palestine Exploration Quarterly 98(1).

Kirkman, James S.

1964   Men and Monuments on the East African Coast. London: Lutterworth Press.

Kleiss, Wolfram (editor)

1988   Bastam II: Ausgrabungen in den urartäischen Anlagen 1977–1978. Teheraner Forschungen 5. Berlin: Gebr. Mann.

Knappett, Carl
1999   Assessing a Polity in Protopalatial Crete. American Journal of Archaeology 103:615–639.
Knibbe, Dieter
1995   Via Sacra Ephesiaca: New Aspects of the Cult of Artemis Ephesia. *In* Ephesos, Metropolis of Asia: An Interdisciplinary Approach to Its Archaeology, Religion and Culture, edited by Helmut Koester, pp. 141–155. Cambridge, MA: Harvard University Press.
Knight, Jeremy K.
1999   The End of Antiquity: Archaeology, Society and Religion AD 235–700. Stroud, UK and Charleston, SC: Tempus.
Knirk, James E.
1993   Runes and Runic Inscriptions. *In* Medieval Scandinavia. An Encyclopedia. Garland Encyclopedias of the Middle Ages 1, pp. 545–552. New York: Garland.
Kolata, Alan L.
1993   The Tiwanaku: Portrait of an Andean Civilization. Cambridge, MA: Blackwell.
Kolb, F.
1984   Die Stadt im Altertum. München: Beck.
Kostof, Spiro
1985   A History of Architecture. Oxford: Oxford University Press.
1991   The City Shaped: Urban Patterns and Meanings through History. Boston: A Bulfinch Press Book of Little, Brown and Company.
1992   The City Assembled: The Elements of Urban Form through History. Boston: A Bulfinch Press Book of Little, Brown and Company.
Kowalewski, Stephen, Gary Feinman, Laura Finsten, Richard Blanton, and Linda Nicholas
1989   Monte Albán's Hinterland, pt. II: Prehispanic Settlement Patterns in Tlacolula, Etla, and Ocotlan, the Valley of Oaxaca, Mexico. Museum of Anthropology, Memoir 23. Ann Arbor: University of Michigan.
Kraeling, Carl H., and Robert McCormick Adams (editors)
1960   City Invincible: A Symposium on Urbanization and Cultural Development in the Ancient Near East. Chicago: University of Chicago Press.
Krapf-Askari, Eva
1969   Yoruba Towns and Cities: An Inquiry into the Nature of Urban Phenomena. Oxford: Clarendon Press.
Krautheimer, Richard
1969   Studies in Christian, Medieval and Renaissance Art. New York: University of London Press.
1983   Rome: Profile of a City, 312–1308. 2nd ed. Princeton, NJ: Princeton University Press.
Kuhrt, Amélie
1995   The Ancient Near East. Vols. 1–2. London: Routledge.
Kusimba, Chapurukha M.
1999a   The Rise and Fall of Swahili States. Walnut Creek, CA: AltaMira Press.
1999b   The Rise of Elites among the Precolonial Swahili of the East African Coast. *In* Material Symbols in Prehistory, edited by John Robb, pp. 318–341. Carbondale: Southern Illinois University Press.
2004   Archaeology of Slavery in East Africa. African Archaeological Review 21:59–88.
Kusimba, Chapurukha M., and Sibel B. Kusimba
2001   Hinterlands of Swahili Cities: Archaeological Investigations of Economy and Trade in Tsavo, Kenya. *In* Africa 2000: Forty Years of African Studies in Prague, edited by L. Kropacek and P. Skalník, pp. 203–232. Prague: Roman Misek Publishers.
2005   Mosaics and Interactions: East Africa, 2000 BP to the present. *In* African Archaeology, edited by Ann B. Stahl, pp. 392–419. Oxford: Blackwell.
Kusimba, Chapurukha M., Sibel B. Kusimba, and David K. Wright
2005   The Development and Collapse of Precolonial Ethnic Mosaics in Tsavo, Kenya. Journal of African Archaeology 3(1):243–265.

Kusimba, Sibel B.
2003   African Foragers: Environment, Technology, Interactions. Walnut Creek, CA: AltaMira Press.

Lakoff, George
1987   Women, Fire, and Dangerous Things: What Categories Reveal about the Mind. Chicago: University of Chicago Press.

Lakoff, George, and Mark Johnson
1980   Metaphors We Live By. Chicago: University of Chicago Press.

Lal, Braj Basi
1975   The Indus Script: Some Observations Based on Archaeology. Journal of the Royal Asiatic Society:173–177.
1997   The Earliest Civilization of South Asia (Rise, Maturity and Decline). Delhi: Aryan Books International.

Lamberg-Karlovsky, Clifford Charles
2001   Comment on *The Bronze Age: Unique Instance of a Pre-industrial World System?* by Shereen Ratnagar. Current Anthropology 42(3):368–369.

Lancaster, Osbert
1949   Drayneflete Revealed. London: Murray.

Lapidus, Ira
1984   Muslim Cities in the Later Middle Ages. Cambridge: Cambridge University Press.
[1967]

Larsen, Mogens Trolle
1976   The Old Assyrian City-State and Its Colonies. Copenhagen: Akademisk Forlag.
2000   The Old Assyrian City-State. *In* A Comparative Study of Thirty City-State Cultures, edited by Mogens H. Hansen, pp. 77–87. Copenhagen: Det Kongelige Danske Videnskabernes Selskab.

Laur, Jean
2002   Angkor: An Illustrated Guide to the Monuments. Translated from the French by Diana Pollin. Paris: Flammarion.

Laurence, Ray
1994   Roman Pompeii: Space and Society. London: Routledge.

LaViolette, Adria, and Jeffrey B. Fleisher
2005   The Archaeology of Sub-Saharan Urbanism: Cities and Their Countryside. *In* African Archaeology, edited by Ann B. Stahl, pp. 327–352. Oxford: Blackwell.

Law, Randall W.
2005   Regional Interaction in the Prehistoric Indus Valley: Initial Results of Rock and Mineral Sourcing Studies at Harappa. *In* South Asian Archaeology 2001, edited by Catherine Jarrige and V. Lefèvre, pp. 179–190. Paris: Editions Recherche sur les Civilisations—ADPF.

Law, Randall W., and S. R. H. Baqri
2003   Black Chert Source Identified at Nammal Gorge, Salt Range. Ancient Pakistan 14:34–37.

Law, Randall W., and J. H. Burton
2006a   Non-destructive* Pb Isotope Analysis of Harappan Galena Fragments Using Ethylenediaminetetraacetic Acid and ICP-MS. (*Practically). *In* Proceedings of the 34th International Symposium on Archaeometry, Zaragoza, 3–7 May 2004 , edited by J. Pérez-Arantegui, pp. 181–185. Zaragoza: Institución Fernando el Católico.
2006b   A Technique for Determining the Provenance of Harappan Banded Limestone "Ringstones" Using ICP-AES. *In* Proceedings of the 34th International Symposium on Archaeometry, Zaragoza, 3–7 May 2004, edited by J. Pérez-Arantegui, pp. 309–314. Zaragoza: Institución Fernando el Católico.

Leeds, Anthony
1980   Towns and Villages in Society: Hierarchies of Order and Cause. *In* Cities in a Larger Context. Proceedings of the Southern Anthropological Society 14, edited by Thomas W. Collins, pp. 6–33. Athens, Georgia: University of Georgia Press.

Lehner, Mark
2000   The Fractal House of Pharaoh: Ancient Egypt as a Complex Adaptive System, a Trial Formulation. *In* Dynamics in Human and Primate Societies, edited by Timothy A. Kohler and George J. Gumerman, pp. 275–354. New York: Oxford University Press.
2002a   The Pyramid Age Settlement of the Southern Mount at Giza. Journal of the American Research Center in Egypt 39:27–74.
2002b   The Workings of a Great Pyramid City. Aeragram 6(1):8–9.
2003   Non-excavation Season 2003 Dig: On the Trail of the Lost City. Aeragram 6(2):6.
2004   Season 2004: A New Neighborhood. Aeragram: Newsletter of the Ancient Egypt Research Associates 7(2).
2006   Three Roads Diverged. Aeragram 8(1):14–15.

León-Portilla, Miguel
1963   Aztec Thought and Culture: A Study of the Ancient Nahuatl Mind. Norman: University of Oklahoma Press.

Levitzion, N.
1988   Islam and State Formation in West Africa. *In* The Early State in African Perspective, edited by Shmuel N. Eisenstadt, M. Abitbol, and N. Chazan, pp. 98–108. Leiden: E. J. Brill.

Levy, Robert I.
1990   Mesocosm: Hinduism and the Organization of a Traditional Newar City in Nepal. Berkeley, Los Angeles, and Oxford: University of California Press.

Licate, Jack A.
1981   Creation of a Mexican Landscape: Territorial Organization and Settlement in the Eastern Puebla Basin, 1520–1605. Chicago: University of Chicago Press.

Li Chi [Li Ji]
1977   Anyang. Seattle: University of Washington Press.

Licordari, Antonio
1984   In margine ai Fasti Ostienses. Archeologia Classica 36:347–352.

Li Ji, Liang Siyong, and Dong Zuobin (editors)
1934   Chengziyai. Zhongguo kaogu baogaoji, vol. 1. Nanjing: Zhongyang Yanjiuyuan.

Lindholm, Charles
1996   The Islamic Middle East: An Historical Anthropology. Cambridge, MA: Blackwell.

Liu Li
1994   Development of Chiefdom Societies in the Middle and Lower Yellow River Valley in Neolithic China: A Study of the Longshan Culture from the Perspective of Settlement Patterns. Unpublished Ph.D. dissertation, Harvard University, Cambridge, MA.
2000   Ancestor Worship: An Archaeological Investigation of Ritual Activities in Neolithic North China. Journal of East Asian Archaeology 2(1–2):129–164.
2004   The Chinese Neolithic: Trajectories to Early States. Cambridge: Cambridge University Press.

Liu Li and Xingcan Chen
2003   State Formation in Early China. London: Duckworth.
2006   Sociopolitical Change from Neolithic to Bronze Age China. *In* Archaeology of Asia, edited by Miriam T. Stark, pp. 149–176. Oxford: Blackwell.

Liu Li, Xingcan Chen, Yun Kuen Lee, Henry Wright, and Arlene Rosen
2002–2004   Settlement Patterns and Development of Social Complexity in the Yiluo Region, North China. Journal of Field Archaeology 20(1/2):75–100.

Liverman, Diana
1999   Vulnerability and Adaptation to Drought in Mexico. Natural Resources Journal 39:99–115.

Lloyd, P. C.
1974   Power and Independence: Urban Africans' Perception of Social Inequality. London: Routledge and Kegan Paul.

Lockhart, James
1992   The Nahuas after the Conquest. Palo Alto, CA: Stanford University Press.

Lohse, Jon C., and Fred Valdez Jr. (editors)
2004 Ancient Maya Commoners. Austin: University of Texas Press.

Loten, Stanley
2003 The North Acropolis: Monumentality, Function, and Architectural Development. *In* Tikal: Dynasties, Foreigners, and Affairs of State: Advancing Maya Archaeology, edited by Jeremy A. Sabloff, pp. 227–252. Santa Fe, NM: SAR Press.

Lothrop, Samuel K.
1924 Tulum: An Archaeological Study of the East Coast of Yucatan. Carnegie Institution of Washington Publication 335. Washington, DC: Carnegie Institution of Washington.

Low, Bobbi S.
2000 Why Sex Matters: A Darwinian Look at Human Behavior. Princeton, NJ: Princeton University Press.

Lumbreras, Luis Guillermo
2001 Uhle y los asentamientos de Chincha en el siglo XVI. Revista del Museo Nacional (Lima) 49:13–87.

Luo Xunzhang
1998 Wulian Xian Dantucun xinshiqishidai yizhi. Zhongguo kaoguxue nianjian 1996, pp. 156–157. Beijing: Wenwu Chubanshe.

Lynch, Kevin
1981 A Theory of Good City Form. Cambridge, MA: MIT Press.

Mabogunje, Akin L.
1962 Yoruba Towns. Ibadan: Ibadan University Press.

Mackay, Ernest J. H.
1938 Further Excavations at Mohenjodaro. Delhi: Government of India.

MacMahon, Ardle
2006 Fixed-Point Retail Location in the Major Towns of Roman Britain. Oxford Journal of Archaeology 25(3):289–309.

Maisels, Charles Keith
1990 The Emergence of Civilisation: From Hunting and Gathering to Agriculture, Cities, and the State in the Near East. London: Routledge.

Malville, John McKim
2000 Introduction. *In* Ancient Cities, Sacred Skies: Cosmic Geometries and City Planning in Ancient India, edited by John McKim Malville and Lalit M. Gujral, pp. 1–10. Delhi: Aryan Books International.

Malville, John McKim, and Lalit M. Gujral (editors)
2000 Ancient Cities, Sacred Skies: Cosmic Geometries and City Planning in Ancient India. Delhi: Aryan Books International.

Mann, Peter H.
1965 An Approach to Urban Sociology. London: Routledge and Kegan Paul.

Manners, Ian R.
1997 Constructing the Image of a City: The Representation of Constantinople in Christopher Buondelmonti's *Liber Insularum Archipelagi*. Annals, Association of American Geographers 87:761–773.

Manzanilla, Linda
1993 Anatomía de un conjunto residencial teotihuacana en Oztoyahualco. México: Instituto de Investigaciones Antropológicas, Universidad Nacional de México.
1996 Corporate Groups and Domestic Activities at Teotihuacan. Latin American Antiquity 7(3):228–246.

Mar, Riccardo
1991 La formazione dello spazio urbano nella citta di Ostia. Mitteilungen des Deutsches Archäologisches Instituts, Römische Abteilung 98:81–109.

2002   Una ciudad modelada por el comercio: La construcción del centro de Ostia. Melanges de l'École Française de Rome, Antiquité 114:111–180.

Mar, Riccardo, Josep M. Nolla, Joaquin Ruiz de Arbulo, and David Vivó
1999   Santuarios y urbanismo en Ostia. La excavación en el campo de Cibeles. Mededelingen van het Nederlands Instituut te Rome, Antiquity 58:20–21.

Marcus, Joyce
1973   Territorial Organization of the Lowland Classic Maya. Science 180:911–916.
1974   Iconography of Power among the Classic Maya. World Archaeology 6(1):83–94.
1976   Emblem and State in the Classic Maya Lowlands: An Epigraphic Approach to Territorial Organization. Washington, DC: Dumbarton Oaks.
1983a   Maya Archaeology at the Crossroads. American Antiquity 48:454–488.
1983b   On the Nature of the Mesoamerican City. In Prehistoric Settlement Patterns: Essays in Honor of Gordon R. Willey, edited by Evon Z. Vogt and Richard M. Leventhal, pp. 195–242. Albuquerque, NM: University of New Mexico Press; Cambridge, MA: Peabody Museum, Harvard University.
1983c   Summary and Conclusions. In The Cloud People, edited by Kent V. Flannery and Joyce Marcus, pp. 355–360. New York: Academic Press.
1984   Mesoamerican Territorial Boundaries: Reconstructions from Archaeology and Hieroglyphic Writing. Archaeological Review from Cambridge 3(2):48–62.
1989   From Centralized Systems to City-States: Possible Models for the Epiclassic. In Mesoamerica after the Decline of Teotihuacan: AD 700–900, edited by Richard A. Diehl and Janet Catherine Berlo, pp. 201–208. Washington, DC: Dumbarton Oaks.
1992a   Dynamic Cycles of Mesoamerican States. National Geographic Research and Exploration 8(4):392–411.
1992b   Mesoamerican Writing Systems: Propaganda, Myth, and History among Four Ancient Civilizations. Princeton, NJ: Princeton University Press.
1993   Ancient Maya Political Organization. In Lowland Maya Civilization in the Eighth Century AD, edited by Jeremy A. Sabloff and John S. Henderson, pp. 111–183. Washington, DC: Dumbarton Oaks.
1995a   Where Is Lowland Maya Archaeology Headed? Journal of Archaeological Research 3(1):3–53.
1995b   Maya Hieroglyphs: History or Propaganda? In Research Frontiers in Anthropology, edited by Carol Ember and Mel Ember, pp. 1–24. Englewood Cliffs, NJ: Prentice-Hall.
1998   The Peaks and Valleys of Ancient States: An Extension of the Dynamic Model. In Archaic States, edited by Gary M. Feinman and Joyce Marcus, pp. 59–94. School of American Research. Santa Fe, NM: SAR Press.
2000 [1983b]   On the Nature of the Mesoamerican City. In The Ancient Civilizations of Mesoamerica, edited by Michael E. Smith and Marilyn A. Masson, pp. 49–82. Malden, MA: Blackwell.
2003a   Recent Advances in Maya Archaeology. Journal of Archaeological Research 11(2):71–148.
2003b   Monumentality in Archaic States: Lessons Learned from Large-Scale Excavations of the Past. In Archaeology in the Mediterranean: Old World and New World Perspectives, edited by John K. Papadopoulos and Richard M. Leventhal, pp. 115–134. Advanced Seminar Series. Los Angeles: Cotsen Institute of Archaeology, University of California.
2006   Identifying Elites and Their Strategies. In Intermediate Elites in Pre-Columbian States and Empires, edited by Christina M. Elson and R. Alan Covey, pp. 212–246. Tucson: University of Arizona Press.

Marcus, Joyce, and Gary M. Feinman
1998   Introduction. In Archaic States, edited by Gary M. Feinman and Joyce Marcus, pp. 3–13. Santa Fe, NM: SAR Press.

Margueron, Jean
1982   Recherches sur les palais Mésopotamiens de l'age de bronze. Paris: Librarie Paul Guethner.

Marshall, John Hubert
1931   Mohenjo-daro and the Indus Civilization. London: A. Probsthain.

Martin, Archer
1996 Un saggio sulle mura del castrum di Ostia (Reg. I, ins: X, 3). *In* "Roman Ostia" Revisited. Archaeological and Historical Papers in Memory of Russell Meiggs, edited by Anna Gallina Zevi and Amanda Claridge, pp. 19–38. London: British School at Rome.

Martínez, Hildeberto
1984 Tepeaca en el siglo XVI. Tendencia de la tierra y organización de un señorío. Ediciones de la Casa Chata no. 21. México: SEP.

Martin-Pardey, Eva
1976 Untersuchungen zur ägyptischen Provinzialverwaltung bis zum Ende des Alten Reiches. Hildesheimer ägyptologische Beiträge 1. Hildesheim.

Martirosjan, A. A.
1961 Gorod Tejšebaini. Erevan: Akademija Nauk Armjanskoj SSR.
1974 Argištichinili, Archeologi eskie Pamjatniki Armenii 8. Erevan: Akademija Nauk Armjanskoj SSR.

Masson, Marilyn A.
2002a Introduction. *In* Ancient Maya Political Economies, edited by Marilyn A. Masson and David A. Freidel, pp. 1–30. Boston: Rowman and Littlefield.
2002b Community Economy and the Mercantile Transformation in Postclassic Northeastern Belize. *In* Ancient Maya Political Economies, edited by Marilyn A. Masson and David A. Freidel, pp. 335–364. Boston: Rowman and Littlefield.

Masson, Marilyn A., and David A. Freidel (editors)
2002 Ancient Maya Political Economies. Boston: Rowman and Littlefield.

Masson, Marilyn A., Timothy S. Hare, and Carlos Peraza Lope
2006 Postclassic Maya Society Regenerated at Mayapan. *In* After the Collapse: The Regeneration of Complex Societies, edited by Glenn M. Schwartz and John J. Nichols, pp. 188–207. Tucson: University of Arizona Press.

Mastache, Alba Guadalupe, Robert Cobean, and Daniel Healan
2002 Ancient Tollan: Tula and the Toltec Heartland. Boulder: University of Colorado Press.

Mattingly, David
1994 Tripolitania. London: Batsford.
1997 Beyond Belief? Drawing a Line beneath the Consumer City. *In* Roman Urbanism: Beyond The Consumer City, edited by Helen M. Parkins, pp. 210–218. London: Routledge.
2004 Being Roman: Expressing Identity in a Provincial Setting. Journal of Roman Archaeology 17:5–25.
2006 An Imperial Possession: Britain in the Roman Empire. London: Allen Lane, Penguin Press.

Mauny, Raymond
1961 Tableau geographique de l'Ouest Africain au moyen Age d'apres les sources ecrites, la tradition et l'archeologie. Dakar: Memoire de l'IFAN.

McAnany, Patricia A.
1993 The Economics of Social Power and Wealth among Eighth-Century Maya Households. *In* Lowland Maya Civilization in the Eighth Century AD, edited by Jeremy A. Sabloff and John S. Henderson, pp. 65–89. Washington, DC: Dumbarton Oaks Research Library and Collection.
1995 Living with the Ancestors. Austin: University of Texas Press.

McAnany, Patricia A., Ben S. Thomas, Steven Morandi, Polly A. Peterson, and Eleanor Harrison
2002 Praise the Ajaw and Pass the Kakaw: Xibun Maya and the Political Economy of Cacao. *In* Ancient Maya Political Economies, edited by Marilyn A. Masson and David A. Freidel, pp. 123–139. Boston: Rowman and Littlefield.

McCracken, G.
1988 Culture and Consumption: New Approaches to the Symbolic Character of Consumer Goods and Activities. Bloomington: Indiana University Press.

McDowell, A. G.
1992 Agricultural Activity by the Workmen of Deir el-Medina. Journal of Egyptian Archaeology 78:195–206.

2001 Village Life in Ancient Egypt: Laundry Lists and Love Songs. Oxford: Oxford University Press.

McEwan, Gordon F.
2005 Pikillacta: The Wari Empire in Cuzco. Iowa City: University of Iowa Press.

McIntosh, Roderick J.
1993 Cities without Citadels: Understanding Urban Origins along the Middle Niger. *In* The Archaeology of Africa: Food, Metals and Towns, edited by Thurston Shaw, Paul Sinclair, Bassey Andah, and Alex Okpopo, pp. 622–641. London: Routledge.
1998 The Peoples of the Middle Niger. Oxford: Blackwell.
2005 Ancient Middle Niger: Urbanism and the Self-Organizing Landscape. Cambridge: Cambridge University Press.

McIntosh, Roderick J., and Susan Keech McIntosh
2003 Early Urban Configurations on the Middle Niger: Clustered Cities and Landscapes of Power. *In* The Social Construction of Ancient Cities, edited by Monica L. Smith, pp. 103–120. Washington, DC: Smithsonian Books.

McIntosh, Roderick J., Joseph A. Tainter, and Susan Keech McIntosh (editors)
2000 The Way the Wind Blows: Climate, History, and Human Action. New York: Columbia University Press.

McIntosh, Susan K.
1997 Urbanism in Sub-Saharan Africa. *In* Encyclopedia of Sub-Saharan Africa, edited by J. O. Vogel, pp. 461–465. Walnut Creek, CA: AltaMira Press.

McIntosh, Susan K. (editor)
1995 Excavations at Jenne-jeno, Hambarketolo, and Kaniana (Inland Niger Delta Mali), the 1981 Season. Berkeley: University of California Press.

McIntosh, Susan K., and Roderick J. McIntosh
1984 The Early City in West Africa: Toward an Understanding. The African Archaeological Review 2:73–98.
1993 Cities without Citadels: Understanding Urban Origins along the Middle Niger. *In* The Archaeology of Africa, edited by Thurstan Shaw et al., pp. 622–641. London: Routledge.

McKillop, Heather
2002 Salt: White Gold of the Ancient Maya. Gainesville: University Press of Florida.
2005 In Search of Maya Sea Traders. College Station: Texas A & M University Press.

Meadow, Richard H.
1991 Faunal Remains and Urbanism at Harappa. *In* Harappa Excavations 1986–1990: A Multidisciplinary Approach to Third Millennium Urbanism, edited by R. H. Meadow, pp. 89–106. Madison, WI: Prehistory Press.
2002 The Chronological and Cultural Significance of a Steatite Wig from Harappa. Iranica Antiqua 37:189–200.

Meadow, Richard H., and Jonathan Mark Kenoyer
1997 Excavations at Harappa 1994–1995: New Perspectives on the Indus Script, Craft Activities and City Organization. *In* South Asian Archaeology 1995, edited by Bridget Allchin and Raymond Allchin, pp. 139–172. Delhi: Oxford University and IBH.
2001 Recent Discoveries and Highlights from Excavations at Harappa, 1998–2000. INDO-KOKO-KENKYU Indian Archaeological Studies 22:19–36.
2005 Excavations at Harappa 2000–2001: New Insights on Chronology and City Organization. *In* South Asian Archaeology 2001, edited by Catherine Jarrige and V. Lefèvre, pp. 207–225. Paris: Editions Recherche sur les Civilisations—ADPF.
2007 The Early Indus Script at Harappa: Origins and Development. *In* Intercultural Relations between South and Southwest Asia. Studies in Commemoration of E. C. L. During-Caspers (1934–1996), edited by E. Olijdam and R. H. Spoor. London: BAR International.

Meadow, Richard H., Jonathan Mark Kenoyer, and Rita P. Wright
1999 Harappa Archaeological Research Project: Harappa Excavations 1999. Report submitted to the Director General of Archaeology and Museums, Government of Pakistan, Karachi.

2001a   Harappa Archaeological Research Project: Harappa Excavations 2000–2001. Report submitted to the Director General of Archaeology and Museums, Government of Pakistan, Karachi.

2001b   Harappa Archaeological Research Project: Harappa Excavations 2001–2002. Report submitted to the Director General of Archaeology and Museums, Government of Pakistan, Karachi.

Meeks, Dimitri, and Christine Favard-Meeks

1996   Daily Life of the Egyptian Gods. Ithaca, NY: Cornell University Press.

Meier, Kristen

2003   The Ballcourt at Chau Hiix: Architectural Insight into Changing Patterns of Political Dominance. Unpublished MA thesis, Indiana University, Bloomington.

Meiggs, Russell

1973   Roman Ostia. 2nd ed. Oxford: Oxford University Press.

Mellaart, James

1967   Çatal Hüyük, a Neolithic Town in Anatolia. London: Thames and Hudson.

Menzel, Dorothy

1959   The Inca Occupation of the South Coast of Peru. Southwestern Journal of Anthropology 15(2):125–142.

1966   The Pottery of Chincha. Ñawpa Pacha 4:77–144.

Meskell, Lynn

2002   Private Life in New Kingdom Egypt. Princeton, NJ: Princeton University Press.

Metcalfe, Jessica

2005   Diet and Migration at Chau Hiix: A Study of Stable Carbon, Nitrogen, and Oxygen Isotopes. Unpublished MA thesis, University of Western Ontario, London, Canada.

Meyer, Jeffrey F.

2001   Myths in Stone: Religious Dimensions of Washington, DC. Berkeley: University of California Press.

Middleton, John

1992   The World of the Swahili: An African Mercantile Civilization. New Haven, CT: Yale University Press.

2004   African Merchants of the Indian Ocean: Swahili of the East African Coast. Long Grove, IL: Waveland Press.

Miles, Susanna W.

1957   The Sixteenth-Century Pokom Maya: A Documentary Analysis of Social Structure and Archaeological Setting. Transactions of the American Philosophical Society 47(4):731–781. Philadelphia.

Miller, George R.

2004   An Investigation of Cuzco-Inca Ceramics: Canons of Form, Proportions and Size. Ñawpa Pacha 25–28(1987–1989):127–149. Berkeley, CA: Institute of Andean Studies.

Miller, Heather M.-L.

1999   Pyrotechnology and Society in the Cities of the Indus Valley. Unpublished Ph.D. dissertation, University of Wisconsin, Madison. University Microfilms, Ann Arbor.

Miller, Laura J.

2003   Secondary Products and Urbanism in South Asia: The Evidence for Traction at Harappa. *In* Ethnobiology and the Indus Civilization, edited by S. Weber and W. R. Belcher, pp. 251–326. Lanham, MD: Lexington Books.

2004   Urban Economies in Early States: The Secondary Products Revolution in the Indus Civilization. Unpublished Ph.D dissertation, New York University.

Millett, Martin

1990   The Romanization of Britain: An Essay in Archaeological Interpretation. Cambridge: Cambridge University Press.

2001   Approaches to Urban Societies. *In* Britons and Romans: Advancing An Archaeological Agenda, edited by S. James and M. Millett, pp. 60–66. Council for British Archaeology Research Report 125. York.

Millon, René
1973 Urbanization at Teotihuacan, Mexico. The Teotihuacan Map, vol. 1, pt. 1. Austin: University of Texas Press.
1981 Teotihuacan: City, State, and Civilization. *In* Supplement to the Handbook of Middle American Indians, vol. 1: Archaeology, edited by Jeremy A. Sabloff, pp. 198–243. Austin: University of Texas Press.
1992 Teotihuacan Studies from 1950 to 1990 and Beyond. *In* Art, Ideology, and the City of Teotihuacan, edited by Janet C. Berlo, pp. 339–429. Washington, DC: Dumbarton Oaks.

Milne, Gustav
1995 Roman London. London: Batsford.

Miner, Horace
1952 The Folk-Urban Continuum. American Sociological Review 17:529–537.
1967 The City and Modernisation: An Introduction. *In* The City in Modern Africa, edited by Horace Miner, pp. 1–20. London: Pall Mall Press.

Mitchell, Peter
2005 African Connections: Archaeological Perspectives on Africa and the Wider World. Walnut Creek, CA: AltaMira Press.

Mithen, Steven J.
1996 The Prehistory of the Mind: A Search for the Origins of Art, Religion and Science. London: Thames and Hudson.

Mols, R.
1955 Introduction a la démographie historique des villes d'Europe de XIVe au XVIIIe siècle 2. Louvain: Gembloux, J. Duculot.

Monzón Estrada, Arturo
1949 El calpulli en la organización social de los Tenochca. Publication of the Instituto de Historia, no. 14. México: Universidad Nacional Autónoma de México.

Morris, Craig
1972 State Settlements in Tawantinsuyu: A Strategy of Compulsory Urbanism. *In* Contemporary Archaeology: A Guide to Theory and Contributions, edited by Mark P. Leone, pp. 393–401. Carbondale: Southern Illinois University Press.
1974 Reconstructing Patterns of Non-agricultural Production in the Inca Economy. Archaeology and Documents in Institutional Analysis. *In* Reconstructing Complex Societies: An Archaeological Colloquium, edited by Charlotte B. Moore, pp. 49–68. Supplement to the Bulletin of the American Schools of Oriental Research, no. 20. Cambridge.
1981 Tecnología y organización inca del almacenamiento de víveres en la sierra. *In* La Tecnología en el Mundo Andino: Runakunap Kawsayninkupaq Rurasqanqunaqa, edited by Heather Lechtman and Ana María Soldi, pp. 327–375. México: Universidad Nacional Autónoma de México.
1982 The Infrastructure of Inka Control in the Peruvian Central Highlands. *In* The Inca and Aztec States, 1400–1800: Anthropology and History, edited by George A. Collier, Renato I. Rosaldo, and John D. Wirth, pp. 153–171. New York: Academic Press.
1986 Storage, Supply, and Redistribution in the Economy of the Inka State. *In* Anthropological History of Andean Polities, edited by John V. Murra, Nathan Wachtel, and Jacques Revel, pp. 59–68. New York: Cambridge University Press.
1987 Arquitectura y estructura del espacio en Huánuco Pampa. Cuadernos Instituto Nacional de Antropología 12:27–45.
2004 Enclosures of Power: The Multiple Spaces of Inka Administrative Palaces. *In* Ancient Palaces of the New World: Form, Function, and Meaning, edited by Susan Toby Evans and Joanne Pillsbury, pp. 299–323. Washington, DC: Dumbarton Oaks.

Morris, Craig, and R. Alan Covey
2005 La Plaza central de Huánuco Pampa: Espacio y transformación. *In* Identidad y transformación en el Tawantinsuyu y en los Andes coloniales. Perspectivas arqueológicas y etnohistóricas. Segunda parte, Boletín de Arqueología PUCP (2003), edited by Peter Kaulicke, Gary Urton, and Ian Farrington. Lima: Fondo Editorial de la Pontificia Universidad Católica del Perú.

2006   The Management of Scale or the Creation of Scale: Administrative Processes in Two Inka Provinces. *In* Intermediate Elites in Pre-Columbian States and Empires, edited by Christina M. Elson and R. Alan Covey, pp. 136–153. Tucson: University of Arizona Press.

Morris, Craig, and Donald E. Thompson
1985   Huánuco Pampa: An Inca City and Its Hinterland. London: Thames and Hudson.

Moseley, Michael E., and Kent C. Day (editors)
1982   Chan Chan: Andean Desert City. Albuquerque: University of New Mexico Press.

Moseley, Michael E., Donna J. Nash, Patrick Ryan Williams, Susan D. deFrance, Ana Miranda, and Mario Ruales
2005   Burning Down the Brewery: Establishing and Evacuating an Ancient Imperial Colony at Cerro Baúl, Perú. Proceedings of the National Academy of Sciences 102(48):17264–17271.

Mote, Frederick W.
1977   The Transformation of Nanking, 1350–1400. *In* The City in Late Imperial China, edited by G. William Skinner, pp. 101–153. Palo Alto, CA: Stanford University Press.

Msemwa, Paul
2001   Archaeology of Upper Rufiji Catchment. *In* People, Contacts, and the Environment in the African Past, edited by F. Chami, G. Pwiti, and C. Radimilahy, pp. 40–52. Dar es Salaam: Dar es Salaam University Press.

Mughal, Mohammad Rafique
1970   The Early Harappan Period in the Greater Indus Valley and Northern Baluchistan. Unpublished Ph.D. dissertation, University of Pennsylvania, Philadelphia.
1980   New Archaeological Evidence from Bahawalpur. Man and Environment 4:93–98.
1990a The Decline of the Indus Civilization and the Late Harappan Period in the Indus Valley. Lahore Museum Bulletin 3(2):1–17.
1990b Further Evidence of the Early Harappan Culture in the Greater Indus Valley: 1971–1990. South Asian Studies 6:175–200.
1991   The Cultural Patterns of Ancient Pakistan and Neighbouring Regions circa 7000–1500 BC. Pakistan Archaeology 26:218–237.
1992a The Geographical Extent of the Indus Civilization during the Early, Mature and Late Harappan Times. *In* South Asian Archaeology Studies, edited by G. L. Possehl, pp. 123–143. Delhi: Oxford University Press and IBH.
1992b Jhukar and the Late Harappan Cultural Mosaic of the Greater Indus Valley. *In* South Asian Archaeology 1989, edited by Catherine Jarrige, pp. 213–222. Madison, WI: Prehistory Press.
1997   A Preliminary Review of Archaeological Surveys in Punjab and Sindh: 1993–1995. South Asian Studies 13:241–249.

Mughal, Mohammad Rafique, F. Iqbal, M. A. K. Khan, and M. Hassan
1996   Archaeological Sites and Monuments in Punjab: Preliminary Report of Explorations: 1992–1996. Pakistan Archaeology 29:1–474.

Mumford, Lewis
1961   The City in History. New York: Harcourt, Brace and World.

Münch, Guido
1976   El cacicazgo de San Juan Teotihuacan durante la colonia (1521–1821). Colección Científica 32. México, D. F.: Instituto Nacional de Antropología e Historia.

Munro-Hay, Stuart
1994   Axum: An African Civilization of Late Antiquity. Glasgow: Edinburgh University Press.

Munson, P. J.
1971   Tichitt Tradition: A Late Prehistoric Occupation in the Southwestern Sahara. Unpublished Ph.D. dissertation, University of Illinois, Urbana-Champaign.
1980   Archaeology and the Prehistoric Origins of the Ghana Empire. Journal of African History 21:457–466.

Murra, John V.
1960   Rite and Crop in the Inca State. *In* Culture in History, edited by Stanley Diamond, pp. 393–407. New York: Columbia University Press.

1962 Cloth and Its Functions in the Inca State. American Anthropologist 64:710–728.
1966 New Data on Retainer and Servile Populations in Tawantinsuyu. *In* XXXVI Congreso Internacional de Americanistas, Spain 1964, vol. 2, pp. 35–45. Seville: Editorial Católica Española.
1972 El Control Vertical de un Máximo de Pisos Ecológicos en la Economía de las Sociedades Andinas. *In* Visita de la Provincia de León de Huánuco en 1562, edited by John Murra, vol. 1, pp. 381–406. Huánuco, Peru: Universidad Nacional Hermilio Valdizán.
1980 The Economic Organization of the Inca State. Greenwich, CT: JAI Press.
1985 The Limits and Limitations of the "Vertical Archipelago" in the Andes. *In* Andean Ecology and Civilization: An Interdisciplinary Perspective on Andean Ecological Complementarity, edited by Shozo Masuda, Izumi Shimada, and Craig Morris, pp. 15–20. Papers from Wenner-Gren Foundation for Anthropological Research Symposium no. 91. Tokyo: University of Tokyo Press.
1986 The Expansion of the Inka State: Armies, War, and Rebellions. *In* Anthropological History of the Andean Polities, edited by John V. Murra, Nathan Wachtel, and Jacques Revel, pp. 49–58. Cambridge: Cambridge University Press.

Murúa, Martín de
1946 Historia del origen y genealogía real de los reyes inças del Perú. Introduction, notes, and
[1590– arrangement by Constantino Bayle. Biblioteca "Missionalia Hispánica," 2. Madrid: Consejo
1609] Superior de Investigaciones Científicas, Instituto Santo Toribio de Mogrovejo.

Mutoro, Henry W.
1998 Precolonial Trading Systems of the East African Interior. *In* Transformations in Africa: Essays on Africa's Later Past, edited by Graham Connah, pp. 186–203. Leicester: Leicester University Press.

Nance, C. R.
1992 Guzmán Mound: A Late Preclassic Salt Works on the South Coast of Guatemala. Ancient Mesoamerica 3(1):27–46.

Nas, Peter J. M.
1993 Urban Symbolism. Leiden: E. J. Brill.

Nath, A.
1998 Rakhigarhi: A Harappan Metropolis in the Saraswati-Drishadvati Divide. Puratattva 28(1997–1998):39–45.
2001 Rakhigarhi: 1999–2000. Puratattva 31(2000–2001):43–46.

Naville, E. H., T. E. Peet, H. R. Hall, K. Haddon, and W. Loat
1914 The Cemeteries of Abydos. London: Egypt Exploration Fund.

Ndoro, Webber
2001 Your Monument, Our Shrine: The Preservation of Great Zimbabwe. Studies in African Archaeology 19, Uppsala: Department of Archaeology and Ancient History, University of Uppsala.

Netting, Robert M.
1993 Smallholders, Householders: Farm Families and the Ecology of Intensive Sustainable Agriculture. Stanford, CA: Stanford University Press.

Niblett, Rosalind
2001 Verulamium: The Roman City of St Albans. Stroud: Tempus.

Niblett, Rosalind, and Isobel Thompson
2005 Alban's Buried Towns: An Assessment of St Albans' Archaeology up to AD 1600. Oxford: Oxbow Books.

Nicholls, C. S.
1971 The Swahili Coast: Politics, Diplomacy and Trade on the African Littoral (1798–1856). London: George Allen and Unwin.
1985 The Swahili: Reconstructing the History and Language of an African Society. Philadelphia: University of Pennsylvania Press.

Nichols, Deborah L., and Thomas H. Charlton (editors)
1997 The Archaeology of City-States. Washington, DC: Smithsonian Institution Press.

Nicholson, Paul T.
2000   Glass [Technology]. *In* Ancient Egyptian Materials and Technology, edited by Paul T. Nicholson and Ian Shaw, pp. 195–224. Cambridge: Cambridge University Press.

Nicolet, Claude
1994   Economy and Society, 133–43 BC. *In* Cambridge Ancient History IX. The Last Days of the Roman Republic, 146–43 BC, 2nd ed., edited by J. A. Crook, Andrew Lintott, and Elizabeth Rawson, pp. 599–643. Cambridge: Cambridge University Press.

Oberg, Kalervo
1940   The Kingdom of Ankole in Uganda. *In* African Political Systems, edited by Meyer Fortes and E. E. Evans-Pritchard, pp. 121–162. London: Oxford University Press.

O'Brien, Michael J.
2005   Evolutionism and North America's Archaeological Record. World Archaeology 37:26–45.

O'Connor, Anthony M.
1983   The African City. London: Hutchinson.

O'Connor, David
1972   The Geography of Settlement in Ancient Egypt. *In* Man, Settlement, and Urbanism, edited by Peter J. Ucko, Ruth Tringham, and G. W. Dimbleby, pp. 681–698. London: Duckworth.
1989a New Funerary Enclosures (Talbezirke) of the Early Dynastic Period at Abydos. Journal of the American Research Center in Egypt 26:51–86.
1989b City and Palace in New Kingdom Egypt. Cahiers de Recherches de l'Institut de Papyrologie de Lille 11:73–87.
1995   Beloved of Maat, the Horizon of Re. *In* Ancient Egyptian Kingship, edited by D. O'Connor and D. P. Silverman, pp. 263–300. Leiden: E. J. Brill.
2005   Cosmological Structures of Ancient Egyptian City Planning. *In* Structure and Meaning in Human Settlements, edited by Tony Atkin and Joseph Rykwert, pp. 55–66. Philadelphia: University of Pennsylvania, Museum of Archaeology and Anthropology.

Ojo, G. J. Afolabi
1966   Yoruba Palaces: A Study of Afins of Yorubaland. London: University of London Press.

Okamura Hidenori (editor)
2000   Chûgoku kodai toshi no keisei. Heisei 9 nendo—Heisei 11 nendo kagaku kenkyûhi hoshokin kihan kenkyû A (2) kenkyû seika hôkokusho. Kyôto: Kyôto Daigaku.

Oppenheim, A. Leo
1969   Mesopotamia—Land of Many Cities. *In* Middle Eastern Cities, edited by Ira M. Lapidus, pp. 3–18. Berkeley: University of California Press.

Organesjan, K. L.
1955   Karmir Blur IV: Architektura Tejšebaini. Archeologi eskie Raskopki ve Armenii no 6. Erevan: Akademija nauk Armianskoj SSR.

Ortiz de Zúñiga, Iñigo
1967   Visita de la Provincia de León de Huánuco en 1562, Iñigo Ortiz de Zúñiga, visitador, edited
[1562] by John V. Murra. Vol. I. Huánuco, Peru: Universidad Nacional Hermilio Valdizán.
1972   Visita de la Provincia de León de Huánuco en 1562, Iñigo Ortiz de Zúñiga, visitador, edited
[1562] by John V. Murra. Vol. II. Huánuco, Peru: Universidad Nacional Hermilio Valdizán.

Orum, Anthony M., and Xiangming Chen
2003   The World of Cities: Places in Comparative and Historical Perspective. Malden, MA: Blackwell.

Osborne, Robin
1998   Early Greek Colonisation? The Nature of Greek Settlement in the West. *In* Archaic Greece: New Approaches and New Evidence, edited by Nick Fisher and Hans van Wees, pp. 251–269. London: Duckworth with The Classical Press of Wales.

Owens, E. J.
1991   The City in the Greek and Roman World. London: Routledge.

Palaima, Thomas
2003 Archaeology and Text: Decipherment, Translation, and Interpretation. *In* Theory and Practice in Mediterranean Archaeology, edited by John K. Papadopoulos and Richard M. Leventhal, pp. 45–73. Los Angeles: Cotsen Institute of Archaeology, University of California.

Palaima, Thomas G., and James C. Wright
1985 Ins and Outs of the Archives Rooms at Pylos: Form and Function in a Mycenaean Palace. American Journal of Archaeology 89:251–262.

Pankhurst, Richard K.
1968 An Introduction to the Economic History of Ethiopia, 1800–1935. Addis Ababa: Haile Selassie I University Press.
1982 History of Ethiopian Towns from the Middle Ages to the Early Nineteenth Century. Wiesbaden: Franz Steiner Verlag, Aethiopische Forschungen 8.
1998 The Ethiopians. Boston: Blackwell.

Park, Robert E.
1915 The City: Suggestions for the Investigation of Human Behavior in the Urban Environment. The American Journal of Sociology 20:577–612.
1952 Human Communities: The City and Human Ecology. Glencoe, IL: Free Press.

Park, Robert Ezra, and Ernest W. Burgess
1924 Introduction to the Science of Sociology. Chicago: University of Chicago Press.

Park, Robert Ezra, Ernest W. Burgess, and Roderick D. McKenzie (editors)
1925 The City. Chicago: University of Chicago Press.

Parpola, Asko
1986 The Indus Script: A Challenging Puzzle. World Archaeology 17(3):399–419.

Parrish, David
2001 Introduction: The Urban Plan and Its Constituent Elements. *In* Urbanism in Western Asia Minor. New Studies on Aphrodisias, Ephesos, Hierapolis, Pergamon, Perge and Xanthos, edited by David Parrish, pp. 8–41. Journal of Roman Archaeology, supplementary series 45.

Parsons, Jeffrey
1971 Prehistoric Settlement Patterns in the Texcoco Region, Mexico. Museum of Anthropology, Memoir no. 3. Ann Arbor: University of Michigan.

Parsons, Jeffrey, Elizabeth Brumfiel, Mary Parsons, and David Wilson
1982 Prehispanic Settlement Patterns in the Southern Valley of Mexico: The Chalco-Xochimilco Region. Museum of Anthropology, Memoir no. 14. Ann Arbor: University of Michigan.

Pauketat, Timothy R.
2003 Materiality and the Immaterial in Historical-Processual Archaeology. *In* Essential Tensions in Archaeological Method and Theory, edited by Todd L. Van Pool and Christine S. Van Pool, pp. 41–53. Salt Lake City: University of Utah Press.

Pavolini, Carlo
1986 La vita quotidiana a Ostia. Rome-Bari: Editori Laterza.

Pearce, John, Martin Millett, and Manuela Struck (editors)
2000 Burial, Society and Context in the Roman World. Oxford: Oxbow Books.

Pearson, Michael N.
1998 Port Cities and Intruders: The Swahili Coast, India, and Portugal in the Early Modern Era. Baltimore: Johns Hopkins University Press.

Pendergast, David M.
1979 Excavations at Altun Ha, Belize, 1964–1970. vol. 1. Toronto: Royal Ontario Museum.
1981 Lamanai, Belize: Summary of the Excavation Results, 1974–1980. Journal of Field Archaeology 8(1):29–53.
1982 Excavations at Altun Ha, Belize, 1964–1970. vol. 2. Toronto: Royal Ontario Museum.
1984 The Hunchback Tomb: A Major Archaeological Discovery in Central America. Rotunda 16(4):5–11. Toronto: Royal Ontario Museum.
1990 Excavations at Altun Ha, Belize, 1964–1970. vol. 3. Toronto: Royal Ontario Museum.

1991   The Southern Maya Lowlands Contact Experience: The View from Lamanai, Belize. *In* Columbian Consequences, vol. 3, edited by David Hurst Thomas, pp. 336–354. Washington, DC: Smithsonian Institution Press.

1992   Noblesse Oblige: The Elites at Lamanai and Altun Ha, Belize. *In* Mesoamerican Elites: An Archaeological Perspective, edited by Diane Z. Chase and Arlen F. Chase, pp. 61–79. Norman: University of Oklahoma Press.

1993   Worlds in Collision: The Maya/Spanish Encounter in Sixteenth and Seventeenth Century Belize. *In* The Meeting of Two Worlds: Europe and the Americas 1492–1650, edited by Warwick Bray, pp. 105–143. London: The British Academy,

1994   The Architecture of Chau Hiix. Appendix to proposal submitted to the National Science Foundation by K. Anne Pyburn.

1998   Intercessions with the Gods: Caches and Their Significance at Altun Ha and Lamanai, Belize. *In* The Sowing and the Dawning: Terminations, Dedications, and Transformations in the Archaeological and Ethnographic Record of Mesoamerica, edited by Shirley B. Mock, pp. 55–63. Albuquerque: University of New Mexico Press.

2003   Teotihuacan at Altun Ha: Did It Make a Difference? *In* The Maya and Teotihuacan: Reinterpreting Early Classic Interaction, edited by Geoffrey E. Braswell, pp. 235–248. The Linda Schele Series in Maya and Pre-Columbian Studies. Austin: University of Texas Press.

Pendlebury, J. D. S.
1951   The City of Akhenaten, pt. III. London: Egypt Exploration Society.

Pensabene, Patrizio
2002   Committenza edilizia a Ostia tra la fine del I e i primi decenni del II secolo. Lo studio dei marmi e la decorazione architettonica come strumento d'indagine. Melanges de l'École Française de Rome, Antiquité 114(1):181–324.

2004   Marmi e classi dirigenti a Ostia tra la tarda repubblica e la prima età augustea. *In* Ostia, Cicero, Gamala, Feasts and the Economy. Papers in Memory of John H. D'Arms, edited by Anna Gallina Zevi and John H. Humphrey, pp. 99–107. Journal of Roman Archaeology, supplementary series 57.

Perring, Dominic
1991   Roman London. London: Seaby.
2002   The Roman House in Britain. London: Routledge.

Petrie, W. M. Flinders
1890   Kahun, Gurob and Hawara. London: Kegan Paul, Trench, Trüber.
1891   Illahun, Kahun and Gurob. London: Nutt.

Petts, David
2003   Christianity in Roman Britain. Stroud: Tempus.

Phillipson, David W.
1998   Ancient Ethiopia. London: British Museum.

Piggott, Stuart
1952   Prehistoric India. Baltimore: Penguin Books.

Pikirayi, Innocent
1993   The Archaeological Identity of Mutapa State; Towards an Historical Archaeology of Northern Zimbabwe. Studies in Africa Archaeology 6. Uppsala: Societas Archaelogica Uppsaliensis.
2001   The Zimbabwe Culture: Origins and Decline of Southern Zambezian States. Walnut Creek, CA: AltaMira Press.

Pinker, Steven
2002   The Blank Slate: The Modern Denial of Human Nature. New York: Viking Press.

Piotrovsky, Boris B.
1967   Urartu: The Kingdom of Van and Its Art. London: Evelyn Adams and Mackay.

Pizarro, Pedro
1917   Descubrimiento y Conquista del Perú. Colección de Libros y Documentos Referentes a la
[1571]   Historia de Perú, edited by Horacio H. Urteaga, vol. 6. Lima: Sanmartí.

Pohl, Mary Deland (editor)
1985 Prehistoric Lowland Maya Environment and Subsistence Economy. Papers of the Peabody Museum of Archaeology and Ethnology, 77. Cambridge, MA: Harvard University.

Polanyi, Karl
1944 The Great Transformation. New York: Farrar and Rinehart.
1957 Marketless Trading in Hammurabi's Time. *In* Trade and Market in Early Empires, edited by Karl Polanyi, Conrad M. Arensberg, and Harry Pearson, pp. 12–26. Glencoe, IL: Free Press.

Polet, J.
1985 Tegdaoust IV: Fouille d'un quartier de Tegdaoust, Mauritanie Orientale: Urbanisation, architecture, utilisation de l'espace construit. Paris: Editions Recherches sur les Civilisations.

Pollock, Harry E. D., Ralph Roys, Tatiana Proskouriakoff, and A. Ledyard Smith
1962 Mayapan, Yucatan, Mexico. Carnegie Institution of Washington Publication 619. Washington, DC.

Polydorides, Nicos D.
1983 The Concept of Centrality in Urban Form and Structure. New York and Bern: Peter Lang.

Possehl, Gregory L.
1990 Revolution in the Urban Revolution: The Emergence of Indus Urbanism. Annual Review of Anthropology 19:261–282.
1997 The Transformation of the Indus Civilization. Journal of World Prehistory 11(4):425–472.
1998 Sociocultural Complexity without the State: The Indus Civilization. *In* Archaic States, edited by Gary M. Feinman and Joyce Marcus, pp. 261–291. Santa Fe, NM: SAR Press
2000 Harappan Beginnings. *In* The Breakout, the Origins of Civilisation, edited by M. Lamberg-Karlovsky, pp. 99–114. Peabody Museum Monographs. Cambridge, MA: Harvard University.
2002a Archaeology of the Harappan Civilization: An Annotated List of Excavations and Surveys. *In* Indian Archaeology in Retrospect, vol. 2: Protohistory: Archaeology of the Harappan Civilization, edited by S. Settar and R. Korisettar, pp. 421–482. Delhi: Indian Council of Historical Research.
2002b Fifty Years of Harappan Archaeology: The Study of the Indus Civilization since Indian Independence. *In* Indian Archaeology in Retrospect, vol. 2: Protohistory: Archaeology of the Harappan Civilization, edited by S. Settar and R. Korisettar, pp. 1–46. Delhi: Indian Council of Historical Research.
2002c The Indus Civilization: A Contemporary Perspective. Walnut Creek, CA: AltaMira Press.

Potter, Timothy W.
1979 The Changing Landscape of South Etruria. London: Elek.

Pracchia, Stefano
1985 Excavations of a Bronze-Age Ceramic Manufacturing Area at Lal Shah, Mehrgarh. New series, East and West 35(4):458–468.

Price, Nancy T.
1995 The Pivot: Comparative Perspectives from the Four Quarters. Early China 20:93–120.

Pwiti, Gilbert
2005 Southern African and the East African Coast. *In* African Archaeology, edited by Ann. B. Stahl, pp. 378–391. Oxford: Blackwell.

Pyburn, K. Anne
1989 Prehistoric Maya Community and Settlement at Nohmul, Belize. Oxford: BAR International Series.
1991 Chau Hiix: A New Archaeological Site in Northern Belize. Mexicon 8(5):84–86.
1996 The Political Economy of Ancient Maya Land Use: The Road to Ruin. *In* The Managed Mosaic: Ancient Maya Agriculture and Resource Use, edited by Scott Fedick, pp. 236–247. Salt Lake City: University of Utah Press.
1997 The Archaeological Signature of Complexity. *In* The Archaeology of City-States: Cross Cultural Approaches, edited by Deborah L. Nichols and Thomas H. Charlton, pp. 155–168. Washington, DC: Smithsonian Institution Press.
1998 Smallholders in the Maya Lowlands: Homage to a Garden Variety Ethnographer. Human Ecology 26(2):267–286.

2003 The Hydrology of Chau Hiix. Ancient Mesoamerica 14(1):123–129.
2004 Ungendering Civilization: Rethinking the Archaeological Record. London: Routledge.
2005 Complex Deposits at Chau Hiix. *In* Archaeological Investigations in the Eastern Maya Lowlands: Papers of the 2004 Belize Archaeology Symposium, edited by Jaime Awe, John Morris, Sherilyne Jones, and Christophe Helmke, pp. 143–154. Research Reports in Belizean Archaeology, vol. 2. Belmopan, Belize: Institute of Archaeology.

Pyburn, K. Anne, Boyd Dixon, Patricia Cook, and Anna McNair
1998 The Albion Island Settlement Pattern Project: Domination and Resistance in Early Classic Northern Belize. Journal of Field Archaeology 25(1):37–162.

Quirin, Hans, and W. Trillmich (editors)
1956 Atlas zur Weltgeschichte, II. Mittelalter. Braunschweig: Westermann.

Quirke, Stephen
2001 The Cult of Ra. Sun-Worship in Ancient Egypt. New York: Thames and Hudson.

Quirke, Stephen G. J., E. Pardey, and B. Haring
2001 Administration and Administrative Texts. The Oxford Encyclopedia of Ancient Egypt, edited by Donald B. Redford, 1:12–29. New York: Oxford University Press.

Quivron, Gonzaque
1997 Incised and Painted Marks on the Pottery of Mehrgarh and Nausharo-Baluchistan. *In* South Asian Archaeology 1995, edited by B. Allchin and R. Allchin, pp. 45–62. Delhi: Oxford University and IBH.

Qunli (pseudonym)
1972 Linzi Qi guo gucheng kantan jiyao. Wenwu 5:45–54.

Rackham, H. (translator)
1932 Aristotle: Politics. Loeb Classical Library. Cambridge, MA: Harvard University Press.

Radimilahy, Chantal
1998 Mahilaka: An Archaeological Investigation of an Early Town in Northwestern Madagascar. Uppsala: University of Uppsala Press.

Railey, Jim A.
1999 Neolithic to Early Bronze Age Sociopolitical Evolution in the Yuanqu Basin, North-Central China. Unpublished Ph.D. dissertation, Washington University, St. Louis.

Rappaport, Roy A.
1971 The Sacred in Human Evolution. Annual Review of Ecology and Systematics 2:23–44.

Rathje, William L.
1971 The Origin and Development of Lowland Maya Civilization. American Antiquity 36(3):275–285.
1972 Praise the Gods and Pass the Metates: A Hypothesis of the Development of Lowland Rainforest Civilizations in Mesoamerica. *In* Contemporary Archaeology: A Guide to Theory and Contributions, edited by Mark P. Leone, pp. 365–392. Carbondale: Southern Illinois University Press.
1975 The Last Tango in Mayapan: A Tentative Trajectory of Production-Distribution Systems. *In* Ancient Civilizations and Trade, edited by Jeremy A. Sabloff and C. C. Lamberg-Karlovsky, pp. 409–448. Albuquerque: University of New Mexico Press.
2002 The Nouveau Elite Potlatch: One Scenario for the Monumental Rise of Early Civilizations. *In* Ancient Maya Political Economies, edited by Marilyn A. Masson and David A. Freidel, pp. 31–40. Boston: Rowman and Littlefield.

Ratnagar, Shereen
1991 Enquiries into the Political Organization of Harappan Society. Pune: Ravish Publishers.
2001 The Bronze Age: Unique Instance of a Pre-industrial World System? Current Anthropology 42(3):351–379.

Rawson, Elizabeth
1987 Discrimina ordinum: The Lex Julia theatralis. Papers of the British School at Rome 55, pp. 83–114.

Reader, John
1997 Africa: A Biography of the Continent. London: Hamish Hamilton.
2004 Cities. London: William Heinemann.

Reddé, Michel (editor)
2003 La Naissance de la Ville dans l'Antiquité. Paris: De Boccard.

Redfield, Robert
1941 The Folk Culture of Yucatan. Chicago: University of Chicago Press.

Redfield, Robert, and Milton Singer
1954 The Cultural Role of Cities. Economic Development and Cultural Change 3:53–73.

Redmond, Elsa M.
1994 Tribal and Chiefly Warfare in South America. Museum of Anthropology, Memoir no. 16. Studies in Latin American Ethnohistory and Archaeology, vol. I. Ann Arbor: University of Michigan.

Reefe, Thomas
1993 The Luba-Lunda Empire. *In* Problems in African History: The Precolonial Centuries, edited by R. O. Collins, pp. 121–126. Princeton, NJ: Marcus Wiener.

Reid, Anthony
2000 Negeri. The Culture of Malay-Speaking City-States of the Fifteenth and Sixteenth Centuries. *In* A Comparative Study of Thirty City-State Cultures, edited by Mogens H. Hansen, pp. 417–429. Copenhagen: Det Kongelige Danske Videnskabernes Selskab.

Reinhard, Johan, and Constanza Ceruti
2006 Sacred Mountains, Ceremonial Sites, and Human Sacrifice among the Incas. Archaeoastronomy 19:1–43.

Reisner, George A.
1931 Mycerinus. Cambridge, MA: Harvard University Press.

Relph, Edward C.
1976 Place and Placelessness. London: Pion.

Renfrew, Colin
1975 Trade as Action at a Distance: Questions of Integration and Communication. *In* Ancient Civilization and Trade, edited by Jeremy A. Sabloff and Carl C. Lamberg-Karlovsky, pp. 3–60. Albuquerque: University of New Mexico Press.
1979a Transformations. *In* Transformations: Mathematical Approaches to Culture Change, edited by Colin Renfrew and Kenneth L. Cooke, pp. 3–44. New York: Academic Press.
1979b Systems Collapse as Social Transformation: Catastrophe and Anastrophe in Early State Societies. *In* Transformations: Mathematical Approaches to Culture Change, edited by Colin Renfrew and Kenneth L. Cooke, pp. 481–507. New York: Academic Press.
1982 Polity and Power: Interaction Intensification and Exploitation. *In* An Island Polity: The Archaeology of Interaction in Melos, edited by Colin Renfrew and Malcolm Wagstaff, pp. 264–290. Cambridge: Cambridge University Press.
1986 Introduction: Peer Polity Interaction and Socio-political Change. *In* Peer Polity Interaction and Socio-political Change, edited by Colin Renfrew and John F. Cherry, pp. 1–18. Cambridge: Cambridge University Press.
1997 Review of *Early Civilizations*, by Bruce G. Trigger. American Journal of Archaeology 101:164.

Renfrew, Colin, and John F. Cherry (editors)
1986 Peer Polity Interaction and Socio-political Change. Cambridge: Cambridge University Press.

Renfrew, Colin, and T. Poston
1979 Discontinuities in the Endogenous Change of Settlement Pattern. *In* Transformations: Mathematical Approaches to Culture Change, edited by Colin Renfrew and Kenneth L. Cooke, pp. 437–462. New York: Academic Press.

Renfrew, A. Colin, and Ezra B. W. Zubrow (editors)
1994 The Ancient Mind: Elements of Cognitive Archaeology. Cambridge: Cambridge University Press.

Restall, Matthew
1997 The Maya World. Yucatec Culture and Society 1550–1850. Palo Alto, CA: Stanford University Press.

Reyes García, Luis
1996   El término calpulli en documentos del siglo XVI. *In* Documentos Nauas de la Ciudad de México del siglo XVI, edited by Luis Reyes García, Eustaquio Celestino Solís, Armando Valencia Ríos, Constantino Medina Lima, and Gregorio Guerrero Días, pp. 21–68. México, D. F.: CIESAS.

Rich, John, and A. Wallace-Hadrill (editors)
1991   City and Country in the Ancient World. London: Routledge.

Ringrose, David R.
2001   Expansion and Global Interaction, 1200–1700. New York: Longman.

Robert, Denise, Serge Robert, and Jean Devisse (editors)
1970   Tegdaoust: Recherches sur Aoudaghost, vol 1. Paris: Arts et Metiers Graphiques.

Robert-Chaleix, D.
1989   Tegdaoust V: Une concession Medievale a Tegdaoust: Implantation, evolution d'une unite d'habitation. Paris: Editions Recherches sur les Civilisations.

Robson, William A., and David E. Regan
1972   Great Cities of the World. Beverly Hills, CA: Sage Publications.

Rogers, Guy
1991   The Sacred Identity of Ephesus: Foundation Myths of a Roman City. London: Routledge.

Rojas Rabiela, Teresa
1986   El sistema de organización en cuadrillas. *In* Origen y Formación del Estado en Mesoamérica, edited by Andrés Medina, Alfredo López Austin, and Mari Carmen Serra P., pp. 135–150. México, D. F.: Universidad Nacional Autónoma de México.

Rosen, Arlene M.
1986   Cities of Clay: The Geoarcheology of Tells. Chicago: University of Chicago Press.

Rosen, Steven A.
1997   Craft Specialization and the Rise of Secondary Urbanism: A View from the Southern Levant. *In* Urbanism in Antiquity, edited by Walter E. Aufrecht, Neil A. Mirau, and Steven W. Gauley, pp. 82–91. Journal for the Study of the Old Testament, supplementary series 244. Sheffield, UK: Sheffield Academic Press.

Rosenthal, Franz (translator)
1958   The Muqaddimah: An Introduction to History (by Ibn Khaldun 1332–1406). New York: Pantheon Books.

Roskams, Steve
1999   The Hinterlands of Roman York: Present Patterns and Future Strategies. *In* The Coloniae of Roman Britain: New Studies and a Review, edited by Henry R. Hurst, pp. 45–72. Journal of Roman Archaeology, supplementary series 36.

Rosselló Verger, Vicens M.
1987   Villas planificadas medievales del Pais Valenciano. Anales de Geografía de la Universidad Complutense 7:509–525.

Rostovtzeff, Michael I.
1957   Social and Economic History of the Roman Empire. 2nd ed. Oxford: Oxford University Press.

Rostworowski de Diez Canseco, María
1970   Mercaderes del valle de Chincha en la época prehispánica: Un documento y unos comentarios. Revista Española de Antropología Americana 5:135–178.
1992   Pachacamac y el Señor de los Milagros: Una Trayectoría Milenaria. Lima: Instituto de Estudios Peruanos.

Rousseau, Jean-Jacques
1762   Du contrat social, quoted after the Pléiade edition, vol. 3. (Paris 1964)

Routledge, Carolyn
1997   Temple as the Center in Ancient Egyptian Urbanism. *In* Urbanism in Antiquity, edited by Walter E. Aufrecht, Neil A. Mirau, and Steven W. Gauley, pp. 221–235. Journal for the Study of the Old Testament, supplementary series 244. Sheffield, UK: Sheffield Academic Press.

Rowe, John H.
1944 An Introduction to the Archaeology of Cuzco. Papers of the Peabody Museum of American Archaeology and Ethnology, vol. 27, no. 2. Cambridge, MA: Harvard University.
1946 Inca Culture at the Time of the Spanish Conquest. *In* The Andean Civilizations, edited by Julian H. Steward, pp. 183–330. Handbook of South American Indians, vol. 2. Washington, DC: Smithsonian Institution.

Roymans, Nico
1995 Romanization, Cultural Identity, and the Ethnic Discussion: The Integration of the Lower Rhine Populations in the Roman Empire. *In* Integration in the Early Roman West: The Role of Culture and Ideology, edited by Jeannot Metzler, Martin Millett, Nico Roymans, and Jan Slosfstra, pp. 47–64. Luxembourg: Musée National d'Histoire d'Art.
1996 The Sword or the Plough: Regional Dynamics in the Romanisation of Belgic Gaul and the Rhineland Area. *In* From the Sword to the Plough: Three Studies in the Earliest Romanisation of Northern Gaul, edited by Nico Roymans, pp. 9–126. Amsterdam: Amsterdam University Press.
2005 Ethnic Identity and Imperial Power: The Batavians in the Early Roman Empire. Amsterdam: Amsterdam University Press.

Russel, Josiah Cox
1958 Late Ancient and Medieval Population. Transactions of the American Philosophical Society 48(3).

Sabloff, Jeremy A.
1977 Old Myths, New Myths: The Role of Sea Traders in the Development of Ancient Maya Civilization. *In* The Sea in the Pre-Columbian World, edited by Elizabeth P. Benson, pp. 67–88. Washington, DC: Dumbarton Oaks Research Library and Collection.
1986 Interaction among Classic Maya Polities: A Preliminary Examination. *In* Peer Polity Interaction and Socio-political Change, edited by Colin Renfrew and John F. Cherry, pp. 109–116. Cambridge: Cambridge University Press.
1990 The New Archaeology and the Ancient Maya. New York: W. H. Freeman.
1992 Interpreting the Collapse of Classic Maya Civilization: A Case Study of Changing Perspectives. *In* Metaarchaeology: Reflections by Archaeologists and Philosophers, edited by Lester Embree, pp. 99–119. New York: Kluwer.
1994 The New Archaeology and the Ancient Maya, paperback ed. New York: W. H. Freeman.
1997 The Cities of Ancient Mexico. Revised ed. New York: Thames and Hudson.
2004 Looking Backward and Looking Forward: How Maya Studies of Yesterday Shape Today. *In* Continuities and Changes in Maya Archaeology: Perspectives at the Millennium, edited by Charles W. Golden and Greg Borgstede, pp. 13–20. New York: Routledge.
2007 It Depends on How We Look at Things: New Perspectives on the Postclassic Period in the Northern Maya Lowlands. Proceedings of the Annual Meeting of the American Philosophical Society 151(1):11–26.

Sabloff, Jeremy A. (editor)
2003 Tikal: Dynasties, Foreigners, and Affairs of State: Advancing Maya Archaeology. School of American Research. Santa Fe, NM: SAR Press.

Sabloff, Jeremy A., and David A. Freidel
1975 A Model of a Pre-Columbian Trading Center. *In* Ancient Civilization and Trade, edited by Jeremy A. Sabloff and Carl C. Lamberg-Karlovsky, pp. 369–408. Albuquerque: University of New Mexico Press.

Sabloff, Jeremy A., and Carl C. Lamberg-Karlovsky (editors)
1975 Ancient Civilization and Trade. Albuquerque: University of New Mexico Press.

Sabloff, Jeremy A., and William L. Rathje
1975 Rise of a Maya Merchant Class. Scientific American 223(4):72–82.

Sabloff, Jeremy A., and William L. Rathje (editors)
1975 A Study of Changing Pre-Columbian Commercial Systems: The 1972–1973 Seasons at Cozumel, Mexico: A Preliminary Report. Cambridge, MA: Peabody Museum of Archaeology and Ethnology, Harvard University.

Sáenz, Cesar
1964a   Ultimos descubrimientos en Xochicalco. Colección Informes, no. 12, México, D. F.:INAH.
1964b   Las estelas de Xochicalco. *In* Actas y Memorias del XXXV Congreso Internacional de Americanistas celebrado en la ciudad de México en 1962, vol. 2, pp. 69–86. México, D. F.: Editorial Libros de México.

Sahagún, Bernardino de
1981   Florentine Codex. Book 2—The Ceremonies. Translated by Arthur J. O. Anderson and Charles E. Dibble. Monographs of the School of American Research, no. 14, pt. III. Santa Fe, NM: School of American Research and University of Utah.

Sahlins, Marshall
1972   Stone Age Economics. Chicago: Aldine.

Sallnow, Michael J.
1987   Pilgrims of the Andes: Regional Cults in Cusco. Washington, DC: Smithsonian Institution.

Sancho de la Hoz, Pedro
1968   The Discovery and Conquest of Peru. Translated by J. M. Cohen. Baltimore: Penguin
[1538]   Books.

Sanders, William T.
1988   The Mesoamerican Urban Tradition. American Anthropologist 90:521–546.
2003   The Population of Tenochtitlan-Tlatelolco. *In* Urbanism in Mesoamerica, edited by William T. Sanders, Alba Guadalupe Mastache, and Robert Cobean, pp. 203–216. México, D. F.: INAH; University Park: Pennsylvania State University.

Sanders, William T., Susan Toby Evans, and Thomas H. Charlton
2001   The Colonial Period Cultural Geography of the Teotihuacan Valley and the Temascalapa Region. *In* The Teotihuacan Valley Project final report, vol. 5: The Aztec Period Occupation of the Valley, pt. 3, edited by William T. Sanders and Susan T. Evans, pp. 891–930. Occasional Papers in Anthropology no. 25. Department of Anthropology, University Park: Pennsylvania State University.

Sanders, William T., Alba Guadalupe Mastache, and Robert H. Cobean (editors)
2003   El Urbanismo en Mesoamérica: Urbanism in Mesoamerica. University Park: Instituto Nacional de Antropología e Historia and Pennsylvania State University.

Sanders, William T., Jeffrey R. Parsons, and Robert Santley
1979   The Basin of Mexico: Ecological Processes in the Evolution of a Civilization. New York: Academic Press.

Sanders, William T., and David Webster
1988   The Mesoamerican Urban Tradition. American Anthropologist 90:521–546.

Sansom, George B.
1963   History of Japan, 1334–1615. Palo Alto, CA: Stanford University Press.

Santillán, Fernando de
1927   Relación del origen y descendencia política de los Incas. Colección de Libros y Documentos
[1563]   Referentes a la Historia del Perú, edited by Horacio H. Urteaga, vol. 9, 2nd series. Lima: Sanmartí.

Savino, Eliodoro
1999   Città di frontiera nell'impero romano. Forme della romanizzazione da Augusto ai Severi. Bari: Edipuglia.

Scarborough, Vernon L., Matthew E. Becher, Jeffrey L. Baker, Garry Harris, and Fred Valdez Jr.
1995   Water and Land at the Ancient Maya Community of La Milpa. Latin American Antiquity 6(2):98–119.

Scargill, David I.
1979   The Form of Cities. New York: St. Martin's Press.

Schaur, Eda
1992   Non-planned Settlements: Characteristic Features, Path System, Surface Subdivision. Stuttgart: K. Krämer.

Schele, Linda, and David A. Freidel
1990   A Forest of Kings: The Untold Story of the Ancient Maya. New York: William Morrow.

Schele, Linda, and Peter Mathews
1998   The Code of Kings. New York: Simon and Schuster.

Scherrer, Peter
1995   The City of Ephesos from the Roman Period to Late Antiquity. *In* Ephesos, Metropolis of Asia: An Interdisciplinary Approach to Its Archaeology, Religion and Culture, edited by Helmut Koester, pp. 1–25. Cambridge, MA, and London: Harvard University Press.
2001   The Historical Topography of Ephesos. *In* Urbanism in Western Asia Minor: New Studies on Aphrodisias, Ephesos, Hierapolis, Pergamon, Perge and Xanthos, edited by David Parrish, pp. 57–87. Journal of Roman Archaeology, supplementary series 45.

Schiffer, Michael B.
1996   Some Relationships between Behavioral and Evolutionary Archaeologies. American Antiquity 61:643–662.
2000   Social Theory in Archaeology: Building Bridges. *In* Social Theory in Archaeology, edited by Michael B. Schiffer, pp. 1–13. Salt Lake City: University of Utah Press.

Schloen, J. David
2001   The House of the Father as Fact and Symbol: Patrimonialism in Ugarit and the Ancient Near East. Studies in Archaeology and History of the Levant, 2. Cambridge, MA: Harvard Semitic Museum.

Schnore, Leo F.
1965   On the Spatial Structure of Cities in the Two Americas. *In* The Study of Urbanization, edited by Philip M. Hauser and Leo F. Schnore, pp. 347–398. New York: John Wiley.

Schowalter, Daniel N.
1999   Honoring the Emperor: The Ephesians Respond to Trajan. *In* 100 Jahre Österreichische Forschungen in Ephesos. Akten des Symposions Wien 1995, edited by Herwig Friesinger and Fritz Krinzinger, pp. 121–126. Vienna: Verlag der Österreichischen Akademie der Wissenschaften.

Schreiber, Katharina J.
1991   Jincamocco: A Huari Administrative Center in the South Central Highlands of Peru. *In* Huari Administrative Structure: Prehistoric Monumental Architecture and State Government, edited by William H. Isbell and Gordon F. McEwan, pp. 199–213. Washington, DC: Dumbarton Oaks Research Library and Collection.

Schuldenrein, Joseph, Rita P. Wright, Mohammad Rafique Mughal, and M. A. Khan
2004   Landscapes, Soils and Mound Histories of the Upper Indus Valley, Pakistan: New Insights on the Holocene Environments near Ancient Harappa. Journal of Archeological Science 31:777–797.

Seidlmayer, Stephan J.
1996   Town and State in the Early Old Kingdom: A View from Elephantine. *In* Aspects of Early Egypt, edited by J. Spencer, pp. 108–127. London: British Museum Press.

Sennett, Richard (editor)
1969   Classic Essays on the Culture of Cities. New York: Appleton-Century-Crofts.

Shaffer, J. G.
1992   The Indus Valley, Baluchistan and Helmand Traditions: Neolithic through Bronze Age. *In* Chronologies in Old World Archaeology, 3rd ed., edited by Robert W. Ehrich, pp. 441–464. Chicago: University of Chicago Press.

Shandong Wenwu Kaogu Yanjiusuo, Shandong Sheng Bowuguan, Jining Diqu Wenwuzu, and Qufu Xian Wenguanhui
1982   Qufu Lu guo gucheng. Jinan: Qilu Shushe. Partially translated as "Archaeological Explorations at the Ancient Capital of Lu at Qufu in Shandong Province." Chinese Sociology and Anthropology 19(1986):9–65.

Shanxi Sheng Kaogu Yanjiusuo Houma Gongzuozhan
1993   Houma zhutong yizhi. 2 vols. Beijing: Wenwu Chubanshe.
1996   Jin du Xintian. Taiyuan: Shanxi Renmin Chubanshe.

Shao Wangping
2000   The Longshan Period and Incipient Chinese Civilization. Journal of East Asian Archaeology 2(1–2):195–226.

Shaw, Ian
1995   The Simulation of Artifact Diversity at el-Amarna, Egypt. Journal of Field Archaeology 22:223–238.

Shelach, Gideon
1999   Leadership Strategies, Economic Activity, and Interregional Interaction: Social Complexity in Northeast China. Fundamental Issues in Archaeology. New York: Kluwer Academic and Plenum Publishers.

Shook, Edwin M.
1952   The Great Wall of Mayapan. Carnegie Institution of Washington, Department of Archaeology, Current Reports, no. 2. Washington, DC.

Sichuan Wenwu Guanliweiyuanhui, Sichuan Sheng Bowuguan, and Guanghan Xian Wenhuaguan
1987   Guanghan Sanxingdui yizhi. Kaogu xuebao 2:227–254.

Silverblatt, Irene
1987   Moon, Sun, Witches: Gender Ideologies and Class in Inca and Colonial Peru. Princeton, NJ: Princeton University Press.

Siméon, Remi
1991   Diccionario de la lengua Náhuatl o Mexicano. México, D. F.: Siglo Veintiuno.

Simonsen, Jørgen Bæk
2000   Mecca and Medina. Arab City-States or Arab Caravan-Cities? *In* A Comparative Study of Thirty City-State Cultures, edited by Mogens H. Hansen, pp. 241–249. Copenhagen: Det Kongelige Danske Videnskabernes Selskab.

Sinclair, Paul
1987   Space, Time and Social Transformation: A Territorial Approach to the Archaeology and Anthropology of Zimbabwe and Mozambique, ca. AD 0–1700. Uppsala: Societas Archaeologica Upsaliensis.

Sinclair, Paul, and Thomas Hakansson
2000   The Swahili City-State culture. *In* Comparative Study of Thirty City-State Cultures, edited by Mogens Hansen, pp. 461–482. Copenhagen: Det Kongelige Danske Videnskabernes Selskab.

Sinclair, Paul J. J., I. Pikirayi, G. Pwiti, and R. Soper
1993   Urban Trajectories on the Zimbabwean Plateau. *In* The Archaeology of Africa. edited by Thurston Shaw, Paul Sinclair, Bassey Andah, and Alex Okpoko, pp. 705–731. London: Routledge.

Singh, Rana P. B.
1994   The Sacred Geometry of India's Holy City, Varnasi: Kashi as Cosmogram. National Geographical Journal of India 40:189–216.

Sjöberg, Gideon
1960   The Preindustrial City, Past and Present. Glencoe, IL: The Free Press.

Skibo, James M., and Gary M. Feinman (editors)
1999   Pottery and People: A Dynamic Interaction. Salt Lake City: University of Utah Press.

Skibo, James M., William H. Walker, and Axel E. Nielsen (editors)
1995   Expanding Archaeology. Salt Lake City: University of Utah Press.

Skinner, G. William (editor)
1977   The City in Late Imperial China. Palo Alto, CA: Stanford University Press.

Slusser, Mary S.
1982   Nepal Mandala. Vol. 1. Princeton, NJ: Princeton University Press.

Smith, Adam T.
2003 The Political Landscape: Constellations of Authority in Early Complex Polities. Berkeley: University of California Press.

Smith, Carol A.
1976a Regional Economic Systems: Linking Geographical Models and Socioeconomic Problems, *In* Regional Analysis, vol. 1: Economic Systems, edited by Carol Smith, pp. 3–67. New York: Academic Press.
1976b Exchange Systems and the Spatial Organization of Elites: The Organization of Stratification in Agrarian Societies. *In* Regional Analysis, vol. 2: Social Systems, edited by Carol Smith, pp. 309–374. New York: Academic Press.

Smith, Michael E.
1979 The Aztec Marketing System and Settlement Pattern in the Valley of Mexico: A Central Place Analysis. American Antiquity 44:110–125.
1989 Cities, Towns, and Urbanism: Comment on Sanders and Webster. American Anthropologist 91:454–461.
1996 The Aztecs. Cambridge, MA: Blackwell.
1997 Life in the Provinces of the Aztec Empire. Scientific American 277(3):56–63.
2003 Can We Read Cosmology in Ancient Maya City Plans? Comment on Ashmore and Sabloff. Latin American Antiquity 14:221–228.
2004 The Archaeology of Ancient State Economies. Annual Review of Anthropology 33(1):73–102.
2005a Did the Maya Build Architectural Cosmograms? Latin American Antiquity 16:217–224.
2005b City Size in Late Postclassic Mesoamerica. Journal of Urban History 31:403–434.

Smith, Monica L.
1999 The Role of Ordinary Goods in Premodern Exchange. Journal of Archaeological Method and Theory 6(2):109–135.
2003a Introduction. *In* The Social Construction of Ancient Cities, edited by Monica L. Smith, pp. 1–36. Washington, DC: Smithsonian Books.
2003b Urban Social Networks: Early Walled Cities of the Indian Subcontinent as "Small Worlds." *In* The Social Construction of Ancient Cities, edited by M. L. Smith, pp. 269–289. Washington, DC: Smithsonian Books.
2006 The Archaeology of South Asian Cities. Journal of Archaeological Research 14(2):97–142.

Smith, Monica L. (editor)
2003c The Social Construction of Ancient Cities. Washington, DC: Smithsonian Books.

Smith, Virginia
1988 The Iconography of Power at Xochicalco, Morelos. Unpublished Ph.D. dissertation, University of Kentucky, Lexington.
2000a The Art and Iconography of the Xochicalco Stelae. *In* The Xochicalco Mapping Project, edited by Kenneth Hirth, pp. 83–101. Archaeological Research at Xochicalco, vol. 2. Salt Lake City: University of Utah Press.
2000b The Iconography of Power at Xochicalco: The Pyramid of the Plumed Serpents. *In* The Xochicalco Mapping Project, edited by Kenneth Hirth, pp. 57–82. Archaeological Research at Xochicalco, vol. 2. Salt Lake City: University of Utah Press.

Snodgrass, Anthony
1986 Interaction by Design: The Greek City State. *In* Peer Polity Interaction and Socio-political Change, edited by Colin Renfrew and John F. Cherry, pp. 47–58. Cambridge: Cambridge University Press.

Sole, Laura
2003 Monumenti repubblicani di Ostia Antica. Archeologica Classica 53:137–186.

Sombart, Werner
1916 Der Moderne Kapitalismus. Leipzig: Duncker und Humblot.
[1902]

Southall, Aidan
1973a   Introduction. *In* Urban Anthropology: Cross-cultural Studies of Urbanization, edited by Aidan William Southall, pp. 3–14. New York: Oxford University Press.
1973b   The Density of Role-Relationships as a Universal Index of Urbanization. *In* Urban Anthropology: Cross-cultural Studies of Urbanization, edited by Aidan William Southall, pp. 71–106. New York: Oxford University Press.
1998   The City in Time and Space. Cambridge: Cambridge University Press.

Southall, Aidan, Peter J. M. Nas, and Ghaus Ansari (editors)
1985   City and Society: Studies in Urban Ethnicity, Life-Style, and Class. Leiden: Institute of Cultural and Social Studies, University of Leiden.

Sparkes, B. A.
1982   The Melian Dialogue of Thucydides. *In* An Island Polity, the Archaeology of Exploitation in Melos, edited by Colin Renfrew and M. Wagstaff, pp. 319–322. Cambridge: Cambridge University Press.

Speakman, R. J., Elizabeth C. Stone, M. D. Glascock, A. Çilingiroğlu, Paul Zimansky, and Hector Neff
2004   Neutron Activation Analysis of Urartian Pottery from Eastern Anatolia. Journal of Radioanalytical and Nuclear Chemistry 262(1):119–127.

Spence, Kate
2004   The Three-dimensional Form of the Amarna House. Journal of Egyptian Archaeology 90:123–152.

Spencer, Charles S.
2006   Modeling (and Measuring) Expansionism and Resistance: State Formation in Ancient Oaxaca, Mexico. *In* History and Mathematics: Historical Dynamics and Development of Complex Societies, edited by Peter Turchin, Leonid Grinin, Andrey Korotayev, and Victor C. de Munck, pp. 170–192. Volgograd: Russian State University for the Humanities.

Spores, Ronald
1967   The Mixtec Kings and Their People. Norman: University of Oklahoma Press.
1984   The Mixtecs in Ancient and Colonial Times. Norman: University of Oklahoma Press.

Steinhart, Edward I.
1978   Ankole: Pastoral Hegemony. *In* The Early State, edited by Henri J. M. Claessen and Peter Skalník, pp. 131–150. The Hague: Mouton.

Stigand, Chaucy H.
1913   The Land of Zinj: Being an Account of the British East Africa, Its Ancient History and Present Inhabitants. London: Constable.

Stone, Elizabeth C.
1987   Nippur Neighborhoods. Studies in Ancient Oriental Civilization 44. Chicago: University of Chicago Press.
1990   The Tell Abu Duwari Project, 1987. The Journal of Field Archaeology 17:141–162.
1995   The Development of Cities in Ancient Mesopotamia. *In* Civilizations of the Ancient Near East I, edited by Jack Sasson, pp. 235–248. New York: Scribners Press.
1997   City States and Their Centers. *In* The Archaeology of City States: Cross-cultural Approaches, edited by Deborah L. Nichols and Thomas H. Charlton, pp. 15–26. Washington, DC: Smithsonian Institution Press.
1999   The Constraints on State and Urban Form in Ancient Mesopotamia. *In* Urbanism and Economy in the Ancient Near East, edited by Michael Hudson and Baruch Levine, pp. 203–227. Cambridge, MA: Peabody Museum of Archaeology and Ethnology, Harvard University.
2005a   The Outer Town of Ayanis, 1997–2001. *In* Anatolian Iron Age V, edited by Altan Çilingiroğlu, pp. 187–194. Ankara: British School of Archaeology in Turkey.
2005b   Mesopotamian Cities and Countryside. *In* A Companion to the Ancient Near East, edited by Daniel Snell, pp. 141–154. Oxford: Blackwell.

Stone, Elizabeth C. (editor)
2007 Settlement and Society: Essays Dedicated to Robert McCormick Adams. Los Angeles: Cotsen Institute of Archaeology, University of California.

Stone, Elizabeth C., D. H. Lindsley, V. Pigott, G. Harbottle, and M. T. Ford
1998 From Shifting Silt to Solid Stone: The Manufacture of Synthetic Basalt in Ancient Mesopotamia. Science 280:2091–2093.

Stone, Elizabeth C., and Paul E. Zimansky
1994 The Second and Third Seasons at Tell Abu Duwari, Iraq. The Journal of Field Archaeology 21:437–455.
1995 The Tapestry of Power in a Mesopotamian City: The Mashkan-shapir Project. Scientific American 272(4):92–97.
2001 Survey and Excavations in the Outer Town, 1997–1998. In Ayanis I: Ten Years' Excavations at Rusahinili Eiduru-kai, 1989–1998, edited by A. Çilingiroğlu and Mirio Salvini, pp. 355–375. Rome: Istituto per gli Studi Micenei ed Egeo-Anatolici.
2003 The Urartian Transformation in the Outer Town of Ayanis. In Archaeology in the Borderlands: Investigations in Cauacasia and Beyond, edited by Adam Smith and Karen Rubinson, pp. 213–228. Los Angeles: Cotsen Institute of Archaeology, University of California.
2004a The Anatomy of a Mesopotamian City: Survey and Soundings at Mashkan-shapir. Winona Lake, IN: Eisenbraun's.
2004b City Planning at Ayanis. In A View from the Highlands: Trans-Caucasus, Eastern Anatolia and Northwestern Iran. Studies in Honour of C. A. Burney, edited by Anthony Sagona, pp. 233–243. Leiden: Peeters Press.

Stone, G., R. M. Netting, and P. Stone
1990 Seasonality, Labor Scheduling, and Agricultural Intensification in the Nigerian Savanna. American Anthropologist 91(1):7–23.

Storey, Glenn
1992 Preindustrial Urban Demography: The Ancient Roman Evidence. Unpublished Ph.D. dissertation, Pennsylvania State University, University Park.

Su Bingqi, with Yan Wenming and Zhang Zhongpei
1994 Zhongguo tongshi, di'er juan: Yuangu shidai. Shanghai: Shanghai Renmin Chubanshe.

Sutton, J. E. G.
1998 Engaruka: An Irrigation Agricultural Community in Northern Tanzania before the Maasai. Azania 33:1–37.

Sweely, Tracy L.
1996 Electromagnetic Induction: A Geophysical Technique for Locating Prehistoric Maya Non-platform Floors. Unpublished MA thesis, Boulder: University of Colorado.
2005 Detecting "Invisible" Dwellings in the Maya Area Using Electromagnetic Induction: Significant Findings of a Pilot Study at Chau Hiix, Belize. Latin American Antiquity 16(2):193–208.

Sweet, Ronald F. G.
1997 Writing as a Factor in the Rise of Urbanism. In Urbanism in Antiquity, edited by Walter E. Aufrecht, Neil A. Mirau, and Steven W. Gauley, pp. 35–49. Journal for the Study of the Old Testament, supplement series 244. Sheffield, UK: Sheffield Academic Press.

Swenson, Edward R.
2003 Cities of Violence: Sacrifice, Power, and Urbanization in the Andes. Journal of Social Archaeology 3(2):256–296.

Tainter, Joseph
1988 The Collapse of Complex Societies. Cambridge: Cambridge University Press.

Tamrat, Tadesse
1972 Church and State in Ethiopia, 1270–1527. Oxford: Clarendon Press.

Thompson, John Eric Sidney
1934 Skybearers, Colors, and Directions in Maya and Mexican Religion. Carnegie Institution of Washington Publication 436, Contribution 10. Washington, DC: Carnegie Institution of Washington.

Thornton, John
1992 Africa and Africans in the Making of the Atlantic World, 1400–1680. Cambridge: Cambridge University Press.
2000 Mbanza Kongo/Sao Salvador: Kongo's Holy City. *In* Africa's Urban Past, edited by David M. Anderson and Richard Rathbone, pp. 67–84. Oxford: James Currey.

Thorp, Robert L.
1991 Erlitou and the Search for the Xia. Early China 16:1–38.

Thür, Hilke
1995 The Processional Way in Ephesos as a Place of Cult and Burial. *In* Ephesos, Metropolis of Asia: An Interdisciplinary Approach to Its Archaeology, Religion and Culture, edited by Helmut Koester, pp. 157–199. Cambridge, MA: Harvard University Press.

Tichy, Franz
1991 Die geordnete Welt indianischer Völker. Wiesbaden: F. Steiner.

Tilley, Christopher
1999 Metaphor and Material Culture. Oxford: Blackwell.

Timm, Stefan
1984– Das christlich-koptische Ägypten in arabischer Zeit. Beihefte zum Tübinger Atlas
1992 des Vorderen Orients, Reihe B, 41/1–6. Wiesbaden: L. Reichert.

Topic, John R., and Theresa Lange Topic
1987 The Archaeological Investigation of Andean Militarism: Some Cautionary Observations. *In* The Origins and Development of the Andean State, edited by Jonathan Haas, Shelia Pozorski, and Thomas Pozorski, pp. 7–55. Cambridge: Cambridge University Press.
1997 Hacia una comprensión conceptual de la guerra andina. *In* Arqueología, Antropología e Historia en los Andes: Homenaje a María Rostworowski, edited by Rafael Varón Gabai and Javier Flores, pp. 567–590. Lima: Institute of Andean Studies.

Torelli, Mario
1984 Lavinio e Roma. Riti iniziatici e matrimonio tra archeologia e storia. Rome: Edizioni Quasar.

Tóvar de Teresa, G.
1987 La Ciudad de México y la Utopia en el Siglo XVI. México, D. F.: Seguros de México.

Trigger, Bruce G.
1985 The Evolution of Pre-industrial Cities: A Multilinear Perspective. *In* Mélanges offerts à Jean Vercoutter, edited by F. Geus and F. Thill, pp. 343–353. Paris: Editions Recherche sur les Civilisations.
1990 Monumental Architecture: A Thermodynamic Explanation of Symbolic Behaviour. World Archaeology 22:119–132.
1993 Early Civilizations: Ancient Egypt in Context. Cairo: American University in Cairo Press.
1998 Archaeology and Epistemology: Dialoguing across the Darwinian Chasm. American Journal of Archaeology 102:1–34.
2003 Understanding Early Civilizations: A Comparative Study. Cambridge: Cambridge University Press.
2006 A History of Archaeological Thought. 2nd ed. New York: Cambridge University Press.

Trombold, Charles D. (editor)
1991 Ancient Road Networks and Settlement Hierarchies in the New World. New York: Cambridge University Press.

Tsetskhladze, G.
1997 A Survey of the Major Urban Settlements in the Kimmerian Bosporos. *In* Yet More Studies in the Ancient Greek Polis, edited by Thomas H. Nielsen, pp. 39–81. Stuttgart: F. Steiner.

Tsipopoulou, Metaxia
1997 Palace-Centered Polities in Eastern Crete: Neopalatial Petras and Its Neighbors. Urbanism in Antiquity, edited by Walter E. Aufrecht, Neil A. Mirau, and Steven W. Gauley, pp. 263–277. Journal for the Study of the Old Testament, supplement series 244. Sheffield Academic Press.

Tuan, Yi-Fu
1968   Discrepancies between Environmental Attitude and Behaviour: Examples from Europe and China. The Canadian Geographer 12(3):176–191.
1978   The City: Its Distance from Nature. Geographical Review 68(1):1–12.

Turner, Victor W.
1969   The Ritual Process: Structure and Anti-structure. Chicago: Aldine.

Tylor, E. B.
1875   Researches into the Early History of Mankind and the Development of Civilization. London: John Murray.

Tyrakowski, Konrad
1989   Autochtone regelmässige Netze vorspanischer Siedlungen im Mexikanischen Hochland. Geographische Zeitschrift 77:107–123.

Underhill, Anne P., Gary M. Feinman, Linda Nicholas, Gwen P. Bennett, Cai Fengshu, Yu Haiguang, Luan Fengshi, and Fang Hui
1998   Systematic, Regional Survey in SE Shandong Province, China. Journal of Field Archaeology 25:453–474.

Upham, Steadman
1990   The Evolution of Political Systems: Sociopolitics in Small-Scale Sedentary Societies. Cambridge: Cambridge University Press

Uphill, Eric P.
1965   The Egyptian Sed-festival rites. Journal of Near Eastern Studies 24(4):365–383.
1969   Pithom and Raamses: Their Location and Significance II. Journal of Near Eastern Studies 28:15–39.
1984   The Temples of Per Ramesses. Warminster, UK: Aris and Phillips.
1988   Egyptian Towns and Cities. Shire, UK: Aylesbury.

Urton, Gary
1993   Moieties and Ceremonialism in the Andes: The Ritual Battles of the Carnival Season in Southern Peru. In El Mundo Ceremonial Andino, edited by Luis Millones and Yoshio Onuki, pp. 117–142. Senri Ethnological Studies no. 37. Osaka: National Museum of Ethnology.

Urton, Gary, and Carrie J. Brezine
2005   Khipu Accounting in Ancient Peru. Science 309:1065–1067.

Usman, Aribidesi
2001   State Periphery Relationships and Sociopolitical Development in Igbomaland, North Central Yoruba, Nigeria. British Archaeological Reports. Oxford: BAR International Series.

Uzzell, Douglas
1979   Conceptual Fallacies in the Rural-Urban Dichotomy. Urban Anthropology 3–4:333–350.

Valbelle, Dominique
1985   Les ouvriers de la Tombe: Deir el-Médineh à l'époque ramesside. Bibliothèque d'Étude 96. Cairo: Institut Français d'Archéologie Orientale du Caire.

Valencia Espinoza, Abraham, and Tatiana Adela Valencia Becerra
2003   Canas y las Batallas Rituales en Chiaraje. In Ritos de competición en los Andes: Luchas y contiendas en el Cuzco, edited by Máximo Cama Ttito, Colección Etnográfica, vol. 1,
        pp. 51–130. Lima: Fondo Editorial de la Pontificia Universidad Católica del Perú.

Valor Piechotta, Magdalena (editor)
1995   El último siglo de la Sevilla islámica (1147–1248). Sevilla: Universidad de Sevilla y Gerencia Municipal de Urbanismo del Ayuntamiento de Sevilla.

Vanacker, C.
1979   Tegdaoust II: Fouille d'un quartier artisanal. Memoires de l'IMRS. Paris: IMRS.

Vance, James E.
1990   The Continuing City: Urban Morphology in Western Civilization. Baltimore: Johns Hopkins University Press.

van de Mieroop, Marc
1997 The Ancient Mesopotamian City. Oxford: Clarendon.
2004 A History of the Near East ca. 3000–323 BC. Oxford: Blackwell.

Vanderhoeven, Alain
1996 The Earliest Urbanization in Northern Gaul: Some Implications of Recent Research in Tongres. *In* From the Sword to the Plough: Three Studies in the Earliest Romanisation of Northern Gaul, edited by Nico Roymans, pp. 189–260. Amsterdam: Amsterdam University Press.

van der Leeuw, Sander E.
1981 Information Flows, Flow Structures, and the Explanation of Change in Human Institutions. *In* Archaeological Approaches to the Study of Complexity, edited by Sander E. van der Leeuw, pp. 229–329. Cingula 6. Amsterdam: Albert Egges van Giffen Instituut voor Prae- en Protohistorie.

Vansina, Jan
1993 Kingdoms of the Savannah. *In* Problems in African History: The Precolonial Centuries, edited by R. O. Collins, pp. 115–120. Princeton, NJ: Marcus Wiener.

van Zantwijk, Rudolf
1985 The Aztec Arrangement: The Social History of Pre-Spanish Mexico. Norman: University of Oklahoma Press.

Vats, Madho Sarup
1940 Excavations at Harappa. Delhi: Government of India Press.

Veblen, Thorstein
1899 The Theory of the Leisure Class: An Economic Study in the Evolution of Institutions. New York: Macmillan.

von Hesberg, Henner
1992 Publica magnificentia. Eine antiklassizistische Intention der frühen augusteischen Baukunst, Jahrbuch des Deutsches Archäologisches Institut 107:125–147.

Vries, Jan de
1981 Patterns of Urbanization in Pre-industrial Europe 1500–1800. *In* Patterns of European Urbanization since 1500, edited by H. Schmal, pp. 79–109. London: Croom Helm.

Wacher, John S.
1995 The Towns of Roman Britain. Revised ed. London: Batsford.

Wachtel, Nathan
1973 Estructuralismo e historia: A propósito de la organización social del Cuzco. *In* Sociedad e ideología: ensayos de historia y antropología andinas, edited by Nathan Wachtel, pp. 21–58. Historia Andina 1. Lima: Instituto de Estudios Peruanos.

Wagstaff, Malcolm, and S. Auguston
1982 Traditional Land Use. *In* An Island Polity, edited by Colin Renfrew and Malcolm Wagstaff, pp. 106–133. Cambridge: Cambridge University Press.

Wagstaff, Malcolm, and John F. Cherry
1982 Settlement and Population Change. *In* An Island Polity, the Archaeology of Exploitation in Melos, edited by Colin Renfrew and Malcolm Wagstaff, pp. 136–155. Cambridge: Cambridge University Press.

Wakefield, T.
1870 Routes of Native Caravans from the Coast to the Interior of East Africa. Journal of the Royal Geographical Society 40:303–338.

Wallerstein, Immanuel
1977 The Modern World System: Capitalist Agriculture and the Origins of the European World Economy in the Sixteenth Century. New York: Academic Press.

Warburton, David
2001 Egypt and the Near East: Politics in the Bronze Age. Paris: Recherches et Publications, Civilisations du Prôche-Orient, IV, 1.

Ward-Perkins, Bryan
2005   The Fall of Rome and the End of Civilization. Oxford: Oxford University Press.

Ward-Perkins, John B.
1974   Cities of Ancient Greece and Italy. New York: Braziller.
1981   Roman Imperial Architecture. Harmondsworth, UK: Penguin.

Watson, Bruce (editor)
1998   Roman London: Recent Archaeological Work. Journal of Roman Archaeology, supplementary series 24.

Weber, Ekkehard
1999   Zu den lateinischen Inschriften von Ephesos. In 100 Jahre Österreichische Forschungen in Ephesos. Akten des Symposions Wien 1995, edited by Herwig Friesinger and Fritz Krinzinger, pp. 139–146. Vienna: Verlag der Österreichischen Akademie der Wissenschaften.

Weber, Max
1947   The Theory of Social and Economic Organization. Translated by A. M. Henderson and T. Persons. New York: The Free Press.
1962   The City. New York: Collier Books.
[1958]
1973   Die "Objektivität" sozialwissenschaftlicher und sozialpolitischer Erkenntnis (1904). Reprinted in Gesammelte Aufsätze zur Wissenschaftslehre. 4th ed., pp. 146–214. Tübingen: J. C. B. Mohr.
1999   Die Stadt. Republished with introduction and commentary by W. Nippel. In Max Weber Gesamtausgabe 1/22.5. Tübingen.

Weber, Steven A.
2003   Archaeobotany at Harappa: Indications for Change. In Ethnobiology and the Indus Civilization, edited by Steven A. Weber and William R. Belcher, pp. 175–198. Lanham, MD: Lexington Books.

Weber, Steven A., and William R. Belcher (editors)
2003   Ethnobiology and the Indus Civilization. Lanham, MD: Lexington Books.

Webster, David
2001   Spatial Dimensions of Maya Courtly Life. In Royal Courts of the Maya, edited by Takeshi Inomata and Stephen D. Houston, pp. 130–167. Boulder, CO: Westview Press.

Wells, Peter S.
1999   The Barbarians Speak: How the Conquered Peoples Shaped Roman Europe. Princeton, NJ, and Oxford: Princeton University Press.

West, Georgia
2002   Ceramic Exchange in the Late Classic and Postclassic Maya Lowlands: A Diachronic Approach. In Ancient Maya Political Economies, edited by Marilyn A. Masson and David A. Freidel, pp. 140–196. Walnut Creek, CA: Altamira Press.

Wheatley, Paul
1971   The Pivot of the Four Quarters: A Preliminary Enquiry into the Origins and Character of the Ancient Chinese City. Chicago: Aldine.
1972   The Concept of Urbanism. In Man, Settlement and Urbanism, edited by Peter J. Ucko, Ruth Tringham, and G. W. Dimbleby, pp. 601–637. London: Duckworth.
1976   Levels of Space Awareness in the Traditional Islamic City. Ekistics 42:354–366.
1978   From Court to Capital: A Tentative Interpretation of the Origins of the Japanese Urban Tradition. Chicago: University of Chicago Press.
1983   Nagara and Commandery: Origins of the Southeast Asian Urban Traditions. Department of Geography Research Papers, nos. 207–208. Chicago: University of Chicago.

Wheeler, Robert Eric Mortimer
1968   The Indus Civilization. Cambridge: Cambridge University Press.
[1953]

White, Roger, and Philip Barker
1998   Wroxeter: Life and Death of a Roman City. Stroud: Tempus.

White, Roger, and Vincent Gaffney
2003 Resolving the Paradox: The Work of the Wroxeter Hinterland Project. *In* The Archaeology of Roman Towns: Studies in Honour of John S. Wacher, edited by Peter R. Wilson, pp. 221–232. Oxford: Oxbow Books.

Whitfield, Peter
1969 Cities of the World: A History in Maps. Berkeley: University of California Press.

Wightman, Edith M.
1985 Gallia Belgica. London: Batsford.

Wilcox, Clifford
2004 Robert Redfield and the Development of American Anthropology. Lanham, MD: Lexington Books.

Wilk, Richard R.
1976 Work in Progress at Colha, 1976. *In* Maya Lithic Studies, edited by Thomas Hester and Norman Hammond, pp. 35–40. Special Report 4. San Antonio: Center for Archaeological Research, University of Texas.
1985 Ancient Maya and the Political Present. Journal of Anthropological Research 41(3):307–326.
1988 Maya Household Organization: Evidence and Analogies. *In* Household and Community in the Mesoamerican Past, edited by Richard R. Wilk and Wendy Ashmore, pp. 135–151. Albuquerque: University of New Mexico Press.
1995 Pageants and Power. *In* Beauty on the Global Stage, edited by Colleen Ballerino Cohen, Richard R. Wilk, and Beverly Stoeltje, pp. 1–12. New York: Routledge.
1996 Economies and Cultures: Foundations of Economic Anthropology. Boulder, CO: Westview Press.
2004 Miss Universe, the Olmec, and the Valley of Oaxaca. Journal of Social Archaeology 4(1):81–98.

Wille, Sarah
2007 Sociopolitics and Community-Building: The Entanglement of Prehispanic Maya Culture, Objects, and Place at Chau Hiix, Belize. Unpublished Ph.D. dissertation, Indiana University, Bloomington.

Wilson, Andrew I.
2000 The Aqueducts of Italy and Gaul. Journal of Roman Archaeology 13:597–604.

Wilson, Edward O.
1978 On Human Nature. Cambridge, MA: Harvard University Press.

Wilson, John A.
1960 Egypt through the New Kingdom: Civilization without Cities. *In* City Invincible: A Symposium on Urbanization and Cultural Development in the Ancient Near East, edited by Carl H. Kraeling and Robert McCormick Adams, pp. 124–164. Chicago: University of Chicago Press.

Winters, Christopher
1981 The Urban Systems of Medieval Mali. Journal of Historical Geography 7:341–355.

Wirth, Eugen
1992 The Concept of the Islamic City—Privacy in the Islamic East versus Public Life in Western Culture. Applied Geography and Development 40:27–38.

Wirth, Louis
1925 A Bibliography of the Urban Community. *In* The City, edited by Robert E. Park, Ernest W. Burgess, and Roderick D. McKenzie, pp. 161–228. Chicago: University of Chicago Press.
1938 Urbanism as a Way of Life. American Journal of Sociology 44:1–24.
1944 Urban and Rural Living: Planning Post-war Ways of Life for American Youth. Washington, DC: National Council for Social Studies.
1969 Human Ecology. *In* Classic Essays of the Culture of Cities, edited by Richard Sennett, pp. 170–179. New York: Appleton-Century-Crofts.

Wolf, Eric R.
1957 Closed Corporate Communities in Mesoamerica and Java. Southwestern Journal of Anthropology 13:1–18.
1966 Peasants. Englewood Cliffs, NJ: Prentice-Hall.

1982 Europe and the People without History. Berkeley: University of California Press.
1986 The Vicissitudes of the Closed Corporate Peasant Community. American Ethnologist 13:325–329.

Woolf, Greg
1998 Becoming Roman: The Origins of Provincial Civilization in Gaul. Cambridge: Cambridge University Press.
2004 The Present State and Future Scope of Roman Archaeology: A Comment. American Journal of Archeology 108:417–428.

Woolley, Sir Leonard, and Sir Max Mallowan
1976 Ur Excavations VII: The Old Babylonian Period. London: British Museum Publications.

Wright, A. C. S., D. H. Romney, R. H. Arbuckle, and V. E. Vial
1959 Land in British Honduras. Colonial Research Publications 24. London: Stationery Office, Colonial Office.

Wright, Arthur F.
1977 The Cosmology of the Chinese City. *In* The City in Late Imperial China, edited by G. William Skinner, pp. 33–73. Palo Alto, CA: Stanford University Press.

Wright, Henry T., and Gregory A. Johnson
1975 Population, Exchange, and Early State Formation in Southwestern Iran. American Anthropologist 77:267–289.

Wright, Rita P.
1996 Technology, Gender, and Class: Worlds of Difference in Ur III Mesopotamia. *In* Gender and Archaeology, edited by Rita P. Wright, pp. 79–110. Philadelphia: University of Pennsylvania Press.

Wright, Rita P., Joseph Schuldenrein, and M. A. Khan
1999 Appendix 2: Old Beas Survey, February 8–May 3, 1999. *In* Harappa Archaeological Research Project: Harappa Excavations 1999, edited by Richard H. Meadow, Jonathan Mark Kenoyer, and Rita P. Wright, pp. 21–24. Cambridge, MA: Harvard University; Madison: University of Wisconsin; and New York: New York University.

Wrobel, Gabriel
2004 Metric and Nonmetric Dental Variation among the Ancient Maya of Northern Belize. Unpublished Ph.D. dissertation, Indiana University, Bloomington.

Xi'an Banpo Bowuguan, Shaanxi Sheng Kaogu Yanjiusuo, and Lintong Xian Bowuguan
1988 Jiangzhai—Xinshiqishidai yizhi fajue baogao. 2 vols. Beijing: Wenwu Chubanshe.

Xu Hong
2000 Xian Qin chengshi kaoguxue. Beijing: Beijing Yanshan Chubanshe.

Yaeger, Jason
2003 Untangling the Ties That Bind: The City, the Countryside, and the Nature of Maya Urbanism at Xunantunich, Belize. *In* The Social Construction of Ancient Cities, edited by Monica L. Smith, pp. 121–155. Washington and London: Smithsonian Books.

Yang, Xiaoneng
2004a Urban Revolution in Late Prehistoric China. *In* Chinese Archaeology in the Twentieth Century, edited by Yang Xiaoneng, vol. 1, pp. 98–143. New Haven, CT: Yale University Press.

Yang, Xiaoneng (editor)
2004b Chinese Archaeology in the Twentieth Century. 2 vols. New Haven, CT: Yale University Press.

Yang Zhaoqing
1997 Shilun Zhengzhou Xishan Yangshao wenhua wanqi gu chengzhi de xingzhi. Hua Xia kaogu 1:55–59, 92.

Yazaki, Takeo
1968 Social Change and the City in Japan. Tokyo: Japan Publications.

Ye Wansong
1992 Jin shinian Luoyang Shi Wenwu Gongzuodui kaogu gongzuo gaishu. Wenwu 3: 40–45, 54.

Yegül, Fikret K.
2000   Memory, Metaphor and Meaning in the Cities of Asia Minor. *In* Romanization and the City: Creation, Transformations, Failure, edited by Elizabeth Fentress, pp. 133–153. Journal of Roman Archaeology, supplementary series 38.

Yoffee, Norman
2005   Myths of the Archaic State: Evolution of the Earliest Cities, States, and Civilizations. Cambridge: Cambridge University Press.

Yoffee, Norman, and Li Min
2005   Cross-cultural Perspectives on the Evolution of the World's Earliest Cities. Paper presented at the International Workshop on Early Chinese Civilization, University of British Columbia, Vancouver, BC, March 10–12.

Yon, Marguerite
1997   La cite d'Ougarit sur le tell de Ras Shamra. Paris: Editions Recherche sur les Civilisations.

Yoneda, Keiko
1991   Los mapas de Cuauhtinchan y la historia cartográfica prehispánica. México, D. F. and Puebla: CIESAS, the State of Puebla, and the Fondo de Cultura Económica.

Zabehlicky, Heinrich
1995   Preliminary Views of the Ephesian Harbour. *In* Ephesos, Metropolis of Asia: An Interdisciplinary Approach to its Archaeology, Religion and Culture, edited by Helmut Koester, pp. 201–215. Cambridge, MA: Harvard University Press.

Zanker, Paul
1988   The Power of Images in the Age of Augustus. Ann Arbor: University of Michigan Press.
2000   The City as Symbol: Rome and the Creation of an Urban Image. *In* Romanization and the City: Creation, Transformations, Failure, edited by Elizabeth Fentress, pp. 25–41. Journal of Roman Archaeology, supplementary series 38.

Zeder, Melinda
1991   Feeding Cities. Washington, DC: Smithsonian Institution.

Zevi, Fausto
1996   Sulle fasi più antiche di Ostia. *In* "Roman Ostia" Revisited. Archaeological and Historical Papers in Memory of Russell Meiggs, edited by Anna Gallina Zevi and Amanda Claridge, pp. 69–89. London: British School at Rome.
1996–   Costruttori eccellenti per le mura di Ostia: Cicerone, Clodio e l'inscrizione della Porta
1997   Romana. Rivista dell'Istituto Nazionale d'Archeologia e Storia dell'Arte Ser. III.
[1998] Vols. 19–20, pp. 61–112.
2000   Traiano e Ostia. *In* Trajano, Emperador de Roma, edited by Julián González, pp. 509–547. Rome: "l'Erma" di Bretschneider.
2002a   Origini di Ostia. *In* Ostia e Portus nelle loro relazioni con Roma, edited by Christer Bruun and Anna Gallina Zevi, pp. 11–32. Acta Instituti Romani Finlandiae 27. Rome: Instituti Romani Finlandiae.
2002b   Appunti per una storia di Ostia repubblicana. Melanges de l'École Française de Rome, Antiquité 114(1):13–58.
2004   P. Lucilio Gamala senior: Un riepilogo trent'anni dopo. *In* Ostia, Cicero, Gamala, Feasts and the Economy. Papers in Memory of John H. D'Arms, edited by Anna Gallina Zevi and John H. Humphrey, pp. 47–67. Journal of Roman Archaeology, supplementary series 57.

Zhang Xuqiu
1994   Qujialing wenhua gucheng de faxian he chubu yanjiu. Kaogu 7:629–634.

Zhao Dianzeng
1989   Jinnian Ba Shu wenhua kaogu zongshu. Sichuan wenwu: Sanxingdui yizhi yanjiu zhuanji (1989):3–10.

Zhongguo Kexueyuan Kaogu Yanjiusuo, and Shaanxi Sheng Xi'an Banpo Bowuguan
1963   Xi'an Banpo: Yuanshi shizi juluo yizhi. Zhongguo tianye kaogu baogaoji, Kaoguxue zhuankan, series IV, no. 14. Beijing: Kexue Chubanshe.

Zhongguo Lishi Bowuguan Kaogubu, Shanxi Sheng Kaogu Yanjiusuo, and Yuanqu Xian Bowuguan
1996　Yuanqu Shang cheng (I): 1985–1986 niandu kancha baogao. Beijing: Kexue Chubanshe.
2001　Yuanqu gucheng dongguan. Huanghe Xiaoliangdi shuiku Shanxi kuqu kaogu baogao, vol. 2. Beijing: Kexue Chubanshe.

Zhongguo Shehuikexueyan Kaogu Yanjiusuo
1994　Yinxu de faxian yu yanjiu. Kaoguxue zhuankan, series I, no. 23. Beijing: Kexue Chubanshe.
1999　Yanshi Erlitou: 1959 nian—1978 nian kaogu fajue baogao. Zhongguo tianye kaogu baogaoji, Kaoguxue zhuankan, series IV, no. 59. Beijing: Zhongguo Dabaikequanshu Chubanshe.
2003　Zhongguo kaoguxue Xia Shang juan. Kaoguxue zhuankan, series 1, vol. 29. Beijing: Zhongguo Shehuikexueyuan Chubanshe.

Zhongguo Shehuikexueyuan Kaogu Yanjiusuo Henan Erdui
1981　Henan Mi Xian Xinzhai yizhi de shijue. Kaogu 5:398–408.

Zhongguo Shehuikexueyuan Kaogu Yanjiusuo and Zhongguo Shehuikexueyuan Gudai Wenming Yanjiu Zhongxin
2003　Zhongguo wenming qiyuan yanjiu. Beijing: Wenwu Chubanshe.

Zhongmei Liangcheng Diqu Lianhe Kaogudui
1997　Shandong Rizhao Shi Liangcheng diqu de kaogu diaocha. Kaogu 4:289–303.

Zimansky, Paul E.
1985　Ecology and Empire: The Structure of the Urartian State. Chicago: Oriental Institute Publication.

Zipf, George K.
1949　Human Behavior and the Principle of Least Effort. Cambridge, MA: Addison-Wesley.

Zorita, Alonso de
1963　Life and Labor in Ancient Mexico. New Brunswick, NJ: Rutgers University Press.
1994　Life and Labor in Ancient Mexico. Norman: University of Oklahoma Press.

Zou Heng
1987　Zhongguo wenming de dansheng. Wenwu 12: 69–74, 85.

Zuidema, R. Tom
1964　The Ceque System of Cuzco: The Social Organization of the Capital of the Inca. Translated by Eva M. Hooykaas. International Archives of Ethnography, suppl. to vol. 50. Leiden: E. J. Brill.

Index

Note: entries in *italics* refer to subject material in figures or tables.

Abydos (Egypt), 326
Acolman (Mexico), 281, 282, *283*
Adams, Robert McC., 46
Addis Ababa (Ethiopia), 234–35
Adiljivaz (Anatolia), 151
Adulis (Ethiopia), 230
Aedui tribe (Gaul), 121
Aeschylus, 30
Africa, and role of early cities in urban and rural interaction spheres, 229–46. *See also* East Africa; Ethiopia; North Africa
agoras, at Ephesos, *105*, 106, *107*, 109
Aix-la-Chapelle (Germany), 86–87
Akamba (Kenya), 239, 241
Akhenaten (pharaoh), 168, 176–80
Aksum (Ethiopia), 230
Alberti, Leon Battista, 89
Aleppo (Syria), 150
Alexandria (Egypt), 103
Allactic form, and transformation of cities, 49
Allegory of Good and Bad Government (Lorenzetti), 31, *32*
alliances, and structure of Inka empire, 318, 319
Al-Muqaddasi, 39
altepetl, and incidental urbanism in Central Mexico, 275, 277–85, 291–93
Altun Ha (Belize): archaeological patterns and historical trajectories of, 255–60; decline and abandonment of, 263–65, 266; disturbance of elite tombs at, 271; smallholders and production at, 265–66; trade and distribution channels of, 270–71
Amarna (Egypt), 48, 49, 176–80, 182
Amiens (France), *123*, 126
Amri (Pakistan), 199
anastrophe, and early state formation, 49
Anatolia, and comparison of Ayanis to Mashkan-shapir in lowland Mesopotamia, 141–64

Ancient City, The (Fustel de Coulanges 1864, 1872, 1963), 4–5, 9
Ancus Marcius, 99
Andorra, as micro-state, 23
Androkos (founder of Ephesos), 98, 99
Anglo-Saxon kingdoms, 69
Ankole (Uganda), 69
Antananarivo (Africa), 233
Antonius Pius (Roman emperor), 112
Anyang (China), 61, 218, *219*
Anyi (China), 223, *224*
aqlla, and Inka empire, 311–12, 332
archaeology: and concept of transformation, 37; and cosmic imagery in ancient cities, 63–64; and evidence for segmental urban structure in Central Mexico, 285–86; and excavation of neighborhoods, 19; and future directions in research on cities and urbanism, 323–36; and identification of "basic needs," 250; and multicultural components of urban experience, 88; and study of urban structure in Mesoamerica, 275–77; and systematic excavation in study of Romano-British towns, 129. *See also* comparative archaeology; historical archaeology; post-processual archaeology; processual archaeology; urban geoarchaeology
archipelago pattern, and structure of urban centers in Inka empire, 301, 312
architecture. *See* monumental architecture; palaces; plazas; public architecture; pyramids; urban planning; walls
Aristophanes, 30, 33
Aristotle, 34–35, 98
Artemis, and ritual pathway at Ephesos, 99–100, 106
Assyria, and Neo-Assyrian empire, 75, 143–44, 150, 160
Aston, Mick, 10
Athens (Greece), 73, 98
Augst (Germany), 128
Augustus (Roman emperor), 83–84, 102, 104–09, 115

Autun (France), 121, 126
Avenches (Germany), *123*, 128
Awdaghoust (Africa), 231, 235
Axayacatl (Mexico), 293
Axum (Ethiopia), 80
Ayanis (Anatolia), 142, 151, 152–64
Aztec: cosmology and quadripartition in cities of, 329; festivals and rites of, 332, 334; and myth of Fifth Sun, 63; and tribute collection from conquered groups, 296

Bairoch, Paul, 72, 74
ball courts, and Maya cities, 263
Baluchistan, 207
Banpo (China), 212
Bantu kingdoms, 69
Bashidang (China), 213
"basic needs," and trade, 250
Bastam (Anatolia), 151, 156
Batavian tribe (Germany), 127
baths, and cities of Roman Empire, 112, 114, 124
Bavay (Gaul), *123*
Begho (Africa), 235
Beidha (Jordan), 331
Bell, E. T., 36–37
Benin City (Nigeria), 233, 235
Bhaktapur (Nepal), 327, 328, 333, 334
Bibracte (France), 121
Bintliff, John L., 37
Bird, James, 11
Blanton, Richard E., 142
Bond, James, 10
Boudicca, and revolt of AD 60/61, 130
Boulogne-Sur-Mer (Gaul), *123*
Britain, and Roman cities, 37, *120*, 121–22, 129–35, 136, 137
Bronze Age, and development of cities in China, 216–27
Buddhism, and urbanism in India, 90
Buhen fortress (Nubia), *18*
bureaucracy: and Early Modern model of secular civil service, 91; and institutional networking in early state formation, 81–82
Burgess, Ernest W., 7, 11, 327–28
burials: and characteristics of Indus urbanism, 195, 206; of elites and smallholders in Maya cities, 271; and necropolises in Chinese cities of Warring States period, 225–26
Bussmann, Richard, 168–69
Butzer, Elisabeth K., 91
Butzer, Karl W., 328

Calakmul (Maya), 335
Calvino, Italo, 45

Carl, P., 49
Carolingian Renewal, 86–87
Carthage (North Africa), 98, 103
case studies, of ancient cities: on character and functions of cities in Inka empire, 299–319; and commentary on methods of analysis, 67–76; and comparison of Mashkan-shapir (Mesopotamia) and Ayanis (Anatolia), 141–64; on development of cities in pre-imperial China, 209–28; on development of Roman cities in Mediterranean, 95–116; on establishment of cities in Roman northwestern provinces, 117–38; on origin and character of urbanism in Indus Valley, 183–207; on role of cities in shaping of urban and rural interaction spheres in early Africa, 229–46; on structure of prehispanic city in Central Mexico, 273–97; on trade and Maya cities of New River Conurbation, 247–72; on types of cities in ancient Egypt, 165–82. *See also* city; urbanism
Cassius Dio, 127
Castor and Pollux, temple of at Ostia, 100, 101, 106
Çatal Höyük (Turkey), 20, 30–31, 69, 326
catastrophe theory, and collapse of state societies, 49
Centinela, La (Peru), 312–18, 319
Central Place Theory: and functional approach to definition of city, 71; and long-distance trade, 75; and processual approaches to study of Maya cities, 54; and studies of urban structure in Mesoamerica, 276
ceramics: and consumption in Chau Hiix (Maya), 262; elites and structure of Cuzco, 305–306; and interpretation of Ayanis (Anatolia), 155–56, 159–60; and urbanism in Indus Valley, 189–90, 192, 198–200, 205
Cerro Tilcajete (Mexico), 335
Chan Chan (Peru), 318
Charlemagne, 86–87
Chau Hiix (Belize): and abandonment of monumental buildings, 264; and burials, 270, 271; compared to Altun Ha, 263; and platforms in Maya architecture, 267; and production by smallholders, 266; and trade networks, 255–62, 269
Chayanov, A. V., 253
Chen Xiangming, 10, 12
Chengtoushan (China), 213
Chengziyai (China), *213*, 215
Cherry, John F., 49
Chiarulli, Beverly, 261
Chicago School, 6–7
Chifeng (China), 214
Childe, V. Gordon, 10, 12, 20, 31, 46–47, 58, 68–71, 74, 82, 86, 165, 326

China: cities as microcosms of universe, 15, 19; and monumental architecture in Shang Dynasty, 61; specialization in cities of late imperial, 251; stages in development of cities in pre-imperial, 209–28

Chincha capital (Inka), 312–18

Chinese language, and semantic range of words for "city," 209–10

Christaller, Walter, 71

Christianity: ideology of and transformation of Roman cities, 84; and Roman cities in northwestern provinces, 136, 137. *See also* religion

chronology, of Indus Valley tradition, 184–85, *186, 189, 199, 202*

Cieza de León, Pedro de, 301

citizenship, and Roman cities in Mediterranean, 109, 111

city: central themes in research on, 323–36; definition of, 12–20, 31, 33, 68–71, 74–76, 275–77, 297; increasing interest in growth and development of, 25; as open systems, 90; review of literature on origins of, 20–21; review of literature on view of by ancients, 22–24; review of past comparative analyses of, 4–12; transformations of through time and space, 29–51; and uniformities in symbolic aspects of cultures, 53–66; and value of comparative studies, 24–25. *See also* case studies; urbanism

city center: and definition of city, 11–12, *16*; and establishment of stratigraphic history, 327–30

city plans, analyzing diversity of, 324–25. *See also* urban planning

city profile, and definition of city, 13, *16*

city-states: and Bronze Age cities in China, 222; definition of, 22–23; dichotomy between territorial states and, 35, 72–74; and locational analysis, 56–58; peer-polity interaction among adjacent, 41. *See also* state

civic identity, formation of Roman at cities in Mediterranean, 102–13, 115

civilization: and cities in context of China, 210; definition of city and, 33; and Roman view of world, 118, 137

Clark-Maxwell, James, 33–34

class. *See* elites; social structure

Claudius (Roman emperor), 129

climate, and cities of greater Indus Valley, 186. *See also* ecology; environmental determinism; floods and flooding

Cluny (medieval monastery), *38*

cognition, cross-cultural uniformities in human, 60

Colchester (England), 124, 129–30

collapse, as part of urban prehistory and history, 78–79

Cologne (Germany), 128

colonialism: and civic identity of Roman cities in Mediterranean, 110–11; and grid-plan towns in Mesoamerica, 89, 90. *See also* Spain

Comhaire, Jean, 24

communication, and urbanism in Inka empire, 318–19

community, and spatial organization of Central Mexican *altepemeh*, 281–85

comparative analyses: and review of literature, 4–12; value of in understanding cities and urbanism, 24–25, 336. *See also* case studies

comparative archaeology, 30

complexity, and urbanism in ancient Egypt, 82

concentric zone model, of city development, 6, 7, 8

Constantinople, as Christian-Byzantine metropolis, 84

consumer city: city-state culture and concept of, 73, 74; and Roman cities in northwestern provinces, 122

consumption: and anthropological analysis of city formation, 268; at Maya city of Chau Hiix, 260–62; monumental architecture and conspicuous, 60, 62; and status of elites, 269. *See also* consumer city

conurbation, definition of, 255

Copán (Honduras), 329

Copenhagen Polis Centre (Denmark), 72

Cordova, Carlos E., 80

cosmic imagery, and archaeological interpretations of ancient cities, 63–64, 329

costs, of urban transformation in Roman cities of Mediterranean, 113–15

countryside, dichotomy of city and, 23. *See also* rural areas

Covey, R. Alan, 309

Cowgill, George L., 29, 31, 35, 71

craft production: building plans and specialization of, 330–31; division of labor and specialization of, 331–32; and urbanism in Indus Valley, 190–91, 194, 200. *See also* manufacturing; production

Crete. *See* Minoan culture

Crumley, Carole L., 142

Crummy, Philip, 130

cuadrilla system, in Central Mexico, 284–85

Cuzco (Peru): compared to Ayanis (Anatolia), 163; cosmograms and form of, 329; elites and administrative palace in, 304–307; and regional centers of Inka empire, 62; Spanish descriptions of, 299; and urban centers of territorial states, 61; and urban planning, 143

Cybele (Anatolian Mother Goddess), 101

cylinder seals, and Mesopotamian cities, 148, *149*. *See also* steatite seals

Dadiwan (China), 212
Dantu (China), *213*, 215
defense: and architecture at Xochicalco (Mexico), 289–90; and fortifications in Roman provincial cities, 136; and functions of city walls, 20, 21. *See also* warfare
Deir el-Medina (Egypt), 83, 174–76
DeLaine, Janet, 82, 117
de Maret, Pierre, 234
DeMatté, Paola, 214
demographics. *See* density; population dispersion; size
de Molina, Fray Alonso, 278
density, of population: and definition of city, 75–76; and diversity of city plans, 324
Dhar Tichitt (Mauritania), 230
Dholavira (India), 183, 188, 193, 201–203, 207
Díaz, Bernal, 273
diversity, of cities as theme, 13
Drayneflete Revealed (Lancaster 1949), 41, *42–43*, 44
Drennan, Robert D., 284
Dublin (Ireland), 69
Dumont, Louis, 119
Durán, Fray Diego, 332
Durrell, Lawrence, 77
Dynamic Model, and cities in territorial states, 39
Dyos, Harold James, 23

Early Modern model, of secular civil service, 91
early-state module, and concept of peer-polity interaction, 40–41
East Africa, and coastal cities, 237–43
ecology, control over arable land and differences in, 142. *See also* climate; environmental determinism; "vertical ecological complementarity"
economics. *See* consumption; costs; household; labor; land and land tenure; production; trade
Edo (Japan), 143
Egypt: bureaucracy and institutional networking in early state formation, 81–82, 91; cosmic imagery in cities of, 63, 329; and dispersed form of villages, 235; residential quarters in pre-Islamic cities, 83; and specialized types of cities, 165–82; and territorial states, 61–62. *See also* Amarna; Deir el-Medina; Memphis
Eliade, Mircea, 63–64
elites: and administrative palace in Cuzco, 304–307; consumption and maintenance of status, 269; lack of evidence for at Harappa, 195; role of in production and trade in Maya cities, 250–52, 266–72. *See also* social structure
emic approaches: to Greek *polis*, 68; to structure of Central Mexican urban centers, 274, 277, 278; to symbolism in early cities, 62–64

empires, imposed structures and similarities in city form, 37–39. *See also* Assyria; Inka; Roman Empire
Emporion (Spain), 98
Engaruka (East Africa), 241
Enlightenment, and distinction between towns and cities, 70
environmental determinism: and historiography on urbanism in Africa, 230–31; and long-term settlement histories, 79. *See also* climate; ecology
Ephesos (Turkey), 95–116
Erligang (China), *217*, 218, 222
Erlitou (China), 218, *219*
Eshnunna (Mesopotamia), 333
Ethiopia: early cities in highlands of, 230; history of urbanism in nineteenth-century, 81
Eurocentricity, and alternative perspectives on urbanism, 92
Europe: and Africa in late fifteenth century, 245; and perspectives on Medieval urbanism, 87–89
evolutionary stages, in life of city, 10–11
Exeter (England), 133–35
experience, and definition of city, 12
explanatory archaeology, 30

Falkenhausen, Lothar von, 21, 69
Faraday, Michael, 33–34
faunal remains, at Ayanis (Anatolia), 161–63
Fentress, Elizabeth, 82
Finley, Moses I., 73
Flannery, Kent V., 34, 54, 55, 264
Fletcher, Roland J., 65, 233
floods and flooding, and urban settlement histories in Spain, 80
Folan, William J., 335
"folk-urban continuum," 23
Forge, Anthony, 65
forum, at Ostia (Italy), 105, 111
Fox, Richard, 275
Freidel, David A., 252
frontiers, and northwestern provinces of Roman Empire, 117
Fry, Robert, 262
functional approach, for study of urban structure in Mesoamerica, 276
Fustel de Coulanges, Numa Denis, 4–5, 9, 54

Galton, Francis, 34
Ganweriwala (India), 188
Gao (Africa), 230
Garner, Barry J., 54–55
Gaul, and Roman cities, 37, 121, *123*, 124, 126–27, 136, 137
Gaya (India), 90

Gedi (Kenya), *234*
Geertz, Clifford, 64, 306
geography, and cities of greater Indus Valley, 186, 187. *See also* topography
Germany, and Roman cities, 127–28, 137
Ghana, kingdom of, 230, 231
Gibson, Charles, 283
Giriama (Kenya), 239, 241
GIS (Geographic Information Systems) analyses, of road systems, 335
Giza (Egypt), 80, 168–72
Gloucester (England), 133
gongcheng, and Warring States period society in China, 225
Gongyi (China), 214
government. *See* bureaucracy; politics; state
Graham, Elizabeth, 251
Great Zimbabwe, *232*, 235, 243–44
Greece: and city-farmers, 72–74; and early urbanization in Archaic and Classical periods, 68; and Hellenistic-style buildings at Roman cities in Mediterranean, 103, 104; and monumental architecture in colonial cities, 69; and urban prototype for Hellenistic city, 82–84. *See also* Minoans; Mycenaeans
grid-plan town, reemergence of in Medieval Europe, 89, 90
Grimal, Pierre, 82

Hadrian (Roman emperor), 111
Hall, Peter, 24
Hancock, Graham, 63
Handan (China), 223, *224*
Hansen, Mogens H., 22, 33, 71, 72, 141, 222, 248
Harappa (Pakistan): and common features of early cities, 50; origin and character of Indus urbanism and, 183, 184, 188–198, 207
Harris, Chauncy D., 8–9, 24
Harth-Terré, Emilio, 310–11
Hassan, Fekri, 236
Hausa (Nigeria), and divisions in cities, 231, 232–33
Hercules, and religious architecture of Ostia, 101, 106
Hermodoros of Ephesos, 98
Hierakonpolis (Egypt), 168, 326
Hinduism, and urbanism in India, 90, 330
hinterland. *See* rural areas
Hirth, Kenneth, 22, 68
Hissoka (Pakistan), 191
historical archaeology, 92
historiography, on urbanism in Africa, 230–31
Hodder, Ian, 30
Houma bronze foundry (China), 224, 225
household, as unit of economic organization, 253

Hoyt, Homer, 7–8, 11
Hoz, Pedro Sancho de la, 299
Huánuco Pampa (Inka), 301, 302–12, 318–19, 333–34
Huey Tozoztli (Aztec festival), 334
humanist approach, to study of early cities, 54
humanitas, and Roman Empire, 117
Husuni Kubwas (Tanzania), *240*
"hypercoherence," and Maya cities, 264

Ibn Khaldun, 10
identity. *See* civic identity; local identity
Ikhmindi (Nubia), *15*
India: religion and urbanism in, 90; and research on border with Pakistan, 207; and size requirements for definition of city, 75; voluntary simplicity and formation of new state, 268
indigenous development, model of for Indus urbanism, 188
individual agents: and comparative approaches to study of city development, 10; roles of in city transformations, 44
Indus civilization, and origin and character of urbanism, 183–207
Inka: character and functions of cities in empire of, 299–319; division of labor and evolution of specialized workers, 311–12, 332; and regional centers, 62. *See also* Cuzco
interaction, and definition of city, 12–13
Ireland, monumental architecture in early Medieval, 69
Islam: and East African coastal cities, 239; urbanism and form of city, 85–86, 87, 91, 328
Italy, relationship between urbanism and government in Renaissance, 31, *32*

Jacobs, Jane, 48
Jalilpur (India), 191
James, Simon, 119
James I of Aragón, 89
Janusek, John Wayne, 251
Japan, and administration of rural estates by elites, 252
Jarmo (Neolithic village), 30
Jenne-jeno (Africa), 68, 230, 235
Jericho (Israel), 30, 31
Jhukar (Pakistan), 199
Jiangzhai (China), 212
Jinancheng (China), *224*, 226–27
Johnson, Gregory A., 34, 54
Julius Caesar, 122, 129

Kahun (Egypt), 172–74
Kalibangan (Pakistan), 193, 195, 204

Index 399

Kano (Africa), 236
Karmir Blur (Anatolia), 151, 157
Karnak (Egypt), 181–82
Kasigau (East Africa), 241, 242
Katsina (Africa), 236
Kemp, Barry, *48*, 166, 173, 177, 178, 180
Kenoyer, Jonathan Mark, 50, 88
Kilwa (Africa), 233
kings and kingdoms, and institutions in central Africa, 237. *See also* Anglo-Saxon kingdoms; Bantu kingdoms
kinship: and social class in Inka empire, 304; and trade in early African cities, 241
Kirongwe (Africa), 242
Kish (Mesopotamia), 146
Kiswahili language (East Africa), 239
Kofyar (Nigeria), and production by smallholders, 253, 254, 270
Koldewey, Robert, 53–54
Kongo kingdom, 235
Kostof, Spiro, 12, 20, 23, 138
Kot Diji (Pakistan), 188, 191, 199
Koumbi Saleh (Africa), 230, 231
Kusimba, Chapurukha M., 69

labor: control of and urban planning in lowland Mesopotamia and highland Anatolia, 142–43; division of as characteristic of urbanism, 69, 75; and economy of Inka empire, 305, 308, 312; and evolution of specialized workers, 331–32; and rotational service at Xochicalco (Mexico), 293–96; and workmen's towns in Egypt, 168–72, 174–76. *See also* craft production; manufacturing; production
Lal Shah (Baluchistan), 192, 196–97
Lamanai (Belize), 255–60, 262–63, 264, 266, 269, 270
La Milpa (Belize), 264
Lancaster, Sir Osbert, 41, *42–43*, 44
land and land tenure: and *altepetl* in Central Mexico, 281, 283–84; and smallholders in Maya context, 266; and urban planning in lowland Mesopotamia and highland Anatolia, 142, 143–44
landscape surveys, 73–74
Larsa (Mesopotamia), 144, *147*
Latin, and inscriptions from Ephesos, 107, 108
Lavinium (Italy), 100
Law, Randall, 191
Leeds, Anthony, 12
Lehner, Mark, 86, 169
Le Mans (France), *136*
Lepcis Magna (North Africa), 95–116
Levy, Robert I., 327

Liangchengzhen (China), 214, 215, 216
Lincoln (England), 133
Linzi (China), *224*, 225–26
Liu Li, 214
Liulihe (China), 220–21
Li Xian (China), 213
local identity, and Roman cities in Mediterranean, 97–102, 115
locational analysis, of distribution and size of settlements in early civilizations, 55–56
Lockhart, James, 279
London: and establishment of Roman cities, 130–32, 135; transformations across space in late Medieval, *48*, 49
Longshan culture (China), 214–15
Lorenzetti, Ambrogio, 31, *32*
Lothrop, Samuel K., 327
Lunda (Africa), 237
Luoyang (China), 223
Lynch, Kevin, 10
Lyon (France), 126

Mackay, Ernest J. H., 200
macro-states. *See* territorial states
Mainz (Germany), 128
Makua (Mozambique), 239
Mallia (Minoan palace), *38*
manufacturing, in Mashkan-shapir (Mesopotamia), 147–48, 150. *See also* craft production
mapping, of city plans, 325
Marcus, Joyce, 35, 39, 49, 53, 54, 56, 62, 249, 265, 277, 278
Marean, Curtis, 161
Marshall, John Hubert, 200
Martínez, Hildeberto, 285
Mashkan-shapir (Mesopotamia), 142, 144–50, 163–64
Masson, Marilyn A., 268–69, 326
Maya: comparisons between social behavior of Roman elite and, 138; and concept of "the four on high," 62; cosmic imagery in cities of, 329; and functional approach to study of urbanism, 276; and monumental architecture, 59; population densities of cities, 75–76; and road systems, 335; trade networks and cities of New River Conurbation, 247–72; and views of cities by ancients, 22
Mayapan (Yucatan), 326
mbanza, and Kongo kingdom, 235
McAnany, Patricia A., 271
McIntosh, Roderick J. & Susan Keech, 24
Mecca (Saudi Arabia), 70
Medina (Saudi Arabia), 70
Medinet Habu (Thebes), 176

Mehrgarh (Pakistan), 188, 190, 193
Mellaart, James, 30
Melos (Greece), 35, 73, 74
Memphis (Egypt), 61–62, 82, 166
Menzel, Dorothy, 313, 318
Meskell, Lynn, 174
Mesoamerica: Spanish colonialism and grid-plan towns, 89–90; and transformations of cities across space and time, 44–46; worldview and principle of quadripartition in cities of, 329. *See also* Maya; Mexico
Mesopotamia: and comparison of Mashkan-shapir to Ayanis in highland Anatolia, 141–64; division of labor and evolution of specialized workers, 331–32; Early Dynastic cities of Egypt compared to cities of, 181
metal working: and early settlement of Harappa, 192; in Mashkan-shapir (Mesopotamia), 147, *149*; and trade in early African cities, 242
Metz (Gaul), *123*
Mexico: environmental context of city construction in Basin of, 80; and specialized production in Oaxaca Valley, 331; structure of prehispanic cities in Central, 273–97. *See also* Aztec; Maya; Mexico City; Tenochtitlan; Teotihuacan
Mexico City, rebuilding of on grid plan, 89
Meyer, Jeffrey F., 329
micro-state, and definition of city-state, 22–23
Miharawa (Africa), 241
Mijikenda (Africa), 241
Miles, Susanna W., 22
military organization, in prehispanic Mesoamerica, 290–91. *See also* warfare
Minanha (Belize), 264
Miner, Horace, 12
Minoan culture: and Bronze Age palaces on Crete, 67, 330
models, of nature and development of cities, 6–9, 188
Mohenjo-daro (Pakistan): and common features of early cities, 50; origin and character of Indus urbanism and, 183, 188, 194, 198–201, 207
Molokwane (South Africa), 235
Mols, R., 76
Monte Albán (Mexico), 328, 334–35
monumental architecture: and Chinese cities during Bronze Age, 224; and definition of city, 69; empires and imposed structures, 37–39; and interaction of religious and political authority in early urban centers, 330; and Lepcis during Augustan period, 107; problems with excavation of, 328; and Roman cities in northwestern provinces, 125; and universalities in early civilizations, 59–60, 62. *See also* public architecture

Moore, Melissa, 159
Morris, Craig, 68, 309, 333–34
mortuary cults, in Egypt, 171
Mote, Frederick W., 24
Msemwa, Paul, 241
Mughal, Mohammad Rafique, 188, 191
multiculturalism, and perspectives on Medieval urbanism in Europe, 87–88, 91
multiple nuclei model, of city development, 8–9
Mumford, Lewis, 10, 47, 48
municipium, and civic identity of Lepcis, 110
Murra, John V., 301, 310
Murúa, Martín de, 304, 306
Mwangia (Africa), 241
Mycenaeans, and palaces, 67–68, 330–31
Mykenai (Greece), 67

Nahuatl language, and *altepetl* in Central Mexico, 278
Nausharo (Baluchistan), 192, 193
Naxos (Greece), 35
neighborhoods, and excavation of cities, 19
Neolithic: and defensive walls of villages, 326; and proto-urban settlements in China, 212–16
Netting, Robert M., 253, 254, 255, 265, 270
New River Conurbation, and Maya cities, 255–60
Nijmegen (Germany), 127
Nile, and settlement patterns in Egypt, 166–68
Nimes (France), 135
Nippur (Mesopotamia), 146
nomes, as "miniature states" in Egypt, 166, *167*
North Africa, and archetype of Islamic city, 85
Novaesium (Germany), *16*
Nubia: cities of, *14*, *15*, *18*; and settlement patterns in Egypt, 168, 181
nucleated settlements: and types of African cities, 233; and structure of Central Mexican urban centers, 278, 279, 296. *See also* settlement patterns; towns
Nyamwezi (Tanzania), 239
Nyon (Germany), 128

O'Connor, David, 63, 232–33
Old Oyo (Nigeria), 231, 235, 237
Oromo (Kenya), 239, 241
Ortiz Zúñiga, Iñigo de, 308
Orum, Anthony, 10, 12
Ostia (Italy), 95–116
Ouagadougou (Africa), 235

Pakistan: and Department of Archaeology, 191; and research on border with India, 207
palaces: administrative palace and elites in Cuzco, 304–307; functions of Mycenaean, 67–68,

330–31; and seats of rulership in Inka empire, 315–16; and urban planning in Mesopotamian cities, 146, 150
Palenque (Maya), 59
Panlongcheng (China), 217
Paros (Greece), 35
peer-polity homologies, and relationship between city and state, 40–41
Per Ramesses (Egypt), 329
Petrie, Flinders, 172, 173, 176–77
Phoenicians, and pre-Roman history of Mediterranean, 97, 98
Pingliangtai (China), 213–14, 215
pious foundations, and towns in Egypt, 168, 169
Pizarro, Pedro, 313
place, and definition of city, 12. *See also* Central Place Theory
Plato, 34–35, 99
plazas, and structure of Inka urban centers, 307–10, 316
Plutarch, 104
Polanyi, Karl, 248, 250
politics: corporate lineages and sociopolitical organization of early Chinese cities, 222–23; interaction with religious authority in early urban centers, 330; warfare and sociopolitical organization of Inka empire, 309–10. *See also* kings and kingdoms; state
Polydorides, Nicos, 11
Pompeii, *17*
population. *See* density; population dispersion; size
population dispersion, and settlement structure of Central Mexican *altepetl*, 284, 286–93, 296. *See also* density, of population
Portugal, and control of Indian Ocean commerce, 239
postmodernism, and approaches to study of cities, 10, 24
Poston, T., 49
post-processual archaeology, 53, 62, 65
power, monumental architecture as way of reinforcing political, 60
Priene (Asia Minor), 35
"principle of centrality," 11
processual archaeology, 53, 65
production: and *aqlla* in Inka empire, 311–12; and elites of urban Maya, 250–55. *See also* craft production; labor
"psychic unity," concept of, 60
public architecture, and structure of urban centers in Central Mexico, 277, 286–89. *See also* monumental architecture

public ceremonial areas, in cities of Inka empire, 302–304

"public magnificence," and Roman Empire under Augustus, 104, 114
public and private spheres, and segregation in Islamic city, 85–86
Pyburn, K. Anne, 69
Pylos (Mycenaean palace), 67, 330–331
Pyramid of the Plumed Serpent (Xochicalco, Mexico), 294–96
pyramids, and workmen's settlements in Egypt, 168–72

quadripartition, and cosmic imagery, 64, 329
Qucun (China), 219, 220
Qufu (China), *220*, 221–22

Ra (Egyptian sun god), 172
radical relativism, and monumental architecture, 59
Rajanpura (Pakistan), 191
Rakhigarhi (India), 183, 188, 203–206, 207
Rathje, William L., 54, 268
Reader, John, 20, 230–31
Redfield, Robert, 23
Red Sea, and establishment of permanent settlements, 182
regional focus, and assessment of interdependence or complementarity of city and hinterland, 333–34
regularities, in urban centers of archaic states, 49–50
Rehmandheri (Pakistan), 193
religion: importance of in study of urbanism, 90–91; and lack of conspicuous temples in Indus cities, 207; and temples in Mesopotamian cities, 145, 146, 150; and temples in Roman colonial cities, 109, 111, 114, 124; and topography of Ostia, 100–102. *See also* Buddhism; Christianity; Hinduism; Islam
Renaissance, relationship between urbanism and government in Italian, 31, *32*
Renfrew, Colin, 13, 20, 30, 39, 49, 53, 69, 70, 71, 73, 74
Rich, John, 82
road systems: of Inka empire, *300*, 301; and linking of cities to hinterlands, 334–35
Roman Empire: case study of development of cities in Mediterranean, 95–116; case study on establishment of cities in northwestern provinces, 117–38; and Greek prototypes for Hellenistic city, 82–84; imposed structures and similarities in city form, 37. *See also* Rome
Rome: Fustel de Coulanges on founding of, 5; and harbor at Ostia, 111; main civic buildings and political structure of, 96; rebuilding of under Augustus, 83–84, 113; and temporal transformations, 41. *See also* Roman Empire

Rosen, Steven A., 331
Rostworowski de Diez Canseco, María, 313
Rousseau, Jean-Jacques, 70
Routledge, Carolyn, 329
Rowe, John H., 309
rural areas: and central plaza of Inka cities, 307–10; dichotomy of rural/urban, 23; regional focus for assessing interdependence or complementarity of cities with, 333–34; and relationships of cities with countryside in early Africa, 236–37, 239–43; and road systems, 334–35
Russel, Josiah Cox, 76

Sackler Colloquium, 20, 30, 34
Sáenz, Cesar, 287
Sahagún, Bernardino de, 332
Sahlins, Marshall, 253
St. Bertrand-de-Comminges (France), 136
St. Gall (medieval monastery), 38
Sallnow, Michael J., 310
Sanders, William T., 275
Santillán, Fernando de, 316
Sanxingdui (China), 217, *218*
Sardis (Turkey), 110
Scargill, David I., 11
Schaur, Eda, 86
Schnore, Leo F., 11
sector model, of city development, 7–8
segmental urban structure, and *altepemeh* of Central Mexico, 285–91, 296
Sesebi (Nubia), *14*
settlement hierarchy, and relationship between city and state, 34–35, *39*
settlement histories, and cycles of city growth and decline, 78–79
settlement patterns: in area of Liangchengzhen (China), *216*; influence of Nile on in Egypt, 166–68; and structure of Central Mexican *altepetl*, 280, 292. *See also* nucleated settlements; population dispersal
Shaba-Kasai (central Africa), 237
shamanism, and cosmic imagery in Upper Paleolithic, 63–64
Shandong University (China), 215
Shixianggou (China), 217–18
Sicily, and city-farmers, 74
Siena (Italy), 31, *32*
Silchester (England), 132
Silverblatt, Irene, 311
size, of population: and definition of city, 75; and difference between towns and cities, 70; of early African cities, 233; of urban centers in Central Mexico, 278
Sjöberg, Gideon, 12, 68, 75

Skinner, G. William, 24–25
slave trade, and trading networks in East Africa, 243
smallholders, and models of production in Maya context, 252–55, 265–66, 268
"small-world" networks, and Indus cities, 206
Smith, Adam T., 62
Smith, Monica L., 19
Smith, Virginia, 70, 71
social structure: and analysis of city space, 125; corporate lineages and sociopolitical organization of early Chinese cities, 222–23; and features of Indus cities, 207; warfare and sociopolitical organization of Inka empire, 309–10. *See also* elites; kinship
sociology, and definition of "city," 12
Sokoto (Africa), 237
Songo Mnara (Tanzania), *233*
Southall, Aidan, 12–13, 30
space: and organization of Central Mexican *altepemeh*, 281–85; transformations of cities across time and, 44–49
Spain: and conquest of Aztec Mexico, 45–46; and descriptions of Inka cities, 299; flooding and urban settlement histories in, 80; and grid-plan towns in Mesoamerica, 89, 90; Medieval archaeology project in sierra of eastern, 91–92; and urban character of Mesoamerican cities, 273. *See also* colonialism
Speakman, R. J., 159
specialization. *See* craft production; labor
stadium, at Ephesos, 109
stamped earth (*hangtu*), and walls in pre-Imperial Chinese settlements, 210, *211*
standardized weights, and urbanism in Indus Valley, 193, 194, 204–205
state: bureaucracies and institutional networking in formation of early, 81–82; consumption and formation of, 268; and definitions of city and civilization, 33–36, 69–70; emergence of in Early Dynastic Egypt, 166; and emergence of urbanism, 23–24; and peer-polity homologies, 40–41. *See also* city-state; micro-state; politics
steatite seals, and inscriptions from Indus cities, *196*, 197–198, 206. *See also* cylinder seals
Stone, G. & P., 254
Stonehenge (England), 30, 69
storage, and urban centers of Inka empire, 302, 310
Storey, Glenn, 235
stratigraphic history, of city center, 327–30
streets, and characteristics of Indus cities, 194
Su Bingqi, 212
Sumeria, as city-state culture, 72

Swahili: and boundaries between "urban" and "hinterland," 231, 241; and urban craft specialists, 236
Switzerland, and production by smallholders, 253
symbolic approaches, and to study of early cities, 58–62. *See also* cosmic imagery
Syria, political organization in Medieval, 143
system mounds, and urban structure in Central Mexico, 286–87, 289

Tacitus, 127, 130
Taita (Africa), 241
Taosi (China), 215, 216
technology, and modern industrial city, 33–34
Tegdoust (Africa), 230
Tell el-Amarna. *See* Amarna
Tengzhou (China), 222
Tenochtitlan (Mexico): and city services, 332; and cosmic imagery, 63, 329; craft specialists and city plan of, 330; "Great Encounter" with Spain and transformation of, 45–46; population of, 278
Teotihuacan (Mexico): building blocks of, 333; and diversity of city plans, 324, 325; population of, 278; and spatial organization of *altepemeh*, 281–82, *283*, 284
Tepeaca (Mexico), 284–85, 291–93
Tepexpan (Mexico), 281, 282–83
terraces, and architecture of Ayanis (Anatolia), 157
territorial states: dichotomy between city-states and, 35, 72–74; and imposed structures, 38–39; and layout of major urban centers, 61; and locational analysis, 57–58
territory disarticulation, and *altepetl* in Central Mexico, 281–84, 286–91, 296
Texcoco (Mexico), 284
Tezcatlipoca (Aztec deity), 332
theaters, and cities of Roman Empire, 105–106, 107, 108, 111, 114, 124
Thebes (Egypt), 67, 176
Thérouanne (Gaul), *123*
Thompson, D'Arcy, 36
Thucydides, 35
Tikal (Maya), 59
Timbuktu (Mali), 87
time, and temporal transformations of cities, 41–49
Tiwanaku empire (southern Andes), 318
Tongeren (Belgium), *123*, 126
topography, changes to natural in Roman cities of Mediterranean, 100–102, 112–13. *See also* geography
towns: and definition of city, 12, 70–71; organization of to function as city, 325. *See also* nucleated settlements
Toynbee, Arnold, 33
trade: as characteristic of city, 74–75; and commercial networks of Roman Mediterranean, 114; and East African coastal cities, 239, *242*; and Great Zimbabwe, 243; and kinship in early African cities, 241; and multiculturalism in Medieval European cities, 87–88; origin and growth of Indus cities and, 184, 191, 192, 197; and rural/urban relationships in Africa, 236, 237, *242*; two-tiered economy of elite and household, 250
Trajan (Roman emperor), 111, 113
transformations: of cities across space and time, 44–49; and city through time, 41–49; concept of, 36–37; and Ephesos under Augustus, 106; and impact of Christian ideology on Roman cities, 84; and impact of warfare on sociopolitical organization of Inka empire, 309–10; Roman cities in Mediterranean and cost of, 113–15; and Roman cities in northwestern provinces, 135–37
Trigger, Bruce G., 29, 33, 35, 40, 47, 50, 69, 71, 72, 74, 75, 138, 141, 142, 143, 251
Tuan, Yi-Fu, 15, 19, 23
Tulum (Maya), 326–27
Turner, Victor W., 306–307
Tylor, E. B., 34
typological approach, to study of prehispanic urbanism in Mesoamerica, 275

Ubii tribe (Germany), 127–28
Ugarit (Mesopotamia), 83
Ullman, Edward L., 8–9, 24
Uphill, Eric P., 329
Ur (Iraq), 59, 146
Urartu (Turkey), 150–52, 163
urban/folk, dichotomy of, 23
urban geo-archaeology, 79–81, 90
urbanism: central themes in research on, 323–36; and characteristics of urban society, 46–47; of conquest and empire, 38; definition of, 54, 67; and emergence of state, 23–24; origin and character of in Indus Valley, 183–207; and parallels with social insects, 30; relationship with government in Renaissance Italy, 31, *32*; and structure of prehispanic city in Central Mexico, 273–97; Western and alternative perspectives on, 77–92. *See also* case studies; city
urban planning, in lowland Mesopotamia and highland Anatolia, 142–45
Uruk (Mesopotamia), 68
Uzzell, Douglas, 277

van der Leeuw, Sander E., 54, 65
Veblen, Thorstein, 60
"vertical ecological complementarity," theory of Andean, 301, 312

Verulamium (England), 130, *131*, 132–33
Vikings, and cities in early Medieval Ireland, 69
Vitruvius, 83, 84
Vries, Jan de, 75

Waata (Africa), 241
Wadi Gawasis (Egypt), 182
Wagstaff, Malcolm, 74
waiguo, and Warring States period society in China, 225
Wallace-Hadrill, A., 82
walls, of cities: and architecture of cities in highland Anatolia, 154; and development of cities in pre-Imperial China, 214, 221–22; diverse functions of, 21; and Indus urbanism, 201, 203; multi-functional roles of, 325–27; and Roman provincial cities, *136*; and stamped earth construction in China, 210, *211*; and urban planning in lowland Mesopotamia, 145, 147
Wangchenggang (China), 215
warfare: and early walled cities, 326; role of in sociopolitical transformation of Inka empire, 309–10. *See also* defense; military organization
Wari empire (central and southern Andes), 318
Warring States period, and development of cities in China, 212, 222, 225, 227
Washington D.C., and quadrants, 329
water transport routes: and Maya cities of New River Conurbation, 258, 259–60; and relationship between city and hinterland, 335
Weber, Max, 54, 72, 276
Webster, David, 275
West, Georgia, 252
Wheatley, Paul, 19, 21, 25, 47, 58, 329
Wheeler, Robert Eric Mortimer, 198
Wilk, Richard R., 271
Wilson, John A., 58, 166
Wirth, Louis, 9, 12, 23, 24, 275
Wolf, Eric R., 15
Wolff, Michael, 23
Woloch, G., 82
women, and *aqlla* of Inka empire, 311–12

Woolley, Leonard, 146
Woolf, Greg, 119
Wright, Henry T., 34
writing systems: and characteristics of urbanism, 68–69; and inscriptions at Indus cities, 184, 193, 194, *196*, 197–98; linking of to archaeological remains, 335–36
Wroxeter (England), 133–35

Xanten (Germany), 127
Xintian (China), 223–24
Xinzhai (China), 215
Xinzheng (China), 222
Xishan (China), 212
Xochicalco (Mexico), 286–91, 293–96
Xu Hong, 212, 214, 215, 219–20, 221, 222, 225
Xunantunich (Maya), 264

Yako (Nigeria), 69–70
Yang, Xiaoneng, 214, 215–16
Yanhuitlán (Mexico), 284
Yao (Tanzania), 239
Yinxu (China), 218, 222
Yoffee, Norman, 72
Yoruba (Nigeria): and corvée labor in city center, 11–12; and distinction between cities and hinterland, 231; kinship and social divisions in cities of, 150; and political organization, 143; size of cities, 233; and spatial data from Mesopotamian and Anatolian cities, 163; and symbolism in city centers, 60, 63; and views of cities by ancients, 22. *See also* Old Oyo
Yuanqu (China), 217

Zanzibar, and nucleated settlements, 233
Zeder, Melinda, 161
Zhongguo (China), 218
Zhou li (*Rites of Zhou*), 221–22
Zhouyuan (China), *219*
Zoumalou (China), 213
Zuidema, R. Tom, 303

Arthur M. Sackler, M.D.
1913–1987

Born in Brooklyn, New York, Arthur M. Sackler was educated in the arts, sciences, and humanities at New York University. These interests remained the focus of his life, as he became widely known as a scientist, art collector, and philanthropist, endowing institutions of learning and culture throughout the world.

He felt that his fundamental role was as a doctor, a vocation he decided upon at the age of four. After completing his internship and service as house physician at Lincoln Hospital in New York City, he became a resident in psychiatry at Creedmoor State Hospital. There, in the 1940s, he started research that resulted in more than 150 papers in neuroendocrinology, psychiatry, and experimental medicine. He considered his scientific research in the metabolic basis of schizophrenia his most significant contribution to science and served as editor of the *Journal of Clinical and Experimental Psychobiology* from 1950 to 1962. In 1960 he started publication of *Medical Tribune*, a weekly medical newspaper that reached over one million readers in 20 countries. He established the Laboratories for Therapeutic Research in 1938, a facility in New York for basic research that he directed until 1983.

As a generous benefactor to the causes of medicine and basic science, Arthur Sackler built and contributed to a wide range of scientific institutions: the Sackler School of Medicine established in 1972 at Tel Aviv University, Tel Aviv, Israel; the Sackler Institute of Graduate Biomedical Science at New York University, founded in 1980; the Arthur M. Sackler Science Center dedicated in 1985 at Clark University, Worcester, Massachusetts; and the Sackler School of Graduate Biomedical Sciences, established in 1980, and the Arthur M. Sackler Center for Health Communications, established in 1986, both at Tufts University, Boston, Massachusetts.

His pre-eminence in the art world is already legendary. According to his wife Jillian, one of his favorite relaxations was to visit museums and art galleries and pick out great pieces others had overlooked. His interest in art is reflected in his philanthropy; he endowed galleries at the Metropolitan Museum of Art and Princeton University, a museum at Harvard University, and the Arthur M. Sackler Gallery of Asian Art in Washington, DC. True to his oft-stated determination to create bridges between peoples, he offered to build a teaching museum in China, which Jillian made possible after his death, and in 1993 opened the Arthur M. Sackler Museum of Art and Archaeology at Peking University in Beijing.

In a world that often sees science and art as two separate cultures, Arthur Sackler saw them as inextricably related. In a speech given at the State University of New York at Stony Brook, *Some reflections on the arts, sciences and humanities,* a year before his death, he observed: "Communication is, for me, the *primum movens* of all culture. In the arts... I find the emotional component most moving. In science, it is the intellectual content. Both are deeply interlinked in the humanities." The Arthur M. Sackler Colloquia at the National Academy of Sciences pay tribute to this faith in communication as the prime mover of knowledge and culture.

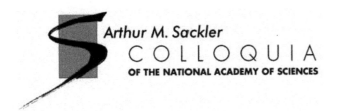

National Academy of Sciences
Sackler Colloquium Series

The Arthur M. Sackler Colloquia of the National Academy of Sciences address scientific topics of broad and current interest, cutting across the boundaries of traditional disciplines. Each year, four or five such colloquia are scheduled, typically two days in length and international in scope. Colloquia are organized by a member of the Academy, often with the assistance of an organizing committee, and feature presentations by leading scientists in the field and discussions with a hundred or more researchers with an interest in the topic. Colloquia presentations are recorded and posted on the National Academy of Sciences Sackler colloquia website and published on CD-ROM. These Colloquia are made possible by a generous gift from Mrs. Jill Sackler, in memory of her husband, Arthur M. Sackler.

CPSIA information can be obtained
at www.ICGtesting.com
Printed in the USA
FFHW011311141119
56060220-62037FF

9 781934 691021